Prepare your students with the power of classroom practice

adopt and assign
MyEducationLab today
www.myeducationlab.com

What is MyEducationLab?

MyEducationLab is a powerful online tool that provides students with assignments and activities set in the context of real classrooms. MyEducationLab is fully integrated in your course and provides practice for your students in an easy to assign format.

Children: "Oo"
Teacher: Good job.

ASSIGNMENTS AND IN-CLASS ACTIVITIES:
Each chapter in MyEducationLab includes assignable Activities and Applications exercises that use authentic classroom video, teacher and student artifacts, or case studies to help students understand course content more deeply and to practice applying that content.

PRACTICE TEACHING: Building Teaching Skills and Dispositions exercises use video, artifacts, and/or case studies to help your students truly see and understand how specific teaching techniques and behaviors impact learners and learning environments. These exercises give your students practice in developing the skills and dispositions that are essential to quality teaching.

> "My students really like the videos, and the articles are interesting and relevant too. I like how the site reinforces the concepts in the textbook in a meaningful way. I am so glad the textbook came with this online resource—it's great!"
>
> — Shari Schroepfer, Adams State College

Does it work?

A survey of student users from across the country tells us that it does!

93% MyEducationLab was easy to use.

70% MyEducationLab's video clips helped me to get a better sense of real classrooms.

79% I would recommend my instructor continue using MyEducationLab.

Percentage of respondents who agree or strongly agree.

Where is it?

- Online at www.myeducationlab.com
- Integrated right into this text! Look for margin annotations and end-of-chapter activities throughout the book.

> "This program will change teaching! Brilliant!"
>
> — Bob Blake, SUNY College at Brockport

What do I have to do to use MyEducationLab in my course?

Just contact your Pearson sales representative and tell him/her that you'd like to use MyEducationLab with this text next semester. Your representative will work with your bookstore to ensure that your students receive access with their books.

What if I need help?

We've got you covered 24/7. Your Pearson sales representative offers training in using MyEducationLab for you and your students. There is also a wealth of helpful information on the site, under "Tours and Training" and "Support." And technical support is available 24 hours a day, seven days a week, at http://247pearsoned.custhelp.com.

> "The ability to track students' performance on the MyEducationLab activities has allowed me to easily keep the students' performance records and devote more time to the development of appropriate in-class activities. The technology has made it possible to design a mastery-based learning system and more easily demonstrate evidence-based practices."
>
> — Daniel E. Hursh, West Virginia University

INCLUSION
Effective Practices for All Students

James McLeskey
University of Florida

Michael S. Rosenberg
Johns Hopkins University

David L. Westling
Western Carolina University

Boston   Columbus   Indianapolis   New York   San Francisco   Upper Saddle River
Amsterdam   Cape Town   Dubai   London   Madrid   Milan   Munich   Paris   Montreal   Toronto
Delhi   Mexico City   Sao Paulo   Sydney   Hong Kong   Seoul   Singapore   Taipei   Tokyo

Vice President and Editor in Chief: Jeffery W. Johnston
Executive Editor: Ann Castel Davis
Development Editor: Heather Doyle Fraser
Editorial Assistant: Penny Burleson
Vice President, Director of Marketing and Sales
Strategies: Emily Williams Knight
Vice President, Director of Marketing: Quinn Perkson
Marketing Manager: Erica DeLuca
Marketing Assistant: Brian Mounts
Senior Managing Editor: Pamela D. Bennett
Production Editor: Sheryl Glicker Langner
Senior Operations Supervisor: Matthew Ottenweller

Operations Specialist: Laura Messerly
Art Director: Candace Rowley
Text Designer: Kristina Holmes
Cover Designer: Diane Lorenzo
Photo Coordinator: Valerie Schultz
Cover Image: Super Stock
Media Producer: Autumn Benson
Media Project Manager: Rebecca Norsic
Composition: S4Carlisle Publishing Services
Printer/Binder: Quebecor/Versailles
Cover Printer: Lehigh-Phoenix
Text Font: Minion

Credits and acknowledgments borrowed from other sources and reproduced, with permission, in this textbook appear on appropriate page within text.

Every effort has been made to provide accurate and current Internet information in this book. However, the Internet and information posted on it are constantly changing, so it is inevitable that some of the Internet addresses listed in this textbook will change.

Photo Credits: Tom Watson/Merrill, pp. 3, 288; Scott Cunningham/Merrill, pp. 9, 13, 35, 53, 86, 108, 178, 190, 192, 221; Bob Daemmrich Photography, Inc., pp. 17, 21, 139, 145, 157 (bottom), 216, 327, 404; Anthony Magnacca/Merrill, pp. 31, 33, 98, 106, 124, 157 (top), 160, 161, 169 (top), 199, 248, 262, 362; George Dodson/PH College, pp. 40, 169 (bottom); Hope Madden/Merrill, pp. 43, 156; Todd Yarrington/Merrill, pp. 50, 291; Ryan McVay/Photodisc/Getty Images, p. 58; Index Open, pp. 63, 121; Richard Hutchings/PhotoEdit Inc., p. 65; Patrick White/Merrill, p. 80; Katelyn Metzger/Merrill, pp. 82, 84, 194, 293; David Mager/Pearson Learning Photo Studio, pp. 90, 258; Michal Heron/PH College, p. 103, David Young-Wolff/PhotoEdit Inc., pp. 105, 323; Paul Conklin/PhotoEdit Inc., pp. 118, 204; Frank Siteman, p. 119; SW Productions/Getty Images, Inc.–Photodisc, pp. 142, 146; Corbis, p. 143; Pearson Scott Foresman, p. 175; Valerie Schultz/Merrill, pp. 180, 324; Getty Images–Digital Vision, p. 210; T. Lindfors/Lindfors Photography, pp. 211, 218, 297, 361, 367, 409; Ryan McVay/Getty Images, Inc.–Photodisc, p. 250; Getty Images–Stockbyte, Royalty Free, p. 254; Doug Menuez/Getty Images, Inc.–PhotoDisc, p. 286; Liz Moore/Merrill, pp. 326, 407; Anderson Ross/Photodisc/Getty Images, p. 332; David Buffington/Getty Images, Inc.–PhotoDisc, p. 364; Bill Aron/PhotoEdit Inc., p. 368; Commissioned by PH Glenview, p. 402; Bob Daemmrich/PhotoEdit, Inc., p. 412.

Library of Congress Cataloging-in-Publication Data

McLeskey, James
  Inclusion: effective practices for all students/James McLeskey, Michael S. Rosenberg, David L. Westling.—1st ed. p. cm.
    ISBN-13: 978-0-13-515403-8
    ISBN-10: 0-13-515403-0
    1. Inclusive education—United States. 2. Special Education—United States. 3. Children with disabilities—Education—United States.
4. Mainstreaming in education—United States. I. Rosenberg, Michael S. II. Westling, David L. III. Title.
    LC1201.M38 2010
    371.9'046~dc22
2009011693

10 9 8 7 6 5 4 3 2 1

www.pearsonhighered.com

ISBN-10:   0-13-515403-0
ISBN-13:   978-0-13-515403-8

To my first mentor, B.T., and all of my students in the "quonset hut," who taught me so much about what it means to be excluded . . . and included.

JM

To Irene and Dan—So much! Still Again, and Always

MSR

To Wendy: For more than 30 years of support.

DLW

Preface

Our Vision

Over the past 30 years, the inclusion of many students with disabilities into our nation's schools has provided learning and social opportunities that have not existed in the past. Nevertheless, inclusion continues to be a source of controversy and poses daily challenges to many educators. Even though most educators are committed to providing an appropriate education in the least restrictive setting for their students, the reality of how to effectively address the academic and behavioral challenges associated with children with special needs is often daunting to school personnel. Clearly, many questions remain regarding how to best design, deliver, support, and evaluate inclusive educational programs. It is our perspective that the responses to these questions are best presented to pre-service and in-service educators in a practical and straightforward fashion, using a format that integrates evidence-based practices with applications and examples that resemble their settings and working conditions.

This text is built upon a pragmatic, 'real-world' approach to inclusion. That is, we assume that all general education classrooms should be designed to accommodate the needs of a diverse range of students, and all students with disabilities should be included to the maximum extent appropriate. Moreover, we take the perspective that many students (including those with and without disabilities) need intensive high quality instruction in general education classrooms, although at times instruction may be delivered to small groups or individually, either in a general education classroom, or outside such a setting.

In this text, we anchor content to three key themes: 1) **Values** underlying inclusion, 2) **Effective Applications** (evidence based practices), 3) the importance of **Professional Educators**. The values theme emphasizes the perspective that students with disabilities should be active participants in the academic and social activities (or communities) of their classrooms and schools. This means that from the beginning, the curriculum and instructional practices of all classrooms should be designed to accommodate and support the academic and social needs of a broad range of students, including those with disabilities. In many instances, students with disabilities should be included as a natural part of the general education classroom, with no need for special accommodations or adaptations.

The second theme, effective applications, emphasizes evidence-based practices that are needed to meet the needs of students with disabilities and others who struggle to learn or adjust socially. These practices may be applied with all students in a general education classroom (e.g., class-wide peer tutoring), or implemented with small groups of students either in the general education classroom or in a separate setting (e.g., intensive reading instruction).

Finally, the third theme emphasizes the importance of highly effective professional educators in meeting the needs of all students. Highly effective professional educators are those who have the knowledge, skills, and dispositions to effectively meet the needs of a broad range of students. These professionals use evidence-based practices, possess in depth knowledge of the content they teach, and continue to learn and grow as they seek to better meet the needs of all students who enter their classrooms and schools.

Organization of Text

To provide a complete picture of inclusion, and to emphasize how it relates to our three key themes, we have organized the text into three parts: Foundations of Successful Inclusion, Meeting the Needs of All Students, and Effective Practices for All Students. The initial Foundations section includes three chapters that provide an introduction to inclusion, an account of how this form of service delivery has evolved, and how the diversity of students in today's schools influences inclusion and education in general. The second part, Meeting the Needs of All Students, includes seven *brief* chapters that provide background information regarding specific disabilities (i.e., definition, identification, characteristics), as well as key issues and challenges for including students with special needs. Part three addresses Effective Practices for All Students. The six chapters within this section provide an overview of key principles related to the topic, followed by the in-depth presentation of 46 key, evidence-based practices.

This three part format allows us to address the needs of the diverse range of teacher preparation students typically enrolled in inclusion coursework: traditional special education students, traditional general education students, and the growing number of alternative certification students. The question that drives each chapter and the text as a whole is: "Regardless of who you are, do you have the necessary knowledge, skills, and dispositions to successfully include students with disabilities in a general education classroom?"

Foundations and Characteristics

Foundations of Successful Inclusion

The three chapters in Part I provide readers with background/foundational information regarding inclusion, address the values that underlie this movement, introduce the three highly successful inclusive schools that will be used throughout the text, and discuss inclusion within the context of more general issues of student diversity in today's schools.

We use a number of pedagogical features to provide examples of the themes throughout the text. Many of these features use examples taken from professional educators in highly effective inclusive schools and classrooms. This ensures that the examples we use are grounded in the real world experiences of teachers, and address both the strengths and challenges of developing inclusive classrooms.

Three Inclusive Schools

A significant amount of content within the text is situated in three highly successful inclusive schools at the elementary, middle, and high school levels. These schools have diverse student bodies, and are located in a variety of settings. We provide a lengthy description of the schools in chapter 1, and teachers, parents, and administrators from the three schools are used in features and as examples throughout the text. These schools provide a foundation for the pragmatic approach we take to inclusion, ensuring that the information we provide is situated in real world settings and across all grade levels.

Meeting the Needs of All Students

Chapters 4–10 are brief and provide descriptive information regarding disability categories, and address general principles and issues regarding the application of effective practices with these students. Whenever a strategy or type of strategy is addressed in the text, you will see a *Strategy Margin Note* directing you to the step-by-step application of the strategy in the Effective Practices section of chapters 11–16. All categorical chapters use the same general outline to facilitate reader comprehension and consistency. Each chapter is written in a clear, succinct, practical, and approachable style and has the same pedagogical elements and themes throughout.

> **Strategy**
>
> For more information regarding a strategy that may be used with students with ADHD to improve note taking, see Strategy 14.5 in Chapter 14.

Perspectives on Education

This feature begins chapters 2–16 in the text and features teachers, parents, and administrators from the three schools (elementary, middle, and high schools) described in Chapter 1. These real life scenarios address the themes of the text and provide readers with an understanding of:

- Teacher, parent, and administrator views regarding inclusion
- Benefits of inclusion and the value of inclusive practices/classrooms/schools

Pause & Reflect Margin Notes

In every chapter of the text we have Pause & Reflect margin notes that focus on specific concepts addressed in the text and ask readers to examine their own perspectives and beliefs on these topics. These notes also are connected to our three themes in the text.

Just the Facts

Because chapters 4–10 are brief, we have provided a "quick facts" feature that addresses definition, identification, assessment, prevalence, and service delivery practices (LRE statistics). This feature will help readers identify the key components on the basic categorical issues covered in each of these chapters.

Teaching Students with Disabilities in Inclusive Classrooms: Challenges and Strategies

This feature, like the chapter opening vignette, addresses a real-world example from one of the three schools featured in the text. In this feature teachers and administrators from these three schools provide their perspectives on teaching students from a given disability category in inclusive classrooms. Through these interviews the teachers share and reflect on the challenges of including all students in the general education classroom and strategies that may be particularly effective with their students. This discussion provides a bridge between the information on the characteristics and the identification of students in a disability category to information on effective instruction.

Effective Practices

Chapters 11–16 address key topical issues for the inclusive classroom and effective practices that can be used with all students. The first half of each chapter discusses the theory and background of each issue (i.e., collaboration, instructional planning, technology, etc.) and the second half of each chapter provides in-depth, step-by-step strategies (up to 10 strategies per chapter topic) related to these issues.

Step-by-Step Strategies

Up to ten effective practices are included in chapters 11–16. These practices present step-by-step evidence-based techniques that provide students with explicit strategies for the topic area discussed in the chapter. You will notice that the pages in this text are perforated and hole punched – this enables students to remove these research-based strategies and put them into a binder for future use as they enter their own classroom.

Each strategy includes the following information:

- Rationale and Research that give the background of the strategy – when and how it should be used and citations for further information
- Step-by-Step instruction on how to use the strategy with students or in the classroom
- Applications and Examples of the strategy in a real-world context
- A Keep in Mind section that helps readers address specific "speedbumps" they may encounter when applying the strategy

Putting It All Together

To connect the theory of the first half of chapters 11–16 with the strategies covered in the second half of these chapters we use a graphic organizer for each chapter called *Putting It All Together*. These graphic organizers are replicated on card stock so developing and new teachers can tear them out and use them in a strategies binder that they can use in their classrooms. These organizers contain the following helpful information:

- A narrative summary of considerations pre-service teachers need to take into account when working in that chapter's particular topical area
- *MyEducationLab*: The MyEducationLab grid directs readers to Activities and Applications and Building Teaching Skills and Dispositions exercises that coordinate with the strategies addressed in the second half of the chapter. Within these assignments and exercises you will find embedded video, cases, strategies, and simulations that will allow you to experience these strategies (or complementary strategies) in a real classroom environment.
- *Effective Practices Grid*: This grid outlines the strategies we cover in the second half of the chapter and gives the reader information regarding each of these strategies at-a-glance. You will find the name of the strategy and page number as well as a brief description and special considerations you should keep in mind when using the strategy.

PEARSON **myeducationlab**

PUTTING IT ALL TOGETHER

At times, particularly early in your career, you will find the process of managing student behavior challenging. You may encounter colleagues who hold flawed views of how best to manage behavior, parents who fail to respond to your well-intentioned efforts to address persistent troubles, and administrators who fall short in supporting your structured management system. If and when these events occur, it is best if you respond in a professional manner:

1. **Remain patient, keep things in perspective, and be aware of the big picture.** Schools are a microcosm of society, and you should not take it personally if events do not go as planned.

2. **Practice diplomacy.** Consider the perspective of those who you find frustrating, and identify the functions of their actions. Try to understand why they believe and act as they do, and seek to negotiate win-win resolutions to conflicts.

3. **Remain poised.** Your comportment during stressful and frustrating circumstances is a reflection of your competence and professionalism. Students look to adults as models of desired behavior, and they will learn from your actions.

4. **Reflect on your own actions, and get help when needed.** Consider how your own actions and belief systems contribute to the development and maintenance of challenging situations. Do not be reluctant to ask for help and support from friends and colleagues.

5. **Show your pleasure when helping your students.** We choose to teach because we enjoy it and derive satisfaction in seeing our students overcome challenges and grow socially. Recognize when challenges are met, and celebrate when students succeed as a result of your efforts.

myeducationlab

We present a series of evidence-based strategies in the second half of this chapter (Strategies 15.1 to 15.8) in a step-by-step format so that you can use them in your classroom right away. In addition, in the following table, we identify some video clips, cases, and simulations that will allow you to experience some of these strategies (or complementary strategies) in a real classroom environment.

EFFECTIVE PRACTICE	MYEDUCATIONLAB CONNECTION	CONSIDER THIS
Strategy 15.1: Developing and Maintaining Rules and Procedures	Go to MyEducationLab, select the topic: Classroom/Behavior Management, and go to the Activities and Applications section. Next, complete the simulation entitled "Who's in Charge?"	As you complete the simulation, reflect on how developing rules and procedures (as discussed in Strategy 15.1) fit into a comprehensive behavior management plan.
Strategy 15.2: Surface Management Techniques	Go to MyEducationLab, select the topic: Classroom/Behavior Management, and go to the Activities and Applications section. Next, read and analyze the case entitled "Hang in There," and answer the accompanying questions.	As you read and analyze the case, consider how you would use the surface management techniques discussed in Strategy 15.2 to help the struggling teacher featured in the case.
Strategy 15.3: Developing Consequences and Delivering Them with Consistency	Go to MyEducationLab, select the topic: Classroom/Behavior Management, and go to the Activities and Applications section. Next, read and analyze the case entitled "Encouraging Appropriate Behavior."	As you read and analyze this case, think about how you can apply the step-by-step techniques discussed in Strategy 15.3 to the multiple instances of problem behavior addressed in the case.
Strategy 15.4: Defusing Confrontations and Responding to Dangerous Behavior	Go to MyEducationLab, select the topic: Classroom/Behavior Management, and go to the Activities and Applications section. Next, complete the simulation entitled "Addressing Disruptive and Noncompliant Behaviors, Part 1."	As you complete the simulation, compare and contrast the strategies discussed in the simulation with these techniques highlighted in Strategy 15.4. Which techniques seem to be most effective in addressing these confrontational behaviors?
Strategy 15.5: Check-In, Connect, and Check-Out Systems	Go to MyEducationLab, select the topic: Classroom/Behavior Management, and go to the Activities and Applications section. Next, watch the video entitled "Schoolwide Positive Behavior Support."	As you watch the video and answer the accompanying questions, reflect on the similarities and differences between the program discussed in the video and the school-wide PBS program discussed in the video.
Strategy 15.6: Behavioral Contracts and Strategy 15.7: Function-Based Thinking, FBAs, & BIPs	Go to MyEducationLab, and select the topic: Classroom/Behavior Management. Next, go to the Building Teaching Skills and Dispositions section, and complete the activity entitled "Multilevel Motivation System."	As you watch the video and answer the accompanying questions in this activity, consider how you might use these specific motivational techniques and strategies to complement the targeted interventions discussed in Strategies 15.6 and 15.7.
Strategy 15.8: Direct Teaching of Social Skills: Social Stories	Go to MyEducationLab, select the topic: Emotional or Behavioral Disorders, and go to the Activities and Applications section. Next, watch the video entitled "Social Skills Lesson," and answer the accompanying questions.	As you watch the video and answer the accompanying questions, compare and contrast the social skills lesson presented in the video to Strategy 15.8. Are these strategies equally effective in teaching social skills? Why or why not?

CLASSROOM MANAGEMENT

377

EFFECTIVE PRACTICES

In the remainder of this chapter, we describe eight effective strategies, which we referred to previously in the chapter, to help you teach effectively to meet the needs of all students.

EFFECTIVE PRACTICE	TYPE OF STRATEGY/BRIEF DESCRIPTION	SPECIAL CONSIDERATIONS
Strategy 15.1: Developing and Maintaining Rules and Procedures	A universal design behavioral support that communicates and defines acceptable behavior and efficient routines associated with success in the classroom.	Rules and procedures must be taught explicitly as well as reviewed and practiced throughout the school year, particularly after breaks for holidays and vacations.
Strategy 15.2: Surface Management Techniques	Commonsense behavior management methods for minor disruptive behavior, surface management techniques overlap with elements of teaching with little disruption to the instructional process.	Surface management requires an awareness of classroom activities and events, multitasking skills that increase with time and experience.
Strategy 15.3: Developing Consequences and Delivering Them with Consistency	A series of teacher-directed events and behaviors that are used to promote compliance to behavioral expectations and to reduce the frequency and intensity of inappropriate behaviors.	For classroom management systems to succeed, it is essential that students complying with expectations are recognized and reinforced for their efforts.
Strategy 15.4: Defusing Confrontations and Responding to Dangerous Behavior	A series of interpersonal communication techniques that can defuse confrontational situations and maintain the safety of students and staff.	Some students use the shock value of extreme behaviors to intimidate and coerce others. It is important to minimize instances of these students' attaining desired outcomes through such behaviors.
Strategy 15.5: Check-In, Connect, and Check-Out Systems	Targeted low-cost interventions that provide students with immediate feedback on behavior, supportive relationships with school personnel, and increased recognition contingent on improvements in appropriate behavior.	The success of check-in systems depends of the quality of adults who coordinate the program. Specifically, coordinators need to interact well with students, work closely with families, proactively address conflict, and believe that positive changes will occur.
Strategy 15.6: Behavioral Contracts	Formal documents that detail the elements of a specific, realistic individualized behavior change initiatives.	Because contracts require students to wait for a specific "payoff," it is important to gauge how long students can maintain their behavior without tangible reinforcement.
Strategy 15.7: Function-Based Thinking, Functional Behavior Assessments, and Behavior Intervention Plans	A process designed to identify possible linkages between student behavior and the events and conditions in classroom and school environments; information identified is used to develop a behavior intervention plan (BIP).	Keep it simple and straightforward: The key element of functional thinking is to identify and intervene on factors that contribute to a student's inappropriate behaviors.
Strategy 15.8: Direct Teaching of Social Skills: Social Stories	Written from the student's perspective, social stories explicitly highlight a course of action that one could take when encountering a challenging social situation.	Social stories work best when they are implemented along with other methods of evidence-based social skill instruction including modeling, role playing, and practice in naturalistic settings.

CLASSROOM MANAGEMENT

378

Supplements for Students and Instructors

The student and instructor support package for *Inclusion: Effective Practices for All Students* includes MyEducationLab, an Online Instructor's Manual with Test Items, Online TestGen assessment software, and Online PowerPoint Presentations.

MYEDUCATIONLAB

Where the classroom comes to life.

"Teacher educators who are developing pedagogies for the analysis of teaching and learning contend that analyzing teaching artifacts has three advantages: it enables new teachers time for reflection while still using the real materials of practice; it provides new teachers with experience thinking about and approaching the complexity of the classroom; and in some cases, it can help new teachers and teacher educators develop a shared understanding and common language about teaching. . . ."[1]

As Linda Darling-Hammond and her colleagues point out, grounding teacher education in real classrooms—among real teachers and students and among actual examples of students' and teachers' work—is an important, and perhaps even an essential, part of training teachers for the complexities of teaching today's students in today's classrooms. We have created a website that provides you and your students with the context of real classrooms and artifacts that research on teacher education tells us is so important. Through authentic in-class video footage, interactive skill-building exercises and more, MyEducationLab offers you and your students a uniquely valuable teacher education tool.

MyEducationLab is easy to use!

In *Inclusion: Effective Practices for All Students*, look for the MyEducationLab logo and directive within the margins at the beginning of chapters 2–10. Additionally, in chapters 11–16 you will find a MyEducationLab strategy grid in the Putting It All Together section that connects the strategies addressed in these chapters to specific ***Activities and Applications*** and ***Building Teaching Skills and Dispositions*** exercises that correspond with the appropriate chapter topics. Follow these directives and the simple navigation instructions to access the videos, simulations, strategies, cases, and artifacts associated with these assignments and activities on MyEducationLab.

- **Activities and Applications:** These exercises offer opportunities to understand content more deeply and are explicitly connected to chapter topics. These exercises present thought-provoking questions that probe the students' understanding of the concept or strategy that is presented in the text through classroom video footage, simulations, strategies, or teacher and student artifacts.
- **Building Teaching Skills and Dispositions:** These application assignments help students practice and strengthen skills that are essential to quality teaching. Students watch authentic classroom video footage or other media and critically analyze how they can apply these skills and strategies and then incorporate them into their teaching repertoire or portfolio.

---

[1]Darling-Hammond, l., & Bransford, J., Eds. (2005). *Preparing Teachers for a Changing World*. San Francisco: John Wiley & Sons.

The rich, authentic, and interactive elements that support the Activities and Applications and the Building Teaching Skills and Dispositions exercises you will encounter throughout MyEducationLab include:

- **Video:** The authentic classroom videos in MyEducationLab show how real teachers handle actual classroom situations. Viewing videos and discussing and analyzing them not only deepens understanding of concepts presented in the book, but also builds skills in observing and analyzing children and classrooms.
- **Simulations:** Created by the IRIS Center at Vanderbilt University, these interactive simulations give you hands-on practice at adapting instruction for a full spectrum of learners.
- **Student & Teacher Artifacts:** Authentic pre-K–12 student and teacher classroom artifacts are tied to course topics and offer you practice in working with the different materials you will encounter daily as teachers.
- **Case Studies:** A diverse set of robust cases illustrate the realities of teaching and offer valuable perspectives on common issues and challenges in education.
- **Strategies:** These teacher-tested, research-based strategies span grade levels pre-K through 12 and all content areas.
- **Lesson & Portfolio Builders:** With this effective and easy-to-use tool, you can create, update, and share standards-based lesson plans and portfolios.

Visit www.myeducationlab.com/ for a demonstration of this exciting new online teaching resource.

Online Instructor's Manual with Test Items and TestGen Software

All of the instructor supplements are available at the Instructor Resource Center. To access the manual, the PowerPoint lecture presentation, and the test bank and TestGen software (see below) go to the Instructor Resource Center at www.pearsonhighered.com and click on the "Educators" link. Here you will be able to login or complete a one-time registration for a user name and password.

The Online Instructor's Manual includes numerous recommendations for presenting and extending text content. It is organized by chapter and contains chapter objectives, chapter summaries, key terms, presentation outlines, discussion questions, application and MyEducationLab activities, and test items. The test item bank contains multiple-choice, short answer, and essay questions that can be used to assess students' recognition, recall, and synthesis of factual content and conceptual issues from each chapter.

The online TestGen is available in both Windows and Macintosh format, along with assessment software allowing professors to create and customize exams and track student progress.

Online PowerPoint Lecture Presentations

The Online PowerPoint Lecture Presentations—available on the Instructor Resources Center—highlight key concepts, summarize content, and provide a presentation outline for each chapter of the text.

Acknowledgments

To make an inclusive classroom function well, professionals must work together, sharing expertise and providing support as it is needed. We have witnessed this firsthand on many occasions in schools, as teachers and administrators work collaboratively to provide extraordinary educational opportunities for all students. The same is true when writing a textbook. While three of us are listed as authors of this text, we had a broad range of support in completing this project. As this text has moved toward completion, the level of support, creativity, and knowledge that colleagues have provided has been extraordinary, and we are extremely privileged and grateful to have had this support.

First, we want to acknowledge the superlative effort of the professionals at Pearson Education for their unparalleled support. Our Executive Editor Ann Davis provided the momentum to get this project started, then used her extensive knowledge of special education textbooks and marketing to provide us with a unique direction for our inclusion text. Throughout the many months we spent writing this text, she continually kept us on-message and encouraged us to produce a unique text with features that were a good fit for the real-world of teaching and inclusive classrooms.

Our many requests for support and information at the Pearson Education offices were cheerfully and quickly addressed in editorial by Penny Burleson and by Kate Romano in marketing. We received great support from Valerie Schultz in selecting the excellent photographs that appear throughout the text and provide support for the content. As we were completing the final drafts of chapters, Luanne Dreyer Elliott provided superlative copy editing, as she kept chapters moving along and ensured the consistency and clarity of content. Finally, we are grateful for the creative coordination of Senior Production Editor Sheryl Langner, who was always there to make sure that the pieces of this project fit together and resulted in a product that was both logical and attractive.

We would like to provide a special thanks to our consistent lifeline at Pearson Education, Senior Development Editor Heather Doyle Fraser. It's no understatement to say that Heather has had to deal with us at our worst, as she has kept us on time, focused, and busy addressing all the details, large and small, that go into writing a textbook. While at times we have dreaded opening the emails from Heather, giving us a new deadline or additional task to complete, she has made this work much more manageable and pleasant. Indeed, Heather's organizational and editorial skills are surpassed only by her wit and grace.

For their fine work on Chapter 3, "A Look at Today's Schools: Teaching Students from Diverse Backgrounds," we want to thank Dorene Ross, Margaret Kamman, and Vivian Correa from the University of Florida, and Jennifer Huber from Clemson University. In this chapter, these colleagues share their expertise and many experiences working with students from diverse backgrounds, and provide much useful information for teachers regarding how to successfully teach these students.

A highlight for each of us as we wrote this book was having the opportunity to interview and observe a group of extraordinarily dedicated teachers and administrators in our three feature schools, Mull Elementary, West Hernando Middle, and Heritage High School. We are very appreciative to these professionals for allowing us to enter their schools, and for their willingness to share their expertise, ideas, and creativity. We are especially appreciative of the following teachers, administrators, and school staff at the three schools.

At Mull Elementary, we especially appreciate assistance provided by Principal Jill King and by many of the teachers and staff in the school, including Anne Vogler, Becky Wyke, Cathy Danford, Debra Bolinger, Jennifer Powell, John Gann, Joyce Flowers, Lisa Church, Madge Goins, Margaret Gordon, and all the others in the school who were kind enough to provide their time and thoughts about successful inclusion.

At West Hernando Middle School, we appreciate the support of Principal Joe Clifford, Counselor Susan Dean, teachers Sue Atkins, Susan Davis, Michelle Duclos, Vicki Eng, Lisa Grover, Lisa Hallal, Laura Scott, Eileen Walls, and Special Education Director Cathy Dofka.

At Heritage High School, we appreciate the support and cooperation of Principal Margaret Huckabee and Dean of Students, Susan Hill. For over a year, these dedicated administrators went above and beyond to make us feel part of their academic community. Also, we are indebted to the dedicated teachers and parents at Heritage, including Melanie Buckley, Sarita Casserta, Denise Pohill, Gina Craun, Anthony Long, Tracey Ludwig, Casey Van Harssel, Steve Kennedy, Jon Preuss, Steve Williams, Kristen Tham, and Shana Watson. Thanks for sharing your expertise and insightful opinions.

The staff at all three of our universities assisted us on a range of tasks, and covered for us when we were hidden away writing chapters. We are most appreciative for this support. Colleagues and staff at the University of Florida included Penny Cox, Shaira Rivas-Otero, Vicki Tucker, Linda Parsons, and Michell York. At Johns Hopkins support was provided by Sharon Lampkin and Shanise Winters. At Western Carolina support was provided by staff members including Jennifer Harwell and Denise Royer, and by colleagues including Karena Cooper-Duffy, David Shapiro and Kelly Kelley.

We sent out many drafts of each chapter for review, and received valuable feedback from a range of colleagues. We appreciate the time these colleagues provided, as well as their willingness to share expertise on topics from each chapter in this text which helped up ensure accuracy and improve the quality of this project. In particular, we would like to thank Joan Bacon, Augustana College; Patricia Bowman, University of California–Los Angeles; Greg Conderman, Northern Illinois University; Michael Dunn, Washington State University; Linda Elksnin, The Citadel (Emerita); Blanche Glimps, Tennessee State University; Yvonne Goddard, University of Michigan; Linda Green, Centenary College; Harold Heller, University of South Florida; Brian Jablonski, University of Virginia; Deborah Johnson, Holy Family University; Darcy Miller, Washington State University; Melissa Miller, University of North Carolina–Chapel Hill; Craig Miner, Southern Illinois University; Kaye Ragland, Pacific Oaks College; Laura Reissner, Northern Michigan University; Linda Seybert, Park University; Qaisar Sultana, Eastern Kentucky University; Mary Ulrich, Miami University; Jane Williams, Arizona State University; and Diane Woodrum, Waynesburg University.

Finally, in spite of our frequent absences while we were completing this project, we continue to have the love and support of our families, and for this we are eternally grateful. This includes our wives, Nancy, Irene, and Wendy; children Gaby, Robby, Matthew, Zeke, Daniel, Jennifer, Jessica, and Meredith; and grandchildren Dylan, Ethan, Hayden, and Riley.

JM
MSR
DLW

Brief Contents

Part I: Foundations of Successful Inclusion, 1

Chapter 1: What Is Inclusion and Why Is It Important?, 2

Chapter 2: Inclusion: Reflections on the Past, Present, and Future, 28

Chapter 3: A Look at Today's Schools: Teaching Students from Diverse Backgrounds, 48

Part II: Meeting the Needs of All Students, 77

Chapter 4: Students with Learning Disabilities, 78

Chapter 5: Students with Attention-Deficit/Hyperactivity Disorder, 96

Chapter 6: Students with Intellectual Disabilities, 116

Chapter 7: Students with Emotional and Behavioral Disabilities, 136

Chapter 8: Students with Autism Spectrum Disorders, 150

Chapter 9: Students with Communication Disorders and Students with Sensory Impairments, 166

Chapter 10: Students with Physical Disabilities, Health Impairments, and Multiple Disabilities, 188

Part III: Effective Practices, 207

Chapter 11: Collaboration and Teaming, 208

Chapter 12: Formal Plans and Planning for Differentiated Instruction, 246

Chapter 13: Effective Instruction in Elementary Inclusive Classrooms: Teaching Reading, Writing, and Mathematics, 284

Chapter 14: Teaching Students in Secondary Content Areas, 320

Chapter 15: Effective Practices for All Students: Classroom Management, 358

Chapter 16: Using Technology to Enhance Inclusion, 400

Glossary, 441

References, 447

Name Index, 465

Subject Index, 473

Contents

Part I: Foundations of Successful Inclusion, 1

Chapter 1: What Is Inclusion and Why Is It Important?, 2

Introduction, 3
Inclusion Is for All Students, 4
Descriptions of Three Highly Effective, Inclusive Schools, 5
Students with Disabilities and Special Education, 9
Other Students Who May Need Support in the General Education
Classroom, 11
Concepts That Support Inclusive Practices, 12
Normalization, 13
Least Restrictive Environment, 14
What Are Effective Inclusive Programs?, 16
Inclusive Programs: Research on Effectiveness, 17
Your Role as a Teacher in an Inclusive School, 19
General Education Teachers, 19
Special Education Teachers, 19
Related Services Professionals, 20
Paraeducators, 21
Teacher Attitudes Toward Inclusion, 21
Being a Good Teacher of All Students, 22
Appropriate Dispositions, 23
Positive Teacher Attitude, 23
Summary, 25

Chapter 2: Inclusion: Reflections on the Past, Present, and Future, 28

Perspectives on Inclusion, 29
Introduction, 30
The Evolution of Inclusive Special Education
Services, 31
From Segregation to Inclusion, 31
Civil Rights and Parent Advocacy, 33
Current Status of Inclusive Practices, 34
Legal Foundations of Special Education and Inclusion, 36
Individuals with Disabilities Education Improvement Act (IDEA 2004), 36
From Law to Classroom: Major Components of IDEA 2004, 37
No Child Left Behind, 40
Elements of NCLB, 40
Section 504 of the Rehabilitation Act of 1973 (PL 93-112) and the
Americans with Disabilities Act, 42

Tomorrow's Challenges, 44
    AYP and Students with Disabilities, 44
    Highly Qualified Professionals, 44
    Evolving Roles in a Changing System, 45
Summary, 46

Chapter 3:   **A Look at Today's Schools: Teaching Students from Diverse Backgrounds, 48**

Perspectives on Teaching Students from Diverse Backgrounds, 49
Introduction, 50
Who Are the Students in Today's Schools?, 51
    Ethnic Groups, 51
    Language, 51
    Poverty, 52
Diversity in Special Education, 53
Student Diversity and Academic Achievement, 54
    Academic Proficiency, 54
    High School Graduation Rates, 56
Teachers, Students, and the Demographic Divide, 56
    Culture and Student Outcomes, 56
    Establishing Connections Across a Cultural Divide, 57
    What Is Culture, and Why Is It So Important?, 57
What Can Teachers Do? Culturally Responsive Teaching in Inclusive Classrooms, 64
    Supporting Resilience and Motivation, 64
    Culturally Responsive Inclusive Pedagogy, 64
    Demonstrating Care, 67
    High Expectations: What Does "No Excuses" Really Mean?, 70
    Using a Diverse Curriculum, 71
Summary, 74

Part II: Meeting the Needs of All Students, 77

Chapter 4:   **Students with Learning Disabilities, 78**

Perspectives on Including Students with Learning Disabilities, 79
Introduction, 80
Who Are Students with Learning Disabilities?, 80
    Identification of Students with Learning Disabilities, 80
    Prevalence, 82
    Service Delivery, 84
Major Characteristics of Students with Learning Disabilities, 86
    Academic Difficulties, 86
    Cognitive Skill Deficits, 87
    Social and Motivational Problems, 87
Effective Instruction for Students with Learning Disabilities, 88
    Effective Instruction for Elementary Students, 88
    Effective Instruction for Secondary Students, 91
Final Thoughts Regarding Effective Practices, 93
Summary, 94

Chapter 5:   Students with Attention-Deficit/Hyperactivity Disorder, 96

Perspectives on Including Students with Attention-Deficit/Hyperactivity
Disorder, 97
Introduction, 98
Who Are Students with Attention-Deficit/Hyperactivity Disorder?, 99
   Definition, 99
   Identification of Students with ADHD, 102
   Prevalence, 103
   Service Delivery, 104
Major Characteristics of Students with ADHD, 104
   Inattentive, Hyperactive, and Impulsive Behaviors, 104
   Social and Behavior Problems, 105
   Academic Difficulties, 106
Effective Instruction for Students with ADHD, 106
   Effective Instruction for Elementary Students, 106
   Effective Instruction for Secondary Students, 109
   The Use of Medication to Address the Symptoms of ADHD, 111
Final Thoughts Regarding Effective Practices, 112
Summary, 112

Chapter 6:   Students with Intellectual Disabilities, 116

Perspectives on Including Students with Intellectual Disabilities, 117
Introduction, 118
Who Are Students with Intellectual Disabilities?, 119
   Definition, 119
   Identification of Students with Intellectual Disabilities, 121
   Prevalence, 122
   Service Delivery, 122
Major Characteristics of Students with Intellectual
Disabilities, 123
   Academic Difficulties, 123
   Cognitive Skill Deficits, 124
   Social and Behavior Problems, 125
Effective Instruction for Students with Intellectual Disabilities, 126
   Effective Instruction for Elementary Students, 126
   Effective Instruction for Secondary Students, 129
Final Thoughts Regarding Effective Practices, 132
Summary, 132

Chapter 7:   Students with Emotional and Behavioral Disabilities, 136

Perspectives on Including Students with Emotional
and Behavioral Disabilities, 137
Introduction, 138
Who Are Students with Emotional and Behavioral Disabilities?, 139
   Definition, 139
Identification of Students with Emotional and Behavioral Disabilities, 140
   Prevalence, 141
   Service Delivery, 141

Major Characteristics of Students with Emotional and Behavioral Disabilities, 142
Externalizing Behavior Problems, 142
Internalizing Behavior Problems, 143
Cognitive, Academic, and Social Behavior, 143
Effective Instruction for Students with Emotional and Behavioral Disabilities, 144
Effective Instruction for Elementary Students, 144
Effective Instruction for Secondary Students, 145
Final Thoughts Regarding Effective Practices, 146
Summary, 147

Chapter 8:   Students with Autism Spectrum Disorders, 150

Perspectives on Including Students with Autism Spectrum Disorders, 151
Introduction, 152
Who Are Students with Autism Spectrum Disorders?, 153
Definition, 153
Identification of Students with Autism Spectrum Disorders, 154
Prevalence, 155
Service Delivery, 155
Major Characteristics of Students with Autism Spectrum Disorders, 156
Primary Characteristics, 156
Secondary Behavioral Factors, 157
Effective Instruction for Students with Autism Spectrum Disorders, 158
Effective Instruction for Elementary Students, 158
Effective Instruction for Secondary Students, 161
Final Thoughts Regarding Effective Practices, 163
Summary, 163

Chapter 9:   Students with Communication Disorders and Students with Sensory Impairments, 166

Perspectives on Including Students with Communication Disorders, 167
Introduction, 168
Who Are Students with Communication Disorders?, 169
Definitions, 169
Identification of Students with Communication Disorders, 169
Prevalence, 172
Service Delivery, 172
Major Characteristics of Students with Communication Disorders, 173
Academic and Cognitive Performance, 173
Behavior Performance and Social Skills, 173
Effective Instruction for Students with Communication Disorders, 174
Effective Instruction for Elementary Students, 174
Effective Instruction for Secondary Students, 175
Who Are Students with Sensory Impairments?, 176
Definitions, 176
Identification of Students with Sensory Impairments, 178

Prevalence, 178
Service Delivery, 179
Major Characteristics of Students with Sensory Impairments, 179
Academic and Cognitive Performance, 179
Behavior Performance and Social Skills, 180
Effective Instruction for Students with Sensory Impairments, 181
Effective Instruction for Elementary Students, 181
Effective Instruction for Secondary Students, 183
Final Thoughts Regarding Effective Practices, 184
Summary, 185

Chapter 10: **Students with Physical Disabilities, Health Impairments, and Multiple Disabilities, 188**

Perspectives on Including Students with Physical Disabilities, 189
Introduction, 190
Who Are Students with Physical Disabilities, Health Impairments, and Multiple Disabilities?, 190
Definitions, 191
Identification of Students with Physical Disabilities, Health Impairments, and Multiple Disabilities, 194
Prevalence, 194
Service Delivery, 195
Major Characteristics of Students with Physical Disabilities, Health Impairments, and Multiple Disabilities, 195
Academic and Cognitive Performance, 195
Behavior Performance and Social Skills, 196
Effective Instruction for Students with Physical Disabilities, Health Impairments, and Multiple Disabilities, 197
Effective Instruction for Elementary Students, 197
Effective Instruction for Secondary Students, 202
Strategies to Achieve Social Success, 203
Final Thoughts Regarding Effective Practices, 204
Summary, 204

Part III: Effective Practices, 207

Chapter 11: **Collaboration and Teaming, 208**

Perspectives on Collaboration, 209
Introduction, 210
Collaboration: What to Expect, 210
What Is Collaboration?, 211
Dispositions Needed for Successful Collaboration, 213
Skills Needed for Successful Collaboration, 215
Collaborative Roles in Inclusive Schools, 216
Collaborative Teams, 216
Co-Teaching, 217
Collaborative Consultation, 218

Students as Collaborators: Peer Assistance in Inclusive Classrooms
and Schools, 220
    The Peer Buddy Program, 221
Summary, 222
Putting It All Together, 225
Strategy 11.1: Key Components of Effective Collaboration, 227
Strategy 11.2: Communication Skills and Successful Collaboration, 229
Strategy 11.3: Teacher Assistance Teams, 231
Strategy 11.4: Co-Teaching, 233
Strategy 11.5: Working with Paraeducators, 235
Strategy 11.6: Working with Families: Home–School Connection, 239
Strategy 11.7: Peer Buddies, 243

Chapter 12:   Formal Plans and Planning for Differentiated Instruction, 246

Perspectives on Planning, 247
Introduction, 248
Response-to-Intervention Plans, 248
Individualized Education Programs, 249
Section 504 Plans, 250
Behavior Intervention Plans, 251
Planning for Differentiated Instruction, 251
    Getting to Know Your Standards, 253
    Level-1 Planning: Identifying Students' Learning Needs, 254
    Level-2 Planning: Preparing for Daily Instruction, 255
    Level 3 Interactive Planning During Instruction, 258
    Monitoring Student Progress, 259
    Grading Students with Disabilities, 260
    Arranging the Classroom for Inclusion, 260
Summary, 262
Putting It All Together, 265
Strategy 12.1: Contributing to Individualized Educational Programs, 267
Strategy 12.2: Procedures for Developing a 504 Plan, 269
Strategy 12.3: Planning for Differentiated Instruction, 271
Strategy 12.4: Identifying Instructional Needs for Students with Disabilities
                or Special Needs in General Education Classrooms, 273
Strategy 12.5: Planning for Basic Skills Instruction in an Inclusive
                Classroom, 275
Strategy 12.6: Planning for Academic Content Instruction in an Inclusive
                Classroom, 277
Strategy 12.7: Using Curriculum-Based Measures to Measure Student
                Academic Progress, 279
Strategy 12.8: Procedures for Developing a Personalized
                Grading Plan, 281

Chapter 13:   Effective Instruction in Elementary Inclusive Classrooms:
               Teaching Reading, Writing, and Mathematics, 284

Perspectives on Effective Instruction, 285
Introduction, 286

Effective Instruction in an Inclusive Classroom: What to Expect, 287
Principles and Practices to Support Effective Instruction, 288
  Effective Instruction: Teacher Behaviors in Delivering Instruction, 288
  Grouping Students to Support the Delivery of Effective Instruction, 290
  Individual Tutoring, 292
  Peer Tutoring, 292
Effective Instruction in Reading, Writing, and Mathematics, 293
  Reading Instruction, 293
  Writing Instruction, 295
  Mathematics Instruction, 298
Summary, 300
Putting It All Together, 303
Strategy 13.1: Success for All, 305
Strategy 13.2: Cooperative Learning, 307
Strategy 13.3: Reading Recovery, 309
Strategy 13.4: Peer-Assisted Learning Strategies, 311
Strategy 13.5: Beginning Reading: Tiers of Instruction and Response
      to Intervention, 313
Strategy 13.6: Self-Regulated Strategy Development and Writing
      Instruction 315
Strategy 13.7: Cognitive Strategy Instruction for Teaching Math Problem
      Solving, 317

Chapter 14:   Teaching Students in Secondary Content Areas, 320

Perspectives on Teaching Secondary Content to Students
with Disabilities, 321
Introduction, 322
Content Learning Differences: What to Expect, 323
Prerequisites for Inclusive Content-Area Instruction, 324
  Understanding Curriculum, 324
  Working Collaboratively, 325
Models and Approaches for Inclusive Content-Area Instruction, 326
  Universal Design for Learning, 326
  Direct Instruction, 327
  Guided Discovery Learning, 327
  Cooperative Learning, 328
  Learning Strategies, 328
  Content Enhancements, 329
Content Survival Strategies, 330
  Content-Area Reading, 331
  Note Taking, 331
  Test Taking, 332
  Time and Assignment Management, 332
Content-Area Instruction for Students with Severe Disabilities, 333
Summary, 335
Putting It All Together, 337
Strategy 14.1: Content Enhancement: Unit and Lesson Organizers, 339
Strategy 14.2: Improving Expository Writing Across Content-Area
      Classes, 343
Strategy 14.3: Mnemonic Strategies, 347

Strategy 14.4: Content-Area Reading, 349
Strategy 14.5: Developing and Supporting Note Taking, 351
Strategy 14.6: Developing Effective Test Taking, 355

Chapter 15:   Effective Practices for All Students: Classroom Management, 358

Perspectives on Classroom Management, 359
Introduction, 360
Student Behavior: What to Expect, 361
Behavior Management Readiness, 362
    Classroom Organization, 362
    Effective Instruction, 363
    A Climate of Care and Respect, 364
Addressing Student Behavior: Tiered Management, 365
    Universal Inclusive Practice and Supports, 365
    Targeted Interventions, 368
    Functional Behavioral Assessment, 368
    Behavior Intervention Plans, 368
    Wraparound Supports, 373
Summary, 374
Putting It All Together, 377
Strategy 15.1: Developing and Maintaining Rules and Procedures, 379
Strategy 15.2: Surface Management Techniques, 383
Strategy 15.3: Developing Consequences and Delivering Them with Consistency, 385
Strategy 15.4: Defusing Confrontations and Responding to Dangerous Behavior, 387
Strategy 15.5: Check-In, Connect, Check-Out Systems, 389
Strategy 15.6: Behavioral Contracts, 391
Strategy 15.7: Function-Based Thinking, Functional Behavior Assessments, and Behavior Intervention Plans, 393
Strategy 15.8: Direct Teaching of Social Skills: Social Stories, 397

Chapter 16:   Using Technology to Enhance Inclusion, 400

Perspectives on Using Technology to Enhance Inclusion, 401
Introduction, 402
Educational Technology, 403
    Use of Educational Technology in General Education Classrooms, 403
    Using Educational Technology to Facilitate Inclusion, 403
    What You Can Expect from Educational Technology, 405
Assistive Technology, 407
    AT Devices to Support Academic Activities, 408
    Augmentative and Alternative Communication Devices, 409
    Personal Digital Assistants, 412
    AT Devices for Daily Living, 414
    How Effective Is Assistive Technology?, 415

Universal Design for Learning, 415
    Principles of UDL, 415
    Applying UDL Principles, 415
    Example of the Effectiveness of UDL Applications, 418
Summary, 419
Putting It All Together, 421
Strategy 16.1: Teaching Students to Use Educational Technology
            Programs, 423
Strategy 16.2: Using READ 180 in the Classroom, 425
Strategy 16.3: Using the Computer Game PLATO® Achieve Now on PSP®
            (Mathematics) to Improve Students' Homework
            Performance, 427
Strategy 16.4: Evaluating Educational Technology, 429
Strategy 16.5: A Decision-Making Process for Selecting AT Devices, 431
Strategy 16.6: Using Word Processing and Related Software to Support
            Student Writing, 433
Strategy 16.7: Teaching Students with Disabilities to Use Calculators, 435
Strategy 16.8: Supporting Students Who Use AAC Devices, 437
Strategy 16.9: Supporting Students Who Use Motorized Wheelchairs, 439

Glossary, 441

References, 447

Name Index, 465

Subject Index, 473

PART I
Foundations of
Successful Inclusion

Chapter 1

What Is Inclusion, and Why Is It Important?

Chapter 2

Inclusion: Reflections on the Past, Present, and Future

Chapter 3

A Look at Today's Schools: Teaching Students from Diverse Backgrounds

What Is Inclusion, and Why Is It Important?

KEY TOPICS

After reading this chapter you will:

- Be able to describe the categories and qualities of instruction that characterize special education.
- Be able to identify other students who may need accommodations or supports in a general education classroom.
- Understand concepts that support inclusive practices.
- Describe qualities underlying effective inclusive programs.

- Understand research on the effectiveness of inclusive programs.
- Understand your role as a teacher of students with disabilities in an inclusive classroom.
- Be able to describe attitudes of teachers toward inclusion.
- Understand what it takes to be a good teacher for all students.

chapter 1

Introduction

What does being included in a community mean to you? For most of us, being part of a community means that others care for and respect us for who we are, regardless of our particular strengths and shortcomings. It also means that we have a sense of belonging that brings satisfaction and comfort and tangible indicators of having important connections with and support from others. Most of us go to great lengths to achieve this sense of belonging by moving to certain neighborhoods, joining clubs, and participating in productive and meaningful group activities.

For those of us who work with students with disabilities, being part of the school community is often referred to as *inclusion.* In this text, we take the perspective that inclusion is not a place or a classroom setting but is a philosophy of education. *We define inclusion quite simply as including students with disabilities as valued members of the school community.* This suggests that students with disabilities *belong* to the school community and are accepted by others; that they actively *participate* in the academic and social community of the school; and that they are given supports that offer them the *opportunity* to succeed. In short, they participate in the school community in ways that are much the same as other students.

As you reflect on inclusion and what it means to belong, consider the case of Jacob Hartshorne, a 12-year-old with severe multiple disabilities including deaf-blindness (Hartshorne, 2001/2002). As you read about Jacob in Figure 1.1, consider why it is important to ensure that Jacob is included as a fully participating member of his school community.

We agree with Jacob's mother, Nancy Hartshorne, that the efforts to provide inclusion for Jacob and other students with disabilities are worth the effort. However, we also recognize that providing such programs can be challenging, time-consuming, and frustrating. In fact, the reality of how to effectively address the academic and behavioral challenges associated with students with special needs is often daunting to school personnel. Many questions remain regarding effective practices to design, deliver, support, and evaluate inclusive educational programs.

In this text, we present research-based practices with applications and examples from real-world schools and classrooms. It is our view that the process of designing and delivering inclusion is best presented in a practical and straightforward fashion, using a format that integrates evidence-based practices with applications and examples grounded in the real-world experiences of teachers. Consequently, throughout this text, you will notice that we explain a significant amount of content within the context of three successful inclusive schools: Mull Elementary, West Hernando Middle School, and Heritage High School. These schools serve students of different age and grade levels and have diverse student bodies.

myeducationlab

Go to MyEducationLab, select the topic *Inclusive Practices,* and go to the Activities and Applications section. As you complete the simulation entitled "What Do You See?" think about how your perception of students with special needs might impact your teaching.

Pause & Reflect

What does it mean to you to be *included* as part of a community? Perhaps reflecting on instances of when you have been excluded will provide insight into why being included is so important.

Students with disabilities are included in most general education classrooms.

Figure 1.1	Why Include Jacob?

Jacob is a 12-year-old sixth-grade student with severe multiple disabilities including deaf-blindness (Hartshorne, 2001/2002). From ages three to five, Jacob was educated in a classroom for students with severe multiple impairments that was segregated from peers without disabilities. Jacob received all services (including lunch) in the classroom, and the individualized nature of the instructional activities precluded socialization with other children. Furthermore, because physical and language skills were not taught in natural contexts, Jacob had limited opportunities for practicing these skills with peers and limited generalization and maintenance of the skills.

Because of these shortcomings, Jacob's mother, Nancy, advocated for changes in Jacob's education. Consequently, since kindergarten, Jacob has received his educational program in the natural context of his school and classroom beside his same-age peers. How is this done? As a sixth grader, Jacob participates in all classroom activities with the assistance of a one-on-one intervener (a paraeducator with particular skills in addressing the needs of a student who is deaf-blind). Related services such as physical therapy and occupational therapy are delivered in natural contexts (e.g., during physical education). Language is taught and practiced naturally throughout the school day, and Jacob is an active participant in extracurricular activities such as school plays, music concerts, and talent shows. Perhaps most important, Jacob has a strong, active group of friends.

Clearly, in Jacob's case, educators can provide supports for inclusion. However, are all of the creative, high-energy efforts of Jacob's team worth the effort? Jacob's mother is convinced that without inclusive programming, Jacob would not be

- Walking independently and using signs to communicate
- Responding to invitations to birthday parties and having classmates attend his annual birthday bash
- Attending Cub Scout campouts and earning honors for his outstanding participation
- Enjoying the sincere support of his Circle of Friends, which includes 18 students, many of whom have been friends since first grade

Source: From Hartshorne, N. (2001/2002). It sounds nice, but is inclusion really worth it? *Deaf-Blind Perspectives,* 9(2), 12–13. Adapted with permission.

It is important to note that we do not present these schools as examples of ideal inclusive practices. Indeed, the work of developing an inclusive school is never done (McLeskey & Waldron, 2000, 2006), as school professionals must adapt to the ever-changing needs of students. These three schools are no exception, as they continue to actively strive to meet the needs of all of their students. You will hear from the teachers and administrators from these schools throughout this text, as they provide a real-world perspective on their continuing quest to provide effective, inclusive programs for their students. We introduce you to these schools in the accompanying box, "Descriptions of Three Highly Effective, Inclusive Schools."

Inclusion Is for All Students

If you reflect back on your experiences in K–12 general education classrooms, you'll readily recognize that many students have difficulty making academic and social progress in these settings or do not fit in well and need supports or accommodations to succeed. We say this because inclusion is not just about students with disabilities. While much of our focus in this text is on students with disabilities, many of the interventions we describe are useful for a wide range of students who need support in general education classrooms.

This philosophy is illustrated by the perspective taken toward inclusion by teachers and administrators at one of our feature schools, West Hernando Middle School. Principal Joe Clifford says,

> Our philosophy is that when a kid comes into West Hernando Middle School, our teachers and other staff engage in collaborative decision making to decide how to support the kid and help him fit in. We don't have programs for students with certain labels. We look at the individual student, and figure out what will work so the student will fit in. They're everyone's kids and part

Mull Elementary School

Located in Burke County, North Carolina, near the small town of Morganton, Mull Elementary School is housed in a 100+ year-old building and has much of the warmth and charm that are often associated with historic rural schools. Personal relations among professionals, students, and family members are considered important and form a central value in the way education is provided. The cordial greeting that all receive as they walk into the front office sets the tone for the friendly atmosphere that permeates the school.

Jill King, Mull's principal, leads a staff of over 50, including teachers and other professionals, paraeducators, and noninstructional personnel. Statistically, the 400 students in grades K–5 at Mull reflect the demographics of the region. The large majority, 89%, are non-Hispanic European American children, while African American, Hispanic, and Asian students about evenly represent the remainder. Approximately half of the students are eligible for free or reduced lunch, and about 12% are identified with disabilities.

Until a couple of years ago, Mull used a very traditional approach to special education. Students who were struggling academically or behaviorally were referred for evaluation and tested to determine their eligibility for special education services. Typically, these students were making inadequate academic progress but were not identified until their problems became so formidable that they failed in general education. They were then referred for possible special education services, and many were identified with a mild disability (i.e., a learning disability, a mild intellectual disability, or an emotional and behavioral disability). Once identified, most of these students received special education services in a separate classroom.

The administration and special education faculty at Mull were concerned about three significant problems with this approach. First, they had to "wait for failure" before they could begin to offer the students the help they needed. Second, the separate-class, or pull-out, model wasn't providing enough direct instruction to students after they had been identified. Finally, a number of students who were challenged by the grade-level curriculum and needed assistance remained ineligible for special education services.

As these problems were recognized, the North Carolina Department of Public Instruction initiated a pilot program in which a number of schools throughout the state were asked to participate in the evolving response-to-intervention (RTI) model for determining eligibility for special education. RTI models are developed based on the assumption that as students fall behind academically in the early grades, they should receive the necessary intensive instruction to catch up with peers rather than waiting to fail to receive services. Interventions are initially provided as part of the general education curriculum and increase in intensity only if a student continues to lag behind peers. (We describe the RTI approach to student identification and service delivery in more detail in Chapters 4 and 13.)

The administration and staff at Mull saw many advantages to using the RTI model and decided to get on board with it. As they did so, they also realized that if their special education teachers and general education teachers could work together as co-teachers in general education classrooms, they not only could increase the amount of appropriate instruction provided to students with special needs but also could better serve those students who were experiencing difficulty but were not eligible for special education. So Mull melded together the concepts of RTI and inclusion.

Under the leadership of Principal Jill King, a Student Success Team (SST) was formed to oversee the RTI model and to facilitate the inclusion of students with disabilities in general education classrooms. Besides the principal, the team includes two special education teachers, Cathy Danford and Becky Wyke; the school counselor, Anne Vogler; and Margaret Gordon, the school speech–language therapist. The SST works closely with classroom teachers to implement the RTI procedures. Additionally, Cathy and Becky work in the inclusive classrooms as co-teachers with a number of the school's general education teachers.

This model has been quite successful. "The greatest thing is that we don't have to wait for them to fail," explained Jill. "As soon as we see a problem, we jump on it." This has resulted in success for most students, and a reduction in the number of students identified with disabilities. Furthermore, those students who are identified with disabilities continue to be included in general education classrooms. In most reading and math classes, the special education teacher and the classroom teacher co-teach using whole-group instruction as well as small-group and individualized instruction as students need additional support. Within the class, no distinctions are made between those in special education and those who simply need high-quality instruction.

Although at first glance Mull Elementary might seem like an "old-fashioned" school, in reality the staff works to provide high-quality instruction based on individual student needs. The RTI program and inclusive classrooms allow children to receive effective instruction before years of failure. The goal is to have every student, whether identified with a disability or not, achieve success and remain an accepted member of the Mull school community. It's a goal many schools can emulate.

West Hernando Middle School

West Hernando Middle School is located outside the small town of Brooksville, Florida, in rapidly growing Hernando County, a suburban area 50 miles north of Tampa. West Hernando enrolls approximately 1,100 students in grades 6 through 8 and is the county's cluster school for

students with disabilities. About 75% of the shcool's students are European American, while the remaining 25% are Hispanic, African American, multi-ethnic, or Asian. Over 20% of the students have disabilities, while 51% qualify for free or reduced lunch, making West Hernando a Title I school.

Joe Clifford has been the principal of West Hernando for the past 9 years. He came to the school as an energetic, popular assistant principal, who brought many of his own teachers and administrators to the school to build on an already existing philosophy of including and supporting all students. An inclusive philosophy pervades the West Hernando school community in all activities and is reflected in the belief statement that guides the work of the school improvement team and all school staff. This statement follows:

WHMS students soar with WINGS (W—Wise choices, I—Innovative learning, N—new challenges, G—Good citizenship, S—Strong positive attitudes). WHMS faculty and staff work to create an environment where all community stakeholders embrace innovative learning strategies and new challenges. We intend to accomplish this by encouraging strong positive attitudes, good citizenship and by recognizing students' wise choices. We are dedicated to providing a rigorous curriculum delivered through research-based programs and practices with differentiated instruction to insure that all students can and will learn.

Joe Clifford describes how these beliefs play out every day as the "West Hernando Way." This is obvious to a visitor when entering the school, as a quote by Booker T. Washington is prominently displayed on the building opposite the entry: "If you want to lift yourself up, lift up someone else." It is also obvious from observing students walking in halls, congregating in the large courtyard, or interacting in classrooms. Teachers and students at West Hernando are a community of learners who support one another in a range of ways, formal and informal, large and small. Joe Clifford notes that this leads to a philosophy that teachers collaborate to ensure that all students fit in, without differentiating students by using labels or by determining who is "your" student and who is "my" student. As Joe Clifford says, "All students at West Hernando are *our* students!"

Throughout the chapters that follow, we'll discuss many of the instructional approaches used at West Hernando to support students with disabilities in general education classrooms and as part of the school community. These activities include co-teaching, peer buddies, differentiated instruction, grouping practices, collaborative teaming, and a range of other effective practices. However, the most powerful aspect of the education students receive at West Hernando Middle School is the dedication of the school staff and students to build a community that supports and includes all students and the pride that staff and students feel in being part of this special community. The large, open courtyard at West Hernando where students congregate and build community perhaps best illustrates this.

Over each of the past 9 years, a major project has been undertaken to add to the courtyard, under the leadership of Mr. Clifford, teachers, and parents. These projects take several months to complete and require the active engagement of a large part of the school community. Projects have included building an aviary, a butterfly garden, a bridge, cisterns, and a hydroponic greenhouse. This year the school community is working with Mr. James Gibson from Tampa, one of the well-known Florida artists who have been called the "Highwaymen." Mr. Gibson has given his permission for the construction of a mosaic of one of his works of art and will attend a ceremony to dedicate the mosaic later in the school year. Students benefit academically by participating in these projects, but perhaps as importantly, the projects help to build community and pride in their school.

The success of West Hernando can be measured in several ways, including the awards the school has received (an "A" school in Florida, meeting 97% of NCLB goals, and receiving an award from the governor of Florida as one of the Top 50 Combination Schools for Making Progress in the state); the rates at which students with a range of disabilities are included in general education classrooms (50% above the state average); or by student academic progress, as measured by several state and local tests. By any of these measures, WHMS excels. It also excels as an extraordinary middle school, where all students belong to a school community that provides academic and social support, and strives to ensure that every student is successful. As Principal Joe Clifford says, "My responsibility is not just to create an environment where students are academically successful, but also to create an environment where students learn to become caring, patient, loving, tolerant human beings. And to create this environment for all kids. That's why, while most things are negotiable at WHMS, inclusion is not."

Heritage High School

Heritage High School, a modern comprehensive high school of approximately 1,750 students, is located in Leesburg, Virginia. Leesburg, the county seat of Loudoun County, is a historic area, having once, during the War of 1812, been the temporary location for the U.S. government and its archives. The areas surrounding the town center are also known for their Civil War battlefields (e.g., Antietam). Located at the far end of the densely populated Washington, DC, and Northern Virginia corridor, Leesburg has experienced tremendous growth in population, particularly among Hispanic and Asian immigrant groups. Reflecting the influx of families from these cultures, Heritage High School is considerably diverse, with 17% of its students of Hispanic origin, 14% African American, and 9% of Asian descent. The remaining 60% are European American. Among all students enrolled, approximately 16% are eligible for free or reduced lunch, and 12.6% have identified disabilities.

Margaret Huckaby, the founding principal of Heritage, had the rare and challenging opportunity of developing the school's administrative structure, climate, and culture from the ground up. With an energetic, positive, and creative interactive style, she garnered considerable input from all of the school's stakeholders—from cafeteria workers to psychologists—to articulate a mission statement for the school. This statement has served as the foundation for developing student-centered approaches and procedures to provide sustained success for all students.

Visitors to Heritage can readily see the results of these efforts: Collaboration and empowerment pervade the school's administrative, instructional, and extracurricular policies and activities. Teams of administrators, teachers, and professional staff work together, ensuring that all students have opportunities to receive supportive instruction and caring related services. This teaming is not left to chance: Margaret and her administrative staff are sensitive to interpersonal dynamics and form teams that build on how teachers' strengths can be combined to improve student outcomes.

Heritage High's efforts at collaborative teaming have resulted in a number of impressive outcomes. The school routinely scores well above the state average on Virginia State Report Card measures, resulting in the all-important designation of adequate yearly progress (AYP). Numerous Advanced Placement courses are offered, and approximately one third of graduating students receive the Governor's Seal on their Advanced Studies Diploma.

Perhaps the most notable element of teaming at Heritage is the day-to-day operation of its inclusive education philosophy. Monitored and nurtured by Dean of Students Susan Hill, special education services are delivered in a variety of individualized ways, depending on the unique needs of the student. Most students at Heritage receive their special education services within general education content classrooms. Depending on the instructional and behavioral profile of the student, special education teachers either consult or co-teach with general education content area specialists. Teachers often use universal designed instructional techniques (adaptations and accommodations that are useful for students with and without disabilities) or curricular supports in lessons and unit plans. In many other cases, classes are actively co-taught by both highly qualified general and special education teachers. Because co-teaching has been a mainstay of the Heritage instructional delivery system since the school opened, it is not viewed as strange or unusual: It is just the way things are done at Heritage.

Some students at Heritage require supplemental supports in addition to what is provided in their general education classrooms. For these students, small-group sessions are arranged and delivered in a private area of the school (i.e., the library) or another classroom. Students with significant disabilities are included in general education classrooms for social, behavioral, and general knowledge exposure and also may spend time receiving direct instruction in separate class settings. Peer Teams are employed to support these students in their classrooms and during extracurricular activities.

Things are not perfect at Heritage. Situations arise that require swift action, creative problem solving, and sometimes difficult decision making. However, with a solid foundation of administrative support and collaborative teaming, staff feel empowered and supported in their attempts to address the many issues typical of teaching and managing large numbers of developing adolescents.

of our community. We're all responsible for making sure they're successful. This is inclusion for us.

We provide information that illustrates the diversity of the general education classroom in the following sections. In addition to students with disability, students in general education classes who contribute to this diversity and may need accommodations include students who are at risk for difficulty in school, students from diverse cultural and linguistic backgrounds, students who are eligible for services under Section 504, and students identified as gifted and talented.

Many students with and without disabilities need supports to succeed in general education classrooms.

Students with Disabilities and Special Education

In the most basic sense, special education consists of services and supports that teachers provide to meet the needs of students who are identified with disabilities. While the categories used to define disabilities vary across states, most use some variation of the federal definitions of disability categories. Table 1.1 includes the terms used by the federal government in the Individuals with Disabilities Education Improvement Act, or PL 108-446 (IDEA, 2004), as well as brief descriptions of disability categories.

As you will note, these disability categories include a broad range of students with abilities and disabilities related to cognitive, social, physical, and sensory skills. To simplify disability categories, some states use more general categories such as *mild-to-moderate disabilities* and *significant disabilities*. The mild-to-moderate category includes most students who are identified with learning disabilities and speech or language impairment and some students from other categories (e.g., autism, other health impairments, intellectual disabilities). About 90% of students with disabilities are included in the mild-to-moderate category. The significant disability category includes about 10% of all students, and most students who are identified with multiple disabilities and deaf-blindness fall into this category. In addition, some students in several other categories may be identified with significant disabilities (e.g., autism and intellectual disabilities).

On average, about 11.4% of students are identified with disabilities (U.S. Department of Education, 2007a). Special education services and supports are specially designed to meet the needs of these students. Several factors make special education "special," including the following (Kauffman & Hallahan, 2005):

- **Intensity.** Special education instruction may involve adjusting the intensity of instruction provided to a student. More time for direct instruction and practice are critical elements of more intense instruction. This may involve a lower teacher–pupil ratio, using strategies such as class-wide peer tutoring, cooperative learning, or co-teaching.
- **Structure.** Students with disabilities are provided with learning conditions that are more organized, explicit, and predictable.
- **Curriculum.** While almost all students with disabilities learn based on the general education curriculum, many of these students require specialized supports and accommodations to access this material. Some students with significant disabilities require an alternative

Table 1.1   Disability Categories and Definitions from PL 108-446, IDEA 2004

Disability Category	Brief Definition
Learning disability (called specific learning disability in IDEA, 2004)	This very diverse category includes students who have difficulty making adequate academic progress in school, especially in basic skill areas such as reading, writing, and/or mathematics.
Speech or language impairment	Most students in this category have mild speech disorders (e.g., difficulty articulating certain speech sounds) and are included in general education classrooms for most of the school day.
Other health impairments	Includes a range of health impairments (e.g., epilepsy, diabetes) that adversely affect a student's educational performance. Attention-deficit/hyperactivity disorder (ADHD) is also included.
Intellectual disabilities (called mental retardation in IDEA, 2004)	Includes a broad range of students, from those with mild impairments in intellectual and adaptive skills to those with significant impairments.
Emotional disturbance	Includes a group of students who exhibit aggressive behavior as well as those who have more internalized emotional disorders (e.g., pervasive unhappiness or depression).
Autism	Autism (often referred to as *autism spectrum disorders*) is a developmental disability significantly affecting verbal and nonverbal communication and social interaction. The number of students identified with autism has grown rapidly in recent years, largely due to the identification of increasing numbers of students with milder forms of autism, such as Asperger's syndrome.
Multiple disabilities	Includes students who have disabilities in more than one area (e.g., intellectual disability and blindness, intellectual disability and orthopedic impairment) that often result in severe impairments and significant educational needs.
Developmental delay	This category is used at the discretion of states, and is thus not used in every state. It is typically used to identify children before they enter first grade but can be used from ages 3 through 9. *Developmental delay* may describe students who experience delays in physical, cognitive, communication, emotional, or adaptive development.
Hearing impairments and deafness	Students with hearing impairments have some residual hearing that may be used to understand oral speech (i.e., they are not deaf). In contrast, children who are deaf lack such residual hearing.
Orthopedic impairments	Students with orthopedic impairments have physical limitations and may use a wheelchair. These students have a range of intellectual abilities but may have difficulty demonstrating this ability without specialized supports.
Visual impairments including blindness	Includes students who are blind and those with significant visual impairments.
Traumatic brain injury	This is the only category limited to students who acquire a disability after birth. Traumatic brain injury means an acquired injury to the brain caused by an external physical force, resulting in total or partial functional disability or psychosocial impairment, or both, that adversely affects a child's educational performance.
Deaf-blindness	This is the smallest disability category, and only includes individuals with significant educational needs.

Note: Complete federal definitions for each category of disability are provided in Chapters 4 to 10.

curriculum for some part of the school day that addresses basic life skills, alternative communication skills, or social skills.

- **Collaboration.** For a successful educational experience, professionals from general and special education must combine their expertise to address the needs of students with disabilities.
- **Monitoring/assessment.** Teachers monitor the students' progress in an academic area, and adjust instructional methods based on this information. Thus, teachers may use a variety of approaches if a student with a disability has difficulty learning critical elements of the curriculum.

Other Students Who May Need Support in the General Education Classroom

As we noted previously, many students who do not have disabilities may need supports to succeed in general education classrooms. Indeed, many teachers and other school professionals have noted that the effective practices used in inclusive classrooms are beneficial for many students who do not have disabilities but struggle academically or socially. As Cathy Dofka, Director of Special Education in Hernando County Florida (and for West Hernando Middle School), notes, "Inclusion benefits all students academically and socially. Effective teaching methods are good for all students who struggle, not just those with disabilities." Students who benefit from these practices may include students who are at risk for difficulty in school, students from diverse cultural and linguistic backgrounds, students who are eligible for services under Section 504, and students identified as gifted and talented.

Students at Risk for Difficulties in School. Students who grow up in poverty are at greater risk than other students for having academic or social difficulty in school. Of course, many students who have risk factors in their backgrounds do quite well in school, while for others these factors may contribute to difficulty in school. At least five factors related to growing up in poverty influence student performance in school (Kauchak & Eggen, 2008). These factors are:

Fulfillment of basic needs, including sufficient nutrition, medical care

Family stability, including parent frustration and marital stability related to economic struggle

School-related experiences, including exposure to educational experiences (e.g., visits to museums, libraries) or educational activities (e.g., computer classes, dance lessons) outside of school

Interaction patterns in the home, including the use of less elaborate language, and the tendency to "tell" rather than to "explain"

Parental attitudes and values, including the value placed on getting a good education and reading in the home

Students who are at risk in school are placed in general education classrooms and are the responsibility of general education teachers. We provide a more detailed discussion of issues related to growing up in poverty in Chapter 3. In addition, in Chapters 11 to 16 we include separate sections entitled "Effective Practices," which describe many practices that teachers may use to address the needs of students who are at risk for school failure.

Students from Diverse Cultural and Linguistic Backgrounds. Another major component of diversity in general education classrooms relates to students from culturally and linguistically diverse backgrounds. These students often come from backgrounds that are different from their teachers, who most often are European American. In 2004 (National Center for Educational Statistics, 2007), approximately 43% of all school-aged students in the United States were from non-European American backgrounds. This includes 18.9% of students who are of Hispanic or Latino origin, and 17.0% who are African American. Further adding to the diversity in classrooms across the United States is the range of languages that are spoken. The U.S. Census Bureau (2007) reported that in 2006, a language other than English was spoken in 17.9% of all homes.

Educators and researchers (Ross, Kamman, & Coady, 2008) have recommended that to better meet the needs of individuals from diverse language and cultural backgrounds, all teachers should

- Better understand the students' cultural and linguistic backgrounds.
- Learn to adapt teaching based on this information to ensure positive student outcomes.

We provide additional information regarding students from culturally and linguistically diverse backgrounds in Chapter 3. We intend this information to help you better understand the backgrounds of these students and how this information affects instruction in general education classrooms.

Students with Disabilities Who Are Eligible Under Section 504. As you have seen in Table 1.1, definitions of disability categories from IDEA include criteria for identifying students, as well as the stipulation that the disability adversely affects educational performance. When a student is eligible for special education services based on one of these definitions, she will have a written individualized education program (IEP) that describes the special educational services to which she is entitled. However, students who are not eligible for services as part of IDEA may still be eligible for classroom accommodations as part of Section 504 of the Rehabilitation Act of 1973.

Section 504 is not an education act, but a civil rights law that was passed to protect the rights of persons with disabilities, and to prevent discrimination. This act has a broader definition of disability than IDEA 2004, which stipulates that the student must be determined to (1) have a physical or mental impairment that substantially limits one or more major life activities, (2) have a record of such an impairment, or (3) be regarded as having such an impairment (U.S. Department of Education, 2007b).

Students who are frequently provided accommodations in many states based on Section 504 include students with attention-deficit/hyperactivity disorder (ADHD). For example, if a student is identified with a mild attention-deficit disorder that does not adversely affect educational performance, the student may be eligible for certain accommodations (e.g., added time to complete a test) under Section 504. The specific accommodations will typically be carried out in a general education classroom and will be described as part of a 504 Plan. Many of the instructional practices described in the "Effective Practices" sections (see Chapters 11 to 16) may be used to address the needs of students who have 504 Plans.

Students Who Are Gifted and Talented. Children who are identified as gifted or talented are those who learn academic content in one or more areas much more rapidly than most other students, or have high levels of performance ability in visual or performing arts, creativity, or leadership. In some states, students who are identified as gifted or talented must meet a cutoff for IQ and/or achievement (e.g., an IQ cutoff of 130 or higher) that is significantly higher than average performance by peers (Jones & Southern, 2008).

Gifted and talented is not a category of disability, and is thus not addressed in IDEA 2004. Identification criteria and funding for programs for these students are typically addressed in state law. The level of support for gifted and talented programs across the United States varies widely. Many general education classrooms have students who achieve at a level that is much higher than most other peers in the class. Some of these students are assigned to separate classes (e.g., advanced mathematics) for part of the school day. Further, many schools have teachers who provide support for gifted and talented students in general education classrooms.

Pause & Reflect

When someone says, "special education," what words come to mind? Historically, most of the words that have come to mind for many have been negative. Why is this the case? How are attitudes changing as a result of the inclusion of increasing numbers of persons with disabilities in schools and the community?

Concepts That Support Inclusive Practices

Two critical concepts provide the foundation on which inclusive practices are built. These concepts are *normalization* and the *least restrictive environment*.

Normalization

The concept of normalization originated in Scandinavia and was initially used to address individuals with intellectual disabilities or mental retardation. This concept has since been applied to all people with disabilities. Bengt Nirjie defined *normalization* as "making available to all mentally retarded people patterns of life and conditions of everyday living, which are as close as possible to the regular circumstances and ways of life of society" (p. 6, cited in Biklen, 1985). This suggests that persons with disabilities should have the opportunity to live their lives as independently as possible, making their own life decisions regarding work, leisure, housing, and so forth. See Figure 1.2 for an example of this principle.

Inclusion is intended to provide students with disabilities a school experience that is as typical as possible.

This concept sharply contrasts perspectives on people with disabilities that were previously held by many educators and the general public. For example, people with intellectual disabilities were long held to be "eternal children," who needed to be protected and could not live independently or make their own life decisions. In contrast, the concept of normalization suggests that people with disabilities should be self-determined, making their own life decisions, and should be accorded the dignity of risk, rather than protection, in making decisions about their lives as they grow older, similar to other individuals. Furthermore, a goal of schooling for people with disabilities should be to provide them with the knowledge and skills needed to lead as typical a life as possible, and to live as independently as possible, with a job, a place to live in the community, and leisure activities that result in a full, enjoyable, productive life.

Cathy Dofka, Director of Special Education in Hernando County, Florida, emphasizes the importance of this perspective, when she states, "Students with disabilities have been too isolated in separate classes, where they only see other students with disabilities. They don't learn to get along with other people in these settings. You don't have (a special education) Wal-Mart or Publix. Students with disabilities need to learn to get along in a community with everyone else."

The wide acceptance of the concept of normalization led to increased expectations for life outcomes and increased value for the lives of people with disabilities. This has led disability rights advocates to demand the use of more respectful language when discussing persons with disabilities, including the use of people-first language. (For more information regarding people-first

---

Figure 1.2   An Example of the Principle of Normalization

Nirje has described one of his favorite illustrations of the principle of normalization (Biklen, 1985). While he was president of the Swedish Association for Retarded Children, Nirje asked a group of adults with intellectual disabilities what requests they would make to change national policies that affect their lives. These individuals did not ask to be given special privileges (e.g., preference for housing during a housing shortage that all Swedes faced at the time). Presumably, they already received enough treatment that they viewed as "special." Rather, they said that they wanted to go on outings (e.g., shopping) in groups of two or three rather than in large groups. Further, they did not want to go to camps for persons with intellectual disabilities, but rather wanted to vacation like everyone else, in vacation resorts in Europe. In short, persons with intellectual disabilities wanted to be treated like everyone else, and have the same opportunities as others, and not to receive special activities or privileges because of their disability.

Pause & Reflect

Is people-first language important, or is it an over-reaction to a minor concern? What language have you heard being used in schools to describe people with disabilities? In social settings outside of school? What does this language say about our attitudes toward people with disabilities?

language, see Figure 1.3.) Furthermore, inclusive practices in schools are built on the assumption that the principle of normalization should be applied in school settings; that is, students with disabilities should have school experiences that are as typical as possible, and student differences should be accommodated in as typical a manner as possible. Further, it is assumed that this type of school experience will be more effective in preparing a person with a disability to live an independent, self-determined life as an adult.

Least Restrictive Environment

A second concept that provides support for inclusion in federal law is the **least restrictive environment (LRE)** mandate. This mandate was included in the IDEA when the U.S. Congress initially passed it in 1975 (the law was then called the Education for All Handicapped Children Act). The LRE mandate states that "To the maximum extent appropriate, children with disabilities . . . are educated with children who are non-disabled; and special classes, separate schooling, or other removal of children with disabilities from the regular educational environment occurs only if the nature or severity of the disability is such that education in regular classes with the use of supplementary aids and services cannot be achieved satisfactorily" (PL 108-446, IDEA, 2004, Regulations Part 300, Sec. 300.114).

While the term *inclusion* is not included in federal law, the LRE mandate creates a presumption in favor of educating students with disabilities in the general education classroom (Williamson, McLeskey, Hoppey, & Rentz, 2006). The law is interpreted to mean that every

Figure 1.3	People-First Language

People-first language emphasizes that persons with disabilities are just that: people who happen to have an intellectual, sensory, physical, or emotional disability. Language should be used that is respectful of people with disabilities. For example, language should not be used to express pity for persons with disabilities, nor should words that are used to describe people with disabilities be used in negative ways. For example, "He's a *retard.*" Some terms have taken on such a negative connotation that they are no longer used to describe people with disabilities (e.g., *retarded* or *handicapped,* suggesting a person begging with "cap in hand"). Language describing a disability should be used only when necessary. It often isn't necessary to point out that a person has a disability. Suggestions for using respectful, people-first language include the following:

People-First Language	Inappropriate Language
Disability	Handicap
Intellectual disability	Retarded or mental retardation
John has an intellectual disability.	John is retarded.
Nancy uses a wheelchair.	Nancy is wheelchair bound (or confined to a wheelchair).
Dane has cerebral palsy.	Dane suffers from cerebral palsy.
Karson has Down syndrome.	She's Down's.
The boy with a learning disability	The learning disabled boy

Source: For more information on people-first language, see www.disabilityisnatural.com.

student with a disability has a right to be educated in a classroom with peers without disabilities, if they can succeed in that setting with appropriate supports. Thus, students with disabilities should be placed in more restrictive settings (i.e., a separate, special education class, or separate school) only if they do not succeed in the general education classroom with supports and if the separate class can lead to more success than the general education placement.

To ensure that the needs of all students with disabilities are met, IDEA 2004 requires provision of a continuum of services for students with disabilities. Figure 1.4 provides a description of the continuum of services as it exists in most school systems. As you will note in this figure, placement options differ based on the time students with disabilities spend in the general education classroom with peers without disabilities.

General Education Classroom. Approximately 54% of students with disabilities are provided services in a general education classroom for most of the school day. If separate special education services are provided, the student is in a separate classroom for no more than 20% of the school day. This placement includes students who are in a general education classroom full-time, with only consultation services from a special education teacher; students who are served in a general education classroom that is co-taught by a general and a special education teacher; and students who are provided short-term, intensive instruction in particular content areas (e.g., reading, learning strategies) or instructional support in specific content areas (e.g., science, social studies) in separate, special education settings.

Part-Time Special Education Classroom. Located in the local school, part-time special education classrooms are often referred to as *resource classes*. In these settings, a small number of students with disabilities (e.g., three to eight) are provided instruction for short periods of time in basic skills (i.e., reading, writing, mathematics), tutorial support in specific subjects, or instruction in the use of learning strategies. Students with disabilities who are in part-time special education classes spend from 21% to 60% of the school day in these settings, and the remainder of the day in a general education classroom. A special education teacher and/or a paraeducator, under the supervision of a special education teacher, provide services in these part-time classes. Approximately 25% of all students with disabilities are served in these settings.

Full-Time Special Education Classroom. Approximately 17% of all students with disabilities are served in full-time special education classrooms on local school campuses. These students with disabilities spend most of the school day (60% or more) in a classroom with other students

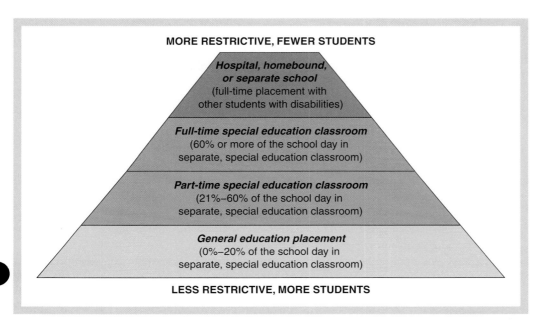

MORE RESTRICTIVE, FEWER STUDENTS

Hospital, homebound, or separate school
(full-time placement with other students with disabilities)

Full-time special education classroom
(60% or more of the school day in separate, special education classroom)

Part-time special education classroom
(21%–60% of the school day in separate, special education classroom)

General education placement
(0%–20% of the school day in separate, special education classroom)

LESS RESTRICTIVE, MORE STUDENTS

Figure 1.4

Continuum of Educational Services for Students with Disabilities

with similar disabilities. These classrooms typically include a small number of students (5–15, depending on the severity of the disabilities and the number of professionals in the classroom), a special education teacher, and one or more paraeducators. Students most often served in these settings include those with intellectual disabilities, emotional disturbance, multiple disabilities, deaf-blindness, and autism.

Hospital, Homebound, Separate Residential Schools, and Separate Day Schools. Students who are educated in these settings attend school full-time in a placement other than their neighborhood schools. These schools may be separate settings in the local school system, or residential schools in another city where students live full-time during the school year. Separate schools are designed to provide highly specialized instruction and supports for students with disabilities and often include students from a single disability category (e.g., deaf or hearing impaired, blind or visually impaired, significant intellectual disabilities, serious emotional disturbance), or a limited number of disability categories. Approximately 4% of all students with disabilities are served in these settings.

What Are Effective Inclusive Programs?

You will note that none of the service-delivery settings we described are called "inclusive." This is because inclusion is not a place or a setting. As we noted previously, we view inclusion as a philosophy of education, and we define *inclusion* quite simply as including students with disabilities as valued members of the school community. This suggests that students with disabilities *belong* to the school community and are accepted by others; that they actively *participate* in the academic and social community of the school; and that they are given supports that offer them the *opportunity to succeed*. In short, they participate in the school community in ways that are much the same as other students.

Not all educators define *inclusion* in the same way. It is important to seek clarification when discussing inclusion to ensure a clear understanding of the intended meaning of the term. For example, much controversy has surrounded the use of the term **full inclusion**, and the perspective taken by some that all students with disabilities should be included in general education classes for the entire school day (Fuchs & Fuchs, 1994; Kauffman, 1993; McLeskey, 2007). Still others have engaged in inclusion that could be characterized as irresponsible, as they have moved students with disabilities into general education classrooms with little planning and with little support for general education teachers (Dymond & Russell, 2004; Kauffman, Lloyd, Baker, & Riedel, 1995; Pivik, McComas, & Laflamme, 2002), resulting in poor outcomes for students with and without disabilities, and much frustration on the part of their teachers.

When we discuss inclusive programs or classrooms in this text, we refer to well-designed, effective inclusive programs. We thus assume the following regarding these programs:

1. All students with disabilities are part of the academic and social community of the school. They are valued members of the school, and participate in the school community in much the same way as all other students.
2. Most students with disabilities are educated for most of the school day in general education classrooms, while instruction is provided in separate settings as needed.
3. Student academic and social progress is monitored to ensure improved student outcomes. Educational materials, instruction, and/or placement are changed as needed to ensure improved student outcomes.
4. Resources, including both personnel and materials, are available to provide appropriate supports for students in general education classrooms.
5. Time is available to allow general and special education teachers and other professionals to collaboratively plan the delivery of services and their instructional roles. This time is available to

Pause & Reflect

Does it surprise you that persons with disabilities want the same things from school that all other students want? Do you think these students want the same things from life? What does this say about the importance of inclusive programs in schools?

plan the inclusive program before it begins, as well as to conduct ongoing planning once the program is implemented.

6. Teachers are provided professional development to learn new skills needed to provide students with appropriate services.

7. Teachers adapt the general education curriculum to meet the needs of all students. This may include providing supports to ensure access to the general education curriculum or providing alternative curriculum for some students with highly specialized needs.

8. Teachers plan instruction so that most student needs are met as a natural part of the school day.

9. Teachers provide classroom supports in a manner that is natural and unobtrusive. These supports are used with a range of students, not just those with disabilities, and serve to make student differences a natural part of the school day.

Most of the needs of students with disabilities should be met as a natural part of the school day.

10. The rhythm of the school day for students with disabilities is similar to the rhythm of the day for all students. The schedules of students with disabilities are similar to those of other students, and their school day is not identifiable because they have a disability.

Inclusive Programs: Research on Effectiveness

Much controversy has surrounded research on the effectiveness of inclusive programs (Fuchs & Fuchs, 1994; Kauffman, 1993; Kavale & Forness, 2000; McLeskey, 2007; McLeskey & Waldron, 1996). This controversy largely relates to how effectiveness is defined. Some have argued that researchers, educators, and policy makers have all placed too much emphasis on providing students with disabilities access to general education classrooms in neighborhood schools and too little emphasis on improving student outcomes (Fuchs & Fuchs, 1994; Kavale & Forness, 2000). These criticisms have taken on added importance with the passage of the No Child Left Behind (NCLB) Act (2001), which mandates that all schools must be held accountable for educational outcomes for all students, including those with disabilities.

With the passage of the NCLB Act, local schools now must ensure access to the general education classroom for students with disabilities and also ensure improved student outcomes. As we're sure you would speculate based on the previous information in this chapter, as well as any previous experience you've had with inclusion, it is not a simple task to develop an effective, inclusive program. However, research evidence supports the effectiveness of well-designed inclusive programs (e.g., Cole, Waldron, & Madj, 2004; Salend & Garrick Duhaney, 2007). These programs allow students with disabilities to benefit from access to the general education curriculum, as well as to have intensive, focused instruction in critical skill areas (i.e., reading, writing, mathematics). They also provide a context for developing social skills, making friendships, and so forth, that serve to prepare all students, including those with disabilities, for a successful, independent life beyond their school years. Key findings from research regarding the academic and social benefits of inclusive programs are included in Figure 1.5.

As Figure 1.5 reveals, many students with disabilities benefit from well-designed inclusive programs in a range of ways. However, three caveats should be noted regarding this research. First, several studies have revealed that students with disabilities do not make improved academic progress when inclusive programs are not well designed (Baines, Baines, & Masterson, 1994; Dymond & Russell, 2004; Fox & Ysseldyke, 1997; Pivik, McComas, & Laflamme, 2002).

Figure 1.5	Research on Academic and Social Outcomes for Students in Inclusive Placements

- Students with disabilities do at least as well, and often better, on academics in inclusive programs than when they are educated in resource or self-contained classrooms (Cole, Waldron, & Madj, 2004; Freeman & Alkin, 2000; Rea, McLaughlin, & Walther-Thomas, 2002; Ryndak, Morrison, & Sommerstein, 1999; Salend & Garrick Duhaney, 2007; Waldron & McLeskey, 1998; Waldron, McLeskey, & Pacchiano, 1999).
- Students with disabilities in inclusive programs benefit from improved work habits, increased self-confidence, increased willingness to take risks, and more on-task or attentive behavior (Dore, Dion, Wagner, & Brunet, 2002; Foreman, Arthur-Kelly, Pascoe, & King, 2004; Waldron, McLeskey, & Pacchiano, 1999).
- Students without disabilities do at least as well, and often better, academically when educated in a well-designed inclusive classroom (Cole, et al., 2004; Manset & Semmel, 1997; Salend & Garrick Duhaney, 2007).
- Given appropriate supports, inclusive placements have been shown to improve self-esteem, increase interactions with other students, improve social competence, result in students' developing richer and more long-lasting friendships, and improve social status of students with disabilities (Boutot & Bryant, 2005; Freeman & Alkin, 2000; Salend & Duhaney, 1999; Salend & Garrick Duhaney, 2007).
- Students without disabilities benefit socially from inclusion through increased personal growth, appreciation and acceptance of other children, feelings of accomplishment as they provide assistance to others, development of friendships with students with mild and significant disabilities, and improved understanding of disability-related issues (Boutot & Bryant, 2005; Burstein, Sears, Wilcoxen, Cabello, & Spagna, 2004; Carter & Hughes, 2006; Gun Han & Chadsey, 2004; Idol, 2006; Lee, Yoo, & Bak, 2003; Peck, Staub, Galucci, & Schwartz, 2004; Salend & Duhaney, 1999).

In fact, these investigations reveal that poorly designed inclusive programs may have negative effects on academic outcomes for students with disabilities as well as their peers without disabilities.

A second caveat relates to the fact that no matter how well an inclusive program is designed, most research has revealed that some students with disabilities do not make as much academic progress as we'd like them to make (McLeskey, 2007; McLeskey & Waldron, 1995; Zigmond et al., 1995a). To improve outcomes of inclusive programs, some researchers have studied the use of well-designed, intensive, small-group instruction to support inclusive program placements (Madden & Slavin, 1983; Manset & Semmel, 1997; Marston, 1996; Rashotte, MacPhee, & Torgesen, 2001; Torgesen, 2000; Zigmond et al., 1995b). Several of these programs have resulted in improved student achievement outcomes. This instruction occurs for brief periods of time, includes small groups of students (e.g., two to five students) who have similar academic needs, focuses on the development of certain academic skills (e.g., phonemic awareness), and includes frequent assessment of student progress to ensure the effectiveness of the intervention (S. Deno, 2007; Marston, 1996).

Finally, research has revealed that simply placing students with disabilities in general education classrooms does not improve social skills or social status (Dore, Dion, Wagner, & Brunet, 2002). It is often necessary for teachers in inclusive classrooms to provide instruction and support to ensure that social interactions for these students are successful and beneficial. If this does not occur, placement of some students with disabilities in general education classrooms can result in limited social interactions (Dore et al., 2002) and may produce negative outcomes such as social isolation and negative interactions with peers that are characterized by teasing, negative comments, staring, and isolation (Pavri & Monda-Amaya, 2001; Pivik, McComas, & Laflamme, 2002).

Pause & Reflect

Why do you think students with disabilities often do better academically in general education classrooms? What is it about general education classes that leads to higher achievement levels?

Your Role as a Teacher in an Inclusive School

If you work as a general education teacher in a well-developed inclusive school, such as Mull Elementary, West Hernando Middle School, or Heritage High School, you will very likely teach in an inclusive classroom with a range of students with disabilities and other students from diverse backgrounds (e.g., different language and cultural backgrounds) for much or all of the school day. Moreover, in any school, you will likely spend at least part of the day teaching in an inclusive setting. Let's look at the data for a moment to put this in perspective. In an average school with 1,000 students, about 114 students will be identified with disabilities (U.S. Department of Education, 2007a). About 106 of these students will have mild disabilities (e.g., learning disabilities, speech and language impairments, and other health impairments, e.g., ADHD), while about 8 will have significant disabilities (e.g., significant intellectual disability, multiple disability).

These data suggest that if you are a general education teacher, it is very likely that you will have one or more students with mild disabilities in your classroom each year. In addition, over a number of years, you will likely have a student with a significant disability in your class. Successfully meeting the needs of students with disabilities presents a range of challenges and requires that school professionals work collaboratively to meet these needs. In Chapter 11 we will focus on ways teachers and others can collaborate and work as a team effectively. For the present, we'll look at different professionals within schools and see how they can contribute to successful inclusion.

General Education Teachers

Whether an elementary or secondary educator, the general education teacher is expected to have knowledge of the curriculum content students are to learn and to design instruction with an expectation that all students will be successful learners. The practice of including students with disabilities in general education classrooms and encouraging their participation in the general curriculum places the general education teacher in a critical role. To ensure that all students succeed, the general education teacher often works closely with the special education teacher and other professionals to develop accommodations and supports for students with special needs.

Although the special education teacher continues to play a central role with students with disabilities included in general education classrooms, the general education teacher *shares* in the responsibility for providing instruction to these students. An important ingredient for the general education teacher to succeed in this role is an open mind and a willingness to collaborate. The teacher not only needs to help students with disabilities feel that they belong with their nondisabled peers but also needs to be a catalyst for acceptance.

Special Education Teachers

Special educators are usually professionally prepared to work with students who have specific types of disabilities or special needs. These may be students with mild disabilities, or students with more significant disabilities. Still other special educators may be prepared to work with students with sensory disabilities.

When working with students with special needs in general education classrooms, special educators may provide direct support to students by working with the general education teacher as a co-teacher. When working as co-teachers, the general and special education teacher plan instruction collabortively, and their roles in the classroom are often indistinguishable to the students because both teach all of the students at different times.

Special education teachers may also provide indirect support by observing in the classroom and working with the general education teacher as a consultant to plan instruction and related supports for students with special needs. This may also include supervision of a paraeducator who works in the general education classroom to support students with special needs.

Related Services Professionals

Related services are special supports required by federal law for students in special education that are necessary to help the students benefit from other school services. For example, if a student needs physical therapy to participate in learning activities, then physical therapy must be provided. The result of this legal requirement is that public schools employ many professionals besides general education or special education teachers to serve students with special needs.

According to data from the U.S. Department of Education (2007a), U.S. public schools employ approximately 19,000 social workers, about 47,800 speech–language pathologists, more than 7,600 physical therapists, and nearly 15,900 occupational therapists to work with students with disabilities. Additionally, educational administrators, counselors, rehabilitation specialists, and school psychologists play significant roles in the education of students with special needs. While we can't fully describe all of these professionals, Table 1.2 lists and briefly describes the roles of some who often work with students with special needs.

In many schools where students with special needs are included in general education classrooms, related services professionals work closely with special education teachers and general education teachers to support students. They do this in several ways. For example, a speech–language pathologist might help the student work on communication skills that allow more participation in class activities, while a physical therapist might help design the layout of a classroom so it will be accessible to students with physical disabilities. Similarly, a school psychologist might help develop a behavior intervention plan to improve a student's challenging behavior.

Table 1.2   Other Professionals Who Work with Students with Disabilities

Professional	Role
School psychologists	The primary role of the school psychologist is to conduct assessments to determine the present level of cognitive, academic, social-emotional, and adaptive behavioral functioning of students with disabilities.
Physical and occupational therapists (PTs and OTs)	The PT evaluates, plans, and develops interventions to improve posture and balance; to prevent bodily misformations; and to improve walking ability and other gross-motor skills. The PT works primarily with students who have significant disabilities. The OT has knowledge and skills similar to the PT's but has an orientation toward purposeful activities or tasks such as the use of fine-motor skills related to daily living activities.
Speech–language pathologists (SLPs)	The SLP evaluates a student's speech and language abilities and develops appropriate goals in this area if necessary. SLPs also may work with students with more significant disabilities to develop alternate or augmentative communication systems.
Social workers	Social workers address many issues that occur outside of the school. They may deal with family matters and will often make home visits to help resolve conflicts or improve parent–child interactions. They also can arrange for other service agency support.
School guidance counselors	Guidance counselors can help provide direction for academic or behavioral improvements. They will work one on one with students or with groups.
Art, music, and recreational therapists	These professionals use their particular specialties to help improve students' functioning in several areas, such as communication or social skills.

Paraeducators

Teacher assistants, often referred to as *paraeducators*, *paraprofessionals*, or *teacher aides*, also play a major role in the education of students with special needs in general education classrooms (Giangreco & Doyle, 2002; Giangreco, Edelman, Broer, & Doyle, 2001; Giangreco, Smith, & Pinckney, 2006). Paraeducators perform a range of instructional and noninstructional activities under the supervision of the special and general education teachers. These activities may include tutoring a student after a teacher provides primary instruction, preparing instructional materials and games, reading a story to students, and a range of other activities (Correa, Jones, Thomas, & Morsink, 2005).

When paraeducators are assigned to work with students with disabilities included in general education classrooms, they are in a position to have a very positive influence, as they help students to learn successfully and adapt to an inclusive setting. In most cases, it is preferable for the paraeducator to work with *all* students within the general education classroom, not only a single student or students with disabilities.

Paraeducators often provide support to students with disabilities. Specialists provide support for some students with physical disabilities.

Teacher Attitudes Toward Inclusion

One of the most important issues in determining whether an inclusive program will be effective and sustained over time is support for the program by teachers who are involved in implementing inclusive practices in their classrooms. Working in an inclusive setting can be challenging for a teacher, but many teachers find this work very rewarding.

Consider the perspective of Vicki Eng, a seventh-grade teacher at West Hernando Middle School.

Teaching in an inclusive classroom can be frustrating at times, but it's not what's best for me, it's what's best for the child. I can make a difference in their lives during the 7 1/2 hours a day they're in school. And that's what I tell myself; that's what keeps me going. And you know what, we make progress, and it's exciting to make progress, and to know that you've helped somebody by including them and helping them learn. And inclusion is more like real life. You're going to meet people with all types of abilities and disabilities, no matter where you are. That's what we're preparing them for. We're not just teaching them academics; we're preparing them for life.

In the well-developed inclusive schools that we described previously, most teachers are strongly supportive of inclusive programs. But how did they get to this point? What were their concerns as they began discussing the development of inclusive programs? When such major changes occur, teachers are often anxious about these changes, and have many questions that need to be answered. This area has been extensively researched, providing insight into the nature of teacher attitudes toward inclusion and factors that influence these attitudes.

Although some have contended that teachers are not supportive of inclusion (Coates, 1989; Semmel, Abernathy, Butera, & Lesar, 1991), most research has not supported this perspective, instead indicating that most teachers support the concept of inclusion and find it a desirable practice (Scruggs & Mastropieri, 1996). However, while most teachers tend to support inclusion, many have concerns regarding how these programs are implemented. These concerns do not relate to social prejudice or negative attitudes toward students with disabilities, but rather are related to whether they could make inclusion work in their classrooms and to concerns regarding the substantial changes necessary to make these efforts succeed (Waldron, 2007). These concerns must be addressed if inclusive programs are to succeed and be sustainable. The primary questions teachers express regarding inclusive programs are included in Figure 1.6.

As you can see from reviewing the questions teachers have regarding inclusion, all of the concerns that are raised are justified and reflect teacher concerns regarding whether they will be effective in an inclusive classroom. Indeed, these are questions any responsible teacher should ask when major changes are occurring in classroom practices (Waldron, 2007). For example, teacher concerns regarding whether they are well prepared for teaching students with disabilities and have the resources and support to ensure that the inclusive program succeeds are basic questions that must be addressed when any change occurs in classroom practice. Similarly, when teachers express concern regarding the need for support in addressing highly specialized student needs, it is reasonable to assume that professionals with this knowledge will be available to provide support to the teacher. Indeed, given the diversity of the needs of students with disabilities, it is not possible for any single teacher to have all the knowledge and skills that are needed to meet every student's needs.

Pause & Reflect

Are you surprised that teachers are generally supportive of the concept of inclusion? As you review the questions teachers ask about inclusion in Figure 1.6, do these questions seem reasonable and appropriate? What other questions do you think teachers may ask about inclusion?

As this research suggests, teachers' attitudes toward inclusion provide insight into issues that arise when inclusive programs are developed. When inclusion programs are poorly designed, as has been the case in some settings (Dymond & Russell, 2004; Fox & Ysseldyke, 1997; Pivik et al., 2002), teachers express justifiable concerns regarding these programs, and raise questions regarding whether students benefit from these programs. However, when these programs are well developed, teachers tend to be very supportive of having students with disabilities in general education classrooms.

Being a Good Teacher of All Students

There is no doubt that the success of inclusion for students with special needs rests largely on the collaborative efforts of general education and special education teachers. We can state it no more simply than to say that without teachers of high quality who are committed to teaching *all* students, inclusion will not succeed.

So what does it take to be a good teacher for all students? What personal qualities are important? What areas of knowledge and sets of skills must teachers learn? We propose that the following attributes and characteristics are necessary for teachers who wish to be effective for *all* of their students.

Figure 1.6	Questions Teachers Ask Regarding Inclusive Programs

1. Do students with disabilities benefit from inclusion?
2. Do students without disabilities benefit from inclusion?
3. Do students with disabilities have a negative effect on the classroom environment, especially related to disruptive behavior?
4. Do teachers have enough time to effectively teach all students?
5. Do teachers have sufficient knowledge and skills to address the needs of all students?
6. Is sufficient professional development available to ensure teachers are well prepared for inclusive classrooms?
7. Do teachers have sufficient instructional materials?
8. Do teachers have sufficient personnel support in the classroom?
9. Do teachers have consultative support for highly specialized student needs from a team of professionals?
10. Do teachers have sufficient time to collaborate with other professionals?

Sources: Carter & Hughes, 2006; McLeskey, Waldron, So, Swanson, & Loveland, 2001; Scruggs & Mastropieri, 1996; Waldron, 2007; Werts, Wolery, Snyder, & Caldwell, 1996.

Appropriate Dispositions

To be most effective as a teacher, you should have a disposition that values the nature of human differences and recognizes the importance of being a good teacher for *all* students. Teacher dispositions are just as important as having appropriate content knowledge and pedagogical skills. If you plan to be a professional educator, you must accept that you have a responsibility to teach all students regardless of their different challenges or special needs.

Having an appropriate disposition to be a teacher means having an outlook that maintains that all students are important and should be valued as members of the learning community. Without a disposition of this nature, the quality of a teacher is likely to be diminished. Inclusive schools have a philosophy that supports teachers who have these types of dispositions.

Principal Joe Clifford, West Hernando Middle School, illustrates this point when he says,

> At West Hernando, inclusion is part of the culture of our community. We all have a common goal, and common interests, to treat everyone in our school community with respect and dignity, to make sure everyone belongs, fits in, participates, and succeeds. Not everyone buys into this for every single minute of the school day. But this is the underlying theme that runs through the school. We have the school structures with procedures, rules, and regulations for kids, and we make sure supports are there that the kids need to fit in and succeed.

Positive Teacher Attitudes

Teachers sometimes are frustrated because certain students don't have positive attitudes toward learning. But teachers themselves should reflect on their own attitudes to see how they might influence their teaching. Here we examine some critical attitudes that are necessary for an effective teacher.

Caring, fairness, and respect are not just good qualities for teachers to have; they are essential. A teacher who cares about his students is more likely to have a positive impact because most students will be more responsive to a caring teacher (Bell, 2003). Fairness and respect are also important attitudes for teachers. Fairness means that teachers provide the instruction and support that individual students need without bias. Respect means that a teacher interacts with students in ways that acknowledge their humanity and strengths. Stronge (2002) reports that students feel most strongly about the following:

- They expect teachers to treat them as people.
- They view effective teachers as those who do not ridicule students or allow them to be embarrassed in front of their peers.
- They believe effective teachers are fair with regard to gender and ethnicity.
- They see teachers who are consistent and allow students to have input into the classroom as fair and respectful.
- They believe effective teachers offer all students opportunities to participate and to succeed.

Enthusiasm, motivation, and dedication suggest that students' interest in what is being taught is affected by the teacher's interest. Teachers who are excited about what they are doing tend to increase the excitement and interest of their students (Stronge, 2002). If you are enthusiastic about teaching, you will probably also be motivated to be an effective teacher. Your enthusiasm and motivation can sustain you through challenging times and improve your students' motivation and interest in what is being taught.

If you are a person who is dedicated to teaching, you will have interest in both your students' learning and your own. You will always be searching for better ways to teach and more effective ways to get your students to learn. You will take courses, participate actively in professional development sessions, and attend professional conferences. You will also collaborate with other professionals, share and receive ideas, and often volunteer to contribute to needs in the school or community. This is what it means to be dedicated to teaching.

Teacher expectations and personal teaching efficacy are final yet necessary and important attitudes of effective teachers. These attitudes imply that a teacher can have a positive impact on students, *regardless* of the nature or degree of the students' needs. Your view of your potential for success as a teacher is known as your "personal teaching efficacy." Teachers with high levels of personal teaching efficacy believe that they can positively influence student achievement and motivation. These attitudes correlate positively with student achievement and with teachers' willingness to implement innovations in order to be more effective teachers (Carlson, Lee, & Schroll, 2004; Tschannen-Moran et al., 1998).

Using Evidence-Based Teaching Approaches. While we cannot underestimate the importance of appropriate dispositions and positive attitudes for teachers, we also need to tell you that these qualities are not enough. Successful teaching requires using the most effective teaching practices. This is especially true when the student has learning difficulties or special needs.

To be most effective, teachers must seek and use evidence-based instructional approaches whenever possible. Evidence-based practices are those that are supported by scientific research and have been shown to demonstrate a high degree of success in terms of student learning outcomes.

Pause & Reflect

Review the qualities of a good teacher for all students. Do you have these qualities? Are any of these qualities a particular concern for you? Which do you think are most important?

To be a successful teacher, you must learn about the most effective ways to teach and promote your students' learning. Although research cannot claim to produce the only effective ways to teach, for much of what we do, we can find evidence that is either supportive or critical of our methods. Obviously, finding this evidence is an ongoing process, one that should be a part of your development as a professional. In Chapters 11 to 16, we present a number of evidence-based practices that teachers can use to support successful inclusion.

Differentiated Instruction: Making Instruction Work for All Students. Inclusive schools and classrooms work because teachers create instructional settings in which the needs of all students can be met. A term that is widely used and that provides a perspective on assuring that this occurs is differentiated instruction, which has been defined as "shaking up what goes on in the classroom so that students have multiple options for taking in information, making sense of ideas, and expressing what they learn" (Tomlinson, 2001, p. 1). In a general sense, all of the methods we discuss in this text relate to differentiated instruction. These are methods that result in significant benefits for all students, but especially those with disabilities. For a perspective on how students with disabilities (and others) benefit from these supports as they are educated in inclusive settings, see the following comments from teachers at West Hernando Middle School.

How Do Students Benefit from Being Taught in Inclusive Settings? Interviews with School Staff at West Hernando Middle School

We interviewed several teachers and staff at West Hernando Middle School regarding how students benefit from inclusion. Here's what they had to say.

The school counselor, Susan Dean, said "all students benefit from inclusion. Students who have trouble with academics have the opportunity to work with their same-age peers, and they are challenged more to be the best that they can be." Vicki Eng (a seventh-grade special education teacher) added, "Inclusion teaches all students tolerance and sensitivity. They learn that everybody has something they're good at, and some things they're not so good at. Everybody has strengths and weaknesses. And we try to help them recognize what their strengths and weaknesses are." Susan Dean continued by stating, "Including students with more significant disabilities benefits all students even more. The general education student that volunteers in our peer program, for example, gains by learning about these students, knowing these students, understanding these students. They gain as much as the students with disabilities."

Several teachers noted benefits of placement in general education classrooms that would not occur if students with disabilities were educated in a separate setting. For example, a sixth-grade teacher, Lisa Grover, noted that inclusion helps "kids realize that everyone is different. When they are all in general education classrooms, they tend not to make fun of one another. Kids can be very cruel to one another. When the kids with disabilities are separated, that's when the kids tend to pick on them. When they're included in their classrooms, you see those kids trying to help them out a lot."

Several teachers noted that the quality of the instruction in the general education classroom is often better. For example, Eileen Walls (Behavior Specialist) said, "Even the best special education teacher can never reproduce the richness of what happens in [the general education] classroom in terms of class discussion and student interaction, the stuff that naturally occurs. You have more teachable moments that occur in a class discussion in a regular class, when the kid finally gets it." In a similar vein, Principal Joe Clifford stated that students with disabilities "also benefit from the opportunity to be challenged at a higher level than if they had been in a separate class. The key is finding the level of ability and pushing them just beyond that, with the supports that are necessary."

Finally, everyone we talked with mentioned the importance of being in a class with models for good academic and social behavior. Joe Clifford made this point when he said that it is very "important to provide students with the opportunity to model appropriate strategies to gain knowledge, to participate in groups where different strategies are being used on a regular basis to enrich and enhance content mastery."

Eileen Walls eloquently expanded on this point, as she said, "When you take a group of kids and put them with others with similar types of problems, they think that's what normal is. Kids with disabilities in separate settings learn from other kids in that setting. Take a kid who's not a desk thrower and put him in a class with desk throwers, he's going to become a desk thrower. When that's the only thing you know in the separate environment, you don't have a chance to practice more appropriate behaviors to behave or learn, or know more appropriate behaviors. You develop a self-fulfilling prophecy that is so destructive in preventing kids from reaching their potential. That's a very strong casualty of separate classes, and an argument for more inclusion."

Summary

This chapter addressed the following topics:

The categories and qualities of instruction that characterize special education

- IDEA 2004 includes 13 categories of disability, ranging from mild-to-moderate disabilities such as learning disabilities and speech and language impairments, to significant disabilities such as deaf-blindness and multiple disabilities. Some categories include students with disabilities that range from mild-to-moderate to significant disabilities, including intellectual disabilities and autism.
- About 90% of students with disabilities have mild-to-moderate disabilities.
- Special education services and supports are "special" because of the intensity of instruction, the structure used during instruction, the specialized supports and accommodations, collaboration among professionals to meet student needs, and close monitoring of student performance.

Other students who may need accommodations or supports in a general education classroom

- Students who are at risk for difficulties in school, including those with risk factors in their backgrounds that largely relate to growing up in poverty, may need supports or accommodations in general education classrooms.
- About 43% of school-aged students are from diverse cultural and linguistic backgrounds that are often different from their teachers. Accommodations may need to be made to address the language and cultural backgrounds of these students.
- Some students may be identified with disabilities and determined to be eligible for classroom accommodations under Section 504 of the Rehabilitation Act of 1973 if the disability substantially limits a major life activity.
- Students who are gifted or talented may achieve at a level that is much higher than most of their peers and may need accommodations in the general education classroom.

Concepts that support inclusive practices

- The key concept underlying inclusion in federal law is the least restrictive environment (LRE), which requires that all students be educated with typical peers to the maximum extent appropriate.
- *Normalization* is a concept that has influenced inclusion. This concept suggests that all persons with disabilities should have the opportunity to live their lives in as typical a manner as possible.

Qualities underlying effective inclusive programs

- Not all educators define inclusion the same way. Some educators have developed programs that were called "inclusive" that did not meet student needs.
- Effective inclusive programs are designed to ensure that all students with disabilities are part of the academic and social community of the school.
- Effective inclusive schools are designed to ensure that teachers receive needed support and all students benefit.

Research on the effectiveness of inclusive programs

- Research has shown that academic outcomes for students with disabilities are at least as good, and sometimes better, in well-designed, effective, inclusive settings.
- Research has shown that academic outcomes for students without disabilities are at least as good, and sometimes better, in well-designed inclusive settings.
- Research has shown that simply placing a student in an inclusive setting does not improve social outcomes. Teacher instruction and support are needed to improve social outcomes.
- Research has shown that students without disabilities often benefit socially from inclusive placements.

Your role as a teacher of students with disabilities

- Most general education teachers will have one or more students with disabilities included in their classes.
- General education teachers share responsibility with special education teachers for educating students with disabilities in their classes.
- Special education teachers are responsible for providing intensive, specialized instruction to students with disabilities to improve performance in basic skill areas.
- Related services professionals (e.g., school psychologists, speech–language pathologists, physical therapists) are available to provide support to students with disabilities who are educated in inclusive settings.
- Paraeducators often work with students with disabilities and general education teachers in inclusive settings.

Attitudes of teachers toward inclusion

- Most general education teachers support the concept of inclusion but have concerns regarding how these programs are implemented.
- Concerns of general education teachers relate to the need for appropriate levels of support to meet student needs and to ensure that all students benefit from inclusion.

What it takes to be a good teacher for all students

- Good teachers have attitudes toward teaching all students that reflect caring, fairness, respect, enthusiasm, motivation, and dedication.
- Good teachers have high expectations regarding their ability to teach all students.
- Good teachers use effective, evidence-based teaching approaches.

Addressing Professional Standards

At the end of each chapter we will include professional standards that are addressed in that chapter. These standards are used to design teacher education programs, and are widely viewed as necessary for effective teaching. Standards are taken from the Council for Exceptional Children (CEC), the largest organization for special education teachers and other professionals; Interstate Teacher Assessment and Support Consortium (INTASC), a group of state education agencies and national professional organizations that have developed widely used standards for teacher education; and Praxis™ II, which is a battery of standardized tests that are designed to measure many of these standards.

Standards addressed in Chapter 1 include:

CEC Standards: (1) foundations, (2) development and characteristics of learners, (3) individual learning differences.

INTASC Standards: Principle 1—Understand central concepts of the discipline.

Praxis™ II Standards: Knowledge-based core principles: (1) understanding exceptionalities and (2) legal and societal issues.

Inclusion: Reflections on the Past, Present, and Future

KEY TOPICS

After reading this chapter you will:

- Know how the evolution of inclusive education has been shaped by social history, civil rights, and parent advocacy.
- Understand the major components of the Individuals with Disabilities Education Improvement Act (IDEA 2004), and know how historic legislation and litigation influenced its development.
- Know the five components of the No Child Left Behind (NCLB) Act, and understand how these requirements influence the education of students with disabilities.

- Recognize how Section 504 of the Rehabilitation Act and the Americans with Disabilities Act (ADA) influence educational service delivery to school-aged children and youth with disabilities.
- Be able to identify three issues that challenge educators and policy makers seeking to improve inclusive educational programs: adequate yearly progress (AYP) and students with disabilities, the need for a highly qualified workforce, and changing roles in a changing system.

Perspectives on Inclusion

Interview with Sarita Casserta, Parent of a Student at Heritage High School

Sarita Casserta could hardly believe her ears. At the family dinner table, her daughter Krista, then a tenth grader at Heritage High School, mentioned that for the first time in her life she was enjoying school. The reasons for Krista's positive feelings: she had a group of friends and was participating in extracurricular activities. Most important, she didn't feel strange when she needed help in her classes. Most of the subject area classes were co-taught by two teachers, and students had easy access to support and assistance within the usual procedures of the classroom. Sarita had suspected that things were going well. Krista seemed less depressed and was no longer making excuses to avoid going to school. Morning discussion now centered on what Krista wanted to wear rather than on why it was essential that she attend school.

What accounted for Krista's change in attitude and behavior? Sarita believes it is the inclusive education program at Heritage High School. Krista was referred for special education services when she was a second grader due to reading and attention problems. She was identified as having a learning disability and was placed in segregated pull-out programs for significant portions of the school day. Although Krista was "mainstreamed" for many of the nonacademic parts of the school day, she didn't feel part of the school community. She always felt sick and had few friends and limited opportunities to participate in the school's social activities.

This changed when Krista entered Heritage. Both Krista and Sarita were impressed with the faculty and staff's commitment to providing support in subject area classes. In some classes (e.g., math, biology), support was provided through co-teaching. In others, peer-tutoring structures were developed, leading to relationships that benefited Krista academically and socially. Sarita was especially impressed with the level of support provided by the administration: A case manager monitored Krista's progress in all of her classes and, when necessary, study halls were provided to supply intensive one-to-one instruction. The administration was also receptive to new ideas and welcomed Sarita's observations of Krista's progress and attitude toward school.

Sarita noticed that inclusion at Heritage provided Krista with a comprehensive and caring system of supports. Seeing the difference in her daughter's behaviors and attitude toward school has made her a believer in this method of special education service delivery. "Inclusion is the best

program for a student with learning difficulties to achieve academically, develop a social life, and build self-esteem. A well-developed inclusive model shows that people really care and that you are really part of the community." Krista is now a senior at Heritage, enjoying her friends, participating in school activities, and looking forward to graduation.

Introduction

Our society's desire for knowledgeable and responsible citizens is reflected in the numerous laws and public policies that promote education for our children and youth. For example, as early as 1918, every state in the union passed compulsory school attendance laws providing, and requiring, a free public education for all children (Yell, Rogers, & Rogers, 1998). Ironically, these *universal* attendance laws did not apply to all students. Those with disabilities could be, and often were, denied the opportunity to receive their free public *compulsory* education. Until the 1970s, access to school could be withheld if a school district claimed it was unable to accommodate a student with special needs, an exclusionary practice that was usually upheld in the courts.

Two cases illustrate the extreme insensitivity of these exclusionary practices (Yell et al., 1998). In 1919, the Wisconsin Supreme Court allowed the exclusion of a fifth-grade student who had a disability that caused speech problems, facial contortions, and drooling. The reasons for the exclusion: The school district claimed that the student's presence *nauseated* teachers and students and impacted discipline and academic progress negatively. Although the student was not hearing impaired, the school district recommended that the student attend a special day school for students who were deaf. In 1958, the Supreme Court of Illinois held that the state's compulsory attendance laws did not apply to those whose limited intelligence precluded the ability to benefit from a good education. This included students who were considered "feeble-minded" and "mentally deficient." The message was clear: those with intellectual disabilities would not benefit from education, so why provide one to them.

Fortunately, several significant legislative acts, including the landmark PL 94-142, the Education for All Handicapped Children Act of 1975 (EAHCA), provide access to a free and appropriate public education (FAPE) for all children regardless of their disability status. No longer are students denied an education because of their special needs and behavioral characteristics. The *total* exclusion of students with disabilities from educational settings was stopped by the historic litigation and federal legislation of the 1970s.

However, access to schooling alone does not automatically result in an appropriate education. Even though students with disabilities are provided full access to schools, practices in some schools actually limit full participation in appropriate academic and social activities. Some students with disabilities are *functionally excluded,* meaning that they occupy the same locations as their peers without disabilities, but they do not truly participate in the academic and social activities of the school. Moreover, they are not given supports that offer an opportunity to thrive and succeed in general education settings (Turnbull, 1993). They appear superficially to be part of the general education environment but are never fully integrated into the academic and social fabric of the school community. Unfortunately, many of these practices are so institutionalized and subtle that well-intentioned educators fail to notice when they occur. Consider how the following examples of placement in the general education environment do not allow for truly inclusive educational opportunities:

- Placing students with behavioral challenges in segregated classrooms with few opportunities to interact with normally achieving peers.
- Assigning secondary students with disabilities to large subject area general education classes with no organizational supports, peer assistance, or curricular accommodations.

- Relegating students with disabilities to segregated lunch, physical education, and recess periods and locations that are removed from their age-appropriate peers.
- Placing elementary students with disabilities in general education classrooms and having a special education teacher provide them with instruction in separate groups away from their classmates.

Although we have clearly moved beyond the total exclusion of students with disabilities, more work needs to be done to minimize instances of functional exclusion. As noted by Sarita Casserta, her daughter Krista believed she was truly part of her subject area classes when she was provided with naturally occurring peer tutoring. Clearly, access to inclusive environments is not enough to ensure belonging and academic success. We believe that the first steps in facilitating true involvement—the *functional inclusion* of all students—are an understanding of the evolution of special education service delivery, the legal foundations of inclusive special education, and an awareness of emerging issues and controversies that impact typical school and classroom practices.

The Evolution of Inclusive Special Education Services

Placing students with disabilities in general education classes without organizational supports, peer assistance, or curricular accommodations is not effective inclusion.

> ### Pause & Reflect
>
> Think of an instance when you were part of an activity or event, but felt that you were *functionally excluded* from full participation. Describe the elements of the situation that made you feel uncomfortable or uneasy. Could you have been made to feel truly part of the activity? How?

The current delivery of inclusive education has been shaped by special education's rich social history, landmark litigation and legislation, significant political events, and the courageous advocacy of parents. An awareness of the evolution of inclusive education will enable you to understand why practices such as appropriate dispositions, collaboration, and positive behavioral supports (discussed in later chapters) are essential to successful student outcomes.

From Segregation to Inclusion

Until the 1960s, most students with disabilities were educated in settings that were segregated from peers without disabilities for most or all of the school day. Those educated on regular school campuses were typically isolated from other students in separate wings or in basements of the main school building. Others were educated in separate schools that served only students with disabilities (McLeskey, 2007). Many criticized these segregated settings as ineffective, stigmatizing, and resulting in low expectations for those students (Deno, 1970; Dunn, 1968; Johnson, 1962). Furthermore, a disproportionate number of students who were identified with mild disabilities and educated in these settings were poor children from diverse backgrounds. Such findings led to a call to mainstream students with mild disabilities into general education classrooms for at least part of the school day (Dunn, 1968).

As educators were mainstreaming students with disabilities, they made several assumptions regarding these students and their education (see Figure 2.1). Mainstreaming addressed only students with mild disabilities, not those with severe disabilities. Moreover, students with disabilities were assumed to belong to special education and were simply visiting the general education classroom, primarily to improve their social skills or improve academic skills if they could work at grade level. The responsibility for student outcomes remained with special education.

Figure 2.1	**Comparisons of Assumptions Underlying Mainstreaming and Inclusion**

Mainstreaming addresses the needs of students with mild disabilities.

Inclusion addresses the needs of all students with disabilities who benefit from inclusive placements.

Mainstreaming is provided to students as a privilege.

Inclusion is a student's basic right.

General education teachers volunteer to teach students with disabilities who are **mainstreamed.**

All general education teachers are expected to teach students with disabilities who are **included.**

To be **mainstreamed,** students are expected to fit into the general education classroom.

The general education classroom is changed to support students who are **included.**

Special education is responsible and accountable for students who are **mainstreamed.**

When students are **included,** general and special education share responsibility and accountability.

At the same time, policies of normalization and deinstitutionalization were being implemented (Nirje, 1972; Wolfensberger, 1972). Normalization required agencies to provide persons with disabilities with living and learning experiences that were as "normal" as possible. Skills to be taught were those that would allow greater independence and life patterns that were parallel to those of people without disabilities. And the instructional procedures for teaching these skills were to be as close to "normal" as possible. The policy of deinstitutionalization resulted in a decline in the number of persons living in large residential institutions and an increase in the number living with their families and in smaller community-based residences. Community facilities were intended to be homelike and included foster homes, group homes, intermediate-care facilities, and sheltered apartments. In these smaller facilities located in neighborhood communities, individuals were to receive services traditionally provided only in the institutions (Westling & Fox, 2008).

By the 1980s, advocates and researchers were concerned about the effectiveness of mainstreaming (Reynolds, Wang, & Walberg, 1987; Stainback & Stainback, 1984). Even with efforts such as the regular education initiative (REI)—a largely special education effort to have general and special teachers share the responsibilities of educating students with disabilities in mainstream settings (Will, 1986)—concerns regarding mainstreaming continued, as a result of the following:

- Students with disabilities were not making adequate academic progress.
- Only the needs of students with mild disabilities were addressed; thus, many students with more severe disabilities did not have access to the general education classroom and curriculum.
- Few changes were occurring in general education classrooms to accommodate for the needs of students with disabilities.
- Additional collaboration was needed between general and special education to provide more support for students with disabilities in general education classrooms.

In response to these concerns, the inclusion movement began in the mid-1980s, resulting in major changes (see Figure 2.1). You will note that the assumptions underlying inclusion differ significantly from those underlying mainstreaming. For example, advocates of inclusion consider the education of students with disabilities in general education classrooms to be a fundamental right for all students with disabilities and the instruction of these students to be the responsibility of every general education teacher. Furthermore, proponents of inclusion assume that general and special educators will share the responsibility and accountability for educating students with disabilities and that students with disabilities will be as much a part of the educational community of the school as are other students who do not have disabilities. Finally, the collaboration between general and special educators is expected to ensure that students with disabilities receive appropriate supports, ensuring adequate progress academically and socially.

While increasing numbers of students with disabilities have been included in general education classrooms since the mid-1980s (McLeskey, Hoppey, Williamson, & Rentz, 2004; Williamson, McLeskey, Hoppey, & Rentz, 2006), controversy continues to surround the movement. The major concern relates to positions taken by some advocates regarding full inclusion (Fuchs & Fuchs, 1994; Kauffman, 1993; McLeskey, 2007). Full inclusion suggests that all students with disabilities be educated for the entire school day in general education classrooms. In recent years, however, educators have placed less emphasis on full inclusion and more on including all students with disabilities as members of the school's academic and social community. Furthermore, policy makers and administrators have increasingly emphasized student outcomes as a key element of inclusive efforts.

Proponents of inclusion assume that general and special educators share the responsibility for educating students with disabilities.

Civil Rights and Parent Advocacy

The civil rights movement of the mid-20th century had a monumental effect on the lives of many members of disenfranchised groups, including individuals with disabilities. Until the mid-1970s, no guarantee existed that a child with a disability would receive a free and appropriate public education. Schools educated only one in five children with disabilities, and many states had laws that explicitly excluded students with certain types of disabilities. Mirroring the earlier efforts of civil rights workers for African American schoolchildren, advocates for people with disabilities used the schools as a prominent battleground in efforts to achieve equal rights and due process of law. In fact, many of the original decisions rectifying the exclusion and segregation of students based on race were expanded to include students with disabilities (Murdick, Gartin, & Crabtree, 2002).

Pause & Reflect

How does the advocacy for the education of students with disabilities parallel the civil rights movement of the mid-20th century? Describe how schools served as a major battleground for equal rights and due process.

In the courtroom, as well as in the court of public opinion, parents and civil rights advocates took on state governments and school districts to ensure that students with disabilities had access to a FAPE (Weintraub & Abeson, 1976). Using the precedent of *Brown v. Board of Education* of Topeka, Kansas (1954)—in which the U.S. Supreme Court ruled that African American students attending segregated schools were not receiving an equal education—disability rights advocates made the case that access to an appropriate education was being denied because of the students' disabilities. The *Brown* plaintiffs and those advocating for children with disabilities were very similar. Both groups (1) challenged segregation in education, (2) proved they were denied equal educational opportunities, and (3) advanced an enduring public policy that views the function of school as meaningfully educating all students (Turnbull, Stowe, & Huerta, 2007).

One constant in the enduring legal processes of gaining access to education for students with disabilities has been active parent advocacy. Although many parents would have preferred to invest this time into their own quality of life efforts (Soodak et al., 2002), significant legislative gains such as the original passage of EAHCA (PL 94-142) would not have been possible without these efforts. Today, it is likely that you will encounter many parents of students with disabilities actively advocating for the inclusion of their children. The majority of parents of students with disabilities support inclusion and believe it contributes positively to social, emotional, and academic development (Duhaney & Salend, 2000). With greater access to appropriate role models and friendships, parents like Sarita Casserta at Heritage High School see inclusion contributing positively to their children's socialization, self-image, happiness, and confidence.

You will also find that parents have several realistic concerns about inclusion. Among the more prominent issues are the availability of qualified personnel and the ability of teachers in general education settings to provide needed supports. Many parents, particularly those of children with severe disabilities, fear that too many educators do not have the necessary skills and resources to implement inclusion effectively. Consequently, many parents believe they must be extremely vigilant, ensuring that their children are not mistreated, isolated, or just not receiving the services to which they are entitled when placed in general education settings (Duhaney & Salend, 2000; Erwin & Soodak, 2000).

Current Status of Inclusive Practices

Today, most students with disabilities are educated in their neighborhood schools and in general education classrooms. Table 2.1 represents the extent to which students who are identified with different disabilities are served in inclusive or in more restrictive settings. These data reveal that students with mild disabilities (i.e., speech–language impairments, developmental delays, visual impairments,

Table 2.1   Percentage of School-Aged Students with Disabilities Served in Different Placement Settings in the 2005–2006 School Year

Disability	Percentage of Time Served Outside of General Education Classroom			
	<21%	21%–60%	>60%	Separate School
Speech–language	88.7	6.2	4.6	0.5
Developmental delay	59.5	23.4	15.8	1.3
Visual impairment	58.2	15.2	14.2	12.4
Other health impairments	56.0	28.0	12.8	3.2
Learning disabilities	54.5	33.7	10.9	0.9
Orthopedic impairment	49.5	18.1	25.7	6.7
Hearing impairment	48.8	18.3	19.5	13.4
Traumatic brain injury	40.0	27.5	24.5	8.0
Emotional disorders	34.7	21.6	26.8	16.9
Autism	31.4	18.2	39.8	10.6
Deaf-blindness	22.8	15.1	33.6	28.5
Intellectual disabilities	14.1	29.1	52.3	4.5
Multiple disabilities	13.3	16.9	45.1	24.7
All disabilities	**54.2**	**25.1**	**16.7**	**4.0**

Source: U.S. Department of Education (2007).

other health impairments, and learning disabilities) are educated in general education classrooms for most or all of the school day. Students who are placed in the more restrictive settings include those who are identified with multiple disabilities, intellectual disabilities, deaf-blindness, autism, and emotional disturbance.

On average, across the United States, about 4 of every 5 students with disabilities spend a substantial portion of the school day (40% or more) in a general education classroom; the remaining 1 in 5 students spends very little time in a general education classroom (U.S. Department of Education, 2007). Wide variation, however, exists among states, local school districts, and even across schools within districts in the percentage of students with disabilities who are educated in inclusive settings. For example, up to 65% of all students with intellectual disabilities are educated in general education settings for most of the school day in one state, while in other states, very few of these students are educated in these settings (Williamson, McLeskey, Hoppey, & Rentz, 2006). The rate of inclusion appears to depend on the extent to which inclusion is a priority in the individual schools and districts.

Most students with disabilities—about 80%—spend a majority of their school day in general education settings.

Clearly, more and more students are being educated in neighborhood schools and general education classrooms. Nonetheless, as many parents of students with disabilities know, access—and the official numbers used to index integration into the inclusive environment—is not enough. As mentioned earlier, access to general education settings must not functionally exclude students from successful participation but truly result in significant involvement in the school community. To meet this goal, inclusion cannot be viewed strictly as a disability issue. Efforts to improve services and include students with disabilities require initiatives that benefit all children and schools (Bricker, 2000).

Pause & Reflect

How would you convince others that inclusion is not only a disability "problem" that requires solving? What strategies would you employ to ensure that inclusion is viewed as a core value applied to all students and integrated in schools?

Dianne Ferguson, a special education scholar and parent of a child with a disability, related how her thinking of inclusion changed as a result of her family's efforts to secure a more "normalized" school experience for her son Ian (Ferguson, 1995). With severe and multiple disabilities, Ian was in self-contained classrooms with few opportunities for contact with nondisabled peers. Through her research and advocacy, Ferguson found that typical efforts to mainstream or integrate students with disabilities did little to fully facilitate full participation in the learning community. Inclusion efforts merely relocated the special education but did little to change the perception that the students were "irregular," even when they were in "regular" classrooms. The challenge was to find out how to truly create an environment where a person with a disability is part of the community (an experience Ian had when in a drama class).

Ferguson realized that if inclusion were to really work, tactics would need to change. Rather than merely "adding on" to the existing systems to accommodate a few students, inclusion had to be viewed as a core value that applied to all students, regardless of disability status. For inclusion to really work, it must be viewed as

a process of meshing general and special education reform initiatives and strategies in order to achieve a unified system of public education that incorporates all children and youth as active, fully participating members of the school community; that views diversity as the norm; and that ensures a high quality education for each student by providing meaningful curriculum, effective teaching, and necessary supports for each student. (Ferguson, 1995, p. 285)

Legal Foundations of Special Education and Inclusion

Four major legislative acts influence how schools structure, and how individual teachers deliver, special education services in inclusive schools:

- The Individuals with Disabilities Education Improvement Act of 2004 (IDEA 2004)
- The No Child Left Behind (NCLB) Act of 2001
- Section 504 of the Rehabilitation Act
- The Americans with Disabilities Act (ADA)

In our discussions of each of these acts, we describe the major components of the legislation and consider how these laws impact the delivery of inclusive education programs.

Individuals with Disabilities Education Improvement Act (IDEA 2004)

IDEA 2004 is arguably the most significant piece of legislation supporting the education of children and youth with disabilities. Because of IDEA, most children and youth with disabilities are educated in their neighborhood schools in general education classrooms with their nondisabled peers. Moreover, postschool employment rates for people with disabilities, although not where they should be, are twice those of older adults with similar profiles who did not have the rights and protections of the law. Even more heartening are the numbers of students with disabilities who attend college; compared to 1978, the number of first-year college students with disabilities has more than tripled (U.S. Department of Education, n.d.).

IDEA 2004 updates and amends earlier legislation that served as the legal basis for the education of those with disabilities: EAHCA of 1975; the 1983 and 1986 EAHCA amendments; and the Individuals with Disabilities Education Act (IDEA) of 1990, 1992, and 1997. Keep in mind that legislation is temporary, fluid, and subject to the influence of political pressure. Reauthorizations of the law have sought to improve the law by strengthening the role of parents, encouraging nonadversarial resolution of disputes, and requiring participation in the general education curriculum and state- and district-wide assessments. "Just the Facts: IDEA 2004" provides an overview of the major components of the current IDEA. "Just the Facts: Evolution of 1975 Legislation" illustrates how the original 1975 legislation evolved into the current statute.

In addition to evolving legislation, litigation (legal cases in which a judge or a jury interprets the law in situational disputes) influenced the initial passage and prompted improvements in the provisions of IDEA 2004. Following are several legal principles that have had the most influence in the development of special education law:

- **Due process.** The due process clauses of both the 5th and 14th Amendments of the Constitution require that laws be applied to all with sufficient safeguards. For students with disabilities, this means fair and specific procedures related to assessment, identification, and placement of children in special education (Turnbull, Stowe, & Huerta, 2007).
- **Equal protection.** The equal protection clause of the 14th Amendment forbids states from denying anyone equal protection of the laws without justification. Therefore, states must provide the same rights and benefits (e.g., opportunities to have qualified teachers, go on field trips, and participate in extracurricular activities) to students with disabilities as to those without disabilities.
- **Zero reject.** No child with a disability can be excluded from school, and all school agencies are to follow a policy of not excluding students from school.
- **Free and appropriate public education.** Individual students must be provided with a full range of appropriate direct and related educational services at no cost to students or their families.
- **Least restrictive environment (LRE).** Students with disabilities should be educated, to the maximum extent appropriate, with students who do not have disabilities, and they should be

Just the Facts   IDEA 2004 Components

Free and appropriate public education	• All children regardless of severity of disability can learn and are entitled to a FAPE. • Special education and related services are provided at public expense in conformity to an IEP.
Nondiscriminatory assessment	• All testing and evaluation used to identify and assess students with disabilities are not racially or culturally discriminatory. • Evaluations requiring tests are in the child's native language or appropriate mode of communication, validated, and administered by trained personnel.
Least restrictive environment	• Preferred placement for students with disabilities is the general education classroom. • When success in the general education classroom cannot be achieved even with significant alterations, alternatives on the continuum of placements are considered.
Individualized education program	• An IEP is developed for each student with a disability and includes (1) current levels of performance, (2) annual goals, (3) extent of participation in general education programs, (4) beginning dates and anticipated duration of service, and (5) evaluation methods. • Participants in IEP planning include at least one special and general educator, a local education agency (LEA) representative, an evaluation specialist, related service specialists, and parents.
Parent participation	• Written permission from parents is needed for all testing, evaluation, and changes in services. • Parents are entitled to active participation in IEP development and annual reviews.
Procedural safeguards	• Adequate notice must be provided to parents for meetings. • Allow for the settling of disagreements through mediation and due process hearings.

removed from a general education classroom only when the curriculum and instruction cannot be adapted to achieve satisfactory results.

- **Nondiscriminatory assessment.** Biased evaluation instruments and/or procedures constitute a denial of equal access to education. Students can be harmed by assessments that wrongly label them and mistakenly place them in environments that deprive them of opportunities for advancement.

From Law to Classroom: Major Components of IDEA 2004

The components of IDEA reflect what all teachers and service providers should know and be able to do when teaching students with disabilities (Rosenberg, O'Shea, & O'Shea, 2006).

Nondiscriminatory Identification, Assessment, and Evaluation. IDEA requires schools and community agencies to locate and evaluate students who may have disabilities. The goal is to determine if there is the presence of a disability and, if so, to identify the full spectrum of educational services needed for the student to succeed in school or preschool settings. When conducting such evaluations, the law requires that a multidisciplinary team:

1. Employ testing materials and procedures in the student's primary language or mode of communication.
2. Use more than one test or procedure to determine disability or placement status.
3. Provide a full-scale evaluation in all areas of functioning related to the suspected disability, including intelligence, achievement, social skills, language, motor skills, and adaptive behavior.
4. Have only qualified personnel administer those tests, and use tools validated for the purpose of assessing students' functioning in classroom situations.
5. Ensure that tests and procedures are not racially, culturally, or ideologically biased or discriminatory.
6. Secure written consent and input from parents and guardians for both initial evaluation and reevaluations; summarize data into a format that is readily accessed and understood.

Just the Facts   Evolution of 1975 Legislation into IDEA 2004

PL 94–142, Education for All Handicapped Children Act (EAHCA, 1975)	The precursor to IDEA 2004, EAHCA is often referred to as the Bill of Rights for students with disabilities. This law guaranteed the availability of a free and appropriate public education, due process, and IEPs to all students with disabilities.
PL 98–199, Parent Training and Information Centers (1983)	Provided for training and provision of information to parents and volunteers.
PL 99–457, Education of the Handicapped Students Act Amendments (1986)	Extended the mandate from PL 94–142 to include special education and related services beginning at age three and created a discretionary early intervention program to serve students from birth through age two.
PL 101–476, Individuals with Disabilities Education Act (IDEA, 1990)	Further amended the provisions of PL 94–142 and PL 99–457, renamed the act IDEA, and mandated that the IEP include a statement of transition services.
PL 101–336, Americans with Disabilities Act (ADA, 1990)	Prohibited discrimination based on disabilities in the areas of employment, public services, transportation, public accommodations, and telecommunications.
PL 101–392, Carl D. Perkins Vocational and Technology Education Act (1990)	Provided resources for improving educational skills needed in a technologically advanced society, guaranteeing full vocational educational opportunities for all special populations.
PL 103–239, School-to-Work Opportunities Act (1994)	Encouraged partnership models between school-based and employment-based sites at the local level by encouraging schools and employment site personnel to plan, implement, and evaluate integrated school-based and work-based learning. It encouraged interagency agreements, technical assistance, and services to employers, educators, case managers, and others.
PL 102–476, Individuals with Disabilities Education Act (IDEA)	Passed in 1990 and amended in 1997 **(PL 105–17)**. It established a number of new provisions designed to improve outcomes for students with disabilities. Provisions inherent in the reauthorized law, IDEA '97, include requirements that students with disabilities must be included in state- and district-wide assessments, that students' IEPs address the issue of students' access to general education curricula, and that states establish performance goals and indicators for students with disabilities.

Least Restrictive Environment. Would it surprise you to learn that IDEA does not use the terms *mainstream, include, segregate,* or *integrate*? The language used in the law requires that the education of students with disabilities occur in the LRE, which has the following implications:

- Education placement is determined at least annually and is based on an individual student's educational needs.
- To the greatest degree possible, students with disabilities receive services close to their home, are educated with nondisabled peers, and have access to the general education curriculum and extracurricular activities.
- Removal from the general education environment occurs only when the nature and the severity of the disability preclude the satisfactory delivery of educational services with appropriate supplemental aids and services (Murdick et al., 2002).

Placement is not permanent, and service providers work to move students to less restrictive— and in our view, functionally inclusive—levels of service. However, when the needs of a student require more intensive levels of service, movement to more restrictive situations is both necessary and appropriate.

Individualized Education Programs. IDEA 2004 requires that each student identified as having a disability receive an individualized education program (IEP), a document that informs and guides the delivery of instruction and related services. Requirements for the development of an IEP are quite specific in terms of information included and the individuals who develop the plan. The IEP requires six categories of information: (1) the student's current levels of academic and functional performance; (2) measurable annual goals related to meeting the student's needs resulting from the disability and enabling progress in the general education curriculum; (3) a description of how the student's progress toward meeting annual goals is measured and reported; (4) a statement of special education and related services and supplementary aids and services provided for or on behalf of the student; (5) the extent, if any, to which the student will not participate with nondisabled students in the general education environment; and (6) the projected date for the beginning of services and the anticipated frequency, location, and duration of those services and modifications.

The IEP team also addresses postsecondary transition issues for students turning 16 (or younger, if deemed necessary by the team). Consequently, the IEP must include measurable goals and corresponding services based on appropriate transition assessments. Finally, as the student approaches the state's legal age, the IEP must include a statement that the student has been informed of his or her rights in regard to IDEA 2004. (IEP development is detailed in Chapter 12.)

Successful development and implementation of IEPs require input from a team of informed stakeholders. Consequently, IDEA 2004 requires that the IEP process involve

- At least one general education teacher of the student (if the student is participating, or is planning to participate, in general education activities)
- At least one special educator of the student
- A school district representative who is knowledgeable about available service-delivery options and programs as well as the general education curriculum and related-service availability
- An evaluation specialist who can interpret the instructional implications of assessments
- Other specialists who can provide important information, such as related-service providers, transportation specialists, physicians, lawyers, and advocates
- Parents, guardians, surrogate parents, and, when appropriate, the student

Individual team members can be excused from attending if their area is not being discussed or if there is agreement that written input is acceptable.

> ## Pause & Reflect
>
> Although IEPs are a critical element of IDEA, their use in classrooms has been limited. Why are they not used more frequently? Can you think of ways to make IEPs more user-friendly?

Procedural Safeguards. IDEA 2004 requires that schools ensure that parents, guardians, or surrogates have the opportunity to participate in every decision related to the identification, assessment, and placement of their child. In addition to providing adequate notice for meetings and scheduling them at a mutually agreed-on time and place, schools are to notify parents when considering changes in educational programming or related services.

If parents believe that their rights have been violated or if they disagree with educators regarding the development of their child's IEP, they can appeal specific decisions. One step is **mediation**, a voluntary process in which a qualified, impartial facilitator works with the parties to come to resolution. If mediation does not satisfy the parties, IDEA 2004 mandates the convening of a due process hearing. These hearings allow dissenting parties to question decisions and actions. Parties also have the right to appeal due process hearing decisions in federal court if they remain unsatisfied. To reduce the need for protracted and costly legal activities associated with due process hearings and appeals, IDEA 2004 urges states to strengthen their mediation procedures.

Suspensions and Expulsions. For those inappropriate behaviors deemed not a manifestation (i.e., caused by or substantially related to the disability or a failure to implement IEP procedures) of the student's special needs, schools can apply disciplinary actions in the same manner as they do for students without disabilities (as long as special education services continue). However, schools cannot remove a student with a disability from his or her current placement for more than 10 days if it is determined that the problem behaviors are a function of the disability. Nonetheless, for violations such as (1) bringing a dangerous weapon to school, (2) selling or possessing illegal drugs, and (3) inflicting serious bodily injury on another person while at school

IDEA guarantees parents, guardians, and surrogates participation in all of their child's identification, assessment, and placement decisions.

or at a school function, IDEA 2004 provides schools with the authority to consider unique circumstances on a case-by-case basis. In such cases, the school district may unilaterally place a student in an interim alternative placement for up to 45 school days.

Confidentiality and Access to Information. IDEA 2004 requires that one official in each school district assume responsibility for ensuring confidentiality of school records and ensuring that those who have contact with student records are trained in records-management procedures. Parents by law have the right to inspect and review all information on their child, and it is not unusual for them to request an explanation regarding the information in the records.

Services to Infants, Toddlers, and Preschoolers. It was not until 1986, and an early reauthorization of IDEA, that preschool special education services were mandated for children ages 3 to 5, and incentives were provided to states encouraging the development of programs for infants, toddlers, and their families. Preschoolers are afforded the same services and protections available to school-aged children. Because infants and toddlers with disabilities often require medical, psychological, and human service interventions, as do members of the entire family, the federal government has encouraged the development of statewide, multidisciplinary, interagency programs by offering increased grant support.

No Child Left Behind

The NCLB Act of 2001 is a comprehensive federal initiative designed to improve the educational performance of *all* students. A reauthorization of earlier Elementary and Secondary Education Acts (ESEA), NCLB explicitly mandates compliance to high standards and sanctions states and schools that fail to meet set criteria (Hardman & Mulder, 2004; Yell & Drasgow, 2005). In enacting NCLB, the federal government asserted that states were not doing enough to ensure that all students were performing adequately in school. The act requires states to reduce the disparity in performance between those groups of students who typically achieve and those students who have had difficulties meeting standards, often due to economic disadvantage, linguistic differences, or disability status. Figure 2.2 offers a brief introduction to NCLB.

Elements of NCLB

Five core principles form the foundation of NCLB: (1) strong accountability for results; (2) expanded flexibility and local control of schools; (3) an emphasis on teaching methods based on scientific

Figure 2.2	The No Child Left Behind Act of 2001

Accountability for Results

- States create assessments to measure what children know and learn.
- Annual report cards on school performance allow parents to know of the quality of the children's schools, the qualifications of teachers, and progress in key subjects.
- Statewide performance reports are disaggregated according to race, gender, and other relevant criteria to assess closing of achievement gap.

Expanded Options for Parents

- Parents with children in failing schools are allowed to transfer their children to a better-performing public school, including charter schools.
- Parents can request schools to use Title I funds to provide supplemental educational programs (e.g., tutoring, after-school services, summer school) for children in failing schools.
- Federal support for charter schools is expanded.

Strengthening Teacher Quality

- A highly qualified teacher will be in every public school classroom by 2005.

Teaching Methods Based on Scientific Research

- Requires use of programs that have demonstrated effectiveness.

Flexibility and Local Control

- Demonstrates greater sensitivity to the needs of local schools by allowing flexibility in the use of federal funds without prior government approval.

research; (4) expanded options for parents, particularly those whose children attend low-performing schools; and (5) highly qualified teachers.

Strong Accountability for Results. NCLB requires states to develop clearly defined goals, or proficiency standards, and then assess whether individual students and schools meet these targets. Comparing student performance data to the standards allows parents to know how their child is doing at school. In turn, policy makers and school leaders can assess how individual schools and school districts are performing in relation to state standards. In addition to measures of performance for all students across schools and districts, states are required to parse out, or disaggregate, data for specific groups of students, including those who are economically disadvantaged, members of varying culturally and linguistically diverse groups, and students with disabilities. The goal is making **adequate yearly progress (AYP)**—the minimum standard, or benchmark, expected of every student and school. Schools that meet their goals receive positive public acknowledgement of effort. Those that do not meet their goals for 2 years running are designated in need of improvement.

Historically, students with disabilities were excluded, both formally and informally, from school and district assessments, perpetuating low expectations throughout their educational careers. Now they are included in assessments. Although many have welcomed this inclusion in accountability policies, questions remain regarding the appropriateness of including students with cognitive disabilities in overall determinations of school effectiveness. To address this concern, NCLB allows school districts and states to exempt 1% of all students from the usual assessments. This 1% represents about 9% of those with disabilities and includes those with the most severe disabilities. Responding to concerns voiced by state and local officials, the U.S. Department of Education (2008) allows additional flexibility: An additional 2%, those students identified as needing modified standards and assessments, can be assessed through alternate means rather than the usual tests.

Expanded Flexibility and Local Control. Local school personnel have greater sensitivity to the needs of neighborhood schools than do federal administrators. Consequently, NCLB provides the freedom for school districts to transfer up to 50% of federal funds among a number of programs without the need to obtain prior government approval. The act also allows school districts to consolidate funds from several programs and to enter into flexible state–local partnerships.

Teaching Methods Based on Scientific Research. Far too often, educators adopt programs and teaching methods based on fads, bandwagons, anecdote, and personal whim, usually with dismal results (Kauffman, 1981; Yell & Drasgow, 2005). With NCLB, federal support is targeted to only those programs that have a proven track record, demonstrating effectiveness through rigorous scientific research.

Expanded Options for Parents. What would happen if a parent had a ninth-grade child who attended a low-performing school that continually experienced significant discipline issues? Under NCLB she would have options. First, if the school did not meet state goals for two consecutive years, she could choose to transfer her child to a better-performing school in the district, with transportation provided. Second, if the school failed to meet goals for three consecutive years, her child would be eligible for a range of supplemental activities, including free tutoring and after-school instruction.

Highly Qualified Teachers. NCLB requires that all teachers be highly qualified. This means being appropriately licensed and having the requisite qualifications in core academic subject areas. For content-area teachers, this requirement is fairly straightforward. To continue teaching one must (1) have a college degree; (2) have full state certification or licensure; and (3) demonstrate competency in the areas he teaches by passing subject-specific, state-administered tests. Being highly qualified is not so clear-cut for special educators. In addition to developing their special education skills, those who teach at the elementary level must pass a test of subject knowledge and teaching skill in the standard elementary curriculum (e.g., reading, writing, mathematics). Special education teachers at the middle and high school levels must be highly qualified in special education as well as in each of the core subject areas they teach. Not surprisingly, these requirements can be overwhelming and burdensome for many thinking of a special education teaching career.

Pause & Reflect

Some believe that the requirements of NCLB are admirable but in some cases unattainable. What do you think? Can all teachers be highly qualified? Is it possible that all students will meet state-mandated standards of proficiency?

Section 504 of the Rehabilitation Act of 1973 (PL 93–112) and the Americans with Disabilities Act

Section 504 is a component of the Rehabilitation Act that authorizes federal support for the rehabilitation and training of individuals with physical and mental disabilities. Section 504 is significant for students with special needs because it provides protections for those whose disabilities do not match the definitions under the IDEA statute. In addition to using a categorical approach to disability, Section 504 protects students with (1) communicable diseases; (2) temporary disabilities arising from accidents; and (3) allergies, asthma, or environmental illnesses. Students who do not qualify for services under IDEA may qualify under Section 504. In essence, under Section 504 a student has a disability if he or she functions as though having a disability (Murdick et al., 2002), and the law provides these students with equal opportunities to obtain the same results, benefits, and levels of achievement as those without disabilities. Section 504 also extends protections against discrimination beyond school settings to employment and social and health services.

The major differences between Section 504 and IDEA are in the flexibility of the procedures and the reduced procedural criteria required of school personnel. Schools typically offer less assistance and monitoring with Section 504 because fewer federal regulations address compliance. Indeed, no IEP is required for students. Still, Section 504 levels the playing field by eliminating barriers that exclude those with disabilities from full participation in activities (Rosenfeld, 2005). These barriers can be physical (e.g., architectural impediments that stop a person with a physical or sensory disability from accessing a building), or they can be programmatic (e.g., not giving a student with attention-deficit/hyperactivity disorder [ADHD] supports and accommodations so that he can benefit from instruction).

Section 504 ensures that appropriate educational services are delivered to children with disabilities. Appropriate services are educational activities designed to meet the needs of those with disabilities to the same extent that the needs of those without disabilities are met. Eligibility for Section 504 services is based on a team's determination of whether there is a substantial limitation to major life activities resulting from a physical or mental impairment. Once a determination is made, an individual accommodation plan is developed. The accommodation plan is not as extensive as an IEP but should include clear information on how school personnel can implement accommodations to meet individual student needs. We discuss how to develop Section 504 Plans in Chapter 12.

Examples of situations that may require a Section 504 Plan include:

- Providing an acoustical amplification system and distraction-free seating for a student with ADHD who has difficulty attending to instruction
- Developing a management plan that trains school personnel to meet the needs of a student with diabetes including specialized snacks, lavatory access, and exercise opportunities
- Providing appropriate training to those who work with a student with bipolar disorder; providing the student with the disorder opportunities for time-out when unpredictable mood swings occur
- Creating a health care plan for management of acute and chronic phases of student illnesses such as cystic fibrosis and epilepsy, or hypersensitive allergic reactions to certain foods (e.g., peanuts) or environmental events (odors, noise, etc.)

> ## Pause & Reflect
>
> Can you think of other circumstances that would require the development of a 504 Plan? How do these plans promote the successful inclusion of all students?

Similar to Section 504, the ADA, PL 101–336, is civil rights legislation for those with disabilities. Passed in 1990, the ADA requires nondiscriminatory protections such as equal opportunity to participate fully in community life, equal opportunity to live independently, and accessibility of all buildings and physical facilities to individuals with disabilities. The ADA applies to all segments of society—employment, education, and recreation services—with the exception of private schools and religious organizations. Similar to Section 504, the ADA uses a functional definition of disability. Rather than listing all possible conditions, a person with a disability is defined as someone with a physical or mental impairment that limits participation in major life activities (Moses, 1990).

Viewed by many as the Emancipation Proclamation for individuals with disabilities, the ADA prohibits discrimination in employment, governmental entities, and public accommodations (Smith, 2001). Consider the frustration experienced by a student with a physical disability unable to play with peers because of an architectural barrier precluding entry to the gymnasium or playground. The ADA requires removal of existing physical barriers or the provision of alternative means of service implementation.

Section 504 Plans allow for acoustical amplification systems for students with ADHD who have difficulties attending to lessons.

Many of the ADA requirements for schools were already addressed by Section 504. However, the ADA did clarify certain lingering issues. For example, the ADA ensures that students with contagious diseases, such as HIV/AIDS, are protected from discrimination as long as they do not threaten the health and safety of others (Murdick et al., 2002). Also, protections are extended to those who are associated with a person with a disability. Specifically, a child whose parent or sibling has a communicable disease cannot be prevented from attending school.

Tomorrow's Challenges

In this chapter, we described the history of service delivery to students with disabilities by tracing the evolution of inclusive services and then describing the laws that guide current educational programming. As a result of the tireless efforts of disability advocates and landmark legislative efforts such as IDEA and NCLB, considerable progress has been made in the education of students with disabilities. How successful have these efforts been? Consider these findings from a study commissioned by the National Council on Disability (2008) assessing the impact of IDEA and NCLB on special education outcomes. Since the laws were (re)authorized, students with disabilities are doing better academically, with fewer scoring in the "below-basic" proficiency level and more attaining "proficient" or higher levels, than were in previous years. Moreover, students with disabilities are graduating with diplomas and certificates at higher rates than in the past. Equally important, attitudes and expectations of key stakeholders—policy makers, teachers, parents, and students—have been changing in a positive direction. Students with disabilities have increased access to higher-level curricula, and a culture of high expectations for these students has taken root.

> ## Pause & Reflect
>
> Consider the major accomplishments of IDEA and NCLB as they relate to the delivery of inclusive educational programming. Have these laws fulfilled their promise of providing a FAPE to students with disabilities in the least restrictive environment? What, if any, challenges remain to be addressed?

Still, as students with disabilities gain greater access to challenging academic environments, several issues continue to pose challenges to teachers and policy makers. Three of the more prominent issues are (1) how to best assess AYP of students with disabilities, (2) building and sustaining a highly qualified workforce, and (3) the evolving roles of teachers in changing educational delivery systems.

AYP and Students with Disabilities

In our earlier discussion of NCLB, we noted that states determine AYP by adopting or designing content-specific standardized tests and setting proficiency score benchmarks that students are required to attain. Although NCLB requires 100% proficiency by 2014, it is generally accepted that some students with disabilities will not be able to meet the same standards and time frame as their peers without disabilities. Currently, schools are allowed to have 1% of their students (typically, students with serious cognitive disabilities) take alternate assessments. Alternate achievement standards are based on performance expectations that differ in complexity from grade-level achievement standards. An additional 2% of students with disabilities—from any category under IDEA—are eligible for assessments that are based on modified achievement standards. These standards are aligned with typical grade-level standards but with reduced depth and breadth of content coverage. It is presumed that alternate and modified assessments are technically sound and reflect grade-level content (Yell et al., 2006).

In addition to the challenges involved in designing alternative assessments for students under the "1% and 2% options," some professionals believe these exemptions from traditional AYP requirements to be inadequate. Large numbers of students receiving special education services have disabilities that interfere with their learning. These students typically perform at much lower levels on state tests, making it far more likely that schools with a large special education subgroup will fail to make AYP (Olson, 2005). While special education advocates welcome being part of inclusive assessments, some fear that failures to make AYP, due to the limited performance of students with disabilities, could increase the "already existing anti-special education bias" (Allbritten, Mainzer, & Ziegler, 2004, p. 157). Not surprisingly, a number of teacher groups (e.g., American Federation of Teachers, 2006) are advocating that the numbers of students with disabilities assessed under alternative and modified standards not be limited by arbitrary federal percentages. Rather, knowledgeable IEP teams should determine how students participate in required assessments.

Highly Qualified Professionals

The quality and skill of a student's teacher are critical factors in the development of academic proficiency, and as required by NCLB, a well-prepared, highly qualified teacher is needed in every classroom. Unfortunately, in several areas such as math, science, and special education, a severe and chronic shortage of fully credentialed teachers continues to plague our nation's schools. Consider some of the special education numbers: 98% of the nation's school districts report shortages of special education teachers, and approximately 11.4% of those teaching students with disabilities lack special education certification. Moreover, in spite of this serious shortage, the number of people interested in pursuing a career in special education has gradually declined (Cook & Boe, 2007; McLeskey, Tyler, & Flippin, 2004).

Among the many unfortunate effects associated with the shortage of highly qualified and certified teachers is a lack of skill in providing collaborative and supportive inclusive programming. As you will note throughout this text, successful inclusive practices require that teachers possess general and specialized skills in both instructional and interpersonal domains. In the chapter-opening "Perspectives" interview, for example, Sarita Casserta noticed a positive difference in the education of her daughter when she entered Heritage High School, which is adequately staffed with highly qualified professionals. Lacking sufficient numbers of personnel who possess the needed skills to implement inclusive programs can ultimately derail successful efforts of educating students in high-demand general education environments.

As you can imagine, addressing teacher quality in a time of persistent shortages is complex. For example, although few argue with the need to increase the number of highly qualified special education teachers, many educators and policy makers are concerned that additional requirements can exacerbate current shortages. At the same time, apprehension exists that exempting special education teachers from some of the highly qualified standards could widen the achievement gap between students with and without disabilities and promote separate systems of teacher qualifications and accountability (Rosenberg, Sindelar, & Hardman, 2004).

The dilemma of enhancing quality at a time of teacher shortages has led policy makers to consider **alternative routes to certification** and streamlined teacher preparation programs (Rosenberg, Boyer, Sindelar, & Misra, 2007). These nontraditional teacher preparation efforts vary in terms of breadth of coverage and level of support. Although these programs remain controversial, most agree that the programs need to be evaluated in terms of long-term retention rates and measures of teacher quality.

Evolving Roles in a Changing System

Throughout this text you will see frequent references to a process referred to as **response to intervention (RTI)**. As we will fully describe in later chapters, RTI is an integrated, school-wide method of delivering general and special education that promotes academic and behavioral success. Increasingly, educators are considering RTI as a framework for addressing the needs of all students who experience academic, social, or behavioral difficulties in school. The central element of RTI is a continuum of services, typically referred to as tiers, available to all students—those with and without disabilities—based on an assessment of individual needs. Typically, the first tier is a high-quality universal general education program that employs research-based instructional practices. Tier-2 instruction supplements Tier-1 instruction with focused, targeted interventions for those students who do not meet expected patterns of growth and achievement. Tier-3 instruction is highly intensive intervention—often provided by special education teachers—designed for students who do not respond to Tier-2 efforts (Council for Exceptional Children, 2007; Hoover & Patton, 2008; Martinez, Nellis, & Prendergast, 2006).

How will the roles and responsibilities of teachers change as increased numbers of students receive instruction within a multitiered framework? Currently, this remains unclear. General educators likely will be responsible for delivering research-based Tier-1 instruction. This would require that all teachers remain current on what constitutes effective practices for a range of learners in a variety of skill and subject areas (Mastropieri & Scruggs, 2005). Special educators would likely support students at risk and with disabilities in all three of the tiers. According to Hoover and Patton (2008), this would require that special education teachers assume a multitude of roles including (1) modeling data-driven decision making, (2) being a resource for

Pause & Reflect

Special education has evolved from segregated to more inclusive modes of service delivery. How have the roles and responsibilities of general and special educators changed as a result of this evolution?

evidence-based practices, (3) providing differentiated instruction and behavioral supports, and (4) being a model of collaborative practice. There are concerns that many general and special education teachers are not fully prepared to fulfill these new roles. A major challenge may be to ensure that gaps in training are provided as RTI becomes more prominent in schools.

Summary

Providing an inclusive education for all students requires an understanding of the evolution of special education service delivery, the legal foundations of special education, and an awareness of emerging issues. We presented the following major points in this chapter.

The evolution of inclusive service delivery

- Until the 1960s, the majority of students with disabilities were educated in segregated settings for most or all of the school day.
- Mainstreaming was a policy of integrating students with mild disabilities into general education settings, although those students still "belonged" to special education.
- The inclusion movement, founded on the assumption that general and special educators share responsibility and accountability in educating students with disabilities, gathered strength in the mid-1980s.
- Parents and civil rights advocates used the precedent of *Brown v. Board of Education* (1954) to achieve access to education and due process of law.
- Parents of students with disabilities tend to support inclusion but remain concerned that too many educators lack the skills to implement such programming effectively.
- Today, most students with disabilities are educated in their neighborhood schools and in general education classes.

Legal foundations: IDEA

- The Individuals with Disabilities Education Improvement Act (IDEA 2004), the most recent iteration of the landmark Education for All Handicapped Children Act (EAHCA) of 1975, is the most significant legislative effort supporting the education of students with disabilities.
- IDEA, a confluence of significant legal decisions and principles, ensures that all students, regardless of their disability, receive a free and appropriate public education (FAPE) in the least restrictive environment (LRE).
- An individualized education program (IEP) containing current students' levels of functioning, annual goals, special education and related services, projected dates of services, and the extent of participation in the general education environment guides instructional efforts.
- Students and their families have procedural due process protections and are ensured of receiving a nondiscriminatory assessment of strengths and weaknesses.

Legal foundations: NCLB

- No Child Left Behind (NCLB), a comprehensive federal initiative designed to improve the educational performance of *all* students, mandates compliance to high standards and sanctions states and schools that fail to meet set criteria.
- The major components of NCLB are strong accountability for results, expanded flexibility and local control, scientifically based teaching methods, expanded options for parents, and highly qualified teacher requirements. These components are having a substantial impact on how all students are being educated.

Legal foundations: Section 504 and the ADA

- Section 504 and the Americans with Disabilities Act (ADA) are significant pieces of legislation that provide protections for students with disabilities who do not match the definitions provided under the IDEA statutes.
- Section 504 considers a child with a disability to be one who functions as having a disability.
- ADA expands protections to prohibit discrimination in employment and public accommodations.

Tomorrow's challenges

- Although it is generally accepted that some students with disabilities are unable to meet the same standards as their peers, educators and policy makers continue to struggle with determining how to best set high standards and assess academic progress.
- A severe and chronic shortage of highly qualified and fully certified special education teachers may derail efforts to deliver collaborative and supportive inclusive programming.
- Response to intervention (RTI), considered to be a useful framework for the delivery of educational services, may result in changing roles and responsibilities for both general and special educators.

Addressing Professional Standards

Standards addressed in Chapter 2 include:

CEC Standards: (1) Foundations, (8) assessment, (9) professional and ethical practice

INTASC Standards: Principle 1: Understand central concepts of the discipline; Principle 9: Reflect on practices and seek opportunities to grow professionally

Praxis™ II Standards: Special education knowledge-based core principles: (2) Legal and societal issues

Praxis II Standards: Special education application of core principles across categories: (5) Professional roles/issues/literature

A Look at Today's Schools: Teaching Students from Diverse Backgrounds

KEY TOPICS

After reading this chapter you will:

- Understand how the demographics of public school students are changing.
- Know how the demographics of students with disabilities compare to the demographics of the public school population at large.
- Be able to explain the significant discrepancies in educational outcomes for students who vary by ethnicity, culture, socioeconomic status, language, and learning differences.

- Understand the importance of inclusive classroom teachers' becoming knowledgeable about differences in students' backgrounds and experiences in the areas of culture, ethnicity, socioeconomic status, and language.
- Know what successful teachers believe and do to enhance the educational futures of all students.

Dorene Ross and Margaret Kamman, *University of Florida*
Vivian Correa and Jennifer Huber, *Clemson University*

Perspectives on Teaching Students from Diverse Backgrounds

An Interview with Melanie Buckley, English Teacher and Department Chair, Heritage High School

Melanie Buckley knows that cultural diversity is not just an urban issue. As an English teacher and department chair at Heritage High School in suburban (some may even say rural) Leesburg, Virginia, Melanie has observed that too many students from culturally and linguistically diverse (CLD) backgrounds have difficulty meeting academic and behavioral standards. This is a major challenge: Approximately 40% of the Heritage student population comes from CLD backgrounds, as one in four students are Hispanic or Asian.

Melanie Buckley has considerable teaching experience at both the high school and community college level. Her experience has taught her that "all teachers must be culturally aware and culturally responsive. This means that teachers must be cognizant of their students' lives outside of school, actively learning of their varied cultural backgrounds and the media-saturated popular culture contexts in which they live." She and her team have initiated a number of professional development activities to assist teachers at Heritage. These activities—known as *purposeful pedagogy*—have helped teachers connect elements of the secondary curriculum to the lives of their students from CLD backgrounds. One of the curriculum development sessions, "Beyond Dead White Men and Why You Should Diversify Your Literature Curriculum" was useful and popular with the faculty of the English department.

Melanie recognizes that professional development for teachers must be supplemented by specific actions that engage students and families from CLD backgrounds. Recognizing that school personnel need consistent family support to address the learning needs of their students, Melanie and the Heritage team developed "Success Nights," a strategy to involve families that had a history of limited contact with the school. To engage these families, Success Nights recognized the accomplishments of students and showcased how modest achievements could serve as a foundation for greater academic and social success. In addition to recognizing student accomplishments, guest speakers presented important topical information in an accessible, jargon-free fashion. Instead of being formal and authoritative, Success Nights were social occasions for community team building and letting families know that their input was welcome and needed by the school faculty and administration.

Melanie and her colleagues know that being culturally responsive requires problem solving and experimentation. For example, after reviewing the Heritage standardized test data, it was discovered that students from the English Language Learner subgroup were failing to meet minimum levels of performance at a disproportionately high rate. Recognizing that merely assigning more work would not address the challenge, Melanie and her colleagues wrote a grant proposal to examine various ways of motivating this group of learners. A similar group process was used to hypothesize a series of ways to increase homework completion among these same students.

Melanie Buckley recognizes that far too many students from diverse backgrounds struggle to meet academic expectations. This results in an achievement gap between these students and European American students and higher dropout rates and special education placements for students from CLD backgrounds. Through understanding, reflection, and creative experimentation, Heritage High School remains committed to navigating the intersection of ethnicity, language, and disability and enhancing cultural responsiveness across all aspects of the school community.

Students with disabilities come from a diverse range of cultural, language, and ethnic backgrounds.

Introduction

Imagine that you are about to begin working in an inclusive school with students who are from very diverse backgrounds. In most schools, you will have a significant number of students who come from homes of poverty and many students of color. Unfortunately, as Melanie Buckley observed in the opening interview for this chapter and as available evidence indicates, many of these students likely will be behind in both reading and/or mathematics on state assessments (California Department of Education, 2007). Some of these students will be learning English as a second language, others will have disabilities, while some will qualify for gifted and talented programs. A classroom context such as this challenges the skills of any teacher who is committed to ensuring that all students achieve at high levels. Success will require finding ways to engage students who may have begun school resistant to learning. Success will also require meeting the individual needs of each student with special needs and finding ways to communicate with students and families whose backgrounds vary considerably from yours.

It is important to note that a widespread misconception is that diverse schools exist only in urban settings. Heritage High School, in Leesburg, Virginia, is one of many schools that refute this perspective. In fact, the population of the United States is changing rapidly and dramatically, and understanding the needs of diverse learners is critical to the success of all teachers in all settings, particularly teachers with a commitment to inclusive education. Teachers in inclusive schools are responsible for the learning of all students and hold an important responsibility to advocate for students with disabilities to ensure that their needs are met. Students with disabilities are just as diverse as—and in some cases more so than—the general population of students. Students with disabilities are also from diverse cultures and ethnic groups (i.e., non–European American backgrounds, where standard English is often not spoken in the home). In addition, some of these students are in foster care, are homeless, or are from low-income families.

To better meet the needs of students with disabilities from diverse backgrounds within inclusive schools and classrooms, researchers recommend that all teachers should achieve the following:

- Better understand students' cultural and language backgrounds.
- Learn how they can adapt their teaching based on information about students' cultural and language backgrounds.
- Provide supports to ensure each student's success and ensure that all students are active participants in the academic and social community of the school (Banks et al., 2005; Gay, 2002; Ginsburg, 2005; Irvine, 2002).

In this chapter we provide information that addresses the cultural, language, ethnic, and economic backgrounds of students and how these factors affect teaching practices and student learning. Understanding your own background provides a context for reading about the backgrounds and experiences of students from diverse backgrounds that we discuss in this chapter. Before reading the rest of the chapter, please take a moment to reflect on your background in the "Pause & Reflect" exercise.

myeducationlab

Go to MyEducationLab, select the topic *Cultural and Linguistic Diversity*, and go to the Activities and Applications section. As you complete the simulation "Teachers at the Loom," think about how you can address the individual learning needs of your students while also taking into account how their cultural background may impact their learning.

Who Are the Students in Today's Schools?

Are today's students different from the students who entered school 15 to 20 years ago? Are schools more diverse? Next we'll examine how individual characteristics of the student population have changed and continue to change.

Pause & Reflect

Our choice of the words we use to describe ourselves is one way we define our identity. Take a moment, and list every word that you would use to describe yourself. Include words that define your physical characteristics, but be sure to go beyond that and list words that describe who you are and the various roles you play. Share your list with a peer, and discuss your commonalities and differences.

Ethnic Groups

Throughout the history of the United States, the ethnic composition has been majority European American (although we use this term, the U.S. Census Bureau and the U.S. Department of Education use the term *non-Hispanic Whites*). This ethnic composition is still the case today, with 67% of the country identified as European Americans. However, minority percentages have been rising and continue to rise (U.S. Census Bureau, 2006). Already, nearly 1 in 10 of the nation's 3,141 counties has a population that is more than 50% minority (U.S. Census Bureau, 2007). Additionally, California, New Mexico, and Texas do not have any group that represents a majority of the state's population, and three other states, Maryland, Georgia, and Nevada, are not far from joining this group (U.S. Census Bureau, 2006). Hispanics make up almost 19% of the school-age population in the United States and are the largest and fastest-growing minority group (U.S. Census Bureau, 2007). The U.S. Census Bureau estimates that Hispanics will make up 1 of every 3 U.S. residents by 2050 (U.S. Census Bureau, 2008). The second-largest minority group, African Americans, make up about 17% of the school-aged population (U.S. Census Bureau, 2007). The minority population is expanding so rapidly that by 2025 it is likely that half of all students will be non–European American (Hussar, 2005).

Language

Factors related to language have been changing and continue to change rapidly. Currently, almost 10 million students, 1 of 5, speak a language other than English when they are at home (Crawford, 2002). U.S. Census Bureau 2000 figures estimate that by 2030, 40% of school-aged children will not have English as their first language (National Center for Education Statistics, 2005). This creates a challenge for schools committed to making the changes in instruction and curriculum necessary to meet the needs of second-language learners and therefore has profound implications for educational programming. In the 2003–2004 school year, 11% of the total student enrollment were designated as **English-language learners (ELLs)** and entitled to general educational services to address their limited-English proficiency (LEP). As the number of second-language learners increases, the need for services will also increase, and the majority of teachers entering the profession will need to be prepared to meet their needs. Indeed, this is already true in some states. For example, in Florida, all teachers are required to have proficiency in addressing the needs of students who are ELLs.

Not surprisingly, extreme differences exist among the states in the numbers of students designated ELL. According to the National Center for Education Statistics (2005), California and Texas have the largest reported number of students receiving ELL services, 26% and 16%, respectively. The 100 largest districts in the United States report even more astonishing figures. The Los Angeles Unified School District serves 307,594 students designated ELL, 41.8% of their total student population. Complicating this further is the fact that students designated ELL represent more than 400 languages.

Poverty

Family situations have changed significantly since the 1970s. Characteristics such as single-parent homes illustrate this change. According to a U.S. Census Bureau report, in 1970, only 3 million children lived in single-mother households. By 2003 this number more than tripled, to 10 million (Fields, 2004). At the forefront of these family situations is the incidence of children (1) living in poverty, (2) living in foster care, and (3) who are homeless.

Economic segregation plagues our country and, therefore, our schools. The poverty rates in the United States may surprise you. According to the National Center for Children in Poverty (Fass & Cauthen, 2007), in 2006 nearly 13 million children, or 17%, lived in families with incomes below the federal poverty level, up 1.2 million since 2000. Even more problematic are the across-state differences. Thirteen states have a child poverty rate above 20%, and two have a rate under 10%. Additionally, ethnicity is intertwined with poverty. Thirty-three percent of African American children, 27% of Latino children, and 40% of Native American children live in poor families (Fass & Cauthen, 2007). Figure 3.1 gives additional and more detailed information on ethnic disparities in poverty rates.

In addition to living in poverty, a large number of children face a home life in foster care. In 2006 the U.S. Department of Health and Human Services reported that 510,000 children were in foster care in the United States, with 129,000 waiting to be adopted. Twenty-four percent of these

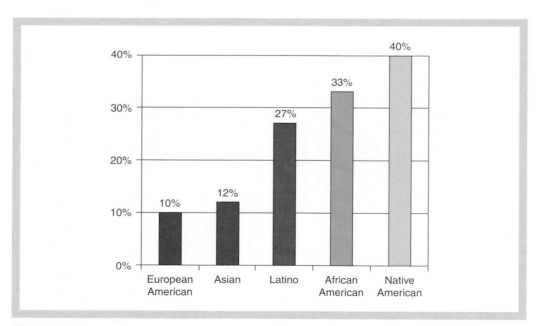

Figure 3.1

Statistics on Children Living in Poverty by Ethnicity in 2006
Source: Data from Fass, S., & Cauthen, N. (2007). *Who are America's poor children? The official story. The National Center for Children in Poverty.* Retrieved May 17, 2008, from http://www.nccp.org/publications/pub_787.html

children have been in the foster care system for more than 3 years. Moreover, an even greater number of children live with relatives as a result of a private arrangement and, therefore, are not connected to social service agencies (Murray, Macomber, & Geen, 2004). Together, the children in foster care and those raised by relatives are often referred to as *no-parent children*. Research on this group of children has shown that they often have poor academic outcomes (Harden, 2004; Sun, 2003).

One final family situation requiring attention is families without a home. The fastest-growing segment of the homeless population is families with children, and an estimated 2% of all children (1.35 million) experience homelessness over the course of a year (Institute for Children and Poverty, 2003). Homelessness has a devastating impact on educational opportunities. Issues such as residency requirements and immunization records often prevent homeless children from enrolling in school, and those who are able to enroll face barriers to regular attendance. Additionally, homeless children change schools often, as approximately one half of these children attend three or more schools each year (Institute for Children and Poverty, 2007).

Diversity in Special Education

Now that you have a picture of the demographics of the student population in general, we describe how these demographics intersect with students in special education. In the 2005–2006 school year, 6,796,274 students with disabilities aged 3 to 21 were served under IDEA (ideadata.org, 2007). European American students made up 58.7% of students with disabilities; 20% were African American; 17.5% were Hispanic; 2.2% were Asian/Pacific Islander; and 1.6% were Native American/Alaska Native. Additionally, 7.04% of students who are second-language learners, 30% of children who are abused or neglected, 16% of children in foster care, and an estimated 30% to 40% of homeless children were identified with a disability (ideadata.org, 2007; Smithgall, Gladden, Howard, Goerge, & Courtney, 2004; Wingerden, Emerson, & Ichikawa, 2002).

Understanding the intersection of ethnicity, language, and disability is important, but it goes deeper than overall statistics. Some groups of students are over- or underrepresented in special education. This means that for some demographic groups, the proportion of students identified for special education is higher than the proportion of that group in the general population. Specifically, a significantly greater proportion of African American and Native American/Alaska Native students are identified with disabilities. Table 3.1 highlights the breakdown of selected disability categories for several ethnic groups. While overrepresentation of some minorities in special education is a persistent problem, underrepresentation in gifted and talented programs is an equal concern. According to the National Center for Education Statistics (2007), gifted and talented

It is important that teachers understand the cultural, ethnic, and language backgrounds of students

Table 3.1   Special Education Demographics Within Five Ethnic Groups

	Percentage of Students with Disabilities by Ethnic Group				
Disability	Non-Hispanic European American	African American— Non-Hispanic	Hispanic	Asian/ Pacific Islander	Native American/ Alaska Native
Learning disability	45.6	44.9	57.3	39.4	54.5
Speech or language impaired	20.1	14.3	18.1	26	16.0
Intellectual disability	7.9	16.1	4.9	8.9	7.5
Emotional disturbance	7.9	11.2	1.9	4.6	8.0
All other disabilities	18.5	13.5	17.8	17.5	14.0

Percentages shown are based on the total number of students with disabilities within each ethnic group. For example, these data reveal that 45.6% of all non-Hispanic European American students with disabilities are identified with learning disabilities but that 57.3% of all Hispanic students with disabilities are identified with learning disabilities.

Source: Data from National Center for Education Statistics. (2007). *Percentage of gifted and talented students in public elementary and secondary schools, by sex, race/ethnicity, and state: 2002 and 2004.* Retrieved May 30, 2008, from http://nces.ed.gov/programs/digest/d07/table/dt07_051.asp

students represent 6.7% of the total enrolled population. However, large differences in prevalence exist when broken down by ethnicity. For example, 7.9% of European Americans are identified as gifted compared to 3.5% of African Americans, 11.9% of Asians, 4.3% of Hispanics, and 5.2% of Native American/Alaska Natives.

Further complicating this issue are the specific placements and outcomes for different student demographics. Regardless of over- or underrepresentation, the ethnicity or language of a student strongly influences their classroom placement. For example, African American, Hispanic, Native American/Alaska Native, and ELL students with disabilities are more likely to be taught in separate classrooms or schools than students who are European American or Asian and Pacific Islander (deValenzuela, Copeland, Huaqing, & Park, 2006). Additionally, although all students with disabilities have low graduation rates, Hispanic, Native American/Alaska Native, and African American students with disabilities have substantially lower graduation rates than do European American students (ideadata.org, 2007). See "Just the Facts" for more information regarding diversity and students with disabilities.

The population of students entering the classroom today differs substantially from students in the 1990s and is predicted to further increase in diversity in the future. Moreover, the disproportionate number of these students with disabilities necessitates that educators adapt their inclusive classroom practices to meet the particular needs of students from diverse backgrounds. This need becomes especially obvious when examining the low academic achievement levels and higher than expected dropout rates for many of these students, including both those with and without disabilities.

Student Diversity and Academic Achievement

In this section we discuss how students from diverse backgrounds struggle to meet academic expectations, resulting in an achievement gap between these students and European American students, and higher dropout rates for students from diverse backgrounds.

Academic Proficiency

The achievement gap is the disparity in performance on achievement tests among groups of students based on ethnicity, language, and socioeconomic status. As the opening interview with Melanie Buckley revealed, such a gap was found at Heritage High School, as a large number

Just the Facts — About Student Diversity and Disability

What is the prevalence of disability by diversity factors? That is, what percentage of all students from each group is identified with a disability?	• Homeless 30% to 40% • Native American/Alaska Native 13.8% • Foster Care 16% • African American 12.4% • European American 8.7% • Hispanic 8.2% • English Language Learners 7% • Asian/Pacific Islander 4.5%
Are there differences in ethnicity by disability category?	• Significantly more African American and Native American/Alaska Native students are identified with disabilities than are students from other ethnic groups. • African American and Native American/Alaska Native students are overrepresented in the categories of intellectual disability, learning disability, and emotional and behavioral disability
How do graduation and dropout rates compare?	• Only 36.2% of African American students with disabilities graduate with a standard diploma, compared to 59.1% of European American students with disabilities. The dropout rate for students with disabilities by ethnic background is 29.9% of European American students, compared to 48.4% of Native American/Alaska Native students, 41.7% of African American students, and 38.9% of Hispanic students.
Where are students educated?	• African American students with disabilities are the least likely of any ethnic group to be educated in a general education classroom. Of these students, 38.6% are educated in general education settings for most of the school day, compared to 54.7% of European American students. • While 14% of European American students with disabilities are educated in separate special education classes or schools for most of the school day, 22.9% of Hispanic and 28.1% of African American students with disabilities are educated in these settings.
Who is living in poverty?	• Students with disabilities are more likely to be poor than are students in the general population. • About 25% of elementary and secondary students with disabilities live in poverty, compared with 20% of the general population.

of students from diverse backgrounds did not meet performance standards. Unfortunately, this finding is common across many schools. For example, achievement results from the 2006 California Standards Test show large differences in student proficiency when examined by subgroup. In English/language arts, 27.4% of Hispanic and 29% of African American students were rated proficient or better, compared to 60% of European American students (California Department of Education, 2007). Even more troubling, only 15% of students designated ELLs were at or above proficiency. The results for math are not any better, with 25% of African American students and 30% of Hispanic students rated as proficient, compared with 53% of European American students.

The achievement gap also exists among high-achieving youth. According to a 2004 report published by the National Center on the Gifted and Talented, African American, Hispanic, and Native American students are significantly underrepresented among the nation's highest achieving students (Miller, 2004). For example, 17% of European Americans and 14% of Asian Americans earned mostly A's, but only 7% of African American, 10% of Hispanic, and 8% of Native American students did (Horn, Peter, & Rooney, 2002). These same disparities exist for Advanced Placement (AP) exams and Scholastic Aptitude Test (SAT) scores (Miller, 2004).

Poverty also poses a serious challenge to children's potential to succeed in school. Research has suggested that growing up in poverty can negatively impact children's mental and behavioral development as well as their overall health, which can make it more difficult for them to learn (Duncan, Brooks-Gunn, & Klebanov 1994; Pollitt, 1994). As such, the achievement gap is often pronounced for students living in poverty.

High School Graduation Rates

The 27th Annual Report to Congress (U.S. Department of Education, 2007) reported that only 51.9% of students with disabilities graduated from high school with a regular diploma. About 1 in 3 of these students drop out of school. Graduation rates were the lowest for African American students with disabilities, at 36.2%. In general, students from culturally and linguistically diverse backgrounds are "three times more likely to be low achievers than high achievers, two times more likely to be at least one grade level behind in schools, and four times more likely to drop out than their native-English-speaking peers" (American Association of Colleges for Teacher Education, 2002, p. 3).

Teachers, Students, and the Demographic Divide

As you may know, the diversity that exists in the student population does not exist in the teaching force. A severe and chronic shortage of teachers from culturally and linguistically diverse (CLD) backgrounds exists. According to data collected by the National Education Association (2003), the teaching workforce in the United States is largely European American (86%), female (more than 75%), and middle-aged (median age 46). Furthermore, the proportion of African American teachers has declined from 8% to 6% since the 1990–1991 school year.

This lack of teachers from diverse backgrounds creates a demographic divide in many schools. According to the National Commission on Teaching and America's Future (2003), individuals of African American, Hispanic, Latino, Asian, and Native American/Alaska Native descent make up only 14% of the K–12 teachers, while 36% of the students are from these backgrounds. In the nation's largest schools, students from diverse backgrounds make up 69% of the population, while only 35% of their teachers are from similar backgrounds (National Education Association, 2003).

We do not mean to suggest that teachers from the majority culture cannot successfully teach students from diverse backgrounds. This is certainly not the case. However, it is important that the teacher workforce include at least a reasonable proportion of teachers who share the cultural and language experiences of their students. These teachers can serve as a rich resource for other teachers and ensure that the diverse backgrounds of students are used to enrich the lives of everyone in the school (Tyler et al., 2004). In the next section, we discuss how all teachers can bridge the demographic divide by learning about a student's background and experiences, and how these cultural experiences influence student behavior in school.

Culture and Student Outcomes

Clearly, significant differences in educational outcomes exist for students who vary by class, ethnicity, and home language. However, we are not suggesting that the demographic divide between teachers and students or any other single factor determines educational outcomes. Students within and across these groups achieve amazing success. For example, you may have seen the movie *Homeless to Harvard* (Mahoney, Kern, & Levin, 2003), which documents the educational and personal success of Liz Murray. Similarly, the book *And Still We Rise* (Corwin, 2001) documents the outcomes for 12 gifted high school students living in the Watts neighborhood of Los Angeles. Despite what most of us would consider overwhelming odds (i.e., poverty, second-language background, gang culture, teenage pregnancy, homelessness), the youth in these stories demonstrate the capacity to succeed and move toward promising futures.

Additionally, it is important to remember that each student has a complex history that encompasses varied factors such as social class, ethnicity, language, family structure, medical history, school history, ability, and disability. School experience and probable educational outcomes are influenced by the interplay of such factors. Think for a moment about how and why the importance of teachers and school might vary in determining the educational futures of two students with similar, mild learning disabilities. One student comes from a European American, upper middle-class family with resources to provide tutors. The other is a recent immigrant, a student designated ELL, whose parents do not understand the U.S. educational system and have little disposable income. Resources and knowledge of how to work within the system (social capital) are critical factors that provide advantages to some students over others. Teachers and schools play a significant role for all children, but particularly for students whose families lack social capital. The connections (or lack of connections) between students and their teachers often make the difference between academic success and failure.

Establishing Connections Across a Cultural Divide

A critical issue is whether teachers view differences as "normal." A frequently occurring human tendency is to perceive difference as dividing people and behavior into two groups, "normal" and "abnormal," rather than perceiving human variation along a continuum (Baglieri & Knopf, 2004). We all tend to perceive those most like us as "normal" and those who differ from us in significant ways as "abnormal." For most of us, these perceptions are implicit feelings. Try a little experiment to help you think about your perceptions of "normal" and how hard it is to alter perceptions.

Cross your arms across your chest in the way that you habitually cross them. Notice which hand is on top. Now cross your arms so that the *other* hand is on top. Many find this so "abnormal" that it takes several tries to cross their arms in the nonhabitual way, but there is nothing inherently "normal" about having one's left (or right) hand on top. Yet even when you *know* that there is nothing abnormal about the new position, it feels weird. Without deliberate intention, you will habitually return your arms to their accustomed position.

In school, teachers often define "normal" students as those who come prepared to behave in particular ways and to handle a specific type of academic structure. A number of culturally specific behaviors have been identified that often are challenging for teachers (Lewis & Doorlag, 2006). Consider whether the following behaviors, which are "normal" behaviors within specific cultural contexts, might seem problematic for you:

- Students talk out, often talking over you or other students in a form of communal participation.
- Students are very reticent to participate, or to ask and answer questions.
- Students come to school or school functions late.

European American, middle-class teachers who have spoken English from birth may expect all students to exhibit behaviors such as taking turns speaking in class, looking teachers in the eye when reprimanded, and asking questions when they don't understand. Yet, each of these behaviors is outside the norm for one or more cultural groups. This can mean that the teacher perceives actions that fall within the norms for a certain student's culture as "abnormal."

These implicit judgments can lead teachers to blame students or their families for lack of success in school, disrupting their connections with students and creating barriers to success. As Chamberlain has noted, "What we learn through our culture becomes our reality, and to see beyond that is often difficult" (2005, p. 199). *When a teacher's cultural assumptions lead to the conclusion that a student's academic or social behavior is outside the norm of appropriate, the teacher may make well-intended decisions that undermine the student's educational success.*

What Is Culture, and Why Is It So Important?

Culture is a concept that helps teachers understand the implicit evaluations they make and the reasons behind some of the student behaviors that "seem" atypical or abnormal. *Culture* has been defined as "the values, traditions, worldview, and social and political relationships created, shared, and transformed by a group of people bound together by a common history, geographic location, language, social class, religion, or other shared identity" (Nieto & Bode, 2008, p. 171). As this

Cultural background can influence how students interact and work together in school.

definition suggests, culture is dynamic, or changing, and is socially constructed by those who participate in it. Culture has also been referred to as an iceberg (Oetzel & Ting-Toomey, 2006). The part that we see and hear on the surface includes such variables as dress, music, food, and language. What is below the surface includes the deeper culture such as traditions, beliefs, values, norms, and worldviews. It is this invisible part of the iceberg that can confuse people as they interact with different cultural groups.

Cultural Norms and School: Some Examples. Culture can influence how students interact in schools, especially students who are new to the United States. Dimensions of culture include styles of communication and interaction, concepts of self, behavioral expectations and management styles, time, and spatial proximity (Oetzel & Ting-Toomey, 2006; Storti, 1999). It is important to note that cultural dimensions are not characteristics that students either have or don't have but are aspects that fall along a continuum (Salend & Duhaney, 2005). For example, some groups tend toward an *individualist orientation* in their culture and communication style, while others tend toward a *collectivist orientation.* Individualist cultures emphasize individual achievement and initiative and promote self-realization (Gudykunst & Kim, 2003). Students in individualist cultures typically are motivated by individual recognition. For example, the teacher might create a public display of achievement by hanging stellar student work on the wall. A common manifestation of this orientation in schools is the selection of a citizen of the week.

In collectivist cultures, working for the common good is more highly valued than individual achievement. Students from collectivist cultures may prefer to work in groups, and each member's contribution is judged "successful" only to the degree that it enhances the whole group. Individuals from collectivist cultures may not be motivated by individual awards, praise, or displays of accomplishment; instead, they may be motivated by group productivity and accomplishment (Trumbull, Rothstein-Fisch, & Greenfield, 2000). Although cultural groups have tendencies toward individualism or collectivism, these cultural traits fall along a continuum, and all cultures have both individual and collective traits. In addition, individuals within cultures differ with regard to these traits.

Pause & Reflect

Can you think of examples of classroom practices, folk tales, or historical figures that represent an individualist orientation in U.S. culture? How about practices, tales, and figures that represent a collective orientation? Why is it important to examine these examples?

The Impact of Culture on Education. Cultural tendencies impact the way students participate in education. Figure 3.2 describes several classroom situations and some cultural dimensions to consider. This figure will help you see how a teacher might misinterpret the behavior of a student from a diverse culture. Cultural differences may cause educators to inaccurately judge students as poorly behaved or disrespectful. Consider also that as adults, teachers must accept the responsibility for learning about cultural differences and helping build bridges between home and school cultures. Because cultural differences are implicit, students may have a great deal of difficulty perceiving that their actions are inconsistent with teacher expectations and may find themselves reprimanded by teachers but fail to understand what they did that caused concern.

The influence of culture on beliefs about education, the value of education, and participation styles cannot be overestimated. Some newly arrived immigrant students, for example, tend to be quiet in class and view making eye contact with teachers as inappropriate (Bennett, 2006). In contrast, most European American students are taught to value active classroom discussion and to look teachers directly in the eye to show respect. Their teachers view participation as a sign of engagement and competence (Cartledge, Gardner, & Ford, 2009).

Figure 3.2   Cultural Perspectives on Education

Classroom Situation

Cultural Dimensions to Consider

Cultural Dimension: Styles of Communication

A student nods his head "yes" when asked in front of the whole class if he understands the solution to the math problem. Yet the student clearly did not understand the concept, because he is unable to even successfully complete any problems on an individual practice assignment.

Consider that the student comes from a culture where he would be embarrassed to admit that he did not know the answer. The student's culture may not encourage direct communication and "calling attention" to individuals. The teacher could wait and ask the student, individually, to show him how to solve the problem or use response cards during small group instruction.

Cultural Dimension: Concept of Self

Students in a small group are asked to play "Jeopardy" as a way of solving social studies questions. The winner will receive an award and be allowed to choose a toy from the class store. Lucia, a student from the Ukraine, does not attempt to answer any of the questions.

Consider that the student comes from a culture that promotes collaboration and collectivism. The nature of the competition may make this student uncomfortable. The teacher could set up small teams to work together in answering the "Jeopardy" questions.

Cultural Dimension: Management Style

A new student arrives from Central America. The teacher uses a lot of cooperative learning strategies in the classroom. The student seems confused and does not want to leave his desk.

Consider that the student came from a class where the teacher lectures and the students' roles are more passive. The teacher can use a buddy system to help the new student adjust to more "open" classroom activities.

Cultural Dimension: Time

A student arrives to class late and without his notebook. He's visibly upset. His friend offers to let him borrow a notebook, but the student refuses and remains distracted throughout the class period.

Consider that the student might come from a culture that has a monochromic perspective, in which time commitments are taken very seriously and so is personal property. Borrowing or lending is seen to intrude on privacy.

Cultural Dimension: Proximity

A new student who speaks very little English is having a problem getting along with the other students. He has fights on the playground every day, which he seems to provoke by constantly touching the other boys.

Consider that the student might come from a culture where it is appropriate to get close in personal space and touch each other. The other students do not feel comfortable with the close proximity and touching and respond with anger. The teacher needs to speak to the students about personal space and encourage students to express their comfort with proximity.

Another contrast involves the role of parents in education. Parents from some cultures tend to regard teachers as experts and will often defer educational decision making to them (Harry, 2008). In contrast, European American parents are often more actively involved in their children's classrooms. These cultural differences may cause educators to make inaccurate judgments regarding the value that non–European American families place on education. While it is important to keep in mind that different cultural groups *tend* to follow particular language and interaction styles, tremendous variability exists within cultural groups (Gutiérrez & Rogoff, 2003). Thus, educators need to understand individual histories and ideologies regarding education and learning as well as the cultural patterns and beliefs of groups. Next we'll look at a couple of cases to examine in more detail how culture impacts educational interactions.

Understanding Culture Through the Lens of Ethnicity and Student Behavior. To help you think about the role of ethnicity in student behavior, we'll consider a study of the pattern of discipline referrals in a large, urban high school (Gregory, 2007). It is well documented that African American youth receive a disproportionate number of school sanctions such as referrals and suspensions (Wald & Losen, 2007). In one high school, researchers examined referral data for 1 year to provide a better understanding of the issues behind this disproportionality (Gregory, 2007). The data revealed that the majority of referrals were for student defiance of adult authority. It is noteworthy that 80% of the African American students who received referrals received at least one for defiance as compared to fewer than 50% of the European American students who received referrals.

> ### Pause & Reflect
>
> Is it possible that defiance exists in the interaction between the student and the teacher, not in the student? Can you think of a time when the way another person reacted to something you said or did led you to do something you might not otherwise have done?

Although African American students were referred more often for defiance, students were not uniformly defiant (Gregory, 2007). That is, a student who was defiant with one teacher might have been cooperative with another. The difference was in the quality of the relationship between the teacher and the student. Students were "more cooperative and less defiant in one classroom compared to another. This suggests that defiance referrals often arise as situation- or relationship-specific for most students, with only a small number of students consistently defiant in most or all of their classrooms" (p. 2).

Understanding and addressing the overrepresentation of African American students in discipline-related incidents requires an examination of the problem of negative interactions between African American students and their teachers, particularly around issues of authority (Gregory, 2007). The acceptance of teacher authority is grounded in students' perceptions that teachers care about them, genuinely believe in their academic potential, and are acting in their best interest (Gay, 2002). Furthermore, at times teachers who lack knowledge regarding certain cultural issues may create power struggles by ordering compliance instead of using their relationship with a student to help support the student in resolving a problem (Marks, 2005). When teachers do not have positive relationships with African American students, this may place these students at risk for lower achievement because of "missed instructional time, loss of adult advocacy, lower adult support for achievement, and the stigmatizing label of being a behavior problem" (Gregory, 2007, p. 3).

> ### Pause & Reflect
>
> You have learned that Shawn, an African American in your eighth-grade visual arts class has been referred to the teacher assistance team (TAT) due to his hyperactivity and verbally aggressive behavior. You are surprised because your impression is that Shawn may be gifted in music and art. What could you do to assist the TAT in addressing Shawn's needs?

Understanding the possible cultural sources of student resistance or defiance requires that teachers look at their own and their students' behavior in new ways. It is important to note, however, that the ability to attend to cultural differences does not require that the teacher share the same culture as the student (Bondy, Ross, Gallingane & Hambacher, 2007; Gregory, 2007).

Understanding Culture Through the Lens of Language and Disability. Linguistically diverse students face the complex task of acquiring English as a second or sometimes third language. Because acquiring a second language is a long and often arduous process, educators may find it difficult to determine whether a student is following the typical progression in development of a second language or struggling with a language disability. Two errors are possible. Teachers may misinterpret typical language acquisition as a language disability, or they may fail to perceive a language disability that does exist (Artiles, Klingner, & Tate, 2006; Coady & Escamilla, 2005; Klingner, Artiles, & Barletta, 2006). Moreover, it is important that educators communicate with parents in a language that they understand so that the student's developmental and educational needs can be well understood and successfully addressed.

In the United States, some view bilingualism as a deficit (Baca & Cervantes, 2004; Connor & Boskin, 2001). This may lead to the misidentification of students who are acquiring English as having a learning disability or a communication disorder (Connor & Boskin, 2001; Cummins,

2001). In contrast to the assumption that bilingualism is a deficit, research has shown that young bilingual children generally have a "far more advanced linguistic schema than that of the monolingual child" (Connor & Boskin, 2001, p. 26). If these cultural and linguistic strengths are recognized and built upon in the classroom, they can be used to enhance academic achievement (Baca & Cervantes, 2004). The following vignette provides an example regarding how a culturally responsive teacher addressed issues related to language and a possible disability for Reynaldo, an 8-year-old student from Mexico.

Learning About Student Culture and Language: An Example

We explore another set of cultural factors as we consider the experiences of Reynaldo Muñoz, an 8-year-old student from Mexico. Reynaldo's mother enrolled him in school a couple of months after they arrived in the United States. After 4 months in a "newcomers' classroom," Reynaldo was put in a second-grade classroom with 24 students and provided 1 hour daily of English instruction with the English as a second language (ESL) teacher. Shortly after being placed in Ms. Kahn's second-grade classroom, he began struggling academically and seemed very anxious. On a few occasions, Reynaldo cried and needed to be consoled by the bilingual family liaison. He rarely spoke, even with the three other Hispanic class members. He played by himself most of the day, appearing shy and nervous around his peers. Ms. Kahn thought that Reynaldo was showing signs of social isolation and possibly a learning disability. She wondered whether he was receiving academic support or encouragement from home.

The teacher assistance team suggested that an important first step was for Ms. Kahn to learn more about the family. Ms. Kahn and the family liaison scheduled multiple home visits, structured as conversations with the family. Ms. Kahn had learned about the "funds of knowledge" approach to learning about and connecting with families from culturally and linguistically diverse backgrounds (Moll, Amanti, Neff, & Gonzalez, 1992), and used this framework as a guide for the interviews. She was interested in understanding more about Reynaldo's family history, networks, educational history, language use, and child-rearing ideologies. Here are some of the things Ms. Kahn learned: Reynaldo's parents both had graduated from high school, and his father had run his own plumbing business in Mexico while Mrs. Muñoz had stayed at home to raise Reynaldo and his younger sister, Sonia. The family moved to the United States in hopes of finding better health care for Reynaldo, who was diagnosed with severe asthma when he was 3 years old.

The family, including one grandmother who provided childcare, share a small apartment with Mr. Muñoz's brothers. All family members work long hours in jobs in maintenance and housekeeping at a local resort. During their time off, Reynaldo's uncles often take him to local soccer matches and teach him about soccer. In turn, Reynaldo helps his uncles with English. Reynaldo shows off his newfound reading skills by reading library books to them and helps them with words in the newspaper. He checks out preschool-level books at his weekly trips to the library with his mother, who is also learning English through classes at her job.

Ms. Kahn observed Reynaldo taking care of his *hermanita,* Sonia. He was gentle with her, fed her, changed her diaper, and played with her patiently. Mrs. Muñoz commented on how responsible he was, "un buen hijo"! The family attended the local Catholic church, which provided mass services and Bible school in Spanish. Mrs. Muñoz reported that Reynaldo loved Sunday school and enjoyed playing and talking with the other children. The family was also involved with the church's community outreach efforts, volunteering to help others who were newly emigrated from Mexico.

Ms. Kahn also learned that Reynaldo had experienced severe asthmatic attacks while at school in Mexico and had become fearful of going to school. His mother reported that he had been absent from school for most of the first year in elementary school and believed this caused him to fall behind academically. The family spoke of wanting Reynaldo to do well in school. They hoped he would attend college and become a teacher. His *abuelita* spoke little English but was adamant about her grandson becoming "bien educado," or well socialized and well mannered.

As Ms. Kahn drove home from one of her home visits, she reflected on all she had learned. She appreciated this new view of Reynaldo because she realized he was not withdrawn outside of school. Instead, he was proud to share all he was learning with his uncles, grandmother, and parents. Ms. Kahn thought about the meaningful interactions she had witnessed as Reynaldo read to his family and giggled and snuggled close to his mother, grandmother, father, or uncles. Ms. Kahn also was impressed at the closeness of his family, the social support they gained from their church and community, and their high aspirations for Reynaldo. She wondered how she would figure out whether he had a learning disability or was behind because of his asthma-related absences. She wondered how she could apply all these new insights to better meet Reynaldo's needs.

How Culture Mediates School Experience. Looking at school achievement through different cultural lenses demonstrates the ways in which teacher and student behaviors are mediated by their culturally derived values, experiences, and beliefs (Chamberlain, 2005; Garcia, Méndez Perez, & Ortiz, 2000; Gay, 2002). The challenge for teachers is that students vary in so many ways, and the examples we provide describe just a few of these variations. Furthermore, as we've noted throughout this chapter, students and their families also differ significantly within a given cultural group, and no two students from a given cultural group are the same. While keeping this variation in mind, two areas of cultural difference are so significant that they warrant special attention. One is the issue of poverty, and the second is the interface between culture and parental expectations.

The Significance of Poverty. Does money impact a parent's ability to support her children's school achievement? Perhaps one could argue that it doesn't take money to read to a child, take him to the library, or help him with homework. There is some logic to this perspective. However, research reveals that the lack of economic resources can severely limit the ability of parents to support their children. Poverty impacts access to medical care, prenatal care, early childhood education, therapy, tutors, after-school and summer enrichment programs, stable housing, and sufficient quantities of healthy food (Rothstein, 2002). In all of these ways, poverty persistently diminishes opportunities for success. Consider just two of the ways in which poverty undermines achievement.

Pause & Reflect

What role do you think family income plays in access to mental health services? How do you think needing but not receiving mental health services might impact referral to and placement in special education?

Many children and youth from impoverished backgrounds lack access to preventive mental health services. Although access to services varies, current practices tend to focus on treatment rather than prevention of problems, and by a margin of 3 to 1, states fund treatment of adults over treatment of children (J. L. Cooper, 2008). In addition, fewer than 13% of youth who need drug or alcohol treatment receive it, and fewer than 20% of children and youth needing mental health services receive them (J. L. Cooper, 2008).

Similarly, educational needs often go unmet for students from high-poverty backgrounds. Consider the lack of access to summer programs. Numerous studies suggest that differences in student's experiences during the summer account for a significant amount of the achievement gap. For example, a review of 13 studies of the impact of summer vacation on learning revealed that middle-class children made significantly greater gains in reading and language achievement during the summer than lower-class children did (H. Cooper et al., 1996). A second review of this research found that students from all economic classes make comparable gains during the school year, but that students from poverty backgrounds lose ground in reading and mathematics achievement over the summer (Alexander, Entwistle, & Olson, 2001). Data from other sources reveal that the life circumstances of children living in poverty mean they begin school behind and all too often do not catch up (Books, 2007). These findings are not intended to dismiss the significant role that schools can play in creating opportunities for children. Powerful education can alter the life circumstances for students in poverty; however, solving the achievement gap requires social policy that directly tackles the challenges of poverty rather than suggesting that schools alone can solve the problem.

Culture, Parent Expectations, and Disability. Cultural values and beliefs influence how people view disability (Skinner & Weisner, 2007; Wilder, Dyches, Obiakor, & Algozzine, 2004).

Some Latino parents, for example, may view caring for a child with a disability as a form of devotion or a gift from God. Religiosity plays a major role in the family's adaptation to having a child with a disability, with many families reporting that personal faith provided more support than church (Skinner, Correa, Skinner, & Bailey, 2001).

This one example regarding Latino parents only begins to suggest the range of beliefs and perspectives of different cultural groups regarding disability. It is important to keep in mind that groups exhibit tremendous variation in beliefs (i.e., not all Hispanic families have the same beliefs regarding disability). As Correa and Tulbert (1993) suggest, "cultural profiles of ethnic groups will be effective [for professionals only if they] can affirm that the cultural pattern does indeed exist within the individual family" (p. 256). Thus, it is very important for teachers to know their students, learn about students' lives outside of school, and understand an individual family's cultural perspectives about disability. This information is crucial in guiding interactions with parents. In the opening interview of this chapter, Melanie Buckley describes one strategy that teachers may use to begin to address this need, "Success Nights," which are informal social gatherings to recognize students and get to know parents. Figure 3.3 provides a framework that outlines several strategies that educators should consider in working with African American families. As you review this framework, keep in mind that many of the strategies also apply to other culturally and linguistically diverse families (Boyd & Correa, 2005).

It is important that teachers learn about the lives of their students outside of school.

Pause & Reflect

What questions could you ask family members to help understand their logistical, emotional, informational, and community supports? What community resources could you turn to in assisting families who are new to the area?

Although students vary in many ways both within and across cultures, and although the problems of poverty are pervasive, we want to be clear that schools and teachers play a critical role in making a difference for students from these backgrounds. Furthermore, teachers differ significantly in their capacity to make a difference in the lives of these students. In fact, teachers who accept the responsibility to make a difference with *every* student can have a powerful impact on achievement. This difference is magnified when teachers and administrators in entire schools take this perspective (Bempechat, 1998; Corbett, Wilson, & Williams, 2002).

Figure 3.3	Culturally and Family-Centered Supports
Logistical Support Schedule meetings when families can attend, and provide transportation and child care for the meeting.	**Emotional Supports** Conduct information-gathering interviews with families, asking about their goals, needs, priorities, values, and beliefs related to their child, and incorporate the extended family.
Informational Supports Provide information in family-friendly written formats, and convey a sense of cooperation and joint responsibility for solving problems.	**Community Supports** Establish networks with leaders in the community, and invite them to serve on school advisory councils.

Source: Adapted from Boyd, B., & Correa, V. (2005). Developing a framework for reducing the cultural clash between African American parents and the special education system. *Multicultural Perspectives, 7*(2), 3–11.

What Can Teachers Do? Culturally Responsive Teaching in Inclusive Classrooms

The remainder of this chapter draws on the literature about culturally responsive teaching and culturally responsive classroom management to suggest guiding principles for inclusive classrooms that help to ensure the success of students from diverse backgrounds. As you know, an inclusive classroom is designed to meet the needs of all students. Ginsberg (2005) reminds us that,

> across all cultural groups, all students are motivated, even when they are not motivated to learn what a teacher has to offer. Determination to find ways to encourage motivation is fundamental to equity in teaching and learning and is a core virtue of educators who successfully differentiate instruction. (p. 219)

Students who struggle in school, including those with disabilities, need strong motivation and interest to sustain the high level of effort necessary to master skills and content that come more easily to other students. Sustained effort requires a strong *will to learn*. In an effort to help students achieve at high levels, it can be tempting to focus only on the skills they need. However, effective teachers in inclusive classrooms focus simultaneously on the factors that support motivation to ensure that they meet the needs of all learners, particularly those from diverse backgrounds. The information that we provide in Chapter 3 complements and extends the information in other chapters addressing effective instruction and classroom management regarding specific pedagogy for including students with disabilities.

Supporting Resilience and Motivation

The No Child Left Behind (NCLB) Act has had a powerful impact on education since it became law in 2002. A clear and positive impact of this law is that school districts, schools, and teachers are now clearly focused on the learning of every child. This results because NCLB evaluates schools based on the learning of several subgroups of students in a school (e.g., students from low-income backgrounds and minority ethnic groups, students with disabilities, and students who are second-language learners). However, despite the intent of NCLB, the achievement gap persists along lines of ethnicity, social class, language, and disability. The unintended impact of NCLB in some instances is that schools and teachers have become more narrowly focused on raising test scores, and some advocates of NCLB would argue that this is the point—to raise test scores. We certainly agree that improving students' achievement is important, but raising scores is not enough.

The real goal is to help students develop achievement motivation and the capacity to be resilient; that is, we want to enhance students' strengths in order to support their capacity and motivation to learn and their beliefs that they are capable. Resilience has been defined as the "capacity for or outcome of successful adaptation despite challenging or threatening circumstances" (Masten, Best, & Garmezy, 1990, p. 425). Resilience is not the result of innate abilities but is a capacity available to all students that is bolstered by supportive factors (Bempechat, 1998; Benard, 2004).

A critical goal, then, is to assess the strengths students bring to school and build on those strengths by tailoring instruction toward them while building capacity in weaker areas. This type of instruction helps to build resilience, as the teacher works to ensure that each student becomes more autonomous, has a strong sense of purpose, is socially competent, has a problem-solving orientation, and has a strong achievement motivation (Morrison & Allen, 2007). A key to ensuring that this occurs is to provide instruction that is responsive to students' cultural backgrounds.

Culturally Responsive Inclusive Pedagogy

Culturally responsive teachers are simultaneously curious about culture and introspective (Irvine, 2003; Stormont, 2007). They know that culture impacts people's perceptions, knowledge, and interactions, and that the impact of cultural assumptions is often implicit. They strive to learn more about themselves, what they believe, and how their beliefs and experiences influence their perceptions of and interactions with students and their families.

Learning About Culture and Difference. No teacher will possess comprehensive knowledge about all of the possible cultures, languages, disabilities, and economic influences on learning. A teacher's underlying curiosity about individuals, culture, and difference is vitally important (Banks et al., 2005). As Melanie Buckley notes in the opening interview in this chapter, "All teachers must be culturally aware and culturally responsive. This means they must be cognizant of their students' lives outside of school, actively learning of their varied cultural backgrounds." A teacher who is culturally curious and responsive recognizes that all people are influenced by their background, culture, and experience, and that variations within cultures are as significant as variations across cultures. Reflect on the vignette earlier in this chapter and how Ms. Kahn learned about Reynaldo by being curious about his home, family, and culture.

While we are all inevitably influenced by our culture, the pervasiveness and dominance of one's own culture (European American, heterosexual, middle-class for a large proportion of teachers) can make certain cultural characteristics invisible to many who have grown up inside that culture. Remember your response to the "Pause & Reflect" exercise that addressed understanding your own background. If you are female, your list may include *sister, friend, sorority member, runner, good student, motivated, strong-willed*. Look back at your list to see if you also listed any descriptive words such as *White, middle class, monolingual, heterosexual, Christian, European American*. Persons from European American, middle-class backgrounds seldom include these terms when describing themselves, suggesting parts of their culture may be invisible to them.

Pause & Reflect

Are certain parts of your culture largely invisible to you or taken for granted? Discuss with a friend or classmate from a different cultural background how this might influence your interactions with friends or your interactions with students in a classroom. Why is it important for a teacher to recognize these aspects of her culture?

The culturally responsive teacher actively strives to see the world through alternative lenses. At times it is necessary for teachers to be willing to "step out of their skin" in order to critically examine the impact of their differences from others (Klug, Luckey, Wilkins, & Whitfield, 2006). In this chapter you have learned about some of the ways that people from various cultures view parenting, teachers, authority, social interaction, and disability. Our hope is that this has made you curious enough about other perspectives to initiate dialogue with those whose perspectives might differ from yours. You may be surprised to find that even friends you know very well will have different views of the world based on their background.

Using material from different cultural groups for instruction can motivate students to learn.

All Students Have the Capacity to Achieve. While almost all teachers believe that all students can succeed, what teachers do about these beliefs differs (Scheurich & Skla, 2003). In a study of diverse, urban classrooms and schools where students succeed at high levels versus those where they do not, researchers note that

> important distinctions [exist] in [teachers'] interpretations of the phrase's meaning. . . . Some said that all students could succeed and it was the teacher's job to ensure this happened. . . . Others took exception to such an idealistic philosophy. . . . One portion maintained that students had to show some effort first; another group stressed that home environments had to be more supportive of education. (Corbett, Wilson, & Williams, 2002, p. 12)

It is important to keep in mind that low expectations exist when low achievement is excused because students are poor, live in foster care, are second-language learners, don't try hard enough, or have a disability. Have you had contact with teachers who excuse behavior because of any of these reasons? Many of these teachers are often well intentioned and may feel sorry for students or believe the students face insurmountable challenges. Holding high expectations is particularly important for gifted students from diverse backgrounds. Kitano (2003) argues underrepresentation of diverse learners in gifted education may be a result of lowered expectations by teachers due to ethnic bias and students' internalization of these lowered expectations for their performance. For more information regarding gifted and talented students from diverse backgrounds, see Figure 3.4.

Teachers who have overcome challenges in their own lives may find it easier to believe in the capacity of every student. For example, one teacher draws on her own history with homelessness in working with students who face challenges. She tells her students with pride how far she has come and communicates that success requires hard work. This teacher's background enables her to communicate a "deep belief in the possibility of transcendence" (Gay, 2002, p. 52), an important characteristic of teachers who communicate culturally responsive caring to their students.

Teachers from more advantaged backgrounds may have to work to teach themselves to "really believe" any obstacle can be overcome by learning the stories of individuals who have overcome

---

Figure 3.4   Meeting the Needs of Gifted and Talented Students from Diverse Backgrounds

Students in inclusive classrooms represent the full range of abilities. Meeting the needs of every student means accommodating the needs of students who have been identified as gifted and talented, and students who have talents that have not been formally identified. Many of the strategies described in this chapter are important in meeting the needs of these students. In addition to these general strategies, you should consider the following important cautions and strategies to address the needs of students from diverse backgrounds.

Keep in mind that gifted and talented students are not all the same, just as students from any given culture are not all the same (Vaughn, Bos, & Schumm, 2007). It is all too often the case that within a specific classroom, the most able students are those who learn the least. This can be because of low expectations, but it can also be because teachers assume the most able students don't need scaffolding or emotional and academic support. Boredom and perfectionism, which can both interfere with effort and engagement, are two specific challenges these students might face (Vaughn et al., 2007).

The strategies suggested in this chapter for learning to know your students, holding high expectations, and facilitating engagement are very important for students who are gifted and talented. In addition, it is especially important that teachers examine possible stereotypes and preconceptions. This requires confronting beliefs about issues such as whether a test score defines giftedness, whether IQ tests represent the knowledge of all cultural groups equally, and whether we should give priority to identifying a few students with gifts and talents, or emphasize the development of talents within all students (Milner & Ford, 2005). Believing that some students have talents and others do not puts teachers in the position of sorting their students rather identifying strengths and talents and building on them.

Numerous additional suggestions can help teachers make accommodations or enrich the curriculum to meet the needs of students who are gifted and talented (Friend & Bursuck, 2006; Lawrence-Brown, 2004; Van Tassel-Baska & Stambaugh, 2005; Vaughn et al., 2007). Here are a few possibilities:

- Accelerate the curriculum, or provide additional activities that add complexity.
- Incorporate creative tasks (e.g., have students create representations of core content through graphic arts, song, dance, sculpture, plays).
- Provide activities and problems with multiple solutions.
- Provide opportunities for long-term projects around topics that intrigue students.
- Provide an environment where it is safe to take risks so that perfectionist students will tackle challenges.
- Pre-assess student knowledge, and adapt the curriculum scope and pace so that all learners are mastering new knowledge and skills. For example, this could involve providing some students with more difficult texts and/or more challenging application problems, or enabling a student to tackle an independent project that extends his learning.

hardships (e.g., Corwin, 2001; Mahoney et al., 2003; Mooney & Cole, 2000) or reading about teachers who are successful in helping students overcome seemingly insurmountable odds (e.g., Esquith, 2007; Gruwell, 1999). Gruwell's description of her work in Watts is a powerful story of how a teacher with determination and skill engages high school students when everyone else has given up. School officials viewed their chances of success to be so poor that they refused to provide books for them to read. Despite homes of poverty and communities riddled with gang violence and drugs, the students not only succeeded—*their* writing is featured in Gruwell's book. She helped them discover a passion for learning. In the process they graduated from high school, and *all* of them went on to college.

All school systems have teachers whose success with students is legendary. Gloria Merriex is a fifth-grade teacher in Florida whose low-income, minority students consistently make among the highest gains on the state math assessment. Ms. Merriex succeeds with students with disabilities and students with a history of low achievement because she communicates that she believes in them and uses innovative pedagogy to ensure they succeed. If you find and visit teachers like Ms. Merriex, this can help you understand how success is possible for all students. Effective teaching for *all* students is not magic. Simply put, effective teaching for *all* students is about believing that success is possible and working relentlessly to make it happen.

Reflecting on Beliefs. Working effectively with students from diverse backgrounds requires us to constantly question our reactions to students and their families and to check the human tendency to judge different as "abnormal." This is difficult to do. Recall how weird it felt to cross your arms in an abnormal way. Even though you know (a cognitive reaction) that there is nothing abnormal about putting the opposite hand on top, it still feels weird (an affective reaction). Suspending judgment and blame means constantly questioning your reactions to determine when cultural difference might be a factor in your interactions with students.

Unfortunately, there are no road signs to tell you when you are likely to encounter a cultural incongruity with students or with parents. Suspending judgment means you constantly scan your environment through a cultural lens, looking for the possibility that culture could explain a challenge you are facing. Additionally, suspending judgment means you question yourself to identify possible stereotypes that might undermine your expectations for students.

Demonstrating Care

Most teacher education students become teachers because they care about children and youth. The concept of care means developing comprehensive knowledge about students and their lives so that you are able to link new learning to prior experience and use students' strengths to build their capacity to achieve (Gay, 2002). It also means being tough when you need to. Teachers who care treat students with respect, require them to treat others with respect, perceive them as capable, and accept them unconditionally, even as they help them change undesirable behavior (Benard, 2004; Ross, Bondy, Gallingane, & Hambacher, 2008). To do this requires that you know, understand, and value the particular students you teach each year.

Getting to Know Students. Culturally responsive teachers must really *know* their students in order to teach them. For example, in the vignette about Ms. Kahn and Reynaldo, home visits enabled her to develop a more comprehensive picture of Reynaldo and to dispel her inaccurate preconception that he lacked home support for achievement. This example demonstrates that to teach students, we must know them, know how they perceive the world, know their language, know their family traditions and customs, know their interests, know their dreams, know their learning strategies, and know what they care about (Banks et al., 2005).

Acquire information using varied strategies. To get to know students, it is important to spend time in students' communities, visit homes, interact with families, and attend relevant cultural and family-oriented activities. Even those who live outside the community in which they teach find ways to become part of the community. Parents know them and see them in the community, and the teachers know families well enough to know the cultural and experiential resources in students' homes. This has been called knowing the "funds of knowledge" within students' homes, which Ms. Kahn used in her work with Reynaldo, earlier in the chapter (Gonzalez, Moll, & Amanti, 2005).

Culturally responsive teachers also actively seek information about students. For example, many teachers find it useful to have students complete questionnaires. This is particularly effective with older elementary, middle, and high school students. For example, the teacher can ask questions about students' learning preferences: "What would you really like to learn about in this class?" "Describe the way you learn things best." "Is there anything that makes this class especially hard for you?" "Can you think of a way I could help you with this?" (Cushman & Rogers, 2008, pp. 48–49). With younger students, parent surveys or interviews may be more useful. Even as we suggest these strategies, we recognize that getting personal information about students is harder with students from some cultures where privacy is prized (Ginsberg, 2005).

Other strategies for learning about students include informal conversations with students and parents, observation, and analysis of students' work. Moreover, it is important to become a student of children's culture. What are their favorite television shows? Movies? Music? Video games? Where do they go, and what do they do after school? What significant events have happened in the community? The more you know about the students and their communities, the greater your capacity to link schoolwork to their background knowledge and experience.

> ## Pause & Reflect
>
> Adopting an asset orientation matters a great deal. Consider how your interactions with a student would be different if you believed the student to be stubborn (a deficiency) versus determined (an asset), wild versus energetic, or whiny versus sensitive? How can we teach ourselves to see assets instead of deficits?

Using an Asset-Oriented Lens. Once you have knowledge of your students, it's important to maintain an "asset-based" view of your students (Garcia & Ortiz, 2006). All students present an array of strengths and weaknesses. At times it is challenging to see beyond what students do not know to an "asset-based" perspective on the strengths that might be used in teaching them. For example, one teacher encountered a fifth-grade student who had mastered few basic math facts. Prior teachers had tried numerous strategies to get him to learn—urging him to practice, requiring him to complete mad-minute practices, drilling him on fact cards, testing him, failing him, and providing peer tutoring. The teacher learned that he loved video and computer games and loved being a leader. She used these assets to engage him as she created a series of games for the SmartBoard focused on math facts. As the student worked with the teacher to develop the games and helped to guide others in playing the games, he learned the math facts.

Taking an asset-oriented approach may seem obvious, but it is often not easy. As teachers work to develop an asset orientation, they may investigate students' assets. For example, teachers may learn whether students have significant home responsibilities for younger siblings, if they provide translation assistance for adults in their families, or if they have outside jobs or activities. Teachers can then make a list of the skills required to succeed in each academic content area. This type of information helps identify strengths useful in reaching every student.

Developing the Skills and Stance of a Warm Demander. Research suggests that teachers support the achievement motivation of culturally diverse students by adopting the stance of a warm demander. Teachers who are warm demanders are culturally responsive, do not lower their standards, and are viewed as willing to help students (Ware, 2006). Research on positive classroom environments (Patrick, Turner, Meyer, & Midgley, 2003), the development of resilience (Benard, 2004), culturally relevant pedagogy (Irvine, 2002, 2003; Ladson-Billings, 1994), and culturally relevant classroom management (Brown, 2004; Weinstein, Tomlinson-Clarke, & Curran, 2004) indicate that there are four characteristics of classroom environments that support academic achievement (Ross et al., 2008): (1) a respectful relationship between students and the teacher, (2) respectful relationships among peers, (3) a task-oriented environment, and (4) clear and high expectations for achievement. These are consistent with the characteristics of warm demanders (Kleinfeld, 1975).

Care Is the Foundation of the Warm-Demander Stance. The foundation of any effective classroom is that students know the teacher cares about them. This is the "warm" part of being a warm demander. Keep in mind the previous discussion of what it means to care. *Warm* doesn't mean being nice, and it isn't about "gentle nurturing," which often becomes "benign neglect" (Gay, 2002, p. 52). As noted previously, *warm* means the teacher believes in students and cares enough about their futures to create a community where it is safe to take risks, where achievement is valued, and where students are never "let off the hook." Most importantly, it means caring enough to demand that students behave and achieve.

Warm Demanders Create a Respectful Community. Community is a key part of many cultural groups. Within a community, each member's individual needs are met (Gay, 2002). A key task for a culturally responsive teacher is building a community so that it is safe for every student to take the risks necessary to learn. Culturally responsive teachers bring themselves into the classroom and enable students to do the same. The teachers share their families, their interests, and their lives with the students and use structures such as class meetings to enable students to share information and know one another. They communicate that respect for others is highly valued by respecting and listening to students and teaching students to respect and listen to one another.

These classrooms are the opposite of a "collection of strangers," a description that unfortunately fits many American classrooms. When students are strangers, it is impossible to create a network of caring peers who support one another through learning challenges. In addition, classroom-management problems escalate when students do not know one another. Yet, the significance of creating community is often forgotten, particularly in secondary classrooms. For example, a high school teacher initiated a community-building class meeting with a group of ninth-grade students who were in a transition classroom because of poor performance on the eighth-grade state assessment test. Within two meetings, students began to share personal information, and after the second session, the teacher overheard a student say, "Going to this class is like being in a club." The fact that the student saw this class as so different from his other classes suggests how rare it is that some high school students feel a true sense of belonging.

Warm Demanders Explicitly Teach Classroom Rules, Routines, and Procedures. It is critically important to teach expectations, particularly social skills, in diverse, inclusive classrooms (Harriott & Martin, 2004). This means that culturally responsive teachers *never* assume that students know what is expected. Even when teaching high school, culturally responsive teachers teach the behaviors they expect students to demonstrate. In fact, explicitly teaching specific rules and procedures is a long-established principle of effective classroom management (Evertson, Emmer, Sanford, & Clements, 1983). If rules and procedures are not taught, classroom management can become an escalating sequence of consequences and punishments. The result is the development of a negative, often punitive, classroom environment where many fail to thrive.

The following principle may help you: Assume that students will behave respectfully and appropriately if they know and remember what the teacher expects. Culturally responsive classroom teachers teach their academic and behavioral expectations using multiple strategies (Bondy et al., 2007). These strategies include:

- Stating their expectations
- Providing models and demonstrations
- Providing humorous negative examples
- Requiring student restatement of expectations
- Providing opportunities for practice with feedback
- Repeating instructions as necessary
- Reminding students of and reinforcing appropriate behavior

Protecting the Classroom Community Through Teacher Insistence. A key difference between teachers who establish environments that support achievement motivation and those who do not is that effective teachers strategically and respectfully insist that students abide by rules and procedures and that they respect one another and the teacher (Patrick et al., 2003). Yet in their "insistence," they always preserve the respectful and caring connection to each student. As one middle school student commented, "She's mean out of the kindness of her heart" (Wilson & Corbett, 2001, p. 91).

All teachers want their students to abide by classroom rules. Yet, some give multiple "chances" that send inconsistent messages to students. Others become punitive and threatening. These responses undermine the expectation that students must be respectful of one another—the former by allowing disrespectful behavior, and the latter by treating students disrespectfully. Charney (2002) provides guidelines to help teachers say what they mean. In addition to keeping demands simple and short, she directs teachers to clearly communicate what is negotiable and what is not and to remind only twice. An effective "reminder" strategy that she suggests is to ask students to "rewind" when inappropriate behavior surfaces. This gives the student a clear directive and a chance to correct inappropriate behavior but maintains a lighter tone likely to be effective particularly with secondary-level learners.

High Expectations: What Does "No Excuses" Really Mean?

We've already noted that culturally responsive teachers convey a belief in the potential of students that enables them to transcend barriers to learning. Enacting this belief requires that teachers view student learning as a puzzle that they are constantly striving to solve (Banks et al., 2005; Corbett et al., 2002). They use a variety of activities and strategies for instruction and work to match their methods to the students (Cole, 2001).

Teaching Is Guided by Assessment and a Problem-Solving Approach. Culturally responsive teachers use a continual assessment system to determine who is and who isn't learning. (We discuss monitoring student progress in detail in Chapter 12.) They also constantly search for another way to make learning comprehensible (Gay, 2002). If one way isn't working, they modify instruction and reteach (Garcia & Ortiz, 2006). These are teachers who simply refuse to believe there is any student who cannot be reached, and they actively communicate this belief to students. As we will discuss later in Chapter 12, this belief is a guiding principle of inclusive practice and differentiated instruction. Van Garderen and Wittacker (2006) stress:

> The basic premise of differentiated instruction is to systematically plan curriculum and instruction that meets the needs of academically diverse learners by honoring each students' learning needs and maximizing each student's learning capacity. (p. 12)

In short, instruction should be culturally responsive for all students in inclusive classrooms. The guiding principle here is that teaching and learning are not culture free, and therefore, student failure should initially be viewed as a mismatch between the school's culture and environment and the student's needs (Garcia & Ortiz, 2006).

As an example, return to the case of Reynaldo presented earlier in the chapter. The teacher assistance team (TAT) demonstrated a culturally responsive approach by recommending that Ms. Kahn begin her assessment with home visits. Ms. Kahn used the visits to increase her knowledge of Reynaldo and his learning assets. At the end of the vignette, Ms. Kahn wondered how she could apply all these new insights to better meet Reynaldo's needs.

Developing Culturally Responsive Instruction for Reynaldo

Based on what Ms. Kahn learned, the TAT developed instructional recommendations that focused on within-classroom modifications to link instruction more explicitly to Reynaldo's background, experiences, and strengths. Ms. Kahn implemented many of the TAT's recommendations, including (1) modifying her cooperative learning structures so Reynaldo often worked in a small group of classmates with whom he felt more comfortable, (2) initiating a home reading log program so Reynaldo could keep track of the many books he shared with his family in both English and Spanish, and (3) implementing a listening center with books about culturally relevant subjects that may have been too difficult for him to read on his own. Ms. Kahn also began to send books home for the family to read with Reynaldo. She included a special unit on soccer and had Reynaldo show other students some of the special footwork he had learned from his uncles. The team also

PUTTING IT ALL TOGETHER

Today teachers are opening their classroom doors to others as they collaborate to reach increasingly higher expectations for student outcomes. With this in mind, we hope you will embrace collaboration, but keep a few of the following ideas in mind.

1. **Start slowly.** We recommend working with only one or two co-teachers initially. It is important to start slowly with collaborative activities so that you'll have time to develop the skills and reinforce the dispositions you need to make collaboration succeed. Working with a TAT or carefully selecting initial collaborators is often a good way to get started.

2. **Learn and develop the skills needed for collaboration.** You will begin to develop skills as you engage in collaborative activities with peers and observe their behavior during these interactions. Another critical way of gaining these skills is to take advantage of professional development related to collaboration.

3. **Enjoy the collaborative partnerships you develop.** A major benefit of collaboration for teachers is that it reduces the isolation many feel in their profession. Collaboration allows a group of experienced professionals to share and test ideas in a setting where individual and team efforts are recognized and valued and all professionals have opportunities for growth and leadership (Waldron & McLeskey, 2008).

4. **Celebrate the successes of collaboration.** When done well, collaboration leads to the synthesis of available expertise and the discovery of new knowledge and teaching approaches that benefit all students (Kochhar-Bryant, 2008). Be sure to take the time to recognize your successes!

myeducationlab

We present a serious of evidence-based strategies in the second half of this chapter (Strategies 11.1 to 11.7) in a step-by-step format so that you can use them in your classroom now. In addition, in the following table, we identify some video clips, cases, and simulations that will allow you to experience these strategies (or complementary strategies) in a real classroom environment.

EFFECTIVE PRACTICE	MYEDUCATIONLAB CONNECTION	CONSIDER THIS
Strategy 11.1: Key Components of Effective Collaboration	Go to MyEducationLab, select the topic *Collaboration, Consultation, and Co-Teaching*, and go to the Building Teaching Skills and Dispositions section. Next, complete the activity entitled "Building Collaborative Relationships."	As you complete the activity, pay close attention to the views of the teachers featured in the video clips. What components do they think are necessary for effective collaboration? How do these compare or contrast with the components discussed in Strategy 11.1?
Strategy 11.2: Communication Skills and Successful Collaboration	Go to MyEducationLab, select the topic *Collaboration, Consultation, and Co-Teaching*, and go to the Activities and Applications section. Next, read and analyze the case entitled "A Broken Arm."	As you examine the case, focus on how these two teachers communicate and how that is impacting both the success of their collaborative relationship and the student's academic success.
Strategy 11.3: Teacher Assistance Teams	Go to MyEducationLab, select the topic *Collaboration, Consultation, and Co-Teaching*, and go to the Activities and Applications section. Next, watch the video entitled "Team Meeting," and answer the accompanying questions.	As you watch this video, focus on the interactions among the team participants. Compare and contrast these interactions with the components addressed in Strategy 11.3.
Strategy 11.4: Co-Teaching	Go to MyEducationLab, select the topic *Collaboration, Consultation, and Co-Teaching*, and go to the Activities and Applications section. Next, complete the simulation entitled "Focus on the Playbook."	As you complete the simulation, focus on the roles and responsibilities of all the collaborators. How does the situation presented in the simulation compare with the elements discussed in Strategy 11.4?
Strategy 11.5: Working with Paraeducators	Go to MyEducationLab, select the topic *Collaboration, Consultation, and Co-Teaching*, and go to the Activities and Applications section. Next, watch the videos entitled "Collaboration and Communication with Teachers, Paraprofessionals, and Parents" and "Fluency Building: Social Studies Flashcards," and answer the accompanying questions.	As you watch these two videos, first focus on how this teacher views his collaborative relationship with his paraeducators. Then focus on how he incorporates these views into classroom practice.
Strategy 11.6: Working with Families: Home–School Collaboration	Go to MyEducationLab, select the topic *Parents and Families,* and go to the Activities and Applications section. Next, watch the video entitled "Home–School Communication," and answer the accompanying questions.	As you watch the video, reflect on the importance of home–school communication and its role in an effective collaborative relationship between the teacher and the student's caregivers.
Strategy 11.7: Peer Buddies	Go to MyEducationLab, select the topic *Autism,* and go to the Activities and Applications section. Next, watch the video entitled "Social Skills," and answer the accompanying questions.	As you watch the video, reflect on the social skills benefits of this peer buddy situation for Allison, the student featured in the video clip.

EFFECTIVE PRACTICES

In the remainder of this chapter, we describe seven strategies, which we referred to previously in the chapter, to help you plan effectively to meet the needs of all students.

EFFECTIVE PRACTICE	TYPE OF STRATEGY/BRIEF DESCRIPTION	SPECIAL CONSIDERATIONS
Strategy 11.1: Key Components of Effective Collaboration	Collaboration allows teachers to work with other professionals to improve knowledge, teaching skills, and dispositions. The components of effective collaboration provide teachers with the knowledge and skills needed to ensure that they are well prepared for collaborative roles.	When collaborating regarding inclusion, teachers must work to ensure a respectful, equal partnership with their collaborator.
Strategy 11.2: Communication Skills and Successful Collaboration	The most important skills for collaborating successfully with others relate to communication. Communication problems can be overcome through the development of skills related to listening, verbal communication, and nonverbal communication.	Communication is very complex, as it consists of sending and receiving messages simultaneously, sending both verbal and nonverbal messages, and using different types of communication with different people.
Strategy 11.3: Teacher Assistance Teams	A strategy to provide teachers who face problems in their classrooms with a quick, efficient method to seek assistance from well-respected peers. A group of teachers meet with a referring teacher about a specific student problem, brainstorm regarding possible ways to address the problem, and support the teacher in selecting, implementing, and evaluating an intervention.	Most student problems referred to the TAT relate to work habits, classroom behavior, interpersonal behavior, attentional problems, and reading difficulties. Recommended interventions are reported to be successful for almost 90% of students.
Strategy 11.4: Co-Teaching	An approach to collaboration that allows general and special education teachers to share knowledge, dispositions, and skills in an inclusive classroom. Two teachers share responsibility for teaching a diverse group of students in one classroom. Co-teachers take on different roles, depending on the content being taught and student needs.	Co-teaching is a dynamic process that requires teachers to often change roles. Varying teaching roles allows teachers to learn and develop expertise from their teaching partner.
Strategy 11.5: Working with Paraeducators	Paraeducators, who work under the supervision of a certified teacher, provide important support for many students in inclusive classrooms. Effectively supervising a paraeducator requires that the teacher collaborate with the paraeducator to ensure that responsibilities are well defined and the paraeducator is prepared to address these responsibilities.	Paraeducators may provide support such as one-to-one or small-group instruction, support for students with highly specialized needs, grading and other paperwork, preparation of materials for class lessons, etc.
Strategy 11.6: Working with Families: Home–School Collaboration	Effective collaboration between teachers and families can result in significant improvement in student achievement and behavior. Teachers in inclusive classrooms should encourage home–school collaboration and parent involvement in a range of activities. The teacher should get to know parents well and work with parents to determine the types of involvement that will work well for them.	When collaborating with parents, teachers should be knowledgeable regarding the parent's cultural background. This allows the teacher to understand, respect, and take into account cultural background when working with the parent.
Strategy 11.7: Peer Buddies	Adolescents with moderate-to-severe disabilities benefit from peer interactions, just as other students do. Peer buddy programs are designed to provide an opportunity for these peer interactions to occur in natural school settings.	Peer buddy programs have many benefits for both students but require careful planning and consistent support to succeed.

recommended that she conduct language- and curriculum-based assessments in Spanish and that the teacher provide more language supports during instruction. Examples of language supports include using more visuals, gestures, models, and graphic organizers and using drama (Cole, 2001). These modifications demonstrate a culturally responsive approach to addressing learning.

Insisting on Completion and Quality. Insistence is just as important in establishing high academic expectations as it is in establishing a respectful learning community. Culturally responsive teachers do not allow students to do less than their best (Corbett et al., 2002). They insist that students complete and revise their work until it meets high standards. In a study of urban middle school students' perspectives about effective teachers, students valued teachers who made them do their work, even when they didn't want to do it (Wilson & Corbett, 2001). Others have made the same point in stressing that important learning inevitably involves struggle (Weinstein, 2002). Effective teachers not only convey that the struggle is important but insist that students persist through barriers and provide them with support until they succeed. Effective teachers encourage students to try, refuse to allow them to get by with incomplete or sloppy work, give them opportunities to make up work, provide tutoring, make work relevant to students' lives, and reteach using varied strategies until everyone understands and succeeds (Wilson & Corbett, 2001).

> ## Pause & Reflect
>
> Mr. Newsome believes he has high standards. As evidence, he reports that his 10th-grade math students get zeros if they do not turn in homework. He says with pride that he does not just "pass students through." One third of his class got D's or F's last term, and he says, "They earned them." Do these practices suggest that Mr. Newsome has high expectations?

Using a Diverse Curriculum

Motivation to achieve is influenced by factors such as culture, values, and language (Ginsberg, 2005). It also is influenced by the nature of the curriculum. The school curriculum is not culturally neutral. The curriculum as represented in texts, national and state standards, and the experience of most teachers is a reflection of the European American culture. Hollins (1996) explains that the school curriculum "promotes its own (a) cultural values, practices and perceptions; (b) psychological, social, economic, and political needs; and (c) elevated status within the larger society" (p. 82).

Gay (2002) urges teachers to view their curricular materials with a critical eye. The text may include a few multicultural historic figures, but that is often not enough. Gay cautions that when the same few figures are taught repeatedly, students learn that their ancestors really did not contribute much. Similarly, she notes that it is inappropriate to focus more attention on African Americans than on other ethnic groups. In addition, the fiction and nonfiction that students read needs to be diverse so that they see their lives and cultures reflected in the characters, setting, and plot of the stories. When students see themselves in their books, they enjoy reading, make a connection to literature, and build vocabulary and language skills that assist them academically. To be effective, teachers need "wide ranging knowledge of subject matter content, so that they can construct a curriculum that includes multiple representations addressing the prior experiences of different groups of students" (Banks et al., 2005, p. 251).

Literature is not the only strategy to broaden the curriculum. Gay (2002) urges teachers to draw on their communities for curricular content and to take a risk and teach controversial topics such as ethnicity and poverty. Additional strategies for incorporating diversity in the curriculum include ideas such as teaching thematic units organized around countries or languages; studying and comparing fashion, religious and marriage customs, games, and hair styling from around the world; and subscribing to magazines from around the world that help teachers and students learn about students' cultures and provide possible curricular topics (Jones, 2005).

Making Instruction Meaningful. The knowledge that culturally responsive teachers develop about students' strengths, culture, traditions, and interests is critical in linking the curriculum to what students know and the ways that they learn. Making the curriculum meaningful through differentiated pedagogy is a key to keeping students engaged enough to master skills and knowledge.

Using What You Know About Students to Keep Them Engaged. If students see no reason to learn school knowledge, they are unlikely to be engaged in classroom lessons and activities—and half the battle (maybe more than half!) is getting students actively engaged. Engagement has been defined as "active, goal-directed, flexible, constructive, persistent, and focused interactions" with academic tasks (Furrer & Skinner, 2003, p. 149). Unfortunately, academic engagement drops as students move from elementary to high school (Crosnoe, 2001; National Research Council & Institute of Medicine, 2004). It is obviously important to seek to undertand this pattern, yet this is not always a simple matter. For example, Ravet (2007) asked teachers why students were not engaged. In answering, teachers focused on deficits in students (e.g., attention-deficit/hyperactivity disorder, learning disability, lack of motivation). In contrast, 10 students who were interviewed had very different perspectives. They said that the curriculum was boring. The quality and coherence of instruction make a big difference in whether students feel bored or engaged.

When teachers link school knowledge to students' real-world interests and experiences, students are more likely to be engaged and to retain this knowledge. Linking to real-world knowledge and experiences is also important in helping to provide a meaningful context for learning for second-language learners (Lewis & Doorlag, 2006). One strategy to enhance engagement is to teach skills and concepts within an overarching theme that helps students see the big ideas and that stresses critical thinking, respects their curiosity, poses challenging problems for them to solve, and equips them with the skills and knowledge to be successful (National Education Association, 2007). Culturally responsive teachers use pedagogy that provides opportunities for student choice. In this way teachers enable students to become invested in their learning because

> motivation depends on the extent to which teachers are able to satisfy students' needs to feel in control of their learning, feel competent, and feel connected with others. (National Education Association, 2007, sec. 5, p. 3)

Effective teachers provide the explicit instruction students need to succeed and opportunities for meaningful use of their learning (Banks et al., 2005; Delpit, 1995). Explicit instruction is sometimes misunderstood as including only drill of low-level cognitive skills (e.g., math facts). While explicit instruction includes this kind of drill, it involves a great deal more. Explicit instruction should scaffold the development of both skills and higher-order thinking. The most effective teachers find ways to link concepts to everyday experiences and home culture. For example, a local elementary teacher links place value to students' knowledge of families by introducing them to the 100s family, the 1,000s family, the 10,000s family, and so on.

In a more complex example, a high school teacher scaffolds higher-order thinking by drawing on what students already know in Adkins's (2006) study of effective teachers of African American high school students. During a discussion of *Native Son*, the teacher scaffolded students in their thinking about how author Richard Wright portrayed religion. After a student questioned why the preacher is presented as poorly educated, the teacher enhances their comprehension by scaffolding them to think through the text. As part of the conversation, she shares the perspective that "religion is the opiate of the masses." When students are unclear about what "opiate" means, she guides them as follows:

Ms. Lomax: Do you know what heroin is?

> *The students responded that it was a kind of drug.*

Ms. Lomax: Heroin is an opiate. What does heroin do?

Malcolm: It makes you feel better.

Brianna: Takes the pain away.

Ms. Lomax: It makes you slow-witted.

Yusef: You can control them.

Ms. Lomax: Easily controlled. . . . Religion does not tell you to think. They tell you to believe what I'm telling you or you'll go to hell. What is Wright saying [about religion]?

Layla: It can control your mind. As long as you have God in your life, you don't need to be educated. (Shortened from Adkins, 2006, pp. 96–97.)

Using What You Know About Students' Cultures to Keep Them Engaged. Links to students' cultural background and experiences also enhance engagement. For example, African American pedagogy, grounded in characteristics of African American culture, includes characteristics such as teaching at a faster pace, teaching to the verbal strengths of students, and the use of a diversity of multimodal activities (Gay, 2002; Lewis & Doorlag, 2006). An example might be to study the use of language and rhythm in rap music to activate background knowledge and interest as part of an introduction to poetry. The point here is *not* that we should teach rap music. The point is that we link schoolwork to students' culturally derived knowledge to help them access and understand concepts and skills that would otherwise seem to be isolated pieces of "school" knowledge.

Additionally, effective teachers find ways to link to students' families and to link family traditions to instruction. Previously, we noted that parents from some cultures maintain a respectful distance from the school. Yet educators who expand their definitions of involvement find ways to incorporate family traditions into the school. For example, a family traditions event might be used where parents work with their children to help them record family stories to create a family history (Kyle, McIntyre, Miller, & Moore, 2006). Drawing on their knowledge of families, culturally responsive teachers tap the funds of knowledge (Gonzalez et al., 2005) within families to enable parents to share their expertise and enhance the education and experiences of children.

Incorporating Equity and Social Action Projects in the Curriculum. Banks (1988) described four different approaches teachers take in implementing multicultural education. At Level 1, *the contribution approach*, teachers use cultural holidays and heros to teach about diversity. At Level 2, *the additive approach*, teachers "add on" diversity units to the regular curriculum. At Level 3, *the transformative approach*, teachers redesign the curriculum to teach about concepts, events, and themes from diverse ethnic and cultural perspectives. At Level 4, *the social action approach*, teachers engage students in issues of social justice and take actions to solve them. In this chapter, we have described a variety of strategies that move beyond Levels 1 and 2 so that diverse perspectives and pedagogy become an embedded part of the curriculum instead of something that is also taught.

Equity is a particularly important focus for inclusive classrooms, and it is a topic that teachers should address explicitly and regularly. *Equity* is sometimes a difficult concept for students to grasp. Many come into a classroom with the perspective that *fair* means treating everyone the same. As we have emphasized throughout this chapter and in other chapters throughout this text, treating everyone equally is not always fair or equitable and does not result in effective instructional practices or desired educational outcomes. This is especially the case for students from diverse backgrounds and students with disabilities but is true for other students as well.

This chapter has provided many examples of the need to adapt classroom practices based on student characteristics and needs. In later chapters we provide similar suggestions in each chapter that addresses specific disabilities. These suggestions are built on the assumption that fair, equitable treatment of students means giving them what they need, not treating all students the same. We have found that in inclusive classrooms it is often important to directly address this topic with students through discussion. When this is done, most students will readily understand why equity demands that students are at times treated differently within the classroom.

Incorporating social action projects into the curriculum empowers students to tackle problems that are important in their lives and communities. In this way school becomes inextricably linked to the real world, and school knowledge becomes a way to empower students to work for equity. Even preschoolers have a strong sense of fairness and equity. Empowering students to act on these perceptions is a way to strengthen the curriculum, engage students, and pursue an equity agenda in schools.

What might an equity agenda look like? At times, it may be as simple as encouraging a student to speak out when he perceives inequity. Pelo and Davidson (2000) describe a preschool child who became upset when she saw her classmates laughing at two men who were hugging. She knew the men, who were friends with her two mothers, and was angry that her classmates had laughed. Her teacher encouraged her to share her feelings, a strategy that empowered the child to work toward a change she believed should happen and that increased the knowledge and sensitivity of her classmates.

As children mature, lessons related to social justice and equity can be integrated into the curriculum. For example, students can compare the report of historical events and scientific discoveries in their textbook with alternative accounts of these events and scientific discoveries found on the Internet. They could analyze the news coverage of an event through various media to examine how coverage of issues varies and write essays about the possible reasons for discrepancies. Or they could compare pictures and text in magazines from 20 years ago to those in current magazines to analyze portrayals of gender and ethnicity. They might then envision what changes they would like to see in the future and what actions they could take today to move toward that future.

Similarly, students can draw on local and national current events to raise questions related to equity and social justice. For example, national news coverage provides multiple important opportunities for dialogue about issues related to the differential impact of national disasters on low-income families and the role of government versus individuals in responding to citizens' needs. Students can also engage in social action projects, such as taking food to a homeless shelter, raising funds for victims of disasters, or writing to officials about changes they believe would improve their communities. In this way the academic curriculum serves to empower students to believe that they can impact their world and helps them to see school as connected to life.

Summary

This chapter addressed the following topics:

The changing demographics of public school students

- The demographics of public school students are rapidly changing in terms of ethnicity, language, poverty, and disability as classrooms across the United States become more diverse.
- Currently, about 1 of 10 counties in the United States has a population that is more than 50% culturally and linguistically diverse.

How the demographics of students with disabilities compare to the demographics of the school population at large

- Students with disabilities include students from all ethnicities, language backgrounds, and socioeconomic levels.
- Some groups of students are under- or overrepresented in special education. Overrepresentation of some ethnic groups within certain disability categories, as well as underrepresentation in gifted and talented groups, is a persistent concern.

How significant discrepancies in educational outcomes for students who vary by ethnicity, culture, socioeconomic status, language, and learning differences can be explained

- The lowest-performing schools (primarily schools with a high percentage of students from non–European American backgrounds who are living in poverty) typically have lower per-pupil expenditures, fewer highly qualified teachers, and lower-quality curriculum and materials.
- The lack of connection between teachers' and students' background knowledge, experience, and cultural frames (i.e., the demographic divide) is a key contributing factor to this discrepancy.

Why teachers in inclusive classrooms should be knowledgeable about differences in students' backgrounds and experiences, particularly with regard to culture

- Despite the demographic divide and economic disparities, students within and across cultural, language, and socioeconomic groups are achieving substantial success.
- Research on effective teaching across cultural groups provides guidance about how to help students succeed in the classroom and cross the border of language, culture, and disability.

What successful teachers believe and do to enhance the educational futures of all students

- Culturally responsive teaching is designed to foster resilience in students, improve student outcomes, and enhance the educational futures of students.
- Culturally responsive teachers are those who
  - Study culture and the ways that students differ.
  - Believe that every student has the capacity to succeed.
  - Learn to suspend judgment and blame when interacting with students and families.
  - Show students that they sincerely care about them.
  - Develop depth of knowledge about students.
  - Develop the skills and stance of a warm demander.
  - Hold students to high expectations.
  - Make the curriculum meaningful.
  - Connect pedagogy to students' interests and experiences.

Addressing Professional Standards

Standards addressed in Chapter 3 include:

CEC Standards: (1) foundations, (2) development and characteristics of learners, (3) individual learning differences, (4) instructional strategies, (5) learning environments and social interactions, (6) language, (9) professional and ethical practice.

INTASC Standards: Principle 1—Understand central concepts of the discipline; Principle 2—Provide learning opportunities to support the learning and development of all students; Principle 3—Create instructional opportunities for diverse learners; Principle 6—Use knowledge of communication techniques to support students; Principle 7—Plan instruction based on knowledge of the student, curriculum, and community.

Praxis™ II Standards: Knowledge-based core principles: (1) understanding exceptionalities, (2) legal and societal issues. Application of core principles: (1) curriculum, (2) instruction, (4) managing the learning environment, (5) professional roles/issues/literature.

PART II
Meeting the Needs of All Students

Chapter 4 Students with Learning Disabilities

Chapter 5 Students with Attention-Deficit/Hyperactivity Disorder

Chapter 6 Students with Intellectual Disabilities

Chapter 7 Students with Emotional and Behavioral Disabilities

Chapter 8 Students with Autism Spectrum Disorders

Chapter 9 Students with Communication Disorders and Students with Sensory Impairments

Chapter 10 Students with Multiple Disabilities, Physical Disabilities, and Health Impairments

Students with Learning Disabilities

KEY TOPICS

After reading this chapter you will:

- Know the definition and criteria used to identify students with learning disabilities.
- Know how many students are identified with learning disabilities.
- Be able to identify the educational settings in which students with learning disabilities are educated.
- Be able to describe major characteristics of students with learning disabilities.
- Understand key issues and challenges related to including students with learning disabilities in general education classrooms.
- Know effective practices for addressing the needs of students with learning disabilities in elementary and secondary classrooms.

chapter 4

Perspectives on Including Students with Learning Disabilities

Interview with Vicki Eng, Seventh-Grade Special Education Teacher, West Hernando Middle School

We interviewed a seventh-grade special education teacher from West Hernando Middle school, Vicki Eng, who has worked in both inclusive and separate class programs with students with learning disabilities. Ms. Eng sees many advantages related to the inclusion of students with learning disabilities:

> Including students with learning disabilities gives them an opportunity to keep up with the curriculum. They are going to be taking our state test or whatever state achievement test is being used, and the more exposure to the regular curriculum they have, the better off they are going to be.
>
> Related to this, they also benefit from having two teachers who are highly qualified who teach them. One of the teachers has spent more time learning the ins and outs of the academic content that is being taught, and you have another highly qualified teacher who knows the strategies and tricks that will help everybody in the classroom learn all of the material.
>
> This also causes me to set my expectations a little higher. When you're in a pull-out program, you might say, "Oh, well, I don't know if that student can do this right now—let's not even attempt it." In a regular class, you're expecting everybody else to do it, so you set the bar higher, and you often find out that they can meet it and they feel better about themselves, and you take a step back and say, "Hey, they can do anything that everybody else can do."

Ms. Eng also commented on her experience teaching in a separate class and "pulling out" students with learning disabilities from a general education classroom.

> If students with learning disabilities are included in a regular class and are not pulled out, this really helps their self-esteem. Many of these students were pulled out when they were in elementary school, and they didn't like it. It sets you apart when someone comes in and takes you out of class. Students also want to be with their peers, especially at the middle school level. By them being with their peers, then there's not that issue of "there's something different about me."

Finally, Ms. Eng talked about the benefits of inclusion for students with learning disabilities related to their self-advocacy. She noted that many students with learning disabilities do not

understand their disability or why they are provided certain accommodations. She spends time with students so they understand their disability and what accommodations they may need. She also noted that being educated in an inclusive classroom helps these students better understand their disability and gives them the opportunity to learn to advocate with teachers and others for supports or accommodations when they are needed. "I talk with them about appropriate ways to approach the teacher about accommodations. They learn to advocate in a way that is appropriate and doesn't bring negative attention to them."

Introduction

Nearly one half of all students with disabilities are identified with a learning disability. As you might expect, more students with learning disabilities are included in general education classrooms than any other disability. At least one student with a learning disability is included in most general education classes, and many have more than one such student.

Students with learning disabilities are often perplexing to teachers and parents. Perhaps the major reason this occurs relates to the fact that most students with learning disabilities do not have an obvious disability. Many teachers and parents assume that these students should be able to learn the academic content of the classroom with little difficulty. Additionally, students with learning disabilities often have difficulty in a specific academic area (most often reading or math) and perform much better in other areas. If you know a person with a learning disability, you readily recognize how puzzling and sometimes frustrating this disability can be.

In general education classrooms, students with learning disabilities struggle to learn academic content, in spite of high-quality instruction, and often need assistance or support to succeed. As Vicki Eng noted in the "Perspectives" vignette, students with learning disabilities benefit from being in a well-designed inclusive classroom that incorporates the necessary supports to ensure that students succeed. Benefits include greater access to the general education curriculum, higher expectations, and improved self-esteem. In this chapter, we address the characteristics of students with learning disabilities, as well as interventions and supports that many of these students need to ensure they succeed in an inclusive classroom.

Many general education classrooms include students with learning disabilities.

myeducationlab

Go to MyEducationLab, select the topic *Learning Disabilities*, and go to the Activities and Applications section. As you watch the video entitled "Learning Disabilities," think about what you can do as a teacher to help students with learning disabilities feel included in the general education classroom.

Who Are Students with Learning Disabilities?
Definition

A quick review of the learning disabilities category is provided in the accompanying box, "Just the Facts." The most widely used definition of learning disability is included in IDEA (2004), which states:

A) In general—The term "specific learning disability" means a disorder in one or more of the basic psychological processes involved in understanding or in using language, spoken or written, which disorder may manifest itself in the imperfect ability to listen, think, speak, read, write, spell, or do mathematical calculations.

B) Disorders included—Such term includes such conditions as perceptual disabilities, brain injury, minimal brain dysfunction, dyslexia, and developmental aphasia.

Just the Facts — Students with Learning Disabilities

Who are they?	Students with learning disabilities exhibit an uneven pattern of academic development, including unexpected underachievement in one or more academic areas. This underachievement is not explained by another disability or by environmental, cultural, or economic disadvantage. To be identified, the student must need special education services, and the academic problem cannot be overcome in general education without these services.
What are typical characteristics?	• Academic achievement in one or more academic areas that is significantly below grade level. • Cognitive skill deficits related to memory, attention, impulsivity, and/or metacognition. • About 1 in 3 students with a learning disability are also identified with attention-deficit/hyperactivity disorder (ADHD). • Social problems related to social skill deficits and difficulty getting along with others for about 1 in 3 students with learning disabilities. • Motivational problems, especially among adolescents, which result from long-term academic difficulty and can result in passive learning or learned helplessness.
What are the demographics?	• Just over 5% of school-age students (ages 6 to 17) are identified with learning disabilities. • About 45% of all school-age students who have a disability have a learning disability. • About 3 of 4 students with learning disabilities are male.
Where are students educated?	• Almost 9 of 10 students with learning disabilities are educated for some or most of the school day in a general education classroom. • About 1 of 10 students with a learning disability is educated in separate settings for most of the school day.
How are students identified?	• Unexpected underachievement in one or more academic areas is the primary criterion for identifying students with learning disabilities. • A severe discrepancy between expected achievement level (as determined by a standardized test of intelligence) and actual achievement level (as determined by a standardized achievement test) has traditionally been used to identify unexpected underachievement. • After unexpected achievement is documented, the exclusion clause is applied to student identification. This ensures that another disability or environmental, cultural, or economic disadvantage did not cause the underachievement. • IDEA 2004 has mandated that a student's response to a scientific, research-based intervention may be used to identify unexpected underachievement for students with learning disabilities. This response-to-intervention approach is being increasingly used in states for student identification.
What causes learning disabilities?	• The cause of a learning disability in most instances is unknown. • Researchers assume that some type of abnormal brain function causes learning disabilities. • Hereditary factors contribute to learning disabilities, as these difficulties often tend to run in families. • Research using highly effective, research-based practices has demonstrated that some learning disabilities are caused by the lack of opportunity to learn.
What are the outcomes?	• Reading disabilities tend to cause students to have difficulty with other academic areas (e.g., mathematics, social studies, science) as they move through school and content becomes more complex. • About 6 of 10 students with learning disabilities graduate with a standard diploma, while about 3 of 10 drop out of school. • Most learning disabilities persist into adulthood, although many learn to at least partially compensate for the disability. • Many adults with learning disabilities have difficulty finding good employment and achieving satisfaction in life.

Many students with learning disabilities have difficulty in some academic areas but do well in others.

C) Disorders not included—Such term does not include a learning problem that is primarily the result of visual, hearing, or motor disabilities, of mental retardation, of emotional disturbance, or of environmental, cultural, or economic disadvantage. (PL 108-466, Sec. 602[30])

As you review this definition, you will note that the most important consideration in defining a learning disability is low achievement in one or more academic areas such as reading or mathematics. It is assumed that some type of underlying psychological processing disorder causes this difficulty. For example, a student may have difficulty learning to read because of a problem with language, or a student may have difficulty using sound–symbol relationships to sound out words, often referred to as a phonological processing problem (Torgesen, 2002).

The federal definition of learning disability includes several terms that have been used in the past or are currently used by some (e.g., dyslexia, perceptual disabilities) and have been subsumed under this category. A final aspect of the definition is the so-called exclusion clause, which educators use to ensure that the primary reason the student struggles academically is a learning disability and not another type of disability (e.g., visual impairment) or environmental conditions such as poor teaching.

Federal law does not require that states use this definition. Nonetheless, more than 80% of states use the federal definition of learning disability as written in law or with slight alterations. While the remaining states use sections of the federal definition or definitions from other sources, these alternative definitions tend to include underachievement and the exclusion clause as key components (Reschly & Hosp, 2004).

Identification of Students with Learning Disabilities

Since the 1970s, the primary approach that educators have used to identify students with learning disabilities has included the determination of unexpected underachievement. Educators determine this underachievement by examining the discrepancy between a student's actual and expected achievement levels and then using the exclusion clause to eliminate possible causes for the severe discrepancy (e.g., environmental factors or another disability) other than the suspected learning disability. This approach to identification has placed primary emphasis on the determination of a severe discrepancy and less emphasis on the exclusion clause, especially as it relates to poor teaching as a cause for academic deficits.

Identification Using a Severe Discrepancy Approach. When educators use the severe discrepancy approach to identify students with learning disabilities, the primary criterion relates to unexpected underachievement, as determined by a severe discrepancy between the student's expected achievement level and actual achievement level. To illustrate how educators determine a severe discrepancy, consider a student with an average score on a standardized test of intelligence (i.e., 100), who would be expected to achieve on grade level. If this student is in the seventh grade and achieves on a third-grade level in reading on a standardized reading test, the difference between his expected achievement level (seventh grade) and actual achievement level (third grade) in reading would be evidence of a severe discrepancy.

The presence of a severe discrepancy is the primary criterion for the identification of students with learning disabilities. After a determination is made that such a discrepancy exists, however, other factors must be excluded as causes of the unexpected underachievement. This exclusion clause criterion is used to ensure that the severe discrepancy is not the result of another disability, or environmental factors such as the student's cultural background, language used in the home, economic disadvantage, or poor teaching. The primary cause of the underachievement must be the learning disability, and not other, related factors.

In addition to these criteria, a student who is identified with a learning disability must demonstrate a need for special education and related services to an extent that the academic underachievement cannot be overcome in the general education classroom without these services. This requirement relates to the exclusion clause, in that students may not be identified with a learning disability if they have not had the opportunity to learn due to factors such as school absences or poor teaching.

Educators have criticized the severe discrepancy approach to student identification for three primary reasons. First, this method requires that a student fall significantly behind grade level academically before a severe discrepancy exists. Thus, it is difficult for children in the early elementary grades to meet this criterion, when they are learning basic academic skills and can only be 1 or 2 years behind grade level. Furthermore, a student will often fail academic subjects and perhaps be retained in grade before the discrepancy is large enough to be identified with a learning disability. Many professionals have expressed a strong preference for using preventive approaches to addressing student needs rather than this type of "wait-to-fail" approach (Fletcher, Denton, & Francis, 2005).

A second criticism of this approach is that many professionals have found that the methods that are used to determine a severe discrepancy are not reliable or valid (Fletcher, Lyon, Fuchs, & Barnes, 2007). This has resulted in the use of a range of alternatives for determining a severe discrepancy across states that have been called "confusing, unfair, and logically inconsistent" (Gresham, 2002, p. 467). This use of differing methods has contributed to a wide variation in the identification rates for school-age students (ages 6 to 17) with learning disabilities across states, which range from 2% to 7% (U.S. Department of Education, 2007).

A final criticism of this approach to identification is that professionals have lacked a systematic method for determining whether a student's academic difficulty was due to a lack of good teaching or a persistent learning disability. This shortcoming presents a serious problem with regard to student identification, as some students may be struggling with academic content areas because they have not been provided with evidence-based, highly effective instructional strategies, while others have a learning disability and struggle academically in spite of receiving high-quality instruction. Do these criticisms seem extreme enough to change the approach used to identify students with learning disabilities?

> ### Pause & Reflect
>
> Does the severe discrepancy approach to identifying students with learning disabilities seem logical to you? Is the criticism that this approach requires a student to "wait to fail" before identification an important criticism? Why or why not?

As a result of criticisms regarding the severe discrepancy approach to the identification of students with learning disabilities, IDEA 2004 included a stipulation that states must permit the use of a method to identify these students that emphasizes the student's response to scientific, research-based interventions (IDEA, 2004, PL 108-466, Sec. 614 (b)). IDEA 2004 also included a stipulation that states cannot require local schools to use a severe discrepancy to identify students with learning disabilities (PL 108-466, Sec. 614 [b] [6] [A-B]. Educators have developed an alternative approach to student identification, response-to-intervention (RTI), in response to these changes.

Identification Using a Response-to-Intervention Approach. The RTI approach to identifying students with learning disabilities continues to emphasize the use of unexpected underachievement as the primary criterion for student identification. However, this approach is conceptualized differently than when a severe discrepancy is used. Response-to-intervention typically includes the following steps (Reschly, 2005):

1. Students receive high-quality instruction in the general education classroom in core content areas (i.e., reading and mathematics). This is often called Tier 1, or primary prevention.
2. Educators use screening measures to determine students who struggle academically, in spite of high-quality instruction in the general education classroom. For students who struggle

Many students are identified with learning disabilities based on how they respond to high-quality instruction in a general education classroom.

academically, teachers provide secondary prevention, or Tier 2, instruction. This instruction may include systematic, structured teaching, small-group instruction (three to six students), peer tutoring, and so forth.

3. Teachers monitor student progress for those who receive Tier 2 instruction. For those who continue to struggle, teachers provide Tier 3 instruction, which includes intensive, individualized interventions using highly effective instruction and frequent monitoring of student progress.

For students who do not respond to this high-quality instruction, poor teaching has been eliminated as a possible cause of the students' low achievement. These students are then referred to a multidisciplinary team for possible identification with a disability. While several states have adopted an RTI approach to the identification of students with learning disabilities (Bender & Shores, 2007; Jimerson, Burns, & VanDeHeyden, 2007), IDEA 2004 allows states to continue to use a severe discrepancy approach, or a combination of these methods to identify students with learning disabilities.

Prevalence

Learning disability is the largest disability category and includes approximately 45% of all students with disabilities (U.S. Department of Education, 2007). Just over 5% of all school-aged students (ages 6 to 17) in the United States are identified with learning disabilities. To put this information into perspective, in a typical classroom of 25 students, it would be expected that about 1 student would be identified with a learning disability. This number may vary based on a number of factors, including differing identification rates across states and local school districts and clustering of students with learning disabilities in certain schools or classrooms within schools.

It is noteworthy that identification rates for students with learning disabilities vary considerably both across and within states (U.S. Department of Education, 2007). For example, identification rates in states range from a low of 2% in Kentucky to a high of over 7% in Iowa. Several states identify more than 6% of students with learning disabilities, including Delaware, Florida, Illinois, Iowa, Massachusetts, New Jersey, Oklahoma, and the District of Columbia. In contrast, several states identify fewer than 4% of students with learning disabilities, including Colorado, Connecticut, Georgia, Idaho, Kentucky, Louisiana, Maryland, and Minnesota (U.S. Department of Education,

2007). Similar differences exist across school districts within states, likely as a result of differing approaches used to identify students and demographic factors (e.g., poverty rate).

The number of students with learning disabilities grew rapidly from the 1970s until the mid-1990s. This growth likely reflected the newness of the category (the term *learning disability* and a related definition initially appeared in federal law as part of the Learning Disabilities Act of 1969 [Part G, Title VI, PL 91-230]) and a subsequent federal law (i.e., PL 94-142, the Education for All Handicapped Children Act, later renamed IDEA, passed in 1975) mandating that all students with disabilities be identified and provided services. This growth slowed in the mid-1990s. Since that time, the percentage of the school-age population in this category has been relatively stable (U.S. Department of Education, 2007).

Service Delivery

During the 1970s and 1980s, many students with learning disabilities were educated in separate settings for much of the school day (McLeskey, Henry, & Axelrod, 1999; McLeskey & Pacchiano, 1994). More recently, the number of students with learning disabilities who are included in general education classrooms for most or all of the school day has increased significantly (McLeskey, Hoppey, Williamson, & Rentz, 2004). These increases have been influenced by two primary factors: (1) research demonstrating that most students with learning disabilities benefit from spending most of the school day in general education classrooms (Madden & Slavin, 1983; Rea, McLaughlin, & Walther-Thomas, 2002; Salend & Garrick Duhaney, 2007; Waldron & McLeskey, 1998) and (2) federal and state initiatives emphasizing that students with disabilities should be educated in less restrictive settings (e.g., Will, 1986).

The changes in the number of students with learning disabilities who are included in general education classrooms are illustrated in Table 4.1. For example, in the early 1990s, less than 1 in 4 students with learning disabilities spent most or all of the school day in a general education classroom. By 2005–2006, this number had increased significantly, as more than 2 of 4 students with learning disabilities spent most of the school day in a general education setting.

Another important change that is illustrated in Table 4.1 is the decrease in the number of students with learning disabilities who spend very little of the school day in general education classrooms (i.e., students in a separate class and separate setting). In 1990, about 1 in 4 students with learning disabilities were educated in one of these highly restrictive settings. This number declined about 50% by 2005–2006, as many of these students were educated in general education classrooms for an increasing portion of the school day.

Table 4.1   Percentage of School-Age Students with Learning Disabilities Taught in Different Placement Settings, 1990–1991 and 2005–2006

Placement Settings				
School Year	General Education[a]	Resource[a]	Separate Class[a]	Separate Setting[b]
1990–1991	22.6	53.6	22.4	1.5
2005–2006	54.5	33.7	10.9	0.9

[a]General education comprises students who are included in these settings 80% or more of the school day. Resource settings are made up of students who spend from 21% to 60% of the school day in a separate, resource classroom, and the remainder of the day in a general education classroom. Separate class comprises students who spend more than 60% of the school day in a separate, special education classroom.

[b]This setting is made up of several placement settings that are reported by the U.S. Department of Education, including a public separate facility, private separate facility, public residential facility, private residential facility, and home/hospital environment.

Source: Data from U.S. Department of Education. (2007). Individuals with Disabilities Education Act Data. Retrieved December 11, 2007, from https://www.ideadata.org/index.html

The data in Table 4.1 illustrate that schools have rapidly moved toward educating increasing numbers of students with learning disabilities in general education classrooms for much of the school day. While this rapid growth seems to have slowed to some degree in recent years (McLeskey, et al., 2004), we anticipate that the trend toward educating increasing numbers of students with learning disabilities in general education classrooms will continue in the coming years.

Major Characteristics of Students with Learning Disabilities

Perhaps the major characteristic of the learning disability category is its heterogeneity (Mercer & Pullen, 2008). This results in what some researchers have characterized as different subtypes of learning disabilities (Fletcher, Lyon, Fuchs, & Barnes, 2007).

Given the heterogeneity of the learning disability category, it is important to keep in mind that the characteristics we discuss in the following sections apply to some but not all students with learning disabilities. A second point to keep in mind as you review this information is emphasized by Vicki Eng, seventh-grade teacher at West Hernando Middle School: "It's amazing that other students who are not labeled have many of the same characteristics as students with learning disabilities." Many students who are not identified with a learning disability exhibit some of these characteristics at some level, although often not to the extremes exhibited by students with learning disabilities.

Most students with learning disabilities have difficulty learning to read.

Academic Difficulties

As we've noted previously, the main characteristic that educators use to identify students with learning disabilities is underachievement. All of these students share a common characteristic related to academic difficulty in one or more of the following areas: oral expression, listening comprehension, written expression, basic reading skill, reading fluency skills, reading comprehension, mathematics calculation, and mathematics problem solving.

The most common learning disability is in the area of reading. Approximately 80% of students with learning disabilities have difficulty in learning to read (Lerner & Kline, 2006). Evidence seems to suggest that reading difficulties often relate to problems with word recognition and spelling, reading fluency and automaticity, and/or reading comprehension (Fletcher, Lyon, Fuchs, & Barnes, 2007).

As students move through school, reading difficulties can cause problems with all subject areas. For example, in later elementary school, mathematics requires increasing levels of reading skill as the curriculum includes word problems and increasingly complex steps for problem solving. Reading difficulties become increasingly challenging for adolescents with learning disabilities, as the content-area curriculum in all areas becomes more complex, and the gap between student skills and classroom demands increases (Lenz & Deshler, 2004). This contributes to the difficulty students with learning disabilities have in passing high-stakes tests and making passing grades; about 1 in 3 of these students fail content-area courses (Lerner & Kline, 2006).

Some students with learning disabilities also have difficulty in learning mathematics. These problems may relate to difficulty with math computations (e.g., learning math facts at a level that allows quick, automatic responses, or difficulty learning strategies to complete math calculations) or math problem solving (e.g., using strategies to complete word problems) (Bryant & Dix, 1999; Fletcher et al., 2007).

Finally, some students with learning disabilities have difficulty with written expression. These students tend to produce written products with technical errors (i.e., punctuation, grammar), as well as poor organization and limited development of ideas (Lerner & Kline, 2006). As with reading problems, difficulty with written expression tends to cause increasingly more problems for students with learning disabilities as they move through grade levels and as the curriculum becomes more complex.

Cognitive Skill Deficits

Students with learning disabilities have a range of cognitive deficits that contribute to their learning problems. As with academic problems, none of these deficits are common to all students with learning disabilities. We discuss the most common deficits next.

Memory Problems. Memory problems may be manifested in learning relatively simple material such as sight vocabulary or math facts, or they may reflect a lack of effective strategies for learning more complex material. Students with learning disabilities also frequently have difficulty with working memory, which impacts the ability to see something, think about it, and then act on this information (Siegel, 2003).

Attentional Problems. Approximately 25% to 40% of students with learning disabilities also have ADHD (Lerner & Kline, 2006), while as many as 60% may have some mild but noteworthy difficulty with attention (Rock, Fessler, & Church, 1999). These students have difficulty selectively attending to information and sustaining attention over time. They also have problems related to impulsivity (i.e., responding without thinking) when presented with both oral and written problems or questions in class. Finally, these students may have difficulty sitting still in class and may be easily distracted. For more extensive information regarding ADHD, see Chapter 5.

Metacognitive Deficits. Many students with learning disabilities have difficulty monitoring their thinking processes (Mercer & Pullen, 2008; Scott, 1999). These difficulties with metacognition often prevent students from using a series of steps in solving a complex math problem or monitoring their attention to information to ensure that they comprehend written material. Strategies for addressing metacognitive problems have been used effectively with students with learning disabilities, including the use of advance organizers before presenting material, and providing students with strategies for planning and organizing material as they study academic content.

Social and Motivational Problems

Many students with learning disabilities have social and motivational problems that influence school performance. Social problems relate to how well these students get along with others, while motivational difficulties may influence academic progress. This may result in what Susan Davis, eighth-grade teacher at West Hernando Middle School, describes as an "I can't do it attitude" for many students with learning disabilities. Descriptions of the more common social and motivational problems manifested by students with learning disabilities are subsequently provided.

Social Problems. These difficulties relate to how well students get along with teachers and peers. While social skills are a strength for many students with learning disabilities, researchers estimate that approximately one third of these students have social-skill deficits (Lerner & Kline, 2006). These deficits may relate to:

- Lack of skills needed to build social relationships
- Exhibiting aggressive actions or negative verbal behaviors

- More attention-seeking or disruptive behaviors
- Displaying more insensitive, and less tactful or cooperative behaviors when interacting with others (Bryan, Burstein, & Ergul, 2004)

> ## Pause & Reflect
>
> Discuss with a peer in class an activity that is important to you but in which you do not perform well (e.g., music, sports, science, mathematics). How does your poor performance affect your motivation to engage in this task? How does your experience relate to motivational problems exhibited by persons with learning disabilities who repeatedly fail when attempting to learn to read or learn mathematics skills?

These social-skill deficits often lead to social isolation of students with learning disabilities and difficulty getting along with peers and teachers, and they can result in bullying (Weiner, 2004). It is important to note that the low social status of some students with learning disabilities may also relate to the student's low achievement (e.g., placement in a separate class with other students who are low achieving). Thus, when students with learning disabilities are included in general education classes, it is important that teachers recognize and address these social issues, to ensure that they do not increase the student's adjustment problems and contribute to underachievement.

Motivational Problems. Repeated difficulty in learning academic content often leads students to avoid the content, deny that a problem exists, and give up quickly when presented with new information related to the content. In short, the student's motivation is influenced by continued difficulty in mastering content.

As students with learning disabilities move into middle school, motivational problems often become more extreme. For some of these students, repeated failure may cause them to become passive learners and develop an attitude toward learning that has been characterized as learned helplessness (Lerner & Kline, 2006). These students react passively to tasks, do not actively engage in learning, and often wait for the teacher to tell them what to do rather than actively trying to solve a problem.

The most important factors in maintaining a high motivation level for students with learning disabilities involve recognizing when these issues arise and addressing them by providing effective instruction that is appropriate to the students' needs. Teachers may also address these problems by teaching students learning strategies that they can use to actively engage in learning (discussed further in Chapter 14) and by directly teaching social skills (discussed further in Chapter 15).

Effective Instruction for Students with Learning Disabilities

The accompanying box, "Teaching Students with Learning Disabilities in Inclusive Classrooms," provides reflections on the challenges teachers face in addressing the needs of students with learning disabilities and some strategies that three teachers who co-teach at West Hernando Middle School use to support these students. The following sections provide additional information regarding principles for research-based instruction and specific instructional practices that teachers may use to help students with learning disabilities achieve success in inclusive classrooms.

Effective Instruction for Elementary Students with Learning Disabilities

The most critical issue to address in elementary school for students with learning disabilities is learning basic skills in reading, writing, and math. As Susan Davis, Lisa Hallal, and Vicki Eng indicate in the "Teaching Students with Learning Disabilities" box, if these deficits continue into middle school, they can have a very negative influence on students' motivation and ability to learn the general education curriculum. What students with learning disabilities need most as they learn basic reading, writing, and math skills in elementary school is highly effective, research-based instruction. Without this type of instruction, these students fall further and further behind peers in developing basic skills as they move through elementary school.

Teaching Students with Learning Disabilities in Inclusive Classrooms: Challenges and Strategies

We interviewed three teachers who co-teach in inclusive classrooms at West Hernando Middle School regarding the challenges students with learning disabilities face in inclusive settings and strategies to overcome these challenges. Susan Davis and Lisa Hallal are eighth-grade special education teachers, while Vicki Eng is a seventh-grade special education teacher.

One of the major challenges addressed by Susan Davis relates to the higher expectations students with learning disabilities face in general education classrooms.

My students were in separate classes. Our expectations went up when they went into a co-taught, inclusive classroom. They're usually able to fulfill the expectations, but it's not easy In an inclusive classroom, students with learning disabilities see the high expectations and often come in at first with a "can't do it" attitude. You have to give them support to make sure they do get it. You may do some guided practice, and they get it. Or provide them with scaffolding until they get the information. It takes them a while to learn that you'll give them the support that they need and they can do it.

Another challenge is helping the students with learning disabilities understand their disability and how to get things done in spite of it. We tell them there are 15 ways to get to your house, but everybody gets there. It's the same for your work in school. You need to figure out what works for you. Whatever suits you best is the way you need to go.

Lisa Hallal added that there are times when students don't understand the content during a class period, and she doesn't have time to help them so they do get it:

Some students need more than we can give them during class, or they just don't get it during some lessons. It doesn't take much time to help them get it in small groups or one on one. We need to give them time and patience and help them walk through the work with guided practice.

We don't pull students out of academics but find other times to help them that adds to their instructional time. We do an after-school program to give them the extra help they need. Some kids don't get the math lesson during class, so we tutor them after school on what they don't understand during the school day so they do get it. Our help takes a little frustration away from them. Knowing they have the support they need helps them get through things. They don't resist because they know we really want to help them. They learn that it's not easy, but if I put an effort into it, the extra work does pay off.

Finally, Vicki Eng addressed a more general challenge for students with learning disabilities in general education settings, related to the need to self-advocate. This is especially important for students to succeed not only in middle school but also through their college years:

I ask students if they understand their disability. Nine times out of ten, they tell me no, they're not aware they have a learning disability. I sit down with them and explain what a learning disability is, and I tell them what their deficit areas are and explain this to them. If they don't understand what's going on—why they come to see me or go to a class with two teachers—they can't self-advocate. Where would they begin? This knowledge is power.

I also explain to them that they need to know how to self-advocate in a manner that's appropriate and not going to bring negative attention to them. For example, if they need extra time, I talk with them about how to ask the teacher without being inappropriate. I try to give them the knowledge that will lead to the power of them being able to self-advocate. They need to be able to self-advocate all the way through college. When they get to college, they can have the same accommodations made for them, so they need to know that.

Principles of Research-Based Instruction for Students with Learning Disabilities. The following are general principles that are research based and have proven useful when providing instruction to students with learning disabilities, as well as other students who struggle to learn academic content.

- **Provide high-quality core instruction in the general education classroom.** This instruction should be "explicit, well organized, and [should] routinely provide opportunit[ies] for cumulative

Strategy

For more information on providing high-quality core instruction using RTI, see Strategy 13.5 in Chapter 13.

Strategy

For more detailed information on differentiated instruction, see Strategy 12.3 in Chapter 12. And for more information on peer tutoring, see Strategy 13.4 in Chapter 13.

review of previously mastered content" (Fletcher et al., 2007, p. 272). High-quality core instruction in general education classrooms is characterized by good classroom management; balanced teaching of skills; providing students with supports or scaffolding as they learn new content; integration of curriculum across content areas (e.g., teaching reading vocabulary in science) whenever possible; and support for students in developing skills for self-regulation (Foorman, 2007).

- **Increase the time students spend learning key academic content.** Evidence indicates that the time students spend learning academic content has a significant impact on how much they learn (Fletcher et al., 2007). In spite of this finding, students with learning disabilities are often pulled out of elementary reading instruction for instruction in a separate setting. In most, if not all, instances, students with learning disabilities in reading should spend 90 minutes participating in a general education reading block. This instruction should be differentiated to meet the needs of these students. More intensive interventions that are needed and that cannot be provided in the general education classroom should be provided in addition to this instruction and should not supplant high-quality general education instruction.

- **Differentiate instruction in the general education classroom to meet student needs.** All students, including those who struggle learning academic content, will benefit from lessons that provide background information regarding material to be learned (e.g., review of background information and content before reading), or exercises that build skills (e.g., steps for regrouping in math) related to content. However, teachers should provide some instruction in general education classrooms that differentiates activities or instruction based on individual student needs using activities such as peer tutoring and small-group instruction (L. Fuchs & Fuchs, 2007; Vaughn & Roberts, 2007).

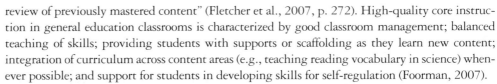

- **Closely integrate interventions with general education practices and curricular content** (Fletcher et al., 2007). Teachers should not use a separate curriculum when providing an intervention in reading, writing, or math for a student with a learning disability. Rather, teachers should use interventions that complement and build on the curriculum of the general education classroom. Teachers should also ensure that the student is learning this curriculum and is being taught the same information in different ways.

- **Employ strategies to increase student attention to and engagement in tasks.** Teachers can support increased attention and engagement using strategies such as the following (Lerner & Kline, 2006):
  - Break a long task into shorter parts.
  - Reduce the length of homework assignments.
  - Use distributed practice (i.e., short periods of practice spread over time).
  - Use strategies to make tasks more interesting, such as building on student interests, using novel activities, or providing students opportunities to work in small groups.
  - Alternate tasks that are high interest for students with those that are low interest.

When students with learning disabilities are pulled out of general education classrooms, teachers should provide them with high-quality, intensive, small-group instruction.

- **Frequently monitor student progress using measures that are directly related to the content being taught.** Educators have developed curriculum-based measurement (CBM) techniques to provide an efficient and effective measure of student progress in basic content areas (Deno, 2003, 2007). The academic progress of students who are struggling should be monitored frequently to determine the effectiveness of instructional strategies and interventions. If students are not making sufficient progress, interventions should be adapted or changed based on data collected from the curriculum-based measures.

Strategy

For more information on CBM, see Strategy 12.7 in Chapter 12.

Increasing Active Student Learning. If you have observed in elementary classrooms, you have seen many commonly used strategies for engaging students. These strategies include hand raising, allowing students to call out answers, and round-robin reading (i.e., one student reads

while others listen and wait their turn). None of these strategies work well for actively engaging all students in class in
learning activities. Moreover, they are especially problematic
for students who struggle to learn academic content, as they
engage one student at a time, provide little or no time to
think about possible responses, assume a high level of student
knowledge regarding the content, offer little opportunity for
student interaction, and are often quite threatening for students (Feldman & Denti, 2004).

In contrast to these approaches, teachers in effective inclusive elementary classrooms frequently use strategies that
actively engage all students. These high-access instructional
strategies are designed to provide thinking time for students, assume different levels of knowledge and skill regarding content, create low levels of threat, carefully structure student interactions, and provide for differentiated instruction based on student skill levels and learning needs
(Feldman & Denti, 2004).

Examples of high-access strategies include the following (Feldman & Denti, 2004):

1. **Thumbs up when you know:** The teacher asks a question and tells students to think
about the answer. Students are further asked to not call out an answer, but put a thumb up when
they have an answer. The teacher then provides thinking time, checks to see that most students
have their thumbs up, then calls on a student or cues students to respond chorally.

2. **Choral responding:** A teacher questions and requests that students not call out answers.
The teacher provides students with thinking time and then gives them an oral or visual cue to
respond as a group or chorally. This strategy works well when teaching basic skills such as sight
vocabulary (e.g., "What is the word I have written on the board?").

3. **Partner strategies:** The teacher assigns students to work in pairs (e.g., a high-achieving
student with a lower-achieving student) and provides participants with specific roles. Then the
group engages in an activity such as *Think–Pair–Share*. This activity begins as the teacher poses
an open-ended question, followed by time for students to think about the question. Students then
form pairs and share answers to the question. The teacher then calls on students to share their
responses.

Another simple partner strategy is *Give one—Get one.* The teacher begins this activity by posing
a question that requires a list of responses. Students then work individually to list responses and draw
a line at the bottom of their list. The teacher then signals the students to move around the class, get
an additional idea from a student, and give at least one idea to another student. Students then
review their lists with either a partner or the entire class.

Teachers can use many other activities to actively engage all students in learning in an elementary classroom. These activities are simple to implement and allow teachers to "capitalize on
the diversity of their classroom without compromising the integrity of classroom expectations"
(Feldman & Denti, 2004, p. 10).

Effective Instruction for Secondary Students with Learning Disabilities

As Vicki Eng, the seventh-grade teacher at West Hernando Middle School, suggests in the
"Teaching Students with Learning Disabilities" box, one of the most important skills that a sec-
ondary student with a learning disability can learn relates to self-advocacy. As Ms. Eng notes,
"Students need to understand their disability and know how to advocate in appropriate ways."

However, if self-advocacy is to succeed, teachers must have strategies that provide students
with disabilities access to the general education curriculum. Many students with learning disabilities can learn much of the general education curriculum, but they need supports and strategies that circumvent their disability to make this information available to them. As teachers
work with students with disabilities and others who struggle with academic content, several

Pause & Reflect

How have you seen teachers in elementary classrooms
engage students? Do they use strategies such as hand
raising, round-robin reading, and loosely structured
group work? Do these strategies actively engage all
students, or do some students disengage when these
activities are used? What alternative strategies have
you seen teachers use that actively engage all
students?

research-based strategies have been developed to ensure that this access occurs (Kame'enui & Carnine, 1998; Kame'enui & Simmons, 1999; Lenz & Deshler, 2004; Schumm, 1999; Vaughn, Bos, & Schumm, 2007).

Effective Strategies for Ensuring Curriculum Access for Students with Learning Disabilities at the Secondary Level:

Focus on Critical Curricular Content. We are currently in the midst of an information explosion, given the ready availability of information via the use of technology. The related growth in the school curriculum has led to difficulties for teachers in covering the material. What results in many schools is students superficially exposed to a wide range of information, while learning very little content in depth. Furthermore, students with learning disabilities have particular difficulty learning content, as they often lack basic skills (e.g., reading or writing) and lack strategies for learning content (e.g., distinguishing important from unimportant content) (Lenz & Deshler, 2004).

Rather than covering extensive content superficially, a better strategy for instruction is to ensure that all students learn the most important academic content in depth (Lenz, Bulgren, Kissam, & Taymans, 2004; Wiggins & McTighe, 2005). This suggests that teachers carefully map curricular content to determine what everyone should learn, what some students should learn, and what only a few students will learn (Lenz & Deshler, 2004; Schumm, 1999; Vaughn et al., 2007). This approach to instruction suggests that not all curricular material is of equal importance and that more important material should be taught in more depth than less important information (Kame'enui & Simmons, 1999).

> **Strategy**
> For more information on content enhancement, see Strategy 14.1 in Chapter 14.

Use Big Ideas to Frame and Guide Instruction. In addition to determining the content that is important for all to learn, teachers should examine the curricular content to determine overriding "big ideas" that provide a framework for learning important content. Big ideas have been defined as "concepts, principles, or heuristics that facilitate the most efficient and broadest acquisition of knowledge" (Kame'enui & Carnine, 1998, p. 8). This information provides students with anchoring concepts that help them learn smaller, related ideas.

To illustrate the use of big ideas to guide instruction, consider the following example for high school students. When studying the Civil War, a big idea might relate to "sectionalism" or how conflicts arose among different geographical regions of the country (Lenz et al., 2004). Teachers would determine what information regarding sectionalism is important for all students, some students, and only a few students to learn. For example, all students might learn about the conflict between the industrialized north and the agricultural south, and examples of issues that contributed to this sectionalism. Fewer students might then learn detailed information regarding how the cotton gin contributed to this conflict. Only a few students might learn detailed information about the invention of the cotton gin and how this invention influenced cotton farming.

> ## Pause & Reflect
> Have you had teachers who kept you guessing regarding which content was important to learn and would be on tests? Why would a teacher use this approach? What are the benefits of being explicit about important content, especially in a diverse classroom? What are the drawbacks?

> **Strategy**
> For more information on content enhancements, see Strategy 14.1 in Chapter 14.

Use Strategies That Explicitly Present Important Content to Students. As accountability becomes an increasingly important issue for teachers and students in secondary schools, it becomes important that teachers explicitly let students know what content is important for them to learn and what content will be tested, and this content should be explicitly taught. This is especially important in inclusive classrooms that include a diverse range of students.

Many strategies have been demonstrated effective in using explicit strategies to ensure that learning occurs and students succeed in inclusive classrooms (Lenz & Deshler, 2004). These strategies emphasize transforming "critical content in ways that help students understand, organize, and remember information . . . in a way that maintains the integrity of the content" (p. 14) and without watering down the curriculum.

Effective secondary teachers often use content-enhancement strategies such as graphic organizers and content maps to explicitly present critical content and make this content accessible to all students. Specific strategies such as content-enhancement routines have also been developed to explicitly present information using graphic organizers, including the unit organizer (a graphic that organizes and highlights critical relationships to be learned in a unit) and concept diagrams (a graphic that introduces critical concepts in a unit and highlights important questions and relationship patterns in the content) (Bulgren, 2006).

Provide Students with Supports by Using Strategies Such as Scaffolding as They Learn Complex Content. While some students quickly learn complex content after a cursory review of information by the teacher, others struggle to learn this content and need support, or scaffolding, to succeed. In mathematics, scaffolding occurs as a teacher breaks down a problem into steps, provides students with background information regarding how to solve each step, and then combines all steps to solve the problem. Effective teachers vary the use of scaffolding, depending on student needs, employ scaffolding only when students need support, and remove scaffolding gradually as students learn complex content (Kame'enui & Simmons, 1999).

Another general support strategy that many secondary teachers use to provide access to the general education curriculum is the guided notes strategy. The teacher provides a handout of an outline or map of the class lecture or other information being addressed and leaves certain critical information blank for students to fill in. This blank information may include critical concepts, facts, definitions, and so forth. The use of guided notes provides students with learning disabilities the scaffolding they need to learn critical information. For example, these students may often have difficulty taking notes quickly and determining the critical information to include in notes. In addition, the blank spaces in the notes allow students practice in learning critical information, as they listen for this information in lectures, search for it in a text, or seek out answers while working with peers.

The guided notes strategy is widely used at West Hernando Middle School to support students in general education classrooms. Michelle Duclos, seventh-grade science teacher at West Hernando, noted that she uses guided notes for students with disabilities and others who struggle learning the content. "For the notes, we take the most important information that they need to know, that will be on the test. Sometimes students get tied up on silly information that's not relevant. We have to refocus them on what's important."

> For more information on note taking, see Strategy 14.5 in Chapter 14.
>
> Strategy

Provide Students with Strategies for Learning Information. Some students naturally generate strategies for learning content. Students with learning disabilities often do not generate these strategies and must be taught them explicitly (Lenz & Deshler, 2004). Conveying knowledge-acquisition "trade secrets" to their students who struggle to learn academic content often has an intuitive appeal for teachers (Kame'enui & Carnine, 1998). Research supports the use of such learning strategies for all students, but those who struggle to learn academic content in particular benefit.

One strategy that has proven effective in improving the memory of students with disabilities is the use of mnemonic devices (Mastropieri & Scruggs, 2007), such as the use of "HOMES" to remember the names of the Great Lakes. Many other strategies have been developed to support students in learning content, solving problems, and completing tasks independently. These strategies address study skills, test taking, writing paragraphs, monitoring errors, following instructions, teamwork, self-advocacy, assignment completion, text comprehension, and many other areas (Deshler, 2005; Lenz & Deshler, 2004; Schumaker & Deshler, 2003).

> For more information regarding the use of mnemonic devices, see Strategy 14.3 in Chapter 14.
>
> Strategy

Final Thoughts Regarding Effective Practices

In Chapters 11 to 16, we provide step-by-step descriptions of many effective practices that are useful for students with learning disabilities and others who struggle in school. For example, many teachers are concerned about effective methods for teaching students with learning disabilities in basic academic skill areas. To address these concerns about teaching basic academic skills to students with learning disabilities, we include effective practices related to teaching beginning reading using RTI and tiers of instruction (Strategy 13.5); teaching reading in content areas at the secondary level (Strategy 14.4); teaching mathematics using cognitive strategy instruction (Strategy 13.7); and teaching writing at the elementary (Strategy 13.6) and secondary (Strategy 14.2) levels. We're sure you will find many of the strategies in Chapters 11 to 16 useful in ddressing the needs of students with learning disabilities in inclusive classrooms.

Summary

This chapter addressed the following topics:

Definition of learning disability and identification criteria

- A *learning disability* is defined as a disorder in one or more of the basic psychological processes involved in understanding or in using language, spoken or written, which disorder may manifest itself in the imperfect ability to listen, think, speak, read, write, spell, or do mathematical calculations.
- Learning disabilities do not include students whose learning problems are the result of another disability or environmental, cultural, or economic disadvantage.
- The primary criterion used to identify students with learning disabilities is unexpectedly low achievement. This criterion is defined by either a severe discrepancy between expected and actual achievement levels, or a procedure that examines the student's response to research-based interventions (i.e., response to intervention, RTI).

Prevalence of students with learning disabilities

- About 45% of all students with disabilities, or 5% of the school-aged population, are identified with learning disabilities.
- Identification rates in states vary from about 2% to over 7%.
- About three of four students with learning disabilities are male.
- The number of students with learning disabilities grew rapidly across the United States until the mid-1990s. Since that time, the number of students in this category has stabilized.
- We do not know what causes most learning disabilities, although it is assumed that these disabilities are somehow related to abnormal brain function. Learning disabilities seem to run in families, and they may be caused by poor teaching.

Educational placements for students with learning disabilities

- Most students identified with learning disabilities are educated for most of the school day in general education classrooms.
- About 1 in 10 students with learning disabilities is educated in a separate setting for much of the school day.

Major characteristics of students with learning disabilities

- The major characteristic of students with learning disabilities is unexpectedly low achievement. About 80% of students with learning disabilities have low achievement in reading. Other common areas of underachievement include mathematics and written expression.
- Students with learning disabilities are heterogeneous. Some of these students, however, are characterized by:
  - Cognitive skills deficits related to memory, attention, and/or metacognition
  - Social problems that result in difficulty getting along with others
  - Motivational problems that often result from prolonged failure in one or more academic content areas

Challenges in including students with learning disabilities in general education classrooms

- Academic skills deficits in reading, writing, or math make it difficult for students with learning disabilities to succeed in general education classrooms without adaptations and support.
- Students with learning disabilities may have difficulty remembering information, attending to important content, and using learning strategies to learn.

- Some students with learning disabilities have difficulty getting along with peers and/or teachers.
- Students with learning disabilities may develop motivational problems related to learning academic content, especially if they have had difficulty learning this content over a period of years.

Principles of effective instruction at the elementary level

- Students with learning disabilities should receive high-quality core instruction in the general education classroom. This should include differentiated instruction that meets the student's particular needs.
- Students with learning disabilities should receive additional instruction in academic areas if they continue to struggle, in spite of high-quality instruction in general education. This instruction should be closely integrated with instruction in the general education classroom.
- Teachers should use strategies to ensure students attend to and actively engage in tasks.
- Teachers should frequently monitor student academic progress and adjust instruction based on these data.

Principles of effective instruction at the secondary level

- Teachers should use co-teaching whenever possible in general education classrooms, ensuring that general and special education teachers combine their knowledge and skills to meet the diverse needs of students.
- Instruction should focus on critical content, ensuring that all students learn this content in depth. Teachers should use curriculum maps and unit plans to determine the content that all students, some students, and a few students should learn.
- Teachers should use big ideas (i.e., concepts, principles, or heuristics that facilitate the most efficient and broadest acquisition of knowledge) to frame and guide instruction. This information provides students with anchoring concepts that help them learn smaller, related ideas.
- Teachers should use strategies such as graphic organizers and content-enhancement routines to explicitly present important content to students. These strategies should maintain the integrity of content and ensure that information is not "watered down."
- Teachers should provide students with supports such as scaffolding when students are learning new information.
- Teachers should explicitly teach strategies to ensure success. These strategies should address areas such as study skills, test taking, following instructions, self-advocacy, and assignment completion.

Addressing Professional Standards

Standards addressed in Chapter 4 include:

CEC Standards: (1) foundations, (2) development and characteristics of learners, (3) individual learning differences, (4) instructional strategies.

INTASC Standards: Principle 1—Understand central concepts of the discipline; Principle 2—Provide learning opportunities to support the learning and development of all students.

Praxis™ II Standards: Knowledge-based core principles: (1) understanding exceptionalities, (3) delivery of services to students with disabilities. Application of core principles: (1) curriculum, (2) instruction, (5) professional roles/issues/ literature.

Students with Attention-Deficit/ Hyperactivity Disorder

KEY TOPICS

After reading this chapter you will:

- Know the definition and criteria used to identify students with attention-deficit/hyperactivity disorder (ADHD).
- Know the number of students who are identified with ADHD.
- Be able to identify the educational settings in which students with ADHD are educated.
- Be able to describe the major characteristics of students with ADHD.
- Understand key issues and challenges related to including students with ADHD in general education classrooms.
- Know effective practices for addressing the needs of students with ADHD in elementary and secondary classrooms.

Perspectives on Including Students with Attention-Deficit/Hyperactivity Disorder

Interview with Eileen Walls, Behavior Specialist, and Laura Scott, Seventh-Grade Special Education Teacher, West Hernando Middle School

We interviewed two teachers from West Hernando Middle School who have worked with many students with ADHD who were included in general education classrooms. Eileen Walls is a behavior specialist, and Laura Scott is a seventh-grade special education teacher.

Eileen Walls noted:

The biggest benefit [for including students with ADHD] is learning to cope effectively in the regular classroom. Why do they need to learn to cope? They don't get to shop at a special education Publix when they graduate from high school. There is no special education line at the bank for them. They have to learn to be successful and be a contributing member to the school community. And when they're out of school, they need to be a contributor to a more global community, whether it is their work environment, or home environment, or church or their own neighborhood. It is important to learn coping strategies so they can be successful later in life and contribute.

Laura Scott addressed academic and social benefits for including students with ADHD:

When we had separate classes, it seemed that the curriculum automatically started getting watered down and covered at a slower pace. We didn't cover the wealth of information that's in the regular curriculum. Students with ADHD benefit academically from being in a general education classroom where there is a general education teacher who is well versed in the curriculum being taught, whether it's math, English, geography, or whatever. So it's better academically to be in general education.

Socially, it's better for them as well. Their day is just like everyone else's day, and that's really important to them. There's a stigma for kids going out of the regular classroom, especially for kids with mild disabilities. All of the students know who the English teachers are,

so it's tough on students when they tell people who their teacher is and they know it's the teacher for the "slow" kids. In the regular class, none of the students really know the function of the special education teacher. We're just co-teaching. We work with all the kids, some one at a time, some in small groups. Sometimes we teach the whole class. So none of the kids are stigmatized.

Laura Scott also discussed two key issues when teaching students with ADHD in inclusive classrooms. One key is to get to know the student well:

The challenges for these students are different, depending on the severity of the ADHD. Some kids are pretty easy to handle; others need more help. The key is really knowing the child, and what they can handle. What are the warning signs that they are going to have a bad day? You can put the label of "ADHD" on lots of kids, but the label doesn't look the same on every child.

A second key is to recognize that academics and the student's ADHD-type behaviors are closely related:

I always keep in mind that much of their behavior is a front or escape from having to do the work that they know they can't do. My job is to make sure there's a lot of academic support, making them sure they *can* do the work. Reassuring them that I will help them, I'm not going to leave them out there hanging on their own. If they think they're going to get help and support, they're much more likely to tackle the work and alleviate some of that behavior that comes from wanting to escape the work.

Many students in general education classrooms have some of the characteristics of ADHD (inattentive, impulsive, highly active).

Introduction

Most of us have a preconceived notion of attention-deficit/hyperactivity disorder (ADHD). You've probably heard friends mention this term, and you may have seen stories on television or in the print media addressing this category of disability. This widespread media coverage likely occurs, at least in part, because the primary characteristics of this category—inattention, impulsivity, and high levels of activity—are so common. Almost all young children exhibit these behaviors at some level, as do many adults. As you have surely noted, circumstances may increase the occurrence of these behaviors for any of us (think of a young child left unsupervised in a grocery store, or a college student who sits through a boring 50-minute lecture). Circumstances may also decrease the occurrence of these behaviors (remember that highly stimulating college class, when time passed so quickly, or that closely supervised young child in a grocery store).

Thus, ADHD seems to be interesting to many people because persons who are given this label are so much like the rest of us. As a special educator once noted, "Students with ADHD are just like everybody else, only more so." This seems to be the essence of the ADHD category. These are students who bring many strengths into the classroom; however, certain aspects of their behavior (inattention, impulsivity, and/or activity level) are so extreme that they interfere with everyday life activities such as school.

Eileen Walls and Laura Scott, teachers at West Hernando Middle School in the "Perspectives" vignette, noted that students with ADHD benefit in many ways when they are included in general education classrooms. These benefits may relate to improved academic skills or social adjustment as well as preparation for coping with life beyond school. Fortunately, many interventions are available to help provide students with supports in the general education classroom that ensure that these benefits are realized. Furthermore, many of these interventions are beneficial for many students, not just those identified with ADHD.

In this chapter, we address the behavior of students who exhibit some combination of inattention, impulsive responses, and overactive behavior. We also discuss interventions and supports that teachers can use to meet the needs of these students (and many of their peers) in a general education classroom.

Who Are Students with Attention-Deficit/Hyperactivity Disorder?
Definition

For a quick overview of the ADHD category, you should review "Just the Facts: Students with ADHD." The definition that is most widely used to identify students with ADHD was developed by the American Psychiatric Association (APA, 2000) and defines ADHD as "a persistent pattern of inattention and/or hyperactivity-impulsivity that is more frequently displayed and more severe than is typically observed in individuals at a comparable level of development" (p. 85). This definition also includes criteria for student identification that are shown in Figure 5.1. This definition and related criteria have been thoroughly researched and revised on several occasions.

As you review Figure 5.1, you should attend to several key issues that are intended to improve the reliability of student identification:

- Students must exhibit six of nine explicit behaviors related to either inattention or hyperactivity-impulsivity.
- These behaviors must be exhibited frequently (e.g., much more often than observed in peers) over a 6-month period.
- The behaviors must be evident across two or more settings (i.e., school and home).
- The impulsive and inattentive behavior was exhibited before the age of 7.
- Students may be identified as having ADHD, predominantly inattentive type; ADHD, predominantly hyperactive-impulsive type; or ADHD combined, who exhibit inattentive and hyperactive-impulsive behaviors.

Another consideration regarding the definition of ADHD is the fact that students exhibit these symptoms in different ways and at different levels as they age. For example, if you observe a group of preschool students in a setting where they are expected to sit and listen to someone read, you will see many examples of all of the behaviors that are used to identify ADHD. As children mature, many learn to monitor and control these behaviors (e.g., inattentive behavior lessens with age for all students) and channel them in more positive directions (e.g., high levels of activity are delayed until time for recess). Furthermore, as West Hernando Middle School teacher Laura Scott noted in the "Perspectives" vignette, every student with ADHD is different, and each of these students exhibits a different pattern of impulsive, inattentive, and hyperactive behaviors.

Given these considerations, how can a definition be developed that can be reliably used to identify students with ADHD? This is the source of much controversy about this category, as professional judgment must be used to determine if behaviors that appear often are manifested frequently enough, at a level that is so extreme when compared to peers, that a student should be identified with ADHD.

myeducationlab

Go to MyEducationLab, select the topic *Attention-Deficit/Hyperactivity Disorder,* and go to the Building Teaching Skills and Dispositions section. As you complete the activity entitled "Self-Monitoring," reflect on how beneficial these strategies are for this student to stay on task.

Pause & Reflect

Do you know someone who exhibits one of the primary characteristics of ADHD with some frequency (i.e., inattentive, impulsive, or highly active)? Do certain circumstances (e.g., a boring college lecture) influence the occurrence of these behaviors? Why does this occur? What does this say about classrooms that might be better (or worse) for educating students with ADHD?

Figure 5.1 *DSM-IV-TR* **Criteria for Identifying ADHD**

A. Either (1) or (2):

   (1) six (or more) of the following symptoms of inattention have persisted for at least 6 months to a degree that is maladaptive and inconsistent with developmental level:

   Inattention

   (a) often fails to give close attention to details or makes careless mistakes in schoolwork, work, or other activities

   (b) often has difficulty sustaining attention in tasks or play activities

   (c) often does not seem to listen when spoken to directly

   (d) often does not follow through on instructions and fails to finish schoolwork, chores, or duties in the workplace (not due to oppositional behavior or failure to understand instructions)

   (e) often has difficulty organizing activities

   (f) often avoids, dislikes, or is reluctant to engage in tasks that require sustained mental effort (such as schoolwork or homework)

   (g) often loses things necessary for tasks or activities (e.g., toys, school assignments, pencils, books, or tools)

   (h) is often easily distracted by extraneous stimuli

   (i) is often forgetful in daily activities

   (2) six (or more) of the following symptoms of hyperactivity-impulsivity have persisted for at least 6 months to a degree that is maladaptive and inconsistent with developmental level:

   Hyperactivity

   (a) often fidgets with hands or feet or squirms in seat

   (b) often leaves seat in classroom or in other situations in which remaining seated is expected

   (c) often runs about or climbs excessively in situations in which it is inappropriate (in adolescents or adults, may be limited to subjective feelings of restlessness)

   (d) often has difficulty playing or engaging in leisure activities quietly

   (e) is often "on the go" or often acts as if "driven by a motor"

   (f) often talks excessively

   Impulsivity

   (a) often blurts out answers before questions have been completed

   (b) often has difficulty awaiting turn

   (c) often interrupts or intrudes on others (e.g., butts into conversations or games)

B. Some hyperactive-impulsive or inattentive symptoms that caused impairment were present before age 7 years.

C. Some impairment from the symptoms is present in two or more settings (e.g., at school [or work] and at home).

D. There must be clear evidence of clinically significant impairment in social, academic, or occupational functioning.

E. The symptoms do not occur exclusively during the course of a Pervasive Developmental Disorder, Schizophrenia, or other Psychotic Disorder and are not better accounted for by another mental disorder (e.g., Mood Disorder, Anxiety Disorder, Dissociative Disorder, or a Personality Disorder).

Code based on type:

314.01 Attention-Deficit/Hyperactivity Disorder, Combined Type: if both Criteria A1 and A2 are met for the past 6 months

314.00 Attention-Deficit/Hyperactivity Disorder, Predominantly Inattentive Type: if Criterion A1 is met but Criterion A2 is not met for the past 6 months.

314.01 Attention-Deficit/Hyperactivity Disorder, Predominantly Hyperactive-Impulsive Type: if Criterion A2 is met but Criterion A1 is not met for the past 6 months

Source: Reprinted with permission from the *Diagnostic and Statistical Manual of Mental Disorders,* Fourth Edition, Text Revision, Copyright 2000. American Psychiatric Association.

Just the Facts   Students with ADHD

Who are they?	Children with ADHD manifest "a persistent pattern of inattention and/or hyperactivity-impulsivity that is more frequently displayed and more severe than is typically observed in individuals at a comparable level of development" (APA, 2000, p. 85). To be identified in a school, these behaviors must significantly impede the student's educational performance.
What are typical characteristics?	• Impulsivity—Responding without thinking. • Hyperactivity—Much more active than other students of the same age. • Inattention—Inability to focus, selectively attend, or maintain attention for sustained periods of time. • Coexisting conduct problems—About 30% to 50% of students with ADHD have significant conduct problems. • Coexisting academic problems—About 80% of these students have some level of academic problem, while about 20% to 25% are identified with a learning disability.
What are the demographics?	• Estimates vary regarding how many school-age students have ADHD. Research indicates that from 3% to 7% of these students (between 2 and 4.5 million students) are identified with ADHD. • Fewer than 1% are identified under IDEA as *other health impaired.* Most students with ADHD are identified under Section 504. • The use of prescription medication varies across states and communities. Overall, about 2% to 4% of school-aged students receive some form of medication (mostly stimulant medications). • About 3 of every 4 students with ADHD are male.
Where are students with ADHD educated?	• Most students with ADHD are educated for a substantial part of the school day in a general education classroom, in less restrictive settings than any special education category other than speech and language impairments. • Most general education classes have from 1 to 3 students with ADHD for most or all of the school day.
How are students identified?	• Criteria from *DSM-IV-TR* (APA, 2000) are widely used to identify students with ADHD (see Figure 5.1 for more information regarding these criteria). • Information from parents and teachers regarding the student's behavior is the most critical information used to identify students with ADHD. This information is collected using interviews, observations in multiple settings, and rating scales.
What causes ADHD?	• The cause of ADHD in most instances is unknown. • ADHD most often seems to result from the complex interaction of many factors. No single factor always results in ADHD. Contributing factors include: • *Brain injury.* Many students who have had documented brain injury exhibit one or more of the symptoms of ADHD. This includes about 5% to 10% of all students with ADHD. • *Brain abnormalities.* Research has shown that students with ADHD often have different brain chemistry when compared to children who do not have ADHD (DuPaul, Barkley, & Connor, 1998). For example, many of these students have deficiencies in neurotransmitters or chemicals in the brain that influence the transmission of signals between nerve cells. • *Hereditary influences.* If a parent or sibling has ADHD, the probability that another sibling will have ADHD increases significantly. • *Family influences.* While poor parenting does not cause ADHD as some have suggested, poor parent behavior management skills can make the symptoms of ADHD worse. Furthermore, extreme stress in a family can temporarily result in the manifestation of symptoms related to ADHD.
What are the outcomes?	• About 1 in 3 students with ADHD has no symptoms of ADHD in adulthood. • About 1 in 4 students with ADHD has conduct disorders in adulthood. • About 1 in 4 students with ADHD develops major depression in adulthood.

Identification of Students with ADHD

As we begin a discussion of the identification of students with ADHD, you should note that this category is unique and somewhat confusing when it comes to identification. This occurs in large part because ADHD is not a separate special education category but is included as part of the other health impairments (OHI) category in IDEA.

Other health impairments are defined in IDEA as follows:

Other health impairment means having limited strength, vitality or alertness, including a heightened alertness to environmental stimuli, that results in limited alertness with respect to the educational environment, that—

   (i) Is due to chronic or acute health problems such as asthma, attention deficit disorder or attention deficit hyperactivity disorder, diabetes, epilepsy, a heart condition, hemophilia, lead poisoning, leukemia, nephritis, rheumatic fever, sickle cell anemia, and Tourette syndrome; and

   (ii) Adversely affects a child's educational performance. (PL 108-446 Regulations, Sec. 300.8(c)(9)(i))

You will note that two terms are used in this definition for students with ADHD: attention-deficit disorder (ADD) and attention-deficit/hyperactivity disorder (ADHD). ADD was formerly used for children with predominantly inattentive behaviors and continues to be used by some to identify these students. Neither of these terms is defined in IDEA. This is also true of the other conditions that are included in the OHI category (i.e., diabetes, epilepsy, etc.). It is thus assumed that these conditions are medically defined and that a physician will make a determination regarding whether the conditions exist.

A physician typically identifies students with ADHD, using information provided by parents, teachers, school psychologists, and others. The American Academy of Pediatrics (Reiff, 2004) has developed guidelines that pediatricians use to identify students with ADHD. The six-step process includes the following:

1. If a child from ages 6 to 12 is described as unusually inattentive, hyperactive, impulsive; underachieving in school; or exhibiting behavior problems, the child should be evaluated for ADHD.
2. To identify a student with ADHD, the *DSM-IV TR* criteria (APA, 2000) should be used.
3. Evidence collected should include information from parents or caregivers regarding the symptoms of ADHD (i.e., impulsivity, inattention, hyperactivity) across settings; the age at which the behaviors were initially noticed; how long the child has exhibited the behaviors; and the degree to which the behaviors interfere with the child's ability to function (i.e., learn in school, get along with peers).
4. The pediatrician should obtain information from the child's teacher or other school professional regarding the symptoms of ADHD that the child exhibits in the classroom, how long the symptoms have been manifested, the degree to which the symptoms interfere with the child's ability to function; and whether any other conditions (e.g., learning disability, emotional/behavior disorder) are suspected.
5. An evaluation of any co-existing conditions (e.g., learning disability, emotional and behavioral disability) should be conducted.
6. Other diagnostic tests (e.g., blood tests, brain scans) or psychological tests are not routinely necessary to identify students with ADHD.

After a student is identified with ADHD, the school-based multidisciplinary team addresses Section (ii) of the OHI definition. This team must determine whether the student's ADHD adversely affects his educational performance. If the multidisciplinary team determines that the child's educational performance is affected (e.g., the child is significantly underachieving in reading or mathematics) and that the child needs special education services, he is then determined eligible as OHI for these services as part of IDEA.

It is noteworthy that eligibility for special education services is not based on the identification of a disability, but rather depends on whether the disability adversely affects the child's educational performance, and whether special education services are required to address this need. With respect to students with ADHD, it is possible that the symptoms of this disability may be very mild, and educational performance is not adversely affected. In still other instances, the symptoms of ADHD may be controlled sufficiently by medication, so that the student does not need special education services. (We will provide more information regarding the use of medication as an intervention for students identified with ADHD later in this chapter.)

If a student is identified as ADHD but is not eligible for special education services, the student still may be eligible for accommodations in the general education classroom as part of Section 504 of the Rehabilitation Act of 1973. This law is a civil rights act, designed to ensure that persons with disabilities receive reasonable accommodations and are not discriminated against as a result of their disability (deBettencourt, 2002). These accommodations may include modification of tests used in a general education classroom to ensure student attention to relevant information or moving the student to a location in the room where distractions will be minimized.

A physician typically determines if a student has ADHD, using information from teachers, parents, school psychologists, and others.

We offer one final cautionary note regarding the identification of students with ADHD and the use of medication to control the symptoms associated with this disability. Much information regarding this disability has appeared in the popular press, resulting in much discussion of this category by parents and teachers. Given this widespread discussion of ADHD, you should keep in mind that a teacher should not recommend to a parent that a child should be referred to a physician to be evaluated for ADHD or suggest that the student could benefit from medication. A school's multidisciplinary team should provide information to parents regarding the nature of a child's difficulty in school and whether these difficulties merit an evaluation by a physician and possible use of medication to address the child's behavior.

Prevalence

For other categories of disability that are part of IDEA, data are collected by the U.S. Department of Education regarding the number of students who are identified and other related information (e.g., the setting in which the student is educated). These data are not collected for students with ADHD, which is not a stand-alone category of disability under IDEA. Although researchers agree that ADHD is the most common behavior problem among school-age students (Barkley, 2006a; Gureasko-Moore, DuPaul, & Power, 2005), specific estimates of the prevalence of students with ADHD vary widely.

The APA (2000) estimates that from 3% to 7% of students are identified with ADHD. Data from studies across settings have supported this estimate (Barkley, 2006b; Costello et al., 2003), although the prevalence rate seems to decline as children move through school (Costello et al., 2003).

The range of prevalence rates suggests that the percentage of students identified with ADHD varies across settings (e.g., schools, school districts, states). However, no matter the setting, a substantial number of students are identified with ADHD (Gureasko-Moore et al., 2005). For example, at least 3 of 100 students are identified as ADHD in most school districts, and from 2 to 4.5 million students are so identified in the United States. This means that most general educators will have 1 to 3 students with ADHD in their classroom each school year.

Far more boys are identified with ADHD than girls. Early in the school years, approximately twice as many boys are identified as having ADHD. This ratio increases to approximately three or more boys to every girl later in the school years (Reiff, 2004; Smith, Barkley, & Shapiro, 2006).

Some evidence also indicates that ADHD is more common among children from low socioeconomic backgrounds; however, it is unclear whether differences exist across different racial groups (Wenar & Kerig, 2006).

Another factor that complicates the determination of how many students are identified with ADHD is that more than 50% of these students are also identified with another disability (Reiff, 2004). For example, the percentage of students who also have ADHD is approximately 20% to 25% of students identified with learning disabilities; 25% to 40% of students with intellectual disabilities; 50% to 60% of students with emotional and behavioral disabilities; and approximately 25% of students with autism spectrum disorder (DuPaul, 2007; Reiff, 2004).

Perhaps the most important point we can make is that while prevalence rates vary significantly across the United States, every general education classroom includes students who exhibit many of the symptoms that are characteristic of these students. Moreover, many of the effective practices that are addressed in relation to effective instruction and classroom management in Chapters 13 and 15 are very useful for addressing these behaviors. We also discuss strategies for addressing the particular behaviors manifested by students identified with ADHD later in this chapter.

Service Delivery

Most students with ADHD spend the majority of the school day in general education classrooms. Those students who are identified with ADHD and receive accommodations as part of Section 504 are typically educated full-time in general education classrooms and have accommodations made in those settings. These are students who have mild symptoms of ADHD, which have a limited impact on the students' educational performance and social interactions. Based on the most conservative estimates of the prevalence rate of ADHD, this amounts to 2% to 3% of the school-age population.

Students who are identified under the OHI category as ADHD, and are in need of special education services, can be assumed to have somewhat more extreme symptoms related to ADHD that affect educational performance. Most of these students are also educated in general education settings for most of the school day. In 2005, 56% of students in the OHI category (most of whom are labeled with ADHD) spent most of the school day (80% or more) in general education classrooms, while only 16% of students identified with OHI spent most of the school day in separate settings (U.S. Department of Education, 2007). The placement settings for these students are the least restrictive of any category of disability other than speech or language impairments.

A final consideration relates to students with ADHD who are identified in another category of disability. As we noted previously, many students identified with learning disabilities, emotional and behavioral disabilities, intellectual disabilities, and autism spectrum disorders also are identified with ADHD. These are often the students with the most extreme symptoms related to ADHD, which interfere with academic progress and social interactions.

When considering all students identified with ADHD, it is likely that most general education teachers will have from one to three students with ADHD in class for most of the school day. This suggests the need for knowledge regarding the characteristics of these students and how to effectively address their needs in the general education classroom.

Major Characteristics of Students with ADHD
Inattentive, Hyperactive, and Impulsive Behaviors

Inattention may take several forms. For example, students with ADHD may have difficulty orienting in an appropriate direction in a classroom (i.e., looking out a window rather than orienting in the direction of the teacher or the board in front of the class). After orienting in an appropriate direction, these students may have difficulty sustaining attention for an appropriate amount of time, or they may be easily distracted by extraneous activities or noises. Finally, even with an appropriate level of sustained attention, some students with ADHD have difficulty selectively attending, or determining just what they should attend to on an overhead (e.g., should the student look at the pictures on the overhead, the words describing the pictures, or both?).

To describe students with ADHD, teachers often use terms such as inattentive; careless; unable to concentrate; disorganized; easily distracted; unable to follow directions; forgetful; and poor at listening, following directions, and completing tasks. Laura Scott, seventh-grade teacher at West Hernando Middle School, described students with ADHD as "having a hard time paying attention, blurting out, saying inappropriate things, or losing control quickly."

Another major characteristic of students with ADHD is hyperactivity, or a high level of activity that is inappropriate for a given setting and is not age appropriate. The level of activity varies significantly among students with ADHD. Some activity levels are annoying to teachers and peers but do not adversely affect the student's educational performance. On the other extreme, some students with ADHD have activity levels that are so high that they disrupt class, interfere with the student's educational progress, and interfere with interactions with teachers and peers.

When teachers describe students who exhibit hyperactive behaviors, they use terms or phrases such as "never slows down," "driven by a motor," "constantly talks out," "cannot sit still," and "wants to do things *now*!" They also note that these students have difficulty following rules, and they engage in behaviors that prevent them from getting along well with others, including peers and teachers.

Impulsivity is often seen as part of a hyperactive-impulsive type of ADHD. Students who are impulsive respond before they think. Thus, teachers often describe students who are impulsive as talking without thinking, refusing to wait for a turn, unable to follow the rules of a game, and intruding on others in social situations.

Students who are hyperactive may present challenges to classroom teachers during instructional activities that require sustained seat work.

Social and Behavior Problems

If you've had the opportunity to interact with someone who is identified with ADHD, or who exhibited some of the symptoms we've discussed previously, you can readily understand why these students might have social problems and difficulty getting along in school. Briefly review the criteria for identifying students with ADHD in Figure 5.1. Do all of these criteria have the potential to create social problems or disrupt classroom activities? Certainly, most do. These are students who have difficulty sustaining attention even during play activities, interfere with the flow of activities during social interactions, have difficulty taking turns, and have difficulty engaging in a two-way conversation with a peer.

Pause & Reflect

Have you had an acquaintance with whom you've talked in a group or individually who had some of the symptoms we've discussed related to ADHD? For example, "talks without thinking." How did you and others react to this person? How would peers react to a person with these symptoms in a general education classroom? How would a teacher react?

Research has indicated that while many students with ADHD get along well with others in school, some may have difficulty and create disruptions. For example, some students with ADHD are more negative and unskilled when interacting with peers, and when introduced to some students with ADHD, peers may notice and react negatively to the student's behaviors (Wenar & Kerig, 2006).

Students with ADHD may also create disruptions in classrooms because of their inattentive, impulsive, and/or hyperactive behaviors. Some of the more extreme difficulties these students exhibit include problems with stubbornness, defiance or refusal to obey requests, verbal hostility, and temper tantrums (Barkley, 2006a). Students who are identified with ADHD who exhibit the

Although many students with ADHD get along well with others, some of these students may be socially isolated because of their behavior.

most extreme disruptive behaviors are often identified with emotional and behavioral disabilities. Approximately 50% to 60% of students with emotional and behavioral disabilities are also identified with ADHD (DuPaul, 2007; Reiff, 2004). For more information regarding emotional and behavioral disabilities, see Chapter 7.

Academic Difficulties

A quick review of the criteria for identifying students with ADHD in Figure 5.1 reveals that many of these behaviors also have the potential to have a negative impact on a student's academic performance. For example, academic classwork, homework, tests, and so forth require concentration for a sustained period of time, attention to details, listening for information and assignments, careful work, and good organizational skills, among others.

These behaviors, as well as the previously noted disruptive behaviors that many students with ADHD manifest, result in approximately 80% of these students having at least some problems with academic achievement in school (Reiff, 2004; Wenar & Kerig, 2006). Researchers have estimated that approximately 20% of these students may have an academic problem that is so severe that they are identified with a learning disability (DuPaul, 2007; Reiff, 2004). (Learning disabilities were discussed previously in Chapter 4.)

Effective Instruction for Students with ADHD

As Laura Scott, a seventh-grade special education teacher at West Hernando Middle School, notes in "Teaching Students with ADHD," the behaviors exhibited by students with ADHD vary significantly. The behavior of some of these students isn't significantly different from other students in a typical middle school classroom, while others have more extreme behaviors. In any form, teachers may find the impulsive, inattentive, and hyperactive behaviors of these students frustrating and perhaps annoying. Fortunately, educators have developed interventions that increase the prospects for success for students with ADHD, and these interventions are also beneficial for many students who are not so identified.

Effective Instruction for Elementary Students with ADHD

Providing Appropriate Structure in General Education Classrooms. As we noted previously, much overlap exists among students with ADHD and those with emotional and behavioral disabilities and learning disabilities. As you might assume, many of the classroom intervention and management strategies that are useful for students with learning disabilities and emotional and behavioral disabilities have proven effective for students with ADHD.

As Laura Scott points out in the "Teaching Students with ADHD" box, one of the keys to success in addressing the needs of students with ADHD in a general education classroom is providing an appropriate level of structure. Several general principles have proven useful for many teachers in organizing and managing a classroom that includes students with ADHD, as well as other students with and without disabilities who have difficulty with impulse control, inattention, and high activity levels (Pfiffner, Barkley, & DuPaul, 2006).

1. The presentation of rules and instructions should be brief, clear, and visual, in the form of charts, lists, and other visual reminders whenever possible. Many children have difficulty remembering rules, and using only verbal reminders is often ineffective.

Strategy

See Strategy 15.1 for more information regarding rules and procedures for use in inclusive classrooms.

Teaching Students with ADHD in Inclusive Classrooms: Challenges and Strategies

Laura Scott, seventh-grade special education teacher at West Hernando Middle School, spoke with us about the challenges of teaching students with ADHD in the general education classroom and described strategies to address some of these challenges. As Ms. Scott noted in the "Perspectives" vignette, students with the label ADHD differ, often significantly, because no two students with ADHD are exactly alike. She also said that one of the keys to successfully teaching these students is to know the particular student well. She elaborates on this idea here:

The teacher has to be very proactive and stay on top of things. When a student has a very hard time paying attention, or blurts out, says inappropriate things, or loses control quickly, you need to be able to see the signs that something is coming. You have to know the child well so you see the signs and you know the child is going to get aggravated. Sometimes another kid will set him off. He might have missed breakfast that morning or had a fight with his brother. You have to catch it before it gets started and redirect the behavior.

Ms. Scott also emphasizes how important it is to praise students when they do things well. But knowing the student well is critical if praise is to be used successfully.

A lot of kids in middle school like to look tough. Maybe they don't respond to verbal praise or don't like you to praise them in front of the other students. They still like positive comments, notes, praise to make it through the class OK. But you may have to save the praise, praise some children quietly, and individually, not in front of the whole class. Maybe they don't want everybody to think that they did the right thing or think that they are a nerd.

We forget, at times, that students in middle school are still just kids. They may be 6 feet tall, but they're only 11 or 12 or 13 years old. Maybe they don't respond to verbal praise. But we have to remember that they're just bigger kids. Ultimately, they want to do well and please their teachers. It's important to praise anything you can, but in a way that works for the child.

Ms. Scott also stresses the need for a "bag of tricks" filled with simple strategies to redirect the student, keep the student focused, and help address inattentive, impulsive, and hyperactive behaviors.

I pay close attention to the student to see when I need to redirect behavior. Sometimes I do this by giving them a little extra attention. It doesn't have to be too long, too wordy or lengthy. Sometimes I walk over and tap on the desk, and say, "You doing ok?" Or I may simply ask the student, "Do you have any questions?" or have them repeat what's just been said in class to make sure they're paying attention.

For some students, the challenges are a matter of giving them something to help them concentrate. We use beads in one class. The teacher made rings with beads and told them to keep the beads in their hand and rub them, fiddle with them, rather than getting out of their seat when they got anxious.

We also do little things with lessons to make sure they're with us. Sometimes I'll write steps on a paper they're working on that tells them what to do. They might listen to instructions but may not remember them or may lose focus. I put simple, concise instructions on their paper, so if I can't sit with them, I can tap on their desk and say look, you need to be on step 2. My co-teacher and I will often tell the student what's coming in the lesson, so they know what to expect. We then break the lesson down and just give them part of it at one time, so they don't get overwhelmed.

Ms. Scott offers some personal comments for new teachers,

Whatever you do with students with ADHD, it's not going to work every time. You fail sometimes. You also should not take things personally. It's easy to get annoyed with a child who is constantly tapping, or moving, or talking out. Some things work one day and not the next. For your own peace of mind, don't take any of these things personally; just keep pulling things from your bag of tricks until something works.

Well-organized, carefully structured instruction often works well for students with ADHD and others who struggle to learn.

Strategy

For more information regarding developing and consistently delivering reinforcers, see Strategy 15.3 in Chapter 15.

2. The approach to consequences must be well organized, thoroughly planned, and systematic. Feedback, rewards, and punishment used to manage a child's behavior must be delivered immediately, at least initially, because many students with ADHD respond better to immediate rather than delayed reinforcement.

3. Frequent feedback when the child follows rules is crucial for maintaining the child's compliance. Catch the student engaging in appropriate behavior, briefly describe the behavior, and provide praise.

4. Children with ADHD are often less sensitive to social praise and reprimands. The consequences for appropriate or inappropriate behavior must be more powerful than those needed to manage the behavior of other children. Occasional praise is not enough.

5. Teachers should use rewards and incentives before punishment (e.g., a reprimand). Significantly more rewards should be used than punishments, by a ratio of at least 3 to 1.

6. Reinforcement systems can be effective over an entire school year, as long as rewards are changed frequently.

7. Anticipation is a key for students with ADHD, especially during classroom transitions. Ensure that students know rules and procedures that are used for transitions before the transition occurs.

8. Students with ADHD should be held even more accountable for their behavior and attainment of goals than students without disabilities. Students with ADHD less frequently monitor their behavior than students without ADHD; thus, their behavior is less regulated by internal information (e.g., self-talk and reflection). Students with ADHD therefore need clear, concise external cues regarding performance expectations.

Pause & Reflect

Students with ADHD who are often off task or respond impulsively in a general education classroom can be very frustrating for teachers. How can you ensure that these student behaviors do not negatively influence how you as a teacher interact with students with ADHD? In other words, how can you ensure that you model appropriate reactions to inappropriate student behaviors?

Facilitating Home–School Communication and Student Support Using Daily or Weekly Report Cards. Parents may be extremely helpful in supporting the teacher in addressing the needs of students with ADHD. One method to address student needs collaboratively with the parent is through the use of a daily (or weekly) report card (Pelham, 2002; Reiff, 2004; Rief, 2005). Daily report cards are brief, very specific reports from a teacher to a parent regarding a child's performance and/or behavior. The teacher sends these either daily or weekly via e-mail, regular mail, or home with the child. Report cards are an effective method to communicate with parents regarding the child's school behavior and performance. "When parents are willing and able to consistently follow through with reinforcement at home for positive performance at school, [the daily report card] is a very powerful motivator for the student" (Rief, 2005, p. 121).

When developing a daily report card, the teacher and parent should explicitly define the goals to be achieved as well as the logistics for monitoring the behavior and procedures for rewarding the student. Possible areas to address include (Reiff, 2004):

Academic performance
Following classroom rules
Relationships with peers
Relationships with teachers
Responsibility for belongings
Homework

Figure 5.2 provides an example of a daily report card. You will note that the daily report card includes simple information, can be quickly completed by the teacher and is easily understood by the parent. You will also note that the items monitored on the Daily Report Card are explicitly defined and easily understood by the child, teacher, and parent.

> For additional information on working with families of students with disabilities, see Strategy 11.6 in Chapter 11.
>
> **Strategy**

Effective Instruction for Secondary Students with ADHD

Many of the strategies for instructing elementary students with ADHD are also applicable to secondary students. Furthermore, the suggestions middle school teacher Laura Scott described in her interview (see the box entitled "Teaching Students with ADHD") may be useful. However, as the material to be learned becomes more complex and longer periods of sustained attention are required, different strategies may be needed. Furthermore, the organization of secondary schools into several periods may cause difficulties for students with ADHD that were not evident in elementary school.

Figure 5.2   Daily Report Card

Daily Report Card

Name: _____

Teacher: _____

School: _____

Date: _____

Behavior	Setting											
	LA			Math			Science			SS		
Raised hand before speaking	A	S	N	A	S	N	A	S	N	A	S	N
Remained in seat when appropriate	A	S	N	A	S	N	A	S	N	A	S	N
Complied with teacher requests	A	S	N	A	S	N	A	S	N	A	S	N
Kept hands to him/herself	A	S	N	A	S	N	A	S	N	A	S	N
Remained on task during seat work	A	S	N	A	S	N	A	S	N	A	S	N
Followed directions	A	S	N	A	S	N	A	S	N	A	S	N
Came to class prepared (e.g., materials)	A	S	N	A	S	N	A	S	N	A	S	N

A = Always   LA = Language Arts
S = Sometimes   SS = Social Studies
N = Never

Strategy

For more information regarding a strategy that may be used with students with ADHD to improve note taking, see Strategy 14.5 in Chapter 14.

Secondary students with ADHD have all of the challenges of other adolescents, as well as several other areas related to the symptoms of ADHD (Rief, 2005). These include:

- Poor skills related to organization, planning, time management, and memory, resulting in difficulty managing assignments and activities in several classes
- Limited study skills that are needed to take notes, complete tests, and so forth
- Learning from instruction that often consists of lecture, a format that is not conducive to successful learning for students with ADHD
- Managing expectations from multiple teachers, including expectations for academic performance, group work in classes, and behavior expectations

Strategies for Addressing the Instructional Needs of Adolescents with ADHD in General Education Classrooms. The American Academy of Pediatrics (Reiff, 2004) has provided several useful recommendations for teachers to support students with ADHD in general education classrooms. These recommendations include:

Keep things simple and doable.

- Break tasks down into steps the student can complete.
- Design the length of tasks to fit the student's attention span, whenever possible.
- Complete academic subjects that require more concentration and sustained attention in the morning, when students are more alert and fresh.

Keep things interesting.

- Encourage class participation, and teach with enthusiasm.
- Vary activities, including lectures, hands-on experiences, and activities.
- When lecturing, provide supplemental activities such as computer games and cooperative activities that address the same material and keep instruction novel, engaging, and motivating.

Keep things organized.

- State, repeat, and post classroom rules in the classroom, and review them often.
- Review the plan for the class period as the period begins.
- Write down information or provide notes for students who may miss information presented verbally or who have difficulty copying from the chalkboard.
- Encourage and monitor the use of simple daily planners that do not overwhelm students.

Strategy

For additional information regarding planning for basic skills instruction in general education classrooms, see Strategy 12.5 in Chapter 12.

Evidence-Based Strategies for Ensuring Student Attention. Zentall (2005) has provided a summary of evidence-based practices that may be used in a general education classroom to address selective attention and to maintain student attention to a task. As we noted previously, selective attention is a problem for many students with ADHD, because they have difficulty ignoring extraneous information and attending to important information. These problems are often of great concern for students at the secondary level, who must attend to complex material for sustained periods of time. Two methods Zentall recommends for addressing selective attention are changing the task and changing the instructions or sequencing of tasks.

Changing the Focus of the Task. Teachers should eliminate irrelevant cues from instructional materials when asking children to respond to a complex task such as reading for comprehension or math problems. The task materials should thus be simplified to include only the material that is to be learned and should not include cartoons or other novel material that may be used to engage some students. Similarly, presenting multiple types of math problems on a single page may result in selective attention problems. Finally, when providing verbal information, added detail and description that is not directly related to the information that is being learned can be distracting for students with ADHD.

Another approach to changing the task for students with ADHD is highlighting relevant information. For example, attention may be focused on the essential elements of a task by highlighting information in written materials, providing an outline of relevant information, or highlighting information in verbal presentations through questions or verbal highlighting through changes in tone and use of pauses.

Changing Instructions or Sequencing of Tasks. Zentall (2005) notes that when learning new material, many students, including those with ADHD, attend to more of the relevant information when simple tasks are presented initially, followed by more complex tasks after a period of practice. Furthermore, self-instructional tasks have proven effective in increasing selective attention. For example, before beginning a task such as reading a complex passage regarding the different types of cloud formations, students ask themselves, "What is my plan for learning this information?" "What do I need to learn?" As they progress, they ask, "Am I following my plan and learning the information?" On completion of an activity, they ask, "How did I do—did I learn the material?"

Zentall (2005) also has identified several evidence-based practices that may be used to maintain attention to a task for students with ADHD. These strategies include changing the task and changing the setting.

Changing the Structure of the Task. Students with ADHD are more successful in maintaining attention if teachers limit the quantity of material to be learned (e.g., practice only two types of math problems) or break the task into parts and instruct students to complete it over time (e.g., a book report). Other changes in the task that teachers can use to maintain attention include using few words to explain tasks, increasing novelty toward the end of a repetitive task, and decreasing the repetitiveness of a task (e.g., practicing a task using different formats). Zentall (2005) notes that these are strategies that improve instruction for many students.

Changing the Setting. Zentall (2005) has also identified several strategies that teachers may use to maintain student attention by changing the setting. One such strategy involves increasing opportunities for the student to move between tasks or engage in self-initiated movement during the task (e.g., active games, filing materials during a task, obtaining materials in the classroom related to the task). Other strategies include adding music, changing the position of the child in the classroom, or introducing novelty (e.g., a video of material being studied).

The Use of Medication to Address the Symptoms of ADHD

Recent data indicate that as many as 1.5 million, or about 3%, of all school-age students are given medication to manage their behavior (Connor, 2006a). It has been reported that more than 50% of students with ADHD are given medication (U.S. Department of Health and Human Services, 2005). The widespread use of stimulant medications to control the symptoms of children with ADHD has produced much controversy. Most of this controversy has addressed concerns regarding the use of powerful medications to control student behavior as well as related concerns that these medications may be used with too many children (Scheffler, Hinshaw, Modrek, & Levine, 2007; Zentall, 2006). Although issues clearly remain in consistently identifying students with ADHD, and some students are likely misidentified, the appropriate use of identification criteria and recommended procedures results in appropriate identification of most students with ADHD (American Academy of Pediatrics [AAP], 2000; APA, 2000; Reiff, 2004).

Pause & Reflect

You have likely seen information in the media regarding the controversy surrounding the use of medication to control the behavior of students with ADHD. Why do you think some parents react negatively to the use of medication? How would you as a teacher address a parent's concerns?

Much research has been conducted regarding the use of medications to control the symptoms of ADHD (Connor, 2006a, 2006b), stimulated in part by the previously noted controversy. This research has revealed that stimulant medications such as methylphenidate (Ritalin or Concerta) or amphetamines (Dexedrine or Adderall) are highly effective treatments for addressing the symptoms of ADHD for 70% to 80% of these students (Connor, 2006a). For students who do not respond to stimulants, other medications such as antihypertensive medications (Clonidine) and antidepressants (Bupropion) have proven effective as second-line options (Connor, 2006b). Finally, recent research has revealed that a nonstimulant, atomoxetine (Strattera), is effective as a first-line treatment for ADHD and reduces symptoms in over 70% of students with ADHD (Smith et al., 2006). It is likely that this medication will be used increasingly in the coming years.

The classroom teacher plays an important role in monitoring student behavior and reaction to medication in the classroom (Rosenberg et al., 2004). For example, the teacher will often be asked by a school psychologist or a physician to monitor the impact of medication on the symptoms of ADHD as the effectiveness of the medication and an appropriate dosage level are being determined. A dosage that is too great may produce unresponsive behavior, or behavior "like a zombie," while a dosage that is too small may produce negligible effects. It is also important to closely monitor the side effects of the medication, which may include insomnia, digestive disorders, headache, and anxiety (Kollins, Barkley, & DuPaul, 2001).

Appropriate levels of medications have been shown to have a significant impact on the negative behaviors of children and adolescents with ADHD (Connor 2006a). These outcomes include increased vigilance, impulse control, fine motor coordination and reaction time; improved social interactions with peers and adults; and reduced hostile and negative behavior toward peers and adults (Connor, 2006a). These improved behaviors also result, as you might expect, in improved reactions of others toward students with ADHD.

In comparing the outcomes of medication with other treatments (e.g., behavioral interventions), medications have proven to be the most effective treatment for the symptoms of ADHD (Multimodal Treatment Study of ADHD [MTA], 1999). However, it is important to recognize that while medication often may be used to control many of the symptoms of ADHD, other interventions are needed if students' academic and social needs are to be effectively addressed (MTA, 1999). Indeed, after medication controls negative student behavior, teachers find behavioral interventions to be most helpful in addressing academic needs and social adjustment of students with ADHD. We described several of these interventions in the previous sections of this chapter, and we will describe others in the effective strategies chapters (Chapters 11 to 16).

> **Strategy**
>
> The use of mnemonics is often a useful strategy for students with ADHD to facilitate remembering important information; see Strategy 14.3, in Chapter 14. Strategy 15.2, in Chapter 15, discusses surface management techniques that are useful for addressing classroom behavior problems.

Final Thoughts Regarding Effective Practices

In Chapters 11 to 16, we provide step-by-step descriptions of many effective practices that are useful for students with disabilities and others who struggle in school. Several of these effective practices are particularly useful for teachers who work with students with ADHD in inclusive classrooms. For example, teachers are often concerned about the classroom behavior of students with ADHD. To address these concerns, we include effective strategies for addressing behavior problems using check-in, connect, check-out systems (Strategy 15.5) and contracting (Strategy 15.6). Teachers are also often concerned about how well students with ADHD regulate their own behavior. To address this concern, we include effective self-regulation strategies for teaching students writing (Strategy 13.6) and math problem solving (Strategy 13.7) at the elementary level and expository writing (Strategy 14.2) at the secondary level. We're sure you will find many of the strategies in Chapters 11 to 16 useful in addressing the needs of students with ADHD in inclusive classrooms.

Summary

This chapter addressed the following topics:

Definition of ADHD and identification criteria

- ADHD is defined as "a persistent pattern of inattention and/or hyperactivity-impulsivity that is more frequently displayed and more severe than is typically observed in individuals at a comparable level of development" (APA, 2000, p. 85).
- The major characteristics of ADHD should last at least 6 months and should be observed across at least two settings (e.g., home and school).

Prevalence of students with ADHD

- Researchers estimate that about 3% to 7% of students have ADHD.
- About 3 times as many boys have ADHD compared to girls.
- Most students with ADHD are also identified with another disability, including emotional and behavioral disability, learning disability, intellectual disability, and autism spectrum disorder.
- We do not know what causes ADHD in the vast majority of cases, but factors that likely contribute to the development of this disability for some students include brain abnormalities, hereditary influences, and family issues.

Educational placements for students with ADHD

- Most students with ADHD are educated for most of the school day in general education classrooms.
- Most general education classrooms will have from one to three students identified with ADHD for much of the school day.

Major characteristics of students with ADHD

- The major characteristics of students with ADHD are impulsivity, inattention, and hyperactivity.
- The characteristics of students with ADHD may lead to difficulty getting along with others, and some of these students develop behavior problems.
- The characteristics of students with ADHD often lead to academic difficulty for as many as 80% of these students, while approximately 20% may develop a learning disability over time.

Challenges of including students with ADHD

- If students with ADHD are to succeed academically in a general education classroom, instruction must be structured so that the student's major characteristics (i.e., impulsivity, inattention, and hyperactivity) are addressed.
- Some students with ADHD exhibit disruptive behavior and/or behavior problems that must be addressed in a general education classroom.

Principles of effective instruction at the elementary level

- Students with ADHD need behavior interventions, such as behavior modification, in addition to medication to address their educational needs.
- Students with ADHD need an appropriate level of structure and predictability in a general education classroom to address their behavior.
- Daily report cards are useful for facilitating home–school communication, as well as for engaging the parents in supporting school behavior and/or academic performance.

Principles of effective instruction at the secondary level

- Secondary-level students with ADHD have difficulty with organizational skills, have limited study skills, and have difficulty managing expectations of multiple teachers and settings.
- Strategies for supporting students with ADHD in general education classrooms include keeping things simple, interesting, and organized.
- Strategies for ensuring that students selectively attend and maintain attention to learning tasks include making alterations in the task, changing instructions or the sequencing of tasks, and changing the setting.

The use of medication to address the symptoms of ADHD

- The use of stimulant medication has been shown to be effective in reducing the symptoms of ADHD for 70% to 80% of elementary and secondary students with this disability.
- While medication is often effective in controlling the symptoms of ADHD, other interventions (e.g., well-structured academic activities, cognitive behavioral strategies) are needed if students' academic and social needs are to be effectively addressed.

Addressing Professional Standards

Standards addressed in Chapter 5 include:

CEC Standards: (1) foundations, (2) development and characteristics of learners, (3) individual learning differences, (4) instructional strategies.

INTASC Standards: Principle 1—Understand central concepts of the discipline; Principle 2—Provide learning opportunities to support the learning and development of all students.

Praxis™ II Standards: Knowledge-based core principles: (1) understanding exceptionalities, (3) delivery of services to students with disabilities. Application of core principles: (1) curriculum, (2) instruction, (5) professional roles/issues/ literature.

Students with Intellectual Disabilities

KEY TOPICS

After reading this chapter you will:

- Know the definition and criteria used to identify students with intellectual disabilities.
- Know how many students are identified with intellectual disabilities.
- Be able to identify the educational settings in which students with intellectual disabilities are educated.
- Be able to describe major characteristics of students with intellectual disabilities.

- Understand key issues and challenges related to including students with intellectual disabilities in general education classrooms.
- Know effective practices for addressing the needs of students with intellectual disabilities in elementary and secondary classrooms.

chapter 6

Perspectives on Including Students with Intellectual Disabilities

Interview with Kristen Tham, Special Education Teacher, Heritage High School

Like most teachers, Kristen Tham expects her students to succeed in school and, ultimately, become active and valued participants in their local communities. The fact that Ms. Tham's students have intellectual disabilities does not in any way diminish her expectations. She points out that all of her students have below-average intellectual abilities, two have Down syndrome, and two others have varying levels of Tourette syndrome and cerebral palsy. Nevertheless, Ms. Tham expects her students to achieve because she and her Heritage High School colleagues collaborate to provide opportunities for students to pursue their own unique interests, have meaningful social interactions, and participate in all facets of school-related activities.

How can students with severe and multiple disabilities achieve these goals in a large comprehensive high school? Ms. Tham, a specialist in providing instruction and supports for students with moderate-to-severe disabilities, is a firm believer in including her students in the school and the community. To achieve this, she promotes and actively initiates frequent interaction among her students and with the rest of the Heritage population. She notes that

> Even though many of my students cannot succeed in many of the highly demanding content classes of the school, all participate in electives and extracurricular activities. Classes such as Art, Chorus, and Health allow my five students to pursue their creative interests while being viewed as active participants in the usual sequence of school activities. Most important, attendance in the classes, along with the socialization that occurs during lunch and extracurricular activities, reinforces that the students are truly part of the Heritage community and really help in the development of friendships.

Learning skills that allow for schoolwide participation requires intensive instruction and practice. Ms. Tham prepares lessons in social skills that employ direct instruction, prompts, and frequent role-playing practice activities with nondisabled peers. According to Ms. Tham, "these activities allow students to learn how specific social conventions such as greeting others and responding to peers during conversations can lead to rewarding and ongoing relationships." These activities also allow

students to learn effective ways to advocate for themselves and request assistance when encountering a troubling situation. To promote successful transitions to work and community living, Ms. Tham provides instruction in life skills such as meal preparation and grooming. Students practice many of these skills in real-world work situations. For example, several of the students participate in highly supervised and supported work experiences in the school's cafeteria and a local Hampton Inn.

Ms. Tham takes great pride in seeing how her students have maintained their involvement at Heritage. They are never hidden from view, and their levels of participation in classes, the cafeteria, and the hallways continue each year. Still, Ms. Tham's most rewarding outcomes have come from her exchanges with general education colleagues. In her early years of teaching, she noticed that her co-workers tended to avoid contact with her students. They had little experience with students with intellectual disabilities and were unsure as to how to interact with them. By modeling positive engagement strategies and encouraging her fellow teachers to "take the time to treat these kids like they are real," Ms. Tham has changed teachers' attitudes and behaviors. No longer are students with disabilities overlooked or considered just the responsibility of special education personnel. All students are treated as members of the Heritage community and provided with frequent occasions for meaningful social contact, opportunities to pursue areas of interest, and socially relevant instruction that facilitates success at school and in the local community.

There are many benefits for students with intellectual disabilities in general education classrooms.

Introduction

Today, almost everyone has had some experience with a person with intellectual disabilities (sometimes referred to as persons with mental retardation or mental handicaps). Perhaps you have a family member, a relative, or a friend with intellectual disabilities; or maybe you went to school with students who had intellectual disabilities. Today, more than at any time in history, people with intellectual disabilities are becoming increasingly visible in schools, neighborhoods, and communities.

Based on your experience, you may have developed a personal perception of what individuals with intellectual disabilities look like, what they can do, and how they act. However, you should be very cautious about adhering to any stereotyped images. Individuals with intellectual disabilities are very diverse in their characteristics, abilities, and needs. Some may have mild-to-moderate disabilities and be able to manage most of their personal daily needs, whereas others may have more severe disabilities and will need more support to participate in various life activities.

Over the last several years, we have learned the same thing through research that Heritage High School teacher Kristen Tham learned through personal experience: Inclusion of students with intellectual disabilities in schools and general education classrooms can be very beneficial. Studies have shown that students with intellectual disabilities, even those with more severe disabilities, can benefit from inclusion in general education classrooms. They can become more attentive, develop better social and communication skills, and demonstrate academic progress (Fisher & Meyer, 2002; Foreman, Arthur-Kelly,

Pause & Reflect

How common is inclusion of students with intellectual disabilities in the schools with which you are familiar? What have been some of the benefits of their inclusion for these students? Have students without disabilities benefited? What is your personal perspective on this issue?

Pascoe, & King, 2004; Ryndak, Morrison, & Sommerstein, 1999). Primarily for these reasons, it is important for general education teachers to collaborate with special education teachers and make every possible effort to include students with intellectual disabilities in meaningful ways in general education classrooms.

Who Are Students with Intellectual Disabilities?

Definition

According to the American Association on Intellectual and Developmental Disabilities (AAIDD, formerly the American Association on Mental Retardation), an intellectual disability is characterized by "significant limitations both in intellectual functioning and in adaptive behavior as expressed in conceptual, social, and practical adaptive skills. This disability originates before age 18" (American Association on Mental Retardation, 2002, p. 1). Similarly, the Individuals with Disabilities Education Improvement Act of 2004 (IDEA) defines the condition in this way: "Mental retardation means significantly subaverage general intellectual functioning, existing concurrently with deficits in adaptive behavior and manifested during the developmental period, that adversely affects a child's educational performance" (20 U.S.C. 1401). According to both definitions, for a person to be considered to have intellectual disabilities, a formal assessment of intelligence must result in a significantly low score (usually an IQ at or lower than 70 to 75 points); the individual must demonstrate an inability to carry out typical daily activities (i.e., the absence of adaptive skills); and the limitations must have originated before the person attained maturity. Additionally, according to IDEA, the condition must result in inadequate educational performance.

In 1992, the AAIDD stopped using the traditional subcategories of intellectual disabilities with which you may be familiar (e.g., mild, moderate, severe, or profound) but instead suggested that an individual who is considered intellectually disabled should be described within a multidimensional context that provides a comprehensive description of the person and necessary supports. The AAIDD theoretical model implies that a person's functioning is not due solely to characteristics

myeducationlab

Go to MyEducationLab, select the topic *Intellectual Disabilities*, and go to the Activities and Application section. As you watch the videos entitled "Who Is Star?" "Guided Notes Study Cards," and "Beyond School: Rachel," compare and contrast the students featured in these videos. How do these students challenge your perception of intellectual disabilities?

Pause & Reflect

Today you often hear people refer to a student as having a "mild" disability or a "severe" disability. What do these terms mean to you? Do you think they help us understand someone better? Do they help us provide better services? Why or why not?

Students with intellectual disabilities require meaningful learning experiences to develop adaptive behavior skills.

Just the Facts   Students with Intellectual Disabilities

Who are they?	Individuals with intellectual disabilities are characterized by significant limitations both in intellectual functioning (generally an IQ below 70 to 75) and in adaptive behavior as expressed in conceptual, social, and practical adaptive skills (or skills for day-to-day functioning). This disability originates before age 18.
What are typical characteristics?	Individuals with intellectual disabilities will often demonstrate: • Low achievement in all academic areas. • General weaknesses in basic learning abilities such as attention, memory, problem solving, and skill generalization. • Weak social skills and sometimes challenging behavior. • Deficits in daily living skills.
What are the demographics?	• Prevalence estimates of persons with intellectual disabilities range between 1% and 3%. • About 1.1% of the school-age population is likely to have intellectual disabilities. Formal classifications may include "mental retardation," "multiple handicaps," or "developmental delay." • Most individuals with intellectual disabilities have "mild" disabilities and are not identified until they begin school. • Persons with more severe degrees of intellectual disabilities can often be identified when they are infants or toddlers.
Where are students educated?	• About 12% of students with intellectual disabilities spend most of their school day in the general education classroom. • Around 82% spend part of the day in the general education classroom and the rest of the day in a special class. • The remaining students, about 6%, are placed in separate schools, residential settings, remain at home, or are in hospitals.
How are students identified?	• Individuals with more severe disabilities can often be identified at birth or as infants or toddlers. • Physical features and behavioral characteristics often lead to assessment by physicians and other clinicians, which determines the presence of a significant developmental delay. • Individuals with milder degrees of intellectual disabilities often do not have obvious physical characteristics and may not be identified until they are in school and begin to display academic and/or social behavior problems.
What causes intellectual disabilities?	• The causes of more severe intellectual disabilities are often physiologically based, including genetic conditions, chromosomal anomalies, maternal illness during pregnancy, or maternal use of toxic substances such as alcohol during pregnancy. • For most individuals with milder levels of intellectual disabilities, the specific cause cannot always be identified. However, the condition often correlates with mild intellectual disabilities in one or two parents, poverty, and inadequate physical and psychological conditions within the home.
What are the outcomes?	Many individuals with intellectual disabilities can enjoy a high quality of life during adulthood. They can work and enjoy leisure activities in the community, and many can live independently or with different levels of support. The outcomes for persons with intellectual disabilities depend largely on the quality of their education as children and adolescents and on the support they receive from key persons in their lives.

of the individual but also to the supportive context in which the person lives and functions. AAIDD therefore looks at intellectual disabilities not as a personal deficiency per se, but in terms of needed supports.

Although the AAIDD eliminated subcategories of intellectual disabilities based on levels of measured intelligence, these (or other) categories are still maintained by many state and local education agencies and in the American Psychiatric Association's (APA) *Diagnostic and Statistical Manual of Mental Disorders, Fourth Edition, Text Revision* (DSM-IV-TR; APA, 2000).

These subcategories also are often referred to in professional writing and discussions. You therefore should be familiar with these levels and their corresponding approximate IQ ranges: mild (50 to 70), moderate (35 to 50), severe (20 to 35), and profound (below 20 to 25) intellectual disabilities.

Identification of Students with Intellectual Disabilities

Identification in the Early Years. We can identify some children with intellectual disabilities when they are very young, even when they are infants or toddlers. These children may have distinctive features (e.g., in the case of Down syndrome) or physical disabilities (e.g., **cerebral palsy**) that suggest the presence of a developmental delay or the possibility that a delay is likely to occur. Usually, their parents or pediatricians are the first to observe that they are not achieving key developmental milestones. For example, language development or motor skills may be below average for their chronological age.

Once children are identified as possibly having a disability, agencies can begin to provide services if assessments by physicians and other skilled clinicians show that a child is truly experiencing a delay. The clinicians will conduct their evaluations using medical and developmental assessments to determine how much of a delay is occurring and in what areas of development. States use different criteria in determining a significant delay, but typically they include a substantial delay in one area (e.g., a 50% delay from the norm) or a significant, but less serious, delay in more than one area (e.g., a 25% delay in two or more areas) (McLean, 2004).

Children identified at a very young age as having intellectual disabilities usually have the condition because of **genetic inheritance**, **chromosomal anomalies**, or various **prenatal causes**. Often professionals refer to very young children as having a "developmental delay"—as opposed to an intellectual disability—because accurate diagnosis of the nature or degree of their disability is difficult.

Pause & Reflect

Providing early intervention to infants and toddlers with developmental delays can have an important effect on later development. Why do you think it is important to provide services as early in life as possible? What kinds of services or specific intervention might reduce the impact of a disability? What kinds might be helpful to families?

Identification in the School Years. The proportion of children who can be identified early in life as having an intellectual or developmental disability is relatively small. Instead, most children in public schools who are classified as having intellectual disabilities are not identified before they begin school; initially they draw attention to themselves in school when they exhibit academic or behavioral challenges. These children usually have a less severe level of the condition and have traditionally been referred to as having mild intellectual disabilities.

Most students with mild intellectual disabilities appear very similar to others in school, except for the fact that they learn academic material much more slowly than most other students and may be less socially mature. Many years ago, the President's Committee on Mental Retardation (1969) originally used the term "six-hour retarded child" in reference to these children because they were labeled as intellectually disabled during the school day but adapted well and often were not readily distinguishable as intellectually disabled at home or in their community.

When a school-age child demonstrates academic or behavioral characteristics that cause concern, the school will first try to find a way to remediate the student in the general education classroom without referring her for special education evaluation. The school will develop and apply a response-to-intervention plan, as described in Chapter 4, and assess whether the child

Most students with mild intellectual disabilities are not identified until the early school years.

improves academically or behaviorally. If the intervention plan succeeds, then the child will not require formal evaluation. However, if the student continues to have difficulty succeeding, the school will refer her for evaluation by a multidisciplinary team.

If as a result of formal psychological evaluation, the student scores at or below 70 to 75 points on a standardized test of intelligence and continues to exhibit weaknesses in academic skills and other conceptual, social, and practical adaptive skills, then school administrators will identify the student as having an intellectual disability and will ask parents to formally endorse this decision. It is important for you to understand that it is primarily the low score on the intelligence test that leads to a classification of intellectual disabilities. Without a significantly low score on this assessment, as well as evidence of a deficit in adaptive behavior, school personnel may place the student in another disability category, such as learning disabilities.

Prevalence

Most authorities have reported the overall prevalence of intellectual disabilities as being somewhere between 1% and 3%, depending on the criteria used to define the condition and the ways in which the numbers are estimated (Beirne-Smith, Patton, & Kim, 2006; Taylor, Richards, & Brady, 2005). According to the U.S. Department of Education (2007b), however, slightly less than 1% (0.87%) of public school students between the ages of 6 and 21 years are classified as "mentally retarded." This may be a little misleading because students with intellectual disabilities may be included in other disability categories. For example, within the same age group (6 to 21), 0.2% of the student population is classified as having "multiple disabilities," and 0.12% is classified as having "developmental delays." Thus, we might estimate that approximately 1.1% of the school-age population has intellectual disabilities.

Across different states, the percentage of students classified by the public schools as having intellectual disabilities varies considerably. Some states are quite a bit below the U.S. Department of Education figure of 0.87%, while others are significantly above it. According to the U.S. Department of Education (2007b), states that report having 0.5% or less of their students classified as students with intellectual disabilities include Alaska (0.44%), California (0.46%), Colorado (0.35%), Connecticut (0.44%), Maine (0.34%), New Hampshire (0.34%), New Jersey (0.34%), New Mexico (0.37%), New York (0.36%), Texas (0.49%), Utah (0.48%), and Washington State (0.41%). In contrast, those reporting that 1.25% or more of their students are so classified include Alabama (1.26%), Arkansas (1.86%), Washington, D.C. (1.63%), Georgia (1.40%), Indiana (1.53%), Iowa (1.80%), Kentucky (1.98%), Nebraska (1.34%), North Carolina (1.51%), Ohio (1.86%), South Carolina (1.58%), and West Virginia (2.47%).

Pause & Reflect

Looking from states with the lowest prevalence of students with intellectual disabilities to those with the highest, proportionally six to seven times more students with intellectual disabilities are in the highest-prevalence states than in the lowest-prevalence states. What do you think accounts for these great differences?

So where does the larger estimate, the 3% figure, come from? Professionals who study the prevalence of conditions such as intellectual disabilities, referred to as *epidemiologists,* often use different criteria of a condition and different data collection methods to arrive at their estimates. Thus, if a very broad criterion were used (e.g., counting all persons in society with an IQ of 75 or less, not just those in public school, and without consideration of adaptive behavior), then the larger percentage would be more likely.

Service Delivery

Based on U.S. Department of Education (2007a, 2007b) data, we know that 52% of public school students between 6 and 21 years who are classified as "mentally retarded" spend more than 60% of their time *outside* the general education classroom. In contrast, only about 12% are taught primarily *in* the general education classrooms, spending less than 21% of their day in a separate setting. As for the remaining students, about 30% spend between 21% and 60% outside the general education class, and the balance, a little more than 6%, spend their school days in public or private special schools (only for students with disabilities), in public or private residential facilities, or in their homes or a hospital. Together, these figures suggest that students with intellectual disabilities are often not placed in general education classrooms, instead spending most of their school day in special classes, on either a full-time or part-time basis.

But the data reveal other information as well. Keeping in mind that nationwide about 12% of students with intellectual disabilities are primarily served in general education classrooms, a great deal of variability around this figure exists from state to state. For example, Colorado, Iowa, Kentucky, Nebraska, New Hampshire, North Dakota, Rhode Island, and Vermont report that *more than 25%* of their students with intellectual disabilities spend most of their time in general education classrooms, whereas the District of Columbia, Nevada, Texas, and Utah report that *less than 5%* of their students with intellectual disabilities spend the same amount of time in the general education classroom. We also know that more students with intellectual disabilities are included at the elementary level and fewer at the middle school and high school level. Additionally, students with multiple disabilities, who are likely to have more severe intellectual disabilities, are more often placed in separate schools, and students who exhibit challenging behavior are more likely to be placed in separate settings if their behavior does not improve.

> ### Pause & Reflect
>
> What do you think accounts for the amount of inclusion of students with intellectual disabilities in different states? Are these philosophical differences, or are there other reasons? How would you describe your state's philosophy on inclusion of these students?

Major Characteristics of Students with Intellectual Disabilities

The diverse range of strengths and weaknesses that we see in students with intellectual disabilities makes it almost impossible to make generalizations about their abilities. While by definition, they all will find learning challenging, you may also be surprised to find that many people with intellectual disabilities have personal strengths and assets that add much value to the world around them. As you will recall from the "Perspectives" interview with Kristen Tham, students often succeed in inclusive environments because others value their participation.

Students with milder intellectual disabilities will often be able to take part in class activities and benefit from the general curriculum, as your other students do. Those with more significant intellectual disabilities can also participate and learn if teachers make accommodations and adjustments to support them.

Academic Difficulties

Students who are identified with mild intellectual disabilities lag behind grade-level peers in developing academic skills and are likely to be delayed in learning to read, learning basic math skills, and learning other academic skills that are based on these building blocks. Although students with mild intellectual disabilities will be behind age-level peers in academic achievement throughout their school years, over time, many will develop basic literacy and math skills, often up to about the fourth-grade level. Also, they should be able to achieve skills necessary for relatively independent functioning, such as using money, telling time, and self-management. The greatest challenges to these students will be skills that require reasoning such as reading comprehension, problem solving, and planning ahead (Beirne-Smith et al., 2006; Taylor et al., 2005).

Students with moderate intellectual disabilities will function somewhat lower than students with mild intellectual disabilities but may still learn a number of basic academic and practical skills. They can master a significant list of letter names and sounds, and most can learn sight words and how to tell time and use money. In terms of norm-referenced abilities, their ultimate academic achievement may be up to about a first- or second-grade level. However, they can learn adequate verbal communication, daily living skills, and domestic skills;

> ### Pause & Reflect
>
> Have you ever reflected on the kinds of academic skills necessary for day-to-day living? In the areas of academics, what do you think would be important for individuals with mild-to-moderate intellectual disabilities to learn?

Students with intellectual disabilities are often challenged by weaknesses in reasoning and problem-solving skills.

and they can learn to operate in the community by doing things such as using public transportation, shopping, and eating at restaurants. As adults, most will be able to work in the community in jobs such as performing basic clerical tasks in offices, or bagging groceries or stocking shelves in stores (Brown, Shiraga, & Kessler, 2006).

Students with more severe intellectual disabilities typically do not possess many academic skills, such as reading or math skills, but they may be able to recognize some words and common signs. They may know that money is of value but may not comprehend the specific value of bills or coins. Communication skills will be very diverse. Many can communicate adequately (with signs, words, or symbols), but some cannot. Some will be able to take care of their personal needs, but others may not. The more severe the disability, the more likely the person is to experience physical or medical conditions in addition to an intellectual disability (Petry & Maes, 2007). Recent advances in assistive technology (AT) have greatly advanced these students' ability to participate in various activities. Assistive technology devices and support services can assist them with communication, daily living skills, and mobility (Westling & Fox, 2009). We describe different types of assistive technology devices in Chapter 16.

Cognitive Skill Deficits

Students with intellectual disabilities experience challenges with a range of cognitive abilities. The following are some challenges that you will likely note in these students.

Language Skills. Individuals with intellectual disabilities will typically have restricted language abilities. Their expressive language limitations may be indicated by problems in articulation, grammar, vocabulary, and general expressive ability. Their receptive language ability, or comprehension, may not be as limited as their expressive ability but will still be problematic. Their difficulties with receptive language may range from having trouble understanding simple verbal directions to being able to engage in a two-part conversation.

Observational and Incidental Learning. *Observational learning* is learning through watching and imitating another person who is serving as a model. *Incidental learning* is learning something that was not taught directly but that might be learned if attended to. Many students with intellectual disabilities do not profit from these forms of learning as well as students who do not have intellectual disabilities.

Skill Synthesis. Most individuals who do not have intellectual disabilities learn separate skills such as reading, writing, and arithmetic, and then pull these skills together in an organized, useful way to undertake a particular activity, such as grocery shopping. For students who have intellectual disabilities, however, the ability to synthesize information and skills is very limited. They often fail to see the relation of one bit of information to another.

Generalization. One of the most significant learning weaknesses of students with intellectual disabilities is their weak ability to generalize acquired skills—to apply what was learned in one situation to another situation. Generalization is usually considered the demonstration of skills with different people, using different objects or materials, in different settings, and at different times.

Social and Behavior Problems

Many students with mild-to-moderate intellectual disabilities can function quite well in social situations, exhibit socially appropriate behavior, and enjoy friendships and acquaintances. For some however, exhibiting socially acceptable behaviors and engaging others in typical, desirable ways can be challenging.

Social Problems. Some students with mild or moderate intellectual disabilities may have difficulty interacting socially, but with instruction and practice their social skills can improve. One problem is that restricted cognitive and language development may cause a student with intellectual disability to have difficulty understanding the content of verbal interactions and understanding social-communicative expectations, such as when to listen and when and how to respond during conversations. Similarly, difficulty with attention and memory can affect social interactions. Students with mild or moderate intellectual disabilities may have difficulties reading social cues and interacting in a socially appropriate manner, especially if they lack support. This may lead to a poor self-concept, a lower social status, and withdrawal in social situations (Beirne-Smith et al., 2006). More positively, as Kristen Tham pointed out, well-constructed social relationships with peers who do not have disabilities can benefit all students.

> ### Pause & Reflect
>
> Should general education teachers have the responsibility of facilitating positive social relationships between students with and without intellectual disabilities? Should this be part of their responsibilities as a teacher? What is your opinion?

Behavior Problems. Some students with intellectual disabilities will demonstrate uncommon, sometimes challenging behaviors. Such behaviors are probably the greatest impediment to social success for students with more severe intellectual disabilities. Some challenging behaviors that students may exhibit include **stereotyped behaviors** (repetitive behaviors, e.g., hand flapping, also referred to as **sterotypies**), **self-injurious behaviors** (SIBs, e.g., head banging), aggressive behaviors (e.g., hitting other people), or noncompliance.

   Although the cause of these behaviors is often difficult to interpret, recently, behavior specialists have recognized the importance of understanding the context in which inappropriate behavior occurs and possible motivating factors. In some cases, the behavior may occur as a basic form of communication; in others, it may occur in order to escape from a demanding situation, one in which the individual does not want to participate. Other causal factors also exist, leading several experts to strongly recommend evaluating both the individual and conditions in the environment to determine factors that may be causing or maintaining the challenging behavior. This type of assessment, called **functional behavioral assessment (FBA)**, can lead to the development of a **behavior intervention plan (BIP)**. These strategies (described in Chapter 15) have proved to be effective in improving the challenging behavior of many persons with severe disabilities (Carr et al., 1999, 2002, Hanley, Iwata, & McCord, 2003).

Strategy 15.7 in Chapter 15 provides directions for conducting an FBA and developing a BIP.

Strategy

Effective Instruction for Students with Intellectual Disabilities

Including students with intellectual disabilities in general education classrooms presents teachers with two major challenges: (1) teaching students so they experience success in both the general academic curriculum and when learning necessary functional skills, and (2) helping students develop appropriate social skills in order to be better accepted by their peers and others in society.

The accompanying box, "Teaching Students with Developmental Disabilities in Postsecondary Settings," discusses an innovative inclusion program at a university.

Effective Instruction for Elementary Students with Intellectual Disabilities

Strategy

Strategy 12.3 in Chapter 12 will be very helpful when planning for students with intellectual disabilities.

Strategies to Achieve Academic Success. We can define academic success for students with intellectual disabilities in different ways, depending on their needs and abilities. For some students, especially those with mild intellectual disabilities, their level of academic potential will be relatively close to that of other students, especially when they are in the earlier grades. For students with moderate or more severe intellectual disabilities, the level of academic achievement will be more limited. We provide several strategies for planning for individualized and differentiated instruction in Chapter 12.

Functional Skills and Systematic Instruction. Functional skill instruction has been the most traditional curriculum for students with intellectual disabilities for many years. Teaching functional skills means that teachers focus on those skills that the student is most likely to need in daily life, such as reading sight words for use in the home and community, learning to tell time, or measuring cooking ingredients.

In addition to functional academic skills, the individualized education program (IEP) team may identify the need for instruction in functional skills in other areas, such as personal care or self-management, and the best way to teach these skills. Very often, instruction on these skills in general education classrooms and in other school settings occurs at different times throughout the school day. In this way these skills can be taught without taking up a great deal of instructional time, and students may learn them in natural contexts, facilitating generalization and better retention of the skills.

Teachers often teach functional skills using systematic instruction. This is a form of instruction that provides very precise directions and prompts, with reduced prompts as students become more proficient in learning the skill. Besides very clear and concise verbal directions, systematic instruction calls for modeling what the student is to do, verbally or physically prompting the student to perform the correct action, and sometimes using full or partial physical guidance to help the student learn the skill (Westling & Fox, 2009).

Academic Skills and Participation in the General Curriculum. Although functional skills are important, federal legislation, including the No Child Left Behind Act (NCLB) and IDEA, requires that all students with disabilities participate as much as possible in the general curriculum. The laws also require that the students be annually evaluated to determine how well and how much they learned (U.S. Department of Education, 2007a).

For students with intellectual disabilities to participate meaningfully in the general curriculum and show progress, their teachers usually have to make adjustments in the curriculum and in their teaching methods. Within the curriculum, a common approach is for teachers to identify the general education curriculum objectives (or benchmarks or milestones) and, based on these, develop extended objectives (or "extensions") for students with intellectual disabilities. Educators must include the objectives based on the general curriculum in the IEP.

To make these instructional adjustments more doable and accessible for teachers, in some states, the state department of education has undertaken the process of converting benchmarks from the general curriculum to curricular extensions for students with intellectual disabilities (e.g., North Carolina State Board of Education, 2007).

Teaching Students with Developmental Disabilities in Postsecondary Settings: Challenges and Strategies

An emerging trend for older students with intellectual and other developmental disabilities is finishing their formal schooling by attending school in traditional postsecondary settings including 2-year and 4-year colleges. One recently developed program was the University Participant (UP) Program at Western Carolina University. Kelly Kelley was the project coordinator and described to us the challenges of including students with developmental disabilities (e.g., cerebral palsy and intellectual disabilities) in university settings and strategies to address some of these challenges.

As Ms. Kelley noted in the interview, students with more visible disabilities often face more isolation and have very individualized needs that instructors must consider. She discussed crucial strategies for successfully implementing this university experience, such as "sharing responsibilities, collaborating effectively, and communicating regularly with one another."

Elaborating on her strategies for collaboration, Ms. Kelley said:

> Getting to know the student's individual preferences and interests, working closely with their families and interagency providers in conjunction with the university personnel are the most critical components for successfully including students with disabilities at the postsecondary level. You must be on the same page with everyone at all times and plan ahead to support what lies ahead. You must develop a sense of community and trust among the team members in order to provide and monitor the specialized support systems needed.

Ms. Kelley also discussed how important it is to coordinate natural supports and educate students on campus about diversity and differences.

> It is amazing what happens when typical college students understand what the students with disabilities are there for and get involved by advocating, supporting, and inviting the individuals to campus organizations and events. Many students find after they get to know each other that there are more similarities than differences among them once they have an opportunity to spend some time together and truly connect.

An improvement in self-determination was noted as a major development by Ms. Kelley.

> They learn so many life skills that they could not experience if they had not had the opportunity to leave home. In this 2-year experience in the UP program, the individuals have learned how to communicate more effectively, improve their personal care skills, access public transportation, manage a budget, learn specific job tasks, participate in university functions such as athletic or musical events, join university clubs and organizations, and attend college courses with their typical peers. Most of all, they have developed friendships with their peers that will last a lifetime.

Of course, there are also challenges.

> One of the main things we are still faced with is locating and sustaining funding sources. The tuition and residential living costs can be burdensome for the families, since these students typically do not qualify for financial aid without having standard high school diplomas. There is also the challenge of funding staff to help support these individuals as they participate in campus activities. We have really had to be creative with limited funding sources and hope there will be future possibilities at the local, state, and federal levels to continue supporting programs similar to this one for individuals with more significant disabilities.

For some students, it is easier to support and include them in university settings while others may need extra supports along the way. It is an adjustment for anyone who makes the transition from high school to college, but it can be more challenging sometimes for individuals with developmental disabilities. Ms. Kelley advised:

> You must teach the students using task analysis, graphic organizers, and role playing how to appropriately socialize, manage their time, and participate to the greatest extent possible with academic content. There will be some activities that will need more support than others. However, it is important to remember age appropriateness and stepping back where you can to allow these individuals to experience the "normality" of life with their peers to

the greatest extent possible. It can be hard to let go of the individual to give them some freedom, but you have to realize when to let go and when to offer support.

Ms. Kelley offered some final words of wisdom for future university programs.

There will be times when you feel you have given all you can give to make things work and are exhausted, but when you remember the true meaning of what you do, it is all worth it. Also remember that taking the time to get to know the individuals with disabilities, their families, and working closely with interagency providers can have the greatest impact for successful results for implementing innovative college-level programs like this.

If states have not created the curricular modifications, this becomes a task for the local education agency or for general educators working with special educators. The general educator serves as the content expert, identifying what students are to learn in areas such as literacy and math. The special education teacher serves as the expert on the learning abilities of the students with disabilities in order to convert objectives so that students with disabilities can achieve them. The teachers must be able to collaborate and to agree that the critical academic content for students with disabilities is aligned with the curricular objectives for the students without disabilities (Browder & Spooner, 2006; Browder, Spooner, Wakeman, Trela, & Baker, 2006).

Pause & Reflect

How important do you think it is for students with intellectual disabilities to participate in the general curriculum as opposed to focusing more on functional academic skills? What are the pros and cons of these different curricular orientations?

Employing Principles of Universal Design for Learning to Improve Student Engagement. Teachers can apply universal design for learning (UDL) principles by using commercial instructional materials or by incorporating UDL into teacher-made materials and lessons, enabling individuals with various ability levels to participate in the curriculum (Center for Applied Special Technology [CAST], 1999–2009; Council for Exceptional Children, 1999; Wehmeyer, 2006; Wehmeyer & Agran, 2006). The CAST (1999–2002) proposed three essential qualities of a curriculum that incorporates UDL:

1. **Multiple means of representation:** Alternative means of presentation can reduce learning barriers, and teachers can adjust presentations to students' differing recognition capabilities. Digital format is the most flexible means for presenting curricular materials because it makes material transformable, transportable, and recordable.
2. **Multiple means of expression:** Students can respond with their preferred means of control. Teachers can accommodate different strategic and motor systems of students.
3. **Multiple means of engagement:** Teachers can match students' interests in learning with the mode of presentation/response; this can better motivate more students.

If the way in which the material is presented, the way the student can respond, and the way the student can be engaged are variable, then it is much more likely that students with intellectual disabilities will be more able to participate in some or all of the curriculum.

Strategies to Achieve Social Success. Because students with intellectual disabilities often have challenges related to interacting acceptably with other students and being accepted by others, learning appropriate social skills is an important aspect of inclusion for these students. There are several effective methods to help students learn these important skills.

Providing Opportunities for Social Success. The first step teachers must use to help students learn social skills is to give them the opportunity to do so. As frequently as possible, students with intellectual disabilities should have contact with other students throughout the school day. This contact provides students with intellectual disabilities the opportunity to observe other students, to communicate with them, to imitate them, and therefore to learn from them. Placing students with intellectual disabilities in pairs or groups with students without disabilities, such as in

Strategy

In Chapter 15, Strategy 15.7 provides an outline for teaching social skills to students with special needs.

peer-tutoring arrangements or in cooperative learning groups, will often give them a useful opportunity to improve social skills and allow them to be a part of the social community.

Unfortunately, sometimes "included" students with intellectual disabilities are secluded by being placed in an isolated part of the room, or they are so attached to a paraprofessional or personal assistant that they have no opportunity to interact with other students.

Direct Instruction of Social Skills. In addition to proximity, achieving social success will sometimes require direct teaching of desired social behavior. Peers without disabilities may also need direct instruction in reinforcing their classmates with intellectual disabilities, especially when they engage in inappropriate behavior. When teaching social skills, teachers verbally instruct students on how they are to act, demonstrate correct behavior, prompt students to act appropriately, reinforce proper social behavior, and redirect them when they engage in inappropriate behavior. If students without disabilities have not had experience interacting with their peers with intellectual disabilities, it may be useful to give them directions and prompt them to interact in appropriate ways. This instruction may take some time and effort, especially at the beginning, but the improvement in students' social behavior will be very beneficial to students and very rewarding to the teacher.

Dealing with Challenging Behaviors. Finally, teachers need to consider how to address students with intellectual disabilities who engage in challenging behavior, such as classroom disruption. Although many times these students will be removed from the inclusive classroom, you should understand that this does not necessarily improve their behavior. When a student exhibits challenging behavior, the first step should be for the teacher to enlist support from a special educator or a behavior specialist to conduct a functional assessment and develop a PBS plan. Very often, appropriate intervention can improve the behavior. In Chapter 12 we provide an overview about BIPs, and then in Chapter 15 we provide more detailed information for using BIPs to improve challenging behavior.

You will recall from our introductory interview with Kristen Tham that initially many general education teachers were not supportive of including students with intellectual disabilities. Certainly, students who exhibit challenging behavior are not likely to be accepted in school or society. It is therefore important for teachers of students with intellectual disabilities to address the issue of challenging behavior.

Cooperative learning groups are discussed in depth in Strategy 13.2 in Chapter 13.

Peer tutoring is discussed in Strategy 13.4 in Chapter 13.

Strategy 11.7 in Chapter 11 discusses how to establish "peer-buddy" relationships.

Strategy 15.7 in Chapter 15 provides directions for conducting an FBA and creating a BIP.

Pause & Reflect

What professional responsibilities do you believe general education teachers should have when addressing challenging behaviors in the classroom? What is your attitude toward teachers' attempting to improve students' behavior?

Effective Instruction for Secondary Students with Intellectual Disabilities

Many of the issues we discussed pertaining to the instruction of students at the elementary level are also relevant when students reach the middle school and high school years. Several other issues, however, are also important for teachers of older students to consider.

Strategies to Achieve Academic Success. The academic gap between students with and without intellectual disabilities will increase as the students grow older. Although students with intellectual disabilities will continue to grow cognitively as their chronological age increases, the rate of their intellectual growth will remain behind that of students without intellectual disabilities. This means that even though their learning potential will increase, it will not reach the same level as that of their peers without disabilities. Still, many of these students likely will be able to learn more academic skills as adolescents and may develop interests in specific subjects and be able to meaningfully participate in various high school classes, with support.

Making Meaningful Curricular Decisions for Transition into Adulthood. As students grow older, they need an increased focus on the achievement of important learning outcomes that will help them succeed after high school. Teachers and members of the IEP team therefore should consider both academic instruction and functional skills instruction that will benefit the student (Beirne-Smith et al., 2006; Westling & Fox, 2009).

When students with intellectual disabilities are in high school, teachers should address four outcomes as they plan for students' transition into the postsecondary school world. Teachers should consider:

- Will the student continue a postsecondary education program?
- Will the student work in a vocational setting?
- What postsecondary living arrangements will be appropriate and possible for the student?
- Based on answers to the preceding questions, what skills should the student learn in order to succeed after high school?

Possible postsecondary outcomes. As you saw earlier in the chapter, in the box entitled "Teaching Students with Developmental Disabilities in Postsecondary Settings," students with intellectual disabilities are increasingly attending community colleges or 4-year colleges and taking part in academic courses (Hall, Kleinert, & Kearns, 2000; Neubert, Moon, & Grigal, 2004). Often, this attendance occurs when students are 18 to 21 years old because, although IDEA allows them to continue as public school students until they are 21, they are beyond the age when most students remain in high school. If students are considering moving from their high school to a postsecondary educational setting, the IEP team and the student need to determine the student's learning activities in that setting.

Another reasonable plan for many students with intellectual disabilities is to seek employment after high school, whether it is typical competitive employment or supported employment. Even if they require a significant degree of support in order to work, many young adults with intellectual disabilities can still work in community settings, and this will be more desirable than working in sheltered settings or only with other adults with disabilities. A key to employment success as an adult is the opportunity to have real-world job experiences while still in high school. Common community learning environments can include office settings, restaurants, and hospitals. Brown et al. (2006) reported on the success of community employment by 50 adults with significant intellectual disabilities. With the support of job coaches and with natural supports provided by their co-workers and employers, these individuals learned employment skills that led to long-term success in community employment.

Planning for a place to live. For a number of students with intellectual disabilities, an important postsecondary school goal will be to move into a community-based house or apartment that will afford them the opportunity for more independence and self-determination. Various supported-living arrangements are possible, but their availability will vary in different locations. Unfortunately, the number of settings is typically limited, so early planning by parents, teachers, community agencies, and the individual with disabilities is extremely important.

Postsecondary outcomes and goals for students with intellectual disabilities have implications for what students must learn while still in high school, the kinds of supports they will need in the present and future, and how professionals and agencies must collaborate to help achieve the desired outcomes. Although the content of formal learning activities in high school may vary based on desired outcomes, it should include a mixture of the following for students with intellectual disabilities:

- Formal academic courses in the general curriculum (with modified standards and assessments), especially courses that might lead to participation in postsecondary education
- Necessary functional, personal care skills that will lead to more independence
- Community-based experiences including vocational skill preparation and skills in areas such as shopping, dining in restaurants, and using public transportation

Strategies to Achieve Social Success. Many of the learning outcomes we've described must also coincide with the continued improvement of social skills and the development of more mature patterns of personal interactions and relations. When students with intellectual disabilities enter adolescence and are approaching adulthood, three critical areas of social learning need special attention: friends and peer relationships, sexuality, and self-determination.

Friendships and Peer Relationships. The quality of life of persons with intellectual disabilities is related to the network of friends and acquaintances that they develop in their schools, workplaces, and communities. The best predictors for the development of relations with others by persons with intellectual disabilities are the same as for those who are not disabled: opportunity, understanding, and common interests. As with elementary-age students, if high school students with intellectual disabilities learn appropriate social skills, including how to interact with others, and are given opportunities to socialize with others, they may be better accepted as individuals.

Studies of social relationships have shown that persons without disabilities are initially somewhat skeptical and cautious about committing themselves to relationships with persons with intellectual disabilities. Often, however, after spending more time together, the relationships mature and become more like typical friendships. Better relationships also tend to develop when the peers share common interests (Green, Schleien, Mactavish, & Benepe, 1995; Pottie & Sumarah, 2004).

In addition to the strategies discussed to improve the social behavior of elementary-age students, teachers at the secondary level can do three things to help improve social relations of high school students with and without intellectual disabilities. First, they can identify any common interests that students may have. Interviews and discussions with students can help find areas of shared interest. Next, teachers can develop opportunities for students to have social interactions. During the school day students interact frequently, and teachers can find natural times to pair students or group them together. Finally, both special educators and general educators can try to support the interactions until students have the chance to discover the quality of their own relationships and real friendships develop.

Sexuality. Another important area of social learning is the area of personal sexuality. Knowledge about sexuality and related issues by most people with intellectual disabilities is limited by their cognitive and social understanding and also by attitudes of others (e.g., parents, caregivers, teachers) and the ensuing restrictions. As a result, adolescents and adults with intellectual disabilities often lack knowledge and experience about sexuality and may hold misperceptions, fears, and negative attitudes toward it (Galea, Butler, Iacono, & Leighton, 2004; Lesseliers & Van Hove, 2002).

Although the desire for love and intimacy is universal, the ways in which people wish to experience these conditions vary. Some people with intellectual disabilities wish to have typical sexual experiences in loving relationships, others prefer closeness but with no (or with limited) physical relationships, and others simply wish to have personal solitude and privacy (Siebelink, de Jong, Taal, & Roelvink, 2006). However, without some form of instruction and support, inappropriate sexual behavior or emotional stress may occur. Therefore, it will be very important for teachers, working closely with parents, to identify and address the level of knowledge and understanding about sexuality required by students with intellectual disabilities. Sexuality is an area that is often neglected but one of great importance (American Association on Intellectual and Developmental Disabilities, 2007).

Self-Determination. Inherent in the areas of social relationships and personal sexuality, along with many other aspects of life, is the need to be able to make certain decisions and choices for oneself. Quite often others have assumed that people with intellectual disabilities are not capable of determining what they want or that their decisions will be inappropriate. Studies have shown, however, that many people with intellectual disabilities do have valid wishes and desires and that, with some guidance and support, they can determine for themselves important life conditions, such as where they would like to live or work and whom they would like for a roommate (Wehmeyer, Kelchner, & Richards, 1996; Wehmeyer & Metzler, 1995; Wehmeyer & Schwartz, 1997).

Self-determination has been defined as "acting as the primary causal agent in one's life and making choices and decisions regarding one's quality of life, free from undue external influence or interference" (Wehmeyer, 1992). High school teachers, working together and with parents, can help adolescents with intellectual disabilities improve their self-determination skills. Some strategies include the following:

- Provide opportunities for them to make important decisions about their daily activities and about longer-term goals—for example, diet, academic goals, and career possibilities.
- Encourage adolescents to see the links between their daily decisions and their ability to achieve important goals for themselves, such as diet, exercise, and physical condition.
- Help them to see how long-term goals can be broken down into smaller tasks that will ultimately lead to the goals.
- Help them to recognize their strengths and weaknesses and how to set and achieve goals in light of this information. "It's great that you love animals, but since science is not one of your strengths, maybe you want to look into animal care instead of vet school."
- Encourage students to recognize different sources of support and to seek it when necessary. For example, you might say, "Don't you think your boss might be able to show you how to clean those parts better? How do you think you could get him to do that?" (Doll, Sands, Wehmeyer, & Palmer, 1996).

Final Thoughts Regarding Effective Practices

In Chapters 11 to 16, we provide step-by-step descriptions of many effective practices that are useful when teaching students with disabilities. You will find several of these practices are particularly effective when teaching students with intellectual disabilities in inclusive classrooms. For example, many general education teachers voice the need for support when teaching students with intellectual disabilities. Therefore, in Chapter 11, we discuss effective methods for collaboration among professionals (Strategy 11.1) and ways to work effectively with paraeducators (Strategy 11.5). In Chapter 12, you will find useful information and strategies for developing formal plans and also for planning for differentiated instruction. In Chapters 13 and 14, you will find specific instructional strategies useful for elementary and secondary students, respectively. You will also find Chapters 15 and 16 very useful, as these include several strategies for improving students' behavior (Chapter 15) and using educational and assistive technology to support students with intellectual disabilities in the general education classroom (Chapter 16).

Summary

This chapter addressed the following topics:

Definition of intellectual disabilities and criteria used for identification

- Intellectual disabilities are defined by the AAIDD as "significant limitations both in intellectual functioning and in adaptive behavior as expressed in conceptual, social, and practical adaptive skills. This disability originates before age 18."
- Educators will evaluate infants and toddlers who may have intellectual disabilities based on lack of achievement of developmental milestones.
- During the school years, educators will use a significantly low score (less than about 70 to 75 IQ points) on a standardized intelligence test and weakness in adaptive behavior to determine that a student has intellectual disabilities.

Prevalence of students with intellectual disabilities

- The overall prevalence of intellectual disabilities is often reported as being somewhere between 1% and 3%.
- Slightly less than 0.88% of public school students between the ages of 6 and 21 years are classified as "mentally retarded."
- Other disability categories including "multiple disabilities" and "developmental delays" may increase the estimate in public schools to a little more than 1%.

Educational placements for students with intellectual disabilities

- About 52% of students with intellectual disabilities spend more than 60% of their education time outside the general education classroom; only 12% are outside the general education classroom for less than 21% of the school day. This suggests most students are served in full-time or part-time special classrooms.
- About 6% of the students with intellectual disabilities are in separate facilities including public or private special schools, residential facilities, or in homes or a hospital.

Major characteristics of students with intellectual disabilities

- Students with mild intellectual disabilities will be below grade level in academic skills but may develop basic academic skills up to about the fourth-grade level.
- The greatest challenges will be the use of reasoning skills in areas such as reading comprehension, problem solving, and planning ahead.
- Students with moderate intellectual disabilities may be able to achieve up to about the first- or second-grade level and learn practical skills such as sight words, how to tell time and to use money, as well as verbal communication, self-help, and domestic and community skills.
- Most adults with moderate intellectual disabilities will be able to work in community jobs.
- Students with severe-to-profound intellectual disabilities will have a wide range of abilities in areas such as communication and self-care.
- Many students with intellectual disabilities may have difficulty understanding the content of verbal interactions and social-communicative expectations.
- Students may develop poor self-concepts and withdraw in social situations.
- Students with more severe disabilities may exhibit challenging behaviors such as stereotyped behaviors, self-injurious behaviors, aggressive behaviors, or noncompliance.

Major challenges of including students with intellectual disabilities

- Facilitating learning in the general academic curriculum, and in learning necessary functional skills.
- Facilitating the development of appropriate social skills at the elementary school level and at the secondary level.

Principles of effective instruction at the elementary level

- Educators must teach students academic skills based on the general curriculum and include these skills on the IEP. They must also teach functional skills when necessary.
- Some states have developed objectives for students with intellectual disabilities based on the general curriculum.
- Educators should use effective instructional strategies such as universal design for learning (UDL) to help students participate in the general curriculum.
- Social skills instruction should focus on increasing opportunities to interact appropriately with peers without disabilities, teaching specific social behaviors, and teaching peers without disabilities how to respond appropriately to the social behavior of students with disabilities.
- Teachers should use functional behavior assessment (FBA) and behavior intervention plans (BIPs) to improve more challenging behavior.

Principles of effective instruction at the secondary level

- Students may continue to learn basic academic skills and also may develop interests in specific subjects.
- Students may participate in general education high school classes with support.
- Students require teachers to focus on objectives for success in different postsecondary environments including educational settings, vocational settings, living facilities, and skills related to success in these settings.
- Social skills should focus on developing friendships and peer relationships, knowledge about sexuality, and improving self-determination.

Addressing Professional Standards

Standards addressed in Chapter 6 include:

CEC Standards: (1) foundations, (2) development and characteristics of learners, (3) individual learning differences, (4) instructional strategies.

INTASC Standards: Principle 1—Understand central concepts of the discipline; Principle 2—Provide learning opportunities to support the learning and development of all students.

Praxis™ II Standards: Knowledge-based core principles: (1) understanding exceptionalities, (3) delivery of services to students with disabilities. Application of core principles: (1) curriculum, (2) instruction, (5) professional roles/issues/ literature.

PUTTING IT ALL TOGETHER

When you have students with disabilities or special needs in your classroom, there is no doubt that your planning responsibilities will increase, but this effort is important.

1. **Collaboration is key.** In this chapter we have discussed several planning needs for students with disabilities and special needs. As you plan to address these needs, you should seek ongoing input from your colleagues in special education.

2. **Get to know your students.** If you know students' needs, their strengths, and their unique challenges, your planning is likely to be much more aligned with their needs. You cannot make "generic" plans that will meet all the needs of students who have such diverse characteristics.

3. **Be more detailed in the beginning.** You will find a lot of variation in the detail that different teachers put into their classroom instructional plans. As a general rule, the more complex the learning needs are of a particular student, the more time you will need to plan for those needs.

4. **Look to different sources for plans.** You can find instructional plans and ideas for plans in many sources. You can attend staff development sessions, confer with your colleagues, take additional courses, attend conferences, and search the Internet to obtain multiple sources of information that will help you plan for your students with special needs.

5. **Save your plans, critically evaluate them, and make revisions.** Learn from your plans. Being an effective teacher will always be "a work in progress." Certainly, in the area of planning, you will improve with experience.

myeducationlab

We present strategies in the second half of this chapter (Strategies 12.1 to 12.8) in a step-by-step format so that you can use them in your classroom right away. In addition, in the following table, we identify some video clips, cases, and simulations that will allow you to experience these strategies (or complementary strategies) in a real classroom environment.

EFFECTIVE PRACTICE	MYEDUCATIONLAB CONNECTION	CONSIDER THIS
Strategy 12.1: Contributing to IEPs	Go to MyEducationLab, select the topic *Pre-Referrals, Placement, and IEP Process*, and go to the Activities and Applications section. Next, watch the video entitled "School Connections: IEP Meeting," and answer the accompanying questions.	As you watch the video, pay close attention to the interaction among the IEP team participants and the role of the general education teacher. How do these interactions compare with the points discussed in Strategy 12.1?
Strategy 12.2: Developing a 504 Plan	Go to MyEducationLab, select the topic *Collaboration, Consultation, and Co-Teaching*, and go to the Activities and Applications section. Next, complete the simulation entitled "Working with Your School Nurse."	As you complete the simulation, focus on the role of the general educator in developing a 504 Plan and collaborating with other professionals.
Strategy 12.3: Planning for Differentiated Instruction	Go to MyEducationLab, select the topic *Inclusive Practices*, and go to the Activities and Applications section. Next, watch the video entitled "Differentiated Instruction," and answer the accompanying questions.	As you watch this video, focus on this teacher's techniques for differentiating instruction for her students. How do her explanation and implementation of this concept compare or contrast with the discussion in Strategy 12.3?
Strategy 12.4: Identifying Instructional Needs	Go to MyEducationLab, select the topic *Collaboration, Consultation, and Co-Teaching*, and go to the Activities and Applications section. Next, read and analyze the case entitled "A Broken Arm."	As you read and analyze the case, focus on the accommodations the co-teacher Ms. King makes for her student Jim. What needs to happen in order for Jim to succeed in this class?
Strategy 12.5: Planning for Basic Skills Instruction	Go to MyEducationLab, select the topic *Instructional Practices and Learning Strategies*, and go to the Activities and Applications section. Next, select the subsection *Direct Instruction*, watch the video entitled "Reading: Direct Instruction," and answer the accompanying questions.	As you watch this video, focus on how this teacher engages her students in this direct-instruction model. Compare and contrast this teacher's techniques with the examples discussed in Strategy 12.5.
Strategy 12.6: Planning for Academic Content Instruction	Go to MyEducationLab, select the topic *Instructional Practices and Learning Strategies*, and go to the Activities and Applications section. Next, watch the video entitled "Cooperative Learning" in the (Cooperative Learning subsection), and answer the accompanying questions.	Using cooperative learning groups in an inclusive classroom setting is a very important component of planning instruction. As you watch the video, reflect on the components of the STAD model of cooperative learning.
Strategy 12.7: Using CBM to Measure Student Academic Progress	Go to MyEducationLab, select the topic *Assessment*, and go to the Activities and Applications section. Next, watch the video entitled "DIBELS: Progress Management," and answer the accompanying questions.	As you watch the video, reflect on how this teacher is using a technology-based curriculum-based measure to monitor student progress in reading.
Strategy 12.8: Developing a Personalized Grading Plan	Go to MyEducationLab, select the topic *Assessment*, and go to the Activities and Applications section. Next, watch the video entitled "Assessment of Special Needs Students," and answer the accompanying questions.	As you watch the video, reflect on how we measure students' progress in the general education curriculum and how this connects with developing a personalized grading system for students who have special needs.

EFFECTIVE PRACTICES

In the remainder of this chapter, we describe eight effective strategies, which we referred to previously in the chapter, to help you plan effectively to meet the needs of all students.

EFFECTIVE PRACTICE	TYPE OF STRATEGY/BRIEF DESCRIPTION	SPECIAL CONSIDERATIONS
Strategy 12.1: Contributing to IEPs	Being an effective member of the IEP team is an important role for the general educator. This strategy offers several ways to help fulfill this important responsibility.	Understanding the required content of an IEP and students' needs will help you be a more effective member of the IEP team.
Strategy 12.2: Developing a 504 Plan	Section 504 plans specify accommodations necessary for some students with special needs. This strategy explains how a 504 committee designs such plans.	504 Plans are used for students who have special needs but do not meet criteria for special education under IDEA.
Strategy 12.3: Planning for Differentiated Instruction	Planning for differentiated instruction can help meet the needs of students with different abilities. This strategy tells you common ways to vary instructional content and delivery.	Besides planning for how to deliver instruction, it is also important to plan how students can demonstrate what they have learned.
Strategy 12.4: Identifying Instructional Needs	This strategy will help you identify the learning needs of students with disabilities based on the general curriculum and also based on their unique learning needs.	Base instructional goals for students with disabilities on the general curriculum, but realize other goals may also be relevant to their needs.
Strategy 12.5: Planning for Basic Skills Instruction	Many students with special needs will need intensive instruction in basic academic skills. This strategy outlines ways to plan for this instruction.	Planning for supplemental forms of instruction can help students learn basic skills.
Strategy 12.6: Planning for Academic Content Instruction	This strategy discusses several planning approaches that can help teachers prepare to teach academic content to students with disabilities.	Modifications in the content and form of delivery can allow many students to benefit from content area instruction (planning pyramids can be useful).
Strategy 12.7: Using CBM to Measure Student Academic Progress	Evaluating student progress is important for students with special needs. CBM allows you to closely monitor students' progress and modify your instruction if necessary in order to improve progress.	Unlike grades, CBMs are quantitative measures of the student's performance within the curriculum.
Strategy 12.8: Developing a Personalized Grading Plan	Many teachers struggle with deciding how to grade students with disabilities. This strategy provides several useful options.	Parents of students with disabilities are often more interested in learning about factors other than how their child compares to others in the classroom.

Students with Emotional and Behavioral Disabilities

KEY TOPICS

After reading this chapter you will:

- Know the definition of emotional and behavioral disabilities (EBD) and the criteria used to identify students with the disability.
- Know the number of students identified with EBD.
- Be able to identify the range of settings in which students with EBD are educated.
- Be able to describe the major characteristics of students with EBD.
- Understand key issues and challenges related to including students with EBD in general education classrooms.
- Know effective practices for including students with EBD in elementary and secondary classrooms.

chapter 7

Perspectives on Including Students with Emotional and Behavioral Disabilities

Interview with Steve Kennedy and Steve Williams, Behavioral Support Program Coordinators, Heritage High School

Steve Kennedy and Steve Williams, known affectionately as "the Steves," coordinate the school-within-a-school (SWAS) behavioral support program at Heritage High School. SWAS is a dynamic, comprehensive program that seeks to reintroduce and successfully maintain students in the general education environment. The majority of the students in the SWAS program have emotional and behavioral disabilities (EBD). Many of the students succeed with the assistance of co-taught content-area classes and brief monitoring on an as-needed basis. Even with supports, however, not all students with EBD are ready for instruction in general education classrooms. For those with more intensive needs, Mr. Kennedy and Mr. Williams provide focused instruction in social skills, immediate recovery room services for crisis management, and personalized content-area instruction in their self-contained setting. In Loudoun County, Virginia, this SWAS continuum is recognized as a model approach for teaching appropriate behaviors and supporting students with challenging behaviors in the neighborhood school.

Why does the program work? Mr. Kennedy and Mr. Williams are quick to attribute the success of the program to teamwork and a positive philosophy of inclusion that starts at the administrative level and pervades all aspects of the school. School administrators ensure that all students are part of the school community and have opportunities to participate in all school activities—required and extracurricular—and that the school provides support to enhance participation. Members of the SWAS clinical team work with individual general educators to make instructional accommodations as well as develop and maintain behavior intervention plans. Most important is the climate of commitment, respect, and trust among members of the faculty and administration, with all doing all they can to help students manage their own behaviors.

Clearly, many challenges are associated with day-to-day administration of the SWAS and the multiple stressors that come with working with students whose behaviors can be volatile and threatening to others. For example, a small, resistant group of students with EBD has resisted all

efforts to become involved in the program. Trying different creative ways to integrate these students is both energizing and, unfortunately, sometimes frustrating. Outreach efforts are not always successful. Mr. Kennedy and Mr. Williams recognize that they must be both persistent and relentless in their attempts to involve their students positively in the culture of the school. They model this behavior by making a special effort to be active in all aspects of the Heritage High School community (Steve Williams is a football coach) and go to great lengths to maintain communication with their colleagues and assistants.

On those inevitable bad days, both teachers make every effort to make sure they do not bring the stress of school home with them. To navigate the tough days, endurance and motivation come largely from the empathy they feel for the students and their families. By recognizing the perspectives of these stakeholders, they humanize the process of education and inclusion, going beyond the often-distant jargon-filled talk of placements, levels, and hours of service delivery. Steve Kennedy and Steve Williams remind themselves that these are real kids, with real families and, unfortunately, with chronic behavioral difficulties. They remind themselves that their program and efforts provide hope and success in an environment of fairness and respect. Their advice for those who will be teaching students with EBD: Always be prepared, adapt lessons for success, work as a member of the team, and remember your commitment to the students.

Introduction

myeducationlab

Go to MyEducationLab, select the topic *Emotional and Behavioral Disabilities*, and go to the Activities and Application section. As you watch the video entitled "Including Students with EBD in General Education," think about the importance of including these students in general education classroom settings.

Is it prudent to include students with extremely challenging behaviors in general education classrooms? Won't these students disrupt the flow of instruction and endanger the safety of other students? What should I do if one of these students has a crisis or acts out repeatedly? Isn't it best for students with **emotional and behavioral disabilities (EBD)** to be assigned to classrooms of their own, environments where they can have sustained opportunities to learn socially appropriate behaviors with professionals specially trained to deal with them?

Questions such as these are typical when educators discuss the inclusion of students with EBD. Because of the frequency and intensity of these students' inappropriate behaviors, many students with emotional and behavioral issues are excluded from key elements of the general education experience. Many students with EBD require focused and individualized instruction in social and emotional skills, lessons that are best delivered in separate settings. However, segregated instruction may be necessary but is usually not sufficient. To practice improvements in social and emotional functioning, students with challenging behaviors require inclusion in typical general education settings. Opportunities to attend one's neighborhood school, to interact with appropriate peer role models, and to participate in high-level content learning are essential elements of educational efforts that lead to generalized and sustained changes in behavior.

Steve Kennedy and Steve Williams of Heritage High School (see the "Perspectives" box) recognize that educating students with EBD requires the availability of a range of specialized supports and accommodations, while simultaneously providing opportunities for students to benefit from general education classes. With their school-within-a-school (SWAS) approach, they respond to individual student needs by offering a balance of separate and inclusive programming with varying levels of behavioral support, mentoring, small-group instruction, and monitoring. Both teachers also recognize the importance of responding to the needs of their general education colleagues, who like most teachers, are at their best when immediate assistance and consultation are available (Shapiro, Miller, Sawka, Gardil, & Handler, 1999). As we present the defining characteristics and effective practices for this group of students with challenging

Pause & Reflect

What fuels general educators' concerns and/or reluctance about teaching students with EBD? Are these apprehensions valid? What actions can educators take to address these concerns?

behaviors, begin thinking of the range of ways that educators can organize schools and classrooms to deliver focused interventions, promote a safe learning environment for all, and maximize the benefits associated with inclusive environments.

Who Are Students with Emotional and Behavioral Disabilities?
Definition

Although frequently faulted for its vague and general terminology, the definition of EBD that we use today is historic and well-worn. It was originally published by Eli Bower in 1960 and included as serious emotional disturbance (SED) in the landmark Education of All Handicapped Children Act (EAHCA) of 1975 and all subsequent reauthorizations (later known as the Individuals with Disabilities Education Improvement Act—IDEA). As you review the following definition, first focus on the positive elements of the definition; then identify the components that are difficult to quantify and/or subject to broad interpretation.

Students with EBD respond well to positive behavior supports and mentoring provided by caring adults.

> The term emotional disturbance means a condition exhibiting one or more of the following characteristics over a long period of time and to a marked degree that adversely affects a student's educational performance: (A) An inability to learn which cannot be explained by intellectual, sensory, or health factors; (B) An inability to build or maintain satisfactory interpersonal relationships with peers and teachers; (C) Inappropriate types of behavior or feelings under normal circumstances; (D) A general pervasive mood of unhappiness or depression; (E) A tendency to develop physical symptoms or fears associated with personal or school problems. The term includes children who are schizophrenic. The term does not include children who are socially maladjusted, unless it is determined that they have an emotional disturbance. (U.S. Department of Education, 2005)

Just the Facts — Students with Emotional and Behavioral Disabilities

Who are they?	Students with EBD have pervasive behavioral and emotional behaviors that differ significantly from appropriate age, cultural, or ethnic norms. These behaviors affect their educational performance adversely.
What are typical characteristics?	• Some students with EBD exhibit primarily externalizing behavioral characteristics such as aggression, rule breaking, and noncompliance. • Others present internalizing behavior problems such as social withdrawal, anxiety, and depression. • Secondary characteristics include social skills deficits and attention deficits.
What are the demographics?	• Researchers estimate that 0.69% of the school-age population (approximately 457,731 students) are identified with EBD. • Approximately 7.6% of all students identified as having a disability are identified as having EBD. Approximately 80% are male, and 50% receive medication.
Where are students educated?	• Approximately one third of students with EBD are educated in neighborhood schools but, on average, are in general education classes 40% of the day. • Over 12% of students with EBD are served in separate day-treatment facilities, or in residential facilities, or in their homes.

Among the positive elements of the definition are the descriptive manifestations of the disability, presented in terms that teachers typically use and understand. Most teachers believe they can recognize *satisfactory interpersonal relationships* and *inappropriate behaviors or feelings.* However, like advocates who have been seeking to strengthen the definition (e.g., Forness & Kavale, 2000), you probably have concerns with the lack of precision surrounding the actual measurement of these descriptors as well as what is meant by the initial qualifying terms *to a marked extent* and *over a long period of time.* Vague terms such as these are prone to a wide range of differing interpretations, resulting in students' being mistakenly included or excluded from this disability category. Not surprisingly, students identified as having EBD vary in characteristics across and within classrooms, schools, and communities.

Keep in mind, however, that developing a truly objective, fail-safe definition of EBD may be difficult if not impossible. Consider the obstacles: First, no single trusted measure of social or emotional functioning is equivalent to those used for assessing intelligence or achievement. Second, the range of behaviors presented by those with EBD often overlaps with the behaviors of those without disabilities. Finally, the variety of theories that attempt to explain the development and maintenance of EBD—such as the behavioral and the psychodynamic models—often conflict.

Pause & Reflect

Although they cannot actually measure it, many teachers believe they know EBD when they see it. Do you agree with this belief? What are the advantages and disadvantages of using teacher judgment in the identification of students with EBD?

Identification of Students with Emotional and Behavioral Disabilities

Educators typically identify and assess students with EBD through a three-step approach that includes screening, identification, and the direct assessment of targeted behaviors. This three-step approach allows for determination of the disability and, more importantly, pinpointing specific behaviors in need of intervention.

Screening is the process of determining if a student has the broad set of behavioral patterns *suggesting* risk for EBD. Most teachers, through their daily instruction, interactions, and observations, informally screen for these patterns on a regular basis. Although these informal activities are practical and straightforward, they can have some negative consequences. Generally, teachers vary greatly in the range and frequency of students they identify. Those teachers with low tolerance levels refer large numbers of students, while those with high tolerance identify fewer students, overlooking a significant proportion of students at risk (Rosenberg et al., 2004). Teachers also tend to identify students who exhibit externalizing and disruptive behaviors, sometimes neglecting those with significant internalizing behavior problems. One way to address these shortcomings is to formalize the screening process. One fairly easy method is to actively rank students on categories of functioning such as appropriate classroom behavior, social interaction, and problem solving. Those at the extreme ends of the classroom distribution are considered for additional, more structured evaluation. Also available are highly structured commercially prepared systems of screening such as the Systematic Screening for Behavior Disorders (SSBD) (Walker & Severson, 1992) and the Early Screening Profile (ESP) (Walker, Severson, & Feil, 1995), which guide teachers through the specific steps of the screening process.

When screening indicates a possible disability, educators refer students for a more in-depth examination. Two types of assessment methods are most often used: behaviorally based rating scales and personality-oriented methods. Behavior rating scales are easy to administer, applied readily across settings and sources (teachers, parents, and students), and serve as efficient summaries of different types of behaviors (Elliott & Busse, 2004). The Child Behavior Checklist (CBCL) (Achenbach & Rescorla, 2001), the Walker Problem Behavior Identification Checklist (Walker, 1983), the Behavioral and Emotional Rating Scale (BERS) (Epstein & Sharma, 1998), and the Social Skills Rating System (SSRS) (Gresham & Elliott, 1990) are among the more frequently used scales.

The goal of personality-oriented methods is to ascertain how a student thinks and feels across situations and over periods of time. Educators use two types of personality measures, objective and projective, in the identification of EBD (Cullinan, 2004). Objective instruments, such as the Piers-Harris Self-Concept Scale (Piers & Harris, 1984), present items in a standard fashion, use a protocol for scoring, and employ normative data to assess differences. Projective measures, such as the Rorschach Ink-Blot test (Rorschach, 1932), require that individuals interpret or project meaning onto ambiguous pictures, images, or statements. It is assumed that these responses reveal an individual's innermost thoughts, feelings, needs, and motives.

Arguably, the most important aspect of the identification process is pinpointing specific instructional and behavioral problems, a prerequisite for the selection or generation of appropriate interventions. The most effective and comprehensive method for instructional and behavioral planning is a **functional behavioral assessment (FBA)**. The logic underlying the FBA is that much of an individual's behavior is supported by the environment, occurs within a particular context, and serves a specific purpose. Specifically, we all behave in ways to satisfy needs or achieve desired outcomes. Unfortunately, many students with EBD use extreme, inappropriate methods to reach their goals. These students require guidance in seeking alternative ways, or *replacement behaviors,* to meet their needs. The FBA is a series of tools that help identify events, activities, and situations associated with a student's problem behaviors and, more importantly, help plan environmental adjustments that can alter the frequency and intensity of such behaviors (Chandler & Dahlquist, 2002; Gable, Hendrickson, & Van Acker, 2001; Scott & Kamps, 2007).

> **Strategy**
>
> Strategy 15.7 in Chapter 15 presents step-by-step information on how to conduct a functional behavioral assessment.

Prevalence

The prevalence, or frequency of occurrence, of students with EBD is less than 1% (0.69%) of the school-age population. This represents approximately 457,731 students, which accounts for 7.6% of all students identified as having a disability. (U.S. Department of Education, 2006). More than three fourths are boys, and those identified with the disability are more likely than other students to live in households with several risk factors, including poverty, single-parent households, unemployed heads of households, and a sibling with a disability (Wagner et al., 2005).

Advocates and teachers alike believe that the actual number of students who need services far surpasses the number who are identified. Nonetheless, while the number of students identified is relatively small, considerable concern exists that certain populations of students are overrepresented. For example, compared to students of European American descent, African Americans are approximately 1.7 times more likely to be identified as having the disability. Still, little consensus exists as to cause of this disproportionality, and unfortunately, many educators are reticent to discuss racial disparity issues directly (Coutinho, Oswald, & Forness, 2002; Skiba, Simmons, Ritter, Kohler, Henderson, & Wu, 2006).

> **Pause & Reflect**
>
> Why are certain groups of students disproportionately represented among students identified as having EBD? Why are issues like this difficult to discuss? What can be done to address this issue in a fair and direct manner?

Service Delivery

With behaviors that can be aggressive, perseverative, and sometimes threatening, students with EBD are educated in restrictive settings more often than any other students with disabilities. Approximately one third of all students with EBD between the ages of 6 and 21 spend more than 60% of their time outside general education classes in their neighborhood schools, 11.1% are served in separate day treatment facilities, and 1.4% are educated in their homes or in hospitals (Henderson & Bradley, 2004). Accordingly, educators continue to debate how best to deliver the variety of special services that students with EBD need. As we mentioned at the beginning of the chapter, this debate is a function of tensions among the desire to provide essential services, the need to maintain these students in the least restrictive environment, and the responsibility of maintaining a safe and orderly instructional environment for all students. Few argue that students with challenging behaviors should garner the benefits of inclusive programming whenever possible. However, many general educators feel unprepapred to deal with students with challenging behaviors and believe they can best serve students by collaborating with knowledgeable special educators. Consequently, the consensus among educators is that students with EBD require team-implemented, individually tailored programs that make use of the full continuum of placement and service options.

Heritage High School's SWAS model is an example of a team-based, full-continuum service-delivery program. As presented briefly in the "Perspectives" vignette, Steve Kennedy and Steve Williams employ a series of activities to support students with EBD (and their teachers) in inclusive classrooms. Some students benefit from the typical co-teaching of general and special education teachers in content-rich classes such as geometry, physics, and biology. In those classes, the co-teaching team adapts instruction to minimize frustration and provides directed encouragement and reinforcement for students to persevere when the going gets tough. Other students at Heritage require the support of one-to-one support personnel, adult mentors, and peer facilitators, all of whom assist the individual student to manage his behavior in the classroom. In all cases, the program emphasizes success with a number of in-class curricular techniques that teachers use to promote inclusive programming. These techniques include self-management, cooperative learning, peer tutoring, and problem-solving training. Teachers monitor data weekly, and students move among levels of support depending on their success. Still, the faculty and staff at Heritage recognize that students with EBD may be easily frustrated and act out, making crisis procedures and protocols for directed social skills necessary and easily accessible.

> **Strategy**
>
> Strategy 11.4 in Chapter 11 presents step-by-step information on how best to implement and maintain a program of co-teaching.

Major Characteristics of Students with Emotional and Behavioral Disabilities

The primary characteristics of students with EBD fall into two major categories: externalizing behavior problems and internalizing behavior problems. We describe the specific patterns of behavior that fall into each of these two categories and also describe common academic and social difficulties.

Externalizing Behavior Problems

Aggression and noncompliance are frightening behaviors that often result in disciplinary removals from the classroom.

Externalizing behavior problems are overt manifestations of defiance and disruption. According to Steve Kennedy and Steve Williams at Heritage High School, these behaviors, most notably aggression and noncompliance, are the most frequent reasons their fellow teachers give for needing support from their SWAS program. These extremely troublesome behaviors are also most responsible for disciplinary removals from classrooms and schools across the nation, as well as for referrals for specialized psychological, psychiatric, and juvenile justice services (Cullinan & Sabornie, 2004; Tobin, Sugai, & Colvin, 1996).

Aggression can be either verbal or physical. Verbal aggression includes yelling, teasing, whining, tantrums, and using profanity, as well as orally threatening or humiliating another person. Physical aggression includes abusive and violent actions such as hitting, kicking, grabbing, and biting (Patterson, Reid, Jones, & Conger, 1975; Rosenberg et al., 2004). You will observe that some students with EBD use aggression to intimidate and manipulate others. Unfortunately, you will also notice that others tend to acquiesce to these students' demands in order to avoid confrontations. Unfortunately, these situations can result in other students' learning that aggressive tendencies can result in desired outcomes.

Students with EBD also frustrate their teachers because they simply refuse to do what is requested of them. *Noncompliance* is the term used to describe those instances when students actively choose not to respond to instructions or requests. A history of these refusals disrupts academic and social development, results in fewer educational opportunities, and often leads to serious patterns of antisocial behavior (Austin & Agar, 2005; Walker & Walker, 1991).

Consider the long-term effects: An individual who fails to respond to requests would be unable to maintain employment and would have a difficult time developing and maintaining friendships.

Internalizing Behavior Problems

In sharp contrast to externalizing problem behaviors, teachers tend to underrefer students with suspected internalizing behavior problems (Gresham & Kern, 2004). Because internalizing problems involve inwardly directed actions, teachers often have difficulty identifying them in classroom situations. Among students with EBD, the more common internalizing behavior problems are social withdrawal, anxiety disorders, and depression.

Students with **social withdrawal** tend to spend an excessive amount of time in solitary play and have low rates of verbalization and positive social interactions with peers and adults (Schreperman, Eby, Snyder, & Stropes, 2006). It is important that teachers identify these students as early as possible, because young children learn from interacting with one another and experimenting on how best to get along with others (Kennedy & Shukla, 1995). Also, not developing appropriate peer relationships in childhood is predictive of social adjustment and psychological problems in adolescence and adulthood, most notably for depression and loneliness (Gresham, Lane, MacMillan, & Bocian, 1999).

Students who do not develop appropriate peer relationships are at risk for later psychological challenges such as depression and social adjustment problems.

Anxiety is the uncomfortable physical signal for concern, thought, and action regarding our daily life challenges. The majority of child and adolescent anxiety is normative and transitory, rarely interfering with typical development. However, approximately 8% of children experience severe anxiety, characterized by excessive worry occurring for a significant amount of time and often requiring clinical intervention (Kauffman, 2001). Common forms of anxiety among children and adolescents (and their symptoms) include (1) generalized anxiety (restlessness, fatigue, irritability, muscle tension, sleep disturbances, and difficulty concentrating); (2) separation anxiety (excessive worry about being separated from primary caretakers); (3) obsessive-compulsive disorder (OCD: ritualistic and repetitive hand washing, thoughts, and checking on events and thoughts); and (4) *social anxiety* (extreme fear of social or performance situations).

Depression is a pervasive and insidious group of symptoms that affect a person's mood, thoughts, and carriage. Although precise incidence rates are unknown, it is estimated that between 2% and 21% of all students experience some symptoms of depression; estimates among students with special education needs range from 14% to 54%. What makes depression particularly frightening is that it often coexists with a range of conduct disorders and is a contributing factor in more than half of all suicides (Maag, 2002; Newcomer, Barenbaum, & Pearson, 1995; Wolff & Ollendick, 2006).

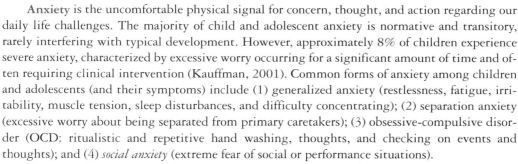

Pause & Reflect

Internalizing behaviors are difficult to identify. What indicators should teachers check for among students, and how should teachers conduct these observations?

Cognitive, Academic, and Social Behavior

Students with EBD tend to have IQ scores in the low-average range (Kauffman, 2001; Mattison, 2004). When compared to the academic profiles of typically developing peers, they present moderate-to-severe academic difficulties in multiple areas that tend not to improve over time. Without appropriate academic supports, students with EBD earn lower grades, fail courses, and are retained in grade more often than their general education peers (Lane, Carter, Pierson, & Glaeser, 2006; Wagner et al., 2005). The presence of these academic deficits is not surprising. As a result of their disability, many students with EBD do not attend to relevant aspects of instruction and disrupt class, responding impulsively with little thought or reflection. Dropout rates for students with EBD are a tragic 58.6%, more than three times that of their peers (Osher, Morrison, & Bailey, 2003; Wagner & Blackorby, 1996).

Students with EBD have consistently and significantly lower social skills than peers with and without disabilities (Wagner et al., 2005). Some students simply have skill deficits and have not acquired the knowledge or skills required to perform essential social behaviors. Others have performance deficits; they have acquired the social behaviors but do not have the opportunity to perform the behavior, or have made a decision not to perform the behavior because of particular circumstances (e.g., not motivated to do so, considerable secondary gain in misbehavior, etc.). Still others are not fluent in social behavior because they have not had adequate exposure to models of social skills and/or have had too few opportunities to rehearse or practice appropriate behavior.

Effective Instruction for Students with Emotional and Behavioral Disabilities

Including students with EBD successfully requires a solid foundation of FBA, evidence-based academic instruction, and highly structured methods of positive behavior management. We provide detailed methods and step-by-step procedures to achieve these essential preconditions in Chapters 11 to 16. Next, we highlight several general case instructional interventions and techniques for elementary and secondary students with EBD.

Effective Instruction for Elementary Students with Emotional and Behavioral Disabilities

Strategy | Strategy 13.4 in Chapter 13 illustrates methods for implementing peer-assisted learning strategies.

Academic Instruction. Because extreme social and emotional behaviors are the defining characteristics of EBD, it is not surprising that little attention is paid to the academic needs of students with EBD. Obviously, it is imperative that students, particularly those in elementary grades, receive appropriate and adequate amounts of academic instruction; anything less would exacerbate gaps in basic reading and math acquisition, essential foundations for ongoing achievement. In inclusive settings, specific teacher and peer actions can enhance academic outcomes. For example, using the results of classroom assessments such as an FBA, teachers can alter task difficulty, provide explicit instructional modifications such as content enhancements, and show students how they can apply specific learning strategies successfully to a range of academic areas.

Additionally, to enhance direct teacher instruction, teachers can use peer-mediated approaches such as cooperative learning and structured tutoring programs that pair higher-performing readers with their lower-performing classmates (e.g., Coleman & Vaughn, 2000; Lane, 2004; Pierce, Reid, & Epstein, 2004).

Token Economy Programs. The token economy is a generic behavior management program that teachers can apply to a number of problematic behaviors associated with EBD. The program is versatile; teachers can apply a range of techniques to increase and decrease behavior to alter behaviors in need of change. Token economy programs are very popular (90% of teachers of students with EBD use some form of it), due in large part to its ease of adminstration and efficacy (Rosenberg et al., 2004). At Heritage High School, for example, the token economy allows student intervention teams to individualize behavioral goals, interventions, and schedules of reinforcement, depending on the nature of the students' behavioral needs.

Setting up a token economy has three basic requirements: tokens, backup reinforcers, and clearly defined contingencies. A token reinforcer can be a checkmark of specific earnings in an elaborate classroom point system. However, for younger students, tangible tokens such as stars, tickets, or smiley faces work best. By themselves, tokens have little reinforcing power (Axelrod, 1983).

Pause & Reflect

Consider the link between a student's classroom behavior and his academic performance. How can academic failure contribute to increased rates of inappropriate behavior? How can teachers prevent some of these behaviors from occurring?

The strength of the token is based on what "backs them up," or what the tokens can obtain. Try to avoid elaborate material reinforcers, as they are not natural to the school or classroom environment. Young children with EBD will work for access to ordinary and usual activities and events such as being the teacher's helper, attending specialized programs and assemblies, as well as fixed amounts of time with favorite adults, peers, and instructional equipment. Finally, clearly defined contingencies will preclude arguments as to what one needs to do in order to earn tokens or backup reinforcers. A good way to define contingencies is to either write them down in a contract or post them in an area that can be accessed by both the teacher and the student.

Peer-mediated approaches to instruction are essential when including students with EBD in general education activities.

Social Skills Instruction. Social skills instruction can be particularly valuable for young students with EBD. Effective instructional sequences are comprehenisve and usually include (1) identification of social skills needing improvement, (2) modeling and explaining the identified skills, (3) providing opportunities for practice while being coached, (4) delivering feedback and reinforcement during practice, and (5) identifying real situations where the skills can be applied (Kavale, Mathur, & Mostert, 2004). Some teachers choose to teach social skills by using a commercially prepared curriculum such as ACCEPTS (A Children's Curriculum for Effective Peer and Teacher Skills) (Walker et al., 1983), Tough Kid Social Skills (Sheridan, 1997), or Skillstreaming (Goldstein & McGinnis, 1997; McGinnis & Goldstein, 1997). Such programs cluster specific skills in groups or domains (e.g., dealing with feelings, friendship-making skills, coping skills) and provide instructional sequences for teaching the skills. Other teachers design their own units, lessons, and activities for teaching social skills, often making use of instruction in replacement behaviors. Replacement behaviors are a series of actions that achieve the same intent as the problem behaviors (Neel & Cessna, 1990). Teachers first determine the intent or functions of the inappropriate behaviors and then focus instructional efforts on teaching appropriate ways to achieve the desired outcomes (Meadows & Stevens, 2004).

> **Strategy**
>
> Strategy 15.6 in Chapter 15 provides step-by-step information for implementing behavioral contracts, an important element of token economies.

Effective Instruction for Secondary Students with Emotional and Behavioral Disabilities

Teaching Self-Control. As we noted previously, many young students with EBD need to learn and master appropriate social skills. The goal for many older students, however, is to regulate their acquired behaviors and apply academic skills independent of teachers and service providers. Self-control is one technique that has helped students with EBD to assume larger and more independent roles in their own academic and behavior change efforts. Self-control develops by prompting students to focus on three activities: self-assessment, goal setting, and self-determination of reinforcement (Polsgrove & Smith, 2004). In self-assessment, students reflect on their own behavior, and they consider whether the behavior of interest is inadequate or inappropriate. Students then reflect on the required behaviors, set goals, and select strategies that help regulate those behaviors. Finally, through the process of self-determination, the students evaluate their performance and consider the nature and scope of reinforcement that they should receive for performance of the target behavior.

> **Strategy**
>
> Strategy 15.2 in Chapter 15 provides a series of surface management techniques that can assist in the development of student self-control.

Vocational Education and Work Experience. Generally, secondary students with EBD do not have a successful transition to postschool life. Approximately one half of students with EBD are unemployed 3 to 5 years after leaving school, and only 40% of those with EBD live

An instructional goal for many older students with EBD is the self-regulation of social behaviors independent of teachers and service providers.

independently (Corbett, Clark, & Blank, 2002; Wagner, Blackorby, Cameto, Hebbeler, & Newman, 1993). On a more positive note, research indicates that vocational education and work experience, alone or in combination, are associated with greater instances of positive postschool outcomes (Cheney & Bullis, 2004; Sitlington & Nuebert, 2004). Vocational education tends to be effective because it centers on the development of a range of work-based competencies such as occupational skills, interpersonal skills, technological literacy, and employability skills associated with particular occupations. Paid work experience during high school, particularly when combined with vocational education, decreases dropout rates and has a significant positive impact on postschool earnings. Many students with EBD who work while in school continue to be workers at those locations when they exit school (Bullis, 2001). In fact, several of the students who completed school-based work projects at Heritage High School have secured service positions offered by the school district.

Wraparound Services. The often pervasive and multifaceted nature of problems faced by students with EBD and their families requires a highly structured, coordinated, and integrated system of service delivery. The term *wraparound* describes this service coordination; it reflects that intervention plans are family and child centered and that services provided go beyond the boundaries of the school building. Wraparound is not a specific program or type of service but a definable planning process that results in a unique set of community services and supports designed to meet the unique needs of children and families (Burns & Goldman, 1998). As a teacher, you will be part of a team of professionals from education, health, and human service backgrounds convened to develop a comprehensive intervention, often based on the results of an FBA. Within most schools, administrators, behavior specialists, counselors, social workers, psychologists, and behavior-support teams implement specialized programs of outreach and intervention. Outside the school, students can be "wrapped around" by services from physicians, mental health service providers, family preservation personnel, and state protective service officers. As students grow older, juvenile justice personnel and even law enforcement officers may be involved.

> **Strategy**
>
> Strategy 11.6 in Chapter 11 provides a series of methods for working with families in team situations.

Final Thoughts Regarding Effective Practices

We recognize that the inclusion of students with EBD requires a number of practices related to effective instruction and behavior management beyond those presented in this chapter. In Chapters 11 to 16, we provide step-by-step descriptions of many effective practices that are useful for students with this disability and others who struggle in school. Several of these effective practices that are particularly useful for teachers who work with students with EBD include effective strategies for the surface management of disruptive behaviors (Strategy 15.2) and the development of effective consequences for appropriate and inappropriate behaviors (Strategy 15.3). Teachers are also concerned about what to do if students engage in confrontation and dangerous behaviors (Strategy 15.4). For those students who require academic supports that preclude frustration with assignments, we provide a series of content enhancements (Strategy 14.1) and peer-assisted learning strategies (Strategy 13.4). We're sure you will find many of the strategies in Chapters 11 to 16 useful in addressing the needs of students with EBD in inclusive classrooms.

Summary

The goal of including students with EBD is to provide specialized supports and accommodations while simultaneously providing all appropriate opportunities to benefit from general education programming. We presented the following major points in this chapter:

Who Are Students with EBD? Definition and Methods of Identification

- EBD is defined as an inability to learn that cannot be explained by intellectual, sensory or health factors; an inability to develop satisfactory interpersonal relationships; inappropriate behaviors and feelings; and the tendency to develop physical symptoms or fears under normal circumstances.
- Because several of the defining characteristics of EBD are vague and imprecise, it is unlikely that a truly objective definition can be developed.
- EBD is identified and assessed through a three-step process that includes screening, identification, and direct assessment of targeted behaviors.

Prevalence of Students with EBD

- The prevalence of EBD is less than 1% (0.69%) of the school-aged population and is about 7.6% of all students with disabilities.
- The number of students who need services for EBD outnumber those who are identified with the disability.
- Certain groups such as African American males are overrepresented in the EBD disability category.

Educational Placements for Students with EBD

- Students with EBD are educated in restrictive settings more often than are students with other types of disabilities.
- Approximately one third of students with EBD spend approximately 60% of their time outside general education classes.
- Over 12% of students with EBD are served in separate day-treatment facilities, or in residential facilities, or in their homes.

Characteristics of Students with EBD

- The primary characteristics of students with EBD fall into two categories, externalizing and internalizing behavior problems.
- Externalizing problems are overt manifestations of defiance and disruption and include aggression and noncompliance.
- Internalizing problems are inwardly directed actions and include social withdrawal, anxiety, and depression.
- As a group, students with EBD tend to have IQ scores in the low-average range, lower social skills than their peers, and without appropriate support, moderate-to-severe academic difficulties.

Principles of Effective Instruction at the Elementary Level

- Specific teacher actions such as explicit instructional modifications, content enhancements, and strategy instruction can assist students with EBD to succeed academically.
- Token economy programs, very popular among teachers of students with EBD, can be applied to a range of behaviors in need of improvement.
- Both commercial and teacher-developed social skills programs can help students with EBD develop and practice skills such as friendship making, coping, and dealing with frustration.

Principles of Effective Instruction at the Secondary Level

- A major goal for secondary students is the application of academic and behavioral skills independent of teachers and service providers.

- Because students with EBD have limited success transitioning to postschool employment, vocational education and work experience are critical components of the secondary curriculum.
- Wraparound programming allows for a team of multidisciplinary professionals to meet the complex and multifaceted needs of students with EBD and their families.

Addressing Professional Standards

Standards addressed in Chapter 7 include:

CEC Standards: (1) foundations, (2) development and characteristics of learners, (3) individual learning differences, (4) instructional strategies.

INTASC Standards: Principle 1—Understand central concepts of the discipline; Principle 2—Provide learning opportunities to support the learning and development of all students.

Praxis™ II Standards: Knowledge-based core principles: (1) understanding exceptionalities, (3) delivery of services to students with disabilities. Application of core principles: (1) curriculum, (2) instruction, (5) professional roles/issues/ literature.

Students with Autism Spectrum Disorders

KEY TOPICS

After reading this chapter you will:

- Know the definition of autism spectrum disorders (ASD) and methods used to identify students with the disability.
- Know the number of students with ASD.
- Be able to identify the range of settings in which students with ASD are educated.
- Be able to describe major characteristics of students with ASD.
- Understand key issues and challenges related to including students with ASD in general education classrooms.
- Know effective practices for including students with ASD in elementary and secondary classrooms.

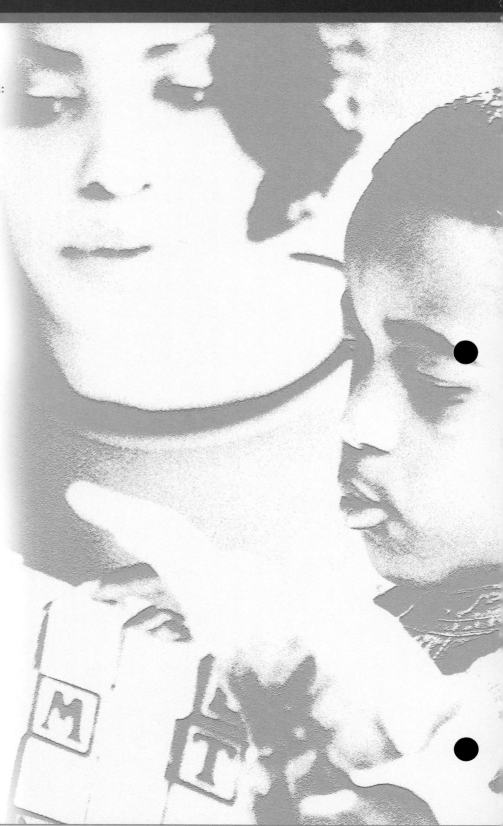

chapter 8

Perspectives on Including Students with Autism Spectrum Disorders

Interview with Eileen Walls, Behavior Specialist, West Hernando Middle School

Eileen Walls, the Behavior Specialist at West Hernando Middle School, has heard the questions, *Can students with autism spectrum disorders (ASD) be included successfully in general education classes? What about their unusual behaviors and their lack of communicative language and socialization? Will there be many disruptions to instruction? Is it fair to the other students? Are there sufficient enough benefits for the students to justify all of effort?*

Among her many responsibilities, Eileen coordinates evidenced-based responses to the learning needs of students with ASD. She has seen, firsthand, how students with the disability can disrupt lessons and fail to interact with peers and teachers when they are not provided appropriate supports and interventions. Regardless of how they appear on television or in movies, students with ASD are challenging in the classroom. Students with severe ASD often appear in a world of their own. They pay little attention to typical routines and procedures, rarely making eye contact with adults or peers. Indeed, it can be quite frustrating when well-meaning approaches and creative initiatives are virtually ignored or sometimes met with bizarre patterns of behavior.

Regardless of the challenges and frustrations, Eileen (and many of her colleagues) is a strong advocate for including students with ASD, as long as the students are provided appropriate supports. Quite simply, she has seen the benefits that come with integrating these students in general education settings, and, yes, it is worth the effort! She attributes some of the success to her collection ("a huge bag") of specific strategies that work in modifying instruction for the students.

How do students with ASD benefit from inclusive programming at West Hernando? According to Eileen, participation in general education provides students with ASD essential experiences with peers who socialize and communicate appropriately. Consistent exposure to these students allows for an endless supply of direct and indirect opportunities to practice communication and friendship-making skills. Moreover, Eileen has observed that explicit instruction in functional behaviors and coping skills delivered in the general education classroom promotes generalization of the students' behaviors to other normative environments. Specifically, she has seen how explicit instruction in sequenced assignment-completion procedures generalizes to successful ordering of

items in a community fast-food restaurant. Such gains contribute to the overall goal of achieving independence. Students with higher-functioning ASD have the additional benefit of acquiring higher-order content as they participate in structured socialization activities.

These benefits do not come easily. Eileen is quick to point out that individualized supports and accommodations require a tremendous amount of planning. Teachers need to identify the essential content of lessons and units and highlight methods for directing students with ASD to that content. In addition to preparing modified unit and lesson plans, Eileen believes that it is critical to make the other students in the class aware of, and sensitive to, the student(s) being included. In the event that the student with ASD engages in self-stimulatory behaviors or makes strange noises during the lesson, students in the class know not to make a big deal of it; that is just the student's way of dealing with things.

Still, Eileen believes that the biggest obstacle in meeting the needs of students with ASD is that many teachers lack sufficient knowledge about the disability. Not only are they unaware of the characteristics typical of ASD, but they also lack experience in how to structure lessons and learning environments. Knowing that an increasing number of students with ASD are being educated in general education settings, Eileen recognizes that all teachers need to be trained to address their instructional needs. In her opinion, students with ASD are the most interesting kids to work with. She views their behaviors as "puzzles" that need to solved, and she recognizes that it is up to her (and her colleagues) to make the personal connections that can get through to them.

Introduction

Autism spectrum disorders (ASDs), also known as pervasive developmental disabilities (PDDs), are among the most mysterious, puzzling, and diverse disabilities you will encounter. Some students with ASD, like those taught by the science team at Heritage High School (see the box entitled "Teaching Students with Autism Spectrum Disorders," later in this chapter), exhibit rigid and awkward patterns of communication and socialization, but usually they can complete academic tasks. Other students with ASD, such as those described by Eileen Walls, the Behavior Specialist at West Hernando Middle School (see the "Perspectives" vignette), exhibit more severe manifestations of the disability, seldom communicating, empathizing, or socializing with others. Although frequently featured in the media, a rare few with the disability have unusual savant-like talents, such as rapidly solving complex equations without the benefit of a calculator or re-creating intricate piano concertos with little or no practice.

As you consider the characteristics of students with ASD and review how educational programming is typically delivered, be aware of three important points: First, as noted previously, the spectrum of behaviors that characterize ASD is wide and variable. Behaviors exist on a continuum, from so-called higher functioning to lower functioning. For example, most students with Asperger's disorder, one type of ASD, do not have extreme delays in language, cognitive development, and acquisition of age-appropriate self-help skills, as do many of those with autistic disorder, another form of ASD. Second, as with other children and youth, students with ASD are ever-changing individuals whose behaviors evolve in unique ways over time. With appropriate supports, accommodations, and encouragement, many students with ASD benefit from instruction in inclusive environments.

Finally, be aware that although teaching students with ASD and providing the necessary supports and accommodations for successful inclusion are rewarding, they can also be time-consuming and challenging. Some students with ASD appear to be in a world of their own, often exhibiting behaviors and facial expressions that separate them from activities, events, and interactions that enrich learning and socialization. Even those who participate in lessons are often hampered by an inability to pick up on the subtle flow of classroom activities, often misunderstanding the communicative intent of lively class discussions. For these reasons, an essential prerequisite for

myeducationlab

Go to MyEducationLab, select the topic *Austism Spectrum Disorders,* and go to the Activities and Applications section. As you watch the video entitled "Tyler Lewis: Progress in the General Education Curriculum," reflect on how important inclusion has been for Tyler and his family.

teaching students with ASD successfully is an awareness of the academic and social behaviors encountered in schools and classrooms.

Who Are Students with Autism Spectrum Disorders?
Definition

Autism spectrum disorder refers to five clinical conditions: autistic disorder, Asperger's disorder, Rett's disorder, childhood disintegrative disorder, and pervasive developmental disorder—not otherwise specified (PDD-NOS). Because autistic and Asperger's disorders are by far the most prevalent, we focus on these two disorders.

Pause & Reflect

In the past few years, media portrayals of individuals with ASD have increased considerably. Have these media accounts impacted how students with the disability are welcomed and educated in inclusive school environments? If so, has the impact been predominantly positive or negative? Explain.

Just the Facts — Students with Autism Spectrum Disorders

Who are they?	• ASD refers to five specific clinical conditions, among which autistic disorder and Asperger's disorder are the most prevalent. • Students with ASD tend to have pervasive, lifelong difficulties in social interaction and deficiencies in communication skills as well as rigid interests and behaviors.

What are typical characteristics?	• Students with autistic disorder often exhibit severe manifestations of the disability, including:
	  • Significant limitations in expressive and receptive language skills
	  • Difficulties in social reciprocity, including a lack of eye contact and little pleasure in the company of others
	  • Repetitive, stereotypical, and ritualistic behaviors
	• Students with Asperger's disorder have similar problems but with less severity including:
	  • Difficulty comprehending and using figurative language
	  • Reduced ability understanding and using implicit rules of social exchanges

What are the demographics?	• Prevalence estimates of ASD range from 3.4 to 6.7 per 1,000 children, leading many to believe we are in the midst of an autism epidemic. • Approximately 225,000 children receive special education services under the autism classification in the Individuals with Disabilities Education Improvement Act, a 500% increase in the past 10 years. • Four times as many boys as girls are identified with ASD.
Where are students educated?	• Although approximately 27% of students with ASD spend less that 21% of the school day outside general education classrooms, most (44%) are educated in separate environments more than 60% of the school day. • Approximately 11.6% of students with ASD are educated in separate environments for the entire school day.
How are students identified?	• Common methods for screening and identification include rating scales, observation protocols, and semistructured interviews. • Functional behavioral assessments provide information for instructional and behavioral planning.
What causes ASD?	• Although the causes of ASD remain uncertain, it likely that they are the product of one or more nature-based factors such as genetic, neurochemical, and neurobiological irregularities.
What are the outcomes?	• The course of ASD is lifelong and chronic, and most students, particularly those with autistic disorder, have ongoing problems with social aspects of life, jobs, and independence. • Success depends on early intervention, the quality and stability of the network of supports, the person's cognitive ability, and symptom severity. • An increasing number of students with high-functioning ASD are transitioning to postsecondary or higher-education settings.

Autistic Disorder. Autistic disorder, routinely referred to simply as *autism,* is a severe developmental disability characterized by an early age of onset, poor social development, impairments in language development, and rigidity in behavior (APA, 2000). In his classic paper "Autistic Disturbances of Affective Content," Kanner (1943) initially detailed descriptions of 11 children "whose condition differs so markedly and uniquely from anything reported so far, that each case merits . . . a detailed consideration of its fascinating peculiarities" (p. 217).

The definition and classification of autism, as it relates to eligibility for special education services, has changed over the years. Earlier iterations of the Individuals with Disabilities Education Act (IDEA) included it with physical and other health impairments (Rosenberg, Wilson, Maheady, & Sindelar, 2004). In more recent reauthorizations, autism received a category of its own and is defined as

> a developmental disability significantly affecting verbal and nonverbal communication and social interaction, generally evident before age 3, that adversely affects a child's educational performance. Other characteristics often associated with autism are engagement in repetitive activities and stereotyped movements, resistance to environmental change or change in daily routines, and unusual responses to sensory experiences. The term does not apply if a child's educational performance is adversely affected primarily because the child has an emotional disturbance. (34 C.F.R., Part 300.7[c] [1][i][1997])

Asperger's Disorder. Asperger's disorder is characterized by severe, sustained, and often lifelong impairments in social interactions and the development of restricted, repetitive patterns of behavior, interests, and activities (APA, 2000). These descriptors resemble those that define autism, except that students with Asperger's tend not to have the same intensity of impairment in language, cognition, and self-help skills. Hans Asperger, an Austrian pediatrician, documented the disorder based on investigations of more than 400 children. Only in the past decade has Asperger's disorder become widely known, in large part because of its increased prevalence (Smith-Myles & Simpson, 2001).

> ## Pause & Reflect
>
> Do you know a person with Asperger's disorder? How does this person behave in social situations? Do you have difficulty communicating with this person? What elements of the person's behavior made socialization and communication challenging?

Identification of Students with Autism Spectrum Disorders

The identification of students with ASD requires measurement of functioning across disciplines, including pediatrics, neurology, psychiatry, speech/language, and education. These assessments are comprehensive processes, requiring time and collaboration among health care and educational professionals as well as families (Hyman & Tobin, 2007).

As with students suspected of having other disabilities, students are first screened for ASD. Screening for ASD is critical: Children who are not identified or provided interventions until they are older lose valuable early intervention opportunities (Coonrod & Stone, 2005). Screening for ASD involves two approaches: nonspecific and ASD-specific. Nonspecific approaches screen for deficits in a wide range of developmental areas, including language, behavior, cognitive skills, and motor skills as well as social and self-help skills. Irregularities in any of these areas can indicate the presence of various disabilities, including ASD. Autism-specific screening approaches, such as the Checklist for Autism in Toddlers (CHAT) (Baird et al., 2000) and the Modified Checklist for Autism in Toddlers (M-CHAT) (Robins et al., 2001), specifically target behavioral manifestations of ASD and help determine whether evidence of that specific disability exists.

Children with results suggesting possible ASD are referred for more intensive evaluations. Typically, multidisciplinary child study teams that include a physician with expertise in ASD, a developmental psychologist, a speech–language specialist, a social worker, and an educator conduct the evaluation. The content of the evaluation typically includes a psychological evaluation and a developmental history of the child; tests of hearing, speech, language, and communication; intelligence testing; medical and neurological exams; and an evaluation of current family functioning (Hyman & Towbin, 2007; Klin, McPartland, & Volkmar, 2005). Evaluators take care to ensure that indicators of performance are assessed over time and in a cross-section of settings.

Prevalence

ASD occurs throughout the world and affects males four times more often than females (Grinker, 2008; Yeargin-Allsopp et al., 2003). *The Diagnostic and Statistical Manual of Mental Disorders, Fourth Edition, Text Revision* (American Psychiatric Association, 2000) reports the prevalence of ASD to range from 2 to 20 cases per 10,000 persons. However, recent estimates indicate that the prevalence is much higher than rates reported in the 1980s and early 1990s, ranging from 3.4 to 6.7 per 1,000 children (Autism Information Center, 2008; Yeargin-Allsopp et al., 2003). Approximately, 225,000 students (0.21% of the school-age population between the ages of 6 and 21) are served under the autism classification for special education services (U.S. Department of Education, 2007). This figure is generally regarded as an understatement of prevalence in schools, because many students with ASD receive special education services through other disability designations and many older individuals are not enrolled in school programs (Autism Information Center, 2008).

Not surprisingly, many believe we are in the midst of an autism epidemic. Although issues surrounding prevalence rates remain controversial, several factors should be considered when comparing rates of ASD over time. First, recent measures of prevalence include all forms of ASD (e.g., Asperger's disorder), while previous studies employed a more narrow definition of autism. Second, in the past, many students with ASD, because of their low IQ scores, were identified as having intellectual impairments. Currently, as a result of improved identification systems and the increased competence of professionals who use them, many of these students are now identified correctly as having ASD (Fombonne, 2003). Finally, as public awareness of ASD increases, parents and clinicians may be looking earlier and more intensively for signs of the disability.

Pause & Reflect

Why are more children and youth identified with ASD? Do you think we are in the midst of an autism epidemic? Defend your response.

Service Delivery

Students with ASD should receive educational services in the least restrictive environment. As with other students with disabilities, educators make placement decisions based on individual student's needs. Among students identified as having autism under IDEA, 61% are included in general education classrooms for 21% to approximately 80% of the school day (U.S. Department of Education, 2007). For higher-functioning students, the least restrictive environment is typically the general education classroom with academic and behavioral supports. For those with more intensive instructional and behavior-management needs, programming is usually provided in more restrictive settings with variable amounts of opportunities for inclusion (Handleman, Harris, & Martins, 2005).

Why are opportunities for inclusion important? Regularly scheduled meaningful contact with typically developing peers augments direct instruction in many of the social and behavioral skills that students with ASD require. Peers are essential models of appropriate behavior and can be enlisted to initiate, prompt, and reinforce important social responses of students with ASD. In instructional situations, classmates without disabilities can clarify instructional requirements, correct inappropriate behaviors, minimize displays of certain symptoms, and include the students with ASD in social events (Ochs, Kremer-Sadlik, Solomon, & Sirota, 2001).

At Heritage High School, students with more severe ASD have numerous opportunities to apply social, behavioral, and academic skills in inclusive settings. Teachers at Heritage ensure that regularly scheduled opportunities occur for students to attend content-area classes for social, behavioral, and general knowledge exposure. Moreover, through the school's Peer Team, a network of

Positive peer interactions are essential elements in the successful inclusion of students with ASD.

peers support students with ASD (and other disabilities) in class, during lunch breaks, as well as at sports events and extracurricular activities. Many of these opportunities succeed because faculty, students, and staff work in collaboration with the special education staff to ensure that student participation is positive, purposeful, and genuinely interactive.

Major Characteristics of Students with Autism Spectrum Disorders

As a spectrum disability, characteristics of students with ASD vary significantly. We focus first on primary characteristics, those manifestations that are universal and specific to the disability. By universal and specific, we mean that these behaviors are found in nearly all students with ASD and are infrequent among those who do not have the disability (American Psychiatric Association, 2000; Rutter, 1978). We then address secondary correlates, those behaviors that often occur along with the primary characteristics.

Primary Characteristics

The three categories of characteristics that are universal and specific to ASD are (1) communication skills difficulties; (2) limitations in social reciprocity; and (3) repetitive, stereotypical, and ritualistic behaviors.

Communication Skills Difficulties. Limitations in communication skills are characteristic of all students with ASD, although levels of severity vary considerably. For those with autistic disorder, impairments in communication skills are pervasive, involving most aspects of expressive and receptive language development. Approximately 50% of these students do not acquire functional language, and many are nonverbal or exhibit echolalia (American Psychiatric Association, 2000). Those who do speak often use speech in a monotonous tone accompanied by unusual pitch, rhythm, and syntax. Because these students rarely use speech for social communication, gestures, body movements, and eye contact are infrequent. Students with autistic disorder also have difficulty understanding spoken language, likely the result of their inability to decipher verbal and nonverbal cues (National Research Council, 2001).

Limitations in communication are not as severe for students with Asperger's disorder. Many have difficulty, however, in comprehending and making use of figurative language—idioms, metaphors, slang, and jokes that add vigor and emotion to communication. When students with Asperger's disorder encounter figurative phrases, they often interpret the words literally and have difficulty deciphering the communicative intent of the message. Also, when these students express themselves, they usually enunciate words and phrases in an odd, robotic fashion accompanied by a limited range of gestures, facial expressions, and eye movements (Rosenberg et al., 2004; Safran, 2002).

Pause & Reflect

Describe a memorable performance, event, or meal *without* using metaphors, slang, or idiomatic phrases. Next, enhance your description incorporating elements of figurative language. List how the two descriptions differ in terms of emotion and utility.

Limitations in Social Reciprocity. Social reciprocity is the multifaceted process of interacting with another person. Because of their reduced ability to understand or use the basic implicit rules that govern social exchanges, students with ASD often experience difficulty in social situations

(American Psychatric Association, 2000). Many with autistic disorder do not respond to familiar faces with a warm, social smile and exhibit little pleasure in the presence of others. They appear aloof, avoid eye contact, and do not attain many of the usual developmental benchmarks such as friendships, play, and expressions of empathy (Rutter, 1978). Limitations in socialization for those with Asperger's disorder are less severe yet still problematic. These students engage others socially, but the quality of their interactions tends to be blunt, rigid, one-sided, and filled with contextually inappropriate verbalizations (Linn & Smith-Myles, 2004). Due to these awkward exchanges, students with Asperger's disorder can become targets of ridicule and become even further distanced from positive social interactions with peers. Some students, seeking to avoid social interactions, may even act out in hope of being sent to a disciplinary time-out setting.

Due to limitations in communication and social skills, students with ASD are often left out of group activities.

Repetitive, Stereotypical, and Ritualistic Behaviors.

At Heritage High School, the most obvious and frequently observed behaviors of students with ASD are repetitive, stereotypical, and ritualistic actions. Students with autistic disorder exhibit several of the more extreme high-frequency motor behaviors—rocking, spinning, arm flapping, and finger flicking; and the school addresses these behaviors in more self-contained settings. Students with autistic disorders often cling to certain objects (e.g., pieces of fabric, dolls, etc.), repeatedly spin toys, or spend large amounts of time lining up objects in a carefully designed, elaborate pattern.

Although less extreme, students with Asperger's disorder present their own unusual forms of ritualistic behavior (American Psychiatric Association, 2000). Many have intense interests in weather systems, maps, or the telephone book as well as schedules for trains, airlines, and television shows (Loveland & Tunali-Kotoski, 2005). Teachers report that it is not unusual for these students to be extremely anxious and upset when daily routines are changed due to unforeseen circumstances. For example, Gina Kraun and Denise Pohill, science teachers at Heritage High School (see the "Teaching Students with Autism Spectrum Disorders" box), noticed that Leon (not his real name), a student with Asperger's disorder, often became agitated when he knew an answer, raised his hand to respond, and was not called on. Leon would tap on his desk and whisper repeatedly "I know, I know, I know. . . ." To address this disruptive, repetitive behavior, his teachers developed a peer response system in which Leon could demonstrate to his partner that he knew the answer. This approach reduced Leon's anxious behavior and increased his levels of appropriate class behavior.

Some students with ASD become anxious and upset when daily classroom routines or procedures are changed.

Secondary Behavioral Factors

Age of Onset and Intellectual Functioning.

Many students with autistic disorder can be identified before reaching 3 years of age. Parents generally report concerns when their child reaches between 15 and 22 months of age, usually because of lack of speech and emergence of ritualistic and repetitive behaviors (Chawarska & Volkmar, 2005; Robins, Fein, Barton, & Green, 2001).

Most children with the Asperger's disorder do not have significant delays in language acquisition, cognitive development, or self-help skills, and limitations are not apparent until the child is in social situations with peers. Consequently, the disorder tends to be identified at a later age, usually when the student is 11 years old (Howlin & Asgharian, 1999).

The measured intelligence of students with ASD ranges from superior to profound intellectual disability (American Psychiatric Association, 2000); however, most students with the disability score in the below-average range (70–85). Higher IQ scores do not mean that other challenging characteristics of ASD are not prominent. Increased measured intelligence does not always lead to corresponding gains in adaptive skills and improvements in the social use of language. However, students with higher IQ scores are less likely to exhibit (1) gross deficits in social interaction and emotional expression, (2) inappropriate play, (3) self-injurious behavior, and (4) delays in motor and language development (National Research Council, 2001).

> ## Pause & Reflect
>
> Why are students with Asperger's disorder identified at such an advanced age? Can you think of any early patterns of behavior that parents and educators can look for that can help screen for the disability?

Self-Injurious Behavior. Self-injurious behavior (SIB) is self-directed aggression manifested by severe head banging, punching, scratching, and/or biting, and it is among the most frightening behaviors exhibited by some students with severe disabilities. More common in children with autistic disorder than those with Asperger's disorder, approximately 10% to 20% of those with the disability engage in SIB. Elimination of these behaviors is a high priority. In addition to the obvious health issues, self-injury precludes placement in inclusive settings and limits access to many learning, working, and community opportunities (O'Reilly, Sigafoos, Lancioni, Edrisinha, & Andrews, 2005). From the behavioral perspective, SIB is believed to be a learned response reinforced by positive and/or negative stimuli. Examples of positive reinforcement include others' attention and sensory gain; negative reinforcement takes the form of escape from demands or situations the individual with ASD wishes to avoid. Fortunately, interventions based on functional behavioral assessment can reduce self-injury, and many structured techniques and programs have been developed to do so (Rosenberg et al., 2004).

Effective Instruction for Students with Autism Spectrum Disorders

Strategy
Strategy 15.7 in Chapter 15 presents step-by-step information on how to conduct a functional behavioral assessment.

As evidenced by the efforts of the Heritage High School science team (in the accompanying box, "Teaching Students with Autism Spectrum Disorders"), collaborative interventions across academic and social domains can have considerable success in meeting the intensive needs of students with ASD.

Interventions are most successful when based on the functional needs of the students. We provide detailed step-by-step descriptions of evidence-based intervention strategies in Chapters 11 to 16. Next, we highlight several general-case instructional interventions and techniques for elementary and secondary students with ASD.

Effective Instruction for Elementary Students

Elementary students with ASD usually require instruction to improve academic performance, social-behavioral functioning, and language skills. Next, we highlight the instructional content typically required of students with ASD and the evidence-based methods used to teach the content in inclusive classrooms.

Instructional Content.

Academics. No specific academic curriculum or methodology exists for teaching academics to elementary students with ASD. State standards, the school district curriculum, assessments of students' needs, and, to some degree, common sense dictate the academic programs for students with

Teaching Students with Autism Spectrum Disorders in Inclusive Classrooms: Challenges and Strategies
Heritage High School Science Co-Teaching Team

Until recently, the majority of students with ASD received most of their academic instruction in specialized, segregated settings. We now know that a significant number of students with ASD can, with appropriate supports and accommodations, succeed in general education classes, even in high-demand subject areas such as math and science. Consider the strategies used at Heritage High School. Denise Pohill (a special educator), Gina Craun (a biology teacher), and Casey Van Harssel (a chemistry teacher) are members of one of several science co-teaching teams. In addition to teaching students with a range of special needs—predominantly students with learning disabilities—the team provides supportive instruction to two students with ASD: Oren and Leon (not their real names) in required biology and chemistry classes. Despite a number of challenges, the team has been pleased with the success of their cooperative instructional efforts. Several strategies have been particularly useful in addressing the needs of Oren and Leon.

First, the team recognizes that the two boys with ASD do not respond well to surprises. The students find support and comfort in specific routines and perform best when explicitly prepared for activities. Therefore, Denise Pohill "primes" all of the students in the class for lessons by using a series of graphic organizers that visually contextualizes objectives and activities into the big picture of instructional unit. This universal technique allows both Oren and Leon to prepare for and focus on the essential aspects of lessons, while also providing useful advance organizers for other students in the class.

Second, knowing that group activities can result in anxiety and withdrawal, the co-teaching team enlists the help of peers to work with Oren and Leon during labs, cooperative learning activities, and guided practice activities. Recognizing that both students have difficulties socializing and communicating, the co-teaching team is very careful when selecting peers, ensuring that they have the social maturity to deal with unusual behaviors. Once selected, the helping peers get a "crash course" on the typical characteristics of ASD and how best to respond to both appropriate and inappropriate behaviors when they occur.

Third, Casey Van Harssel and Gina Craun, the science specialists, ensure that the science lessons modified for Oren and Leon remain rigorous. They work with Denise Pohill to identify essential components of the curriculum and help integrate them into whatever lesson and assignment accommodations and supports are necessary, such as guided notes and study guides. Mr. Van Harssel has also found that the new "high-tech white board" helps cue specific elements of his lessons and, in general, has increased student attention to his presentations.

As you can imagine, the major challenge facing the science co-teaching team is time. Considerable preparation is needed to format units, lessons, guided notes, and assignments for the students. Also challenging are the instances—however infrequent—when Oren and Leon act out and the difficulties the two boys have completing their work. To address the work-completion issue, the team has been thinking of ways to encourage agenda book use, a procedure that the two students have not yet adopted.

The co-teaching team members recognize that to provide supportive instruction they need to understand the typical characteristics of ASD as well as the specific functions that prompt Oren's and Leon's individual behaviors. Although this requires considerable time and energy, the team believes its efforts are paying off. The bottom line: Both Oren and Leon are doing well—better than passing—in their science classes!

autistic and Asperger's disorders (Olley, 2005). Some students with ASD learn academic skills readily, while others struggle with basic preacademic skills. Regardless of their level of functioning, students with ASD have difficulty remembering and organizing information and need instructional supports to increase attention to critical elements of a task. Higher-functioning students with Asperger's disorder also benefit from individualized supports and accommodations, particularly in subjects that require large amounts of oral comprehension encountered in lectures and written assignments.

Strategy 14.1 in Chapter 14 provides step-by-step information on how to employ explicit unit and lesson visual support organizers.

Strategy

Social-Behavioral Functioning. Instruction in social-behavioral functioning typically focuses on age-appropriate behaviors that students must learn to survive and ultimately thrive in the real world. Although based on assessed strengths and needs, lesson content for elementary students with autistic disorder typically involves daily living skills, self-care skills, functional communication skills, and those intangible social graces that enable one to participate in the community. It is not unusual for some students with ASD to need explicit instruction in how to play with peers and, as they grow older, how to deal with the emotions and anxiety of being "different." Students with Asperger's disorder need instruction in understanding facial expressions and gestures, comprehending nonliteral figurative language (i.e., idioms and metaphors), discriminating when others' intentions do not match their words, and understanding the implicit rules of social functioning—those ways of behaving that are not acquired through direct instruction (Smith-Myles & Simpson, 2001).

Language. Teachers determine the content of language instruction based on the student's ability to verbalize along with her corresponding intelligence level. Students who are nonverbal may learn to communicate through the use of pictures, symbols, communication boards, sign language, and electronic devices that enable the child to press a button representing a symbol that is produced verbally. For those who are verbal, instruction often focuses on aspects of language production, including pragmatics, syntax, semantics, and articulation. For students with Asperger's disorder, pragmatics, the social use of language, is one area that usually requires intensive instruction. Specific instruction focuses on recognizing the purpose of communication, speaking in a conversational manner, being sensitive to the needs of the listener, as well as beginning and ending conversations in a socially appropriate fashion (Paul, 2005).

> **Strategy**
>
> Strategy 16.8 in Chapter 16 provides step-by-step information on how to best use augmentative/alternative communication.

Instructional Methods. Instructional methods that teachers commonly use to improve the academic, social, and language skills of elementary students with ASD include applied behavior analysis, augmentative/alternative communication strategies, and social skills instruction.

Applied Behavior Analysis (ABA). ABA is a highly structured behavior-change process that involves (1) conducting a baseline assessment of a targeted behavior, (2) implementing a behavior-change intervention, (3) collecting ongoing data on changes in the targeted behavior during intervention, (4) modifying the intervention based on the data, and (5) generalizing the effects of the intervention to untreated conditions and individuals (Arick, Krug, Fullerton, Loos, & Falco, 2005).

One technique commonly employed as an intervention for students with severe ASD is discrete trial instruction (DTI). DTI is a carefully organized and intensive approach in which teachers identify a specific skill—typically through a functional assessment of behavior. Students then receive skill-acquisition instruction within a highly structured, one-to-one format. Teachers provide prompts as necessary and deliver explicit reinforcement when students perform the skill correctly (Dunlap & Fox, 1999). Teachers often respond to incorrect responses with a neutral "no" or a withdrawal of attention, in an effort to decrease the frequency and intensity of the behavior. Careful data collection allows for progress monitoring and, when necessary, changes in programming (e.g., providing more prompts, increasing the rate of reinforcement).

In inclusive classrooms, teachers enlist peers to initiate appropriate prosocial behaviors from their classmates with ASD. Specifically, teachers instruct peers to initiate play-organizer behaviors such as sharing, helping, affection, and praise. Teachers reinforce both peers and the students with ASD for their efforts: peers,

Students with ASD benefit from role-playing activities in which they practice and receive reinforcement for appropriate social behaviors.

for initiating contact; and the students with ASD, for initially responding and then making contact themselves. By reinforcing both the peers and the students with ASD, teachers increase, maintain, and generalize social contacts beyond the classroom (National Research Council, 2001).

Augmentative and Alternative Communication (AAC) Strategies. Providing alternative modes of communication can be a key element in inclusive lesson participation. Picture boards and picture-exchange procedures, for example, are low-cost visual systems that enable students to receive and express common communicative functions. The Picture Exchange Communication System (PECS) (Frost & Bondy, 2000) is a comprehensive method in which students initiate requests by using icons to request objects or activities. Voice-output communication aids (VOCAs) are portable higher-tech devices that allow messages to be accessed through graphic symbols and words on computerized displays. This technology, with the capacity to store endless combinations of spoken and written text, provides students the opportunity to participate in lessons through more normalized, natural interactions (National Research Council, 2001).

Social Skills Instruction. Higher-functioning students with ASD require instruction in interpreting social skills, the process of understanding the implicit rules of social functioning. Teachers achieve this by explicitly teaching ways to interpret the often unspoken subtleties of social interactions. One method for teaching these skills involves the use of **social stories,** a technique in which students dissect and assess causes and effects that occur during social interactions. The teacher and students discuss strategies to prevent errors and develop plans to minimize occurrences of the errors. In another use of social stories, students create and/or interpret cartoon illustrations that reflect everyday social encounters. Discussions of the visual representations of cartoon characters' actions, verbalizations, and thoughts help students analyze the social exchanges (Smith-Myles & Simpson, 2001). Students with severe difficulties in social skills require highly structured ABA techniques to develop functional communication skills (e.g., initiating interactions, responding to others' inquiries, etc.) as well as naturalistic opportunities to apply those skills in inclusive classrooms.

> ## Pause & Reflect
>
> Low-cost digitized technologies have the potential for providing an increased supply of creative ways to enhance the communication skills of students with ASD. Can you think of how universally designed portable electronic devices (e.g., Palm Pilots, iPods, etc.) can be adapted for use to benefit students with ASD?

Low-cost, higher-tech devices can enhance the communication and academic performance of students with ASD.

Strategy 15.8 in Chapter 15 provides step-by-step information on how to implement social stories interventions.

Strategy

Effective Instruction for Secondary Students

In any given semester, approximately 62% of secondary students with ASD take at least one general education course (Newman, 2007). The majority of students in these classes receive the standard curriculum with functionally appropriate modifications and accommodations. Many of the methods that are effective in teaching elementary students with ASD are also successful at the middle and high school levels. However, in addition to basic academic, language, and social skills (areas in which many students with severe ASD require protracted work through their high school years), secondary-level instruction focuses on subject-area content, vocational training, and transitions to postschool environments.

Content Instruction. In Chapter 14 we provide a number of specific strategies for teaching subject-area content to secondary students with a range of disabilities. Students with ASD, in particular, require explicit organization and structured routines in both lessons and their learning environments. General and special education teachers provide these specialized supports in several ways, including the following:

- Create easily accessed prompts (e.g., flashcards) that clearly and succinctly summarize the critical information of lessons and units.
- Prepare students for new content by sending home lesson and unit organizers that teachers will introduce in days or weeks to come.
- Use visual organizers that introduce key concepts and highlight relationships between and among them.
- Prompt attention to essential content through a series of personalized nonverbal cues (e.g., secret hand signals).
- Facilitate strategic thinking by emphasizing concrete problem-solving steps and actions.
- Introduce mnemonic aids that assist students to remember problem-solving steps and procedures.
- Model step-by-step ways for completing assignments correctly.
- Provide alternative methods for completing assignments that reduce or circumvent extensive written output (e.g., audiotaping or videotaping, computer icons, etc.) (Unok Marks et al., 2003).

> **Strategy**
>
> Strategy 14.3 in Chapter 14 provides step-by-step information on how to best present mnemonic strategies during academic instruction.

Because socialization and communication do not come easily to students with ASD, teachers should take care when configuring seating and group-work arrangements. Students with ASD work best when seated near the teacher or an understanding peer. During group activities, teachers often need to guide the involvement of students with ASD with specific prompts and cues. For example, during cooperative learning activities, it may be best to assign specific student tasks for each of the members of the group. Explicit individual assignments minimize the chance that students with the disability are marginalized and facilitates full participation in activities, even allowing for the showcasing of special talents (Safran, 2002).

Pause & Reflect

Maintaining family involvement in transition planning and instructional activities is essential to the postschool success of students with ASD. What specific actions can teachers take to encourage and support family participation in the transition process?

Transition. Transition planning for students with ASD should begin early in the teen years and should involve teachers, families, and community service providers. Two areas of transition that general and special educators typically collaborate in are vocational training and preparation for postsecondary education.

Vocational Training. Educators use three major approaches to vocational training for students with ASD (Gerhardt & Holmes, 2005). **Supported employment** is a process that recognizes that an individual with ASD can function in the general workforce with ongoing support. Options of supported employment range from intensive one-to-one job-coach assistance models to group-oriented cluster-support arrangements. **Entrepreneurial supports** are business entities that are built on the skills and interests of those with disabilities. They are self-sustaining, for-profit corporations that pay the salaries of workers with disabilities as well as the support staff. **Sheltered workshops** are segregated facilities designed to provide training and employment opportunities for individuals with severe disabilities. Although common, sheltered workshops, by nature of their design, may not be in the best interests of many individuals with ASD. Isolation from normative events with limited supervision and work on repetitive tasks with little feedback are not effective ways to promote personal growth and to foster quality of life for individuals who require interventions in socialization and communication.

What are the roles of the general and special education teacher in vocational training? As members of the instructional team, teachers task analyze the vocational requirements and combine tangible components into doable tasks matching the strengths of individual students. Rather than viewing the actual on-site vocational field experiences as final placements, the instructional team views them as formative learning activities. Consequently, in-class lessons and practice activities address challenges experienced during on-the-job training. In addition to working directly with the students, teachers also provide the students' co-workers and supervisors with practical training and supports to deal with challenging behaviors if and when they occur.

Postsecondary Education. Significant numbers of students with high-functioning ASD are transitioning to postsecondary and higher-education settings. Attending college represents a well-deserved accomplishment that should be celebrated and savored. These successful transitions are also hard-earned victories for families, teachers, and service providers. Still, these milestones signal the need for additional training and support. Not surprisingly, the organizational, functional, and social aspects of college life tend to be most problematic, outweighing the challenges posed by advanced academic content. To best address these issues, peer mentors and college disability personnel help students in the following ways:

- Expand their social circles (e.g., support students in dormitories/dining halls, and initiate conversations during social events).
- Provide guidance in ways to integrate interests into social opportunities (demonstrate the value of clubs and advocacy groups).
- Coach methods of time management, independent living, speaking with professors, and stress management.
- Consider the value of students' having their own rooms where they can reflect, decompress, and reduce the stress associated with managing their idiosyncratic behaviors (Shea & Mesibov, 2005).

Final Thoughts Regarding Effective Practices

The inclusion of students with ASD requires the coordination of a number of practices related to effective instruction and behavior management beyond those presented in this chapter. In Chapters 11 to 16, we provide step-by-step descriptions of many effective practices that are useful for students with this disability and others who struggle in school. Several of these practices that are particularly useful for teachers who work with students with ASD include effective strategies to develop explicit rules and procedures (Strategy 15.1 in Chapter 15) and to facilitate peer relationships through peer-assisted learning strategies (Strategy 13.4 in Chapter 13) and cooperative learning (Strategy 13.2). Teachers also benefit from specific techniques for working with paraeducators (Strategy 11.5 in Chapter 11) and families (Strategy 11.6). For those students who require enhanced technological supports, we provide details on selecting assistive devices (Strategy 16.5 in Chapter 16) and supporting students in the use of devices (Strategy 16.8). We're sure you will find many of the other strategies in Chapters 11 to 16 useful in addressing the needs of students with ASD in inclusive classrooms.

Summary

When provided appropriate supports and accommodations, students with ASD benefit from participation in general education settings. We presented the following major points in this chapter:

Who are students with ASD? Definition and methods of identification

- The two most common forms of ASD are autistic disorder and Asperger's disorder.
- Autistic disorder is a severe developmental disability characterized by an early age of onset, poor social development, impairments in language development, and rigidity in behavior.
- Asperger's disorder is characterized by severe and sustained impairments in social interactions and the development of restricted, repetitive patterns of behavior, interests, and activities.
- The identification of ASD requires measurement of functioning across disciplines. Students are first screened, and those suspected of having the disability are referred to more intensive evaluations.

Prevalence of students with ASD

- Recent estimates indicate that the prevalence of ASD ranges from 3.4 to 6.7 per 1,000 children, much higher than rates reported in the 1980s and early 1990s.
- Approximately 225,000 students, 0.21% of the school-age population between the ages of 6 and 21, are served under the autism classification for special education services.
- ASD occurs worldwide and affects males four times more often than females.

Educational placements for students with ASD

- 11.6% of those identified as having autism under IDEA receive special education in segregated environments.
- Approximately 61% are included in general education classrooms from 21% to approximately 80% of the school day.
- Opportunities for inclusion are important because they allow for meaningful contact with typically developing peers as well as activities that augment instruction in the academic, social, and behavioral skills that students with ASD require.

Major characteristics of students with ASD

- Three characteristics are universal and specific to ASD: communication skills deficiencies; limitations in social reciprocity; and repetitive, stereotypical, and ritualistic behaviors.
- Children with autism are typically identified before the age of 3; Asperger's disorder is typically diagnosed at approximately 11 years of age.
- Approximately 10% to 20% of those with ASD engage in some form of self-injurious behavior (SIB).

Effective instruction for students with ASD

- Although instruction for elementary students with ASD is based on individualized needs, instruction usually emphasizes basic academic skills, social behavioral functioning, and language.
- Instructional methods commonly used in teaching students with ASD include applied behavior analysis (ABA), augmentative and alternative communication (AAC) strategies, and the direct teaching of social skills.
- For many secondary students with ASD, the focus of instruction turns to subject-area content and the transition to postschool activities.

Addressing Professional Standards

Standards addressed in Chapter 8 include:

CEC Standards: (1) foundations, (2) development and characteristics of learners, (3) individual learning differences, (4) instructional strategies.

INTASC Standards: Principle 1—Understand central concepts of the discipline; Principle 2—Provide learning opportunities to support the learning and development of all students.

Praxis™ II Standards: Knowledge-based core principles: (1) understanding exceptionalities, (3) delivery of services to students with disabilities. Application of core principles: (1) curriculum, (2) instruction, (5) professional roles/issues/ literature.

Students with Communication Disorders and Students with Sensory Impairments

KEY TOPICS

After reading this chapter you will:

- Know the definitions and criteria used to identify students with communication disorders and students with sensory impairments.
- Know how many students are identified with communication disorders and how many students have sensory impairments.
- Be able to identify the educational settings in which students with communication disorders and those with sensory disabilities are served.
- Be able to identify major characteristics of students with communication disorders and major characteristics of students with sensory disabilities.
- Understand key issues and challenges related to including students with communication disorders and students with sensory disabilities in general education classrooms.
- Know effective practices for including students with communication disorders and those with sensory disabilities in general education classrooms.

chapter 9

Perspectives on Including Students with Communication Disorders

Interview with Madge Goins, Second-Grade General Education Teacher, Mull Elementary

The benefit of including a student with speech and language difficulties, according to Madge Goins at Mull Elementary, is that inclusion "allows the child to be successful with other peers [and] it allows them to grow at their own pace. It puts them in an environment that allows them to learn from other students' ideas. They can also feel important because they have peers their age, on their level, to share compatible social skills with."

But with Corey, a second grader, at first the teachers experienced some frustration. Ms. Goins explained, "He could be very difficult to understand at times. When we tried to work with him, he was very insecure. Sometimes he would cover his face in social settings when he couldn't express his thoughts." Additionally, his communication disorders interfered with his writing ability. "He was unable to sound out words correctly, which led to frustration with completing thoughts orally and in writing. The challenge was getting him confident enough to express and share his ideas."

Corey, with a lot of teacher support, ultimately experienced some critical success, and, as Ms. Goins said,

> [His success] made a lot of difference in his life. . . . We tried a number of different things and found some especially effective practices . . . with this child. We used raised lined paper, letter tiles, pictures, scripting and copying writings, highlighting words, and paired activities. He seemed more motivated and confident when he was praised for completion of tasks. His peers encouraged him because they understood him and made him a part of the class.

For Madge Goins, her biggest success was seeing his growth in his writing ability.

> He went from having no concept of the meaning of letters and words to being able to write short stories with four to six sentences by the end of the year. The students presented a book they had made as a group. He was able to write, illustrate, and present his page of the book successfully and with confidence.

Being in an inclusive classroom with a supportive teacher made a huge difference for Corey by the end of the year.

We felt like we were effective teachers for this student because of the growth shown in many ways throughout the year. [He] made gains in reading, spelling, writing, math, and social skills. The child went from covering his face and no smiles to smiling and expressing his thoughts freely every day. There was a time in class when we discussed dinosaurs, and he was so excited to stand up in front of the class and share about his dinosaur. This wouldn't have happened at the beginning of the year.

When thinking about Corey's inclusion, Ms. Goins offered some advice to new teachers:

Collaboration in an inclusive setting is important to success for individual issues with children. Always be a learner yourself. You won't have the answers for every student right away, so collaborate and research for new ideas. Our philosophy of teaching is that each child is equally important, and the way any of your students learn depends on the attitude you take into that classroom.

Introduction

myeducationlab

Go to MyEducationLab, select the topic *Communication Disorders*, and go to the Activities and Applications section. As you watch the videos entitled "Who Is George?" and "Communication Disorders: George's Support," think about the accommodations and support that enable George to succeed in academic and social environments.

Students with communication disorders and students with sensory disabilities face unique yet very different kinds of challenges. Successful placements in inclusive classrooms can be advantageous for both groups.

Some students with communication disorders, such as Corey, in the introductory vignette, not only have trouble conveying what they mean, but because of their disability, can experience secondary negative effects such as being embarrassed in front of peers. As a result, they might shut down, participate very little, and consequently may not experience learning opportunities other students enjoy.

To improve communication skills and to counter these other outcomes, teachers like Madge Goins work hard to help students like Corey overcome their communication disorders. Close collaboration with a professional speech–language pathologist (SLP) is an essential component for effective instruction for students with communication disorders. Although in the past, SLPs worked almost exclusively by pulling students out of the classroom for one-on-one therapy, today much of their work is done in general education classrooms and other natural settings. Only rarely will these students leave the classroom for brief periods of time to meet with an SLP. And when this does occur, it becomes critical for the teacher and SLP to communicate closely so the work done outside the classroom can be imported for successful application in the more natural setting of the classroom.

Students with sensory impairments include those who are blind or have a significant vision loss; those who are deaf or have a significant hearing loss; and those who have both a vision and hearing loss, which could result in a classification of deaf-blindness. Like students with communication disorders, these students also face serious challenges, although of a different nature. Their limitations involve obtaining adequate information through residual sensory abilities and/or through the use of their other senses. Students with sensory impairments require strategies to help them gain information easily available to other students.

If you have a student in your classroom with sensory impairments, you will have the benefit of collaborating with a special education teacher with expertise in visual disabilities or

Pause & Reflect

Interestingly, students with communication disorders constitute a "high-incidence" disability, and those with sensory disability are a very "low-incidence" group. How does the relative incidence of a disability affect your personal knowledge and experience? Do you think this affects your ability to understand these groups and be an effective teacher?

hearing impairments. This individual will work closely with you to better ensure an appropriate and successful education for the student.

Sometimes students with communication disorders may avoid participation because of their disability.

Who Are Students with Communication Disorders?

Definitions

The two major types of communication disorders are language disorders and speech disorders. **Language disorders** include problems in formulating and comprehending spoken messages, and **speech disorders** consist of problems related to the verbal transmission of messages. Justice (2006) explained communication disorders in this way:

> *Individuals are normal and effective communicators when they are able to formulate, transmit, receive, and comprehend information from other individuals successfully. A communication disorder or impairment is present when a person has significant difficulty in one of more of these aspects of communication when compared with other people sharing the same language, dialect and culture.* (pp. 21–22)

Speech disorders interfere significantly with the speaker's ability to say something in a way that can be easily understood. A speech disorder can also call attention to the speaker and sometimes cause personal discomfort. The most common speech disorders include phonological and articulation disorders, fluency disorders, voice disorders, and motor speech disorders. Figure 9.1 describes common speech disorders.

An individual can have a language disorder even though her speaking ability may be fine. For example, an elementary school student might have a language disorder if she has a difficult time finding and using the right word or combination of words; using words in the right order; or using the correct words, phrases, or sentences at the right time. Your ability to understand a student's words may be fine, but you may still have a difficult time comprehending what he or she is trying to say. Experts usually divide language disorders into three major categories: disorders of form, content (or semantics), and use (or pragmatics) (Justice, 2006; Owens, Metz, & Haas, 2003; Peña & Davis, 2000). Figure 9.2 provides descriptions of different language disorders.

Identification of Students with Communication Disorders

Children as young as 12 to 18 months old may show signs of delayed or impaired communication development. For some of these children, the delays evolve into disorders that continue into the preschool and school years and perhaps beyond. The communication challenges exhibited by

Pause & Reflect

Speech disorders that are very obvious, such as stuttering, will draw a great deal of unwanted attention to the speaker. How do you think a young child or an adolescent would react to having such a condition? What are some things you think you could do as a teacher to help mitigate this potential embarrassment?

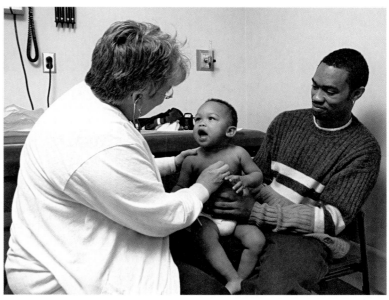

Parents and pediatricians can often recognize communication disorders when children are very young.

Just the Facts   Students with Communication Disorders

Who are they?	Students with communication disorders include those with language disorders, speech disorders, or sometimes a combination of both.
What are typical characteristics?	• Language disorders include (1) form disorders (difficulty making correct sounds, constructing words, or connecting the words correctly); (2) content or semantic disorders (lack of word-meaning knowledge); and (3) use or pragmatic disorders (application of language in social contexts). • Speech disorders include (1) phonological/articulation disorders (distortions, substitutions, or omissions of speech sounds); (2) fluency disorders (the most common is stuttering); (3) voice disorders (e.g., speaking with a harsh or raspy voice); and (4) motor speech disorders (difficulty using the physical components of speech, often due to a neuromuscular disorder).
What are the demographics?	• About 2.3% of children enrolled in public schools are classified as having speech or language disabilities. This does not include other students with speech or language disabilities served under other disability categories. • Totally, about 5% of school-age individuals have speech disorders, and between 2% and 8% have specific language impairments.
Where are students educated?	• Most students with speech disorders are served in general education classrooms and receive speech therapy provided by speech–language pathologists (SLPs). • Communication disorders are common among many students with disabilities who may be in special education or general education classrooms.
How are students identified?	• Speech and language disorders are often identified by parents, preschool teachers, or pediatricians. • Identifying the specific nature of the speech or language problem requires formal assessment by an SLP.
What causes communication disorders?	• Sometimes the cause of a communication disorder can be tied to a specific physiological etiology, an organic cause; sometimes it cannot, in which case it is referred to as a *functional disorder.* • Organic causes of speech disorders can be congenital (present from the time of birth), or they may be acquired later in life.
What are the outcomes?	• Many language and speech disorders improve either without therapy (especially with young children) or with therapy. • Some individuals with these disorders have them throughout life.

children may range from relatively mild to more severe. Parents, pediatricians, and preschool or elementary school teachers may identify communication problems and refer the child to an SLP for formal evaluation.

Because many different types of communication disorders exist, the SLP must use an assessment procedure that will best identify the type of disorder and relevant conditions related to the disorder. Areas of assessment include language, speech, cognition, voice, fluency, hearing, feeding, and swallowing disorders. During the assessment, the SLP will do the following:

- Review existing records to gather relevant historical medical, educational, and psychological information.
- Interview the student, parents, caregivers, and teachers to acquire information about the student's communication history and current condition.
- Ask different individuals, including the classroom teacher, to fill out questionnaires about the student's communication characteristics.

Figure 9.1   Common Speech Disorders

- *Phonological and articulation disorders* impair a person's ability to clearly create speech sounds. Instead of producing standard speech sounds, the speaker produces sounds that include distortions, substitutions, omissions, or additions. A distortion occurs when the speaker produces a nonstandard phoneme, like a lisp. A substitution is the replacement of one phoneme with another, such as "shair" for "chair." An omission is the deletion of a phoneme such as saying "chai" for "chair." An addition is the addition of an extra phoneme such as "chuh air" for "chair" (Owens et al., 2003).
- *Fluency disorders* are interruptions in the normal flow of speech. The most common fluency disorder is stuttering. Stuttering is often affected by environmental and circumstantial conditions and can draw a great deal of attention to the speaker and often cause stress. Definitions of stuttering usually note that it consists of producing an abnormally high number of sound and syllable repetitions, prolongations, or blocks (Shapiro, 1999). People who stutter usually have primary stuttering behaviors and secondary behaviors. The primary behaviors are speech characteristics such as repetitions, prolongations, and blocks. The secondary behaviors are reactions to stuttering that occur as a person tries to deal with the verbalizations such as blinking eyes, opening the jaws, pursing lips, substituting easier words for words that are more difficult, or inserting "uh" before a difficult word (Gillam, 2000).
- *Voice disorders* occur when a person's pitch, loudness, or phonatory quality differs significantly from others of the same sex, age, ethnicity, and cultural background. When compared to peers, the person with a voice disorder has an uncommonly high- or low-pitched voice, or a voice that is too soft or too loud or that has unusual phonatory qualities. To be considered a "disorder," the condition of the voice must be different enough to draw attention to the person or to adversely affect performance in school, at home, or in the community. Speech therapists use a variety of terms to describe a person's voice, but the most commonly used are a harsh or strained voice, a breathy voice, and a hoarse voice (Dalston, 2000).
- *Motor speech disorders* are neurological disorders that affect a person's speech. Speaking requires complex, coordinated movements of very small muscles. Because these movements have a neurological origin, neurological insult or trauma may adversely affect one or more of the building blocks of speech (Maas & Robin, 2006).

Figure 9.2   Language Disorders

- *Form disorders* are disorders in the formation of sounds used to make words and word parts (phonology); disorders in the rules for constructing words and parts of words so that they have meaning (morphology); and disorders in applying rules for connecting the words together correctly (syntax).
- *Content disorders,* or semantics disorders, occur when an individual does not use the specific words or word combinations as language rules require. For example, if a person consistently uses words or phrases that are not meaningful to other people who use the same language, or uses words or phrases that are not valid for the situation, the person is experiencing a content or semantics problem.
- *Use disorders,* or pragmatics disorders, are characterized by individuals who do not use language appropriate for their current social context. A child who has a problem in pragmatics might have difficulty initiating conversations, taking turns with partners, engaging in extensive dialogues, or engaging in a wide range of other language uses in specific situations (e.g., greetings, making requests, or commenting).

- Conduct a systematic observation to assess key skills and abilities such as paying attention, understanding abstract concepts, answering questions, seeking help, or explaining complex details.
- Conduct a speech- or language-sampling procedure with the student to get a clearer picture of the key communication characteristics.
- Use formal tests to learn more about the student's speech and language characteristics. (Justice, 2006; Owens et al., 2003)

Prevalence

According to the most recent U.S. Department of Education (2007) data, almost 1.5 million public school students from 3 to 21 years of age receive speech–language services, about 22% of all students receiving IDEA services. Within the general population, 2.8% of children from 3 to 5 years old and 1.7% of those from 6 to 21 years old receive speech–language services through public schools.

It is important for you to know that the preceding numbers and percentages represent students whose primary IDEA disability category is "speech or language impairment." In addition, many students classified as having other disabilities have communication disorders as secondary disabilities. These students also receive therapy services from SLPs.

Service Delivery

Most young children (3 to 5 years old) who receive services for communication disorders are in early childhood education settings with children without disabilities, although some are also served in early childhood special education programs. During their school years, almost 90% of students with communication disorders are served primarily in the general education classroom (U.S. Department of Education, 2007). Although students with communication disorders are almost always included in general education settings, SLPs will develop individual therapy plans for each of them. The SLP will interpret the results of the assessment and develop an intervention plan designed to be effective, efficient, and easy for the student to follow (Justice, 2006).

SLPs may provide support for students in the general education classroom, or they may work with students in separate therapy settings. The different types of contact an SLP may have with a student, as approved by the American Speech-Language-Hearing Association (2000), are described in Figure 9.3.

Pause & Reflect

Many parents of students with speech or language disorders request frequent, one-to-one therapeutic services from the SLP. But as you can see in Figure 9.3, many types of SLP contacts are possible. How would you explain to a parent that one-to-one therapy sessions are not the only way, or even necessarily the best way, for a child with a communication disorder to improve communication?

| Figure 9.3 | Types of Contacts Between the Speech–Language Pathologist and Students Approved by the American Speech-Language-Hearing Association |

- *Monitor.* The SLP sees the student for a specified amount of time per grading period to monitor or check on the student's speech and language skills. The primary purpose is to determine that the student's communication skills are improving or being maintained.
- *Collaborative consultation.* The SLP, the general and/or special education teacher(s), and parents/families work together to facilitate a student's communication and learning in educational environments. This is an indirect model in which the SLP does not provide direct service to the student.
- *Classroom-based.* This model is also known as integrated services, curriculum-based, transdisciplinary, interdisciplinary, or inclusive programming. Its purpose is to help the student learn effective communication skills within natural environments.
- *Pullout.* This is perhaps the most traditional form of SLP services in public schools. In the pullout model, services are provided to students individually or in small groups in the speech–language resource room.
- *Self-contained program.* Sometimes the SLP is the classroom teacher responsible for providing both academic/curriculum instruction and speech–language remediation.
- *Community-based.* Under this model, the SLP provides communication services to students at home or in the community.
- *Combination.* As you might expect, one of the previously discussed models used alone might not be desirable or sufficient. When this is the case, the SLP will use two or more service-delivery options in combination.

Source: Adapted with permission from *Guidelines for the roles and responsibilities of the school-based speech-language pathologist.* Available from www.asha.org/policy/. Copyright 2000 by the American Speech-Language-Hearing Association.

Major Characteristics of Students with Communication Disorders

Many students with communication disorders will not vary a great deal from their peers except for their specific communication disorder. However, in some cases the student's communication disorder may be related to other characteristics.

Academic and Cognitive Performance

A student can have a speech disorder yet be as capable academically as the student sitting next to him. Although the speech disorder may be of concern, especially from a personal or social point of view, it will not necessarily have an impact on the student's learning ability. Other students may be classified as having a specific language impairment (SLI; Justice, 2006). Although children with SLI have significant variety in their language profiles, Justice reports that you are likely to see the following characteristics:

- Inconsistent skills across language domains (e.g., being strong in phonology but weak in syntax and morphology)
- A history of slow vocabulary development
- Word-finding problems
- Difficulty with grammatical production and comprehension, particularly with the use of verbs
- Problems with social skills, behavior, and attention

Many students who exhibit language disorders at the preschool level successfully overcome them because of either intervention or language growth and development. However, about 50% of these children continue to have language disorders during elementary school and even into high school and adulthood. When language disorders continue beyond the preschool years, the students who exhibit them are likely to be ultimately classified as having learning disabilities, intellectual disabilities, or emotional-behavioral disorders (Owens et al., 2003).

Behavior Performance and Social Skills

Because communication skills are an essential part of social relations, if an individual lacks adequate speech or language skills, social behavior might be affected in different ways. A student may become withdrawn and avoid others, like Corey in the opening vignette. Others may interact inappropriately or may try to compensate for communication weaknesses by undesirable interactions such as aggression or disruption.

Evidence is not entirely clear that communication disorders can *cause* behavioral or emotional disabilities, but researchers have documented a correlation; communication disorders occur very frequently among students classified as having emotional or behavioral disorders. In one review of research, 71% of students who were labeled with emotional and behavioral disabilities had language deficits, and 57% of the students identified with language deficits also were classified as having emotional and behavioral disabilities (Benner, Nelson, & Epstein, 2002). Clearly, having a language disorder places a child at greater risk for emotional and behavioral challenges.

Pause & Reflect

Have you ever experienced a communication problem, even a temporary one, that led to your engagement in some atypical or uncommon behavior? How did others react to your problem? How did you react? Was it emotionally difficult?

Effective Instruction for Students with Communication Disorders
Effective Instruction for Elementary Students

As we discussed previously, an SLP may have contact with and deliver services to students with communication disorders in a variety of ways (see Figure 9.3). In addition, you, as the classroom teacher, can be supportive when working with students with communication disorders in your inclusive classroom.

Strategies to Achieve Academic Success. A major factor for the success of your students who have communication disorders will be your willingness to collaborate with the SLP to provide support for these students when they are in the classroom. The SLP not only will provide direct therapeutic services to students but also will collaborate with you to develop plans that will enhance the effectiveness of direct therapy. Suggestions to help you better work with the SLP in your school are in Figure 9.4. Chapter 11 provides even more information on how to collaborate with professsionals.

> **Strategy**
>
> For step-by-step information on key components for effect collaboration, see Strategy 11.1 in Chapter 11.

Strategies to Achieve Social Success. If a communication disorder draws unfavorable attention to a student, or if the disorder interferes with typical interactions and social relationships, as is sometimes the case, the classroom teacher can play an important role in helping students become more socially successful. In addition to collaborating with the SLP, the following classroom interventions will be helpful:

> **Strategy**
>
> For step-by-step information on how to improve peer buddy interactions, see Strategy 11.7 in Chapter 11.

- Create positive social communication opportunities with peers in pairs and in small groups. Identify peer and grouping arrangements in which the student with the communication disorder can communicate comfortably.
- Promote appropriate social interactions in different situations and the opportunity for positive communicative interactions. This will allow students with communication disorders the chance to improve their communication skills without the threat of criticism from others.
- Reinforce appropriate use of speech and language skills. Encourage students to use their communication skills, and reinforce their efforts to do so. At the same time, avoid putting students into situations that would cause stress or discomfort.
- If social withdrawal or behavior problems occur, use positive behavior support principles to improve student behavior. You and the SLP may need to focus on creating alternative communication systems so that the student may be able to communicate less stressfully.

Figure 9.4	Suggestions for Effective Collaboration with Speech–Language Pathologists

- Discuss with the speech–language pathologist (SLP) any students who appear to be having trouble communicating, whether the problem is with speech or with language. Ask for ways to screen students to help you find those whose communication difficulties might not be readily apparent.
- Ask the SLP to suggest ways to build speech and language exercises into your daily routine, both for students who are receiving SLP services and as ways to improve the communication skills of your entire class. Ask the SLP to look at your lesson plans and offer suggestions, especially for students with communication disorders.
- Make sure you know the specific targeted skills the SLP is working on with individual students. Ask how you can help the students achieve these skills and generalize them.
- Let the SLP know how students with communication disorders are progressing. You may even offer to help keep some type of data on their performance.
- Keep the SLP informed about behavioral challenges the students may exhibit, and work with the SLP to find effective communication skills for students who exhibit such behaviors.

Sources: Hampton et al., 2002; Reed & Spicer, 2003; and Santos, 2002.

Effective Instruction for Secondary Students

Strategies to Achieve Academic Success. The suggestions for working effectively with an SLP in Figure 9.4 are also applicable when teaching older students. Adolescents with persistent speech disorders should continue to receive speech therapy, and classroom teachers should be aware of the nature of the therapy and how they can support it.

Students with communication disorders may need support to achieve social acceptance.

High school students who have language disorders may have difficulty in several areas related to academic performance. They could have trouble expressing ideas, responding appropriately to questions and comments, using appropriate social language, providing sufficient information for listeners, using redundancy in their language, having an inadequate sense of limits or boundaries, expressing their needs and ideas, initiating conversations with peers, and demonstrating appropriate conversational participation (Justice, 2006). Teachers may improve academic success for high school students with communication disorders by use of the following tactics:

- Allow students adequate time to express their ideas, to ask questions, and to comment. At times this could occur during class discussions, although this may depend on the nature of the discussion (i.e., some rapidly flowing discussions may not work well for this purpose). You may also find other opportunities to provide students with sufficient time to communicate, such as during independent work time or small-group activities.
- Reinforce correct language use, and positively redirect students who use inappropriate communication techniques. Especially when asking or answering questions and when commenting, students need to learn to use the correct vocabulary and grammatical structures.
- In separate sessions with small groups or with individuals, directly instruct students in key communication skills such as asking questions and taking turns. Students can also receive support with language skills such as vocabulary development.
- For some students, consider allowing alternatives to oral responding and reports. Students may be able to interact and engage in the subject matter more effectively if they are allowed to use augmentative and alternative communication (AAC) devices or to write responses instead of using oral language.

> **Strategy**
>
> For a step-by-step approach for using augmentative and alternative communication (AAC) devices, see Strategy 16.8 in Chapter 16.

Strategies to Achieve Social Success. Adolescence is a critical time for the development of appropriate social skills, and research has supported a strong link between communication disorders, especially language disorders, and socially inappropriate behavior and even occasionally violent behavior (Ritzman & Sanger, 2007; Sanger, Maag, & Shapera, 1994; Sanger, Moore-Brown, & Alt, 2000; Sanger, Spilker, Williams, & Belau, 2007). To improve the use of appropriate social language by high school students, we suggest the following tactics:

- Don't allow the student's communication disorder to interfere with a positive student–teacher relationship. Encourage students to express their feelings and concerns, and provide them with sufficient time and opportunities to do so. Let students know you are interested in their thoughts and ideas.
- Identify what students perceive as embarrassing situations, and help them to avoid them. Some students may not like to be called on to answer questions or express their opinions during whole-class discussions. Find private situations where they can participate without having other students attend to them. Encourage their participation in larger groups as their self-esteem improves.

- Teach students the meaning of words describing emotions, and give them practice in using them. Being able to use words such as *sad, scared, embarrassed, confused, lonely,* and *disappointed* may help students convey their feelings in a more appropriate manner rather than through classroom disruption.
- Identify students' interests, and encourage them to pursue learning in these and related areas. Use interest areas as a leverage to encourage appropriate vocabulary development and usage. Avoid being judgmental about students' interests. Encourage participation in organizations and activities that are accommodating and in which students show some interest.
- Encourage students to engage in conversations and use appropriate pragmatics. Key situations in which students should learn to use language effectively include getting the teacher's attention, asking for help and explanation of difficult topics, taking turns when speaking with others, staying within a conversational topic, and finding solutions to problems.

Who Are Students with Sensory Impairments?
Definitions

The three classifications of students with sensory impairments are (1) students who are deaf or who have hearing impairments, (2) students who are blind or who have visual disabilities, and (3) students who are deaf-blind.

Deafness and Hearing Impairment. Deafness, as defined under IDEA, means a loss of hearing that is so severe that the student is "impaired in processing linguistic information through hearing, with or without amplification, that adversely affects a child's educational performance" (U.S. Department of Education, 2007, Sec. 300.8[c][3]). In comparison, IDEA defines a hearing impairment as a loss of hearing, "whether permanent or fluctuating, that adversely affects a child's educational performance *but that is not included under the definition of deafness*" (Sec. 300.8 [c][5]).

Hearing loss can be described in terms of the volume required for a person to hear. The unit of measure used to report degree of hearing loss is called **decibels (dB)**. Those who have normal hearing can hear sounds from 0 to 20 dB, that is, at a very low volume. As hearing loss becomes more severe, individuals require progressively higher decibel levels (greater volume) to hear. A mild loss is defined as 20 to 40 dB; a moderate loss, 40 to 60 dB; a severe loss, 60 to 80 dB; and a profound loss, 80 dB or greater (American Speech-Language-Hearing Association, n.d.).

Hearing loss can also be described according to the *type of hearing loss,* which refers to the location in the auditory system where the loss occurs. The types of hearing loss include a conductive hearing loss (in the outer and/or middle ear); a sensorineural hearing loss (in the cochlea, inner ear, or eighth cranial nerve); a mixed hearing loss (both conductive and sensorineural); and a central auditory processing disorder. *Configuration of the hearing loss,* another type of description, describes qualitative aspects of hearing, such as whether both ears are affected or whether different frequencies are differentially affected.

Blindness and Visual Disabilities. According to IDEA, "Visual impairment including blindness means an impairment in vision that, even with correction, adversely affects a child's educational performance. The term includes both partially sighted and blindness" (U.S. Department of Education, 2007, Sec. 300.8[c][13]).

Degree of vision loss is described according to a person's visual acuity. Visual acuity is reported as a fraction (e.g., 20/20), with the top number stating the distance from the object and the bottom number stating the distance at which a person with normal vision could see the same object or figure that is 20 feet away. For example, on a Snellen chart, acuity is measured using letters aligned in rows, and 20/20 is considered normal because you can see from 20 feet as well as another with good vision can see at 20 feet. In contrast, 20/40 means that the line you can correctly read at 20 feet is one that a person with normal vision can read at 40 feet (i.e., you have to be closer to see what others can see at a greater distance). Thus, the larger the bottom number, the worse your

Just the Facts | Students with Sensory Impairments

Who are they?	Students with sensory impairments may include those who are blind or visually impaired, deaf or hard of hearing, or deaf-blind.
What are typical characteristics?	• Students with sensory impairments may have total or partial vision loss, total or partial hearing loss, or a loss of both hearing and vision to a significant degree. • The hearing and/or vision loss must interfere with the student's learning ability in order for the student to qualify for special education.

What are the demographics?	• According to the U.S. Department of Education (2007):
	  • Almost 29,000 students are classified as having a visual impairment as a primary disability (either partially sighted or blind).
	  • Almost 79,000 have hearing impairments (either deaf or hard of hearing).
	  • Nearly 1,900 are deaf-blind (significant loss of both hearing and vision).

Where are students educated?	• Some students with sensory impairments are served in residential schools. • Others are served in general education classes or in special education classes, often in general education schools. • 86% of students with hearing impairments, 88% of students with visual disabilities, and 70% of students with deaf-blindness are in general education classrooms for all or part of the school day. • These students are also served in special classes, special schools, and residential settings.
How are students identified?	• Individuals are often identified at birth or during infancy through testing by medical personnel.
What causes sensory impairments?	• Deafness and hearing loss can be caused by heredity, accidents, or illness; but in many cases the cause is unknown. • Major causes of blindness or low vision in children include congenital cataracts, optic atrophy, albinism, retinopathy of prematurity, rod-cone dystrophy, cortical visual impairment, and optic nerve hypoplasia. • Deaf-blindness may result due to a syndrome, prematurity, low birth weight, or a congenital infection.
What are the outcomes?	• Most persons with visual disabilities will live as adults in integrated society. • Many people who are deaf participate more in the Deaf culture but may also live in an integrated society. • Persons with deaf-blindness will usually require some degree of ongoing support.

visual acuity. A person with 20/200 visual acuity would be standing 20 feet from a figure or an object in order to see it as well as a person with normal vision could see it from 200 feet away.

Along with visual acuity, our vision can be reported according to our visual field, which is the area in front of us that we can see while looking forward and not moving our head. The visual field for each eye is usually measured by a computerized assessment administered by an optometrist or ophthalmologist.

Blindness as defined by IDEA and legal blindness are not necessarily the same. *Legal blindness* refers to a central acuity of 20/200 or less in the better eye with the best possible correction and is used to determine eligibility for various benefits such as a reduction on income tax. The definition of "visual impairment including blindness" under IDEA is broader than the definition of legally blind. Students with visual difficulties who do not meet the requirements of legal blindness may still be served under IDEA because the IDEA definition is concerned more with the educational impact of the vision loss rather than a clinical measure of loss.

Deaf-blindness. According to IDEA, "Deaf-blindness means concomitant hearing and visual impairments, the combination of which causes such severe communication and other developmental and educational needs that they cannot be accommodated in special education programs

A visual disability may be caused by poor visual acuity or a restricted visual field.

solely for children with deafness or children with blindness" (U.S. Department of Education, 2007, Sec. 300.8[c][2]). Most students who are classified as deaf-blind have some residual use of their vision, or hearing, or both. Relatively few individuals are completely without both vision and hearing, which means their ability to function might be better than anticipated.

Identification of Students with Sensory Impairments

Most children with sensory impairments will be identified early in life, usually very soon after birth. Successful early identification means that specialized intervention services can begin earlier in a child's life and thus reduce the impact of the disability.

Any degree of hearing loss can have an adverse effect on language, social, and cognitive development. The earlier the loss is detected, the sooner intervention can begin. In the past, children with hearing loss often were not identified until they were 1 or 2 years old, or even older and had missed important experiences during their development. Today, most states use *universal newborn hearing screening programs* that are designed to assess infants' hearing before they leave the hospital (National Center for Hearing Assessment and Management [NCHAM], 2008). According to NCHAM, the average cost to screen a newborn for hearing impairments is between $10 and $50, depending on the procedure and the technology used. The benefit is that identified children and their families can be referred for early intervention services.

Pause & Reflect

When most people hear the term *deaf-blind*, they think of a person in total isolation. In reality, some degree of vision and/or hearing is usually present. Still, can you imagine living in your world with such sensory restrictions? What are some ways your life might be different if you had severely restricted vision and hearing?

As with deafness and hearing impairments, children who have any degree of visual loss will experience delays in early development. Unless early intervention is provided, they will be impaired in their ability to make visual contact and imitate others, explore their environment, crawl and walk, use fine-motor skills for daily activities such as self-feeding, and experience delayed language development. Pediatricians are most likely to first determine that a child has a visual impairment, and they usually refer children whom they identify to the state's Child Find services. Child Find services are designed to identify children with disabilities and help families identify appropriate early intervention or early childhood education services. Most children with sensory impairments will usually begin receiving special services in infant and toddler programs (0 to 2 years) and continue to receive them as preschoolers (3 to 5 years) and also as school-age students until they are 21 years old.

Prevalence

According to the U.S. Department of Education (2007), individuals with sensory impairments eligible for public school special education services (from age 3 to 21 years) are relatively few in number. The data show that within schools in the United States, approximately 79,000 students are deaf or have hearing impairments; 29,000 are blind or have visual disabilities; and only about 1,900 are deaf-blind. Together, these numbers account for 1 of every 100 students receiving special education services under IDEA, and about 15 of every 1,000 students in the general school-age population.

As you look at these numbers, remember that they represent students within their respective primary special education classifications. This means that these students have no other disability and that their disabilities interfere with their ability to learn under normal conditions. Therefore, other data sources report different numbers:

- The Gallaudet Research Institute (2005) estimates that from 2 to 6 million people have a severe hearing loss or are deaf.
- The American Foundation for the Blind (n.d.) estimates that approximately 10 million blind and visually impaired people are living in the United States, with 1.3 million of these being legally blind.
- The National Technical Assistance Consortium for Children and Young Adults Who Are Deaf-Blind (NTAC) reported that 9,516 students ages 0 to 21 were classified as deaf-blind (NTAC, 2004).

Service Delivery

Services for students with sensory impairments may be provided in different types of settings. U.S. Department of Education (2007) data for children between 3 and 5 years show that the largest percent of children with hearing impairments are in early childhood special education (ECSE) settings (42%), while the others are placed in general early childhood (EC) settings (22%), part-time in ECSE and part-time in EC settings (19%), or full-time in special schools (9%). Preschool children with visual disabilities are served similarly: the greatest percentage are in ECSE settings (38%), followed by EC settings (26%), part-time in ECSE and part-time in EC settings (18%), and in special schools (8%). The pattern for young children with deaf-blindness is nearly the same, except that about twice the percentage, 16%, are served in separate special schools.

When students are older (6 to 21 years), they are likely to be taught, at least to some extent, in general education classrooms. Forty-five percent of the students with hearing impairments are in the general education classroom most of the day (i.e., 80% to 100% of the day), and another 41% are in general education classrooms for at least part of the school day. The placements for students with visual disabilities are similar: 55% are in the general education classroom for most of the day, and another 33% for at least part of their school day.

Almost 14% of students with hearing impairments and about 12% of students with visual disabilities are served either in public or private separate schools or in public or private residential facilities. Additionally, many deaf-blind school-age students are served in separate settings. Only 22% of these students are in the general education classroom for most of the day (80% to 100% of the time), while about 47% spend less than 80% of their day there. Thirty-one percent of students with deaf-blindness are placed in separate schools or residential facilities.

Pause & Reflect

As a group, students with sensory impairments are less frequently included in general education classrooms than many other students with disabilities. Can you think of ways that these students, like others, could benefit from more inclusion?

Major Characteristics of Students with Sensory Impairments

The academic abilities and social behavior of students with sensory impairments depend on a number of factors, including the specific nature of their disability, any associated disabilities that may be present, and previous experiences in different settings. Although we do not want to overgeneralize, some characteristics that occur frequently are important to note. As you become aware of these characteristics, it is important that you understand that the impact of sensory impairments on learning is usually more a function of the lack of sensory input and critical experiences at an early age rather than an inability to learn.

Academic and Cognitive Performance

A sensory impairment per se does not necessarily mean that a student has a reduced level of cognitive or academic ability, and, in fact, many students with sensory impairments are as academically gifted and talented as their peers without disabilities. However, conditions that

Students with hearing impairments may have significant lags in literacy skills.

occur during prenatal development that result in sensory impairments can also affect central nervous system development and thus have a direct impact on cognitive development and learning ability. It is estimated, for example, that about 63% of students who are deaf-blind have intellectual disabilities in addition to their sensory loss (NTAC, 2004). Depending on the specific nature of an individual's disabilities, therefore, learning ability may be impacted to a greater or lesser degree.

Perhaps the most significantly affected academic area for students with hearing impairments is the acquisition of literacy skills, which are based heavily on language development. Although most students who are deaf or who have hearing impairments have the cognitive ability to develop reading and writing skills, their delays in language development will often result in delays in learning to read. Early literacy, which is heavily focused on matching spoken sounds and words to printed letters and words, can be especially difficult. As a result, you are likely to find that children with hearing impairments will be significantly behind their peers in reading. When compared to hearing students, many students who are deaf or hearing impaired will lag in literacy skills during their school years (Schirmer, 2001a, 2001b; Traxler, 2000).

Students who are blind, especially those who are blind from birth or who lost their vision at a very early age, are particularly challenged in learning concepts that are difficult to comprehend without vision. Even though vision specialists provide instructional strategies and materials that allow students to access information through auditory and tactile input (e.g., Braille, large print, assistive and adaptive technology, and audio material), learning many concepts can still be difficult. For example, how do you explain what the sky is like or what water molecules look like? Learning such concepts as these will be challenging for many students with visual disabilities.

Behavior Performance and Social Skills

The social skills of students with sensory impairments will often be impacted, but this is not usually due to an impairment directly related to social development. Instead, it is more often caused by a lack of experiences resulting from the student's sensory loss.

For most of us, social skill development occurs through incidental learning experiences and social reinforcement. In other words, we learn to behave appropriately for our age and culture based on what we see and hear others do and how others react to what we do. Individuals who have sensory impairments are often deprived of this common opportunity, and so their social skills sometimes are atypical. To overcome this lack of natural experiences, students often need direct instruction in appropriate social behavior.

Another serious drawback of having a sensory impairment is that spontaneous relationships and friendships may not occur as frequently as for others. When you cannot hear casual comments or see facial expressions, when you can't determine if someone is serious or joking, or when you don't know if someone is speaking to you or to someone else, your ability to respond in a socially fitting fashion is hampered. In "Teaching Students with Visual Disabilities," you can see the challenges faced by Jennifer Powell, a teacher at Mull Elementary School, when she taught Sam, a fourth-grade student with visual impairments, in her inclusive classroom.

Teaching Students with Visual Disabilities in Inclusive Classrooms: Challenges and Strategies

When we asked Jennifer Powell, a fourth-grade teacher at Mull Elementary, how to succeed as an inclusion teacher, she gave a simple answer: "patience, patience, and more patience." Dealing with real-world conditions in inclusive classrooms certainly requires patience, but it also requires you to be both a competent and a creative teacher. One of Jennifer Powell's biggest challenges was finding a way to include Sam, a girl with both visual disabilities and learning disabilities, who also exhibited a motivation problem that often translated to a problem with completing her work on time.

The first part of the challenge was to create instructional situations to enhance Sam's participation. Jennifer told us about some of the things she did. "Some of the especially effective practices we used with this child were to increase the font size of her papers, sit her at the front of the room, script her work for her to copy from her desk instead of the board, and use a lot of extra praise."

Jennifer found that in math, Sam "seemed to become more comfortable with addition and subtraction using person-to-person contact (touching fingers). She had a really hard time copying anything from the board, so we tried to make it more comfortable for her. One of the ways we did this was by putting a number strip on her desk. These kinds of things sped up her rate of completion."

But a problem with Sam's motivation remained; she just didn't seem to care that much if she finished her work or not. This might not be surprising, given the challenges she faced. "We really were unsure that her impairment was the cause of that," Jennifer said, but it wasn't acceptable. She told us, "She had the capability of completing tasks efficiently, but she just didn't always do it. This child was very strong-willed, and the challenge was getting her motivated to complete her task in a timely manner."

By the end of the year, it was probably the "lots of extra praise" that proved to be most effective. "We felt like we were effective because of the growth Sam showed in many ways throughout the year. She made gains in reading, spelling, writing, math, and social skills. This child went from no smiles to smiling every day."

Effective Instruction for Students with Sensory Impairments

Effective Instruction for Elementary Students

Strategies to Achieve Academic Success. Students with sensory impairments who are in general education classrooms are supported by itinerant or consultant special education teachers with specific professional preparation to meet the students' needs. The main job of the itinerant teacher is to implement strategies and accommodations that will allow the student to participate in the general curriculum. Secondarily, the specialist may design instruction or teach the student to use assistive technology to learn individual skills that will help the student be successful. The general educator's collaboration in this process as the curriculum specialist can be very important.

Like the SLP, the itinerant teacher will work directly with the student and will also consult with the teacher, demonstrating and explaining how the student is to use specific devices, participate in certain activities, or perform academic activities. When working with the student, the itinerant teacher may work on improving communication skills, listening skills, or on forming important, difficult-to-learn concepts.

The suggestions in Figure 9.5 will help general education teachers meet the needs of students who are deaf or hearing impaired in the classroom. Similarly, those in Figure 9.6 will help teachers who have students with visual disabilities.

> **Strategy**
>
> For guidelines for making decisions about the use of assistive technology, see Strategy 16.5 in Chapter 16.

Figure 9.5	Suggestions for Working with Students Who Are Deaf or Have Hearing Impairments in the General Education Classroom

- Always face the class when presenting information. Don't speak to the wall or blackboard! Even students who do not use speechreading will benefit from your facial and body expressions, so make sure they can be seen.
- Allow students to indicate their preferred seating. Many will request to be in the front of the room, but other factors such as lighting and ambient noise can impact this decision.
- The students may have paraprofessional assistance to present auditory information in a visual format. This could be a sign language interpreter, a captioner, an oral interpreter, a cued speech transliterator, and so on. Many forms of auditory assistance exist, but all these professionals have a common characteristic: Their role is to facilitate communication, not to provide instruction.
- Provide visual aids to support information, especially when presenting a new concept. Charts, diagrams, posters, graphic organizers, pictures, and maps are great examples of visual aids that support learning.
- Take time to assess the student's background knowledge. Students who are deaf or hard of hearing may have unexpected gaps in their knowledge base because of incidental learning. Find out what they know, and build from there.
- Do the best you can to reduce the noise distracters in the room. If available, classroom amplification systems will benefit not only the student with hearing loss but the rest of the class as well.

Source: Adapted with permission from Rosenberg, M. S., Westling, D. L., & McLeskey, J. (2008). *Special education for today's teachers: An introduction.* Upper Saddle River, NJ: Merrill/Pearson Education.

Figure 9.6	Suggestions for Working with Students with Visual Disabilities in the General Education Classroom

- Provide opportunities for tactile exploration. When possible, bring real objects to class, or use models or other tangible representations to develop understanding.
- Allow space for specialized equipment. Students may use assistive and adaptive technologies to access printed information, and these items are often large. Plan a space in the room where equipment can be stored when not in use but easily accessed without disrupting others.
- Give verbal descriptions of visual information. Announce the obvious so that the student knows when someone comes and goes, when an unexpected event happens, or when a change in activity occurs. Describe any visual aids you use.
- Learn details about the implications of vision loss for your student. You may need to adjust lighting, colors of bulletin boards, papers, and so on, to maximize what the student can see.
- Allow students to indicate their preferred seating. Many will request to be in the front of the room, but other factors such as field of vision or lighting preferences may impact this decision.

Source: Adapted with permission from Rosenberg, M.S., Westling, D. L., & McLeskey, J. (2008). *Special education for today's teachers: An introduction.* Upper Saddle River, NJ: Merrill/Pearson Education.

Strategies to Achieve Social Success. The most effective approach to improving social skills for students with sensory impairments is through direct instruction. To do this, the teacher may use natural opportunities or create social situations in which students with sensory impairments have the chance to interact with peers who do not have disabilities. In these situations, the teacher will need to interpret the social condition in a way the student can understand, and then explain the correct response and prompt the student to engage in it. Those conditions that we so readily understand, such as voice intonation, volume, facial expression, body language, and spatial relations, may need interpretation and explanation for students with a sensory impairment. In Figures 9.7 and 9.8, we offer suggestions for improving the social skills of students who are deaf or have hearing impairments (Figure 9.7) and the social skills of students who have visual disabilities (Figure 9.8).

Figure 9.7	Suggestions for Improving Social Skills and Relations of Students Who Are Deaf or Have Hearing Impairments

- Provide students with opportunities to become self-advocates and to be more self-determining.
- Assist students in identifying their interests and becoming involved in activities in school and out of school based on those interests.
- Help students without disabilities better understand the student's deafness or hearing impairments, and explain the assistive devices and adaptations the student uses.
- Use literature and instructional units on friendships with the entire class to teach appropriate relationships.
- Provide direct instruction to students on appropriate social behaviors such as how to greet, join a group, express anger, or resolve a conflict.
- Develop a "Circle of Friends" program that will allow students without disabilities to become supportive and assist the student in learning social behaviors.
- Create role-playing activities in which students can enact social situations and learn how they should respond.

Source: Adapted from Luckner, J. L., & Muir, S. (2002). Suggestions for helping students who are deaf succeed in general education settings. *Communication Disorders Quarterly, 24,* 23–30.

Figure 9.8	Suggestions for Improving Social Skills and Relations of Students Who Have Visual Disabilities

- Encourage students to be as independent as possible and to develop confidence in their personal abilities.
- Allow students to practice conversation skills using appropriate social interactions.
- Teach students the appropriate way to express anger and to manage their temper and the difference between assertiveness and aggression.
- Show students how to interact in groups and respect the rights of others in the group.
- Allow students to gradually adjust to new social situations by making initial contacts brief.
- Reinforce improvement; help the student learn by gradually demonstrating more appropriate behavior, but don't let the student continuously avoid social situations.
- Use structured activities to directly teach specific skills.

Source: Adapted with permission from Texas School for the Blind and Visually Impaired. (2007). Dos and don'ts for teaching social skills. Retrieved August 28, 2008, from http://www.tsbvi.edu/Education/do-dont-social-skills.htm

Effective Instruction for Secondary Students

Strategies to Achieve Academic Success. The academic success of students with sensory impairments at the secondary level depends on several factors. Foremost is the degree to which students have developed basic academic skills during earlier school years. If assistive technology devices and accommodations have allowed students to learn how to acquire and understand information, synthesize the information, and demonstrate their knowledge and skills, then you can expect that students will have little difficulty with academic content at the secondary level. Nevertheless, the challenges that they face will be related to those that existed at the elementary level. Many students who are deaf or who have hearing impairments are likely to lag in their reading and literacy skills. Those who are blind may have gaps in comprehending concepts that are difficult to explain or demonstrate through tactile models.

In addition to the strategies listed in Figure 9.5, the following may be helpful when instructing high school students who are deaf or have hearing impairment (Lang, n.d.).

- If the student uses sign language, learn a few basic signs. You do not need to be able to teach through signing, but this will help build rapport with the student and may increase interest.
- Make sure that lessons are logically structured and the structure is followed so that students can keep up with your presentation.

- Use visual graphic organizers, other visuals, and multimedia presentations in order to facilitate the student's understanding.
- Prompt the student to ask questions from time to time and probe the level of comprehension.

Similarly, in addition to the suggestions listed in Figure 9.6, these ideas may be helpful for teaching students with visual disabilities in high school courses (University of Sheffield, 2008).

- Provide handouts in advance of the lecture. If necessary, provide handouts and notes in Braille. (The visual disabilities specialist can prepare these materials for you.)
- Describe any material you are writing down. Talk through any images or diagrams.
- Use printed transparencies, rather than handwritten overheads.
- Speak clearly, and spell out any new or difficult words or names.
- Provide booklists well in advance, because students may have difficulty accessing the library and may read more slowly.
- Provide material such as booklists in electronic format rather than hard copy, which will allow the student to view in their preferred format.

Strategies to Achieve Social Success. Adolescence is often a time when individuals try to discover who they are. In doing so, they will compare themselves to others. Having a sensory impairment can make this difficult. If you cannot see, you do not know how your face and your body compare to others. If you cannot hear, you don't know if you sound like others, if others are saying things that you should say, or if someone is commenting on what you look like or what you are doing. In such cases, being unaware of these aspects of your social situation can be very unsettling. Teachers and other important adults can do much by helping students understand what they cannot see or hear, how they stand within their social world, and how they can participate in social ways like other students (Wolffe, 2006).

Many students with sensory impairments will be shut out of adolescent social situations by the nature of their impairment. For example, they might not be able to drive, play some sports, or know if they look cool or how they should flirt with someone whom they find attractive. Helping the students find ways to remove or work around these barriers, or finding substitutes for them, can be helpful. While doing so, you will find that you can also help improve the student's self-confidence and self-esteem.

Final Thoughts Regarding Effective Practices

In Chapters 11 to 16, we provide step-by-step descriptions of many effective practices that are useful for students with disabilities and others who struggle in school. Several of these effective practices are particularly useful for teachers who work with students with communication disorders, visual disabilities, or hearing impairments in inclusive classrooms, and we have already noted a number of them in this chapter. Other effective practices that you are likely to find especially useful are how to be a good co-teacher (Strategy 11.1), planning for basic skill instruction and for teaching academic content (Strategies 12.4 and 12.5), and strategies for improving student behavior (especially Strategies 15.2, 15.3, and 15.6). You will also find a number of the strategies in Chapter 16 on the use of educational and assistive technology very helpful, especially those on teaching students to use educational technology (Strategy 16.1), selecting assistive technology devices (Strategy 16.5), and using AAC devices (Strategy 16.8). We believe you will find many of the other strategies in Chapters 11 to 16 useful in addressing the needs of students with communication disorders and sensory impairments in inclusive classrooms.

Strategy

Unit and lesson organizers can be helpful for secondary students with sensory impairments. For steps for creating these, see Strategy 14.1 in Chapter 14.

Strategy

Peer buddies can help students with sensory impairments fit in. For step-by-step information on how to develop this type of program, see Strategy 11.7 in Chapter 11.

Summary

Definitions of students with communication disorders and students with sensory impairments

- Communication disorders include students who have language disorders and speech disorders.
- Speech disorders interfere with verbal expression and include phonological and articulation disorders, fluency disorders, voice disorders, and motor speech disorders.
- Language disorders include disorders of form, content (or semantics), and use (or pragmatics)
- *Deafness* means a loss of hearing that is so severe that the student is "impaired in processing linguistic information through hearing, with or without amplification"
- Hearing impairment is a loss of hearing "that adversely affects a child's educational performance but that is not included under the definition of deafness."
- Visual impairment including blindness means an impairment that, even with correction, adversely affects a child's educational performance.
- *Legal blindness* refers to a central acuity of 20/200 or less in the better eye with the best possible correction.
- *Deaf-blindness* means "concomitant hearing and visual impairments, the combination of which causes such severe communication and other developmental and educational needs that they cannot be accommodated in special education programs solely for children with deafness or children with blindness."

Prevalence of students with communication disorders and sensory impairments

- Almost 1.5 million public school students from 3 to 21 years of age receive speech–language services because of their communication disorders.
- Approximately 79,000 students are deaf or have hearing impairments; 29,000 are blind or have visual disabilities; and only about 1,900 are deaf-blind.

Educational settings used by students with communication disorders and sensory impairments

- 90% of students with communication disorders are served primarily in the regular classroom and are provided individual therapy by a speech–language pathologist (SLP).
- 45% of students with hearing impairments are in the general education classroom 80% to 100% of the day; 41% are in the general education classroom for at least part of the school day; and 14% are served in public or private separate schools or in public or private residential facilities.
- 55% of students with visual disabilities are in the general education classroom for most of the day; 33% are in the general education classroom for at least part of their school day; and about 12% of students with visual disabilities are served in public or private separate schools or in public or private residential facilities.
- 22% of students with deaf-blindness are in the general education classroom for most of the day, while the remainder spend less time there (47%). 31% are in separate schools or residential facilities.

Major characteristics of students with communication disorders and of students with sensory impairments

- Students with speech disorders often have typical academic abilities.
- Students with language disabilities may have their learning affected in different ways and may be classified as having a learning disability. They may have mixed language abilities, slow vocabulary development, word-finding problems, and difficulty with grammatical production and comprehension.
- The social behavior of some students with communication disorders might be adversely affected. A student may be withdrawn, may interact inappropriately with others, or may try to compensate for communication weaknesses through aggression or disruption.

- Sensory impairments may impact both academic learning and social development. This impact is largely a function of the lack of sensory input and critical experiences at an early age rather than an inability to learn.
- Sensory impairments often have an adverse effect on developing social relationships, which can be especially difficult during adolescence.

Effective practices for including students with communication disorders and those with sensory impairments

- Strong collaboration among key professionals will best ensure students' success. These professionals include general education classroom teachers, SLPs, deaf educators, and visual disabilities specialists.
- Students with communication disorders may need extra time and practice to improve their communication skills in academic and social contexts.
- Students with hearing impairments benefit from the use of visual images and well-organized presentations. The provision of material in writing is also helpful.
- Students with visual disabilities will require auditory descriptions and tactile models in order to learn much content.
- Many students with sensory impairments will need direct instruction in order to understand correct social behavior and learn to engage in it.

Addressing Professional Standards

Standards addressed in Chapter 9 include:

CEC Standards: (1) foundations, (2) development and characteristics of learners, (3) individual learning differences, (4) instructional strategies.

INTASC Standards: Principle 1—Understand central concepts of the discipline; Principle 2—Provide learning opportunities to support the learning and development of all students.

Praxis™ II Standards: Knowledge-based core principles: (1) understanding exceptionalities, (3) delivery of services to students with disabilities. Application of core principles: (1) curriculum, (2) instruction, (5) professional roles/issues/ literature.

Students with Physical Disabilities, Health Impairments, and Multiple Disabilities

KEY TOPICS

After reading this chapter you will:

- Know the definitions and criteria used to identify students with physical disabilities, health impairments, and multiple disabilities.
- Know how many students have physical disabilities, health impairments, and multiple disabilities.
- Be able to identify the educational settings in which students with physical disabilities, health impairments, and multiple disabilities are served.
- Be able to identify major characteristics of students with physical disabilities, health impairments, and multiple disabilities.

- Understand key issues and challenges related to including students with physical disabilities, health impairments, and multiple disabilities in the general education classrooms.
- Know effective practices for including students with physical disabilities, health impairments, and multiple disabilities in the general education classrooms.

chapter 10

Perspectives on Including Students with Physical Disabilities

Interview with Madge Goins and Jennifer Powell, Mull Elementary

We spoke with Madge Goins and Jennifer Powell about their experiences at Mull Elementary School of including a student with physical disabilities. Because physical disabilities are considered to be a "low-incidence" disability compared to other disabilities, we were not surprised to find that they had very few students with physical disabilities at their school. Sarah was one of the few, and they spoke to us about her and what inclusion meant for her.

Sarah was in the fourth grade and had cerebral palsy, a neurological disorder that affects posture and muscle control in different ways, depending on the nature and the extent of the brain damage. In Sarah's case, cerebral palsy affected her ability to walk, requiring that she use a wheelchair. But Ms. Goins and Ms. Powell considered Sarah's physical disability to be a challenge that created other challenges. Ms. Powell told us, "A frustration that occurred with this student was that at times it was difficult to fulfill all of her physical needs while trying to maintain an entire classroom effectively. She was very bright; however, she struggled to complete task in a timely manner. The challenge was making her surroundings compatible inside and outside the classroom."

The way inclusion helped Sarah mostly was through peer influence. She had a tendency to be withdrawn but ultimately came to be more of a participant. As Ms. Goins said, "At the beginning of the year, a lot of times she chose to sit away from the group. But by they end, {she was} the first to participate with the group." So while inclusion could not directly affect Sarah's physical disability, it did give her an important opportunity to feel more at home socially with her peers.

By the end of the year, the teachers were satisfied with the gains that Sarah had made. "The major success was seeing her growth in her physical mobility," Ms. Powell said. "She went from a wheelchair and a walker to independently playing amongst her peers." Just as important, was that Sarah had developed "a great desire to learn" that resulted in an "always-smiling face."

myeducationlab

Go to
MyEducationLab,
select the topic
*Physical Disabilities
and Health
Impairments,* and go
to the Activities and
Applications section.
As you watch the
video entitled
"Physical
Disabilities," consider
the difference special
education services
have made in this
student's life.

Introduction

As we have seen in earlier chapters, many students are classified as having disabilities because of their cognitive, learning, or behavioral characteristics. For many other students, however, their disabilities are of a physical or medical nature, including students with physical disabilities, health impairments, and multiple disabilities. In Chapter 9 we discussed students with communication disorders, hearing impairments, and visual disabilities, and we discussed how these conditions could adversely affect students' learning. Because of this negative impact, schools can justify the need for special education services for these students. So it is with the students we discuss in this chapter; their physical and health conditions are often of such a magnitude that these can interfere with their learning in schools. When this is the case, special education services are necessary.

As a professional educator, you will readily recognize that some of your students have physical or medical conditions, whereas other such conditions, for the most part, are invisible. For example, some students' physical disabilities are easily noticeable. These include students like Sarah, in the opening vignette, who had cerebral palsy, or others, such as students with muscular dystrophy who are in wheelchairs or using orthopedic devices. But other students' physical disabilities—such as asthma, diabetes, or epilepsy—may rarely catch your attention.

From the perspective of public school education, students with physical disabilities, health impairments, and multiple disabilities fall into one of three categories, requiring (1) no accommodations, (2) some accommodations, or (3) an individualized education program (IEP). For example, a number of these students may attend school without any special services or accommodations. Like a student with poor visual acuity who needs nothing more than to wear corrective lenses, many students with physical or medical conditions simply come to school and manage their own needs.

In the second group of students are those who need some accommodations, but because their condition does not impair their ability to learn, they do not require special education services. These students have Section 504 Plans that list the ways school personnel can meet their needs so that they can participate like other students.

Some students' physical or medical needs will be very apparent; others' will not.

Finally, the third group includes students whose disabilities adversely affect their learning ability and who are therefore considered eligible for special education under the Individuals with Disabilities Education Act (IDEA). These students will have an IEP.

Pause & Reflect

Think about the visibility of a disability. How does it affect a person's life if his or her disability is apparent, such as with cerebral palsy, rather than if it is not, such as diabetes? Do you think the visibility or lack of it makes life easier or more difficult? Why?

Who Are Students with Physical Disabilities, Health Impairments, and Multiple Disabilities?

Strategy

For step-by-step procedures to develop 504 Plans, see Strategy 12.2 in Chapter 12.

In an inclusive classroom, you are likely to encounter students from each of these categories. The accompanying box, "Just the Facts," provides you with basic information about these students. Please keep in mind that as you look at the information in "Just the Facts," and as you read the rest of this chapter, the medical information that we present on the selected conditions is updated regularly. For the most current information, we suggest you visit the

Just the Facts

Students with Physical Disabilities, Health Impairments, and Multiple Disabilities

Who are they?	• *Physical disabilities:* Students with conditions such as cerebral palsy, spina bifida, or other conditions that affect their ability to walk or use their arms or legs. • *Health impairments:* Students with chronic health conditions such as asthma, epilepsy, and HIV/AIDS, which may or may not be terminal, that cause weakness or fatigue or in some other way adversely affect school performance. • *Multiple disabilities:* Students with intellectual disabilities and other physical or sensory disabilities.
What are typical characteristics?	• The conditions of students with physical disabilities may be relatively mild to more severe. • Different body parts may be affected. • Disabilities may be due to central nervous system damage or muscular or orthopedic impairments. • Students with health impairments may be weak and sometimes in pain. Lack of stamina may often be a debilitating factor. They may miss a lot of school due to their illnesses. • Students with multiple disabilities may have sensory and physical impairments and may exhibit uncommon characteristics such as self-stimulatory or self-injurious behavior. Many will have serious medical conditions.
What are the demographics?	Within the school-age population: • About 0.1% have physical disabilities. • About 0.68% have other health impairments. • About 0.2% have multiple disabilities.
Where are students educated?	• The majority of students with physical disabilities and other health impairments are educated in general classes. • Many students with multiple disabilities are placed in special classes.
How are students identified?	• Individuals with physical disabilities, health impairments, and multiple disabilities are initially identified by physicians as having special medical needs. • Educational personnel evaluate these students to determine if special education services or other accommodations are necessary.
What are the causes?	• Physical disabilities may originate before, during, or after birth. They may be genetically based or occur because of trauma or injury. • Health impairments can also be due to inherited conditions or may occur through transmitted viral infections. • Some conditions have unknown causes. • Multiple disabilities are usually due to prenatal causes such as maternal infections, teratogens, or trauma.
What are the outcomes?	• The physical, social, emotional, and health challenges faced by students with physical disabilities, health impairments, and multiple disabilities often continue into their adult years. • Some of these conditions lead to early death.

Websites at the National Institutes of Health (*http://www.nih.gov/*) or the Centers for Disease Control and Prevention (*http://www.cdc.gov/*).

> For guidelines on participating meaningfully in the development of IEPs, see Strategy 12.1 in Chapter 12.

Definitions

Physical Disabilities. Although most of us commonly use the term *physical disabilities*, IDEA uses the term *orthopedic impairments* and defines it as follows:

> Orthopedic impairment means a severe orthopedic impairment that adversely affects a child's educational performance. The term includes impairments caused by **congenital anomaly** (e.g., **clubfoot,** absence of some member, etc.), impairments caused by disease (e.g., **poliomyelitis, bone tuberculosis,** etc.), and impairments from other causes (e.g., **cerebral palsy,** amputations, and fractures or burns that cause contractures).

As you are undoubtedly aware, many different types of physical disabilities exist, and we could not possibly discuss all of them here. However, we will describe four conditions that are seen relatively often in inclusive classrooms, notably: cerebral palsy, muscular dystrophy, spina bifida, and orthopedic and musculoskeletal conditions.

Cerebral palsy can be described according to its physical manifestation.

Cerebral palsy (CP) is a neurological disorder caused by brain damage before, during, or after birth that impairs a person's posture and movement ability. Cerebral palsy is called a "nonprogressive" disability because the brain damage does not continue to worsen with the passage of time. Treatment is necessary, however, to prevent postural deterioration and to improve movement and independence (Best & Bigge, 2005; Griffin, Fitch, & Griffin, 2002; Pellegrino, 2007).

The three major forms of CP are spasticity (characterized by stiff muscles), athetosis (characterized by involuntary muscle movements), and ataxia (characterized by lack of balance and uncoordinated movements). Some persons also have *mixed* CP, meaning that more than one form of the condition occurs in the same person. Physicians also describe CP according to the area of the body that is affected: Hemiplegia means that one side of the body is more affected; diplegia means the legs are more affected than the arms; and quadriplegia means that all four limbs are affected as well as the trunk and the muscles that control the neck, mouth, and tongue.

The brain damage that results in CP can sometimes lead to other problems as well. These may include intellectual disabilities, visual disabilities, hearing impairments, speech and language disorders, seizures, feeding problems, growth abnormalities, learning disabilities, emotional or behavioral disorders, and attention-deficit/hyperactivity disorder (ADHD).

Muscular dystrophy, like CP, is a relatively common physical disability. Unlike CP, however, muscular dystrophy is a progressive disorder that results in ongoing muscle weakness. When children have muscular dystrophy, their muscle tissue gradually degenerates, turning into fatty tissue, and the condition worsens as time passes. Also, unlike CP, the central nervous system is not involved. Duchenne muscular dystrophy is the most common form and is a genetically inherited condition.

Muscular dystrophy first appears during early childhood, between about 2 and 6 years of age, when the calves seem to be growing larger, a condition called pseudohypertrophy. Actually, fat tissue is replacing muscle tissue in the legs as the legs become weaker and weaker. Gradually, the muscle weakness moves up the body, from the legs to the trunk and arms. Often, these children lose the ability to walk and must use a wheelchair. As they become weaker, they can no longer power a manual wheelchair and may require an electric wheelchair for mobility control. Even holding the head erect becomes difficult (Escolar, Tosi, Tesi Rocha, & Kennedy, 2007).

Spina bifida is a break in the spinal cord that can leave a person with a loss of physical ability in the lower part of the body. The extent of loss depends on the location of the break in the spinal column. Different types of the condition exist, but the most severe form, called myelomeningocele, results in a loss of sensation and muscle control in parts of the body below the lesion. Persons with this condition use a wheelchair for mobility and are usually unable to feel touch, temperature, pressure, or pain.

Pause & Reflect

Individuals who have CP can have speech impairments that may be interpreted by some as an intellectual disability. Such an assumption might lead someone to misinterpret the real ability of the person. Do you see any danger in doing this? How might this be avoided?

Strategy

For step-by-step procedures to help students use motorized wheelchairs, see Strategy 16.9 in Chapter 16.

Pause & Reflect

With a condition like muscular dystrophy, the student progressively loses physical ability. How do you think this would affect an individual, and how would you react to a student with a condition that worsens over time?

Orthopedic and musculoskeletal conditions are a variety of conditions in which bodily structures involving the bones and muscles do not develop normally. Some that you may encounter are curvature of the spine (scoliosis), congenital hip dislocations, juvenile arthritis, osteogenesis imperfecta, and limb deficiencies. Individuals with some of these conditions may require surgery; may be fitted with prosthetic devices, such as artificial hands or legs; and usually must use adapted approaches for accomplishing daily tasks.

> **Strategy**
> For guidelines to evaluate different types of assistive technology, see Strategy 16.5 in Chapter 16.

Health Impairments. Like physical disabilities, some chronic health impairments can seriously affect a student's ability to receive an appropriate education. Sometimes these conditions occur in combination with other conditions (e.g., a student with cerebral palsy may also have **epilepsy**); in other cases, however, the health impairment is the primary disability. According to IDEA (2004), a health impairment means

having limited strength, vitality or alertness, including a heightened alertness to environmental stimuli, that results in limited alertness with respect to the educational environment, that— (i) Is due to chronic or acute health problems such as asthma, attention deficit disorder or attention deficit hyperactivity disorder, diabetes, epilepsy, a heart condition, hemophilia, lead poisoning, leukemia, nephritis, rheumatic fever, and sickle cell anemia; and (ii) Adversely affects a child's educational performance.

In Chapter 5, we devoted an entire chapter to provide information about the health impairment ADHD, because this particular health impairment is relatively common. In this section we, briefly describe five other health impairments that you likely will encounter among your students at some time in your career.

Asthma. Asthma is a chronic lung condition that can result in attacks characterized by difficult breathing, wheezing, coughing, excess mucus, sweating, and chest constriction. Attacks may result from different triggers, which may be allergens such as tiny dust particles, cigarette smoke, and pet dander; or even cold, dry air or physical exertion.

Sickle-Cell Disease. In sickle-cell disease, a block in normal blood flow results in episodic pain in the arms, legs, chest, and abdomen as well as priapism (painful prolonged erection). Sickle-cell disease also causes damage to most organs, including the spleen, kidneys, and liver. Young children with sickle-cell disease can be easily debilitated by certain bacterial infections. Sickle-cell disease is most common among those with sub-Saharan African ancestry.

Epilepsy. Epilepsy is a neurological condition that causes seizures. Different types of seizures may occur. The most common type is a tonic-clonic seizure, referred to in the past as a grand mal seizure. During a tonic-clonic seizure, the person loses awareness, ceases to engage in any activity, and loses consciousness. She becomes stiff (tonic), and then jerking (clonic) movements begin. Although the tonic-clonic seizure is the most common type of seizure among persons with severe disabilities who have seizures, other types may also occur. One that you may encounter is called absence seizures, previously referred to as petit mal seizures. During absence seizures, which are very brief, lasting perhaps 1 to 10 seconds, the person experiences a loss of consciousness, but otherwise remains fixed. Observers sometimes assume that a student with absence seizures is simply daydreaming (Weinstein & Gaillard, 2007).

Type-1 Diabetes. Type-1 diabetes, also called juvenile diabetes or insulin-dependent diabetes, is an autoimmune disease that destroys the cells in the pancreas that produce insulin. Type-1 diabetes develops most often in children or young adults but can occur at any age. Children with Type-1 diabetes require insulin shots. Without medication, the student may become very thirsty, need to urinate often, lose weight, and become very weak.

Cystic Fibrosis. Cystic fibrosis is a disease that affects major body organs that secrete fluids. Cystic fibrosis primarily affects the lungs, where airway passages become blocked, and the digestive system, where the mucus interferes with the release of digestive enzymes. The secretions of normal fluids are blocked by the mucus and cysts develop, which become surrounded by scar tissue.

Multiple Disabilities. As defined by IDEA (2004), multiple disabilities are "concomitant impairments (e.g., mental retardation–blindness, mental retardation–orthopedic impairment), the combination of which causes such severe educational needs that they cannot be accommodated in special education programs solely for one of the impairments. The term does not include deaf-blindness."

Students with multiple disabilities have a relatively severe intellectual disability and at least one additional disability, often a physical disability. Additionally, students with multiple disabilities usually have various health problems that complicate and worsen their disabilities. They often develop conditions such as high blood pressure, obesity, brittle bones, depression, and general tiredness. Other conditions include cardiovascular (heart) diseases, respiratory diseases, eating disorders, and growth impairments (Heller, 2004; Thuppal & Sobsey, 2004).

Identification of Students with Physical Disabilities, Health Impairments, and Multiple Disabilities

Parents will often recognize atypical physical or health conditions relatively early in their child's life and will report these conditions to their pediatrician or family doctor, who will then conduct evaluations to establish a diagnosis. Other medical specialists may conduct subsequent evaluations to assess the physical and health status of the child and determine the child's medical needs. As a result of these evaluations, the physicians will prescribe medications or medical interventions, including surgery, to improve the child's physical or health status.

After physicians establish a medical diagnosis, educational personnel must determine through educational assessment whether the condition has a significant negative impact on the student's education. If it does, then the student is evaluated for early intervention or special education services, depending on the child's age. An individual family service plan or IEP is then developed.

When considering the provision of special education services, school professionals must also consider whether related services are necessary for the student to benefit from education. For students with physical disabilities, health impairments, and multiple disabilities, this means that physical therapists and occupational therapists will conduct evaluations, and, if necessary, create intervention programs to meet a student's needs.

A physical or occupational therapist will evaluate students to determine necessary interventions.

Prevalence

According to the most recent data from the U.S. Department of Education (2007), students with physical disabilities, health impairments, and multiple disabilities who are served in public schools under IDEA comprise a very small fraction of the population. At the preschool level (3 to 5 years old), the percentage of children with physical disabilities is 0.08%; those with health impairments is 0.12%; and those with multiple disabilities is 0.07%. During the school years (6 to 21 years), the percentages increase somewhat: physical disabilities increase to 0.10%; health impairments to 0.68%; and multiple disabilities to 0.20%. Nevertheless, all together, the students in these categories make up only about 1% of all students in public schools.

Overall, the number of students identified with these disabilities increases from the preschool to the school years. The greatest increase is in the health impairments category, which increases almost six times. This is likely due at least in part to the fact that students with ADHD, who usually are not identified until the school years, are included in this category.

Service Delivery

As shown in Table 10.1, most students with physical disabilities and health impairments are included in general education classrooms either for most or part of the school day. In contrast, students with multiple disabilities spend less time in the general education classroom, and more attend separate schools or residential facilities for students with severe disabilities (U.S. Department of Education, 2007).

> ### Pause & Reflect
>
> Review the previously described physical disabilities and health impairments. As a classroom teacher, what might you need to do to meet some of these students' educational needs?

Major Characteristics of Students with Physical Disabilities, Health Impairments, and Multiple Disabilities

The range of abilities among students with physical disabilities, health impairments, and multiple disabilities is greater than in the general population. As an educator, you should consider the individual strengths and weaknesses of each of these students. In the following sections, we provide a general description of some of the characteristics that you may observe.

Academic and Cognitive Performance

Students with physical disabilities have a full range of academic abilities and disabilities: Some are gifted, while others have severe intellectual disabilities. For some students, such as a student with severe cerebral palsy, determining the actual degree of cognitive ability is often difficult. Standardized intelligence tests rely on a person's verbal and motor abilities; and because cerebral palsy, for example, often affects these abilities, attaining a precise determination of intelligence level is difficult (Best & Bigge, 2005; Willard-Holt, 1998). Assessment of students with spina bifida faces similar issues: Some of these students may have intellectual disabilities, some may have learning disabilities, and others may have average or above-average intelligence. Even those with higher intellectual abilities may have learning difficulties in the areas of attention, memory, comprehension, organization, and reasoning (Spina Bifida Association, 2008). For many other students with different types

Table 10.1 Public School Placements of School-Age (6 to 21 Years) Students with Physical Disabilities, Health Impairments, and Multiple Disabilities

Disability	Percentage of Students Placed in General Education Classroom for Most of the Day (>80% Time)	Percentage of Students Placed in General Education Classroom for Part of the Day (≤80% Time)	Percentage of Students Placed in Separate Settings (Schools, Residences, Hospitals, or Homes)
Physical disabilities	46.7	47.1	6.2
Health impairments	51.1	45.5	3.4
Multiple disabilities	12.1	63.0	24.9

Source: U.S. Department of Education (2007).

of physical disabilities (particularly those with orthopedic or musculoskeletal disorders), their physical condition likely will not affect their intellectual ability. Those students will be able to readily integrate into the general education classroom and the general curriculum, given adequate supports.

An important consideration for the academic success of students with physical disabilities is the provision of assistive technology (AT) devices and services to meet their needs. As we discuss in Chapter 16, numerous AT devices can be quite helpful to students with physical disabilities, and a number of these devices can make a difference in student success. You are likely to encounter students with physical disabilities who will manage quite well academically if the school has provided them with appropriate AT devices and services.

Most students with health impairments will have adequate cognitive and learning abilities for participation in the general education curriculum, but some may have learning disabilities associated with their health conditions. With others, their health impairment may have an indirect adverse effect on learning. A common difficulty is that the health condition may cause the student to miss an inordinate number of instructional activities because of pain, discomfort, illness, fatigue, or treatment side effects. For example, think of a student who has asthma. Besides being very dangerous, even potentially life-threatening, asthma can affect a student's progress in school. According to the American Academy of Asthma Allergy and Immunology (2005), in 1 year, children with asthma have a total of 10 million absences from school. This obviously translates to a great deal of lost instructional time. Depending on the student, this loss of time can have a significant impact on learning.

A major factor for the academic success of many students with health impairments is how well they can take and respond to prescribed medications. Although most school districts do not allow teachers to administer medications to students, it will sometimes be important for you to be able to monitor students' progress in school and report to parents or the school nurse if the student's participation is declining. This might suggest that the current regimen of medication should be reevaluated.

Students classified as having multiple disabilities will have some degree of intellectual disability in addition to their physical disabilities. This implies that their learning abilities within the general education curriculum will be limited. However, these students *can* participate if the general education curriculum has been adapted in a way that is meaningful to the student yet still reflects the essence of the material (Browder, Spooner, Wakeman, Trela, & Baker, 2006). Special education teachers skilled in working with students with multiple disabilities will provide assistance and support in making these adaptations and ensuring the success of these students in the general education classroom.

Behavior Performance and Social Skills

The personal thoughts, feelings, and social behavior of students with physical disabilities, health impairments, and multiple disabilities can be negatively impacted by the students' conditions. As a result, they may have poor self-esteem or self-worth, and their social interactions with other students may be adversely affected. Their view of the world and their interactions with others are likely to differ from others without disabilities or health conditions.

In one study of high school students with physical disabilities (Doubt & McColl, 2003), the students reported that to be better accepted they tried to avoid calling attention to their disability, sometimes made fun of their own condition, and found a special niche among their peers without disabilities, such as serving in a support role on a sports team. Sometimes, they said, they tried to educate their peers about their condition. Still, certain factors tended to isolate them, including their physical limitations as well as their own decisions to exclude themselves. Sometimes they did this because they could not keep up, but in other cases they excluded themselves because they felt they would not be accepted by others.

The study authors concluded that the students' lack of inclusion resulted from both intrinsic and extrinsic factors. That is, in some cases their own self-views or real physical limitations led to exclusion; and in others, the overt reactions by

Pause & Reflect

Think about a specific physical disability or ongoing health condition we have described. If you had this disability or condition, how well would you fit into your social group? How would the disability or condition affect how you fit in? Do you think your relationships would change?

Teaching Students with Physical Disabilities in Inclusive Classrooms: Challenges and Strategies

When Madge Goins and Jennifer Powell taught Sarah, their fourth-grade student with cerebral palsy, they had the benefit of consulting with a physical therapist (PT) and an occupational therapist about accommodating Sarah in an inclusive classroom. They felt there were many benefits to including Sarah but realized they would have to become creative in order to meet her needs.

Ms. Powell told us that "some especially effective practices that we used were things that the PT suggested. We had to put her in specialized seating, and make some schedule adjustments to allow time for her to get around. We also had to work out her schedule for her physical and occupational therapy needs." Additionally, the teachers had to find the right kinds of materials for Sarah. Ms. Goin said, "We had to get the classroom supplies [that were] adjusted to meet her needs. She struggled with fine motor skills, so we provided her with special scissors and pencils with hand-supported grippers. In her math ability group, she struggled with expressing her answers in writing. She was given manipulatives to use for problem solving, which allowed her to strengthen her fine-motor skills also. She seemed to adapt effectively with the assistance of these modifications."

their peers excluded them. Regardless, the students' physical disabilities meant that they were less socially involved (Doubt & McColl, 2003).

As with physical disabilities, health impairments can sometimes impact normal social behavior, interactions, and relationships. For example, peers may avoid students who experience frequent asthma attacks, and at the same time, parents and teachers may limit play and recreational activities to reduce the chance of an attack (Best, 2005). Similarly, peers may avoid a student with epilepsy who has had a seizure if they are unfamiliar with epilepsy and have not previously witnessed a seizure. Because seizures often first appear during adolescence, this can be very embarrassing for the student, who may be shunned or subjected to taunting and ridicule.

Peers may also react differently to students with chronic health impairments such as cancer or HIV/AIDS. Students with such conditions may miss a great deal of school because of their illness and, when in school, may be weak or tired. As a result, they have limited opportunities to take part in play activities, adolescent bantering, or other typical social activities. Some peers, not fully understanding the nature of a student's condition, may fear it and thus avoid the student. Others may feel sorry for the student and be uncomfortable with normal age-appropriate interactions. In all of these circumstances, the challenge is the same: the student with the condition will not be likely to interact with other students in common ways.

Students who have multiple disabilities may be subjected to these same social conditions. Worse for these students, however, is their proneness to engage in various uncommon behaviors that cause them to appear very different and lead others to avoid them or, even worse, fear them. These behaviors might include repetitive movements (called stereotypies, such as hand-flapping, self-injurious behaviors, such as head-banging), or making loud and atypical vocalizations. Many times these behaviors can be improved through the use of positive behavior support principles (see Chapter 15), but the reaction of other students will usually be problematic.

Effective Instruction for Students with Physical Disabilities, Health Impairments, and Multiple Disabilities

Effective Instruction for Elementary Students

For students with physical disabilities, health impairments, or multiple disabilities to succeed in inclusive classrooms, the teacher should consider several issues beginning with curriculum and instruction. Students with physical disabilities and health impairments who have typical cognitive

For steps to plan appropriate instruction for students with disabilities in the general education classroom, see Strategy 12.3 in Chapter 12.

and learning abilities usually participate in the general curriculum like other students. Their learning goals therefore are the same as others', and most of the instruction provided to others is meaningful to them. As we stated earlier, however, some of these students may have learning disabilities associated with their physical or health impairments and need structured support to participate successfully. On the other hand, students with multiple disabilities have intellectual disabilities, and for these students, modifications in both the curriculum and in instructional methods are necessary.

When designing curriculum for students with physical disabilities, health impairments, or multiple disabilities, in addition to the general curriculum, educators can consider complementary or supplementary instruction such as the following:

- **The general education curriculum with modifications.** Modifications might include changes in the content, desired outcomes, or levels of complexity. This curriculum may be appropriate for a student whose condition impedes success in the general curriculum without modifications—for example, a student with CP who cannot maintain the same pace as the rest of the class.
- **Life skills curriculum.** This curriculum is appropriate for a student who is not acquiring sufficient life skills without specific instruction or for a student who needs to learn to use adaptive devices to participate in different activities. Participation in a life skills curriculum may either complement or supplement participation in the general curriculum with or without modifications.
- **Curriculum modified in communication and task performance.** Those who need explicit instruction in communication skills to participate in home, school, and community life participate in learning activities in this curriculum. These students have relatively severe physical disabilities that may exist with or without concurrent intellectual disabilities (Stump & Bigge, 2005).

Pause & Reflect

Do you think that having a physical disability or a health impairment will significantly interfere with learning? To what extent are you willing to make accommodations to support these students?

For step-by-step guidelines to select appropriate assistive technology devices, see Strategy 16.5 in Chapter 16.

For students with physical disabilities, important accommodations often consist of the use of assistive technology devices including mobility equipment and communication devices. As we describe in Chapter 16, a wide variety of assistive technology is available. Teachers often collaborate with speech–language pathologists, physical therapists, or occupational therapists to ensure the proper fit, use, and support for these devices.

As a professional educator, you should familiarize yourself with any AT devices that your students use. Additionally, if you perceive that a certain type of device, such as an augmentative communication device, might help increase a student's participation, you should discuss this with your colleagues in special education, appropriate therapists, or with members of the IEP team. Beyond understanding your students' devices, it may be important for you to make some adjustments in your classroom so you can better accommodate students' physical needs. These can include changing some of the physical arrangements of your classroom and improving accessibility for students with physical disabilities. Figure 10.1 suggests considerations for educators in classrooms when students with certain physical disabilities or health impairments are present.

Two considerations are especially helpful when teaching students with health impairments. First, these students may need assistance in keeping up with their school work following absences. As mentioned, students' health impairments may sometimes cause them to miss school or attend school feeling tired or unwell. They may also have to leave the classroom on several occasions to use the restroom, to get water or nourishment, to rest, or to take medication. To help these students make up missed instructional time and provide more academic practice, teachers can provide extra time for students to complete their homework, offer supplementary learning activities, or arrange for tutoring from peers, paraprofessionals, or volunteers.

A second consideration for some students with health impairments is the need to take precautions to avoid triggering health-related reactions. For example, students with asthma can have an attack brought on by several different allergens such as tiny dust particles, pet dander, or cold, dry air. Suggestions for accommodating students with health impairments are shown in Figure 10.1.

PUTTING IT ALL TOGETHER

Delivering effective instruction involves not just knowledge of practices, but also much additional information related to collaboration, planning, classroom management, and the use of technology, among other things. With this in mind, we offer several suggestions for your consideration.

1. **Effective instruction depends on collaboration.** In an inclusive setting, a general education teacher often brings a deep knowledge of the content, while the special education teacher brings a toolbox of strategies to ensure that all students learn the material. When teachers combine these areas of expertise, they provide more effective instruction, and all students learn more.

2. **Effective instruction is well organized and depends on good classroom management.** Vicki Eng, from West Hernando Middle School, made this point well: "When you walk into a class with kids with LD or students who struggle, you need to be well organized, you can't wing it, or you lose control of your class. You need to have guidelines, rules posted early, so issues don't become problems you can't control."

3. **Effective teachers have a toolbox of strategies that work.** No effective practice works every time for every student. Effective teachers monitor the effectiveness of instructional approaches and have alternatives available when a strategy does not work with a student.

4. **Effective teachers are lifelong learners.** The best teachers are those who continue to improve and are constantly adding new strategies to help their students who struggle.

myeducationlab

We present strategies in the second half of this chapter (Strategies 13.1 to 13.7) in a step-by-step format so that you can use them in your classroom right away. In addition, in the following table, we identify some video clips, cases, and simulations that will allow you to experience these strategies (or complementary strategies) in a real classroom environment.

EFFECTIVE PRACTICE	MYEDUCATIONLAB CONNECTION	CONSIDER THIS
Strategy 13.1: Success for All	Go to MyEducationLab, select the topic *Instructional Practices and Learning Strategies*, and go to the Building Teaching Skills and Dispositions section. Next, complete the activity entitled "Direct Instruction: Literacy," and answer the accompanying questions.	As you complete the activity, pay close attention to the techniques the teacher uses with her students in the video clips. This teacher is using a teacher-directed program. How would you characterize this program, as compared to the Success for All program discussed in Strategy 13.1?
Strategy 13.2: Cooperative Learning	Go to MyEducationLab, select the topic *Reading Instruction*, and go to the Activities and Applications section. Next, complete the simulation entitled "The Reading Blues."	As you complete the simulation, focus on the CSR strategy and its cooperative learning components. Compare and contrast the CSR strategy with the PALS strategy (Strategy 13.4).
Strategy 13.3: Reading Recovery	Go to MyEducationLab, select the topic *Reading Instruction*, and go to the Activities and Applications section. Next, complete the simulation entitled "Evaluating Reading Progress."	As you complete the simulation, think about how you could use curriculum-based measures in conjunction with the Reading Recovery program to ensure student success in reading.
Strategy 13.4: Peer-Assisted Learning Strategies	Go to MyEducationLab, select the topic *Reading Instruction*, and go to the Activities and Applications section. Next, complete the simulation entitled "See Jane Read."	As you complete the simulation, focus on the different strategies presented. How has the PALS strategy been adapted to meet the needs of kindergartners?
Strategy 13.5: Beginning Reading: Tiers of Instruction & RTI	Go to MyEducationLab, select the topic *Reading Instruction*, and go to the Activities and Applications section. Next, complete the simulation entitled "RTI (Part 3): Reading Instruction."	As you complete the simulation, focus on the three tiers of intervention discussed in Strategy 13.5 and the simulation. How do these gradually increasing interventions ensure success for students who are struggling?
Strategy 13.6: Self-Regulated Strategy Development	Go to MyEducationLab, select the topic *Content Area Teaching*, and go to the Building Teaching Skills and Dispositions section. Next, complete the activity entitled "Scaffolding in Literacy."	As you watch the videos in this activity and answer the accompanying questions, compare and contrast the strategies these teachers use to help their students become successful writers with the points in Strategy 13.6.
Strategy 13.7: Cognitive Strategy Instruction	Go to MyEducationLab, select the topic *Content Area Teaching*, and go to the Activities and Applications section. Next, analyze the strategies entitled "Problem-Solving Self-Monitoring Sheet" and "Self-Monitoring Sheet: Can the Fraction Be Reduced?"	As you analyze these strategies, reflect on how they could help a student who is struggling in math. Could these strategies fit into the cognitive strategy instruction model discussed in Strategy 13.7? Why or why not?

EFFECTIVE PRACTICES

In the remainder of this chapter, we describe seven effective strategies, which we referred to previously in the chapter, to help you plan effectively to meet the needs of all students.

EFFECTIVE PRACTICE	TYPE OF STRATEGY/BRIEF DESCRIPTION	SPECIAL CONSIDERATIONS
Strategy 13.1: Success for All	SFA is an approach to school reform emphasizing early intervention, prevention, and innovative curricula in reading, writing, and language arts. Teachers employ cooperative learning strategies to support student learning.	SFA is only used in schools where 80% or more of the teachers support its use. Teachers are provided extensive professional development, and school-wide changes are required to implement SFA.
Strategy 13.2: Cooperative Learning	A grouping strategy that uses mixed ability groups for instruction. The goal is to ensure all students learn assigned content, which may range from basic academic skills to complex group projects.	Formal approaches using cooperative learning may be used for an extended period of time. However, more informal approaches to cooperative learning may be used to work on specific tasks for brief periods of time.
Strategy 13.3: Reading Recovery	A tutoring approach for beginning readers that employs effective instructional strategies to reduce the number of students who have difficulty learning to read.	Reading Recovery requires special, extensive training for tutors, and it can be expensive to implement. Students can be taught in pairs to reduce costs.
Strategy 13.4: Peer-Assisted Learning Strategies	Peer tutoring that offers an efficient, cost-effective method for providing students with independent practice on the skills they need in order to develop in-depth knowledge of content.	Peer-tutoring programs such as PALS can be used in any subject area, and they are flexible, easy to implement, cost-effective, and time-efficient. These qualities likely account for the acceptance and use of these interventions by many teachers in elementary and secondary classrooms.
Strategy 13.5: Beginning Reading: Tiers of Instruction & RTI	Assumes that a student should be identified with a disability only after high-quality instruction has been provided, and the student has continued to struggle to learn.	In an RTI model, high-quality, effective instruction includes core instruction in the general education classroom (Tier 1), instruction in small groups (Tier 2), and intensive, individualized instruction focusing on specific student needs (Tier 3).
Strategy 13.6: Self-Regulated Strategy Development	An approach used to support students in using writing strategies effectively and independently. Teachers provide explicit instruction as students learn the strategy and how it can be applied.	Many elementary students with disabilities have difficulty planning and regulating writing strategies. SRSD may be used to improve student planning and self-regulation as they learn to write.
Strategy 13.7: Cognitive Strategy Instruction	An approach to support students who struggle to learn mathematics by scaffolding instruction. Includes built-in cues and prompts for students as they engage in strategies for self-regulation, self-instruction, self-monitoring, and self-checking. Supports are gradually faded.	Teachers have developed strategies for solving mathematics problems by talking through how they solve a particular type of problem, or by talking with proficient students to better understand how they solve problems.

Figure 10.1	Classroom Considerations for Students with Physical Disabilities and Health Impairments

Cerebral Palsy

A student's ability to physically engage in class activities depends on the severity and extent of the cerebral palsy (CP). Many can easily participate, but some require adaptations or accommodations. The physical therapist (PT) and occupational therapist (OT) can help teachers design ways to include the student with CP in various learning activities. Sometimes adults assume that the student with CP also has a severe intellectual disability. While this may be true in some cases, it would be a mistake for teachers to approach the student with this assumption. The motor limitations of students with CP often mask their intellectual ability.

Muscular Dystrophy

The child with muscular dystrophy becomes gradually weaker through the childhood years. His intellectual ability does not decrease, but about one third of the boys with Duchene muscular dystrophy have learning disabilities. Instructional activities must take into consideration both physical and academic characteristics. The longer the child can remain upright, active, and mobile, the better. Teachers should maintain positive attitudes about the value of the student as a participating member of the class.

Spina Bifida

The physical ability of the student with spina bifida varies based on where the lesion occurs, but most students require personal assistance to carry out daily activities. These students also commonly use adaptive devices. Many students with spina bifida are cognitively able but challenged by their physical limitations. Many students also experience social isolation from their peers, largely due to their bladder and bowel problems. Relations with the opposite sex can be especially trying.

Orthopedic and Musculoskeletal Conditions

The biggest challenge for these students in the classroom, and for their teachers, is finding ways for them to be physically engaged and involved. Their prosthetic devices, body supports, wheelchairs, and other necessary supports may make it difficult for them to get close to instructional activities. OTs and PTs can help design classroom arrangements and conditions that increase physical closeness and participation. It is also important to address the discomfort that results from the devices so the student is not distracted from learning activities.

Asthma

Teachers should try to keep the classroom free of any antigens that may cause an attack or at least keep the child away from the source. The teacher also needs to be aware of the child's medication and help manage its appropriate use based on home and school guidelines. The child may miss many school days, and the teacher needs to promote a supportive environment to help the child keep up with the other students.

Sickle-Cell Disease

The student with sickle-cell disease may be absent often because of pain episodes and hospitalization, so extra support and homework might help him keep up. Plenty of access to water and the restroom and avoidance of overheating and cold temperatures are important.

Epilepsy

When a student has a seizure, the teacher should help her lie down, turn her to one side to prevent choking on saliva or vomit, loosen clothing around the neck, and place something soft under her head to prevent it from hitting a hard surface. The teacher should not insert anything into the mouth. If the seizure lasts for more than 5 minutes, the teacher should call for emergency assistance. He should also note when the seizure occurred and how long it lasted.

Type 1 Diabetes

Students with diabetes can participate in most activities with other students but need a few special considerations. They may need privacy to test their blood sugar and inject insulin if

(continued)

| Figure 10.1 | **Classroom Considerations for Students with Physical Disabilities and Health Impairments   continued** |

necessary, may need access to the bathroom more frequently than others, and may need to have snacks more often than other students. In the case of hypoglycemia, students may exhibit sweating, paleness, trembling, hunger, and weakness, indicating the need for emergency treatment.

Cystic Fibrosis

Students with cystic fibrosis undergo chest physiotherapy once or twice a day to loosen the mucus in their chests. This may occur before and after school, but while in school they need to take digestive enzymes and other medications. Problems with digestion affect bowel movements, and privacy at this time is an important issue. Teachers may need to take steps to improve social inclusion.

Strategy

For procedures to develop a 504 Plan, see Strategy 12.2 in Chapter 12.

Strategy

For a description of the key components to effective collaboration, see Strategy 11.1 in Chapter 11.

You should note that students with special health needs will usually have an individualized health care plan (IHCP) (Best, 2005). If the student has an IEP, the IHCP is attached to it. On the other hand, if the student is not in special education, the IHCP is incorporated into the student's Section 504 Plan. In either case, teachers who have students with IHCPs should be familiar with their contents and know their responsibilities under the plan.

In contrast to students who have physical disabilities or health impairments, students with multiple disabilities who have intellectual disabilities usually require *systematic instruction* in order to learn to do specific tasks (Westling & Fox, 2009). Various systematic instructional approaches might be useful. One that is commonly used is the least-to-most prompting system. Figure 10.2 describes this process. Close collaboration with a colleague in special education will help you learn to use different systematic instruction procedures successfully.

General educators should be aware of four professionals who can be key contributors to the successful inclusion of the students we discuss in this chapter. These are speech–language pathologists (SLPs), physical therapists (PTs), occupational therapists (OTs), and school nurses.

The SLP is a key individual for determining the most effective mode of communication for students if they have difficulty in this area. SLPs often play an important role with students who have physical or multiple disabilities. The PT evaluates, plans, and develops interventions to improve posture and balance; to prevent bodily malformations; and to improve walking ability and other gross-motor skills. PTs are also very important support persons for students with physical or multiple disabilities. The OT has knowledge and skills similar to the PT's but has an orientation toward purposeful activities or tasks such as the use of fine-motor skills related to daily living activities. The school nurse performs or oversees various treatments for students including evaluating students' health status and administering medications. You will find that collaboration with all of these professionals can be extremely helpful when including students with disabilities.

Sometimes professionals have concerns that students with certain conditions might be contagious and that they may become infected. Discussions about such concerns with the school nurse or

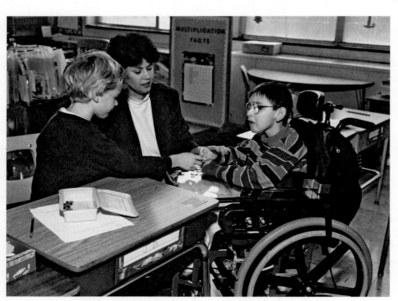

Appropriate adaptive technology devices can allow students with physical disabilities to increase their participation in the general education classroom and curriculum.

Figure 10.2   Systematic Instruction Using Least-to-Most Prompting

- Develop a hierarchy of prompts (see below).
- Provide a prompt on each trial with only the minimum intensity necessary (e.g., start with verbal, the gestural, etc., as necessary to prompt the response).
- At each step of a task, present the target stimulus, and if no response occurs, the next stimulus, and then the next, until finally using a controlling stimulus if necessary.
- Having completed that step, move on to the next step in the chain, and repeat the hierarchical process.

Typical Sequence System of Least Prompts

- No prompt (completion of prior step serves as the cue to do the next step).
- Verbal direction (tell the student what to do).
- Partial physical prompt (e.g., nudge the student's hand in the direction of the action that should occur).
- Full physical assistance (fully guide the student through the behavior that is to occur).

Figure 10.3   Universal Precautions

The Centers for Disease Control and Prevention have established universal precautions to prevent the transmission of infectious diseases. You should always follow these procedures, regardless of whether you know or believe a student has a transmittable condition. Universal precautions include proper hand washing; use of personal protective equipment; safe methods for getting rid of waste, cleaning up spills, and handling laundry; and procedures for dealing with accidental contact to potentially infectious materials. You should use these precautions whenever you have contact with blood, semen, vaginal secretions, or other body fluids that may contain blood (Best, 2005). Your school nurse is a good source of information for how to use universal precautions.

Additional information is available from the Centers for Disease Control and Prevention at http://www.cdc.gov/ncidod/dhqp/bp_universal_precautions.html

---

another health-care provider will be very helpful. This professional may recommend that you adhere to universal precautions, which are procedures developed by the Centers for Disease Control and Prevention to prevent transmission of blood-borne pathogens. Figure 10.3 outlines these procedures.

Strategies to Achieve Social Success. Educators can play a significant role in fostering social success for students with physical disabilities, health impairments, or multiple disabilities. First and most important, teachers and students should develop positive relationships. This provides an important foundation for the students and helps them develop relationships with other students. The actions of the adults also provides an important model for other students to follow.

The second strategy to achieve social success is to nurture communication. The basis of social relationships is communication, and communication by some individuals with physical or multiple disabilities can be difficult (Best & Bigge, 2005). For example, the speech of some persons with CP can be very strained and slow, causing the listener to try to complete the statement or grow tired of waiting to hear it. If this is the case, two tactics are important. First, the teacher should collaborate with an SLP to determine if an alternative or augmentative communication (AAC) device might help the student communicate more effectively and efficiently. The teacher should also try to influence other students to understand why the student has slow or difficult-to-understand speech and encourage and reinforce them to let the student communicate as effectively as possible. By giving the student this type of consideration, social interactions should become more successful.

If students with disabilities are to be social partners with their classmates, we should understand that it means they must take some chances. Teasing, name-calling, and making fun of others is an

For steps to support students who use an AAC device, see Strategy 16.8 in Chapter 16.

Strategy

unpleasant but common part of the transitional process of moving from childhood to adulthood. Students with physical disabilities or health impairments cannot socialize with others without being part of this process. From the point of view of a responsible adult, this is certainly something that one should not condone, but at the same time, you cannot protect the student with special needs from it without causing social isolation. Whatever policy teachers maintain for other students with regard to this issue should be followed for students with disabilities.

Last, to promote successful social interactions and development, we recommend providing all assistance with concern for the student's dignity. The assistance that might be required can range from assisting students through a door to helping them use the bathroom. In all such cases, personal assistance should be provided with as little attention and fanfare as possible, and as discreetly as possible. It is also important that students do as much for themselves as possible and that teachers not convey the notion that the student is helpless or completely dependent.

Effective Instruction for Secondary Students

Strategies to Achieve Academic Success. The majority of middle and high school students with physical disabilities, health impairments, and many with multiple disabilities will have interests similar to their peers. Many will have favorite subjects and will think about their future. Most will also be attracted to members of the opposite sex, think about their real or desired relationships, and have other typical interests within their cultural milieu.

As adolescents, most of the students we have been discussing will enjoy and benefit from subject matter content to an extent similar to that of peers who do not have disabilities. Still, as with elementary-age students, you can expect that they will have some difficulties. As we said earlier, some students will be affected by learning or intellectual disabilities. But for the most part, the biggest challenge for many is finding ways to physically engage them in most learning activities; this is especially true for students with physical and multiple disabilities. Prosthetic devices, body supports, wheelchairs, ventilators, and other necessary supports may make physical closeness to instructional activities difficult in traditional classrooms and school laboratories. PTs and OTs can help design classroom arrangements and conditions that increase physical closeness and participation. These same professionals can help by addressing discomfort resulting from different support devices so the student is not distracted from learning activities.

As people witnessing individuals growing toward maturity, high school teachers should think about the relationship between what they are teaching, what the students are learning, and how this all bears on the student's future. High school students with physical disabilities, health impairments, or multiple disabilities are likely to have one or more of four personal conditions that will affect their future (Clark & Bigge, 2005):

- **Independence difficulties.** High levels of dependency can be a potential barrier to a job or a career. Special needs, such as transportation, accessibility modifications, the use of AT devices, or communication supports, can be problematic.
- **Strength and stamina.** The person's ability to complete the job, side effects due to medications, or the regular need for emergency medical care can pose challenges.
- **Lack of experience in self-care and personal health management.** Generally, people in the workforce expect co-workers to be able to take care of their personal needs. The person who has not learned to do these tasks, or cannot do them, may have difficulties.
- **Limited social experiences.** Most important, people in the workforce expect their co-workers to demonstrate an acceptable level of social ability in the working environment. Persons who have not learned these important skills are at a disadvantage.

Although the primary job of a high school or middle school teacher will be to teach specific subject matter, you can take several small, but not insignificant, actions that can lead to more successful learning at the secondary level for students with physical disabilities, health impairments, and multiple disabilities. These actions will help students participate in your course and at the same time better prepare them to overcome the challenges just described:

- Be aware of the student's cognitive abilities and learning potential, and don't assume that it is less than other students'. Although you may ultimately find that your curriculum or instruction should be modified, assume that the student can learn what you are teaching.
- Look for particular interests that the student may have, and use these to motivate the student and draw her into the subject matter. This, of course, is a useful strategy for all students, but it can especially be helpful for students with disabilities.
- Maintain an awareness of signs of pain, discomfort, or a need for medical or physical support. Make sure you have read the student's IHCP and know what actions to take should the need arise. Don't assume the student has a problem with motivation if you notice a lack of participation, because this lack may be related to the student's physical or health status.
- Use effective teaching methods that are appropriate for all of your students but that will especially benefit students with learning challenges.
- Don't allow the student's physical or health support devices to restrict participation in activities, and also don't allow the student to be isolated by support from a paraeducator or one-on-one support person.

In Chapter 14 we present several step-by-step strategies for increasing the learning success of secondary students with disabilities.

> For a step-by-step strategy to create unit and lesson organizers for secondary students, see Strategy 14.1 in Chapter 14.
>
> Strategy

Strategies to Achieve Social Success

The suggestions we presented in the previous section for supporting the social success of elementary students apply also to adolescents with disabilities. However, during the adolescent years, self-examination and self-perceptions become more intense, and a person's standing in relation to peers often takes on monumental proportions. It is at this age, then, that students with physical disabilities and health impairments are likely to be confused and bewildered about their own development and how they can be socially successful with their peers. Isolation and outright rejection can be a major problem and can have a long-term impact.

> ### Pause & Reflect
>
> If you are, or plan to be, a middle school or high school teacher, to what extent do you think you can or should try to improve social relations for students with disabilities? How might you do this?

A secondary-level teacher may be in a perfect position to observe the social problems of students and perhaps to take an active role in helping the student address them. Although a teacher can't and shouldn't try to solve a student's problems, a teacher can take some actions that may have a positive effect. We suggest the following:

- Help students to focus on their positive abilities wherever they may appear. These might include strengths in academic areas, their sense of humor, or their easygoing disposition. By focusing on these positive aspects, you might provide a counterbalance to feelings of personal devaluation. Please note that any remarks you make should be subtle and never condescending.
- Encourage students' participation in school clubs or organizations and extracurricular activities. You can inform students of opportunities, let them know about organization activities, tell them who current members are, and help them see the benefits of their participation. You might ask a current student member of the organization to invite the student to come as a guest to an initial meeting or activity.
- Encourage self-advocacy and self-determination. Because of their disabilities or health impairments, students may sometimes be less assertive with regard to expressing their needs, wishes, or opinions. You can let students know that everyone has a right to self-expression, and you can reinforce their efforts to positively take a stance with others.
- Report to the parents or the school nurse physical or medical conditions that may inhibit personal interactions with other students. Some students' physical conditions may place them in

Teachers can sometimes play a role in fostering positive social relationships.

social isolation. Unpleasant body odors, bad breath, a disheveled look, or even "uncool" clothing can have such a result, and to the extent that these can be corrected, they should.

Final Thoughts Regarding Effective Practices

In Chapters 11 to 16, we provide step-by-step descriptions of many effective practices that are useful for students with disabilities and others who struggle in school. Several of these effective practices are particularly useful for teachers who work with students with physical disabilities, health impairments, or multiple disabilities. For example, because teachers will especially need to collaborate with professionals such as SLPs, PTs, and OTs, understanding Strategy 11.1, the key elements of successful collaboration, is important. We also recommend close attention to Strategies 11.5 and 11.7, on how paraeducators and peer buddies can be important sources of support for students with disabilities. Some of the most important strategies that educators can use to include students with physical disabilities, health impairments, and multiple disabilities can be found in Chapter 16. We especially recommend that you look at Strategies 16.1 (teaching students to use educational technology), 16.5 (selecting assistive technology devices), 16.8 (using AAC devices), and 16.9 (using motorized wheelchairs).

Summary

Definitions of students with physical disabilities, health impairments, and multiple disabilities

- "Orthopedic impairment [the term used in IDEA instead of *physical disabilities*] means a severe orthopedic impairment that adversely affects a child's educational performance. The term includes impairments caused by congenital anomaly (e.g., clubfoot, absence of some member, etc.), impairments caused by disease (e.g., poliomyelitis, bone tuberculosis, etc.), and impairments from other causes (e.g., cerebral palsy, amputations, and fractures or burns that cause contractures)."

- Health impairment, according to IDEA, means "having limited strength, vitality or alertness, including a heightened alertness to environmental stimuli, that results in limited alertness with respect to the educational environment, that— (i) Is due to chronic or acute health problems such as asthma, attention deficit disorder or attention deficit hyperactivity disorder, diabetes, epilepsy, a heart condition, hemophilia, lead poisoning, leukemia, nephritis, rheumatic fever, and sickle cell anemia; and (ii) Adversely affects a child's educational performance."

- According to IDEA, multiple disabilities are "concomitant impairments (e.g., mental retardation–blindness, mental retardation–orthopedic impairment), the combination of which causes such severe educational needs that they cannot be accommodated in special education programs solely for one of the impairments. The term does not include deaf-blindness."

Prevalence of students with physical disabilities, health impairments, and multiple disabilities

- During the school years, 0.10% of students will have physical disabilities; 0.68% have health impairments; and 0.20% have multiple disabilities.

Educational placements for students with physical disabilities, health impairments, and multiple disabilities

- The large majority of students with physical disabilities and those with health impairments are in the general education classroom for most or part of the day.
- The majority of students with multiple disabilities are placed in special schools or special classes within regular schools for most of the day.

Major characteristics of students with physical disabilities, health impairments, and multiple disabilities

- Academic and cognitive performance
  - Students with physical disabilities: Most of these students have typical cognitive ability and can do academic work with the use of assistive technology. Some may have other disabilities that may affect their abilities.
  - Students with health impairments: Most of these students have adequate cognitive and learning abilities, but some may have learning disabilities. They may also be adversely affected by the amount of school they miss due to their health impairment.
  - Students with multiple disabilities: These students have intellectual disabilities that may be in the severe-to-profound range and require an adapted curriculum.
- Behavior performance and social skills
  - Students with physical disabilities: These students sometimes have difficulty developing social relations with their peers because of differences in their physical characteristics.
  - Students with health impairments: Some of these health impairments may make participation in typical social activities difficult. Sometimes these students may be subjects of discrimination because of their conditions.
  - Students with multiple disabilities: These students often lack the opportunity for social interactions.

Principles of effective instruction at the elementary level

- The general curriculum is appropriate for most students with physical disabilities and health impairments.
- Some students have learning disabilities associated with their conditions and require extra learning support.
- Students with multiple disabilities who also have severe-to-profound intellectual disabilities require a modified curriculum and systematic instruction.
- Assistive technology devices are necessary for many students with physical disabilities and multiple disabilities.
- Students with health impairments may need additional support or instruction to make up for missed instructional time.
- Some students with health impairments need environments free of antigens that may trigger asthma attacks.
- Students may have individualized health care plans (IHCPs) that the teacher will need to be aware of and follow as necessary.
- Teachers will need to collaborate with physical therapists, occupational therapists, and school nurses.

Strategies to promote social skills and relationships at the elementary level

- Show respect for students, and expect an appropriate relation with them.
- Do not demonstrate fear of students or their conditions.
- Promote appropriate language development, including the use of augmentative communication devices if necessary.

- Do not protect students from typical social interactions with other students, even though the interactions may be ill mannered.
- Respect the dignity of students when providing personal assistance.

Principles of effective instruction at the secondary level (in addition to those effective at the elementary level)

- Most students with physical disabilities and health impairments will benefit from content-area instruction.
- Teachers should not allow students' participation to be impaired by special equipment or devices.
- Students will need to consider their individual strengths and weaknesses as they consider future schooling or job possibilities.
- Teachers should use students' interest to promote their participation in the curriculum.
- Teachers should not misinterpret students' discomfort or illness to be a lack of interest or motivation.

Strategies to support students' social development at the secondary level

- Reinforce their personal strengths.
- Encourage their participation in extracurricular activities.
- Encourage self-advocacy and self-determination.
- Identify any personal conditions that may impede social interactions, and work with other professionals to improve them.

Addressing Professional Standards

Standards addressed in Chapter 10 include:

CEC Standards: (1) foundations, (2) development and characteristics of learners, (3) individual learning differences, (4) instructional strategies.

INTASC Standards: Principle 1—Understand central concepts of the discipline; Principle 2—Provide learning opportunities to support the learning and development of all students.

Praxis™ II Standards: Knowledge-based core principles: (1) understanding exceptionalities, (3) delivery of services to students with disabilities. Application of core principles: (1) curriculum, (2) instruction, (5) professional roles/issues/literature.

PART III
Effective Practices

Chapter 11

Collaboration and Teaming

Chapter 12

Formal Plans and Planning for Differentiated Instruction

Chapter 13

Effective Instruction in Elementary Inclusive Classrooms: Teaching Reading, Writing, and Mathematics

Chapter 14

Teaching Students in Secondary Content Areas

Chapter 15

Effective Practices for All Students: Classroom Management

Chapter 16

Using Technology to Enhance Inclusion

Collaboration and Teaming

KEY TOPICS

After reading this chapter you will:

- Know what collaboration is, and why it is important in supporting inclusive classrooms and schools.
- Be able to identify the dispositions needed to effectively collaborate with other professionals.
- Understand the skills needed to effectively collaborate with other professionals.

- Be able to describe the collaborative roles of teachers in inclusive schools.
- Understand how students may be engaged as collaborators to support inclusive programs.
- Possess a series of guided, step-by-step interventions and practices related to working collaboratively to meet the needs of all students.

chapter 11

Perspectives on Collaboration

Why Is Collaboration Absolutely Necessary to Support Inclusion?

An Interview with Susan Davis and Lisa Hallal, Eighth-Grade Special Education Teachers, West Hernando Middle School

Both Susan Davis and Lisa Hallal have backgrounds as elementary general education teachers and have over 20 years of teaching experience. Their primary responsibilities at West Hernando Middle School relate to working as co-teachers or consultants with eighth-grade teachers to support students with disabilities in general education classrooms, and providing small-group or individual instruction to students with disabilities, as needed.

Susan Davis and Lisa Hallal view collaboration as an "absolute necessity" for effective inclusive programs. They note that co-teachers

> bring different skills into the classroom, and collaboration provides the opportunity to share that expertise to benefit all students. Subject matter teachers bring a deep knowledge of the content and strategies for teaching the content in interesting ways. We [special education teachers] often know much less about the content, but bring expertise in making instructional accommodations to make sure that all students learn. . . .
>
> Teachers learn a lot from collaboration. Special education teachers learn a lot about the content, and how to teach it from the content area expert in the general education classroom. We can't know about content in every area in a middle school: English, science, math, social studies. There's no way we can figure out about how to make accommodations in instruction or on tests unless we learn about the content of the class. We learn the content by watching the general education teacher, and then we can teach some of the lessons, do re-teaching for students who don't get the information after going over it in class, and work with the classroom teacher to make accommodations in lessons and on tests.
>
> Content area teachers also learn from us. One of the most important things they learn is to make accommodations for students. They see us making accommodations to help students learn content, or we make suggestions about making accommodations during class lessons. Most content area teachers don't know how to make accommodations for students, but they learn from us and then can do it themselves. We see this because they are comfortable when we have to leave their classroom. They've learned so much about how to make accommodations work. At first

they are nervous to have kids with disabilities in their class when they're alone (or the only teacher). After a while they're very comfortable with that, because they've learned so much about accommodations for all of their students.

Introduction

If you've ever tried to work with peers on a project in a college classroom, you realize that collaboration is not a simple task. Some people readily contribute to projects, while others don't contribute as easily. Some want to complete the project quickly and before the due date, while others want to wait until the last minute. Some attend closely to detail, while others want to focus on the big picture. Given how difficult collaboration can be, why should teachers or other professionals bother collaborating?

The short answer to that question is "two heads (or more) are better than one." That is, two or more persons collaborating on a project or activity can often come up with a better project or answer to a problem than a single person can working alone (Blinder & Morgan, 2000).

Collaboration obviously takes time and effort on the part of all participants. As you reflected on the successful group projects you've worked on in a college classroom, you probably noted that the group members were flexible, cooperative, worked to accommodate the preferences of others, and built on the different areas of expertise that existed in the group. This experience is similar to collaborative roles that teachers assume when they work with teachers or other professionals to solve problems and address student needs.

As Susan Davis and Lisa Hallal from West Hernando Middle School state in the interview at the beginning of this chapter, collaboration is an "absolute necessity" for effective inclusive programs. They note that collaboration is essential primarily because general and special education teachers bring different areas of expertise to the general education classroom, and all of these areas of expertise are needed for inclusion to succeed. For example, general education teachers in a middle school are most often prepared with in-depth knowledge of the content they are teaching and with methods to teach that content to large groups of students. In contrast, special education teachers are typically prepared to differentiate content and adapt instruction to meet the needs of students who struggle to learn the content. Collaboration is all about combining these areas of expertise to meet the needs of all students in the general education classroom.

> ## Pause & Reflect
>
> Consider a group project you completed in a college classroom that was very successful. What qualities of the group made the project successful? Was the content of the project better than any individual could have completed? Does this experience suggest that two heads can often be better than one? Why, or why not?

Teachers collaborate to share knowledge and expertise and improve outcomes for students.

Collaboration: What to Expect

For most of the last century, teachers taught in relative isolation, with their classroom doors closed, and they depended on their own knowledge and expertise to address their students' needs. Since the 1980s, this has begun to change. Two major factors that have contributed to this change are increasing demands for higher levels of student achievement and the increasing diversity of the student population in schools.

Regarding increased demands for student achievement, success in the information age clearly requires all students to achieve higher levels of knowledge and skills, especially related to literacy and numeracy (Kohl, McLaughlin, & Nagle, 2006). States have responded to this need by expecting students to master curriculum at increasingly younger ages. In addition, all states now have accountability measures in place to make certain that students meet expected standards. Thus, teachers are required to ensure that all students achieve increasingly higher levels of achievement.

Part of the accountability system for student achievement is designed to make sure that students who live in poverty, those from different cultural and language backgrounds, and students with disabilities meet achievement standards. The increased diversity of classrooms across the United States has made this task complex. For example, in 2004, about one third of the U.S. population was made up of persons from Hispanic, African American, Asian/Pacific Islander, or Native American/Alaska Native backgrounds (Ross, Kamman, & Coady, 2008). Researchers anticipate that this percentage will grow to 50% by 2025 (Hussar, 2005). Similarly, the number of students in schools who are living in poverty, who speak languages other than English, and who have disabilities is rapidly growing (Rosenberg, Westling, & McLeskey, 2008; Ross, Kamman, & Coady, 2008). This increasing diversity, coupled with increasing demands for student achievement, makes it important that all teachers collaborate and share expertise with others to make certain that all students succeed in school.

What Is Collaboration?

Given the higher demands for achievement and related accountability measures, as well as the increasing diversity of schools across the United States, it is incumbent on teachers that they open their classroom doors and begin to collaborate with other professionals to meet students' needs. As you know, teachers have always collaborated with others to some degree. For example, in the past when a teacher had a problem teaching a student, he often asked a fellow teacher for advice during a break between classes, during lunch, or after school. Now collaboration is more structured, it takes more forms (e.g., co-teaching, working in teams), and teachers are expected to collaborate more frequently regarding all aspects of their jobs.

Collaboration works better as teachers gain trust and respect for one another.

Given the increasing demands for collaboration in schools, many have sought to clearly define collaboration. When we use the term *collaboration* in this book, we refer to "ongoing participation of two or more individuals who are committed to working together to achieve common goals" (Walther-Thomas, Korinek, McLaughlin, & Williams, 2000, p. 5). Several defining characteristics of effective collaboration are important to consider and are summarized in Figure 11.1.

Collaboration is an activity that develops over time. This suggests that initially, the success of collaboration will vary. However, as collaborators gain trust and respect for one another and learn to work together, collaboration will be more successful. Furthermore, this success will ensure that all participants value collaboration and are motivated to participate, because they recognize how much they and their students benefit from these activities.

Pause & Reflect

What are activities that collaborators might engage in to gain the trust and respect of others? What are activities that collaborators might engage in to reduce the level of trust and respect of others? Why are trust and respect so important when collaborating?

Figure 11.1　Defining Characteristics of Collaboration

Collaboration is based on parity: Parity suggests that the contributions of everyone involved in collaboration are equally valued. A critical factor that often influences parity is the power collaborators have or are perceived to have in decision making. For example, collaborators may go along with suggestions from a principal because of the principal's powerful position, evaluating the performance of teachers. In an effective collaborative relationship, all involved must agree to equally respect the input of others. Otherwise, collaboration cannot succeed.

Collaborators share a mutual goal: All participants in collaboration should share a specific, common goal, and this goal should be important to everyone. This ensures that the purpose of collaboration is clear to all participants, and all are motivated to work together to achieve the goal.

Collaborators share participation, decision making, and accountability: All collaborators should actively participate in contributing to decision making, reach a collective decision that all agree to support, and share accountability for the outcomes of the decision. This does not suggest that all participants should contribute to implementing the decision, which may be an intervention that one of the participants implements in his classroom. Rather, this suggests a perspective that "we're all in this together" and we share responsibility for all aspects of collaborative decision making.

Collaborators share their resources and expertise: All participants bring valuable expertise to a collaborative activity. They also bring resources that others may not have (e.g., time, access to computers or curricular materials). It is important that all participants share their expertise and that all participants value the expertise of others. This does not imply that an "expert" will come up with a solution to the problem, but rather that all will share suggestions to ensure that the best possible information and resources are available to make a good decision. It is also important that all share their resources, which are often very limited in a school, to ensure achievement of the best possible solution.

Collaboration is emergent: If collaboration is to succeed, some positive personal characteristics of participants must be present at the beginning of a collaborative activity and must grow and flourish over time. These characteristics include:

1. Value collaboration and believing that "two heads are better than one."
2. Participate in collaboration in ways that ensures participants gain trust and respect for one another.
3. Work together to develop a sense of community, where all share expertise, and work together to maximize the strengths and minimize the weaknesses of all participants.

Source: Adapted from Friend, M., & Cook, L. (2007). *Interactions: Collaboration skills for school professionals* (5th ed.). Boston: Allyn & Bacon.

In any inclusive school, several types of collaboration are needed. As administrators and teachers develop an inclusive school program, they must work together to change their practices, the roles they play, and the very structure of their schools. To achieve these goals, schools develop collaborative teams, which are charged with planning, implementing, monitoring, and supporting the necessary comprehensive changes (McLeskey & Waldron, 2000, 2002).

In addition to this role, teachers in inclusive schools often work collaboratively with other teachers, either in a co-teaching role or as a consultant (i.e., when problems arise, one teacher assists another by problem-solving possible solutions). Still other types of collaborative roles teachers assume include the following:

- Work with other teachers and professionals in building-based support teams to solve classroom or school problems.
- Consult with other professionals regarding highly specialized student needs (e.g., consult with school psychologists, behavior specialists, physical therapists, nurses, physicians).
- Collaborate with parents to address student needs.

As you can see, all teachers in an inclusive school work in a range of collaborative roles to ensure the success of all students. It is safe to say that no single teacher has all of the knowledge and skills to

Figure 11.2	**What Are Dispositions? A Definition from the National Council for Accreditation in Teacher Education (NCATE)**

Dispositions. The values, commitments, and professional ethics that influence behaviors toward students, families, colleagues, and communities and affect student learning, motivation, and development as well as the educator's own professional growth. Dispositions are guided by beliefs and attitudes related to values such as caring, fairness, honesty, responsibility, and social justice. For example, they might include a belief that all students can learn, a vision of high and challenging standards, or a commitment to a safe and supportive learning environment.

Source: Reprinted from National Council for Accreditation in Teacher Education. (2006). NCATE Unit Standards: Glossary. Retrieved October 15, 2007, from http://www.ncate.org/public/unitStandardsRubrics.asp?ch=4

address the needs of any student who might enter her classroom. Thus, working collaboratively provides the opportunity for teachers and other professionals to share expertise, learn from one another, and develop strategies that will result in more successful educational experiences for all students.

While collaboration may seem to be a simple, or even a natural skill for a teacher or other professional to engage in, that is often not the case. Understanding the basic components of effective collaboration is an important beginning point for learning to be a successful collaborator. We discuss these key components and provide more background information regarding collaboration in Strategy 11.1.

> **Strategy**
>
> We discuss key components of effective collaboration in Strategy 11.1.

Dispositions and Skills Needed for Successful Collaboration

Collaboration is not something that comes naturally for most of us. To succeed as collaborators, we need to ensure that we develop and exemplify certain **dispositions** and learn specific skills that lead to success in these roles. See Figure 11.2 for a definition of *dispositions.*

Dispositions Needed for Successful Collaboration

> **Pause & Reflect**
>
> Recall a successful group project you completed in a college classroom. What dispositions of the members of the group contributed to the success of this project? Are the dispositions defined in Figure 11.2 important when working in any collaborative role? Why or why not?

A *disposition* may be characterized as a habitual inclination, an attitude of mind, or a characteristic tendency. See Figure 11.2 for a definition of *dispositions* that is widely used in education. As we attempt to collaborate with others, several dispositions may interfere with collaboration, while others tend to facilitate the process. Consider the following comments from Susan Davis and Lisa Hallal, teachers from West Hernando Middle School, regarding a key disposition for successful collaboration.

A Perspective on an Important Disposition for Collaboration—Flexibility: An interview with Susan Davis and Lisa Halall from West Hernando Middle School

Both Susan Davis and Lisa Halall co-teach with general education teachers in content areas. They take on many roles in these classes—sometimes as an instructor for the entire group and other times providing additional instruction for a small group. They also work at times as a floater in class, while the other teacher delivers instruction, and monitor student work, provide feedback to students, answer questions, make certain students are on task, manage behavior, and so forth. As Lisa Halall said, "There's no end to what you do in that room."

Both teachers feel that dispositions are important to the success of co-teaching.

You have to be flexible, that's the number-one thing. Some teachers prefer to do all or most of the instruction, so you have to deal with that teaching style. We've worked with teachers who like total control of dispensing information, and other teachers who are okay with us doing many of the lessons. You have to be flexible enough to say what works in this classroom, what's good for both of us, and what's going to help these kids learn the best, then that's what we'll do. You just have to do whatever it takes to make sure students are a success.

When we've tested students in classes where the teacher has total control and we float, and compared that to classes where we share teaching, kids came out close to identical on state achievement tests. Even using very different approaches. So in the end, kids benefited from both classes.

When I go into a class and see what works for an individual teacher, I'm going to be flexible and do what that teacher needs. They are a professional in that classroom, and I am, too, so we work together to do it right and meet the students' needs. It takes patience, planning, revamping over and over again, cooperation, and most of all, flexibility.

Flexibility. When you reflected on important dispositions that support successful collaboration, was flexibility one of those dispositions? As Susan Davis and Lisa Hallal noted in the preceding interview, they feel that the most important disposition when engaging in collaborative co-teaching is flexibility. Indeed, perhaps one of the most difficult issues that teachers face when collaborating is that both professionals have much knowledge and skill regarding the issue being addressed and have perspectives on how the problem might be addressed. For successful collaboration, professionals must be willing to:

- Recognize that their solution to a problem may not be the best solution.
- Look at the problem from another person's perspective.
- Compromise regarding an ultimate solution to the problem.

As Susan Davis and Lisa Hallal noted, flexibility is certainly not always easy. However, they are motivated to be flexible because they know that flexibility leads to more successful collaboration and, most importantly, better outcomes for students.

Trust. Collaboration requires trust and respect. For example, two teachers who are co-teaching depend on each other for support when behavior management issues arise or to share responsibility for students who do not learn as much as expected. Similarly, when teacher assistance teams make recommendations to teachers who seek assistance for addressing a concern regarding a student, the teacher must trust that the team has her best interests and those of the student in mind as they work to develop an intervention to address the student's need.

As collaborators depend on one another and become interdependent, trust develops when each member of the team or pair contributes to the achievement of mutual goals by (1) sharing resources, (2) giving help to others, (3) receiving help from others, and (4) dividing the work of the team and taking on a reasonable share of this work (Snell & Janney, 2000).

Trust develops over time, as teachers realize that collaborators are credible; demonstrate empathy for fellow collaborators (i.e., understand issues from another person's perspective); and accept other team members for what they are (Kampwirth, 2006; Snell & Janney, 2000). As you consider how collaborators gain trust, you will readily recognize that while trust is something that takes time to develop, it can be lost in a moment (Kampwirth, 2006) if a collaborator senses that a person is not trustworthy, empathetic, or isn't working in good faith to solve a problem.

Pause & Reflect

When you interact with others, what are personal qualities that influence how much you respect and listen to the person? Are there certain qualities that cause you to shut down when listening to another? How can you address these biases to make sure that collaboration is effective?

Respectful Interactions. Closely related to the development of trust is the need for collaborators to respectfully interact with one another. This suggests that collaborators will work with each other as equal partners, respecting and attempting to understand the perspectives of others. Factors that potentially interfere with parity, or working as equal partners, may include issues such as low- and high-status positions on an organizational chart; university degrees; salary; access to resources (e.g., computers, paraeducators); gender; stature; ethnic background; facility with language; and a range of other factors (Walther-Thomas, Korinek, McLaughlin, & Williams, 2000).

Another aspect of respectful interactions that often influences collaboration is territoriality. That is, a general educator may view co-teaching as an intrusion on her territory, because she must share the classroom with a special education teacher (Kochhar-Bryant, 2008). Similarly, a special education teacher may become territorial when others are assigned to teach "her children" reading. Effective collaborators must closely examine their tendency toward protecting territory and must share responsibility with collaborators, especially when this collaboration can result in better outcomes for students.

Frame of Reference. Every collaborator brings a predisposition to respond to professional situations in a certain way, based on his frame of reference. Many factors influence a person's frame of reference, including disciplinary background and preparation (i.e., general education, special education, school psychology, and so forth); previous work experience; professional socialization; and a range of other factors (Friend & Cook, 2007). For example, general and special education teachers sometimes differ with respect to how reading should be taught. Teachers and other professionals may have different frames of reference regarding the use of certain instructional strategies (e.g., cooperative learning), or who is responsible and accountable for students with disabilities.

Differing frames of reference can result in difficulty collaborating and can contribute to distortions in communication as collaborative interactions occur (Walther-Thomas et al., 2000). Frame of reference may also be influenced by the cultural identity of collaborators. For example, some cultures place great value on individual goals and achievement, while others emphasize interdependence and the well-being of the group as a whole (Friend & Cook, 2007). Reflecting on one's frame of reference, understanding the frames of reference of others, and openly discussing these issues with each other are important in ensuring successful collaboration.

Belief in Collaboration to Meet the Needs of All Students. Beliefs about collaboration and inclusion are important dispositions as you address difficult problems faced by students and their teachers and attempt to solve these problems. First is the belief that students should be included in general education classes to the maximum extent appropriate. Examining and discussing beliefs regarding what inclusion is, why it is important, and how students benefit from inclusion is an important activity for all teachers and administrators (McLeskey & Waldron, 2000, 2002), to ensure that all participants generally agree regarding these issues and support inclusive practices.

Participants in collaboration should also believe in the power of the collaborative process (Kochhar-Bryant, 2008). Confidence that collaboration can improve outcomes for all students is important to convey when working with others, and it can ensure that collaborators take the perspective that even very difficult situations can improve (Kampwirth, 2006).

> ### Pause & Reflect
>
> Examine the dispositions we've addressed in this section, and discuss with a peer whether you have these necessary dispositions. How can you change or improve your dispositions to become an effective collaborator?

Skills Needed for Successful Collaboration

Effective communication is critical for working with other professionals in a collaborative role. Many factors may interfere with effective communication and may result in misunderstandings and poor collaboration. Several of these potential barriers relate to the previously described dispositions. For example, collaborators with different frames of reference will have difficulty communicating and effectively collaborating until they examine and understand the frames of reference that are creating the communication problem. Communication problems can be overcome through the development of effective skills related to listening, verbal communication, nonverbal communication, and addressing conflict. For more information regarding communications skills needed for effective collaboration, see Strategy 11.2.

We discuss communication skills and successful collaboration in Strategy 11.2.

Skills for Managing Difficult Interactions. When collaboration occurs, pairs or teams of professionals can often reach consensus regarding a problem. However, at times, collaborators have very different perspectives on issues, and conflicts arise. When a conflict arises, it is important that collaborators recognize that the problem exists and then actively seek to engage and overcome the issue. Ignoring or avoiding conflict is a sure approach to undermine collaboration in the future.

When conflict occurs, it is important to reaffirm the purpose of collaboration, that is, to improve outcomes for students. How collaborators address challenges depends, to a large degree, on the importance they attach to either achieving a professional goal or maintaining a good relationship with collaborators (Walther-Thomas et al., 2000). For example, when neither of these goals is important, the collaborator may simply avoid the conflict by withdrawing, and letting other collaborators make a final decision. This strategy is fine, if the goal is not important to the person who is withdrawing, or if he is not responsible for decision making. If the goal is very important, the collaborator may attempt to force others to accept a solution, which may increase the level of conflict.

A positive approach to addressing a challenging issue has been described as integrating (Walther-Thomas et al., 2000). When using this strategy, collaborators view the conflict as a problem to solve, and they search for a solution that both addresses the goal of the collaboration and maintains the relationship with collaborators. "This method involves collaboration between people, openness, exchange of information, reduction of tension between parties, and examination of differences to reach a solution acceptable to both parties" (Walther-Thomas et al., 2000, p. 109).

Strategies for addressing conflict include (Correa, Jones, Thomas, & Morsink, 2005):

- Clarify the goal of collaboration.
- Focus on the problem, not the people involved.
- Focus on goals that all collaborators share.
- Insist on using objective criteria to address the problem.
- Examine your feelings, and why they differ from others.
- Generate possible solutions collaboratively that benefit everyone.

Pause & Reflect

Discuss with a peer how you react to conflict. Do you avoid conflict and withdraw? Confront and compete with others? Accommodate others to escape conflict? Or use a collaborative style to address issues directly and professionally? What style will you use when collaborating with other professionals?

Teachers often work in collaborative teams to address the needs of students who are struggling academically or socially.

Collaborative Roles in Inclusive Schools

As we noted previously, inclusive schools increase the necessity for collaboration by all professionals in a variety of roles and types of collaborative relationships. Three key types of collaborative relationships are working in teams, working as a co-teacher, and consulting with others for assistance.

Collaborative Teams

Teams of professionals often work together in schools to address a range of different types of issues and concerns. Most inclusive schools use inclusion-support teams to plan, implement, monitor, and evaluate inclusive school programs (McLeskey & Waldron, 2000, 2002, 2006). These teams consist of a range of professionals in different roles (e.g., teachers, principal, counselor, school psychologist) and other stakeholders (e.g., parents), who all work collaboratively to develop and support an inclusive program.

Inclusion-support teams address schoolwide issues as they seek to develop a plan for school change that uses school resources effectively and efficiently to better meet the academic and social needs of all students. These teams often spend several months planning for inclusion, as they visit inclusive schools, examine their own school, plan professional development for teachers and other school staff, and a range of other activities. (For more information regarding how these teams function, see McLeskey & Waldron, 2000, 2006).

Another type of collaborative team addresses individual student needs. These teams serve a range of differing purposes and may identify and develop individualized education programs (IEPs) for students with disabilities; provide pre-referral interventions for students with possible disabilities (Buck, Polloway, Smith-Thomas, & Cook, 2003); and provide teachers with support in addressing any student problems that may arise (Chalfant & Pysh, 1989; Lane, Pierson, Robertson, & Little, 2004).

The type of team that provides the most direct support for teachers in inclusive classrooms is the **Teacher Assistance Team (TAT)**, which provides teachers with collaborative support in developing interventions to address student academic and social/behavioral needs. Approximately three of every four states require or recommend the use of this type of building-based support team in local schools (Buck et al., 2003) (also called intervention assistance teams, student assistance teams, instructional support teams, schoolwide assistance teams, and teacher support teams). TATs also provide all participating teachers with a form of professional development that is directly related to their classroom practice (Chalfant & Pysh, 1989; Chalfant, Pysh, & Moultrie, 1979). Teachers collaboratively brainstorm possible interventions for addressing student academic and social difficulties and obtain new ideas for their classroom by participating in this process.

Research has revealed that, based on teacher feedback, about 90% of teachers viewed interventions developed by TATs as successful, while about 75% of teachers viewed the teams as very or moderately effective (Safran & Safran, 1996). More recent research has shown that 50% to 60% of teachers view interventions developed by these teams as using acceptable procedures and feel that the interventions were implemented with a high degree of fidelity (Lane et al., 2004).

TATs are relatively simple to implement and can be adapted to fit the particular needs of any school. Many teachers and administrators are highly supportive of the use of these teams. For more information regarding how TATs work, see Strategy 11.3.

> We discuss teacher assistance teams (TATs) in Strategy 11.3.
>
> **Strategy**

Co-Teaching

A second type of collaborative role that is common for teachers in inclusive schools is co-teaching. As Susan Davis and Lisa Halall, teachers from West Hernando Middle School, indicated in the interview in the opening vignette, co-teaching is critical to the success of inclusion in their school. As Susan Davis noted, special education teachers "can't know about content in every area in a middle school: English, science, math, social studies." Similarly, content area teachers don't know all of the strategies that are needed to adapt for the needs of students with disabilities. Thus, having two teachers with different skills working collaboratively results in a combination of skills that benefits all students.

Co-teaching in inclusive classrooms is defined as a general and special education teacher working collaboratively to share responsibility for instructing a diverse group of students in a single classroom. Co-teaching utilizes the expertise of both general and special education teachers and thus provides all students with an improved educational experience.

Several issues are critical to the success of co-teaching (Scruggs, Mastropieri, & McDuffie, 2007). For example, co-teachers emphasize the importance of administrative support to make certain that co-teaching is valued and given the resources and support needed to succeed. Co-teachers also emphasize the need for planning time before the school year begins to prepare for co-teaching; professional development to acquire necessary skills; and common planning time during the school year to continue to support co-teaching (Scruggs et al., 2007).

Perhaps most importantly, teachers emphasize the need for compatibility between co-teaching partners (Mastropieri, Scruggs, Graetz, et al., 2005; Scruggs et al., 2007). When co-teaching relationships work well, they are built on trust and mutual respect for the skills of the co-teaching partner and result in more effective instruction for all students (Mastropieri et al., 2005). Compatibility issues often arise because teachers have different beliefs regarding how to plan for co-teaching, or issues arise related to different beliefs regarding classroom instruction such as classroom routines, discipline, noise levels, and so forth (Friend & Cook, 2007; Mastropieri et al., 2005).

Co-teaching is frequently used in inclusive classrooms to meet a diverse range of student needs.

When co-teaching is done well, many benefits accrue for students with and without disabilities (Scruggs et al., 2007; Thousand, Villa, & Nevin, 2006; Wilson & Michaels, 2006). These benefits include increased student achievement, fewer problems with disruptive behavior, improved student attitudes and self-concepts, and more positive peer relationships.

Co-teaching is effective for students with and without disabilities for three primary reasons. First, co-teaching provides the opportunity to capitalize on the unique knowledge and skills that both teachers bring to the classroom (Thousand et al., 2006). Second, two teachers bring an extra pair of hands to the classroom, which provides the opportunity to structure the class and group students in ways that result in more support for students. For example, teachers can more often:

- Use effective, evidence-based instructional practices.
- Differentiate instruction.
- Employ intensive small-group or individual instruction.
- Provide immediate attention to student needs.
- Monitor student on-task behavior and intervene as needed.

Finally, co-teachers can combine their expertise to determine novel approaches to meet student needs (McLeskey & Waldron, 2000; Thousand et al., 2006). This is necessary in inclusive classrooms when traditional solutions from general and special education do not readily meet the needs of all students.

Some consider co-teaching as synonymous with inclusion, but this is not the case. Many successful inclusive programs use co-teaching as a core strategy for ensuring student success, while others rarely use co-teaching and use other collaborative strategies to support students (e.g., consultative support from a special education teacher, paraeducators). We recommend that teachers in inclusive schools take advantage of co-teaching whenever possible. Co-teaching provides teachers with a powerful opportunity to increase their expertise. For example, special education teachers can learn in-depth information regarding the general education curriculum, methods and grouping strategies that are used in the general education classroom, and which instructional approaches fit into this setting. Similarly, general education teachers can learn methods for making accommodations for diverse student needs, grouping strategies for providing more intensive instruction to students, and so forth. In short, co-teaching provides an excellent opportunity for professional development, and after experiencing co-teaching, teachers often have significantly improved expertise for addressing diverse student needs.

Schools can implement co-teaching in any general education classroom and can use it with any subject matter. Co-teaching takes careful planning, because teacher roles and responsibilities change significantly when using this approach. For more information regarding how co-teaching works, see Strategy 11.4.

Strategy

We discuss co-teaching in inclusive classrooms in Strategy 11.4.

Collaborative Consultation

Collaborative consultation involves two persons working together to seek solutions to a mutually agreed-upon problem or issue. When collaboration involves two professionals, the participants will typically have different areas of expertise and roles. For example, a special education teacher may consult with a general education teacher regarding methods for making accommodations on tests (e.g., allowing more time, breaking the test into several sessions, providing a calculator) to meet the needs of a student with a disability.

When you teach in an inclusive classroom, you will have students with highly specialized needs that you do not fully understand, regardless of whether you are the general or special education teacher. When this occurs, you will need a specialist to provide information and suggest approaches to meet student needs. For example, a special education teacher may need assistance in addressing the physical needs of a student with a severe physical disability and may seek the consultative assistance of a physical therapist. Others that may provide assistance include school psychologists, behavior specialists, curriculum specialists, speech–language pathologists, social workers, nurses, and so forth. (For a list of these professionals and their roles, see Chapter 1, Table 1.2).

The steps that are typically included in collaborative consultation include the following:

- Refer a problem or issue to a consultant.
- Identify the problem to be addressed.
- Brainstorm possible solutions to the problem.
- Select an intervention by the referring teacher.
- Clarify implementation of the intervention.
- Follow up to determine the effectiveness of the intervention.

If the intervention is not effective, or if the collaborators need to address other problems or issues, they repeat the collaborative consultation cycle. Strategy 11.3, "Teacher Assistance Teams," provides a more detailed description of the steps involved in collaborative consultation.

As a teacher in an inclusive classroom, you will not only receive assistance from consultants but also serve as a consultant to others. For example, after you have worked in a successful inclusive program for a period of time, you may be asked to consult with other teachers who are developing inclusive programs. In addition, two of the most critical consultative roles for teachers in inclusive classrooms that you will need to address relate to the work you will do with paraeducators and families.

Paraeducators (also called paraprofessionals, instructional assistants, or teacher's aides) are an important resource for many inclusive classrooms. Paraeducators are individuals who provide instruction and other services to students and who are supervised by teachers responsible for student outcomes (French, 2003). Paraeducators can serve in a variety of roles to support classroom instruction and related activities in an inclusive setting, including (Correa et al., 2005) the following:

- Tutor after a teacher provides primary instruction.
- Float in the classroom to check on student progress and respond to questions.
- Provide skill-and-drill activities to individuals or small groups of students.
- Prepare instructional materials, activities, and games.
- Read stories or content area material.
- Conduct small-group instructional activities.
- Grade, correct homework, and handle other paperwork.
- Work on learning centers, bulletin boards, and so forth.
- Provide support for students with highly specialized needs (e.g., medical or physical needs for students with severe disabilities).

While paraeducators can be a valuable resource in an inclusive classroom, concerns will arise at times regarding paraeducators' roles and responsibilities. For example, in some classrooms, paraeducators are assigned to one student with a disability. This type of assignment raises the possibility that the paraeducator will take on responsibility for the student (i.e., planning student lessons, assessing student progress) that should reside with the classroom teacher, and the classroom teacher will not be familiar with the student and his needs (French, 2003). In addition, if that paraeducator is "velcroed" to the student and does not work with others in the classroom, difficulty developing social relationships may result for the student.

As a teacher in an inclusive classroom, you will at times supervise paraeducators and ensure that their time is used effectively and efficiently. Some local school districts provide training in working effectively with paraeducators. We provide more information in Strategy 11.5 regarding how teachers may work effectively with paraeducators to improve outcomes for students.

We discuss working with paraeducators in Strategy 11.5.

Strategy

Families. Two major factors have contributed to the increased involvement of families in the education of students with disabilities. First, the Individuals with Disabilities Education Improvement Act (IDEA, 2004) mandates that parents work with professionals as partners in ensuring an effective education for students with disabilities. This includes parent participation in every decision related to their child with a disability, including identification, assessment, and placement (Rosenberg et al., 2008). Parents also have extensive rights related to the development and approval of the IEP for school-age students or Individual Family Service Plan (IFSP) for younger children. Parent participation in these activities is designed to ensure that parents and educators work as partners in addressing the needs of students with disabilities and that adversarial relationships are avoided.

A second reason for family involvement is research indicating this involvement can serve to enhance a student's academic achievement and improve behavior and social adjustment.

> More than 30 years of research demonstrate that when families are directly engaged with their children's education, students show increased test scores, higher academic achievement, improved attitudes toward learning, have better social behavior, higher self esteem, fewer placements in special education, higher school attendance rates, and lower dropout rates. (Kochhar-Bryant, 2008, p. 208)

These positive effects have been demonstrated across students from different economic, ethnic, and cultural backgrounds (Kochhar-Bryant, 2008).

Parents and caregivers can be involved in schools in many ways (Correa et al., 2005). For example, families can:

- Share information regarding their children with teachers and other school personnel (e.g., counselor, school psychologist).
- Reinforce and support school programs at home through activities such as a daily report card (Reiff, 2004; Rief, 2005) to address student discipline, or programs to ensure homework completion (Harniss, Epstein, Bursuck, Nelson, & Jayanthi, 2001; Salend, Duhaney, Anderson, & Gottschalk, 2004).
- Advocate for quality services for their child.
- Volunteer to work in schools for part of the school day or in before- or after-school activities.
- Participate in school decision-making groups, such as a school advisory committee.
- Work in the community with businesses and local government to obtain support for the school.

Strategy
We discuss working with families, home–school collaboration, in Strategy 11.6.

For teachers in an inclusive classroom, parent support has the potential to significantly enhance student outcomes and increase the resources available to meet student needs. Research has indicated that interventions can be highly effective when teachers and caregivers work collaboratively to develop and implement interventions to address a range of student needs (Cox, 2005; Fishel & Ramirez, 2005; Lee, Palmer, Turnbull, & Wehmeyer, 2006; Whitbread, Bruder, Fleming, & Park, 2007). We provide more information in Strategy 11.6 regarding the development of effective approaches for home–school collaboration.

Students as Collaborators: Peer Assistance in Inclusive Classrooms and Schools

In many schools, these are days of limited resources, increasing standards for student achievement, and increasing diversity in classrooms. These circumstances require that educators seek cost-effective methods for addressing student needs (Bond & Castagnera, 2006). Teachers who are effective use all available resources to meet student needs, and one readily available resource is the students themselves (Kauchak & Eggen, 2003).

Engaging students in collaborative roles to assist or support peers in addressing the needs of those who are struggling academically or socially is an integral part of many successful inclusive classrooms. Indeed, as we have discussed throughout this text, acceptance and support of students with disabilities is a critical component of any effective, inclusive classroom.

Many peer-assisted strategies have been developed to address basic academic skills, higher-level cognitive skills, and social interactions or skill development (Maheady, Harper, & Mallette, 2001). In Chapter 13, we discuss how teachers can engage peers in supporting students who are struggling to learn academic skills through the use of strategies such as cooperative learning (Aronson, 2004; Slavin & Madden, 2001) and peer tutoring (Fuchs, Fuchs & Burish, 2000; Greenwood, Delquadri, & Carta, 1997). In the following section, we describe a strategy that teachers may use to support students who are struggling academically or socially in inclusive classrooms, the peer buddy program.

The Peer Buddy Program

Several researchers have found a close relationship between academic achievement and the development of friendship skills, behavior control, and self-esteem (Ginsburg-Block et al., 2006). Peer-assisted learning strategies are an intervention that has the potential not only to improve academic achievement but also to improve social skills. For example, in a review of studies related to peer-assisted learning, Ginsburg-Block and colleagues found that these interventions improved student social and self-concept outcomes. This is an important outcome for inclusive classrooms, because the improvement of social skills and the development of friendships are often goals for students with disabilities in these settings.

The need to improve the social skills and acceptance level of students with disabilities in general education classrooms has led to the development of a peer-assisted learning strategy

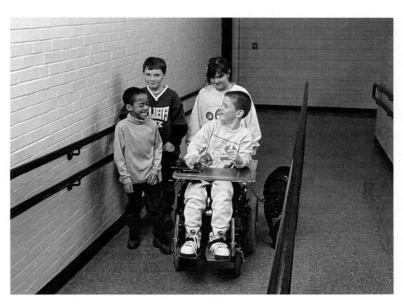

Peer buddy programs can significantly enhance academic and social outcomes for students with disabilities.

called the peer buddy program to directly address this need (Hughes & Carter, 2008). While teachers can use the peer buddy program with any student in a classroom who needs academic support and improved social skills, educators developed it to address the academic and social needs of students with more severe disabilities in middle and high schools (Hughes & Carter, 2008).

Students with severe disabilities in secondary schools who are included in general education classes are often isolated and seldom interact with their peers who do not have disabilities (Carter & Hughes, 2005). This occurs for many reasons, including the limited social and communication skills of many students with severe disabilities; the structure of the school day in secondary schools (e.g., emphasis on lecture and focus on academic material); and concerns among students without disabilities that they lack the skills and knowledge to interact with peers with severe disabilities. Fostering the interactions of students with severe disabilities and their peers in secondary schools requires intentional efforts by educators (Carter & Hughes, 2005).

Hughes and colleagues (Hughes & Carter, 2008; Copeland, McCall, Williams, et al., 2002) developed the peer buddy program to provide a support system for students with severe disabilities in general education classrooms. Peer buddies engage in a range of activities to provide students with severe disabilities with support, including completing assignments, learning ways to interact in social settings, acquiring job skills, participating in extracurricular activities, and so forth (Copeland et al., 2002). For detailed information regarding the peer buddy program, and how such a program is implemented, see Strategy 11.7.

We discuss peer buddies in Strategy 11.7.

Strategy

Summary

This chapter addressed the following topics:

What collaboration is and why it is important in supporting inclusive classrooms and schools

- Collaboration refers to the "ongoing participation of two or more individuals who are committed to working together to achieve common goals" (Walther-Thomas et al., 2000, p. 5).
- Teachers work in a variety of collaborative roles to meet the needs of students in inclusive schools. This collaboration is necessary because no single teacher has all of the knowledge and skills necessary to meet the needs of all students. Thus, teachers and other professionals share knowledge and expertise through collaboration.

The dispositions needed by teachers and other professionals to effectively collaborate

- Dispositions are characteristic tendencies or habitual inclinations.
- Dispositions necessary for effective collaboration include:
  - Flexibility in adapting to work with others in collaborative roles
  - Trust in collaborative partners to share responsibility for addressing student needs
  - Respectful interactions with collaborators
  - A frame of reference that facilitates collaboration
  - A belief in collaboration to meet the needs of all students

The skills needed to effectively collaborate with other professionals

- Effective communication skills for working with other professionals are needed for effective collaboration. Important communication skills include:
  - Listening skills
  - Verbal communication skills
  - Nonverbal communication skills
- Skills for managing difficult interactions with other professionals are also needed for effective collaboration.

The collaborative roles of teachers in inclusive schools

- Teachers often work with teams of other professionals, such as a teacher assistance team (TAT), to collaboratively address student needs.
- Another frequent collaborative role of teachers in inclusive schools is working as a co-teacher.
- Teachers and other professionals may take on a collaborative consultation role. In this role, a professional provides support to another professional to address a specific problem or issue.
- Teachers often work in a collaborative role with paraeducators to provide support for students with disabilities and others who struggle in inclusive classrooms.
- Teachers and other professionals often work collaboratively with families to address the needs of students with disabilities.

The collaborative roles of students to support inclusive programs

- Engaging students to work collaboratively to address the needs of those who struggle academically or socially can be an integral part of successful inclusive classrooms.
- Two types of peer-assisted learning strategies that are often used in inclusive classrooms are cooperative learning and peer tutoring.
- Another effective strategy for engaging students in providing academic and social support for students with disabilities is a peer buddy program.

Addressing Professional Standards

Standards addressed in Chapter 11 include:

CEC Standards: (4) instructional strategies; (5) learning environments and social interactions; (7) instructional planning; (10) collaboration.

INTASC Standards: Principle 2—Provide learning opportunities to support the learning and development of all students; Principle 3—Create instructional opportunities for diverse learners; Principle 5—Create learning environments to support student motivation, behavior, and learning; Principle 6—Use knowledge of communication techniques to support students; Principle 10—Collaborate to support student learning and well-being.

Praxis™ II Standards: Knowledge-based core principles: (3) delivery of services to students with disabilities. Application of core principles: (2) instruction, (4) managing the learning environment, (5) professional roles/issues/literature.

PUTTING IT ALL TOGETHER

Today teachers are opening their classroom doors to others as they collaborate to reach increasingly higher expectations for student outcomes. With this in mind, we hope you will embrace collaboration, but keep a few of the following ideas in mind.

1. **Start slowly.** We recommend working with only one or two co-teachers initially. It is important to start slowly with collaborative activities so that you'll have time to develop the skills and reinforce the dispositions you need to make collaboration succeed. Working with a TAT or carefully selecting initial collaborators is often a good way to get started.

2. **Learn and develop the skills needed for collaboration.** You will begin to develop skills as you engage in collaborative activities with peers and observe their behavior during these interactions. Another critical way of gaining these skills is to take advantage of professional development related to collaboration.

3. **Enjoy the collaborative partnerships you develop.** A major benefit of collaboration for teachers is that it

reduces the isolation many feel in their profession. Collaboration allows a group of experienced professionals to share and test ideas in a setting where individual and team efforts are recognized and valued and all professionals have opportunities for growth and leadership (Waldron & McLeskey, 2008).

4. **Celebrate the successes of collaboration.** When done well, collaboration leads to the synthesis of available expertise and the discovery of new knowledge and teaching approaches that benefit all students (Kochhar-Bryant, 2008). Be sure to take the time to recognize your successes!

myeducationlab

We present a serious of evidence-based strategies in the second half of this chapter (Strategies 11.1 to 11.7) in a step-by-step format so that you can use them in your classroom now. In addition, in the following table, we identify some video clips, cases, and simulations that will allow you to experience these strategies (or complementary strategies) in a real classroom environment.

EFFECTIVE PRACTICE	MYEDUCATIONLAB CONNECTION	CONSIDER THIS
Strategy 11.1: Key Components of Effective Collaboration	Go to MyEducationLab, select the topic *Collaboration, Consultation, and Co-Teaching*, and go to the Building Teaching Skills and Dispositions section. Next, complete the activity entitled "Building Collaborative Relationships."	As you complete the activity, pay close attention to the views of the teachers featured in the video clips. What components do they think are necessary for effective collaboration? How do these compare or contrast with the components discussed in Strategy 11.1?
Strategy 11.2: Communication Skills and Successful Collaboration	Go to MyEducationLab, select the topic *Collaboration, Consultation, and Co-Teaching*, and go to the Activities and Applications section. Next, read and analyze the case entitled "A Broken Arm."	As you examine the case, focus on how these two teachers communicate and how that is impacting both the success of their collaborative relationship and the student's academic success.
Strategy 11.3: Teacher Assistance Teams	Go to MyEducationLab, select the topic *Collaboration, Consultation, and Co-Teaching*, and go to the Activities and Applications section. Next, watch the video entitled "Team Meeting," and answer the accompanying questions.	As you watch this video, focus on the interactions among the team participants. Compare and contrast these interactions with the components addressed in Strategy 11.3.
Strategy 11.4: Co-Teaching	Go to MyEducationLab, select the topic *Collaboration, Consultation, and Co-Teaching*, and go to the Activities and Applications section. Next, complete the simulation entitled "Focus on the Playbook."	As you complete the simulation, focus on the roles and responsibilities of all the collaborators. How does the situation presented in the simulation compare with the elements discussed in Strategy 11.4?
Strategy 11.5: Working with Paraeducators	Go to MyEducationLab, select the topic *Collaboration, Consultation, and Co-Teaching*, and go to the Activities and Applications section. Next, watch the videos entitled "Collaboration and Communication with Teachers, Paraprofessionals, and Parents" and "Fluency Building: Social Studies Flashcards," and answer the accompanying questions.	As you watch these two videos, first focus on how this teacher views his collaborative relationship with his paraeducators. Then focus on how he incorporates these views into classroom practice.
Strategy 11.6: Working with Families: Home–School Collaboration	Go to MyEducationLab, select the topic *Parents and Families,* and go to the Activities and Applications section. Next, watch the video entitled "Home–School Communication," and answer the accompanying questions.	As you watch the video, reflect on the importance of home–school communication and its role in an effective collaborative relationship between the teacher and the student's caregivers.
Strategy 11.7: Peer Buddies	Go to MyEducationLab, select the topic *Autism*, and go to the Activities and Applications section. Next, watch the video entitled "Social Skills," and answer the accompanying questions.	As you watch the video, reflect on the social skills benefits of this peer buddy situation for Allison, the student featured in the video clip.

EFFECTIVE PRACTICES

In the remainder of this chapter, we describe seven strategies, which we referred to previously in the chapter, to help you plan effectively to meet the needs of all students.

EFFECTIVE PRACTICE	TYPE OF STRATEGY/BRIEF DESCRIPTION	SPECIAL CONSIDERATIONS
Strategy 11.1: Key Components of Effective Collaboration	Collaboration allows teachers to work with other professionals to improve knowledge, teaching skills, and dispositions. The components of effective collaboration provide teachers with the knowledge and skills needed to ensure that they are well prepared for collaborative roles.	When collaborating regarding inclusion, teachers must work to ensure a respectful, equal partnership with their collaborator.
Strategy 11.2: Communication Skills and Successful Collaboration	The most important skills for collaborating successfully with others relate to communication. Communication problems can be overcome through the development of skills related to listening, verbal communication, and nonverbal communication.	Communication is very complex, as it consists of sending and receiving messages simultaneously, sending both verbal and nonverbal messages, and using different types of communication with different people.
Strategy 11.3: Teacher Assistance Teams	A strategy to provide teachers who face problems in their classrooms with a quick, efficient method to seek assistance from well-respected peers. A group of teachers meet with a referring teacher about a specific student problem, brainstorm regarding possible ways to address the problem, and support the teacher in selecting, implementing, and evaluating an intervention.	Most student problems referred to the TAT relate to work habits, classroom behavior, interpersonal behavior, attentional problems, and reading difficulties. Recommended interventions are reported to be successful for almost 90% of students.
Strategy 11.4: Co-Teaching	An approach to collaboration that allows general and special education teachers to share knowledge, dispositions, and skills in an inclusive classroom. Two teachers share responsibility for teaching a diverse group of students in one classroom. Co-teachers take on different roles, depending on the content being taught and student needs.	Co-teaching is a dynamic process that requires teachers to often change roles. Varying teaching roles allows teachers to learn and develop expertise from their teaching partner.
Strategy 11.5: Working with Paraeducators	Paraeducators, who work under the supervision of a certified teacher, provide important support for many students in inclusive classrooms. Effectively supervising a paraeducator requires that the teacher collaborate effectively with the paraeducator to ensure that responsibilities are well defined and the paraeducator is well prepared to address these responsibilities.	Paraeducators may provide support such as one-to-one or small-group instruction, support for students with highly specialized needs, grading and other paperwork, preparation of materials for class lessons, etc.
Strategy 11.6: Working with Families: Home–School Collaboration	Effective collaboration between teachers and families can result in significant improvement in student achievement and behavior. Teachers in inclusive classrooms should encourage home–school collaboration and parent involvement in a range of activities. The teacher should get to know parents well and work with parents to determine the types of involvement that will work well for them.	When collaborating with parents, teachers should be knowledgeable regarding the parent's cultural background. This allows the teacher to understand, respect, and take into account cultural background when working with the parent.
Strategy 11.7: Peer Buddies	Adolescents with moderate-to-severe disabilities benefit from peer interactions, just as other students do. Peer buddy programs are designed to provide an opportunity for these peer interactions to occur in natural school settings.	Peer buddy programs have many benefits for both students but require careful planning and consistent support to succeed.

Strategy 11.1

KEY COMPONENTS OF EFFECTIVE COLLABORATION

Rationale and Research

Many professionals take the perspective that collaboration is a skill that should be a natural part of their repertoire as a teacher or school professional (Friend & Cook, 2007). Research evidence indicates that this is not the case (Correa et al., 2005; Dettmer, Thurston, Knackendoffel, & Dyck, 2009; Friend & Cook, 2007). While some teachers may be natural collaborators, many teachers need to learn the skills for working effectively with others.

Consideration of key components of collaboration can improve the likelihood that teachers and other professionals will succeed when engaged in these activities. For example, teachers must be well prepared for their collaborative roles, roles should be carefully delineated, support should be provided for structuring the roles, and outcomes should be evaluated to ensure that collaboration has succeeded (Dettmer et al., 2009; Friend & Cook, 2007).

Key References

Correa, V., Jones H., Thomas, C., & Morsink, C. (2005). *Interactive teaming: Enhancing programs for students with special needs.* Upper Saddle River, NJ: Merrill/Education Pearson.

Dettmer, P., Thurston, L., Knackendoffel, A., & Dyck, N. (2009). *Collaboration, consultation, and teamwork for students with special needs.* Upper Saddle River, NJ: Merrill/Pearson Education.

Friend, M., & Cook, L. (2007). *Interactions: Collaboration skills for school professionals* (5th ed.). Boston: Allyn & Bacon.

Kampwirth, T. (2006). *Collaborative consultation in the schools* (3rd ed.). Upper Saddle River, NJ: Merrill/Pearson Education.

Kochhar-Bryant, C. (2008). *Collaboration and system coordination for students with special needs.* Upper Saddle River, NJ: Merrill/Pearson Education.

Step-by-Step

As you engage in collaboration with other professionals, you should address several key components of these activities to enhance the collaborative activities and improve student outcomes.

(1) Prepare for collaboration. Most of us must learn collaboration skills. As we noted previously in this chapter, some of the key skills in collaboration relate to effective communication and addressing conflict. Participants in a collaborative relationship should participate in professional development activities together to ensure that they have the knowledge, skills, and dispositions needed for effective collaboration. Possible topics for professional development (addressed later in this chapter) include co-teaching, teaming, working with parents, and working with paraeducators. Other areas of professional development that may be useful include methods for problem solving and working collaboratively to develop inclusive classrooms.

(2) Define roles. A key to the success of any collaborative endeavor is ensuring that all participants are clear regarding their roles. For example, co-teachers can take on a range of roles (see Strategy 11.4 for more information on co-teaching roles), and these roles can change over time. Similarly, when professionals work on collaborative teams that address curriculum in a content area or across disciplines, or address individual needs of students and teachers, they must clearly define their roles to ensure that they provide well-coordinated, seamless support for students (Dettmer, et al., 2009).

(3) Achieve role parity. For collaboration to succeed, all participants must feel that they are important contributors, that they are equal partners in decision making, and that their contributions are valued (Friend & Cook, 2007). This becomes difficult at times when a collaborator is a principal or other professional who is in a supervisory role or is viewed as more knowledgeable than others regarding a particular topic (e.g., inclusion, classroom management). In inclusive settings, professionals often bring different expertise to collaborative deliberations (e.g., a general education teacher may have deep knowledge of a content area, while a special education teacher has skills in adapting and differentiating content). While collaborating, participants must agree to have parity and work as equal partners, even if this is not the case outside of the collaborative relationship (e.g., with a principal) or if knowledge levels regarding the content being addressed differ.

(4) *Address key considerations when collaborating.* As you collaborate with other professionals, keep the following in mind (Kampwirth, 2006):

a. Reach out to your collaborators to make them feel comfortable and accepted as equal partners.

b. Make it clear to your collaborators that you strongly prefer to work collaboratively.

c. Use time efficiently, so that no one feels that time is being wasted.

d. When a problem arises, clearly define the problem, and focus on finding solutions.

e. Try to understand the collaborative relationship from the perspective of other participants.

f. Continue to work on any problems until they are resolved.

(5) *Evaluate the collaborative relationship frequently.* Collaborative relationships change over time, making it important for participants to frequently evaluate whether the collaboration is working and how it might be changed to work better. This is true with co-teaching, which may change as student needs evolve over time or as demands on the teacher for content knowledge or differentiation of instruction change. Collaborative colleagues can use discussions to address the evolving nature of collaboration and to ensure that all participants continue to be committed to the collaborative relationship.

Applications and Examples

Teachers who are good collaborators continue to gain skills and dispositions that facilitate their work. For example, collaborators must be open to new ideas and must demonstrate willingness to others to explore new perspectives, even when they contrast with your point of view. This shows respect for other collaborators and can prevent potential problems with collaborative interactions. Several essential behaviors to consider when working toward a respectful, equal partnership with a collaborator include (Dettmer et al., 2009):

- Really listen, and talk, together with collaborators.
- Describe your perspectives, but give objective examples whenever possible.
- Work toward resolutions or compromises together.
- Provide a collective summary of discussion points and tentative agreements.
- If the process is stalled, seek input from others.
- Talk after completing a plan, to reflect on outcomes and how to improve collaboration next time.

Keep in Mind

As you collaborate regarding inclusion, keep in mind that professionals often do not share common definitions of inclusion or inclusive practices. Given this variability, it is important to discuss individual perspectives on inclusion with other collaborators and to ensure that all understand your perspective and that you understand those of others. Successful collaborators determine common ground on which they can focus (e.g., improving outcomes for all students, making all students part of the academic and social community of the school), emphasize similar perspectives, and downplay differences.

Strategy 11.2

COMMUNICATION SKILLS AND SUCCESSFUL COLLABORATION

Rationale and Research

The most important skills for effectively working with others relate to communication (Correa et al., 2005; Friend & Cook, 2007). Collaboration can be effective only if those involved understand each other, convey both verbal and nonverbal (e.g., body language) information intentionally, and avoid misunderstandings. Many factors may interfere with effective communication and result in misunderstandings and poor collaboration. Several of these potential barriers relate to the dispositions we discussed previously in this chapter. For example, collaborators with different frames of reference will have difficulty communicating effectively until they examine and understand the frames of reference that are creating the communication problem. As we noted previously, collaboration skills, including communication skills, are often taken for granted by professionals. However, it is important for collaborators to learn these skills to facilitate effective collaboration and improve student outcomes.

Key References

Correa, V., Jones, H., Thomas, C., & Morsink, C. (2005). *Interactive teaming: Enhancing programs for students with special needs.* Upper Saddle River, NJ: Merrill/Pearson Education.

Friend, M., & Cook, L. (2007). *Interactions: Collaboration skills for school professionals* (5th ed.). Boston: Allyn & Bacon.

Kochhar-Bryant, C. (2008). *Collaboration and system coordination for students with special needs.* Upper Saddle River, NJ: Merrill/Pearson Education.

Vaughn, S., Bos, C., & Schumm, J. (2007). *Teaching students who are exceptional, diverse, at risk in the general education classroom* (4th ed.). Boston: Allyn & Bacon.

Walther-Thomas, C., Korinek, L., McLaughlin, V., & Williams, B. (2000). *Collaboration for inclusive education.* Boston: Allyn & Bacon.

Step-by-Step

Collaborators can overcome communication problems by developing effective communication skills to ensure communication of the desired information. Perhaps the most important communication skills for collaborators relate to listening, verbal communication, and nonverbal communication.

(1) Listen. Many factors may interfere with effective listening when collaborating (Friend & Cook, 2007). These factors include:

- Filtering certain messages that you do not want to hear. The listener hears the topic of the message and then tunes out.
- Being distracted by details that are tangential to the main point.
- Rehearsing a response while a collaborator is talking.
- Reacting to "hot" words that cause you to react strongly, such as whole language, direct instruction, inclusion, accountability, behaviorism.

Monitoring your reactions to words or topics as communication occurs and recognizing that you are engaging in these behaviors are important steps in moving beyond these barriers to communication. Other listening skills that will improve communication include (Vaughn, Bos, & Schumm, 2007; Walther-Thomas, Korinek, McLaughlin, & Williams, 2000) actively listening for the real content of the message you're hearing; attending to the feelings that may be in the message; paraphrasing what you've heard, including the content of the message and the feelings behind the message; and providing the speaker with the opportunity to clarify your perspectives.

(2) Develop verbal communication skills. Your verbal communication skills are also important to consider as you work in a collaborative relationship. You may use several strategies to be clearly understood as you interact with others (Vaughn et al., 2007; Walther-Thomas et al., 2000), including:

a. Repeat messages through multiple modes, including restating a message in a different manner (e.g., summarizing the key points of a previous message), and providing a written summary of a message.

b. Practice empathy, or placing yourself in the other person's shoes, in an attempt to understand the frame of reference or perspective on a topic being discussed.

c. Ensure understanding by using clear and concise language that is understandable by collaborators (e.g., avoiding the use of professional jargon and acronyms such as IEP, LRE, ADHD, NCLB).

d. Use questions to clarify, better understand, seek further information, and convey acceptance to the speaker.

e. Summarize the content to make certain that all agree regarding what has been discussed.

Michelle Duclos, a seventh-grade science teacher at West Hernando Middle School, notes that at times, she and her co-teacher will only have a few minutes to plan before beginning a team lesson. Frequent, clear, effective communication is needed to ensure that she and her co-teacher share ideas and "play off each other, emphasizing our strengths" during the class. She also emphasizes the importance of teachers reading one another as they move through the class period, by either talking briefly or picking up on nonverbal cues as "an amazing idea comes to one of us during the lesson."

③ ***Address nonverbal communication.*** Many teachers who are initially involved in collaboration with other professionals and parents overlook the importance of **nonverbal communication,** which may be a more accurate representation of the intent of what is being communicated than the verbal message (Correa et al., 2005). Certain negative, nonverbal messages are sent to others by appearing to be bored, inattentiveness to comments made by certain collaborators, facial expressions or eye rolling, sighing, tone of voice, lack of eye contact, and so forth.

Effective collaboration requires that participants use nonverbal communication to convey attention, respect, and understanding when others are speaking. Strategies for conveying positive messages through nonverbal communication include leaning toward the speaker and maintaining eye contact, appearing relaxed and interested in the speaker, maintaining appropriate proximity to the speaker, using an appropriate tone of voice, and monitoring negative nonverbal messages (e.g., sighing, facial expressions) (Correa et al., 2005; Friend & Cook, 2007).

Applications and Examples

Several issues may result in barriers to effective communication as you work with other professionals. These potential blocks include (Kochhar-Bryant, 2008):

- Verbal or nonverbal messages that convey unequal status or lack of parity. These messages convey the perspective that "I don't view you as an equal partner or respect your point of view."
- A communication mismatch, when one collaborator needs to vent while another wants to discuss how to address a particular child's needs.
- Communications that send mixed messages. For example, a teacher says "I'm not frustrated," but body language suggests otherwise.

- Distractions or interruptions that convey to a collaborator that his perspective is not respected.
- Focusing on the past with statements such as, "We tried that before, and it didn't work."
- Moralizing or preaching, advising, and conveying that "I know how to solve your problems."

Collaborators need to be vigilant in monitoring their own behavior as well as others' to ensure that these barriers do not arise and have a negative influence or result in a total breakdown of collaboration.

Keep in Mind

Think for a moment about how difficult it is to communicate effectively. We all have experienced times when we thought we communicated clearly, but the person to whom we were sending the message did not receive the intended message. The complexity of communication is illustrated by several factors, including (Friend & Cook, 2007) the following:

- Communication consists of sending and receiving messages simultaneously.
- Messages are sent using both verbal and nonverbal information.
- The environment in which the message is sent influences communication (e.g., noise or distractions in the setting, others who are present).
- Different types of communication are used by different people.
- Different modes of communication are used to convey information (e.g., verbal, electronic, written messages).

Given the complexity of communication, it is critically important that collaborators frequently check with each other to ensure that they are sending and receiving messages clearly. This requires collaborators to send information in different formats, check understanding by using different words, and ask collaborators to rephrase information to ensure all understand the information.

Strategy 11.3

TEACHER ASSISTANCE TEAMS

Rationale and Research

When teachers need assistance, they have typically sought out help from respected colleagues by walking down the hall during a break, or catching the colleague during lunch or after school. Teacher assistance teams (TATs) formalize and simplify this source of assistance. These teams are also a source of professional development, as teachers who participate on the team learn from others about strategies to address a range of student needs.

Teacher assistance teams consist of a group of well-respected professionals who meet two to four times per month to provide assistance using collaborative consultation to other teachers who are having difficulty with a student or group of students. These teams have been called by a number of names, including intervention assistance teams, student assistance teams, and building-based teams. Research has shown that, when TATs are well designed and supported by teachers and the building principal, referring teachers often receive assistance that they can use in their classroom to address the identified student need (Lane, Pierson, Robertson, & Little, 2004).

Key References

Chalfant, J., & Pysh, M. (1989). Teacher assistance teams: Five descriptive studies on 96 teams. *Remedial and Special Education, 10*(6), 49–58.

Chalfant, J., Pysh, M., & Moultrie, R. (1979). Teacher assistance teams: A model for within building problem solving. *Learning Disability Quarterly, 2*(3), 85–96.

Lane, K., Pierson, M., Robertson, E., & Little, A. (2004). Teachers' views of prereferral interventions: Perceptions of and recommendations for implementation support. *Education and Treatment of Children, 27*(4), 420–439.

Snell, M., & Janney, R. (2000). *Collaborative teaming.* Baltimore: Brookes.

Walther-Thomas, C., Korinek, L., McLaughlin, V., & Williams, B. (2000). *Collaboration for inclusive education.* Boston: Allyn & Bacon.

Step-by-Step

TATs typically begin their work when a teacher refers a student with a particular need to the TAT. Once the referral occurs, the team goes through the following steps:

1. *Team members read the referral,* which includes specific information regarding the child's challenges. For example, the referral form could include a request for information regarding what the referring teacher wants the student to be able to do that she is not currently doing, what the teacher has already tried to address this problem, and the student's assets and deficits. If necessary, one team member observes the child in the referring teacher's class to provide more in-depth information regarding the problem.

2. *The team meets with the teacher* for about 30 minutes. The first step in this meeting is to explicitly identify the problem the team will address. The team discusses the problem until all members agree about the definition of the problem.

3. *The team, including the referring teacher, brainstorm possible solutions* to the problem. During this time, no comments are made regarding the possible solutions to the problem. A recorder lists a recommendation, and then the team moves on to additional recommendations. Teams generate anywhere from 10 to 50 recommendations for addressing most problems.

4. *The referring teacher selects several of the recommendations* that might fit into her classroom and approach to teaching, and asks for further clarification regarding the recommendations, as necessary.

5. *The referring teacher selects a recommendation he will use in his classroom* to address the student's problem. The team works with the teacher to clarify any aspects of the recommendation that are unclear and options for using the intervention in the teacher's classroom.

6. *The team and the teacher discuss goals for determining the success of the intervention* (e.g., a specific reduction in out-of-seat behavior, handing in homework 90% of the time), and arrange a time for a follow-up meeting.

(7) *During the follow-up meeting, the teacher provides the TAT with feedback* regarding how the recommended intervention worked. If the intervention did not work, the team will begin at step 1 and generate an additional recommendation, or the teacher will select a recommendation from the list generated in the previous meeting.

Applications and Examples

Members of TATs may be appointed by the principal, may be elected by teachers, or may volunteer. No matter how they are selected, all teachers on the TAT should be well-respected members of the faculty who are trusted by other faculty. In most instances principals do not serve on TATs, because they are in a position to evaluate teachers, and this may result in a reduction in the number of referrals to the team. To address this concern in one school, a principal (who was not on the TAT) was vocal in support of the TAT and told teachers that referrals to the TAT would be viewed in a positive way for their yearly evaluations, indicating that they were trying to improve their teaching. This resulted in an increase in referrals to the TAT.

TATs are designed to use the time of participants efficiently. For example, the referral form should be one page long and should include only information that is absolutely necessary for team decision making (see Figure 11.3 for a sample referral form). Furthermore, procedures for running the TAT meeting are designed to focus the group quickly on the problem and efficiently brainstorm and select possible interventions to address the problem. For more information regarding this process, see Walther-Thomas et al. (2000).

REQUEST FOR ASSISTANCE—SOUTHSIDE ELEMENTARY SCHOOL.

Name of Student   Age   Grade

Name of Parent

Referred by

What would you like the student to be able to do that s/he cannot currently do?

Describe what the student does well (assets).

Describe what the student does not do well (deficits).

Additional information that is relevant for the TAT to consider

---

Figure 11.3

Teacher Assistance Team Sample Referral Form

Keep in Mind

Most student problems that are referred to the TAT relate to work habits, classroom behavior, interpersonal behavior, attentional problems, and reading difficulties. The recommended interventions are reported to succeed for almost 90% of all referrals. Some students for whom recommendations are not successful may be referred to special education (if they are not already identified with a disability), to determine if they need more intensive interventions. It is noteworthy that the TAT process often significantly reduces the number of referrals to special education. Furthermore, when students are referred to special education after being referred to the TAT, they are most often identified with a disability.

Strategy 11.4

CO-TEACHING

Rationale and Research

When used to support inclusion, the primary purpose of co-teaching is to make sure that instruction for students with disabilities (and other students who struggle academically and/or socially) is adapted to meet individual student needs. Co-teaching thus provides students with more intense and individualized instruction, which is built on the general education curriculum.

Co-teaching has several strengths. When teachers share responsibility for teaching a diverse group of students in one classroom, they can combine their expertise to meet the needs of all students. For students with disabilities in particular, co-teaching provides access to the general education curriculum, reduces the fragmentation of the curriculum that results when students are pulled out of general education classrooms for instruction, reduces the stigma attached to pullout programs, and often results in improved student outcomes. Teachers also report that co-teaching provides a professional support system and leads to less feeling of professional isolation, especially for special education teachers.

Key References

Correa, V., Jones, H., Thomas, C., & Morsink, C. (2005). *Interactive teaming: Enhancing programs for students with special needs* (4th ed.). Upper Saddle River, NJ: Merrill/Pearson Education.

Friend, M. (2008). *Co-Teach!* Greensboro, NC: Marilyn Friend.

Friend, M., & Cook, L. (2007). *Interactions: Collaboration skills for school professionals* (5th ed.). Boston: Allyn & Bacon.

Villa, R., Thousand, J., & Nevin, A. (2004). *A guide for co-teaching.* Thousand Oaks, CA: Sage.

Walther-Thomas, C., Korinek, L., McLaughlin, V., & Williams, B. (2000). *Collaboration for inclusive education.* Boston: Allyn & Bacon.

Step-by-Step

During the first year of co-teaching, develop a maximum of one to two new partnerships. Sufficient time to plan for the co-teaching partnerships should be available during the spring and summer before beginning to co-teach. Planning for co-teaching should address the following:

1 *Determine common goals for co-teaching* that both teachers understand, agree to, and value. These goals facilitate buy-in from the co-teachers and ensure interdependence in addressing and meeting the goals.

2 *Discuss the strengths both teachers bring to the classroom,* and how both teachers will use these strengths to make co-teaching succeed. Also address how teachers will share expertise (e.g., observation, coaching).

3 *Define roles and responsibilities for both co-teachers.* Roles should vary, depending on student needs and the content being taught. Figure 11.4 describes possible teacher roles.

Team Teaching—Both teachers share equal responsibility for instructing the whole group and teach the group as equal members of a team.

One teach, one support—One teacher teaches the content of the class, while the other teacher floats, responds to student questions, keeps students on task, and so forth.

Complementary teaching—The class is divided based on student needs, and both teachers teach a group. This may include different content for the groups, review of material that a group of students has not mastered, and intensive instruction for a small group of students.

Figure 11.4

Co-Teaching Options

4 *Participate in professional development* related to co-teaching, collaboration, communication skills, problem solving, and instructional strategies. This allows partner teachers the opportunity to develop the common skills they need to enhance the success of co-teaching.

5 *Develop a master plan for instruction and a general format for daily lessons* that is predictable but flexible. This should make certain that lessons are lively, logical, and well organized.

6 *Develop a plan for classroom management,* including how to address behavior issues proactively, rules for student behavior, consequences (both positive and negative), and who will handle delivery of consequences.

7 *Create a common planning time for co-teachers* during the school year. During this time, co-teachers address student progress, instructional content, teachers' roles, accountability, and so forth. Teachers should also use this time to reflect on how co-teaching is working and make changes as needed. Teachers should agree on how to efficiently use this planning time. For example, planning routines may be developed to include activities such as the following:

- Celebrate the successes of co-teaching from the previous week's instruction.
- Discuss student needs based on the previous week's instruction.
- Plan instructional content and related student accommodations for the coming week.
- Plan teacher responsibilities for the coming week, to make sure that students receive support as needed.

Applications and Examples

Co-teaching is a dynamic process, and you will need to continue to make decisions with your teaching partner regarding a variety of logistical issues over the first year of co-teaching and beyond. As you enter into a co-teaching relationship, continue to acquire skills to support co-teaching and learn about your partner teacher. This makes it important that you and your co-teacher agree that it is fine to ask questions about any issues or misunderstandings that arise. You will likely need to continue to work on sharing responsibility with another professional and communicating effectively regarding student issues, as well as the logistics of co-teaching.

Another issue that you will continue to address is the roles that you and your teaching partner play as co-teachers. Student learning and related needs change over time, and you will find that student-grouping patterns and teacher responsibilities must also change. It is likely that as the year progresses, you will use the one-teach, one-assist model of co-teaching less often, and the complementary teaching and team-teaching models more often to ensure that students receive the individual support that they need.

Keep in Mind

It is easy to fall into a pattern of often grouping low-achieving students together and assuming certain teaching roles that are traditional for general and special education teachers. For example, the general education teacher may always assume the role of content teacher for the large group, while the special education teacher always assumes the role of attending to the needs of low-achieving students. As we've noted previously, a critical aspect of effective inclusion programs is that differences become an ordinary part of the school day. Furthermore, varying the teaching roles allows teachers to learn and develop expertise from their partner teacher and to use their expertise with all students. If co-teaching is to work well, partner teachers must not revert to traditional teaching roles and grouping patterns. Rather, teachers should seamlessly share roles in the classroom, and students who are struggling should be grouped into small, homogeneous groups for only brief periods of intensive instruction. Otherwise, the grouping patterns for these students should be similar to that of their peers.

Strategy 11.5

WORKING WITH PARAEDUCATORS

Rationale and Research

The number of paraeducators working in schools has increased dramatically since the advent of inclusion (French, 2003; Wallace, 2003). Many of these paraeducators have been hired to provide support for students with disabilities in inclusive classrooms. Many students with disabilities in general education classrooms require more attention and individual support than the classroom teacher can provide (French, 2003). One approach to providing this support is the use of paraeducators.

Paraeducators work under the supervision of a certified teacher and provide support such as one-to-one or small-group instruction (e.g., tutoring or drill and practice) on material already taught by the teacher, support for students with highly specialized needs, grading and other paperwork, preparation of materials for class lessons, and so forth. In short, paraeducators provide support for certified teachers in much the same way paralegals provide support to lawyers or paramedics provide medical support.

Key References

Causton-Theoharis, J., Giangreco, M., Doyle, M., & Vadasy, P. (2007). Paraprofessionals: The "Sous-Chefs" of literacy instruction. *Teaching Exceptional Children, 40*(1), 56–62.

French, N. (2003). Paraeducators in special education programs. *Focus on Exceptional Children, 36*(2), 1–16.

Friend, M. & Cook, L. (2007). *Interactions: Collaboration skills for school professionals* (5th ed.). Boston: Allyn & Bacon.

Riggs, C. (2005). To teachers: What paraeducators want you to know. *Teaching Exceptional Children, 36(5),* 8–12.

Wallace, T. (2003). *Paraprofessionals.* (COPSSE Document No. IB–3). Gainesville, FL: University of Florida, Center on Personnel Studies in Special Education.

Step-by-Step

Paraeducators can provide invaluable assistance in an inclusive classroom if their responsibilities are well defined and they are well prepared for the responsibilities. The supervising teacher is responsible for ensuring that this occurs. When a paraeducator is assigned, the teacher should follow several steps to ensure that they are well prepared. These steps include:

(1) *Welcome and acknowledge the paraeducator.* This includes activities such as introducing the paraeducator to other professionals as part of the teaching team (and not a helper for a specific student); providing a space for personal belongings; putting the paraeducator's name on the classroom door; and sharing routine responsibilities that communicate authority (e.g., taking roll, writing on the board) (Causton-Theoharis et al., 2007). These types of activities serve to welcome the paraeducator and communicate that she is a valued part of the professional team.

(2) *Orient the paraeducator to the school.* This includes activities such as a thorough tour of the school; introductions to important staff (e.g., office staff, librarian); a review of classroom procedures, policies, and rules; provision of information regarding location of supplies and technology; and access to IEPs and support in reading and interpreting these documents (Causton-Theoharis et al., 2007).

(3) *Provide training related to assigned instructional activities.* While the school district may provide general training for paraeducators, the supervising teacher is in the best position to provide training on specific curricular materials and methods used in the inclusive classroom. This may include training related to the use of methods for tutoring, the use of packaged programs for reading or math instruction, and so forth. As the year progresses, the supervising teacher monitors the skills of the paraeducator, provides individual training and support, and discusses possible training opportunities offered by the district that meet the specific needs related to the paraeducator's responsibilities.

(4) *Plan a schedule with the paraeducator.* A critical task of the supervising teacher is to ensure appropriate use of a paraeducator's particular skills in assigned duties. The supervising teacher and paraeducator should discuss these issues and develop a weekly schedule that includes who the paraeducator will support and what the paraeducator's role will be. Addressing what the paraeducator's role should not be may also be important. For example, paraeducators should not be fully responsible for any student and should not be responsible for planning programs or lessons, but rather should carry out plans developed by the supervising

teacher. The teacher may develop these plans collaboratively with the paraeducator, but ultimately, plans are the responsibility of the supervising teacher. After developing a schedule, the supervising teacher and paraeducator should meet frequently to evaluate how the schedule is working, and make adjustments as necessary.

(5) *Communicate effectively with the paraeducator.* Teachers need regularly scheduled meetings to facilitate effective communication with paraeducators. These meetings may occur during common planning time or at other times during the school day, but they should allow adequate, uninterrupted time to address important issues and concerns. For example, it is important to use the time of the paraeducator effectively, to develop appropriate roles and responsibilities, to address any training needs, and to adjust the paraeducator's schedule as necessary. In addition to regular meetings, communication may be enhanced by the use of daily notebooks, e-mail, and checking in at the beginning and end of each day. Finally, it is important to be open to the ideas and perspectives that the paraeducator provides and to engage in active listening to ensure that these perspectives are clearly understood (Causton-Theoharis et al., 2007).

(6) *Supervise the paraeducator appropriately.* The supervising teacher is responsible for supervising the work of the paraeducator. Roles related to supervision include (Friend & Cook, 2007) the following:

- Monitor how well paraeducators are performing assigned tasks.
- Provide feedback, and point out strategies to improve performance or those that are not working.
- Model effective instructional strategies and ways to interact with students.
- Problem solve as disagreements arise with the paraeducator and other teachers.
- Make certain that the paraeducator understands school policies and ethical practices and adheres to these policies and practices.
- Support paraeducators by responding to any questions they may have and providing support and training.
- Publicly acknowledge the work of paraeducators.

Applications and Examples

A key to working effectively with paraeducators is to build a relationship that includes open communication and reflects respect and trust. Collaborating with paraeducators in determining their role, needed training, weekly assignments, and so forth is an important step in ensuring that this occurs. Furthermore, the effective skills for collaboration that we discussed earlier in this chapter are important when working with paraeducators.

Cathryn Riggs (2005) surveyed paraeducators and asked them what is essential for teachers to be good partners with paraeducators. The results of this survey are summarized in Figure 11.5. The results of this survey provide much insight into how you can work effectively with paraeducators. As we noted previously, key issues seem to be working collaboratively with paraeducators in an atmosphere of trust and respect, clearly defining the paraeducator's role, and ensuring that the paraeducator receives appropriate training to meet students' needs.

Keep in Mind

Paraeducators can serve in a variety of roles in an inclusive classroom. For example, they can be especially effective in providing tutoring for students using well-structured materials, or engaging students in teacher-developed skill-and-drill activities. Nonetheless, some teachers are hesitant to delegate responsibilities to paraeducators. Some of the reasons this occurs relate to concerns regarding the quality of the paraeducator's work, the need for training if the paraeducator is to engage in certain tasks, the feeling that the teacher doesn't want to be bossy, or the perspective that the teacher can do it faster herself (Friend & Cook, 2007).

Teachers should work through these concerns and learn to delegate increasing levels of responsibility to paraeducators. This ensures the efficient use of resources to meet student needs, empowers paraeducators, allows them to learn new skills, and helps to create a team committed to student success (Friend & Cook, 2007).

1. **Know and use the paraeducator's name.** Paraeducators are not "Kasey's helper" or invisible! They are a valuable member of the professional staff and should be recognized and treated as such. This is an important first step in building trust, respect, and good communication.

2. **Be familiar with rules and policies in your district regarding paraeducators.** It is important that the supervising teachers and others understand the ground rules regarding paraeducators. A special education supervisor should have this information readily available.

3. **Work with the paraeducator as a team.** The working relationship that develops between a paraeducator and teacher should reflect professionalism, cooperation, and camaraderie. It logically follows that teachers should recognize paraeducators as valued members of the professional team.

4. **Explicitly share your expectations.** Paraeducators want to know what to do, as well as what not to do in the classroom. Teachers should clearly share information regarding expectations, including classroom management, student behavior, and expectations for certain students.

5. **Define roles and responsibilities for paraeducators and teachers.** Avoid disagreements and conflicts by explicitly defining the role of the paraeducator in a job description and ensuring that their role is clearly differentiated from the role of the teacher.

6. **The teacher should supervise and direct paraeducators.** Paraeducators are often confused regarding who should provide them with direction in a co-taught, inclusive classroom. Teachers should be explicit regarding who provides direction and supervision.

7. **Ensure effective communication.** Determining effective methods to provide formal and informal feedback to paraeducators regarding their work is a critical role for the supervising teacher.

8. **Recognize that paraeducators have knowledge and experience to share in the classroom.** Paraeducators often gain extensive information regarding students as they perform tasks across a range of settings. Furthermore, paraeducators gain valuable skills as they work with teachers and students over a number of years. Respecting and valuing the knowledge and skills paraeducators bring to their jobs helps to create a good working relationship and can have a positive effect on student learning.

9. **Take ownership of all students.** Teachers should be classroom leaders for all students and not put paraeducators in the position of taking responsibility of some students (e.g., a student with a disability). When a paraeducator works individually with a student for a long period of time, the teacher may not be familiar with the student and his needs. It is important to make sure that this does not occur, and the teacher knows and works with all students in the classroom.

10. **Respect paraeducators.** If teachers model respect for paraeducators, students will likely model this same behavior. In addition, the job satisfaction and retention of paraeducators are influenced by the extent to which they are valued and respected for the work that they perform.

Figure 11.5

What Paraeducators Want Teachers to Know

Source: Adapted from Riggs, C. (2005). To teachers: What paraeducators want you to know. *Teaching Exceptional Children, 36*(5), 8–12.

Strategy 11.6

WORKING WITH FAMILIES: HOME–SCHOOL COLLABORATION

Rationale and Research

Extensive evidence reveals that home–school collaboration can result in significant improvement in student achievement and behavior. Home–school collaboration is defined as a teacher and parent or significant caregiver working collaboratively to develop interventions to address student needs. Interventions that have proven effective include simple activities such as parent monitoring of homework or dispensing consequences based on a daily report card, to more extensive interventions that require parent training, such as parent tutoring in reading and math or improving a student's self-determination skills (Cox, 2005; Fishel & Ramirez, 2005; Kochhar-Bryant, 2008). A critical aspect of successful home–school interventions has been school personnel's collaborating with caregivers and treating them as equals (Cox, 2005).

Family involvement and support are especially important for inclusive programs. Moreover, caregivers for students with disabilities are in a unique position to become involved in their child's education and to work as a partner with educators, given the high level of parent involvement that is required as part of IDEA (Correa et al., 2005; Whitbread et al., 2007). Unfortunately, many parents are not engaged in their child's education. Some of this lack of engagement can be explained by a parent's choice not to become involved, while other parents want to be involved but may have family responsibilities and stressors that make it impossible to be involved (Kochhar-Bryant, 2008). Still other parents may not be involved because of cultural issues that impede clear, effective communication between school and home (Matuszny, Banda, & Coleman, 2007).

Key References

Correa, V., Jones, H., Thomas, C., & Morsink, C. (2005). *Interactive teaming: Enhancing programs for students with special needs* (4th ed.). Upper Saddle River, NJ: Merrill/Pearson Education.

Cox, D. (2005). Evidence-based interventions using home–school collaboration. *School Psychology Quarterly, 20*(4), 473–497.

Fishel, M., & Ramirez, L. (2005). Evidence-based parent involvement interventions with school-aged children. *School Psychology Quarterly, 20*(4), 371–402.

Kochhar-Bryant, C. (2008). *Collaboration and system coordination for students with special needs.* Upper Saddle River, NJ: Merrill/Pearson Education.

Matuszny, R., Banda, D., & Coleman, T. (2007). A progressive plan for building collaborative relationships with parents from diverse backgrounds. *Teaching Exceptional Children, 39*(4), 24–31.

Step-by-Step

An important responsibility you will have as a teacher in an inclusive classroom is to encourage home–school collaboration and other forms of parent involvement in their children's education. The following steps will help ensure that parents have an opportunity to participate and serve as a resource to improve their children's education:

1. *Get to know parents as individuals, build trust, and open lines of communication.* While some parents may immediately want to become involved in their child's education, for others, you will need to get to know the parent before you can develop home–school collaborative inter-

ventions. It is important to engage parents in informal settings early in the school year to begin this process. For example, the school might sponsor a kick-off-the-year event that allows teachers and parents to meet in an atmosphere that is informal, comfortable, and stress free (Matuszny et al., 2007). Talking with parents before and after school about topics unrelated to their child is also helpful in this regard.

After initially getting to know the parents, you should engage in activities such as inviting parents into the classroom and providing information the parents will find useful to further build a positive relationship. Finally, you could give parents choices regarding alternatives for participating in school-related activities and ask them for input in decision making (Matuszny et al., 2007).

(2) *Try to understand, respect, and take into account the parent's perspective.* Most families have some difficulty adjusting to the needs of a child with a disability. For example, after determining that a child has a disability, some parents may deny that a disability exists and need time before they can accept the disability. Other parents may have stressors in their lives, and these stressors may be exacerbated by having to address the child's disability in home and in school. Understanding the parent's perspective by talking with the parent and/or visiting in the home will lead to the conclusion that some parents do not have the time to participate in home–school collaboration, while others choose not to participate, often for very understandable reasons.

(3) *Determine the types of involvement that will work for particular parents.* A group of parents likely will be willing and prepared to engage in home–school collaboration on an intervention that will improve student achievement and/or behavior. We advise beginning with a small group of parents who are interested in using a single intervention. This allows teachers the opportunity to "work out the bugs" with the intervention while working with a group of parents who will provide feedback and aren't likely to be discouraged if some aspects of the intervention need to be adjusted.

(4) *Design, implement, and evaluate* the intervention collaboratively with parents. The intervention should be well structured and easily understood by participating parents, and resources should be available to support the intervention, as needed. Information on possible interventions related to homework, student behavior, tutoring, self-determination, and so forth are widely available. For more information, see the resources listed previously.

Applications and Examples

When engaging parents in home–school collaboration, or otherwise encouraging parent involvement in school activities, an important consideration is the parent's cultural background. To ensure that teachers understand, respect, and take into account a parent's cultural background, we recommend the following activities (Correa et al., 2005; Harry, Kalyanpur, & Day, 1999):

- Identify cultural values that are embedded in the teacher's interpretation of a student's difficulties or in recommendations for services such as independence and individuality.

- Explore whether the family understands and values how teachers interpret the student's difficulties, and, if not, have the family share how their values differ from the teacher's.
- Respect any differences that exist regarding the student that are embedded in the cultural background of the family.
- Determine ways to adapt the teacher's recommendations or interpretations to the value system of the family.

For guidelines for how teachers can encourage involvement of parents from culturally diverse backgrounds, see Figure 11.6.

1. **Empower families with knowledge and skills to:**
   - Adapt and cope with the school system, which will likely be very different from their previous experience.
   - Work with their children and reinforce educational programs at home in ways that are natural and functional.

2. **Provide the family with assistance in moving from their native culture to the mainstream culture,** recognizing that cultures vary significantly within such groups as Hispanics or Asians.

3. **Work as a culture broker,** and support the family in contacts with the school. This may involve serving as an advocate or mediator for students from certain ethnic backgrounds, and/or linking with community leaders to enhance home–school collaboration.

4. **When communicating with families, determine the preferred means of communication** that will remove barriers related to cultural, language, and communication differences and will enhance communication between school and home.

5. **Collect information regarding the family related to:**
   - The role of extended family members and siblings.
   - The amount of available community support.
   - Religious, spiritual, and cultural beliefs.
   - Parenting practices related to discipline and independence.

6. **Provide the family with information** in written and/or oral forms that enable family members to understand exactly what is being conveyed. Ensure that linguistic and cultural barriers do not impede this communication.

Figure 11.6

Guidelines for Encouraging Involvement of Parents from Diverse Cultural
and Language Backgrounds in Their Child's Education.

Source: Adapted from Correa, V., Jones, H., Thomas, C., & Morsink, C. (2005). *Interactive teaming: Enhancing programs for students with special needs* (4th ed.). Upper Saddle River, NJ: Merrill/Pearson Education.

Keep in Mind

While home–school collaboration is especially important for teachers in inclusive settings, it is only one type of interaction teachers have with parents. Teachers often will be involved in providing information to parents regarding their children, legal issues, and so forth. Teachers may also be involved in reporting and interpreting evaluation and test results for parents; encouraging and preparing parents to work as volunteers in school activities (e.g., working in an after-school tutoring program or participating in a school decision-making group); and/or providing training to build parenting skills (e.g., communicating with children, discipline). Of course, all of these activities are important and should be done while keeping in mind the step-by-step guidelines for effectively working with parents.

Strategy 11.7

PEER BUDDIES

Rationale and Research

As students enter adolescence, they spend more time with peers, increasing the influence of these interactions on adolescent development (Carter & Hughes, 2005). Adolescents with moderate-to-severe disabilities benefit from peer interactions, just as other students do, while they make friends, learn social skills, and experience an enhanced quality of life. Unfortunately, even when students with moderate-to-severe disabilities are included in general education classes and participate in daily activities in a school (e.g., lunch), they often remain substantially isolated socially from their peers without disabilities. Thus, students with moderate-to-severe disabilities need teachers to intervene and facilitate social interactions with peers (Carter & Hughes, 2005).

Many middle and high schools across the United States have implemented peer buddy programs, which have proven effective in increasing social interactions between students with disabilities and their peers. These programs offer students the opportunity to earn course credit and participate in service learning, as they interact with students with disabilities in school, leisure, and/or work settings.

Key References

Carter, E., & Hughes, E. (2005). Increasing social interaction among adolescents with intellectual disabilities and their general education peers: Effective interventions. *Research & Practice for Persons with Severe Disabilities, 30*(4), 179–193.

Copeland, S., Hughes, C., Carter, E., Guth, C., Presley, J., Williams, C., & Fowler, S. (2004). Increasing access to general education: Perspectives of participants in a high school peer support program. *Remedial and Special Education, 25*(3), 342–352.

Hughes, C., & Carter, E. (2006). *Success for all students: Promoting inclusion in secondary programs through peer buddy programs.* Upper Saddle River, NJ: Pearson Education.

Hughes, C., Guth, C., Hall, S., Presley, J., Dye, M., & Byers, C. (1999). "They are my best friends": Peer buddies promote inclusion in high school. *Teaching Exceptional Children, 31*(5), 32–37.

Westling, D., & Fox, L. (2004). *Teaching students with severe disabilities* (3rd ed.). Upper Saddle River, NJ: Merrill/Pearson Education.

Step-by-Step

Peer buddy programs are a strategy for "promoting inclusion in the high school, ensuring a positive experience both for the students with severe disabilities and their general education peer buddies" (Hughes et al., 1999, p. 32). These programs may also be effective for students with mild-to-moderate disabilities. Hughes and colleagues (Hughes & Carter, 2006; Hughes et al., 1999) suggest the following steps in developing a peer buddy program in a middle or high school.

1 **Develop a course** that offers students course credit and an opportunity to fulfill service-learning requirements for participating in the peer buddy program. This course provides time for peer buddies to spend at least one class period per day with their partners. Course credit also offers participants the opportunity to learn about persons with disabilities and gain knowledge and skills necessary for successfully interacting with and supporting their peer buddies.

2 **Recruit peer buddies** to participate in the program. This involves promoting the program to teachers, administrators, school staff, and students. Students may be recruited in inclusive classrooms that include a student who would benefit from a peer buddy, or in classes where disability-related issues are being discussed (e.g., health, civics, literature). Once the program is in place, peer buddies can provide support in recruitment.

3 **Screen students** who apply to be peer buddies. Screening criteria may include good attendance (always a key criterion), an adequate grade-point average, recommendations of teachers, written applications, and interviews. Peer buddies should be willing to take the initiative and require minimal supervision, should be open-minded and tolerant regarding individual differences, and they should demonstrate personal qualities such as caring, flexibility, responsibility, and so forth. Keep in mind that peer buddies may not

be the highest-achieving students, and students with disabilities may be peer buddies.

 4 *Match students* with peer buddies. Students should be tentatively matched by a teacher or counselor based on common interests, student preferences, and so forth. Students should then have the opportunity to interact, observe in classes, and clarify the role of the peer buddy to determine if the match is a good one. Students, teachers, and/or counselors should participate in making the final matches for peer buddies.

5 *Develop expectations,* and communicate those expectations to peer buddies. Teachers should communicate expectations to peer buddies through an orientation session. Peer buddies from previous years may assist with this session. Expectations should address attendance, role and responsibilities of the peer buddy, and other program procedures and expectations.

6 *Prepare peer buddies* to ensure success. Training sessions should address topics such as student information (regarding each student's peer buddy) and confidentiality, disability awareness, instructional strategies, interaction and communication strategies, suggestions for activities, addressing challenging behaviors, and handling emergencies.

Applications and Examples

On the entrance to West Hernando Middle School is a quote from Booker T. Washington: "If you want to lift yourself up, lift up someone else." The school lives this quote in many ways, including its peer buddy program. West Hernando has 63 peer buddies, making the peer buddy course students take the second-most popular elective in the school. Students who serve as peer buddies include those with and without disabilities. Teachers and administrators at West Hernando have noted that these students provide the teacher in an inclusive classroom with invaluable support, as they support the students during academic activities and build natural social relationships with students with disabilities.

Benefits of peer buddy programs are included in Figure 11.7. It is noteworthy that these benefits accrue not only for the student with a disability but for the peer buddy, teachers, and administrators. However, the most important benefits of peer buddy programs are for students with disabilities. As Lisa Hallal, a teacher at West Hernando, noted, "We have seen so many benefits. Like Zak, who now goes to the lunchroom. He never went to the lunchroom. Now he goes with his peers, not his peer buddy. He's like a normal kid; he gets to do what everybody else is doing. That's the beauty of it."

Keep in Mind

While peer buddy programs have many benefits, to realize these benefits, the program must be carefully planned and consistently supported. Students who have participated in these programs recommend the following to ensure success (Copeland et al., 2004):

- Offer activities for all students that increase awareness of students with disabilities.
- Ensure that peer buddies receive information about their partner, as well as training regarding how to provide effective support.
- Encourage friendships between students with disabilities and their peers, to increase participation in academic and social activities.
- Provide structures that support the peer buddy program. Sources of structure that are beneficial include a daily schedule of suggested activities, a peer buddy manual that includes information about disabilities, regular conversations with a supervising teacher regarding the peer buddy experience, and writing in a reflective journal.

For general education students . . .

- Develop new friendships
- Increase their advocacy skills and awareness of disability issues
- Gain additional knowledge about people in general and those with disabilities
- Learn enhanced interpersonal skills
- Experience personal growth and a sense of accomplishment
- Develop an interest in pursuing a career in human services
- Increase their expectations of peers with disabilities
- Learn from students with disabilities who are positive role models
- Have fun

For students with disabilities . . .

- Develop new friendships
- Gain opportunities for social interactions with peers
- Acquire important academic, social, and life skills
- Spend time with age-appropriate role models
- Receive effective peer support in general education settings
- Increase their independence and self-confidence
- Have fun

For teachers . . .

- Receive additional assistance from peer buddies in individualizing instruction for students with disabilities
- Experience professional growth and personal satisfaction
- Provide socializing opportunities for all students
- Experience increased diversity in the classroom

For administrators . . .

- Improve the school climate by supporting practices that foster a caring school community
- Align school practices with school reform efforts and legislation related to inclusion

For parents . . .

- Experience increased enthusiasm for their children's schooling
- Appreciate their children's growth and expanded social interactions and friendships

Figure 11.7

Benefits Associated with Peer Buddy Programs

Sources: Copeland et al. (2004, 2006); Helmstetter, Peck & Giangreco (1994); Hughes et al. (2001); Longwill & Kleinert (1998).
Reprinted with permission from Hughes, C., & Carter, E. (2006). *Success for all students: Promoting inclusion in secondary programs through peer buddy programs.* Upper Saddle River, NJ: Pearson Education.

Formal Plans and Planning for Differentiated Instruction

KEY TOPICS

After reading this chapter you will:

- Know about four formal plans required for students who are at risk or who have disabilities, and know the general educator's role in their development.
- Be able to plan for differentiated instruction in a classroom with diverse learners.
- Be able to monitor the progress of individual students in order to make instructional decisions.
- Know about an adaptive grading system that you can use for grading students with disabilities.
- Be aware of ways to plan a classroom's physical layout to accommodate students with disabilities.
- Possess eight detailed effective planning strategies to help you meet the needs of all the students in your classroom.

chapter 12

Perspectives on Planning

Thoughts on the Importance of Planning for Inclusion

Interview with Jill King, Principal, and Cathy Danford, Special Education Teacher, Mull Elementary School

If students with special needs are to be served well in inclusive classrooms, it won't just happen magically. We need to understand that by including these students with others we create a much more diverse population in terms of educational (and other) needs. To meet these needs, effective planning is essential. Jill King, the principal at Mull Elementary School in Burke County, North Carolina, and Cathy Danford, one of the special education teachers, offered their thoughts about effective planning.

"Communication is key," Jill said. "Becky [the other special education teacher], and Cathy, and their inclusion partners are continuously communicating concerning whole-group needs and individual needs. We do grade-level planning for whole-group instruction as a grade-level team, and this happens weekly or bi-weekly per subject area. Becky and Cathy work with their particular teachers if they cannot sit down at the time that the grade level is planning to get the plans and add their input. Cathy and Becky, a lot of times, are doing very specific needs instruction, which is their expertise, utilizing SRA, Reading-First strategies, math activities. These remedial needs are scheduled into the instructional block for the whole group. This instruction meets the IEP goals."

"Inclusion planning is a *constant*," Jill continued, emphasizing "constant." The planning with different teachers, focusing on different students in different classrooms, is necessary because the needs vary so much from one class to another. "Cathy may be teaching a reading lesson to the whole group while Lisa Church [a second-grade teacher] is running interventions or Madge Goines [a first-grade teacher] is working with an individual student or small group. For Becky and Cathy to have a planning period that coincides with each grade level would be ideal, [but it is] just not realistic with their schedules. They do a great job keeping up with what their inclusion teachers are planning. What amazes me is these ladies can walk into any classroom and fit and go with instruction," she concluded.

Cathy Danford agreed with Jill, "Constant collaboration is key. We divide up instructional skills that each grade level has determined that grade needs to work on based on county pacing guides. I'm teaching whole group when I'm in the inclusion group, while the grade-level teacher is providing data-driven individual instruction or progress monitoring students at Tier 1, 2, [in the response-to-intervention model] EC students or any student that needs specific skill drill. Inclusion is a win-win, because I've learned more about grade-level curriculum than I knew before, and I hope grade-level teachers have learned strategies for providing success for struggling students."

Introduction

Whether we do it formally or informally, for our immediate needs or long-term wishes, most of us engage in planning of some nature. In the morning we plan what we will wear today; this afternoon we might think about what we are doing this weekend; and tonight, maybe we will get out maps and travel brochures and mull over some plans for our vacation. When you think about it, many of us spend a good part of our life planning for the other parts of our life.

If we are looking for effective ways to achieve important goals, planning is an absolute necessity. That is why, as Jill King and Cathy Danford explained in their interview, planning is critical if students with disabilities and special needs are to achieve success in inclusive academic settings. We cannot expect these students to achieve sufficiently unless we make plans for it to happen.

Besides direct engagement in teaching and learning activities, teachers' most persistent responsibility is instructional planning. You are probably aware of your state's or school district's general curriculum or standard course of study (SCOS) and the grade-level curricular benchmarks that they include. Many of these are online, such as Florida's Sunshine State Standards (*http://www.fldoe.org/bii/curriculum/sss/*) and North Carolina's Standard Course of Study (*http://www.dpi.state.nc.us/curriculum/*). Standards such as these provide the basis of what students are expected to learn. Planning allows teachers to use their knowledge, experience, and creativity to design effective instruction that will lead to the desired learning outcomes included in the standards. Most students with disabilities or special needs are expected to acquire the same knowledge reflected in the SCOS as students without disabilities, but, in addition, these students may also need to achieve other learning objectives.

Pause & Reflect

Some teachers and other educational professionals think that we have too many "formal" plans that require too many meetings and too much paperwork. What is your thought on this issue? After learning a little more about the plans, decide if you think some can be eliminated.

Teachers may participate in developing four types of formal plans for students who have academic learning difficulties, who exhibit challenging behavior, or who have other special needs: *response-to-intervention* (RTI) plans, *individualized educational program* (IEP) plans, *Section 504 Plans*, or *behavior intervention plans*. In addition, teachers must create plans for differentiated instruction that can effectively meet the needs of all the students in their class, including those students with special educational needs. In this chapter we first discuss the formal plans, then we address how to develop instructional plans that will meet the variety of abilities you are likely to find in your classroom.

Plans and planning constitute an important part of a teacher's responsibilities.

Response-to-Intervention Plans

Today, planning for a student with special needs is likely to begin before the student receives special education services. Because many educators believe that every effort must be made to offer effective instruction in the general education classroom before a student falls too far behind, and thus prevent the need for special services, many school districts today use an RTI model. (Some state and local education agencies use the term *response to instruction*.) The RTI model allows the school to begin more structured interventions with students even though students have yet to be identified as being eligible for special education.

School districts use RTI for two reasons. The first is to determine if a struggling student might be able to improve performance if the teacher provides more concentrated instruction. Jill King and many of the teachers at Mull Elementary pointed out to us that RTI means that teachers do not have to wait until the student fails but can try to prevent failure by increasing the intensity or directness of instruction.

A second purpose of RTI is as an alternative means of determining whether a student really needs special education, instead of, or in addition to, formal testing. Educators reason that if a student receives increasingly intensive instruction on key areas of weakness and still does not make adequate progress based on a dynamic assessment process (i.e., does *not respond to the instruction*), then the student probably needs special education services (D. Fuchs & Fuchs, 2006; Hilton, 2007).

RTI models usually consist of three or four "instructional tiers," with each tier requiring more intensive instruction and usually involving more expertise. For example in Tier 1, the teacher may meet with a student's parents and work out an instructional procedure that they agree might be more effective. When providing the newly planned instruction, the teacher also uses instructional probes (direct assessments of student performance) in the areas in which the student needs to improve in order to determine whether progress is adequate. If after a sufficient period of time, the first tier of RTI is not effective, then the teacher assistance team (TAT; sometimes called a student support team [SST]) meets to discuss a more intense form of intervention, and this becomes the second tier of intervention. This team generally includes a special education teacher, a school guidance counselor, a school psychologist, and perhaps other specialists. The team then designs a plan for the student or recommends an existing protocol (a strategy, material, and teaching process) for the general education teacher to implement. After initiating Tier 2, the teacher continues to measure student progress to determine whether progress is occurring. If progress is still not adequate, educators may evaluate the student for special education eligibility, and the student may begin receiving special education services. This is usually considered the final or uppermost tier in the RTI model.

The RTI model has tremendous implications for general educators, because they are the primary instructional agents delivering RTI instruction and monitoring student progress. As noted, the general educator is supported by members of the school's TAT or SST, who will help in identifying the form of instruction and the instructional targets for monitoring. However, the general educator is expected to work directly with the student under the RTI model.

Pause & Reflect

RTI models are a new way to identify students for special education. What do you see as the advantages and disadvantages of this model over traditional testing approaches?

Individualized Education Programs

In many cases, we can expect that the RTI approach will result in students being served adequately without being identified as a student with a disability. However, if this is not the case, and the student is found to be eligible for special education services, an IEP planning team must create an IEP.

As you saw in Chapter 2, an IEP is a document that lists the educational goals for students with special needs, the special education and related services the student is to receive, the educational placement of the student, and other important information. As noted, the IEP team develops and approves the IEP. The team includes professionals, the student's parents, and whenever possible, the student for whom the IEP is being written. According to IDEA 2004, an IEP must include the following parts:

1. **A statement of the student's present level of educational achievement and functional performance.** The IEP must contain information about the student's educational skills and how they affect her ability to make progress in the general curriculum.

2. **A statement of measurable annual goals and, for students evaluated through alternate assessments, benchmarks, or short-term objectives.** These goals must be related to meeting the child's needs that result from her disability in order to enable the child to be involved and progress in the general curriculum or, for a preschool child, to participate in appropriate activities. The goals must also address each of the child's other educational needs that result from her disability.

3. **A statement of the special education and related services and supplementary aids and services that teachers will provide to the child.** This part of the IEP must also include a

statement of the program modifications or supports for school personnel that educators will provide for the child so that she can advance appropriately toward attaining annual goals, participate and progress in the general curriculum, and participate in extracurricular and other nonacademic activities with children with and without special needs. The services provided must be based on "peer-reviewed research to the extent practicable" (IDEA 2004, Sec. 614[d][1][a]).

4. **An explanation of the extent, if any, to which the child will not participate with nondisabled children in the general education classroom and in other school activities.** The assumption implicit in IDEA 2004 is that a child with a disability *will* be included in the general education classroom, participate in the general curriculum, and in other ways be involved in school activities. If this is not to occur, educators must include an explanation on the IEP.

5. **A statement about the child's participation in state- or district-wide assessments of student achievement.** This statement must include any individualized modifications in the administration of state- or district-wide assessments that the child needs in order to participate in the assessment. If the IEP team determines that the child will not participate in a particular state- or district-wide assessment, the IEP must state why that assessment is not appropriate for the child and how the child will be assessed.

6. **The projected dates for beginning services and modifications.** These dates refer to services described in item 3 and their anticipated frequency, location, and duration.

7. **A statement of how educators will measure the child's progress toward the annual goals described in item 2 and how the child's parents will be regularly informed.** Parents of children with special needs must be informed of their children's progress at least as often as other parents are informed of their children's progress. The progress reports must tell parents about a child's progress toward her annual goals and the extent to which that progress is sufficient to enable the child to achieve the goals by the end of the year.

A general education teacher usually is a part of the IEP planning team, especially if the student receives instruction in the general education classroom. Strategy 12.1 provides some suggestions for being an effective member of the IEP planning team.

> **Strategy** Strategy 12.1 outlines step-by-step procedures for successfully contributing to IEPs.

Pause & Reflect

The laws did not always require classroom teachers to be a part of the IEP team; this requirement was added in a later revision of IDEA because of inclusion. You also saw that teachers were key to the RTI model. With so much involvement by general education teachers with students who have special needs, how do you think this should affect the role of the special educator?

Section 504 of the Rehabilitation Act as well as the Americans with Disabilities Act are intended to allow participation in public settings by all persons.

Section 504 Plans

Educators develop a Section 504 Plan for a student who, under Section 504 of the Rehabilitation Act or under the Americans with Disabilities Act (ADA), is considered to be a person with a disability but who under IDEA does not qualify for special education services. Students who qualify for services under Section 504 have the right to plans that specify any accommodations or adaptations that they need in order to participate in school activities. The Section 504 Plan ensures that schools respect the civil rights of students with disabilities who are entitled to accommodations so they can participate in school. Under Section 504, individuals with special needs, who are otherwise qualified, cannot be excluded from activities or services that are available to all others.

Because public schools receive federal funds, they must comply with Section 504. However, because a disability is more broadly defined under the Rehabilitation Act and ADA than under IDEA legislation, many students in public schools who are not in special education may still be considered to have a mental or physical disability that "substantially limits a major life activity." For example, a student who has asthma may not need special education services because his school performance may be adequate. However, he may still qualify for supports and services under Section 504. Therefore, Section 504 covers all students with special needs, including those receiving services under IDEA and those who qualify according to the Rehabilitation Act (U.S. Department of Education, Office for Civil Rights, n.d.). If a student with a disability has an IEP, the IEP will meet the requirement for an intervention plan under both IDEA and Section 504. However, if the student is not in special education but is eligible for services under Section 504, then a 504 Plan is required.

For the most part, Section 504 Plans affect the development of accommodations for students in general education. General education teachers often have students with 504 Plans in their classrooms or may have students who should have a 504 Plan. Strategy 12.2 outlines procedures that schools usually follow when developing a 504 Plan, and Figure 12.1 displays a sample 504 referral form.

> **Strategy**
>
> Strategy 12.2 discusses procedures for developing a 504 Plan.

> ## Pause & Reflect
>
> Why do you think different criteria define *disability* under Section 504 of the Rehabilitation Act or ADA and IDEA? Isn't a disability a disability no matter the law?

Behavior Intervention Plans

A small number of students exhibit challenging behavior to such an extent that school personnel must develop a formal plan that they can implement to improve the student's behavior. This plan, called a behavior intervention plan (BIP), is required by law for students with disabilities if the challenging behavior threatens to lead to a more restrictive placement. For example, if a student in a general education classroom exhibits behavior that might require the student to be placed in a separate classroom or school, then educators must write a BIP. Most districts also develop BIPs for any student who regularly engages in inappropriate behavior. The general education classroom teacher is expected to provide information to help develop the plan and also is asked to implement the plan as carefully as possible in order to help the student improve the behavior.

The lead person who develops the BIP is usually a school psychologist or behavior specialist who has training in the area of *applied behavior analysis* and *positive behavior supports*. This person completes a *functional behavior assessment* (FBA) by interviewing the teacher and directly observing the student. Based on this assessment, the behavior specialist develops a BIP and reviews it with the teacher to determine if the teacher understands the intervention process and feels able to implement it in the classroom. Chapter 15 provides additional information on conducting FBAs and developing BIPs.

Although it is important for you to understand and be able to participate in developing and implementing the formal plans we have just described, the most challenging form of planning that you will face will be preparing for instruction in your classroom.

Planning for Differentiated Instruction

As you think about planning for classroom instruction, think about how you would plan for an important event. For example, suppose you wanted to throw a party to celebrate graduation. Most likely, you would think about the following:

- Who will come to the party? Should I invite all my friends or keep it small?
- What time will the party start and when should it end? If I'm serving food, when should I do that?
- What kind of supplies will I need? How about food and drinks?
- What kind of music will people like? Should I have the TV on? Should I have a DVD on?
- How should I arrange the furniture, and will I need to borrow some additional tables and chairs?
- Should I try to plan some party games or just let everybody hang out?

Figure 12.1 Sample Section 504 Referral Form

Student Information

Name:		Date of birth:	
Address:		Grade level:	
Phone:		School:	

Parent Information

Name:	
Address:	
Phone:	

Person Making Referral

Name:	
Relationship to Student:	

Reason for Referral

Identified disability (if any):

Treating Physician

Name:
Address:
Phone:

Other persons who may have information that can be used in determining 504 eligibility (e.g., psychologist or counselor)

Name: Address: Phone:	Name: Address: Phone:
Name: Address: Phone:	Name: Address: Phone:

Permission to contact and receive records from the persons listed above should be requested of the student's parent/guardian.

Principal/Date	Referring Party/Date

Now consider planning for instruction in your classroom, where you are likely to have students with a diverse range of abilities, including some with disabilities or special needs. Here are some questions you will need to answer:

- How big is my class, how many students have disabilities or special needs, and how might their personal conditions affect their participation and learning?
- Will the students with disabilities be in my class all day or part of the day? How will I fill the time with meaningful activities for them?
- Do I have all the materials and supplies that I will need to provide instruction and meet students' learning needs? If not, what else will I need? How will I obtain the materials I need?
- What types of instruction and learning activities should I plan? Will students be able to participate and learn like my other students, will they understand my directions and explanations, or do I need to offer some special form of instruction?
- Should I rearrange my furniture and other classroom fixtures in order to better accommodate them? Are different classroom arrangements necessary?

The planning processes we discuss in this section will help you address these issues and help you to offer differentiated instruction to your students. Differentiated instruction is based on the premise that, within a given group of students, the range of individual strengths, abilities, and needs will preclude a "one size fits all" approach to instruction. Instead, differentiated instruction calls for teachers to offer students different ways to take in information, to process the information so that it makes sense to them, and to demonstrate what they have learned (Tomlinson, 2005).

> **Strategy 12.3** discusses planning for differentiated instruction.
>
> **Strategy**

> ## Pause & Reflect
>
> Reflect back to earlier chapters on students with different disabilities and on your personal life experience. Are there some students whom you think would be easier or more difficult to include in your classroom? Why? How do you think you could plan to meet their needs?

Getting to Know Your Students

In earlier chapters, we discussed various categories of students with disabilities so that you might develop an overview of their conditions. However, getting to know your individual students, including those with and without special needs, will allow you to develop a much more personalized understanding of their strengths and weaknesses, an understanding that will exceed categories and labels. Although the depth of knowledge teachers can develop for each student may vary, ultimately, the more you learn about your students, the better you will be able to teach them. By reviewing students' records, including the formal plans discussed previously, talking to the students, and meeting with their other teachers, you will be able to learn important personal information such as the following:

- The age and birthday of each student
- The student's specific disability and associated conditions
- The approximate developmental level of the student and general learning ability
- Personal social strengths and past academic achievements of the student
- The names of family members and relevant cultural information, and any special concerns of parents or caregivers
- Any medications or other medical needs of the student; also any relevant dietary restrictions
- Likes and dislikes of the student and possible sources of positive reinforcement for appropriate behavior
- Any challenging behaviors the student may exhibit, the effectiveness of past specific behavioral interventions, and how the student reacts to discipline

As you learn about your students, try not to focus only on their limitations or special needs, but also on their strengths. This may help you develop a positive relationship with the student and thus become a more effective teacher.

Working collaboratively with your colleague(s) in special education, you can begin planning for differentiated instruction as you acquire important knowledge about your students and their needs. This planning should occur at different levels and at different times (Rosenberg, O'Shea,

& O'Shea, 2006). We propose three key levels of planning: a strategic level where you focus on students' learning needs, a tactical level where you plan daily instruction, and an interactive level where you engage in moment-to-moment planning as you teach.

Level-1 Planning: Identifying Students' Learning Needs

At Level 1, you consider what students are to learn, whether basic skills, such as reading, writing, and math, or specific content areas, such as science and social studies. During this planning, you should look first at the common needs of your whole class and then at the special needs of individual students.

Focus on the General Curriculum for All Students. The general curriculum, or SCOS, provides the basis of instruction for all your students, including students with disabilities. According to IDEA and No Child Left Behind (NCLB), students with disabilities are expected to participate in the general curriculum. Therefore, as a general rule, you should always try to consider how you can apply the principles of differentiated instruction so that these and all students can learn the material you are presenting to the maximum extent possible. Depending on the nature and degree of students' disability, three critical adjustments can help students achieve successful outcomes in the general curriculum: accommodations, supplemental instruction, and modifications of the curriculum. (Note that if a student should receive any of these adjustments, the student's IEP will specify them.)

Accommodations. Students may receive accommodations or special supports to facilitate learning, as well as supports for evaluation to determine their achievement on general curriculum outcomes. Instructional accommodations might include any number of changes such as using word processing software with spell checkers, listening to audio books, or learning and applying learning strategies, for example. Students may receive testing accommodations for class tests or for end-of-grade or end-of-course assessments. An example of a testing accommodation could be having the test read to a student in order to assess his knowledge of the content.

The important thing to remember about an accommodation is that it is not intended to allow the student to achieve an easier standard, but to help the student achieve and demonstrate the same standard as others. Therefore, teachers cannot use an accommodation if it changes the validity of a particular standard. For example, if a standard requires that a student orally read a list of vocabulary words, the teacher cannot read the words for the student. On the other hand, if the standard requires that the student demonstrate an understanding of a key concept in political science, then the student can listen to a lecture or a pre-recorded passage about the concept and then verbally explain the concept to demonstrate knowledge.

Planning for the use of different accommodations may help students participate in the general curriculum.

Supplemental Instruction. Teachers can often improve the success of students on academic skills by providing supplemental instruction in key areas. This type of instruction usually focuses on improving basic skills, such as reading, writing, and math skills. These skills would be taught to better help the student be more successful on advanced skills. Alternatively, students may learn to use effective learning strategies, such as note taking and organizational skills, to help them succeed when learning in content areas. Supplemental instruction is not intended to supplant other instructional areas in the general curriculum but to help students better achieve standard outcomes.

Curriculum Modifications. In some cases it will not be reasonable to expect students to master the same general curriculum objectives as other students, even if teachers provide one or more accommodations or forms of supplemental instruction. (This will often be true if a student has a more significant degree of intellectual or behavioral disability.) In such cases the IEP team will probably indicate that the student is to take part in a state's or school district's "alternate-assessment" program. The student will demonstrate skills parallel to those of same-grade peers but qualitatively different in nature. A central tenet for making the general curriculum accessible to these students is structuring standards or outcomes within the general curriculum that have been originally developed for students without disabilities so that they may be achieved by learners with more significant disabilities. This process is referred to as *linking* or *aligning* the standards for students with disabilities so that they require a different form or degree of performance but are still based on grade-level standards (Westling & Fox, 2009).

Strategy 12.4 discusses identifying instructional needs for students with disabilities or special needs in general education classrooms.

Strategy

Identify Nonacademic Goals or Objectives. Although general classroom instruction must focus on academic instruction, some students' formal plans will also include goals or objectives in other areas and instruction such as improving social skills, self-determination skills, and personal-care skills. Level-1 planning, therefore, should include a review of students' IEPs and other formal plans in order to learn not only how the students participate in the general curriculum but also whether they should achieve other important goals or objectives. Strategy 12.4 provides a step-by-step plan for identifying the instructional needs of students with disabilities or special needs.

Pause & Reflect

Today the primary focus of education is to achieve important academic outcomes, and teachers have a strong focus on this goal. What is your opinion about general education teachers trying to help students achieve nonacademic goals?

Level-2 Planning: Preparing for Daily Instruction

At the second, or tactical, level of planning, you will write detailed plans for daily instruction. This is the most involved part of planning, but it rests greatly on what you learn during Level-1 planning. When at Level 2, your daily plans should cover the following:

- Who? Which students will you involve in the lesson? Everyone? A small group? Individual students?
- What? What do you want students to learn? What are your instructional objectives?
- Why? You should note the source of the objectives such as the standard in the state general curriculum the lesson will address.
- When? On what day and at what time of day will the instruction occur? How long will the lesson last?
- Where? In what part of your classroom (or elsewhere) will the lesson occur?
- How? What will happen during the lesson? What will the teacher, teacher assistant(s), and students do?

The plan will list all teaching and learning activities including whole-class instruction, group and individual learning activities, instructional materials, and the kinds of educational or assistive technology that some students will be using.

Although no firm guidelines exist, to some extent, the instructional approaches you must plan for depend on the nature of the learning material. If you are planning to teach basic skills, you are more likely to incorporate some tactics; whereas if you are planning for academic content instruction, you might use others.

Strategy 12.5 discusses planning for basic skills instruction in an inclusive classroom.

Strategy

Planning for Basic Skills Instruction. Successful basic skills instruction in inclusive classrooms often incorporates four key tactics: direct instruction, flexible ability grouping, peer tutoring, and the use of assistive and/or educational technology devices and programs. In Figure 12.2, we give an overview of these four components of basic instruction, and in Strategy 12.5, we provide a detailed process for planning for basic skills instruction.

Figure 12.2	Key Tactics for Planning Basic Skills Instruction
Tactic	**Description**
Direct Instruction	Direct Instruction (DI) is a model for teaching that emphasizes well-developed and carefully planned lessons designed around small learning increments and clearly defined and prescribed teaching tasks. It is based on the theory that clear instruction eliminating misinterpretations can greatly improve and accelerate learning (National Institute for Direct Instruction, n.d.).
Flexible Ability Grouping	When teaching basic academic skills, same-ability groups are often very effective and work well with direct instruction. Same-ability grouping allows teachers to focus more intensely on what students need because students within the groups have about the same skill level and thus approximately equal learning needs. Ability groups should be flexible and used for specific targeted learning, such as acquiring reading or math skills. As students demonstrate adequate skill acquisition, teachers should move them from lower groups to higher groups. Ability grouping should not be full-time. Students should spend as much time as possible in heterogeneous groups.
Peer Tutoring	Peer tutoring, and especially classwide peer tutoring (CWPT), provides a useful tactic for practicing basic academic skills. CWPT provides students with increased opportunities to improve skills by receiving immediate feedback from a peer tutor. Pairs of students take turns tutoring each other to reinforce concepts and skills initially taught by the teacher. CWPT requires the teacher to instruct all students how to tutor, to give material appropriate for practicing skills, and to allow time on a regular basis (three to five times per week) for tutoring.
Educational and Assistive Technology	Educational technology and assistive technology can be used by students with and without disabilities. For example, assistive technology may include the use of word processing software to help students write better and more creatively. Educational technology might be specific computer programs designed to teach select reading and math skills.

Planning for Academic Content Instruction. Planning for instruction in academic content areas such as science or social studies is likely to be very challenging when teaching students with mixed academic abilities. Unlike basic skills instruction, during which teachers usually can provide direct instruction to students with similar abilities, content instruction often presents a wide range of information that can be difficult to grasp for many students. Additionally, content instruction often relies on comprehending spoken and written material and demonstrating learning through written tests and student papers.

Four tactics can help teachers prepare to teach academic content to students with disabilities or special needs in inclusive classrooms: Plan units of instruction, use the planning pyramid, use principles of universal design for learning (UDL), and use cooperative learning groups. These tactics are described in Figure 12.3. In Strategy 12.6, we provide a detailed process for planning for academic content instruction.

> **Strategy**
>
> Strategy 12.6 discusses planning for academic content instruction in an inclusive classroom.

Selecting Instructional Materials. The instructional materials that your students use will play an important role in students' success. As you and your colleagues consider the selection of materials, you should keep in mind the appropriateness of the materials for students with

Figure 12.3	Key Tactics for Planning Academic Content Instruction
Tactic	**Description**
Units of Instruction	A unit of instruction focuses on a theme and provides a framework for students to acquire knowledge of the subject matter and also improve academic skills. Units may include activities such as watching DVDs, reading related material, or conducting individual research. Students may also hear a presentation by a guest speaker, participate in whole-group or small-group discussions, play games relevant to the material, or engage in independent learning activities. Students may write reports, prepare presentations, create products, or take oral or written exams. Units of instruction can be an effective instructional approach for students with disabilities because they allow variation in instructional activities for different ability levels.
Planning Pyramid	The planning pyramid calls for the teacher to identify "degrees of learning," which implies that within any content area, different students may acquire more or less information than others. *All students* may learn some of the material, *most students* (but not all) may learn more of the material, and a *few students* will learn more of the material than all others. The teacher's main goal, therefore, is to identify three degrees of learning: (1) the major concepts, facts, or information that all of the students must learn (the base of the pyramid); (2) additional information and more complex material that most of the students should learn (the middle part of the pyramid, and (3) less central information that a few students may learn, often through self-directed learning activities.
Universal Design for Learning (UDL)	The intent of UDL is to create instruction planned from the outset and accessible to learners of different ability levels while maintaining high standards of instructional outcomes. UDL consists of the following key elements: • *Alternative modes of presentation* means that you will plan for different ways to present content to students, so all students will have a better chance of understanding the material you are presenting. • *Alternative modes of responding* suggests that all students will be able to demonstrate their understanding of the material in some fashion consistent with their ability. • *Multiple ways of participation* means that all students can be active learners by engaging in whole-group or small-group discussions, participating on discussion teams, playing educational games, using educational technology, participating in learning centers, being involved in literature circles, or working individually on assignments.
Cooperative Learning	Cooperative learning activities, especially using the Jigsaw method (see Chapter 13, Strategy 13.2), involves every participant by providing each one with a unique assignment. Cooperative learning allows students with different abilities to participate in the activity and gain knowledge from it. The important benefit about using cooperative learning groups is that students can help each other and acquire more appropriate social skills.

special needs. The principles of UDL (see Figure 12.3) are useful when searching for materials. CAST (the Center for Applied Special Technology, at *www.cast.org*) is an important resource for finding and developing instructional materials based on UDL principles. For example, in the online *CAST UDL Book Builder* section, you can "create, read, and share engaging digital books that build reading skills for students. Your universally designed books will engage and support diverse learners according to their individual needs, interests, and skills" (see *bookbuilder.cast.org*).

In a recent effort to make traditional text-based material more accessible to all students, the U.S. Department of Education supported a project by CAST to develop a *National Instructional Materials Accessibility Standard* (NIMAS, 2008). According to CAST,

> NIMAS is a technical standard used by publishers to produce source files that may be used to develop multiple specialized formats (such as Braille or audio books) for students with print disabilities. The source files are prepared using Extensible Markup Language (XML) to mark up the structure of the original content and provide a means for presenting the content in a variety of ways and styles. For example, once a NIMAS fileset has been produced for printed materials, the XML and image source files may be used to create Braille, large print, HTML versions, DAISY talking books using human voice or text-to-speech, audio files derived from text-to-speech transformations, and more.

Digital reading material provides a new resource for teachers to consider during planning.

Ultimately, all material that is contained in elementary and high school textbooks will be available to students in forms and formats that they will be more able to access and learn from. Clearly, this will make learning for many students in inclusive settings much more viable.

For the present, many schools may continue to use more traditional, text-based materials. When these materials are designed to improve reading skills or require reading skills for learning academic content, you should think about the appropriateness of the material for your students who have weak reading skills. Not all such materials that require reading skills are created equally, and some may be more appropriately designed than others (Sperling, 2006; Wanzek, Dickson, Bursuck, & White, 2000). Figure 12.4 provides a checklist for evaluating the reading requirements of textbooks used by students with disabilities. A careful review of this checklist may help you select appropriate reading materials.

Pause & Reflect

Instructional materials, like this textbook and important Websites, are important media to help learners acquire information. Can you see how the structure or accessibility of some materials might make them more or less useful learning tools for some students?

Level-3: Interactive Planning During Instruction

The final aspect of planning is the dynamic creation of plans that usually occurs as teachers present lessons and carry out activities. By the time you reach this point, you have carefully considered your students' current learning needs and have created written, detailed lesson plans that choreograph the actions you will take and the ways you expect groups and individual students to participate.

Most effective teachers will use a lesson presentation format such as the following:

- **Introduction.** Tell students what they will learn and why it is important. Motivate students to pay attention and do their best during instruction.
- **Review.** Remind students of previously learned material, and show them how it relates to the current lesson.
- **Presentation.** Explain the new material (the concept or the academic skill), and probe students to find out if they are developing an initial understanding of the material.
- **Demonstration.** Show, tell, and give examples of the correct way to perform tasks within the lesson.

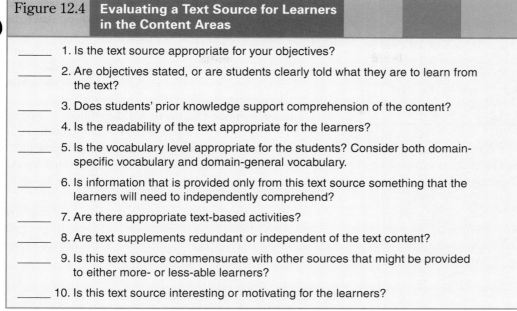

Figure 12.4 **Evaluating a Text Source for Learners in the Content Areas**

_____ 1. Is the text source appropriate for your objectives?

_____ 2. Are objectives stated, or are students clearly told what they are to learn from the text?

_____ 3. Does students' prior knowledge support comprehension of the content?

_____ 4. Is the readability of the text appropriate for the learners?

_____ 5. Is the vocabulary level appropriate for the students? Consider both domain-specific vocabulary and domain-general vocabulary.

_____ 6. Is information that is provided only from this text source something that the learners will need to independently comprehend?

_____ 7. Are there appropriate text-based activities?

_____ 8. Are text supplements redundant or independent of the text content?

_____ 9. Is this text source commensurate with other sources that might be provided to either more- or less-able learners?

_____ 10. Is this text source interesting or motivating for the learners?

Source: Reprinted with permission from Sperling, R.A. (2006). Assessing reading materials for students who are learning disabled. *Intervention in School and Clinic, 41*(3), 138–143. Copyright 2006 by Sage Publications.

- **Demonstrate incorrect responses.** Show students examples of incorrect responses and the types of errors they need to avoid.
- **Allow practice.** Give students time to practice their new skills or use their new knowledge.
- **Provide feedback.** As students practice, reinforce correct responses, and correct incorrect responses.
- **Review and summarize.** At the end of the lesson, review what has been learned, and summarize the important points.
- **Evaluate.** During some lessons, build in an evaluation process to determine student learning.

During the lesson, good teachers often attune themselves to their students' actions and try to maintain student engagement. Some students with special needs present a challenge at this point. They may drift off in another direction, appear confused, not show interest, and sometimes even show a degree of noncompliance while instructional and learning activities occur. The recommendations for improving student behavior in Chapter 15 will be especially useful when you must engage in Level-3 planning to address these students' behavioral patterns.

Monitoring Student Progress

Progress monitoring is a procedure that allows teachers to regularly and directly measure how well students are performing on key academic skills. Curriculum-based measurement (CBM) is one of the most common forms of progress monitoring. Teachers use CBM primarily to monitor student progress in key areas including reading, writing, and math (Deno, 2003). CBM is based on a simple yet ingenious idea: If teachers can clearly define what students should learn (as contained in the student's curriculum) and create an easy, quick progress-monitoring process, then teachers can make frequent decisions about whether or not progress is occurring. With this knowledge, teachers can decide if their instructional procedures are effective.

Research has shown that CBM is useful for many current trends in general and special education. It is commonly used to measure student performance in RTI models, to determine if students in inclusive or special classes are making adequate progress, and to predict how students will do on end-of-grade assessments (Deno, 2003; Zimmerman & Dibenedetto, 2008).

CBM relies on brief, frequent (weekly or bi-weekly), direct measures of student performance. Using material based on the curriculum in which the student is currently working, or using *general outcome measures,* on a regular basis, the teacher or a paraprofessional will sit one-to-one with the student and give the student a brief test or probe. For example, the student will read for 1 minute

Strategy 12.7 discusses using CBM to measure student academic progress.

Pause & Reflect

Monitoring student performance is necessary if we are to really know whether or not students are learning. Are you familiar with ways to monitor student learning other than direct monitoring, such as CBMs? How would you describe them?

from grade-level text while the evaluator marks the words the student misses on a separate data-collection sheet. After the reading session is finished, the teacher will count the number of words read correctly and the number read incorrectly and record the student's performance on a piece of graph paper. Because a similar measure is taken every week from the same-level material (but reading from a different passage), the evaluator can monitor whether or not the student is making progress. If progress is on target, the instruction continues until the student reaches the desired criterion. The student then moves into a higher or more difficult level in the curriculum. If progress is not adequate, the teacher can examine various aspects of the instructional process and make modifications. (In RTI, for example, the SST may decide to move the student to a higher-intervention tier if progress is insufficient.)

Using CBM, teachers can readily evaluate performance on academic objectives for students with disabilities. As part of their collaborative efforts, general education and special education teachers can arrange regular times and conditions to assess student performance. Guidelines for using CBM are contained in Strategy 12.7.

Grading Students with Disabilities

When teachers use standard grading procedures for students with disabilities, as you might expect, the procedures almost always result in lower grades than other students receive. Although standard grades may reflect the normative academic performance of students with disabilities (i.e., indicate that they are below average among other students), the grades fail to evaluate the student on other important outcomes such as the amount of effort by the student, the process the student used to reach a correct answer, or the improvement in the student's performance from the previous grading period (Munk & Bursuck, 2004; Silva, Munk, & Bursuck, 2005).

Many school districts have developed grading adaptations for students with disabilities that allow them to be graded based on different criteria. Five types of grading adaptations are relatively common (Silva et al., 2005):

- Progress on IEP objectives
- Improvement over past performance
- Performance on prioritized content and assignments
- Use of process and effort to complete work
- Modified weights and scales

Strategy 12.8 discusses procedures for developing a personalized grading plan.

By using one or more of these adaptations, teachers may develop a "personalized grading plan" for students and document this plan in the student's IEP (Munk & Bursuck, 2004). Figure 12.5 lists the different types of grading adaptations and gives examples of how they might be used to form grades. Strategy 12.8 provides an outline for developing a personalized grading plan for students with disabilities.

Arranging the Classroom for Inclusion

As you undertake other parts of planning, it will be very helpful for you to consider the physical arrangements of your classroom and how they might impact students with disabilities or special needs (Wadsworth & Knight, 1999). Here are some of the more important conditions for you to think about:

- **Furniture arrangement and spacing.** Placing furniture too close together can make movement difficult for students with poor motor control or physical disabilities. Remember that both students and teachers need to be able to move about easily in the classroom; make sure there is sufficient space for them to do so.
- **Lighting.** Generally, adequate lighting is necessary for students to learn. Keep in mind, however, that some lighting, and the buzz emitted by fluorescent lights, may be aversive to some students with disabilities. You should make sure all lighting is sufficient, have noisy lights replaced, and if possible, create some space that uses indirect lighting.

Figure 12.5	Types of Grading Adaptations	

Adaptation	Example
Progress on IEP objectives	*Daily work* If a student's IEP objective states, "The student will use a strategy to solve math problems with 85% accuracy," then the student's use of the math strategy on an assignment with 85% accuracy might result in the student receiving an A on the assignment. *Report card grade* A percentage of a student's report card could be determined by progress on an IEP objective.
Improvement	*Daily work* If a student raised his or her test scores average from 50% to 65%, the teacher could add the 15% that would allow the student to raise his or her grade from an F to a D. *Report card grade* A student could be given bonus points for each correct paragraph the student writes beyond the three paragraphs required. So, if the student attempted to write an additional paragraph, he or she could receive bonus points.
Prioritization of educational content and assignments	If you believe that one of the two social studies units being covered during the marking period is more important than the other, then the student will spend more time and receive more support on these assignments and they will count more toward the grade.
A balanced grading system: processes	Editing is a process that a student might use in the writing process, so a portion of a student's grade could come from the effective use of an editing strategy.
A balanced grading system: effort	An example of basing part of a student's grade for an assignment on the student's effort would be to base part of the grade for a math homework assignment on the number of word problems attempted.
Modified weights and scales	*Daily work* A teacher could change the grading scale so that a student must earn 90 out of 100 points (90%), rather than the 93 points (93%) indicated in the school-wide grading policy, to earn an A. *Report card grade* A teacher could change the weights assigned to different performance areas by changing the weights assigned to tests and homework to reduce the penalty to a student who struggles with tests but benefits from doing homework.

Source: Adapted with permission from Silva, M., Munk, D. D., & Bursuck, W. D. (2005). Grading adaptations for students with disabilities. *Intervention in School and Clinic, 41*(2), Table 1, Types of Grading Adaptations, pp. 92–93. Copyright 2005 by Sage Publications.

- **Noise control.** Most classrooms can be expected to have a certain level of auditory stimuli. For some students, however, this can be distracting or even lead to challenging behavior. You can use book cases, room dividers, carpeting, and acoustic tiles to reduce noise levels, as well as set an expectation that students use "indoor voices" in the classroom.
- **Ventilation and temperature.** Although we all desire to be in a space that has a comfortable temperature, for some students with disabilities this can be even more important. Some students may simply be more difficult to manage in extreme temperatures, while others may be physically sensitive due to physiological conditions such as hypothermia.

A well-planned classroom can be important for including students with special needs.

- **Visual accessibility.** As you arrange your classroom, remember that you need to see your students at all times, and they need to see you much of the time. Avoid placing bookcases, room dividers or other structures that might interfere with making visual contact.
- **Materials storage.** In an orderly classroom, materials and equipment not in use must be stored out of the way so as not to be distracting. For materials that students themselves must retrieve, be sure that they are easily accessible.
- **Plants and animals in the classroom.** Many teachers enjoy using plants and animals for their educational purposes. If you intend to have live creatures in the classroom, remember that some students will need to learn how to interact with them and care for them appropriately. Also remember that you may have some students with allergies or asthma who could be adversely affected by live creatures.

These arrangements will help meet the needs of most students with disabilities in your classroom. In some cases, students with special conditions (either with IEPs or 504 Plans) may require a little more attention. Often you can find help in meeting the needs of these students in your classroom by consulting with the special education teacher, the school nurse, or the occupational or physical therapist who works in your school.

Summary

In this chapter we have addressed the following topics:

Four formal plans required for students who are at risk or who have disabilities

- *RTI plans.* Students who are having difficulties but who have not yet been placed in special education may require RTI plans.
- *Individualized education program (IEP).* Students in special education require IEPs, which list annual goals, the types of services the student will receive, and other specific components of the special education procedures.
- *Section 504 Plans.* Educators prepare Section 504 Plans for some students who have disabilities as defined by the Rehabilitation Act but are not considered to have disabilities under IDEA. These plans list the accommodations and supports for students.
- *Behavior interventions plans (BIPs).* Educators write BIPs for some students who exhibit significant behavioral issues.

Planning for differentiated instruction

- Understanding students and their characteristics is a key component of differentiated instruction.
- Level-1 planning requires the teacher to identify learning goals based on the general curriculum and individual goals for students with special needs.
- Teachers should incorporate accommodations, supplemental instruction, and curriculum modifications into Level-1 planning for students with special needs.

PUTTING IT ALL TOGETHER

With increased academic standards required of all students, more students with disabilities are being included in high-demand content-area classes and many arrive unable to respond to the academic demands. Teams of general and special education teachers are required to design and apply instructional procedures that simultaneously meet the individual needs of students with learning differences as they deliver engaging, challenging, and provocative lessons to entire classes.

To maximize your efforts, we recommend that you keep in mind the following factors—central to successful student outcomes:

1. **Content-area instruction in inclusive settings is a team effort** requiring the active participation of subject-area experts and special education learning specialists.

2. **The primary role of the content-area specialist is to select carefully the subject matter** that is essential for all students to learn and to format the material for access and acquisition; the role of the special education specialist is to provide supports and teach students the strategies and skills to enhance their effectiveness as efficient learners (Deshler & Putnam, 1996).

3. **When presented well, content-area subject matter is interesting, engaging, and motivating.** Consequently, if provided with opportunities and support for interacting with the material, students will respond positively and participate in class discussions and activities.

4. **Methods that support and enhance accessibility** such as universal design, content enhancements, and learning strategies can be integrated into classroom activities with little negative impact on the instruction of other learners.

5. **Remember the affective elements of teaching when providing specialized supports.** Encouragement, positive self-statements, and skills for coping with difficult situations should always supplement content and strategy instruction.

myeducationlab

We present a series of evidence-based strategies in the second half of this chapter (Strategies 14.1 to 14.6) in a step-by-step format so that you can use them in your classroom right away. In addition, in the following table, we identify some video clips, cases, and simulations that will allow you to experience these strategies (or complementary strategies) in a real classroom environment.

EFFECTIVE PRACTICE	MYEDUCATIONLAB CONNECTION	CONSIDER THIS
Strategy 14.1: Content Enhancements: Unit and Lesson Organizers	Go to MyEducationLab, select the topic *Instructional Practices and Learning Strategies*, and go to the Activities and Applications section. Next, go to the subsection *Developing Learning Strategies and Conceptual Understanding*, and watch the video entitled "Graphic Organizer."	As you watch the video and answer the accompanying questions, compare and contrast this graphic organizer and the accompanying cooperative activity with the discussion in Strategy 14.1. Do you think the graphic organizer and this activity (depicted in the video) are successful in helping all students access this content? Why or why not?
Strategy 14.2: Improving Expository Writing Across Content-Area Classes	Go to MyEducationLab, select the topic *Content-Area Teaching*, and go to the Building Teaching Skills and Dispositions section. Next, complete the activity entitled "Scaffolding in Literacy."	As you complete the activity and watch the videos, focus on the techniques these teachers use to teach and scaffold successful writing for their students. Although these students are in elementary school, they are receiving the basic instruction on how to improve their expository writing. Compare and contrast these strategies with Strategy 14.2.
Strategy 14.3: Mnemonic Strategies	Go to MyEducationLab, select the topic *Instructional Practices and Learning Strategies*, and go to the Activities and Application section. Next, complete the simulation entitled "Using Learning Strategies."	As you complete the simulation, reflect on the importance of learning strategies such as mnemonics in the general education classroom. Consider the usefulness of the strategies discussed in the simulation as well as in Strategy 14.3.
Strategy 14.4: Content-Area Reading	Go to MyEducationLab, select the topic *Reading Instruction*, and go to the Activities and Applications section. Next, go to the subsection *Comprehension*, and watch the video entitled "Context Clues."	As you watch this video and answer the accompanying questions, consider how you could adapt the techniques this teacher uses for older students using a textbook.
Strategy 14.5: Developing and Supporting Note Taking	Go to MyEducationLab, select the topic *Attention-Deficit/Hyperactivity Disorder*, and go to the Activities and Applications section. Next, read and analyze the strategy entitled "Split-Page Note Taking," then go to the topic *Intellectual Disabilities*, and watch the video entitled "Guided Notes Study Cards."	As you read and analyze the strategy and then watch the video, consider the similarities and differences between these two note-taking strategies. How do these strategies support the discussion in Strategy 14.5?
Strategy 14.6: Developing Effective Test Taking	Go to MyEducationLab, select the topic *Instructional Practices and Learning Strategies*, and go to the Activities and Applications section. Next, read and analyze the strategies entitled "Strategies for Taking Objective Tests" and "PIRATES Test-Taking Strategy."	As you read and analyze these strategies, compare and contrast the major components of these strategies with the discussion in Strategy 14.6. How would you use these strategies in your classroom to help students who are struggling with taking tests?

EFFECTIVE PRACTICES

In the remainder of this chapter, we describe six effective strategies, which we referred to previously in the chapter, to help you plan effectively to meet the needs of all students.

EFFECTIVE PRACTICE	TYPE OF STRATEGY/BRIEF DESCRIPTION	SPECIAL CONSIDERATIONS
Strategy 14.1: Content Enhancements: Unit and Lesson Organizers	A universal design instructional support that highlights unit and lesson content, how elements of the content are related, and the knowledge and assignments required for success.	Components of the organizers must be taught explicitly to mastery; without such instruction, students may be confused by the graphical components.
Strategy 14.2: Improving Expository Writing Across Content-Area Classes	The most important skills for writing thoughtful and informative narratives involve an awareness and strategic application of the three-stage writing process: prewriting, production, and reviewing.	Writing is very complex, and students need to understand that it is a process that cannot be completed thoughtlessly. Successful writing is focused, multiphased, and iterative, requiring considerable planning, adequate source material, and an organizational framework.
Strategy 14.3: Mnemonic Strategies	A versatile series of techniques that produce meaningful recall-enhancing connections that do not exist naturally in content.	Mnemonics can be a labor-intensive, time-consuming instructional activity, and the relative cost-benefit of using the technique needs to be monitored regularly.
Strategy 14.4: Content-Area Reading	A series of supports and strategies that assist students in understanding textbook content. Specific techniques include textbook exploration activities, adapted vocabulary, structured comprehension strategies, study guides, and visual maps.	The development of effective reading accommodations for secondary content can be challenging. However, the extent of text-driven content instruction necessitates that teachers devote time to the development of these supports and accommodations.
Strategy 14.5: Developing and Supporting Note Taking	To facilitate the coordination of the myriad skills required for effective note taking, teachers provide explicit instruction in specific techniques and strategies as well as infuse supports in their lessons.	The complexity of skills required for successful note taking may require that some students receive intensive practice in small groups with enhanced teacher guidance.
Strategy 14.6: Developing Effective Test Taking	A series of strategies that ensure that student test performance reflects true understanding including appropriate test accommodations and the direct teaching of test-taking skills and strategies.	In addition to teaching test-taking strategies, it is important to ensure that test accommodations provided are acceptable and appropriate for individual students.

- Level-2 planning is planning for two types of daily instruction: basic skills instruction and instruction in academic content areas.
- Level-3 planning is moment-to-moment planning conducted as you provide classroom effective instruction.

Monitoring student progress

- Progress monitoring is a procedure that allows teachers to regularly and directly measure key academic skills.
- Curriculum-based measurement (CBM) is one of the most common forms of progress monitoring.
- CBM relies on brief, frequent (weekly or bi-weekly), direct measures of student performance.
- If progress is on target, the instruction will continue; if progress is not adequate, the teacher can make modifications.

Using an adaptive grading system for students with disabilities

- Grades usually fail to evaluate students with disabilities on important outcomes such as amount of effort, the process used to reach a correct answer, or the improvement in the student's performance.
- The following grading adaptations are relatively common:
  - Progress on IEP objectives
  - Improvement over past performance
  - Performance on prioritized content and assignments
  - Use of process and effort to complete work
  - Modified weights and scales
- Personalized grading plans may be created for students using different types of grading adaptations.

Planning a classroom's physical layout to accommodate students with disabilities

- The following physical arrangements of a classroom might impact students with disabilities or special needs and should be modified appropriately:
  - Furniture arrangement and spacing
  - Lighting
  - Noise levels
  - Ventilation and temperature
  - Visual accessibility
  - Materials storage
  - Plants and animals in the classroom

Addressing Professional Standards

Standards addressed in Chapter 12 include:

CEC Standards: (1) foundations; (4) instructional strategies; (5) learning environments and social interactions; (7) instructional planning; (10) collaboration.

INTASC Standards: Principle 2—Provide learning opportunities to support the learning and development of all students; Principle 3—Create instructional opportunities for diverse learners; Principle 4—Understand and use a variety of instructional strategies; Principle 5—Create learning environments to support student motivation, behavior, and learning; Principle 7—Plan instruction based on knowledge of the student, curriculum, and community; Principle 8—Use assessment strategies to ensure continuous progress; Principle 10—Collaborate to support student learning and well-being.

Praxis™ II Standards: Knowledge-based core principles: (2) legal and societal issues; (3) delivery of services to students with disabilities. Application of core principles: (3) assessment; (4) managing the learning environment.

PUTTING IT ALL TOGETHER

When you have students with disabilities or special needs in your classroom, there is no doubt that your planning responsibilities will increase, but this effort is important.

1. Collaboration is key. In this chapter we have discussed several planning needs for students with disabilities and special needs. As you plan to address these needs, you should seek ongoing input from your colleagues in special education.

2. Get to know your students. If you know students' needs, their strengths, and their unique challenges, your planning is likely to be much more aligned with their needs. You cannot make "generic" plans that will meet all the needs of students who have such diverse characteristics.

3. Be more detailed in the beginning. You will find a lot of variation in the detail that different teachers put into their classroom instructional plans. As a general rule, the more complex the learning needs are of a particular student, the more time you will need to plan for those needs.

4. Look to different sources for plans. You can find instructional plans and ideas for plans in many sources. You can attend staff development sessions, confer with your colleagues, take additional courses, attend conferences, and search the Internet to obtain multiple sources of information that will help you plan for your students with special needs.

5. Save your plans, critically evaluate them, and make revisions. Learn from your plans. Being an effective teacher will always be "a work in progress." Certainly, in the area of planning, you will improve with experience.

myeducationlab

We present strategies in the second half of this chapter (Strategies 12.1 to 12.8) in a step-by-step format so that you can use them in your classroom right away. In addition, in the following table, we identify some video clips, cases, and simulations that will allow you to experience these strategies (or complementary strategies) in a real classroom environment.

EFFECTIVE PRACTICE	MYEDUCATIONLAB CONNECTION	CONSIDER THIS
Strategy 12.1: Contributing to IEPs	Go to MyEducationLab, select the topic *Pre-Referrals, Placement, and IEP Process*, and go to the Activities and Applications section. Next, watch the video entitled "School Connections: IEP Meeting," and answer the accompanying questions.	As you watch the video, pay close attention to the interaction among the IEP team participants and the role of the general education teacher. How do these interactions compare with the points discussed in Strategy 12.1?
Strategy 12.2: Developing a 504 Plan	Go to MyEducationLab, select the topic *Collaboration, Consultation, and Co-Teaching,* and go to the Activities and Applications section.Next, complete the simulation entitled "Working with Your School Nurse."	As you complete the simulation, focus on the role of the general educator in developing a 504 Plan and collaborating with other professionals.
Strategy 12.3: Planning for Differentiated Instruction	Go to MyEducationLab, select the topic *Inclusive Practices,* and go to the Activities and Applications section. Next, watch the video entitled "Differentiated Instruction," and answer the accompanying questions.	As you watch this video, focus on this teacher's techniques for differentiating instruction for her students. How do her explanation and implementation of this concept compare or contrast with the discussion in Strategy 12.3?
Strategy 12.4: Identifying Instructional Needs	Go to MyEducationLab, select the topic *Collaboration, Consultation, and Co-Teaching,* and go to the Activities and Applications section. Next, read and analyze the case entitled "A Broken Arm."	As you read and analyze the case, focus on the accommodations the co-teacher Ms. King makes for her student Jim. What needs to happen in order for Jim to succeed in this class?
Strategy 12.5: Planning for Basic Skills Instruction	Go to MyEducationLab, select the topic *Instructional Practices and Learning Strategies*, and go to the Activities and Applications section. Next, select the subsection *Direct Instruction,* watch the video entitled "Reading: Direct Instruction," and answer the accompanying questions.	As you watch this video, focus on how this teacher engages her students in this direct-instruction model. Compare and contrast this teacher's techniques with the examples discussed in Strategy 12.5.
Strategy 12.6: Planning for Academic Content Instruction	Go to MyEducationLab, select the topic *Instructional Practices and Learning Strategies*, and go to the Activities and Applications section. Next, watch the video entitled "Cooperative Learning" in the (Cooperative Learning subsection), and answer the accompanying questions.	Using cooperative learning groups in an inclusive classroom setting is a very important component of planning instruction. As you watch the video, reflect on the components of the STAD model of cooperative learning.
Strategy 12.7: Using CBM to Measure Student Academic Progress	Go to MyEducationLab, select the topic *Assessment*, and go to the Activities and Applications section. Next, watch the video entitled "DIBELS: Progress Management," and answer the accompanying questions.	As you watch the video, reflect on how this teacher is using a technology-based curriculum-based measure to monitor student progress in reading.
Strategy 12.8: Developing a Personalized Grading Plan	Go to MyEducationLab, select the topic *Assessment*, and go to the Activities and Applications section. Next, watch the video entitled "Assessment of Special Needs Students," and answer the accompanying questions.	As you watch the video, reflect on how we measure students' progress in the general education curriculum and how this connects with developing a personalized grading system for students who have special needs.

EFFECTIVE PRACTICES

In the remainder of this chapter, we describe eight effective strategies, which we referred to previously in the chapter, to help you plan effectively to meet the needs of all students.

EFFECTIVE PRACTICE	TYPE OF STRATEGY/BRIEF DESCRIPTION	SPECIAL CONSIDERATIONS
Strategy 12.1: Contributing to IEPs	Being an effective member of the IEP team is an important role for the general educator. This strategy offers several ways to help fulfill this important responsibility.	Understanding the required content of an IEP and students' needs will help you be a more effective member of the IEP team.
Strategy 12.2: Developing a 504 Plan	Section 504 plans specify accommodations necessary for some students with special needs. This strategy explains how a 504 committee designs such plans.	504 Plans are used for students who have special needs but do not meet criteria for special education under IDEA.
Strategy 12.3: Planning for Differentiated Instruction	Planning for differentiated instruction can help meet the needs of students with different abilities. This strategy tells you common ways to vary instructional content and delivery.	Besides planning for how to deliver instruction, it is also important to plan how students can demonstrate what they have learned.
Strategy 12.4: Identifying Instructional Needs	This strategy will help you identify the learning needs of students with disabilities based on the general curriculum and also based on their unique learning needs.	Base instructional goals for students with disabilities on the general curriculum, but realize other goals may also be relevant to their needs.
Strategy 12.5: Planning for Basic Skills Instruction	Many students with special needs will need intensive instruction in basic academic skills. This strategy outlines ways to plan for this instruction.	Planning for supplemental forms of instruction can help students learn basic skills.
Strategy 12.6: Planning for Academic Content Instruction	This strategy discusses several planning approaches that can help teachers prepare to teach academic content to students with disabilities.	Modifications in the content and form of delivery can allow many students to benefit from content area instruction (planning pyramids can be useful).
Strategy 12.7: Using CBM to Measure Student Academic Progress	Evaluating student progress is important for students with special needs. CBM allows you to closely monitor students' progress and modify your instruction if necessary in order to improve progress.	Unlike grades, CBMs are quantitative measures of the student's performance within the curriculum.
Strategy 12.8: Developing a Personalized Grading Plan	Many teachers struggle with deciding how to grade students with disabilities. This strategy provides several useful options.	Parents of students with disabilities are often more interested in learning about factors other than how their child compares to others in the classroom.

Strategy 12.1

CONTRIBUTING TO INDIVIDUALIZED EDUCATIONAL PROGRAMS

Rationale and Research

IDEA requires general education teachers to participate as a member of the IEP planning team if all or part of the student's time in school is spent in the general education classroom. The law requires this participation so that the teacher can provide input regarding the curriculum and instruction used in the general education classroom.

Sometimes general education teachers do not like to participate in IEP planning meetings because they do not see the relevance of the process to their job; do not understand the terms, forms, and paperwork; and feel that they are not valued as a team member.

In fact, general educators have a great deal to contribute to planning an IEP. Under current IDEA guidelines, all students with disabilities are expected to participate in the general curriculum, and teachers are held accountable for their learning. Therefore, in order for students to achieve objectives based on the general curriculum, general education teachers should be considered as key partners from the beginning. Their involvement on the IEP team, then, is essential.

Key References

Kamens, M. W. (2004). Learning to write IEPs: A personalized, reflective approach for preservice teachers. *Intervention in School and Clinic, 40*(2), 76–80.

Lytle, R. K., & Bordin, J. (2001). Enhancing the IEP team: Strategies for parents and professionals. *Teaching Exceptional Children, 33*(5), 40–44.

Martin, J. E., Marshall, L. H., Maxson, L. M., & Jerman, P. L. (1996). *The self-directed IEP.* Longmont, CO: Sopris West.

Menlove, R. R., Hudson, P. J., & Suter, D. (2001). A field of IEP dreams: Increasing general education teacher participation in the IEP development process. *Teaching Exceptional Children, 33*(5), 28–33.

Werts, M. G., Mamlin, N., & Pogoloff, S. M. (2002). Knowing what to expect: Introducing preservice teachers to IEP meetings. *Teacher Education and Special Education, 25*, 413–418.

Step-by-Step

(1) *Recognize the importance of your role.* Consider yourself an equal member of the team and a collaborator. General education teachers are expected to participate and contribute, especially with regard to issues related to inclusion and participation in the general curriculum. Many general education teachers feel that they need more preparation in developing IEPs. For this reason, we encourage you to take advantage of all opportunities for staff development in this area.

(2) *Become familiar with the terms, forms, and procedures.* Don't be intimidated by words and acronyms that you do not understand. If you have not developed knowledge through various learning experiences, ask your colleagues to be kind enough to explain the meaning of their statements.

(3) *Be prepared for the IEP meeting.* Your job will be to discuss the student's status and progress in your classroom, or to discuss the curriculum and instruction that will occur and how the student might participate. If the student is currently in your

class, collect information and student work samples to demonstrate current skill level. Formal or informal assessments will also be useful. If the student is not in your class, bring examples of the curriculum and work that will be required.

(4) *Involve students in the IEP session.* Whenever possible, students should participate in their own IEP planning meetings. General educators and special educators can help students become involved participants by preparing before the meeting to identify and state their own goals. Available curricular material, such as the *Self-Directed IEP* (Martin, Marshall, Maxson, & Jerman, 1996), can help teachers prepare students for more active participation.

(5) *Leave with a clear understanding of your role and that of others.* After the IEP meeting, you should know the student's goals and how you will address these in the general education classroom. You should also understand the type of instructional interaction you are to have with the student and the support you will receive in the classroom. Additionally, you should know if the student is going to use any assistive technology or other special equipment or material.

Applications and Examples

IEP meetings may be scheduled at different times but will generally occur before or after school or during a teacher's planning period if the teacher is expected to attend. Regardless, you should be informed about the meeting enough in advance so that you are prepared and able to attend. When you learn about the meeting, you should inquire about its purpose (to determine eligibility, to plan goals, to review performance) and what you are expected to

6 ***Respect confidentiality.*** The material and information discussed in IEP and other meetings about students are always confidential. Remember to respect this confidentiality after you leave the meeting.

contribute. Then you should gather the necessary documentation, review it before the meeting, and make any notes to yourself about issues you feel are most important to remember. When the meeting begins, ask for an agenda if one is not provided, and if there is none, ask the meeting coordinator to let you know when you will be expected to participate. Be professional, cordial, and attentive throughout the meeting.

Keep in Mind

Unfortunately, many teachers and school administrators today view the IEP planning process with a degree of disdain, feeling that it requires an unnecessary degree of bureaucracy and paperwork. While there is no doubt some truth to this perception, a well-developed IEP can provide the basis for a meaningful education for a student. Your role in this process can make the difference in simply complying with the law and improving the quality of a student's education.

Strategy 12.2

PROCEDURES FOR DEVELOPING A 504 PLAN

Rationale and Research

Millions of public school students in the United States have conditions such as attention-deficit/hyperactivity disorder (ADHD), asthma, epilepsy, or different physical disabilities that present them with unique challenges. They may need extra time to rest, may need privacy to take their medication, or may require assistance with personal needs. If their conditions do not interfere with their learning ability, they will not be eligible for, nor do they need, special education services as required under IDEA. However, because in our society we have laws against discrimination, schools must provide these students with reasonable accommodations in the school and classrooms so that their opportunity to participate like other students is not adversely affected.

A Section 504 Plan states the specific accommodations and modifications that a student will receive in order to have equal access to educational services. A school 504 Plan coordinator and an ad hoc committee that includes the student's general education teacher form the plans. All general education teachers, therefore, should be knowledgeable about the contents of 504 Plans and how they are developed.

Key References

Madaus, J. W., & Shaw, S. F. (2008). The role of school professionals in implementing Section 504 for students with disabilities. *Educational Policy, 22,* 363–378.

U.S. Department of Education, Office of Civil Rights. (n.d.) *Questions and Answers on Disability Discrimination under Section 504 and Title II.* Retrieved on June 17, 2008, from http://www.ed.gov/about/offices/list/ocr/qa-disability.html

Wrightslaw. (1998–2008). *Discrimination: Section 504 and ADA.* Retrieved July 11, 2008, from http://www.wrightslaw.com/info/sec504.index.htm

Step-by-Step

1 **Identify the student who may require a 504 Plan.** Any student who has a physical or emotional disability, or who is recovering from a chemical dependency, or who has a condition that interferes with one or more life activity is eligible for a 504 Plan. Major life activities include caring for one's self, performing manual tasks, walking, seeing, hearing, speaking, breathing, working, and learning. Sometimes students returning to school after a lengthy absence due to illness will require a 504 Plan.

2 **Identify the 504 Plan coordinator and committee.** Every school must have a 504 Plan coordinator. This is often an assistant principal or guidance counselor, but not a special educator. If you suspect that a student requires a 504 Plan, you should contact the coordinator and complete a referral form. The coordinator should then form a committee to address the student's needs. The committee should include the coordinator, one or more teachers, the parents or guardians, and the student if appropriate. It may also include other personnel with specific knowledge about a student's needs such as a nurse or physician.

3 **Participate on a 504 planning committee.** As the person referring the student, you should serve on the 504 planning committee so that you can express your concerns about the student's needs. Your focus should be on developing accommodations so the student can participate successfully in your classroom and elsewhere.

4 **Develop the 504 Plan.** Members of the committee should identify the accommodations the student requires to participate in school activities. Examples of accommodations might include:

- A seat assignment to accommodate the student.
- A diabetic student may be permitted to eat in the classroom.
- A student may be permitted to go to the office for the administration of medication.
- A student's assignments or testing conditions may be adjusted (i.e., extensions of time, modification of test questions).

After developing the plan, all committee members are required to sign it in order to show their agreement with it.

5 **Inform key persons of the contents of the plan.** Once the plan has been developed, it is important that all key school personnel are aware of its provisions. The plan constitutes a legal document, so teachers and other professionals do not have the option to accept or reject it. The provisions are mandatory, and the 504 Plan coordinator should make sure that all key persons are aware of it.

 6 *Set a review date to review and revise the plan if necessary.* As the plan is approved, it should be scheduled for review at a later time to determine if it is serving its intended purpose. The review date may come at any time, but it should not be longer than 1 year. When the plan is reviewed, if necessary, it should be revised accordingly.

Applications and Examples

An example of the need for a 504 Plan might be a student with diabetes. Type-1 diabetes, also called juvenile diabetes or insulin-dependent diabetes, is an autoimmune disease that destroys the cells in the pancreas that produce insulin. Children with Type-1 diabetes require insulin shots. Without medication, the student may become very thirsty, need to urinate often, lose weight, and be very weak. Students with diabetes can participate in most activities with other students but need a few special considerations. They may need privacy to test their blood sugar and inject insulin if necessary, may need access to the bathroom more frequently than others, and may need to have snacks more often than other students. In the case of hypoglycemia, the student may experience sweating, paleness, trembling, hunger, and weakness, indicating the need for emergency treatment. A 504 Plan for a student with diabetes lists specific supports in the following categories (see *http://www.theparentaladvocate.com/sample-504-plan.htm* for a detailed version of this plan):

- Health-care supervision
- Training of personnel
- Student's level of self-care
- Snacks and meals
- Water and bathroom access
- Treating high or low blood sugar
- Glucose testing
- Insulin injections
- Field trips and extracurricular activities
- Tests and classroom work
- Daily instructions
- Equal treatment and encouragement
- Parental notification and emergency procedures

Keep in Mind

Most students who require 504 Plans will be able to participate in school activities like other students, given that educators provide appropriate accommodations. It is important for general educators to refer students for 504 Plans if they believe one may be necessary and to be aware of existing plans and their responsibilities under the plans. Failure to do so could have serious implications for students and teachers.

Strategy 12.3

PLANNING FOR DIFFERENTIATED INSTRUCTION

Rationale and Research

Differentiated instruction is an approach to teaching that is intended to meet the learning needs of students with diverse abilities. It allows teachers to consider different strengths and weaknesses of students and devise instruction based on these characteristics. The instruction is varied, so that students can take in information, in different ways, use different approaches to understanding key aspects of the information, and express or demonstrate what they have learned according to their personal skills and abilities.

Differentiated instruction assumes that different students will learn material to different breadths and depths, but it focuses on all students learning the most essential components, or the most powerful ideas, of the material. To accomplish its desired outcomes, differentiated instruction uses flexible grouping patterns; sometimes whole-class instruction occurs, and sometimes students work in small groups. Groups are never static but may change based on student progress.

Meeting the needs of diverse students during the elementary years is especially important, because these young students form critical attitudes about school and its value. This is also the time when it will be most important for students to learn critical foundational skills.

Key References

Broderick, A., Mehta-Parekh, H., & Reid, D. K. (2005). Differentiating instruction for disabled students in inclusive classrooms. *Theory into Practice, 44*, 194–202.

Cox, S. G. (2008). Differentiated instruction in the elementary classroom. *Education Digest: Essential Readings Condensed for Quick Review*, 73(9), 51–54.

Levy, H. M. (2008). Meeting the needs of all students through differentiated instruction: Helping every child reach and exceed standards. *Clearing House: A Journal of Educational Strategies, Issues and Ideas, 81*(4), 161–164.

Tomlinson, C. A. (2005). *How to differentiate instruction in mixed-ability classrooms* (2nd ed.). Upper Saddle River, NJ: Merrill/Pearson Education.

Step-by-Step

1 *Vary the instructional content based on student performance level and need.* Consider the instructional content and how it might be quantitatively or qualitatively varied based on student entry level. The idea is not to change the essential aspects of the content but to offer it in different ways or degrees based on current student performance. Students must succeed at the building blocks of content before moving on to more complex aspects of the learning material. On the other hand, students who are more advanced should not be held back from more advanced learning. You will often need to conduct some type of pre-assessment to learn students' familiarity with the content that you are about to teach.

2 *Vary the instructional approach, lessons, and grouping based on student characteristics and need for support.* The learning processes that students use differ, and therefore different students need different amounts and types of support. Teachers should consider how they might modify instruction, or create tiered lessons, and then group students in ways for the different types of instruction to be delivered. Teachers may place students in a whole-class grouping for initial instruction and then in different grouping arrangements based on the nature of the instruction and learning activities. You will derive your knowledge of how students learn from your experience with the students and from reports of previous teachers.

3 *Consider different ways for students to demonstrate what they have learned.* For some students, more traditional forms of assessment are the best ways to determine their mastery of content knowledge; for others, alternative forms of assessment such as oral assessments or reports might be more appropriate. The important point is that you objectively evaluate how well the student has acquired the desired content through a summative assessment.

④ *Use formative assessment to monitor student learning.* While it is important to know if students have acquired the necessary knowledge and skills (determined through summative assessment), it is also important to monitor their progress as instruction is occurring. This is called formative assessment. Through monitoring student progress, we can make decisions about current instructional processes and whether certain students might be regrouped for more basic or more advanced forms of instruction. Instructional grouping should be flexible and based on student needs, given the current learning context.

Applications and Examples

The purpose of differentiated instruction is to maximize learning for each student based on the student's individual characteristics and learning potential. One way to do this is through flexible grouping. For example, a teacher can use whole-class instruction, small-group instruction, and individual instruction, grouping students based on current knowledge, ability, or interests. Care should be taken so that students are challenged to move beyond their current knowledge level but are always given adequate instructional support in order to advance.

One particularly useful approach to differentiated learning is providing tiered activities. The teacher wants all the students to learn the same concepts and skills but provides different routes of access that vary in complexity and abstractness.

Tiered assignments can be carried out through cube activities, in which the teacher writes different assignments on the six faces of a cube. Cubing allows teachers to plan different activities for different students or groups based on student readiness, learning styles, and/or interests. All cube activities reflect the same content, but each activity differs. One cube would have six different assignments based on a single topic. Cubes can also be color coded to ensure assignments are on the appropriate level for a particular group of students.

Another way to provide differentiated instruction is through anchor activities, such as journal writing, reading, math games, or vocabulary skills. These are activities that extend the curriculum. Teachers can also use interest centers, learning centers, and learning stations as anchor activities.

Keep in Mind

Differentiated instruction is meant to replace "one size fits all" instruction, but it is clearly a more complicated process that requires more teacher time, thought, and energy. A beginning point is to examine the curriculum standards for your class, and then see how you might differentiate the content for students at different levels. As you work more with your students, you will come to better understand their abilities, strengths, and weaknesses. Ultimately, you will become more proficient at maximizing learning for *all* of your students.

Strategy 12.4

IDENTIFYING INSTRUCTIONAL NEEDS FOR STUDENTS WITH DISABILITIES OR SPECIAL NEEDS IN GENERAL EDUCATION CLASSROOMS

Rationale and Research

We cannot say that students with disabilities are successfully included in general education classrooms unless their instructional needs are being met. Some instructional needs for these students will resemble those of other students, but others will extend beyond common learning needs. Today, the instructional needs of students with special needs are somewhat complex to identify. Most of these students should be able to participate in the general curriculum and show progress in it, but to do so, they may need to have special arrangements. In addition, many students with special needs may need instruction in other areas such as improving their social skills.

We know that many students with disabilities and special needs can learn in the general education classroom, but without adequate planning, students may be physically present but not succeeding as learners. The first planning step for successful inclusion is to identify students' instructional needs. This will require that the classroom teacher work with the special education teacher in a continuous, collaborative process to identify students' needs and then plan ways to meet them.

Key References

Kilgore, K., Griffin, C. C., Sindelar, P. T., & Webb, R. B. (2002). Restructuring for inclusion: Changing teaching practices (Part II). *Middle School Journal, 33*(3), 7–13.

Levy, H. M. (2008). Meeting the needs of all students through differentiated instruction: Helping every child reach and exceed standards. *The Clearing House, 81*(4), 161–164.

Saint-Laurent, L. (2001). The SIO: An instrument to facilitate inclusion. *Reading and Writing Quarterly: Overcoming Learning Difficulties, 17*(4), 349–355.

Schwarz, Patrick A. (2007). Special education: A service, not a sentence. *Educational Leadership, 64*(5), 39–42.

Voltz, D. L., Brazil, N., & Ford, A. (2001). What matters most in inclusive education: A practical guide for moving forward. *Intervention in School and Clinic, 37*(1), 23–30.

Step-by-Step

(1) *Participate in the student's IEP meeting.* A good starting point to learning about the educational needs of a student with a disability is to attend the student's IEP meeting. Often, general education teachers are invited to these meetings in order to explain their teaching philosophy, curriculum, or the progress of the student if he is already in the classroom. If you have or will be receiving a student with disabilities, you can learn more about the student and his needs by attending the IEP meeting.

(2) *Study the general curriculum.* You should begin with an assumption that students with disabilities in your classroom will take part in and learn content from the general curriculum. Therefore, as a classroom teacher, your starting point in planning for these students is to carefully study the curriculum required by your local or state education agency for the course(s) and grade level you teach.

(3) *Identify learning goals from the general curriculum for each student with disabilities.* For many students with disabilities, you can expect that they will achieve learning outcomes like students without disabilities. For some students, however, it may be necessary to identify high-priority learning goals from the curriculum. Often, this is done at the IEP planning meeting in conjunction with the special education teacher and the student's parents. As you look at the scope and sequence of the general education curriculum, make sure you know the high-priority outcomes for each student with disabilities in your classroom.

(4) *Decide how students with disabilities can participate in the general curriculum.* Students will be able to participate more fully in the curriculum if teachers provide accommodations (e.g., listening to an audio book if unable to read), use supplemental instruction (e.g., improving basic skills or teaching the student to use strategies), or make curriculum modifications (e.g., learning skills or developing knowledge that reflects a goal in the general curriculum but that the student is more likely to achieve). Collaboration with the special education teacher can help you identify more ways for the student to participate.

(5) *Identify other relevant learning objectives for students with disabilities as listed on their IEPs.* Students with disabilities and special needs, although participating in the general curriculum in an inclusive classroom, often will have other nonacademic learning needs that adults should address.

These needs may be identified by parents, special education teachers, or related services professionals such as a speech therapist. You should learn about these other priorities by studying the student's IEP and talking to parents and other professionals.

(6) *Create a classroom list of important IEP goals and objectives for all students with disabilities in your classroom.* A master list of goals and objectives for all the students with disabilities in your classroom, which is accessible and easy to review, will help you keep track of your learning priorities for these students.

Applications and Examples

Before the beginning of an academic year (and in some schools, as the year is ending), many schools begin assigning students to their next grades. In schools where inclusion is commonly practiced, students with disabilities or with other special needs will be assigned to their classes. Sometimes this occurs as part of the IEP planning process so that the student attends a classroom that parents and teachers believe will be most beneficial.

Once you know the students you will have in your class, special planning for those students should begin. You will need to consider (1) how they will be able to learn the same content as other students and (2) other special content they will need to learn. You will find that successful planning for these students will be best done through discussions with the special education teacher about each individual student.

Keep in Mind

Sometimes teachers feel that they are not adequately prepared to teach students with disabilities in their classrooms, and sometimes this is true. The first step in overcoming this issue is to know what the students should learn. Once you have determined this, then your challenge is to find the best way to teach them.

Strategy 12.5

PLANNING FOR BASIC SKILLS INSTRUCTION IN AN INCLUSIVE CLASSROOM

Rationale and Research

The most common problem of students with disabilities and students who are at risk is a significant weakness in basic academic skills including reading, writing, and/or math. Students who demonstrate weaknesses in one or more of these areas at a young age often fall further and further behind their peers as they grow older. Without adequate acquisition of these skills, many students will have great difficulty acquiring more advanced knowledge and skills in academic content areas such as science and social studies.

Research has demonstrated that more intense and frequent direct instruction often can help young students improve basic skills. Direct instruction requires that regular scripted interactions occur between the teacher and a small group of students with about the same level of ability. Additionally, students will need the opportunity for increased practice, and teachers should carefully monitor their progress in order to make decisions about the level and form of continued instruction.

Key References

Deno, S. L. (2003). Developments in curriculum-based measurement. *Journal of Special Education, 37*(3), 184–192.

Maheady, L., Mallette, B., & Harper, G. F. (2006). Four classwide peer tutoring models: Similarities, differences, and implications for research and practice. *Reading & Writing Quarterly, 22*(1), 65–89.

National Center on Student Progress Monitoring. (n.d.). *Review of progress monitoring tools.* Retrieved July 7, 2008, from http://www.studentprogress.org/default.asp

National Institute for Direct Instruction. (n.d.). *What is direct instruction?* Retrieved July 30, 2008, from http://www.nifdi.org/#Tools

Stecker, P. M., Lembke, E. S., & Foegen, A. (2008). Using progress-monitoring data to improve instructional decision making. *Preventing School Failure, 52*(2), 48–58.

University of Kansas. (1999–2005). *An introduction to classwide peer tutoring.* Retrieved July 30, 2008, from http://www.specialconnections.ku.edu/cgi-bin/cgiwrap/specconn/main.php?cat=instruction&section=cwpt/main

Step-by-Step

1 **Determine students' current skill level.** Teachers often assess the academic abilities and needs of students at the elementary level through end-of-grade testing or screening assessments. Using these assessments, teachers can identify students who are significantly behind their peers on academic skills. Teachers can then use individual diagnostic assessments to confirm specific weaknesses that will then be the target for remediation.

2 **Group students into flexible same-ability groups for instructions.** Teachers should place students with similar strengths and weaknesses into small groups of five to seven students for instruction. The groups should not be static. Teachers should move students between groups as performance data indicate changes in their skill level.

3 **Use direct instruction methods to teach specific skills.** Different formal, commercial instructional programs, such as Reading Mastery, use direct instruction methods. Determine the program(s) used in your district for use in direct instruction. Your district may offer staff-development sessions that will help you learn how to use direct instruction. You will need to plan to spend 20 to 30 minutes each day on direct instruction with each group.

4 **Supplement direct instruction with peer tutoring.** Class-wide peer tutoring (CWPT) provides extra practice time for students to work in pairs on basic skills. Pairs of students take turns tutoring each other to reinforce concepts and skills initially taught by the teacher. CWPT requires that the teacher must instruct all students on how to tutor and must give students material appropriate for practicing skills. CWPT should occur three to five times per week.

5 *Supplement direct instruction with educational technology.* Individual students can work on developing basic skills by using educational technology. Many of these programs allow students to work on individually prescribed skills, provide a great deal of practice and feedback for students, and monitor students' progress.

6 *Monitor students' progress.* Performance monitoring is important when focusing on basic skills. This process uses brief measures of performance (1 or 2 minutes) called "curriculum-based measures" to directly assess each student's progress. Schools using direct instruction will usually have probe material available to collect performance data. Performance monitoring should occur once a week for each student, but it only takes a few minutes per student.

7 *Plan for skill maintenance and generalization.* As students show mastery of basic skills, teachers should advance them to higher skill levels in the curriculum. Students should then practice previously learned skills in the classroom through different exercises so that the skills may be useful and applicable in different ways and at different times.

Applications and Examples

In inclusive classrooms where teachers must work with some students on basic skills, there will typically be a time when small groups of students huddle with the teacher to receive direct instruction. While the teacher is providing direct instruction to one small group, the other students may be working independently, practicing previously learned skills, or working quietly on a group project for an instructional unit under the supervision of another teacher or an assistant. After the direct instruction for the small group is finished, the students return to the ongoing classroom activities.

Another small group, working on different basic skills, then meets with the teacher for instruction. Once a week, such as on Friday, instead of pulling together the small groups, the teacher asks individual students to meet with her for a few minutes so she can administer a performance-monitoring assessment. The teacher records how the students perform on basic skills, such as sounding out letters, within a brief time period (such as 1 minute), and charts their performance on a piece of graph paper in order to watch their progress over time.

Keep in Mind

Providing direct instruction, using CWPT, and using prescriptive educational technology can be very powerful in improving students' basic skills. The greatest challenge, however, is coordinating all such activities. This requires teachers to conduct a great deal of planning in order to have a smoothly operating classroom.

Strategy 12.6

PLANNING FOR ACADEMIC CONTENT INSTRUCTION IN AN INCLUSIVE CLASSROOM

Rationale and Research

When students with disabilities or students who are at risk learn academic content, they are often at a disadvantage. They may have difficulty attending to lectures and comprehending important concepts, reading assignments and comprehending what they read, and writing reports or taking written tests related to the instructional content. For these reasons, many students with disabilities either do not successfully participate in instructional activities to learn specific content or benefit only marginally from their participation.

This situation frustrates many general education teachers. Sometimes they feel that students are not properly motivated to learn, and other times they feel that these students should not participate in general curriculum learning. However, neither of these is necessarily true. If academic content instruction is planned and presented correctly, many students who are challenged by academic content can benefit from instruction and accomplish a number of intended learning outcomes.

Key References

Gardner, J. E., & Wissick, C. A. (2002). Enhancing thematic units using the World Wide Web: Tools and strategies for students with mild disabilities. *Journal of Special Education Technology, 17*(1), 27–38.

Gardner, J. E., Wissick, C. A., Schweder, W., & Canter, L. S. (2003). Enhancing interdisciplinary instruction in general and special education: Thematic units and technology. *Remedial and Special Education, 24*, 161–172.

NIMAS at CAST. (2008). What is the National Instructional Materials Accessibility Standard (NIMAS)? Retrieved August 5, 2008, from http://nimas.cast.org/about/nimas

Schumm, J. S., Vaughn, S., & Leavell, A. G. (1994). Planning pyramid: A framework for planning for diverse student needs during content area instruction. *Reading Teacher, 47*, 608–615.

Sperling, R. A. (2006). Assessing reading materials for students who are learning disabled. *Intervention in School and Clinic, 41*(3), 138–143.

Step-by-Step

1 *Determine what students should learn.* Identify the learning goals that all students should achieve by examining your local or state general curriculum requirements for the content area of interest. What must students know and be able to do, and what is the order of learning? Decide the sequence of instruction and which learning goals students should achieve at what time.

2 *Consider using a thematic instructional unit approach.* After you determine what students should learn, think about developing a thematic unit, such as "Transportation in Modern Europe." The unit can incorporate content from science (e.g., the development of transportation machinery), social studies (e.g., the effects of labor unions on transportation), as well as basic skills such as vocabulary development, spelling, and math applications and problem solving. You can easily adjust goals for students with disabilities within a thematic unit, and students can still participate.

3 *If using a more traditional instruction....* You will develop your whole-class lessons, identify the textbook reading students will complete, develop individual report assignments, and develop classroom tests to determine students' level of success in learning the material.

4 *Use a planning pyramid (Figure 12.6) to consider the learning needs of your students.* When you plan your instruction, imagine a pyramid as you think about what you want students to learn. At the base of the pyramid is the content, or big ideas, that you want all students to learn, including those with disabilities or special needs. In the middle is the content you want most students to learn, but it is not necessary for all students to do so. At the top of the pyramid is more specialized knowledge about the topic that a few students will learn. Develop your instructional plan to proportionally cover all levels of the pyramid.

5 *Determine any special arrangements that can help students access the instructional material.* When

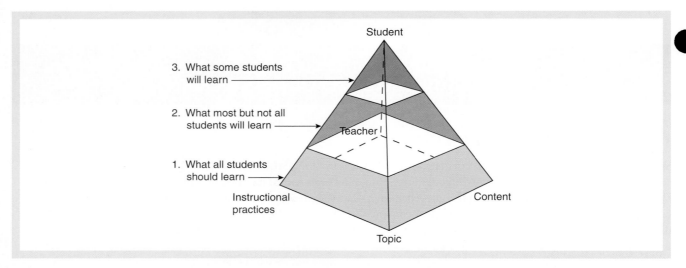

Figure 12.6

Basic Components of the Planning Pyramid, Including Three Degrees of Learning and Five Points of Entry
Source: Reprinted with permission from Schumm, J. S., Vaughn, S., & Leavell, A. G. (1994). Planning pyramid: A framework for planning for diverse student needs during content area instruction. *Reading Teacher, 47,* p. 610. Copyright 1994 by International Reading Association.

planning the content that students with disabilities can learn, consider how you can increase their learning potential. Teachers often can achieve this by offering accommodations, supplemental instruction, or curriculum modifications.

6 *Identify the materials and resources you will need.* As you think about your instructional materials, consider the ability levels of your students with disabilities. With the special education teacher, identify alternative materials that may facilitate their learning such as audio books,

text-to-voice software, and video presentations. Check out organizations such as CAST (*http://www.cast.org/*) to find materials that can be accessible for all students.

7 *Use cooperative learning groups.* Teachers can often improve students' learning of content material by placing students in mixed-ability groups and allowing them to work as a group to complete a project or develop a product. Cooperative learning lets students help each other and acquire more appropriate social skills.

Applications and Examples

The following is an abridged statement from an SCOS for sixth-grade social studies:

> The focus for sixth grade is on considering, comparing, and connecting those studies about the United States to the study of South America and Europe, including Russia. As students examine social, economic, and political institutions, they analyze similarities and differences among societies.

To plan lessons to meet this standard so that students with disabilities could participate, a teacher would first

review the objectives in the standard using the planning pyramid to see which would be most appropriate for all students. Next, the teacher would plan instructional lessons and activities and select materials. In considering students with special needs, the teacher would try to determine if students should use accommodations, curriculum modifications, or supplemental instruction and if any accessible materials for students exist. The teacher would also consider cooperative learning groups and other ways that students could be engaged in learning activities.

Keep in Mind

As you learn more about your students with special needs, you will learn more about their strengths and weaknesses. Your goals should be to find the best way to present information to them—and to all students—so that it is most comprehensible; to find activities in which your students will maintain a high degree of engagement; and to develop assessment procedures that will help you best determine what they have learned.

Strategy 12.7

USING CURRICULUM-BASED MEASURES TO MEASURE STUDENT ACADEMIC PROGRESS

Rationale and Research

Curriculum-based measures (CBMs) are progress-monitoring tools designed to directly measure academic skills. The value of CBMs and similar progress-monitoring systems is that they allow decisions to be made about changes in instruction before failure occurs. CBMs use repeated measures of student performance over time in order to note progress in the student performance. The measurement is based on the curriculum the student is working on. For example, if the student is trying to improve oral reading skills, the CBM measures oral reading; if the student is working on improving math computation skills, the CBM measures computational skills. The measurement is also direct. In the reading example, the teacher would listen to the student's oral reading and make a record of the words read correctly and incorrectly; in the math example, the teacher might give the student a page of addition or subtraction problems and record the number of correct and incorrect answers. Research has shown that CBM has a high degree of validity and reliability. A student's performance on CBM correlates with how well she will perform on standardized tests, on end-of-grade tests, and on other measures of academic achievements.

Key References

Busch, T. W., & Reschly, A. L. (2007). Progress monitoring in reading: Using curriculum-based measurement in a response-to-intervention. *Assessment for Effective Intervention, 32*(4), 223–230.

Deno, S. L. (2003). Developments in curriculum-based measurement. *Journal of Special Education, 37*(3), 184–192.

Fuchs, L. S., Fuchs, D., & Hamlett, C. L. (2007). Using curriculum-based measurement to inform reading instruction. *Reading and Writing: An Interdisciplinary Journal, 20*(6), 553–567.

Stecker, P. M., Lembke, E. S., & Foegen, A. (2008). Using progress-monitoring data to improve instructional decision making. *Preventing School Failure, 52*(2), 48–58.

Step-by-Step

(1) *Identify the students and the learning targets that are to be monitored.* Teachers can use CBM to measure the progress of any student on various tasks. However, CBM is most useful for measuring the performance of students with disabilities or students who are at risk on key academic areas.

(2) *Identify measurement materials to be used, and evaluate their technical quality.* The most common use of CBM is for basic reading skills; however, teachers can also use CBM to measure other skills, including writing and math skills. Some researchers also use CBM to measure performance on academic content at the secondary level. Several commercial measurement systems are available. You can examine several of these at the Website of the National Center on Student Progress Monitoring (www.studentprogress.org). At this same Website, you can also find information about the technical quality (the validity and reliability) of the measurement tools.

(3) *Administer the assessments, score, and graph the outcomes.* If the students have disabilities or are at risk, the teacher should administer the measures once or twice a week.

Most measures take only one or a few minutes to administer. It is extremely important that the teacher administer the measures in the same way and for the same amount of time at each occurrence. Only in this way will the observed outcomes maintain their reliability and validity. The teacher records and graphs the results of the student's performance each time a measurement is taken.

(4) *Compare outcomes to target outcomes.* Many school districts maintain the norms of the performance of students without disabilities at the end of the year on the CBMs. If this is the case, the goal will often be for the targeted student to reach this point by the end of the school year. By drawing a line from the beginning level of performance (i.e., the baseline) to the desired outcome across the 36 weeks of the school year, and by noting whether or not performance is keeping up with the target line, the teacher can monitor whether or not progress is sufficient for a particular student. For example, the target line may indicate that every week the student should be able to read two to three more words correctly (see Figure 12.7).

⑤ *Evaluate and modify instructional approaches.* If adequate progress is not occurring, the teacher should make changes in the instructional process. This could include a change in skill instruction, the amount of instructional time, the size of the instructional group, the instructional materials, the educational technology program, or the reinforcement strategies. When a teacher makes a change, he should make a notation on the chart in order to determine whether progress has improved. If not, then the teacher should attempt subsequent changes.

⑥ *Continue to measure student progress.* Over the course of the school year, the teacher should continue to monitor the student's progress and make any necessary changes.

Applications and Examples

Direct measurement should occur once or twice a week. As mentioned in Step 4, the teacher should then compare the student's outcomes to the target outcomes. The teacher places the measured outcomes on a piece of graph paper in order to see the student's progress (see Figure 12.7). On that same graph paper, the teacher draws a line to indicate the student's learning target. By comparing the student's progress to the target, the teacher (as well as the teacher assistance team, the parents, or other key persons) can determine whether or not to continue with the same instructional procedures (if adequate progress is being made), modify the instruction (if progress is not sufficient), or move on to a higher target (if progress exceeds the current target). To create a CBM for a particular skill, the teacher develops brief oral or written tasks for the student that last about 1 or 2 minutes. Then the teacher (or an assistant) sits one-to-one with the student and gives the student the brief task (which is sometimes called a *probe*). For example, the student reads for 1 minute from grade-level text, while the evaluator marks the words the student misses on a separate data-collection sheet. After the reading session is finished, the teacher counts the number of words read correctly and the number read incorrectly and records the student's performance on a piece of graph paper such as in Figure 12.7.

Keep in Mind

For CBM to be useful, the teacher must measure the academic skill on a regular basis. Then the teacher must examine the data (as presented on the graph in Figure 12.7) and make decisions about whether or not adequate progress is occurring. If it is not, then a change in instruction may be necessary to improve performance.

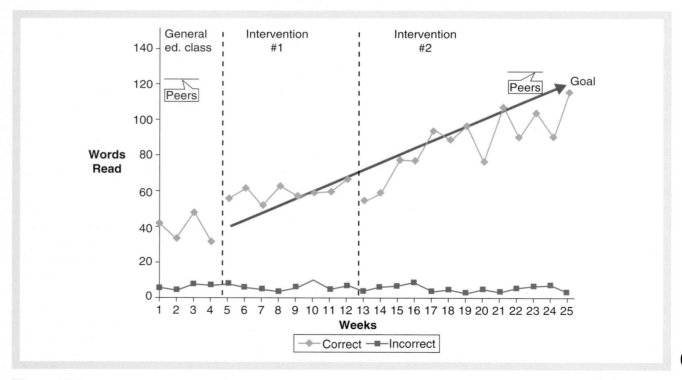

Figure 12.7

Curriculum-Based Measure Progress Graph

Strategy 12.8

PROCEDURES FOR DEVELOPING A PERSONALIZED GRADING PLAN

Rationale and Research

Many students with disabilities will not earn acceptable grades based on traditional grading systems. Their daily grades and report cards will often indicate that they have failed or at least are below average in their performance. Most grades used in public schools are assumed to be norm-referenced; that is, the grades report the status of a student on a particular academic skill in relation to other students. Those who are well above the average earn an A or a B; those below earn a D or an F.

It stands to reason that most students with disabilities or students who are at risk will have below-average grades when considering the population of all of the students in a school. If they did not, it is doubtful that they would be designated with disabilities or at risk. Therefore, what useful purpose comes from giving them a grade based on their performance as it relates to other students, when that grade is usually already highly predictable? Such grades not only tell us little about the students or their work, but they can serve to reduce the students' confidence and punish their efforts to achieve standards that may be very challenging for them. For all of these reasons, educators have developed personalized grading plans (PGPs).

Key References

Bursuck, W. D., Munk, D. D., & Olson, M. M. (1999). The fairness of report card grading adaptations: What do students with and without learning disabilities think? *Remedial and Special Education*, 20(2), 84–92, 105.

Munk, D. D., & Bursuck, W. D. (1998). Report card grading adaptations for students with disabilities: Types and acceptability. *Intervention in School and Clinic, 33,* 306–308.

Munk, D. D., & Bursuck, W. D. (2001). Preliminary findings on personalized grading plans for middle school students with learning disabilities. *Exceptional Children*, 67, 211–234.

Munk, D. D., & Bursuck, W. D. (2004). Personalized grading plans: A systematic approach to making the grades of included students more accurate and meaningful. *Focus on Exceptional Children, 36*(9), 1–11.

Silva, M., Munk, D. D., & Bursuck, W. D. (2005). Grading adaptations for students with disabilities. *Intervention in School and Clinic, 41*(2), 87–98.

Step-by-Step

1. **Review school district policies on adaptive grading.** Many school districts have developed clearly articulated adapted grading standards for students with disabilities. You should inquire about these and determine processes used for grading before giving students assignments that you will evaluate. If the school district does not have its own adapted grading policies, you may work with your school administration and fellow teachers if you think one is necessary.

2. **Decide if adaptive grading is necessary.** If teachers can provide accommodations or supports in curriculum and instruction for students with disabilities, adaptive grading may not be necessary. The teacher should discuss this issue with the other teachers, parents, and student, who may feel that the playing field has already been sufficiently leveled and no change to the grading process for other students is necessary.

3. **Decide on the purposes of grading.** Teachers, parents, and students should discuss what they believe grades should mean and come to a common understanding about their meaning. Unless all can agree on what information a grade should convey, then it will be difficult to create a personalized grading plan for a student.

4. **Examine learner characteristics in the context of classroom demands.** It is important to know the requirements in the classroom that will be especially challenging to the student, given her particular strengths and weaknesses. One outcome of this process may be the identification of an accommodation that might help the student succeed in areas that are known to be difficult.

5. **Review current classwide grading practices, and decide if a grading adaptation would be helpful.** By knowing about specific student weaknesses and the classwide

grading practices for forthcoming assignments, teachers, parents, and students can determine their probable impact on the students' grades. If the impact is significant, they may then decide that adaptive grading would be appropriate, in that it might lead to a higher and more meaningful grade.

6 *Determine the grading adaptation to be used.* A PGP may include adaptations in grading both for individual daily work and assignments, and for report cards. Adaptations may vary depending on what is agreed upon, but the most commonly used PGPs base grades on (1) progress on specific IEP objectives; (2) improvement in performance over time; (3) performance on select, prioritized content and assignments; (4) correct procedure use despite an incomplete assignment or test or, similarly, demonstration of a high level of effort although not achieving a desired outcome; or (5) modified grading scale.

Applications and Examples

When many students with disabilities advance to more rigorous subject matter, they have difficulty, not because of the material, but because they lack some of the basic skills necessary to perform well. For example, a student in an eighth-grade Algebra I class might have insufficient basic arithmetic skills (memorization of basic facts in addition, subtraction, multiplication, and division). One approach to this problem is to provide the student with a calculator (an accommodation) so that he could work the more complex math problems without relying on memorized facts. However, as trends change, many math teachers are now moving away from the use of such devices, and even though the student has a unique need, the teacher might not feel that the calculator is the answer.

A teacher might develop a PGP that incorporates two adaptations. For example, the teacher could grade based on the extra effort of the student to learn basic math facts during the year, so the the student could apply those to the algebra problems. The teacher could also reduce the number of problems required until the student's speed became more comparable to other students'.

Keep in Mind

The IEP team must specify grading adaptations on an IEP, and grading adaptations should coincide with other curricular and instructional adaptations. In the preceding case, a calculator may have actually eliminated the need for an adaptive grading plan. It is also important at the secondary level to consider postsecondary plans of the student. Grading adaptations will not be recognized by some postsecondary institutions. Finally, it is important to keep the issue of fairness in mind. If the adaptation is viewed as creating an unfair advantage for the student, it will not be well accepted.

Effective Instruction in Elementary Inclusive Classrooms: Teaching Reading, Writing, and Mathematics

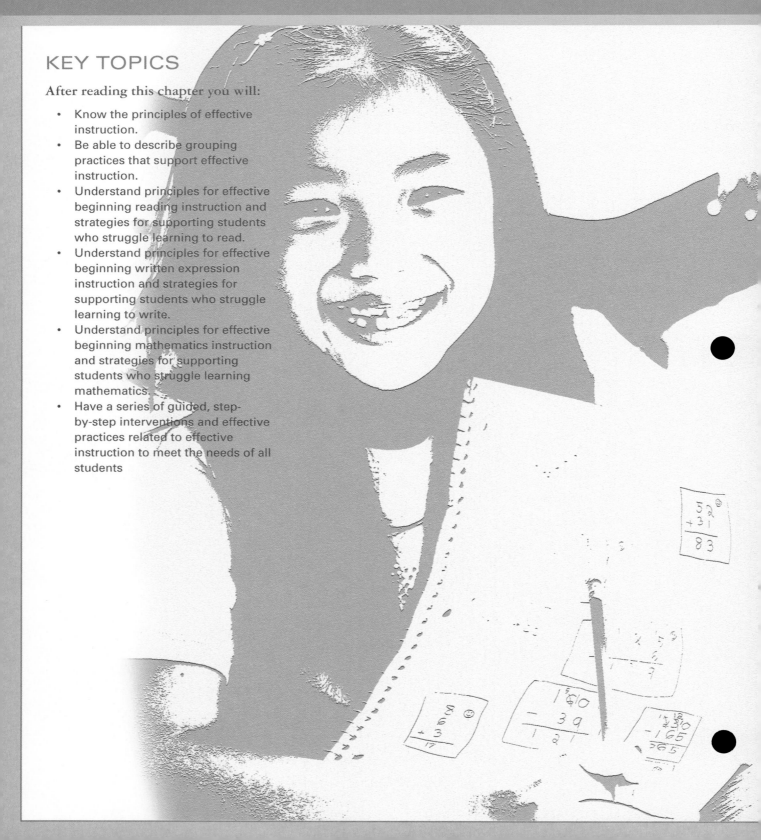

KEY TOPICS

After reading this chapter you will:

- Know the principles of effective instruction.
- Be able to describe grouping practices that support effective instruction.
- Understand principles for effective beginning reading instruction and strategies for supporting students who struggle learning to read.
- Understand principles for effective beginning written expression instruction and strategies for supporting students who struggle learning to write.
- Understand principles for effective beginning mathematics instruction and strategies for supporting students who struggle learning mathematics.
- Have a series of guided, step-by-step interventions and effective practices related to effective instruction to meet the needs of all students

Perspectives on Effective Instruction

Interview with Lisa Grover, Sue Atkins, Laura Scott, Eileen Walls, and Vicki Eng, West Hernando Middle School

We interviewed several teachers at West Hernando Middle School regarding effective instruction in inclusive classrooms. Here's what they had to say.

A sixth-grade teacher, Lisa Grover emphasized the importance of getting to know the student. "We do pretesting, talk with the students, review their work, for much of the first month of school. We look at what kind of work they hand in, what type of motivation they have. We look at whether they have a behavior problem as well. You really need to get to know them and their levels and what they understand." She also stressed the importance of communication with parents as she gets to know her students. "I send a letter to the parents at the beginning of the year, and say, 'in a million words or less, tell me about your child.' This is a very good learning opportunity for me. The parents really open up more when they're writing something down about the child. I get to know about their child's strengths and weaknesses, what the family relationships are. I keep the letters on file all year, and go back to them often."

Ms. Grover also emphasized that an important part of effective instruction is providing extra instruction for students who struggle and reviewing skills they've already learned to make sure they retain this information. "My co-teacher and I break them into small groups and teach the skills they need to learn. We also do centers and independent stations. The teacher center is always where I work with them on skills they need, while the other stations review skills they've already learned."

Sue Atkins, also a sixth-grade teacher, noted the importance of making content relevant to students. "I try to make the content relevant to their lives and tie things to the real world whenever I can. Mixing up instruction also helps, spending time learning basic skills, then spending 1 or 2 weeks on an interdisciplinary project applying things they've learned."

Laura Scott, a seventh-grade teacher, talked about the need for planning a lesson well and letting students know what's coming. "It's good to give students a heads up in the morning about the schedule for the day to keep them focused. For some children, it's really important for them to know what's going to happen during a class period, even if it's written on an index card that says we're going to do 1, 2, and then 3, so that they see what's coming and know what the period looks like. Sometimes it's a matter of having very specific expectations for the student, and they know they have to work for a certain amount of time."

Ms. Scott also talked about the need to involve students in the lesson. "The more you can get the student involved in the lesson, the more active the lesson is, the better for most students. It's really important to change things up a bit or you're going to lose them. If you lecture for 35 minutes, they'll miss most of what you say because they're not going to be with you. We review for a few minutes, have them work with partners, do a hands-on activity, then work independently."

Eileen Walls, a behavior specialist, extended the idea of actively involving students. "Visual aids are very powerful, when they can look at it, touch it, pass it around. That helps. We do charts, maps. Sometimes we have them draw their own map, and a lot of other 'do-it-yourself' activities. When we're talking about weather, in the book is a weather map from years ago in another part of the country. I'll tell them, when you go home, look at the weather outside, and make yourself a weather map. Why is the weather like it is now?"

Finally, Vicki Eng, a seventh-grade teacher, noted the importance of having a classroom where expectations are clear, and lessons are carefully planned and well organized. "It helps students to have guidelines and rules posted. This helps get the class under control, and they know what to expect. Lessons also need to be well planned, what you're going to teach them and how. Then they can make progress in learning, and I can make a real difference in their lives."

Pause & Reflect

Discuss with a peer your experiences in a class in which you learned a lot. What were factors that contributed to this effective instruction? What were the characteristics of a class in which you learned very little? How did these classes differ?

Introduction

As you reflected with a peer on effective and ineffective teachers you have had, the importance of an effective teacher was likely obvious. You may be surprised to know that it has only been in recent years that educators have realized just *how* important an effective teacher is, especially for students who struggle to learn academic basic academic skills (i.e., reading, writing, and arithmetic). This research has shown that students who are assigned to the most effective teachers 3 years in a row score as many as 50 percentile points higher on achievement tests when compared to students who are assigned to the least effective teachers (Sanders & Rivers, 1996).

For students with less effective teachers, this level of difference in achievement is sufficient to lead to failing statewide accountability measures, grade retention, and even, in some extreme cases, a label of learning disability. Over a period of years, the quality of the teacher contributes more to student achievement than any other factor, including class size, class composition, or student background (Rivkin, Hanushek, & Kain, 2001; Sanders & Horn, 1998).

Fortunately, research has documented many of the effective practices that teachers may employ to ensure that students who struggle academically learn to read, write, and use math skills. While some of these practices may be new to you, others are surprisingly simple and obvious, as the interview with teachers from West Hernando Middle School at the beginning of this chapter illustrated.

The most important single factor influencing student learning is an effective teacher.

For example, as seventh-grade teacher Laura Scott said, lessons should be carefully planned so students know what is expected of them, and students should be actively involved in the lessons whenever possible. A related part of effective instruction is described by sixth-grade teacher Lisa

Grover, as she notes that the teacher needs to know her students well, understand what they know and don't know, and provide extra instruction in areas where students are struggling.

A key concept that we often use when describing effective instruction is that many students seem to learn basic skills in reading, writing, and math by osmosis; they just soak up this information and readily learn it. However, students who struggle to learn these skills, including many who have disabilities, are different. It seems that they must be taught everything, using direct, explicit methods. This is a bit of an oversimplification (e.g., all students struggle at times, and all students seem to learn at least some things by osmosis), but we have found this concept useful as we consider what works when teaching students who struggle to learn basic academic skills.

In this chapter, we address effective instruction for basic skills in reading, writing, and mathematics for elementary-level students. We do this by addressing high-quality core instruction in general education classroom (called Tier 1 instruction in response-to-intervention [RTI] models), as well as supplementary instruction that teachers may provide in general education classrooms when students struggle to learn this content (i.e., Tier 2 instruction). These instructional practices provide a critical foundation of knowledge and skills that you will need in order to effectively meet the needs of all students and to ensure that they learn basic academic skills in reading, writing, and mathematics, and make adequate yearly progress as they move through school.

Effective Instruction in an Inclusive Classroom: What to Expect

As you know from your years in school, students in *any* classroom have skill levels in reading, writing, and mathematics that vary dramatically. It is not uncommon in an elementary classroom to have some students who read well above grade level, while others struggle to read and learn from material presented in class. This same range of skill levels is also common in writing and mathematics. Providing effective instruction for the full range of students in an elementary classroom while addressing the needs of students who struggle to learn basic skills is not a simple matter.

However, the importance of providing instruction to ensure that students learn basic skills in early elementary school is widely recognized by elementary teachers, parents, and policy makers (i.e., by the U.S. Congress in the No Child Left Behind Act of 2001). More specifically, basic skills in reading, writing, and mathematics are building blocks for later learning, and students must master these skills to ensure success as they move through school and learn more complex content.

Providing effective instruction for all students is a major purpose of inclusion and is why most general education teachers support well-designed inclusive programs. These teachers realize that they will be much more successful in providing effective instruction to all students if they have a special education teacher as a collaborator. To make inclusion successful, general and special education teachers share their skills and knowledge of students, instructional methods, and classroom organization to effectively meet student needs. This collaboration thus provides the opportunity to creatively group students and differentiate instruction so that teachers can more effectively address the needs of all students.

The reality of elementary classrooms is that teachers engage in what one teacher called a juggling act, trying to figure out how to distribute their time among students to ensure that they provide effective instruction and address students' needs. As Lisa Hallal, an eighth-grade teacher at West Hernando Middle School, noted, "One of my biggest challenges is finding the time in the day to give students who struggle as much teaching as they need." Working with a special education teacher or paraeducator may address this need to some degree, because this allows teachers to regroup students and provide intensive, small-group instruction to those who struggle to learn basic skills. But even under the best of circumstances with support in a general education classroom, time is at a premium. Given this shortage of time, many teachers in inclusive programs use strategies such as cooperative learning and peer tutoring to engage students in learning together collaboratively to better address student needs.

Finally, a reality of many elementary general education classes is that instructional services are being reorganized to provide seamless tiers of instruction to better meet student needs as part of RTI models. These models are designed to provide high-quality, effective core instruction in the general education classroom (Tier 1 instruction), and supplementary instruction in the general education classroom for students who struggle to learn basic skills (Tier 2 instruction). Well-designed RTI models can provide the foundation for effective instruction in inclusive schools and classrooms, ensuring that all students have the necessary supports to learn basic skills in reading, writing, and mathematics.

Principles and Practices to Support Effective Instruction

Delivering effective instruction in basic skill areas is not a simple task. In this section, we present information on research-based practices for delivering instruction that is effective with many students who struggle to learn basic skills in reading, writing, and mathematics. We begin by addressing teacher behaviors in delivering instruction, and then describe grouping practices that may be used to deliver effective Tier 1 and Tier 2 instruction.

Effective Instruction: Teacher Behaviors in Delivering Instruction

Research and the experiences of teachers have shown that when a teacher engages in effective instruction in teaching basic skills in reading, writing, and mathematics (or teaching new skills in any content area), certain instructional behaviors are consistently observed (Rosenshine & Stevens, 1986). These behaviors relate to effective Tier 1 or core instruction and include the teacher's actions when beginning a lesson, presenting information during the lesson, guiding student practice after instruction, correcting student work and providing feedback, planning and carrying out student seat work, and following up the lesson. Each of these components is briefly described in Figure 13.1.

You will note from Figure 13.1 that effective instruction is well organized; focuses student attention on well-defined, critical information; provides multiple opportunities to learn material with feedback; and includes follow-up monitoring to ensure that the information is retained over time. These components of effective instruction and related lesson structure provide a foundation for effective core instruction in the general education classroom. If you review the interview with teachers from West Hernando Middle School at the beginning of this chapter, you'll see that they address many of these principles, including providing clear expectations, ensuring that lessons are well organized, varying activities during a lesson, and reviewing material frequently for students who struggle. Although these components do not include everything a teacher needs to know about effective instruction, they provide a good foundation, especially for teaching basic skills in reading, writing, and mathematics.

Educators have incorporated the components of effective instruction in Figure 13.1 into materials that use **direct instruction** or an explicit approach to instruction. Teachers can use direct instruction as part of Tier 2 instruction for students who struggle learning basic skills. *Direct instruction* is defined as "a model that uses teacher explanation and modeling combined with student practice and feedback to teach concepts and procedural skills" (Eggen & Kauchak, 2006, p. 292). For example, Reading Mastery (Engelmann & Bruner, 2003) is a complete instructional program to teach reading that is built on the principles

Effective instruction requires careful planning and organization of classroom activities.

| Figure 13.1 | **Components of Effective Instruction: Lesson Delivery and Follow-Up** | |

1. Daily review and checking homework
    Establish routines for students to check each other's homework.
    Review and question regarding past learning.
    Reteach when necessary.
    Review relevant prerequisite skills.

2. Presentation of material, information
    Provide a short statement of objectives.
    Provide overview or advance organizer.
    Proceed at a rapid pace, but in small steps.
    Check for understanding by asking questions.
    Highlight main points.
    Provide concrete examples and illustrations.
    Provide models and demonstrations.
    As necessary, provide detailed and redundant instruction and examples.

3. Guided practice
    Initially guide student practice.
    Frequent questions and overt student practice (from teacher or materials).
    Evaluate student responses to check for understanding.
    When checking for understanding, give additional explanation, process feedback,
        or repeat explanation, as needed.
    All students respond and receive feedback; teacher ensures all students participate.
    Initial student practice is sufficient so students can work independently.
    Guided practice continues until students firmly grasp content and achieve a success
        rate of at least 80%.

4. Correctives and Feedback
    Quick, firm, correct response can be followed by another question or a brief
        acknowledgment of correctness (e.g., "That's right").
    Follow hesitant correct responses with process feedback (e.g., "Yes, Linda, that's right
        because . . .").
    Student errors indicate a need for more practice.
    Monitor student work for systematic errors.
    Attempt to obtain a substantive response to each question.
    Corrections can include sustaining feedback (i.e., simplify the question, give clues),
        explaining or reviewing steps, giving process feedback, or reteaching the last steps.
    When the first response is incorrect, try to elicit an improved response.
    Continue guided practice and corrections until the group can meet the objectives
        of the lesson.
    Use praise in moderation; specific praise is more effective than general praise.

5. Independent practice (seat work)
    Provide sufficient practice.
    Practice should be directly relevant to the skills and content being taught.
    Practice to overlearning, and responses are firm, quick, and automatic.
    During independent practice, the correct response rate should be 95% or better.
    Students should know that seat work will be checked.
    Students should be held accountable for seat work.
    Seat work should be actively supervised, whenever possible.

6. Weekly and monthly review
    Systematically review material previously learned.
    Include review of homework.
    Test frequently.
    Reteach material missed on tests.

Source: Adapted from Rosenshine, B., & Stevens, R. (1986). Teaching functions. In M. C. Wittrock (Ed.), *Handbook of research of teaching* (3rd ed., pp. 376–391). New York: Macmillan.

of direct instruction. This program includes highly structured material for students in grades K–6, with related scripts for teachers as they teach material to students. Similar programs are available to teach reading to older students (Corrective Reading, Engelmann, Hanner, & Johnson, 2008, for students in grades 4–12), writing (Reasoning and Writing, Engelmann, 2001, for students in grades K–12); and mathematics (Connecting Math Concepts, Engelmann, Carnine, Bernadette, & Engelmann, 2003, for grades K–8; and Corrective Math, Carnine, Engelmann, & Steely, 2003, for grade 4 to adult).

As the previous sections reveal, effective instruction should be well planned, systematically delivered, and closely monitored. In addition, the instructional content (the curriculum or objectives for instruction) must be well planned with adaptations for individual student needs (see Chapter 12), and the classroom must be well organized and orderly (see Chapter 15). Once these basics are in place, teachers can use effective instruction to enhance student learning and address more complex content.

Pause & Reflect

Consider the ways you were grouped for instruction when you were in school. What were the most common grouping arrangements in elementary school? Secondary school? Which grouping arrangements made it easier for you to learn content? Why?

Grouping Students to Support the Delivery of Effective Instruction

As you reflected on your experiences with grouping arrangements in school, you likely recalled many examples of a teacher's providing instruction to an entire class. This approach to instruction is efficient, as the teacher conveys information to a large number of students quickly. You (and most teachers) very likely have been quite successful in learning information using this grouping format. However, for some students, especially those who struggle to learn basic academic content, this approach often does not work well.

In recent years, many teachers have begun to use alternatives to whole-group instruction in general education classrooms to ensure that they better meet the needs of all students (Good & Brophy, 2008; Vaughn et al., 2003). This change in practice has occurred as teachers have recognized that if only whole-class instruction is used, "individual student needs are not met or, worse yet, that selected children, often the most needy, may be denied access to knowledge, instruction, and an opportunity to learn" (Reutzel, 2003, p. 243).

These alternative grouping strategies are designed to allow teachers to use components of effective instruction (see Figure 13.1) that may be difficult to employ when using whole-group instruction. For example, teachers may use these grouping strategies to reduce the number of students being taught and offer the teacher the opportunity to provide intensive, explicit instruction that is tailored to the individual needs of students and closely monitored to ensure effectiveness (Elbaum, Vaughn, Hughes, & Moody, 1999; Vaughn, Gersten, & Chard, 2000).

Options for grouping students who do not learn content via whole-group instruction include homogeneous ability groups; mixed-ability groups (e.g., cooperative groups); individual tutoring; and peer tutoring. These grouping options may be used in a general education classroom or in a separate classroom. In order to determine whether groups of students require instruction in the classroom or in separate locations, teachers should address logistical considerations related to the size of the general education classroom, the type of activities that are occurring across groups, student characteristics (e.g., attention to task), and similar issues.

Ability Grouping. Perhaps the most intuitively appealing approach for grouping students who struggle to learn academic content, and indeed the most widely used strategy in schools for most of the last century (Haager & Klingner, 2004), has been to group students based on their perceived ability or skill level. This ability grouping, or tracking strategy, has been (and continues to be) an appealing approach because it ostensibly allows teachers to group students based on common needs, and it simplifies planning and teaching so that teachers may focus on specific student needs.

Much evidence indicates that when students in low-skill or low-ability groups are grouped together *for much or all of the school day,* they often do not benefit academically (Freeman & Alkin,

2000; Good & Brophy, 2008; Oakes, 1992; Reutzel, 2003; Salend & Garrick Duhaney, 2007). This type of ability grouping has been particularly negative for students from low socioeconomic status backgrounds and those with disabilities (Freeman & Alkin, 2000; Good & Brophy, 2008; Salend & Garrick Duhaney, 2007). The lack of effectiveness of this type of grouping has been attributed to a number of factors (Good & Brophy, 2008; Reutzel, 2003), including:

- Fewer students assume leadership roles.
- More students engage in disruptive behavior.
- Assignment to lower groups tends to be long term.
- Contact between students across different skill levels is limited.
- The quality of instruction in these groups tends to be poor.

Cooperative learning is an alternative grouping strategy that can lead to improved student learning.

While long-term ability groups are often not effective, this does not mean that students should never be grouped by skill or ability for instruction. When used appropriately, this type of instruction has been demonstrated to be highly effective. For example, teachers may use ability grouping to provide struggling readers the intensive instruction they need to make adequate academic progress. However, when using ability grouping, teachers should attend to guidelines for effective practice (summarized in Figure 13.2) that help to avoid many of the pitfalls that have arisen in the past.

Strategy 13.1 discusses student ability grouping using Success for All (Slavin, 2004).

Mixed-Ability Grouping Using Cooperative Learning. At least in part in response to problems that exist when grouping students with similar skills or ability, educators developed strategies for delivering instruction using mixed-ability groups (Aronson, Blaney, Stephan, Sikes, & Snapp, 1978; Johnson & Johnson, 1974; Slavin, 1977). These strategies are primarily based on the use of small groups of students (usually three to six) who work in cooperative groups to learn academic content. Cooperative learning involves students working together to learn and to ensure that others in their group learn as well (Slavin, 1995). While cooperative learning groups

Strategy 13.2 discusses cooperative learning.

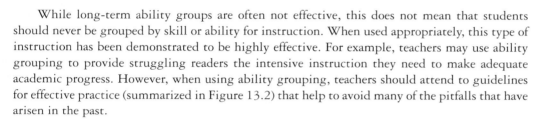

Figure 13.2 Guidelines for Student Grouping

1. The number, size, and composition of groups should be flexible and should vary according to content and student needs.
2. Teachers should periodically create, modify, and disband groups, depending on student needs.
3. Groups should vary in size, from 2 to 10, depending on the purpose and format of instruction.
4. Grouping should lead to more effective instruction and improved achievement, not simply differential pacing through the curriculum.
5. Group scheduling and instruction should be flexible and should depend on the content of instruction and students' instructional needs.
6. Students should spend the majority of the day in mixed-ability groups.
7. Teachers should limit the extent to which membership in an ability group determines other school experiences.
8. Teachers should organize groups so that struggling learners receive the extra instruction they need. Groups for these students should typically be smaller and should meet for more instructional time with the teacher.
9. Teachers should use an explicit strategy for closely supervising the work of groups.

Sources: Adapted from Good & Brophy, 2008; McLeskey & Waldron, 2000; Unsworth, 1984.

Pause & Reflect

Cooperative learning groups are at times frustrating for students. Have you experienced this frustration? Why? How can frustrating experiences for students when using cooperative groups be minimized?

Strategy 13.3 discusses reading recovery.

vary widely in type, they share common characteristics that are described in Figure 13.3 (Marzano, Pickering, & Pollock, 2001; Putnam, 1998).

Individual Tutoring

Several researchers contend that individualized tutoring is the optimal instructional method for meeting the needs of students who are struggling academically (D'Agostino & Murphy, 2004; Elbaum et al., 2000; Good & Brophy, 2008). Tutoring is especially effective when done by teachers who are highly skilled and can provide instruction and engage in flexible decision making that other tutors lack.

Several teacher tutoring programs have been developed that focus on helping students develop early reading skills (Clay, 2001; Hayes, Lane, & Pullen, 2005; Hoover, 2001). The most widely used of these programs is Reading Recovery (Clay, 2001), which has been documented as effective for many students. This program is highly specialized and requires extensive training and related materials. For more information on Reading Recovery, see Strategy 13.3.

Peer Tutoring

Peer-assisted tutoring strategies are a more cost-effective approach to providing individual tutoring for students who struggle to learn academic content. These strategies have consistently been shown to increase the academic achievement of struggling readers and are academically beneficial for the tutor as well (Bond & Castagnera, 2006; Elbaum et al., 1999; Greenwood, Arreaga-Mayer, Utley, Gavin, & Terry, 2001; Rohrbeck, Ginsbury-Block, Fantuzzo, & Miller, 2003). Furthermore, teachers have effectively used these activities across grade levels and content areas (Bond & Castagnera, 2006; Rohrbeck et al., 2003; Stenhoff & Lignugaris/Kraft, 2007).

Peer-assisted learning strategies entail the use of same-age or cross-age peers to provide academic and/or social assistance to students who are struggling in school (Ginsburg-Block, Rohrbeck,

---

Figure 13.3   Common Characteristics of Cooperative Learning Groups

- Positive interdependence: The accomplishment of the group goal depends on all group members working together. Thus, each group member must be concerned about the performance of all of the other group members. Students do not succeed until the group has achieved its goal and each individual has attained his or her goal.
- Individual accountability: The teacher holds all students individually accountable for their own learning, as well as for their contributions to the group. The teacher uses individual evaluations to determine whether each student has mastered the content.
- Cooperative skills: Students must learn and practice social and cooperative skills within the group. These are social skills that are commonly used in group activities, such as sharing materials, turn taking, and encouraging others.
- Face-to-face interaction: In cooperative learning groups, students interact with one another as they are working. They may seek assistance from others, offer assistance, plan activities, learn different aspects of the content, teach content to others, and so forth.
- Student reflection and goal setting: At the end of a cooperative activity, students evaluate how the group functioned, and whether the group's goals were met. Students then engage in reflective discussion and individual goal setting to improve their work in cooperative groups.
- Heterogeneous grouping: Most often cooperative groups should be heterogeneous, as students are mixed based on ability, skills, interests, and student characteristics (e.g., gender, ethnicity, ability or disability, language spoken in the home). At times, however, homogeneous groups are formed based on student interest (e.g., students interested in a particular topic in science might work together) or for instruction in particular skills.

Sources: Marzano, Pickering, & Pollock, 2001; Putnam, 1998.

& Fantuzzo, 2006; McMaster, Fuchs, & Fuchs, 2006). The most widely used and thoroughly researched peer-assisted learning strategy is class-wide peer tutoring (CWPT) and a variation on this strategy, peer-assisted learning strategies (PALS) (Abbott Greenwood, Buzhardt, & Tapia, 2006; D. Fuchs, Fuchs, Thompson, et al., 2001; Greenwood et al., 2001; Mathes, Grek, Howard, Babyak, & Allen, 1999; McMaster et al., 2006). For more information regarding a form of peer tutoring that is used to teach reading in grades 2–6, see Strategy 13.4, "Peer-Assisted Learning Strategies."

> **Strategy 13.4 discusses peer-assisted learning strategies.**
> *Strategy*

To ensure that peer tutoring is effective, tutors require training, and teachers must address other procedural guidelines. Good and Brophy (2008) have provided guidelines for implementing peer tutoring programs. These guidelines begin by noting that the learning outlook in the class must change to a "we learn from one another" mind-set. They also describe several important procedural matters, including:

1. Provide clearly specified times of the day for tutoring.
2. Clearly describe specific assignments, and provide related materials for tutors.
3. Tutors should work with tutees long enough to complete a sequence of assignments (over 1 to 2 weeks), and not start anew each day.
4. Tutoring assignments should be changed every couple of weeks to prevent tutors from developing an "I'm your teacher" perspective.
5. Tutors should not administer tests or be responsible for other student evaluation.
6. All students should be both tutors and tutees.
7. Developing a peer-tutoring program takes time. The teacher should spend the first week or so modeling tutoring behaviors, making sure instructions for tutoring are clear, having students model appropriate tutoring, and so forth.
8. Let parents know that peer tutoring will be used and that all students will be both tutors and tutees.

Peer tutoring can be a highly effective instructional strategy.

Effective Instruction in Reading, Writing, and Mathematics

> ## Pause & Reflect
>
> What are the instructional strengths of each of the different types of instructional groups? Weaknesses? Why is the flexible use of different types of groups so important?

In the sections that follow, we address high-quality, effective core instruction (Tier 1) in the general education classroom in reading, writing, and mathematics. This instruction forms the foundation of any effective, inclusive classroom, and it ensures that students have the opportunity to learn basic skills that form the foundation for later learning in school. However, as we've discussed previously, even with high-quality Tier 1, or core, instruction, some students continue to struggle to learn basic skills in reading, writing, and/or mathematics. We also address Tier 2 research-based instructional strategies and programs that teachers need in order to meet the needs of these students in the general education classroom.

Reading Instruction

While most students seem to learn to read with little effort, some students in all schools struggle to learn to recognize words, read fluently, and comprehend what they read. Students who struggle learning to read often experience difficulty in two areas (Torgesen, 2000). First, they encounter difficulty in understanding how words they know orally are represented in print. This problem is often manifested in difficulty connecting sounds and letters in words, and it results in difficulty sounding out words. For example, a child may not recognize a beginning sound in a word, or that beginning sounds in two words match (e.g., *dog* and *duck,* or *fat* and *fox*).

Many children who struggle learning to read also often have a second problem related to a limited sight vocabulary. That is, the words they recognize immediately by sight are limited in number and range (Torgesen, 2000). For example, students in first grade may have difficulty quickly recognizing high-frequency words such as *him, walk,* and *open,* even after often reviewing the words over a period of several weeks.

These difficulties must be addressed explicitly if beginning readers are to make adequate progress in learning to read. Research related to why children struggle as they learn to read has led to a better understanding of critical components of beginning reading instruction that teachers need in order to address these difficulties.

Effective Beginning Reading Instruction. Most educators agree on the crucial components of beginning reading instruction that are needed to address the difficulties faced by children who struggle learning to read (National Reading Panel, 2000; Pressley, 2002). These components address learning the sounds of letters in spoken words (phonological awareness), learning how letters correspond to sounds and applying this information (phonics), learning to read quickly and accurately (fluency), and understanding what is read, including single words (vocabulary) and the text (comprehension). These components of beginning reading are included in many beginning reading programs and basal reading series.

Students who struggle learning to read often have difficulty with these components of reading. Explicit instruction that focuses on these components and uses effective instructional strategies can significantly reduce the number of students who struggle when learning to read (Foorman & Torgesen, 2001). Many activities that teachers may use in the general education classroom to address each of these areas have been developed by the Florida Center for Reading Research (FCRR) and are available at *www.fcrr.org/Curriculum/studentCenterActivities.htm.*

Teachers can use activities from the FCRR Website to address difficulties with beginning reading related to phonological awareness, phonics, fluency, vocabulary, and comprehension. See Figure 13.4 for examples of these activities.

Beginning reading instruction is typically delivered to whole groups. This strategy is effective for many students (Reutzel, 2003), especially if lessons are well designed and the components of effective instruction are used in the lesson. (We addressed these topics previously in this chapter.) These strategies ensure that information is taught explicitly and that teachers provide students supports or scaffolding as they learn material.

In addition, during whole-class instruction, teachers can use several activities that engage students who struggle learning to read. These activities include storytelling, reading aloud, sharing student-authored material (stories, poems, songs), and reading books together (Reutzel, 2003). Other strategies to engage students who struggle during large-group instruction include asking questions regarding reading material and pairing students to discuss the answer; having students provide a summary of the main points of a presentation; and checking frequently with students to determine if they have a question about a point made or material presented (Vaughn, Hughes, Moody, & Elbaum 2001).

After completing a lesson, it is important that students who struggle learning the content have opportunities for practice with high-quality feedback based on their specific needs (Coyne, Zipoli, & Ruby, 2006). This may occur as part of instruction on specific skills in a small group, which provides students opportunities to respond and interact with the teacher that were not available during large-group instruction. Another strategy for feedback involves pairing students or having them work in cooperative groups to ensure that all have mastered lesson content.

Supporting Students Who Struggle Learning to Read. If students continue to struggle when provided high-quality, effective core instruction (Tier 1), it may be necessary to provide additional, Tier 2 instruction to small, homogeneous groups (e.g., 1–3 students) or individual students. This instruction should not take the place of regularly provided reading instruction but should be additional instruction, closely coordinated with the general education classroom

Figure 13.4	Activities to Support Student Learning of Critical Skills in Beginning Reading Instruction

- **Phonological Awareness.** Rhyme Recognition: The teacher shows the student a picture, and the student names the object in the picture ("A box"). The student views a second picture, names the object ("A fox"), and is asked if the words rhyme.
- **Phonological Awareness.** Syllables Segmenting and Blending: Students working in pairs receive a picture of a harmonica and the written word *harmonica*. One student says the word, "harmonica," and pauses between syllables. The second student counts the syllables and says "Harmonica has four syllables." The students then exchange roles and complete another word.
- **Phonological Awareness.** Phoneme matching: Students view pictures of three objects and match initial sounds in the words. Students name each object, then mark the object that does not have the same sound as the other two objects.
- **Phonics.** Letter recognition: Students use a board with a grid of letters of the alphabet and magnetic letters. The teacher asks the students to choose a magnetic letter, say the letter name, and match the letter to the grid.
- **Phonics.** Letter–sound correspondence: The teacher gives the student several objects and a grid of letters that match the initial sound of each object. The student chooses an object and places the object on the letter that matches the initial sound ("Glove," /g/).
- **Fluency.** Fast match of high-frequency words: Students work in pairs with 20 cards of high-frequency words. One student says a word, "large," and counts to 5 while the second student finds the matching word among the cards. Students then reverse roles.
- **Vocabulary.** Word Identification, Memory Word Match: Students have 20 words on cards, placed face down on a table. One student turns over two cards. If the cards match, the student keeps them for her pile. If they do not match, she turns the cards face down in their original place, and the other student turns over two cards. Students continue until they find matches for all cards.
- **Comprehension.** Sentence structure and meaning: The teacher gives the student pictures and sentences written on strips of paper. The student reads the sentence, then matches the meaning of the sentence to one of the pictures. This continues until all sentences and pictures are matched.

Source: Adapted from Florida Center for Reading Research. (2008). *Curriculum and instruction: Student center activities, grades K–1.* Retrieved May 13, 2008, from www.fcrr.org/Curriculum/studentCenterActivities.htm

curriculum. This instruction should be intensive and focused on specific skills that students are struggling to learn.

One of the most widely researched areas in education is beginning reading instruction. This research has resulted in a number of research-based programs that teachers can use for instruction to improve student skills in phonological awareness and phonics (also called *alphabetics*), fluency, comprehension, and general reading achievement (Institute of Education Sciences, 2008). Several of these programs are briefly described in Figure 13.5.

Teachers often use the types of intensive instructional programs that are described in Figure 13.5 as they deliver high-quality Tier 2 instruction to students who struggle learning to read. Educators develop these instructional tiers to provide high-quality instruction as part of a school's RTI program and as a framework for identifying students with disabilities (Reschly, 2005). For more information regarding the development of an RTI program and tiers of instruction for reading, see Strategy 13.5.

> **Pause & Reflect**
>
> How were you taught to read? Discuss this topic with a peer. If you learned to read with ease, how do the structured, intensive methods of reading instruction described here differ from how you were taught? Why are these methods needed for students who struggle?

> Strategy 13.5 discusses beginning reading tiers of instruction and response to intervention.

Writing Instruction

Writing is a very complex process that requires the integration of many skills related to content knowledge, the mechanics of writing (i.e., handwriting, spelling, punctuation), self-regulation, attention, and planning and organization. Most teachers focus on the process of writing rather than the end product when teaching writing (Gardner & Johnson, 1997). Thus, students learn to write by engaging in planning, writing, revising, and editing their work.

Figure 13.5	**Research-Based Programs for Providing Beginning Reading Instruction**

Effective for Addressing Alphabetics (Phonological Awareness and Phonics), Fluency, and Comprehension

- **KaplanSpellRead** formerly known as *SpellRead Phonological Auditory Training*. This program is designed for students in grades 2 and above who are 2 or more years below grade level in reading. The *KaplanSpellRead* program emphasizes mastering specific skills through explicit instruction, consists of 130 lessons, and takes from 5 to 9 months to complete (Kaplan, 2008). Teachers offer the program for 60 to 90 minutes per day to groups of five students.
- **Ladders to Literacy** has been documented as effective for kindergarten students and includes 20 activities addressing each of three areas: print awareness, phonological awareness, and oral language (Ladders to Literacy, 2008). This program is published as part of *Ladders to Literacy: A Kindergarten Activity Book.*
- **Peer-Assisted Learning Strategies (PALS)** (D. Fuchs, Fuchs, & Burish, 2000) is a peer-tutoring program that incorporates the existing curriculum to address student needs in reading. Students typically participate in PALS tutoring three times per week for 30 to 35 minutes. For more information regarding PALS, see Strategy 13.4.

Effective for Alphabetics and Fluency

- **Corrective Reading** (Engelmann, Hanner, & Johnson, 2008) is a direct instruction program that is designed to address alphabetics, fluency, and comprehension for students in grades 3 and higher. Lessons are highly structured and scripted and can be used with an entire class or small groups (four to five students). This program is used 4 to 5 times per week for 45 minutes.

Effective for Alphabetics and Comprehension

- **Reading Intervention for Early Success** (formerly called *Early Intervention in Reading* [*EIR*]) (Houghton Mifflin, 2006) is used with the entire class and small groups to address the needs of students who are struggling learning to read. *Early Success* uses picture books to provide instruction related to phonemic awareness, fluency, sight vocabulary, and reading comprehension for students in grades K–4.

Effective for Alphabetics

- **Lindamood Phonemic Sequencing Program (LIPS)** (Lindamood & Lindamood, 1998), formerly called Auditory Discrimination in Depth. This program is designed for use with small groups or one child in grades K–4. LIPS offers direct instruction regarding decoding words, identifying individual sounds, and blending in words, letter patterns, sight words, and using context clues. The program is used for 1 hour a day and lasts for 4 to 6 months.
- **Earobics** (Houghton Mifflin, n.d.) is used to supplement a language arts program. The program uses interactive software for students in pre-K through grade 1 (Earobics Foundations) and grades 2–3 (Earobics Connections), to provide systematic instruction in basic literacy skills, including phonemic awareness, phonics, and comprehension. Multimedia support materials for the software are available, as well as books, leveled readers, manipulatives, and card sets.

Source: Information on selected programs adapted from Institute of Education Sciences. (2008). *What works clearinghouse.* Retrieved March 12, 2008, from http://ies.ed.gov/ncee/wwc

Effective Beginning Writing Instruction. The stages of process writing typically include the following (Gardner & Johnson, 1997; Lipkewich & Mazurenko, 2008):

1. **Prewriting.** This stage provides the writer with the opportunity to gain information regarding the topic through a review of written material (e.g., magazines, books, newspapers), online information, media, personal experiences, and so forth. Students may also collaborate with other students to discuss and brainstorm regarding a topic or content area. To assist students in organizing information during prewriting, teachers often use strategies such as graphic organizers or brainstorming webs. Prewriting prepares students with the information needed to write about a topic and organizes information to facilitate writing.

2. **Writing a draft.** Students learn to write by writing. At this stage, teachers encourage students to get something on paper to work with. Teachers emphasize producing content and not the mechanics of writing at this stage. Students need a nonthreatening setting to encourage them to begin exploring a content area without fear that they lack the skills to write. Teachers encourage students to pick their best ideas to write about and to continue writing rather than stopping to edit (that comes later).

3. **Revising the draft.** Teachers initially encourage students to read their drafts aloud for flow and content. Teachers then encourage students to work with a peer or in a small group to obtain feedback on their draft. Students may read their draft to others and note if the paper is clear, logical, contains sufficient detail, and so forth. Teachers may provide students with a framework for reviewing the paper. For example, teachers may ask students to review the paper using the following rubric:

Students should write each day in a setting where they are comfortable and motivated to write.

    a. Any additional information the reader needs to know?
    b. Is the information in a logical, effective order?
    c. What information or details are not needed?
    d. What words or details could you replace with better or clearer words?

4. **Editing the draft.** After receiving feedback, the student then edits the draft for content and organization. Students work together to edit for mechanics (spelling, punctuation, capitalization). The teacher may provide assistance to students, as needed. Revision and editing continue until the student has a final draft that is acceptable to the student and teacher.

5. **Publishing.** The students then publish the final draft of their work. Students then may read their work aloud and share the final product with peers, parents, and others.

Several additional features of exemplary writing instruction are included in Figure 13.6. These features emphasize that students learn to write by writing each day in a setting where they

---

Figure 13.6   Features of Classrooms with Effective Writing Instruction

- Student work is displayed prominently; writing and reading materials are abundant.
- Students work on a range of writing activities daily.
- Students are motivated to write by a risk-free setting, as well as by selecting their own topics for writing or modifying teacher assignments, being reinforced for their writing accomplishments, and having a positive attitude that all can learn to write successfully.
- The teacher regularly meets with students concerning their writing and establishes goals and criteria to guide the students' work.
- Students use a predictable writing routine as they reflect on and revise their work.
- The teacher models the process of writing and a positive attitude toward writing.
- Students work cooperatively with others to assist with the writing process.
- Students present their work in process or completed work to peers for feedback.
- The teacher provides instruction that addresses necessary skills, including phonological awareness, handwriting, spelling, writing conventions, sentence-level skills, text structure, the functions of writing, and planning and revising.
- The teacher provides follow-up, targeted instruction to ensure that all students master necessary writing skills.
- Writing skills are integrated across the curriculum.
- Teachers provide students opportunities to self-regulate their writing by working independently, arranging their own space, and seeking help from others.
- The teacher frequently assesses writing progress, strengths, and needs.
- Teachers conduct conferences and use other communication with parents regarding the writing program and students' progress as writers.

Source: Adapted from Graham, S., Harris, K., & Larsen, L. (2001). Prevention and intervention of writing difficulties for students with learning disabilities. *Learning Disabilities Research & Practice, 16*(2), 74–84.

are comfortable and motivated to write and where they receive the supports necessary to succeed in the writing process.

Supporting Students Who Struggle Learning to Write. While many students learn to write successfully using process writing in a setting that emphasizes the features of exemplary writing instruction, many students with disabilities who receive this effective instruction continue to struggle. These students produce written products that are less coherent, expansive, polished, and effective than those produced by peers without disabilities (Harris, Graham, & Mason, 2003).

To effectively teach students with disabilities who struggle as they learn to write, research suggests that an effective teacher should develop the attitudes and practice the behaviors described next (Graham, Harris, & Larsen, 2001):

1. **Expect that every child will learn to write.** When students struggle learning to read and have difficulty with the mechanics of writing, it may not be easy for a teacher to remain optimistic that the student will succeed in learning to write. Negative attitudes may result in less interaction and feedback with students, more criticism, and less praise. Children with disabilities can be taught to write, but they need added support to succeed. It is important to focus on what the student can do as the writing process progresses and to build on the student's strengths.

2. **Identify and address obstacles that impede the student's success.** Students with disabilities may minimize the role of planning in writing, use ineffective strategies when revising their writing (e.g., focus on mechanical errors and not the content), struggle with the mechanics of writing, or place too much emphasis on handwriting, punctuation, or spelling. The particular obstacles that face a student who is learning to write should be identified so that writing instruction can be tailored to the student's individual needs.

3. **Intervene early.** Providing supplemental instruction addressing areas of weakness as students begin to learn to write can prevent or reduce the effects of difficulties later on. For example, research has shown that early instruction in areas such as spelling and handwriting can have a positive impact on a student's compositional fluency later on.

4. **Provide** balanced instruction. Students who struggle learning to write need a balance of informal instructional methods (i.e., process writing) and formal instruction in specific skill areas that are weak (e.g., writing form and structure, strategies for planning). Students need a balance because too much formal instruction can have a negative impact on the students' motivation to write, while too much emphasis on informal methods may leave students without the skills critical to success.

5. **Use technology to support writing.** The writing of many students with disabilities can be significantly facilitated and enhanced by using technology. For example, the use of word processing reduces the need to recopy when revising, reduces demands related to handwriting for students with motor problems, and results in papers produced in attractive, professional formats. For more on this topic, see Chapter 16.

> **Strategy**
>
> Strategy 13.6 discusses Self-Regulated Strategy Development and writing instruction.

Perhaps the most important skill for students who struggle learning to write relates to strategies for regulating their own writing, from prewriting activities through the finished product. For example, some students benefit from explicit instruction in an approach to improve planning as they are writing. Harris, Graham, and colleagues (Harris, Graham, Mason, & Friedlander, 2007; Harris et al., 2003; Graham, Harris, & MacArthur, 2006) have developed an instructional approach called Self-Regulated Strategy Development (SRSD) that teachers can use to formally teach students strategies that improve writing.

Mathematics Instruction

Many students with disabilities have difficulty keeping up with grade-level peers in math. This occurs for a range of reasons, depending on the characteristics of the disability and the nature of the mathematics content. For example, some students with reading problems do not have difficulty with math until later elementary grades, when word problems are prevalent and the demands of reading make it difficult for them to make adequate progress. Other students with disabilities have difficulty learning basic math skills because of memory problems, while some have difficulty with math concepts (e.g., number sense) that may occur because of a mathematics disability or a cognitive deficit. Of course, some students with disabilities do quite well in math, so you'll see a wide variation of strengths and weaknesses when working with students with disabilities in mathematics.

Effective Beginning Mathematics Instruction. As you know, mathematics is a unique subject matter in that content is relatively simple to sequence, with skills building on one another. Thus, if a student misses information regarding one aspect of division, she will likely have difficulty with higher-level division skills until mastery of the prerequisite skill occurs or accommodations are provided.

Given the nature of mathematics content, effective mathematics instruction depends on lessons that are well designed, using effective instructional practices (we discussed these practices and effective lesson design previously in this chapter). Key components of effective instruction in mathematics include ensuring that students have prior or prerequisite knowledge, teacher modeling, and providing sufficient time for student practice with teacher feedback.

Researchers have examined mathematics basal series that are widely used in elementary schools to determine if important features of instructional design that support effective instruction are built into these materials (Jitendra, Salmento, & Haydt, 1999). These features of instructional design are included in Figure 13.7.

These instructional design features are included in most basal mathematics series. However, at times a text may place insufficient emphasis on one of the criteria (e.g., not enough distributed practice on skills learned), making it necessary for the teacher to add instructional activities to ensure that students learn and retain the skills taught (Jitendra et al., 1999).

Supporting Students Who Struggle Learning Mathematics. Even with highly effective Tier-1, or core, instruction in the general education classroom, some students will continue to struggle in learning mathematics. When this occurs, several research-based strategies are available for teaching these students more effectively and efficiently and include the following:

1. **Teachers should instruct students in small groups or individually, using systematic, explicit instruction.** Explicit instruction in math has been defined as "a teacher demonstrating a specific plan (strategy) for solving the problem types and students using this plan to think their way through a solution" (Gersten & Clarke, 2007). This type of instruction works most efficiently when used with a small group of students (no more than three to six) who need to learn the same skill. The teacher should present instruction using the components of effective instruction (discussed previously in this chapter). Instruction should provide highly explicit modeling of the steps to solve problems (Gersten & Clarke, 2007).

2. **Instruction should be fast paced, use varied activities, and ensure student engagement** (L. Fuchs & Fuchs, 2001). Using rapid pacing in a lesson ensures that students will complete

Figure 13.7	**Features of Instructional Design That Support Effective Instruction in Mathematics**

- Objectives state what students will do and address behaviors that are observable, clear, and complete.
- One new concept or skill is taught at a time.
- An adequate amount of review activities of background knowledge is provided.
- Explicit explanations of problems or concepts to be learned are provided.
- Lessons are carefully constructed for efficient use of instructional time and maximum student achievement.
- Sufficient and appropriate teaching examples are provided.
- Adequate opportunities for practice are provided.
- Reviews of skills learned are appropriately distributed over time.
- Feedback procedures are in place that allow quick, effective feedback when errors are made.

Source: Adapted from Jitendra, A., Salmento, M., & Haydt, L. (1999). A case analysis of fourth-grade subtraction instruction in basal mathematics programs: Adherence to important instructional design criteria. *Learning Disabilities Research & Practice*, *14*(2), 69–79.

more activities in a lesson. Using varied instructional activities (e.g., modeling, discussion, hands-on examples, problem solving) and quick pacing increases the level of student involvement and engagement in the lesson.

3. **Teachers should use concrete, representational (pictures) and abstract examples of problems in lessons** (L. Fuchs & Fuchs, 2001; Gersten & Clarke, 2007; Miller & Hudson, 2007; Smith & Geller, 2004). Students with disabilities and others who struggle to learn math skills and concepts benefit from using manipulatives as they are learning concepts that underlie math problems (e.g., bundles of 10 sticks to illustrate regrouping). Using manipulatives to help students learn math concepts facilitates mastery of the concepts and improves maintenance of the skills learned (L. Fuchs & Fuchs, 2001). Mathematics instruction is most effective when teachers provide multiple graphic or manipulative examples that are specific to a set of problems and when students then practice using their own graphic organizers with teacher guidance (Gersten & Clarke, 2007).

4. **Teachers should encourage students to use self-questioning or think-aloud strategies** (L. Fuchs & Fuchs, 2001; Gersten & Clarke, 2007; Montague, 2007; Smith & Geller, 2004). Students with disabilities and others who struggle to learn math often have difficulty with multistep problems. When this occurs, these students may randomly use strategies rather than a step-by-step approach. Research has demonstrated that encouraging students to verbalize their thinking (i.e., talking through a problem) is consistently effective in improving math problem solving (Gersten & Clarke, 2007). For a detailed example of the use of self-talk as a self-regulation strategy in math instruction (Montague, 2007), see Strategy 13.7.

> **Strategy**
> Strategy 13.7 discusses cognitive strategy instruction for teaching math problem solving.

Summary

This chapter addressed the following topics:

Important principles of effective instruction

- Effective instruction is well organized; focuses student attention on well-defined, critical information; provides multiple opportunities to learn material with feedback; and includes follow-up monitoring to ensure that the information is retained over time.
- The components of effective instruction have been incorporated into materials that use an explicit or direct instruction approach.
- Effective instruction requires well-planned instructional content, with adaptations for individual student needs.

Grouping practices that support effective instruction

- Alternatives to whole-group instruction are needed to meet the needs of some students.
- Alternative grouping strategies allow teachers to use components of effective instruction that they may not be able to use during whole-group instruction.
- Grouping alternatives include homogeneous ability groups, mixed-ability groups (e.g., cooperative groups), individual tutoring, and peer tutoring.
- Long-term ability groups are often ineffective. However, short-term, small-group, intensive instruction using ability groups may be very effective.

Principles for effective beginning reading instruction and strategies for supporting students who struggle learning to read

- When students struggle learning to read, critical components of beginning reading programs include phonological awareness, phonics, fluency, and comprehension (including understanding both single words and the text).
- Explicit instruction should be used to teach beginning readers who struggle learning to read.
- After a group reading lesson, it is important that students who struggle learning to read have opportunities for high-quality feedback based on their specific needs.
- Students who continue to struggle when provided high-quality core instruction in reading should be provided more intensive, explicit instruction in small groups or individually.

Principles for effective beginning writing instruction and strategies for supporting students who struggle learning to write

- Writing requires the integration of skills related to content knowledge, the mechanics of writing, self-regulation, attention, and planning and organization.
- Stages of effective writing instruction include prewriting, writing a draft, revising the draft, editing the draft, and publishing.
- Students who continue to struggle when provided high-quality core instruction in writing should be provided more intensive, explicit instruction in small groups or individually.
- For struggling writers, teachers should identify obstacles to learning to write, intervene early, provide balanced instruction, and use technology to support writing.

Principles for effective beginning mathematics instruction and strategies for supporting students who struggle learning mathematics

- Key components of effective mathematics instruction include ensuring that students have prerequisite knowledge, teacher modeling of information being taught, and providing sufficient time for student practice with teacher feedback.
- Students who continue to struggle when provided high-quality core instruction in mathematics should be provided more intensive, explicit instruction in small groups or individually.
- High-quality instruction in mathematics should be fast paced, use varied activities, and ensure student engagement; present concrete, representational (pictures), and abstract examples of problems during lessons; and encourage students to use self-questioning or think-aloud strategies.

Addressing Professional Standards

Standards addressed in Chapter 13 include:

CEC Standards: (3) individual learning differences; (4) instructional strategies; (5) learning environments and social interactions; (7) instructional planning.

INTASC Standards: Principle 2—Provide learning opportunities to support the learning and development of all students; Principle 3—Create instructional opportunities for diverse learners; Principle 4—Understand and use a variety of instructional strategies; Principle 5—Create learning environments to support student motivation, behavior, and learning; Principle 7—Plan instruction based on knowledge of the student, curriculum, and community.

Praxis™ II Standards: Knowledge-based core principles: (3) delivery of services to students with disabilities. Application of core principles: (1) curriculum, (2) instruction, (4) managing the learning environment.

PUTTING IT ALL TOGETHER

Delivering effective instruction involves not just knowledge of practices, but also much additional information related to collaboration, planning, classroom management, and the use of technology, among other things. With this in mind, we offer several suggestions for your consideration.

1. **Effective instruction depends on collaboration.** In an inclusive setting, a general education teacher often brings a deep knowledge of the content, while the special education teacher brings a toolbox of strategies to ensure that all students learn the material. When teachers combine these areas of expertise, they provide more effective instruction, and all students learn more.

2. **Effective instruction is well organized and depends on good classroom management.** Vicki Eng, from West Hernando Middle School, made this point well: "When you walk into a class with kids with LD or students who struggle, you need to be well organized, you can't wing it, or you lose control of your class. You need to have guidelines, rules posted early, so issues don't become problems you can't control."

3. **Effective teachers have a toolbox of strategies that work.** No effective practice works every time for every student. Effective teachers monitor the effectiveness of instructional approaches and have alternatives available when a strategy does not work with a student.

4. **Effective teachers are lifelong learners.** The best teachers are those who continue to improve and are constantly adding new strategies to help their students who struggle.

myeducationlab

We present strategies in the second half of this chapter (Strategies 13.1 to 13.7) in a step-by-step format so that you can use them in your classroom right away. In addition, in the following table, we identify some video clips, cases, and simulations that will allow you to experience these strategies (or complementary strategies) in a real classroom environment.

EFFECTIVE PRACTICE	MYEDUCATIONLAB CONNECTION	CONSIDER THIS
Strategy 13.1: Success for All	Go to MyEducationLab, select the topic *Instructional Practices and Learning Strategies*, and go to the Building Teaching Skills and Dispositions section. Next, complete the activity entitled "Direct Instruction: Literacy," and answer the accompanying questions.	As you complete the activity, pay close attention to the techniques the teacher uses with her students in the video clips. This teacher is using a teacher-directed program. How would you characterize this program, as compared to the Success for All program discussed in Strategy 13.1?
Strategy 13.2: Cooperative Learning	Go to MyEducationLab, select the topic *Reading Instruction*, and go to the Activities and Applications section. Next, complete the simulation entitled "The Reading Blues."	As you complete the simulation, focus on the CSR strategy and its cooperative learning components. Compare and contrast the CSR strategy with the PALS strategy (Strategy 13.4).
Strategy 13.3: Reading Recovery	Go to MyEducationLab, select the topic *Reading Instruction*, and go to the Activities and Applications section. Next, complete the simulation entitled "Evaluating Reading Progress."	As you complete the simulation, think about how you could use curriculum-based measures in conjunction with the Reading Recovery program to ensure student success in reading.
Strategy 13.4: Peer-Assisted Learning Strategies	Go to MyEducationLab, select the topic *Reading Instruction*, and go to the Activities and Applications section. Next, complete the simulation entitled "See Jane Read."	As you complete the simulation, focus on the different strategies presented. How has the PALS strategy been adapted to meet the needs of kindergartners?
Strategy 13.5: Beginning Reading: Tiers of Instruction & RTI	Go to MyEducationLab, select the topic *Reading Instruction*, and go to the Activities and Applications section. Next, complete the simulation entitled "RTI (Part 3): Reading Instruction."	As you complete the simulation, focus on the three tiers of intervention discussed in Strategy 13.5 and the simulation. How do these gradually increasing interventions ensure success for students who are struggling?
Strategy 13.6: Self-Regulated Strategy Development	Go to MyEducationLab, select the topic *Content Area Teaching*, and go to the Building Teaching Skills and Dispositions section. Next, complete the activity entitled "Scaffolding in Literacy."	As you watch the videos in this activity and answer the accompanying questions, compare and contrast the strategies these teachers use to help their students become successful writers with the points in Strategy 13.6.
Strategy 13.7: Cognitive Strategy Instruction	Go to MyEducationLab, select the topic *Content Area Teaching*, and go to the Activities and Applications section. Next, analyze the strategies entitled "Problem-Solving Self-Monitoring Sheet" and "Self-Monitoring Sheet: Can the Fraction Be Reduced?"	As you analyze these strategies, reflect on how they could help a student who is struggling in math. Could these strategies fit into the cognitive strategy instruction model discussed in Strategy 13.7? Why or why not?

EFFECTIVE PRACTICES

In the remainder of this chapter, we describe seven effective strategies, which we referred to previously in the chapter, to help you plan effectively to meet the needs of all students.

EFFECTIVE PRACTICE	TYPE OF STRATEGY/BRIEF DESCRIPTION	SPECIAL CONSIDERATIONS
Strategy 13.1: Success for All	SFA is an approach to school reform emphasizing early intervention, prevention, and innovative curricula in reading, writing, and language arts. Teachers employ cooperative learning strategies to support student learning.	SFA is only used in schools where 80% or more of the teachers support its use. Teachers are provided extensive professional development, and school-wide changes are required to implement SFA.
Strategy 13.2: Cooperative Learning	A grouping strategy that uses mixed ability groups for instruction. The goal is to ensure all students learn assigned content, which may range from basic academic skills to complex group projects.	Formal approaches using cooperative learning may be used for an extended period of time. However, more informal approaches to cooperative learning may be used to work on specific tasks for brief periods of time.
Strategy 13.3: Reading Recovery	A tutoring approach for beginning readers that employs effective instructional strategies to reduce the number of students who have difficulty learning to read.	Reading Recovery requires special, extensive training for tutors, and it can be expensive to implement. Students can be taught in pairs to reduce costs.
Strategy 13.4: Peer-Assisted Learning Strategies	Peer tutoring that offers an efficient, cost-effective method for providing students with independent practice on the skills they need in order to develop in-depth knowledge of content.	Peer-tutoring programs such as PALS can be used in any subject area, and they are flexible, easy to implement, cost-effective, and time-efficient. These qualities likely account for the acceptance and use of these interventions by many teachers in elementary and secondary classrooms.
Strategy 13.5: Beginning Reading: Tiers of Instruction & RTI	Assumes that a student should be identified with a disability only after high-quality instruction has been provided, and the student has continued to struggle to learn.	In an RTI model, high-quality, effective instruction includes core instruction in the general education classroom (Tier 1), instruction in small groups (Tier 2), and intensive, individualized instruction focusing on specific student needs (Tier 3).
Strategy 13.6: Self-Regulated Strategy Development	An approach used to support students in using writing strategies effectively and independently. Teachers provide explicit instruction as students learn the strategy and how it can be applied.	Many elementary students with disabilities have difficulty planning and regulating writing strategies. SRSD may be used to improve student planning and self-regulation as they learn to write.
Strategy 13.7: Cognitive Strategy Instruction	An approach to support students who struggle to learn mathematics by scaffolding instruction. Includes built-in cues and prompts for students as they engage in strategies for self-regulation, self-instruction, self-monitoring, and self-checking. Supports are gradually faded.	Teachers have developed strategies for solving mathematics problems by talking through how they solve a particular type of problem, or by talking with proficient students to better understand how they solve problems.

Strategy 13.1

SUCCESS FOR ALL

Rationale and Research

One of the most effective approaches to school reform that improves student achievement and supports inclusive programs is Success for All (SFA) (Slavin & Madden, 2001). Elementary schools that use this program engage in comprehensive restructuring to better serve students who struggle learning to read. SFA emphasizes early intervention; prevention; innovative curricula in reading, writing, and language arts; and extensive professional development support for teachers (Slavin, 2004).

Research on SFA indicates that this approach has been highly effective in improving reading achievement of students who are struggling. This includes students with disabilities, as well as students from high-poverty backgrounds and those who are English language learners (Slavin & Madden, 2006). Additional benefits of SFA include reduced numbers of students assigned to special education, increased student attendance, and reduced rates of retention (Slavin & Madden, 2006). Finally, teachers have been found to be supportive of SFA and feel that this program is effective for their students (Slavin & Madden, 2006).

Key References

Borman, G., & Hewes, G. (2003). Long-term effects and cost effectiveness of success for all. *Educational Evaluation and Policy Analysis, 24(2)*, 243–266.

Koh, M., & Robertson, J. (2003). School reform models and special education. *Education and Urban Society, 35(4)*, 421–442.

Slavin, R. (2004). Built to last: Long-term maintenance of Success for all. *Remedial and Special Education, 25(1)*, 61–66.

Slavin, R., & Madden, N. (Eds.). (2001). *Success for all: Research and reform in elementary education.* Mahwah, NJ: Erlbaum.

Slavin, R., & Madden, N. (2006). *Success for all: Summary of research on achievement outcomes.* Baltimore: Johns Hopkins University, Center for Data-Driven Reform in Education.

Step-by-Step

The underlying assumption of SFA is that all students should be reading on grade level by the end of third grade. To achieve this goal, SFA focuses on early intervention and prevention, as elementary schools are reorganized to provide high-quality, systematic instruction to all students during a 90-minute reading block. Success for All is typically implemented with the following components:

1 *Teachers assign students across all grade levels into reading groups* of 15 to 20 students who read at the same level. A research-based curriculum is included as part of SFA in reading and writing, and teachers employ cooperative learning strategies to support student learning.

2 *All students participate in a daily 90-minute reading block.* In grades K–1, students engage in activities to support the development of language, comprehension, and alphabetic skills (e.g., phonemic awareness). Teachers begin the reading block by reading children's literature and discussing the story with students. Students also read phonetically regular stories in pairs, among other activities.

3 *In grades 2–6, students read novels or other engaging reading material and do not use workbooks.* Activities used during the reading block include cooperative learning, partner reading, story summarization, writing, and direct instruction of comprehension skills.

4 *Family support teams, consisting of school professionals, are used in each school* to engage parents in their children's school success. Parent education and involvement activities focus on topics such as student behavior and school attendance. In addition, all students are expected to read a book they have selected at home each evening for 20 minutes.

5 *Students are assessed every 8 weeks* to ensure that they are making appropriate progress in reading. If a student is not making desired progress, the teacher uses alternative teaching or grouping strategies to provide additional support.

6 *Students who continue to struggle learning* to read are provided tutoring daily for 20 minutes, in addition to the 90-minute reading block. Well-trained teachers or paraeducators provide this tutoring using materials that are well coordinated with classroom instruction.

Applications and Examples

Success for All is implemented only in schools where at least 80% of teachers vote by secret ballot to support the program. Teachers receive extensive professional development in the use of SFA materials and instructional strategies. This includes 3 days of professional development during the summer before the program is implemented and 12 days of on-site support during the school year. Professional development activities address such topics as cooperative learning, classroom management, pacing of instruction, and direct instruction.

In addition to this support, SFA programs have an on-site facilitator who works with teachers as they have questions regarding implementation of components of SFA. This includes organizing meetings where small groups of teachers discuss problems and address individual student needs. The facilitator also conducts student assessments every 8 weeks, works with the family support team, and provides other program support as needed.

Keep in Mind

Success for All has been implemented in hundreds of schools in 48 states. This program produces dramatic changes in how teachers go about their work, the curriculum and instructional methods they use, how they group students for instruction, and so forth. In spite of these changes, most evidence indicates that 80% to 90% of teachers support SFA after 1 to 3 years of implementation, while a small number of teachers do not support these programs. The teachers who do not support SFA often have concerns that the prescribed nature of the program does not allow them the flexibility that they desire.

Strategy 13.2

COOPERATIVE LEARNING

Rationale and Research

Cooperative learning is a grouping strategy that uses mixed-ability groups for instruction. The goal of this strategy is to ensure that all students learn assigned content, which may range from basic academic skills to complex group projects. Teachers can use two general types of cooperative groups in general education classrooms, depending on the purpose of the lesson and student needs (Johnson & Johnson, 1999; Marzano, Pickering, & Pollock, 2001). Teachers may use informal groups (ask your neighbor, Think-Pair-Share) to work on specific, well-defined tasks for brief periods of time. These groups help students understand expectations, provide additional time for learning content with support, and focus students' attention on important content (Marzano et al., 2001). Teachers may use more formal cooperative groups for several days or weeks to complete a complex task or to learn more extensive content.

Research on cooperative learning has revealed that this approach may be used to improve the achievement of students across a range of content areas and often results in greater achievement gains than traditional, whole-group instruction (Good & Brophy, 2008; Johnson & Johnson, 1999; Slavin, Hurley, & Chamberlain, 2003). Other benefits of cooperative learning include improved prosocial interactions among students who differ with regard to achievement, gender, or ethnicity; improved acceptance of students with disabilities among peers without disabilities; and improved affective outcomes related to student self-esteem, academic self-confidence, motivation for learning, and value for shared academic work (Good & Brophy, 2008; Johnson, Johnson, & Stanne, 2000; Slavin & Madden, 2001).

Key References

Aronson, E. (2008). *Jigsaw classroom: Jigsaw in 10 easy steps.* Retrieved February 20, 2008, from http://www.jigsaw.org

Good, T., & Brophy, J. (2008). *Looking in classrooms* (9th ed.). Boston: Allyn & Bacon.

Johnson, D. W., Johnson, R., & Holubec, E. (1998). *Cooperation in the classroom* (7th ed.). Edina, MN: Interaction Books.

Kagan, S. (1994). *Cooperative learning.* San Diego, CA: Kagan Cooperative Learning.

McMaster, K., & Fuchs, D. (2005). *Cooperative learning for students with disabilities.* Retrieved February 20, 2008, from www.teachingld.org

Slavin, R., & Madden, N. (Eds.). (2001). *Success for all: Research and reform in elementary education.* Mahwah, NJ: Erlbaum.

Step-by-Step

Jigsaw (Aronson, 2004, 2008) is a cooperative learning strategy that is widely used by teachers. This strategy uses mixed-ability groups to learn content, solve a problem, or complete a project. Each member of the group is given an assignment or assigned to specialize in one aspect of a unit of instruction. Each assignment is a piece of the overall puzzle required to solve the problem, complete the project, or learn the content. Thus, each student's contribution is critical, and assignments are tailored to the strengths of the particular student. Teachers typically implement Jigsaw using the following steps:

1 *The teacher divides the class into four- to six-person Jigsaw groups.* Group composition should be based on the individual strengths of each student, and groups

should be diverse in relation to gender, ethnicity, and ability. One person should be appointed as the group leader, typically a responsible, mature student.

2 *The teacher divides the day's lesson into four to six components.* A history lesson in which students are to learn about Eleanor Roosevelt might consist of the following independent segments: (1) her childhood, (2) her family life with Franklin and their children, (3) her life after Franklin contracted polio, (4) her work in the White House as First Lady, and (5) her life and work after Franklin's death.

3 *Each student is then assigned to learn one segment.* The teacher ensures that each student has access only to information regarding her segment of the assignment.

(4) *Each student reads her assignment at least twice* and becomes familiar with the information. Students then form temporary expert groups, by having one student from each group join other students who are assigned to learn the same segment. Students in these expert groups then discuss their segment, and rehearse the presentations they will make to their Jigsaw group.

(5) *Students return to their Jigsaw groups* and present information regarding their segments to the other group members. All group members are encouraged to ask questions for clarification.

(6) *During these activities, the teacher floats from group to group,* observes, and intervenes if any group is having difficulty (e.g., one group member is dominating or disruptive).

(7) *At the end of the session,* students may be required to produce a product with their completed work or take a quiz regarding the content of the lesson.

(Adapted from Aronson, E. [2008]. *Jigsaw classroom: Jigsaw in 10 easy steps.* Retrieved February 20, 2008, from http://www.jigsaw.org)

Applications and Examples

Cooperative learning methods are often adapted to meet particular classroom needs. For example, Jigsaw has been adapted for use with narrative material that all students are assigned to learn (Slavin, 1990). When using this Jigsaw II approach, heterogeneous groups of students all receive the same assignment (e.g., reading a section of a chapter in a history class that addresses the Civil War). The teacher selects topics from the assignment, and each student from a group is assigned to become an expert on one topic. After reviewing the material, students across groups meet to discuss and learn about their topic with others who have the same assigned topic. After all become experts on their topics, they return to their Jigsaw II group and teach the information to their peers. Students are then prepared to take individual tests on the content (Slavin, 1990).

Keep in Mind

Many informal structures are also available for using cooperative learning (Good & Brophy, 2008; Kagan, 1994). For example, when using Think-Pair-Share (Good & Brophy, 2008), the teacher asks a question, students are given time to think individually, students then discuss their ideas with a partner, and the teacher then asks some students to share their ideas with the class. Another cooperative structure is called Numbered Heads Together (Kagan, 1994). When using this structure, students are assigned to small groups of three or four, and each student in the group is given a number. The teacher then asks a question or poses a problem, students think about the problem individually, and then put their heads together to discuss the problem. Finally, the teacher asks all students with a certain number to stand and asks some of these students to share and discuss their answer with the class. This strategy is good for reviewing and checking student understanding of material (Good & Brophy 2008).

Strategy 13.3

READING RECOVERY

Rationale and Research

Some researchers have contended that the most effective approach to rapidly increasing student academic achievement in basic content areas is having a well-trained teacher work with a student one-on-one using highly effective instructional materials and strategies (D'Agostino & Murphy, 2004; Good & Brophy, 2008). Reading Recovery is a tutoring approach for beginning readers that employs effective instructional strategies with a goal of reducing the number of students who have severe difficulty learning to read.

Reading Recovery was developed in New Zealand by Marie Clay in 1976 (Clay, 1993), has since spread to the United States, and is widely used in most states. Research on Reading Recovery reveals that this approach is highly effective in improving the reading skills of many struggling beginning readers, and these improvements are sustained beyond the tutoring sessions at least until the end of second grade (D'Agostino & Murphy, 2004). Evidence indicates that students improve alphabetic skills, fluency, comprehension, and general reading achievement (Baenen, Bernhole, Dulaney, & Banks, 2004; Elbaum, Vaughn, Hughes, & Moody, 2000; Pinnell, 1989).

Key References

Clay, M. (1993). *Reading recovery: A guidebook for teachers in training.* Portsmouth, NH: Heinemann.

Clay, M. (2001). *An observation survey of early literacy achievement* (2nd ed.). Portsmouth, NH: Heinemann.

D'Agostino, J., & Murphy, J. (2004). A meta-analysis of Reading recovery in United States schools. *Educational Evaluation and Policy Analysis, 26(1),* 23–38.

Ehri, L., Dreyer, L., Flugman, B., & Gross, A. (2007). Reading rescue: An effective tutoring intervention model for language-minority students who are struggling readers in first grade. *American Educational Research Journal, 44(2),* 414–448. (Reading Rescue is a tutoring program that is used in some states and is similar to Reading Recovery.)

Elbaum, B., Vaughn, S., Hughes, M., & Moody, S. (2000). How effective are one-to-one tutoring programs in reading for elementary students at risk for reading failure? A meta-analysis of the intervention research. *Journal of Educational Psychology, 92(4),* 605–619.

Iverson, S., Tunmer, W., & Chapman, J. (2005). The effects of varying group size on the reading recovery approach to preventive early intervention. *Journal of Learning Disabilities, 38(5),* 456–472.

Step-by-Step

Teachers offer Reading Recovery to students who are among the lowest 10% to 20% of struggling readers. Reading Recovery involves daily tutoring sessions that continue for 12 to 20 weeks, or until the student meets program criteria for discontinuation (that is, his reading improves significantly, closing the achievement gap with peers). Students who struggle the most with reading are the first to receive tutoring in a school. Reading Recovery is built on several assumptions, including (1) reading is more than reading words; (2) reading is a social activity; (3) children begin to read by attending to various aspects of printed text; (4) the tasks children must attend to most closely when they are learning to read require less attention as their reading improves (Clay, 2001; D'Agostino & Murphy, 2004). Reading Recovery is typically implemented with the following components:

(1) *Students who are identified by teachers as struggling readers in the first grade are assessed* on their skills related to letter identification, hearing and recording sounds in words, print concepts, word skills, writing, and text reading. Typically, students who score at or below the 20th percentile on a test of these skills are eligible for Reading Recovery tutoring.

(2) *Selected students receive tutoring daily for 30 minutes,* for as many as 20 weeks or until the student's reading achievement improves to a level similar to peers, and the child is discontinued.

③ *Tutoring sessions for the first 2 weeks consist of "roaming around the known,"* including activities such as sharing reading and writing, building trust, and determining the student's strengths.

④ *Reading Recovery lessons then begin* and include a fixed set of activities, as the child (1) reads from one or more familiar books; (2) independently reads the previous day's book as the teacher keeps a running record of student responses (e.g., miscues, omissions); (3) identifies letters and engages in a word making/breaking activity using plastic letters and a magnetic board; (4) writes a sentence or brief story, which is cut into pieces; (5) reassembles the cut-up sentence or story; (6) reads a new book with teacher support.

⑤ *Children are discontinued when they read at an average level for their grade.* Other students continue for up to 20 weeks of tutoring.

Applications and Examples

Reading Recovery is only one of several approaches to tutoring that teachers may use with students who are struggling to learn to read. Another approach that teachers use in some states is Reading Rescue (Hoover, 2001; Hoover & Lane, 2001). Reading Rescue is similar to Reading Recovery, except that it places more emphasis on teaching phonemic awareness and phonics (Ehri, Dreyer, Flugman, & Gross, 2007). Research has revealed that Reading Rescue is an effective intervention for struggling readers, and paraeducators may implement this approach with results that are nearly as effective as when teachers conduct the tutoring (Ehri et al., 2007). Other tutoring programs are available that use volunteers who are not fully certified teachers as tutors, and research has shown that these programs are effective with many students who struggle learning to read (Baker, Gersten, & Keating, 2000; Hayes et al., 2005; Pullen, Lane, & Monaghan, 2004).

Keep in Mind

Some educators have criticized Reading Recovery and other teacher tutoring programs because of the high cost of these interventions (Grossen, Coulter, & Ruggles, 1996; Mathes & Denton, 2002). The estimates of the cost per student vary widely, from $2,500 to $10,000. A related consideration is that as many of 50% of students who complete Reading Recovery continue to struggle learning to read (Mathes & Denton, 2002). Some evidence indicates that the expense of Reading Recovery may be reduced by teaching students in pairs (Iversen, Tunmer, & Chapman, 2005). However, there is no doubt that individual tutoring by a teacher is expensive and that tutoring by peers or volunteers and small-group instruction may be more cost-effective. Still other evidence has shown that small, homogeneous groups of students (from two to five) who are taught using highly effective instructional methods learn as much as students who are taught using one-to-one tutoring (Elbaum et al., 2000). The key issues in this research seem to relate to the quality and the intensity (brief, focused on specific skills) of the instruction.

Strategy 13.4

PEER-ASSISTED LEARNING STRATEGIES

Rationale and Research

An issue teachers often face in inclusive classrooms is having enough time and hands to provide students with the instruction they need, especially in basic skill areas (i.e., reading and math). Once a teacher has initially taught new material, peer tutoring offers an efficient, cost-effective method for providing students with independent practice on the skills that are needed to develop in-depth knowledge regarding the content. Extensive research has revealed that peer tutoring has positive academic and social outcomes for both the tutor and tutee across grade levels and content areas (Ginsburg-Block et al., 2006; McMaster et al., 2006; Rohrbeck et al., 2003; Stenhoff & Lignugaris/Kraft, 2007).

Peer-assisted learning strategies (PALS) is one form of peer tutoring that researchers have demonstrated to be effective, and many teachers have found that it fits well into their classroom routines. PALS uses "structured activities that require peers to engage in frequent interaction, provide each other with immediate corrective feedback, and take turns as tutor and tutee" (D. Fuchs, Fuchs, & Burish, 2000, p. 85). Teachers have used PALS with students from kindergarten through grade 12, in the areas of reading and math. This approach to tutoring is based on another method that has been demonstrated effective, classwide peer tutoring.

Key References

Fuchs, D., Fuchs, L., & Burish, P. (2000). Peer-assisted learning strategies: An evidence-based practice to promote reading achievement. *Learning Disabilities Research and Practice, 15*(2), 85–91.

Fuchs, D., Fuchs, L., Thompson, A., et al. (2001). Peer-assisted learning strategies in reading: Extensions for kindergarten, first grade, and high school. *Remedial and Special Education, 22*(1), 15–21.

Fuchs, L., Fuchs, D., Karns, K., Yazdian, L., & Powell, S. (2001). Creating a strong foundation for mathematics learning with kindergarten peer-assisted learning strategies. *Teaching Exceptional Children, 33*(3), 84–87.

Fulk, B., & King, K. (2001). Classwide peer tutoring at work. *Teaching Exceptional Children, 34*(2), 49–53.

Greenwood, C., Delquadri, J., & Carta, J. (1997). *Together we can: Classwide peer tutoring to improve basic academic skills.* Longmont, CO: Sopris West.

Step-by-Step

The use of PALS in reading is one example of the PALS approach. Teachers use this particular strategy with students in grades 2–6, and it addresses activities to increase student fluency and comprehension. This program is implemented using the following steps:

1 **The teacher provides an orientation and trains students** in the use of peer-tutoring strategies. PALS materials (available at *http://kc.vanderbilt.edu/pals/*) provide structured lessons lasting from 30 to 60 minutes that teachers can use to train students. Teachers instruct students how to use the PALS instructional strategies, how and when to respond to peers when errors are made, and so forth. They are also informed that two teams will be formed, each with one half of the tutoring pairs, and the teams will be awarded points.

2 **The teacher selects pairs of students** based on their reading level, matching higher- and lower-level readers.

For example, the teacher might rank-order all students based on their reading level, split the list in half, and pair the student on top of the first list with the student on top of the second list. Some variation in this procedure may occur based on teacher judgment regarding students who are a good match and those who are not.

3 **The teacher schedules** three, 35-minute PALS sessions per week. These sessions may be in addition to current reading instructional time or could take the place of reading activities that are currently used.

4 **PALS sessions begin with partner reading.** For this activity, the student with the higher reading level always initially reads a selected reading passage that is at the reading level of the lower reader. The lower-level reader then reads the passage. As the passage is read, the tutor notes when a reading error occurs, stops the reader, points out the word that was missed, and asks the reader to figure out the word. If the reader does not respond within 4 seconds, the tutor provides the word, and reading continues.

(5) **Students engage in paragraph shrinking.** This activity requires readers to monitor their comprehension and make judgments regarding the selection and reduction of the material being read. More specifically, students read a paragraph and stop to identify the main idea. They are assisted by tutors, who guide main idea statements by asking who or what the paragraph is mainly about, and to identify the most important thing related to the *who* or *what.* Students then express the main idea in 10 words or less.

(6) **Prediction relay** is the final PALS activity. In this activity, the reader makes a prediction about the information on the next one-half page, reads this information aloud as the tutor corrects errors, confirms or disconfirms the prediction, and summarizes the main idea. The tutor provides feedback regarding the prediction and summarized main idea.

(7) **Points are awarded** by students for correct responses and by the teacher as students demonstrate appropriate tutoring behavior. At the end of the week, the points for each team are tallied, the winning team is announced, and students applaud. Thus, PALS combines competition among teams with cooperation as pairs of students work together.

Applications and Examples

Several forms of peer tutoring are available, but CWPT and PALS are the most widely used and have been demonstrated as effective by extensive research. Teachers can use these approaches to peer tutoring with any subject area, and these approaches are flexible, easy to implement, cost-effective, and time-efficient. These qualities likely account for the acceptance and use of these interventions by many teachers in elementary and secondary classrooms.

An important research finding to note is that the effectiveness of peer tutoring is significantly enhanced if tutors are thoroughly trained before the intervention. In addition, it is important that teachers monitor the behavior of tutors to ensure that tutors use appropriate procedures consistently (Stenhoff & Lignugaris/Kraft, 2007). Research has also revealed that peer tutoring can have a positive effect on student social skills and self-concept (Ginsburg-Block et al., 2006).

Keep in Mind

In spite of increasing emphasis on accountability measures and ensuring that all students learn to read by grade 3, evidence suggests many students do not meet these goals (Rohrbeck et al., 2003). The most effective method for rapidly catching these students up in basic skills is one-to-one or small-group instruction (Elbaum et al., 2000). Unfortunately, most schools do not have the resources to provide this type of instruction to students on a regular basis. Peer tutoring offers an excellent alternative to small-group or one-to-one instruction provided by teachers or paraeducators. Students who provide peer tutoring are a readily available resource, and with appropriate training, they can significantly improve student outcomes.

Strategy 13.5

BEGINNING READING: TIERS OF INSTRUCTION AND RESPONSE TO INTERVENTION

Rationale and Research

As we noted in Chapter 4, response to intervention (RTI) was included in IDEA 2004 as an alternative for identifying students with disabilities (Reschly, 2005). Student identification using RTI is based on the assumption that a student should be identified with a disability only after high-quality instruction has been provided, and the student has continued to struggle to learn. This high-quality instruction typically includes core instruction in the general education classroom (Tier 1), instruction in small groups (Tier 2), and intensive, individualized instruction focusing on specific student needs (Tier 3) (L. Fuchs & Fuchs, 2007).

Research indicates that the use of tiered interventions for students who struggle learning to read are effective in preventing reading difficulties for many students who are at risk or who struggle in the early elementary grades (Torgeson, Alexander, Wagner, Rashotte, Voeller, & Conway, 2001; Vellutino, Scanlon, Small, & Fanuele, 2006). For example, after providing kindergarten and first-grade interventions consisting of small-group and individualized tutoring for students who were at risk for reading problems, Vellutino and colleagues (2006) found that well over one half of these students were no longer at risk and continued to achieve at this level through third grade. This suggests that a tiered approach to delivering high-quality instruction may prevent many reading problems and reduce the number of students who are identified with disabilities.

Key References

Fuchs, L., & Fuchs, D. (2007). A model for implementing responsiveness to intervention. *Teaching Exceptional Children, 39*(5), 14–20.

Gersten, R., & Dimino, J. (2006). RTI (response to intervention): Rethinking special education for students with reading difficulties (yet again). *Reading Research Quarterly, 41*(1), 99–108.

Jimerson, S., Burns, M., & VanDeHeyden, A. (Eds.). (2007). *Handbook of response to intervention: The science and practice of assessment and intervention.* New York: Springer.

Kamps, D., & Greenwood, C. (2005). Formulating secondary-level reading interventions. *Journal of Learning Disabilities, 38*(6), 500–509.

Reschly, D. (2005). Learning disabilities identification: Primary intervention, secondary intervention, and then what? *Journal of Learning Disabilities, 38*(6), 510–515.

Vaughn, S., & Roberts, G. (2007). Secondary intervention in reading: Providing additional information for students at risk. *Teaching Exceptional Children, 39*(5), 40–46.

Step-by-Step

The primary purpose of RTI is to provide high-quality early intervention for students who are at risk for academic difficulties, while a related purpose is more valid identification of students with disabilities (Gersten & Dimino, 2006). The advantages of an RTI approach "include earlier identification, a stronger focus on prevention, and assessment with clearer implications for academic programming" (L. Fuchs & Fuchs, 2007, p. 14). Many approaches to implementing RTI are available. One such approach (adapted from recommendations by L. Fuchs & Fuchs, 2007, and Vaughn & Roberts, 2007) includes the following steps:

1. *The foundation for an effective RTI approach is high-quality core instruction in the general education*
classroom. In reading, this instruction is typically built on a curriculum that includes the basic components of early reading instruction (i.e., phonemic awareness, phonics, reading fluency, and comprehension). Many schools use a basal reading series such as *Open Court Reading* (SRA/McGraw-Hill, 2005), a "phonics-based K–6 curriculum that is grounded in the research-based practices cited in the National Reading Panel Report" (Borman, Dowling, & Schneck, n.d.), to provide a framework for high-quality instruction. Other schools use a program such as Success for All (Slavin, 2004). We described effective instructional practices to meet student needs previously in this chapter.

② *Teachers use a universal screening of all students to identify students who struggle to learn to read when provided high-quality instruction in the general education classroom* Teachers then monitor the reading progress of those identified with possible reading problems on a weekly basis using a curriculum-based measure (CBM) (for more on CBMs, see Chapter 12). Students identified with a reading problem based on the CBM results then receive a Tier-2 intervention (L. Fuchs & Fuchs, 2007).

③ *A Tier-2 intervention is more intensive than instruction that is typically provided in the general education classroom.* Teachers deliver these interventions in small groups (1:4 or 5) for brief periods of time (e.g., 15 to 30 minutes) each day, for up to 20 weeks. Tier-2 interventions should be provided in addition to core instruction in the general education classroom, coordinated with the curriculum of the general education classroom, targeted to specific student skill deficits, and include progress monitoring two to four times per month to ensure adequate progress (L. Fuchs & Fuchs, 2007; Vaughn & Roberts, 2007).

④ *While many students with early reading difficulties have skill deficits, others may have motivational problems.* For these students, a school psychologist may work with the teacher to problem solve regarding individualized interventions that the teacher can use to increase the student's motivation (L. Fuchs & Fuchs, 2007). Interventions may include the use of books or other reading material addressing topics that are high interest for the student, group reading activities with peers, or employment of reinforcement systems that reward the student for reading.

⑤ *During Tier 2, teachers monitor student progress on targeted skills using a CBM system or other measure of student progress from two to four times per month.* Teachers use these measures to determine if a student has progressed sufficiently to ensure success in the general education classroom. For students who continue to struggle, a multidisciplinary team meets to discuss the student's eligibility for special education, and, as appropriate, to develop a Tier-3 intervention.

⑥ *A Tier-3 intervention consists of instruction delivered by special education.* This intervention should be more intensive and focused on individual student needs than instruction provided in Tier 2; closely coordinated with general education instruction; provided in addition to general education reading instruction; and frequently monitored using CBM to ensure that the intervention is working (L. Fuchs & Fuchs, 2007; Vaughn & Roberts, 2007). Teachers should deliver Tier-3 instruction in groups of 2 to 3 students, and it should last longer than Tier-2 instruction (for 50 minutes or more) (Vaughn & Roberts, 2007).

Applications and Examples

An important characteristic of well-designed tiers of instruction is coordination of curriculum across tiers, and close alignment of instruction with the general education curriculum. Curriculum coordination has often presented difficulty across general and special education classrooms, because different materials are used and different student skills are emphasized across settings. Well-aligned instruction provides the student with multiple opportunities to master needed skills and increases the effectiveness of interventions.

For example, *Reading Intervention for Early Success* [formerly called *Early Intervention in Reading EIR*] (Houghton Mifflin, 2006), is designed to use with basal reading series that emphasize evidence-based instructional practices. Teachers can use *Reading Intervention for Early Success* with small groups (five to seven students) to address reading weaknesses as a Tier-2 intervention. Research has proven this program to be effective in addressing early reading difficulties (Wahl, 2003). Teachers use *Early Success* for 30 minutes per day to address skill development related to phonics, fluency, sight vocabulary, and reading comprehension.

Keep in Mind

Response to Intervention is an approach to delivering effective instruction in other basic skill areas (e.g., mathematics [L. Fuchs, Fuchs, Compton, Bryant, Hamlett, & Seethaler, 2007] or writing [Graham et al., 2006]), and teachers can also use RTI to provide support for students with behavior problems (Fairbanks, Sugai, Guarding, & Lathrop, 2007; Gresham, 2005). The use of RTI in writing or mathematics is similar to the steps used with reading intervention. The use of this framework to address student behavior problems is somewhat different. For example, a Tier-1 intervention for students with possible emotional and behavioral problems might consist of a school-wide system that requires schools to "identify and explicitly teach school-wide expectations; implement a system to acknowledge expectation-compliant behavior; define and consistently apply consequences for inappropriate behavior; and regularly review progress towards school-wide goals. Such a universal system reflects the features of positive behavior support" (Fairbanks et al., 2007, p. 289). Teachers then use Tier-2 interventions to develop specific social behavior and skills for small groups of students; Tier 3 addresses individualized intervention. For more information regarding the use of a tiered system of behavior management, see Chapter 15.

Strategy 13.6

SELF-REGULATED STRATEGY DEVELOPMENT AND WRITING INSTRUCTION

Rationale and Research

Many elementary students with disabilities have difficulty planning and regulating the strategies they use as they write (Harris et al., 2003). Harris and Graham have developed several strategies that teachers may use to improve student planning and self-regulation as students learn to write. One of these strategies begins with a three-step framework for planning and writing called POW (Pick my idea; Organize my notes; Write and Say more). POW may be coupled with a strategy for composing called TREE (Topic sentence—Tell what you believe; Reasons—3 or more, Why do I believe this? Will my readers believe this?; Ending—Wrap it up right; Examine—Do I have all my parts?). The POW and TREE strategies provide students with a framework for both planning and composing as they learn to write.

Research has revealed that self-regulation strategies can be successfully taught, are used by students in their writing, and result in improved written products (Graham & Harris, 2006). Teachers have successfully used Self-Regulated Strategy Development (SRSD) with classes, small groups, and individual students to develop writing strategies for a range of genres (Harris et al., 2003).

Key References

Graham, S., & Harris, K. (2006). Cognitive strategy instruction. In C. MacArthur, S. Graham, & K. Harris (Eds.), *Handbook of writing research* (pp. 187–207). New York: Guilford.

Graham, S., Harris, K., & Larsen, L. (2001). Prevention and intervention of writing difficulties for students with learning disabilities. *Learning Disabilities Research & Practice, 16*(2), 74–84.

Graham, S., Harris, K., & MacArthur, S. (2006). Explicitly teaching struggling writers: Strategies for mastering the writing process. *Intervention in School and Clinic, 41*(5), 290–294.

Harris, K., Graham, S., & Mason, L. (2003). Self-regulated strategy development in the classroom: Part of a balanced approach to writing instruction for students with disabilities. *Focus on Exceptional Children, 35*(7), 1–16.

Harris, K., Graham, S., Mason, L., & Friedlander, B. (2007). *Powerful writing strategies for all students*. Baltimore: Brookes.

Step-by-Step

Teachers use SRSD to support students in using writing strategies effectively and independently. The teacher provides explicit instruction as the student learns the strategy and provides the student with instruction related to how they can apply the strategy. Instruction in these strategies entails the use of six steps.

1 ***Ensure background knowledge.*** Initially, the teacher determines the background knowledge and skills (e.g., vocabulary, concepts) the student needs in order to learn and use the strategy. The teacher presents this information to students and determines how to organize and structure instruction, given the particular students who are being taught. Students are also typically given one or more self-statements or self-speech, which is a powerful form of self-regulation, and they begin learning to use this powerful from of self-regulation. For

example, they may use a self-statement such as "I can do this if I use my strategy and take my time." The teacher discusses with students why these statements are important, as well as how and when they should be used.

2 ***Discuss the strategy.*** The teacher and student then discuss the strategy to be learned. For example, the teacher describes the POW + TREE strategies and how the student can use them to guide her writing. The teacher explains each step in the strategies as well as how the mnemonics can help the student to remember the strategies. The teacher may also examine with the student her current level of writing performance, and how the strategy might help improve her writing.

3 ***Model the strategy.*** The teacher or a peer then models the use of the strategy for the student, using self-instruction

while writing on a class assignment. The modeling and self-instruction should be spontaneous and natural.

(4) *Memorize the strategy.* Students then memorize the steps in the strategy and the mnemonic that facilitates learning. Memorization typically begins in the previous two steps and may continue into the next step. This repetition and distributed practice is important for students who have difficulty remembering information, because students can't use the strategy if they can't remember it.

(5) *Provide support.* Students then use the strategy as they plan, compose, write, revise, and edit class writing assignments. The students use the self-regulation strategy to support this work, and the teacher provides support or scaffolding as needed through prompts, interactions, and guidance.

(6) *Student independent use.* The teacher should fade or discontinue use of supports as quickly as possible, so that students independently use the self-regulation strategy. The teacher should plan to periodically review the strategy with students to ensure continued use. Over time, the teachers and students may determine that the self-regulation strategy should be discontinued as the students' reading skills and self-regulation skills improve.

(Adapted from Graham, Harris, Mason, & MacArthur, 2006; Harris, Graham, & Mason, 2003; Harris, Graham, & Friedlander, 2007.)

Applications and Examples

Another strategy that Harris and Graham have developed is W-W-W WHAT=2 HOW=2 (Harris et al., 2003). Teachers use this strategy as a framework for students who are engaged in story planning. This framework includes the following:

Who is the main character?
When does the story take place?
Where does the story take place?
What does the main character do or want to do? What do other characters do?

What happens then?
How does the story end?
How does the main character feel? How do the other characters feel?

Teachers can pair this strategy with the POW strategy and can use graphic organizers to outline the information produced as prewriting planning takes place. For more information regarding this strategy, see Harris and colleagues (2003).

Keep in Mind

The overall goals of SRSD relate to assisting students in developing skills and strategies to support planning, writing, revising, and editing; to support students in monitoring and managing their own writing; and to promote positive attitudes toward writing. To ensure effective use of SRSD, teachers have noted several important considerations (Harris et al., 2003). First, these activities should be collaborative among teachers and students. As instruction continues, students should take increasing responsibility for self-regulation strategies. Second, teachers should tailor strategy instruction to the individual student's approach to writing. Strategies will work well with or fit some students and not others. Teachers should adapt strategies to fit individual student's needs. Third, the teacher should give each student the time he needs to master a strategy, rather than only a fixed amount of time to teach a strategy. Finally, to teach a strategy well, teachers should help students understand the meaning and significance of the strategy.

Strategy 13.7

COGNITIVE STRATEGY INSTRUCTION FOR TEACHING MATH PROBLEM SOLVING

Rationale and Research

The most powerful interventions for students who struggle to learn mathematics are the use of direct instruction (discussed previously in this chapter), and cognitive strategy instruction (Montague, 2007). Cognitive strategy instruction can be as simple as a teacher's modeling and encouraging students to verbalize their thinking as they work on a math problem (self-talk) or having students draw a graphic representation of the steps needed to solve a computation problem (Gersten & Clarke, 2007). Still other self-regulation strategies consist of teaching students several steps to follow when solving word problems (L. Fuchs & Fuchs, 2001; Montague, 2007).

Researchers suggest that the use of strategy instruction such as think-alouds or self-regulation is often effective because this approach helps students control the impulsive, often random approach they use to problem solving (Gersten & Clarke, 2007). This instruction is also useful in teaching students the steps needed to solve a problem and ensuring that students maintain this information over time (Montague, 2007).

Key References

Fuchs, L., & Fuchs, D. (2001). Principles for the prevention and intervention of mathematics difficulties. *Learning Disabilities Research and Practice, 16*(2), 85–95.

Gersten, R., & Clarke, B. (2007). *Effective strategies for teaching students with difficulties in mathematics: Instruction research brief.* Reston, VA: National Council for Teachers of Mathematics.

Maccini, P., & Gagnon, J. (2005). *Math graphic organizers for students with disabilities.* Retrieved March 11, 2008, from www.K8accesscenter.org

Montague, M. (2007). Self-regulation and mathematics instruction. *Learning Disabilities Research and Practice, 22*(1), 75–83.

Montague, M., Warger, C., & Morgan, T. (2000). Solve it! Strategy instruction to improve mathematical problem solving. *Learning Disabilities Research and Practice, 15*(2), 110–116.

Step-by-Step

Strategy instruction is designed to support students who struggle to learn mathematics by scaffolding instruction so that students can think and respond like successful learners. This instruction includes built-in cues and prompts for students as they engage in strategies for self-regulation, self-instruction, self-monitoring, and self-checking (Montague, 2007). Teachers gradually fade supports as students become proficient. The major components of strategy instruction are described in the following example (adapted from Dunlap & Dunlap, 1989; Montague, 2007; Montague, Warger & Morgan, 2000):

1 *Assess the student* to determine if he has mastered the prerequisite knowledge and skills. For example, if completing subtraction problems with regrouping, the student must understand the concepts underlying addition, subtraction, and place value. The student also must either know basic math facts or be able to use a fact chart efficiently (Fahsl, 2007).

2 *Develop and explicitly teach the student a strategy for problem solving.* For example, for solving subtraction problems, the teacher could provide the following steps to the student, who checks off the strategies as they are completed (Dunlap & Dunlap, 1989):

a. Did I copy the problem correctly?
b. Did I regroup when needed?
c. Did I borrow correctly?
d. Did I subtract all the numbers?
e. Did I subtract correctly?

3 *Model the strategy.* As part of explicit instruction of the problem-solving strategy, the teacher should model the strategy while engaging in self-talk through each step. The student then repeats this process with support from the teacher. The student may also practice the problem-solving strategy with peers, who provide feedback as needed.

④ *Fade the prompts.* As students practice the problem-solving strategy, they become more proficient, and the teacher may fade the prompts (verbal cues, checklist of strategies).

⑤ *Provide students with specific feedback* regarding their performance as they use the problem-solving strategy. Teachers should also praise students for their performance, as appropriate, to maintain motivation and convey that they are making progress and can learn to successfully solve problems.

Applications and Examples

Recently, educators have placed more emphasis on solving mathematics problems that are applicable to the student's real world (Montague et al., 2000). Many students struggle to solve complex mathematics word problems and benefit from strategies that provide a systematic structure for addressing such problems. Self-regulation strategies help students to control their own actions and become more independent as they learn to solve complex problems (Montague, 2007). Steps used in a self-regulation strategy for mathematics word problems may include the following (Montague, 2007; Montague et al., 2000):

1. Read the problem for understanding, then ask if you understand the problem.
2. Put the problem into your own words. First underline important information, then ask yourself if you understand this information.

3. Make a drawing or diagram of the problem. Teachers can use a graphic organizer with built-in prompts (i.e., some of the information provided) to support students (Maccini & Gagnon, 2005).
4. Develop a plan to solve the problem by deciding the operations that should be used and how many steps are needed, then check to see if the plan makes sense.
5. Predict the answer by rounding numbers and doing the problem in your head. Check to make sure you used the important information in the problem.
6. Complete the operations in the problem in the correct order. Does your answer compare to your estimate?
7. Check to see if you correctly completed all the computation steps and in the correct order.
8. Ask for help if needed.

Keep in Mind

Many sources may be useful for a wide range of strategies for solving particular types of mathematics problems. Elementary and secondary mathematics texts are sources of these strategies. Another option is applying general problem-solving strategies that have proven useful for students in other academic areas. For example, SRSD (described previously as a strategy for improving written expression in Strategy 13.6) has also proven useful as a strategy for improving student skill development in mathematics (Case, Harris, & Graham, 1992).

Many teachers have developed their own problem-solving strategies by engaging in self-talk as they solve a particular type of mathematics problem or by talking with proficient students to better understand how they solve problems. (Try Googling "math problem-solving strategies," and you'll find the results of this work). Remember, think-alouds or problem-solving strategies are simply how proficient learners solve mathematics problems. Sharing these strategies with students who struggle learning mathematics is a powerful approach to improving skill development.

Teaching Students in Secondary Content Areas

KEY TOPICS

After reading this chapter you will:

- Be able to identify the learning characteristics typical of students with disabilities.
- Understand core prerequisite considerations that contribute to successful inclusive content-area instruction.
- Identify and describe a range of models and approaches for inclusive content-area instruction including
  - Universal design for learning
  - Direct instruction
  - Guided discovery learning
  - Cooperative learning
  - Learning strategies
  - Content enhancements
- Describe the essential elements of four content survival strategies: content-area reading, note taking, test taking, and time and assignment management.
- Know why content-area instruction is important for students with more severe disabilities and how it can be done successfully.
- Possess a series of guided step-by-step effective practices for teaching students with disabilities in content-area classes.

chapter 14

Perspectives on Teaching Secondary Content to Students with Disabilities

Interview with Susan Hill, Dean of Special Education, Heritage High School

Susan Hill, Dean of Special Education at Heritage High School, is always on the move. With her active involvement in almost all aspects of special education at the school, it is rare when Ms. Hill has time to sit down and catch her breath. She would have it no other way: Ms. Hill spends considerable time on important legal and compliance issues, ensuring that parents understand and remain part of their child's special education program. Still, she is primarily an instructional leader, devoting most of her efforts to coaching and providing consultative service to content-area general educators, special education teachers, and co-teaching teams. Being the instructional resource "person" is among the most rewarding aspects of her position. Ms. Hill receives great satisfaction suggesting evidence-based practices to her colleagues, and she enjoys having opportunities to model specific techniques that help students with disabilities succeed in their subject-area classrooms. Along with the many rewards, however, Susan feels that developing and implementing instructional supports for her students are also among the most challenging and frustrating aspects of her job.

What is so challenging? Ms. Hill has observed that many ninth-grade students with disabilities enter Heritage with a wide diversity of background knowledge, academic skills, and learning strategies. As a result of this diversity, students require significant amounts of remedial instruction in how to access, engage, and use secondary content material. Some students lack the reading skills to benefit fully from established textbooks and cannot prepare written assignments that reflect understanding of the curriculum. In fact, the level of skill deficiencies—in reading, writing, and math—are so severe that Heritage has developed a highly structured elective course to remediate basic skills for all ninth graders with disabilities. Recognizing that a special course in skills is necessary but clearly not sufficient, Ms. Hill and her general and special colleagues regularly assess the learning needs of individual students, determine which elements of each subject area curriculum are essential for the student to acquire, and find methods that can help students learn that content. The overwhelming challenge is to ensure that the content deemed essential is not watered down, or weakened. Students must receive rigorous instruction in much of the standard curriculum in order to pass the state-mandated exit exams, Standards of Learning Tests (SOLs), required for students seeking an academic diploma.

How do Ms. Hill and her team meet these challenges? As with most activities at Heritage, collaborative planning teams determine how teachers can best address the content learning of the students. For some students, Ms. Hill and other special educators provide consultative services to general education content specialists. In other cases, co-teaching teams coordinate the delivery of instruction and support. For students with more severe cognitive disabilities, content-area specialists assist special education teachers to identify elements of the curriculum that can be presented in a more functional and concrete fashion.

In terms of specific techniques, Ms. Hill urges her teachers to augment their instruction with content enhancements, explicit tools that help organize lessons and assist when demonstrating difficult concepts to struggling learners. She also recognizes the need to reduce the reliance on textbooks for students with disabilities. Many have difficulty reading and comprehending high-level textual material and benefit from alternative high-interest, easier-readability reading materials as well as technology-based supports such as audio recordings and white boards. Ms. Hill has also observed the value of universally designed instructional techniques, and she urges all of her teachers to use routines that help students organize their daily class notes and assignments. For students with more severe cognitive impairments, she urges care in selecting the aspects of the curriculum to emphasize and increased amounts of teacher directed instruction. Although this often requires novel ways of deploying personnel, both teachers and paraprofessionals, she has noted that increased adult support results in fewer behavioral disruptions and greater academic performance.

Susan Hill recognizes that aligning essential elements of the secondary curriculum and specific instructional supports to the learning needs of individual students is not a perfect science. It is detective work, an exercise of daily problem solving to determine which evidence-based practices work for specific students. More often than not, the process works. Assisted considerably by the work of Ms. Hill and her colleagues, students at Heritage High School, those with and without disabilities, continue to perform well on their SOLs and have achieved AYP (adequate yearly progress) for the past 4 years.

Introduction

When presented with effective, motivating instruction, most secondary students learn their subject-area content material: science, history, math, and so on. Although students vary in their acquired levels of proficiency, they succeed, in large part, because they read fluently, attend to presentations selectively, and devise strategies to organize and remember major elements of their lessons. They perform well on assessments (papers and exams) because they know how to access and retrieve what they have learned. Moreover, in seemingly automatic fashion, these students organize new learning; connect new content to old; store material in ways that make future use easy; and take time to actually *think about their thinking* (Bransford, Brown, & Cocking, 2000; Ellis, 1993).

Unfortunately, not all students experience content-area learning in this way. As observed by Susan Hill, the Dean of Special Education at Heritage High School, in the opening vignette, some students enter secondary classrooms lacking the basic skills—often reading and writing—and strategies to benefit fully from the curriculum. In some circumstances, students present themselves as unorganized, unmotivated, uninterested, and disruptive. More often than not, these behaviors are functions of a learning problem or disability and reflect years of frustration being unable to understand important and interesting subject matter.

In addition to their need for motivating material, these students need explicit guidance and support in how best to access subject-area content. Moreover, they need clear instruction in how to organize and manage their own learning. Meeting the instructional needs of these students is the challenge facing content-area general and special education teachers in inclusive settings. By pooling their efforts and expertise, teachers can make secondary content interesting subjects, (e.g., biology, history, physics, and geometry) accessible to all levels and types of learners.

How can teachers identify students who lack adequate information processing skills? How can subject-area content be made accessible to students with learning differences and disabilities? Is it possible to differentiate content instruction for such students and still maintain high standards for other students in the classroom? Many teachers, such as those on the faculty at Heritage High School, recognize that universal and individualized instructional practices help all students access and acquire subject-area knowledge. These instructional practices are *engineered* (Dukes & Lamar-Dukes, 2009)—designed and delivered collaboratively by general and special education teachers. In this chapter, we focus on strategies and techniques that provide students with explicit strategies for reading, organizing, storing, and retrieving content, practices that result in enhanced subject-area achievement.

Students who have learning problems and disabilities often mask their inability to understand lesson content by appearing uninterested or being disruptive.

Content Learning Differences: What to Expect

Consider what it is like for learners who lack the skills to acquire the material presented in secondary-content classes. First and foremost, many of these students have difficulty understanding incoming information because of receptive language difficulties, reading comprehension problems, organization deficits, as well as shortcomings in short- and long-term memory functioning (Anderson-Inman, Knox-Quinn, & Horney, 1996). Along with poor spelling, handwriting skills, and a tendency toward easy distractibility, essential skills such as note taking, studying, and test taking fail to develop adequately. Not surprisingly, frustration builds, motivation falls, and students experiencing continued failure often engage in inappropriate behaviors to mask their academic weaknesses.

Pause & Reflect

Think back to a situation where you were unable to perform a skill, complete a task, or engage in an activity to your (or other's) satisfaction. Describe your frustrations, and identify several of the feelings you experienced in relation to your inability to meet the requirements adequately. What could have been done to help you?

Many of these learners also lack the tools for approaching and managing the complex requirements of academic tasks. They either lack specific strategies for dealing with subject matter, or select—sometimes randomly—instructional approaches that are inappropriate for the assigned task. When facing complex content, these students do not actively interface with the learning process. Specifically, they do not reflect on previous lessons, rarely think of alternative ways to think about the content, or evaluate and revise their initial thinking.

As these issues often involve metacognition or "the thinking about thinking," you should anticipate that content-area instruction goes beyond curriculum standards and basic skills. To reach all students, teachers need to enrich lessons and learning resources with strategic enhancements and provide instruction that is sensitive to information processing. How do teachers make these adjustments to lesson development? Research has found that successful teachers differentiate instruction to best meet the needs of individual learners. Simultaneously, successful teachers ensure that instruction sensitive to individual learners is also appropriate for the entire class (Lenz, Deshler, & Kissam, 2004).

No one understands the need to provide supports and accommodations for challenging content more than Jon Pruess, a general science and physics teacher at Heritage High School.

Identified as having a learning disability for most of his middle and high school years, Mr. Pruess had few teachers who understood the way he processed their subject-area lessons. Currently, along with special education co-teacher Tracey Ludwig, Mr. Pruess sees firsthand that stimulating content and enthusiastic presentations are not enough for some of his students. Every day, Mr. Pruess and Mr. Ludwig make critical decisions as to which elements of the curriculum to emphasize and how much of their instruction should target specialized methods and supports that help students connect with the content. In the remainder of this chapter, we describe evidence-based supports and accommodations that you can readily implement in inclusive secondary content-area classes.

Prerequisites for Inclusive Content-Area Instruction

Like Jon Pruess and Tracey Ludwig, most general and special education subject-area teachers make decisions about which aspects of the curriculum to emphasize, consider effective ways to present that material, and suggest ways for students to interact with the content. To make these types of instructional decisions, teachers must first understand the nature of curriculum and what it takes to work collaboratively in the delivery of the curriculum.

Understanding Curriculum

Among the most critical decisions made by parents, educators, and policy makers is the composition of the curriculum: the content, skills, and processes students learn in school. With state government policy makers mandating core curricular standards for schools, teachers in recent years have had reduced input in the selection of course content. However, teachers remain central in the allocation of topics emphasized in their classes, as well as the materials, resources, and methods used to deliver the content. More important, teachers make daily decisions regarding adaptations and accommodations to the curriculum to address the individual needs of their students.

What do teachers of inclusive content-area classes need to understand about curriculum? First, with federal (e.g., No Child Left Behind [NCLB]) and statewide accountability systems, most students with disabilities are expected to make progress in all aspects of the general education curriculum. Second, because students vary in their ability to learn, retain, and apply information, not all students will learn all aspects of a given subject area. Specifically, some enduring elements of subject material must be learned to proficiency by all students, while other aspects of the material will be learned by only a smaller proportion of students. Finally, teachers typically need structured routines for instructional planning in order to determine which elements of the curriculum specific students require.

In Chapter 12 we presented planning pyramids (see Figure 12.6) (Schumm, 1999; Vaughn, Bos, & Schumm, 2007), one of several methods that allow teachers to visually represent the content of the curriculum to be learned by all of the students, most of the students, and some of the students. Figure 14.1 provides a specific illustration of the technique, a typical middle school science pyramid lesson plan addressing weathering and erosion. Notice how the base of the pyramid includes content important for all students to learn, such as the forces that change the earth's crust. At the next level is content that most but not all students will learn, including how humans cause weathering. Finally, the top

Teachers work collaboratively to make curricular adaptations that address the individual needs of students.

THE PLANNING PYRAMID UNIT PLANNING FORM

UNIT PLANNING FORM

Date: *Sept 1–30*   **Class Period:** *1.30 – 2.30*
Unit Title: *Weathering and Erosion*

What some students will learn.	• *How Earth looked during Ice Age* • *Disasters caused by sudden changes* • *Geographic examples of slow and fast changes*
What most students will learn.	• *Compare and contrast weathering and erosion* • *How humans cause physical and chemical weathering* • *Basic types of rocks*
What ALL students should learn.	• *Basic components of Earth's surface* • *Forces that change crust are weathering and erosion*

Materials/Resources:

Guest speaker an volcanoes
Video erosion and weathering
Rock samples
Library books — disasters, volcanoes, etc.
Colored transparencies for lectures

Instructional Strategies/Adaptations:

Concept maps
Cooperative learning groups to learn material in textbook
Audiotape of chapter
Study buddies to prepare for quizzes and tests

Evaluation/Products:

Weekly quiz
Unit test
Learning logs (daily record of "What I learned")
Vocabulary flask

Figure 14.1

A Planning Pyramid for a Middle School Science Lesson on Weathering and Erosion

Source: Reprinted with permission from Vaughn, S., Bos, C., & Schumm, J. (2007). *Teaching students who are exceptional, diverse, and at-risk in the general education classroom* (4th ed., p. 218). Boston: Allyn & Bacon.

of the pyramid includes content that only some students will learn, such as how the earth looked during the Ice Age. In addition to planning content, the unit-planning form prompts decisions regarding materials and resources, instructional strategies and adaptations, and evaluation and products to meet the needs of all students in the science class.

Working Collaboratively

Throughout this text, we discuss repeatedly the importance of collaboration in the delivery of inclusive educational programs. Not surprisingly, when teaching subject-area content, a solid working partnership between the content-area expert and the special educator is essential. How do such partnerships work? At Heritage High School, for example, the nature and style of collaborative teaming arrangements vary from class to class, often a function of the teachers' expertise, instructional styles, comfort levels, and, of course, the needs of the students. For example, in the inclusive physics class co-taught by Jon Pruess and Tracey Ludwig, Mr. Pruess, a natural storyteller and accomplished scientist, delivers the majority of the large-group direct instruction. Mr. Ludwig, the special educator, circulates among the students, providing efficient and timely support in the form of suggested strategies, content enhancements, and encouragement. In the geometry class co-taught by Anthony Long and Shana Watson, Ms. Watson, the special educator, assumes a greater share of the large-group direct instruction responsibilities. Ms. Watson, certified in both math and special education, also provides guided notes and individualized support to students when Mr. Long provides the direct instruction.

Pause & Reflect

What does the phrase "working collaboratively" mean to you? Knowing that individuals have varying definitions of "collaboration," identify how teachers can arrive at a common operational definition of this process.

Each of these co-teaching teams uses a slightly different collaborative approach to instruction and support. Still, each of their collaborative efforts is effective because they orchestrate their planning and instruction in ways that maximize individual pedagogical strengths, they are sensitive to preferred instructional roles, and they address the needs of students. Although roles and responsibilities change, the co-teaching partners make sure that they plan lessons together as well as review their instructional processes and student outcomes frequently. Most important, regardless of their co-teaching approach, the special educators are not put in the position of being classroom assistants. They regularly provide substantial instruction and support, to the entire group, small groups, or individual students.

Models and Approaches for Inclusive Content-Area Instruction

When teaching secondary content in inclusive classes, successful teachers select from a variety of evidence-based models and approaches. Typical practices include universal design for learning, direct instruction, guided discovery learning, cooperative learning, strategy instruction, and content enhancements.

Universal design for learning is a way of making instruction accessible by building supports and accommodation into typical modes of instructional delivery.

Strategy 14.1 discusses content enhancements: unit and lesson organizers.

Universal Design for Learning

Universal design for learning is a way of making instruction accessible to all students by building supports and accommodation into the original mode of teaching rather than making adaptations after the fact. Universal design is all around us, most noticeably in architecture and product development (Hitchcock, Meyer, Rose, & Jackson, 2002; Orkwis & McLane, 1998). Currently, it is typical practice for architects to use universal design to build in accommodations to buildings from their initial design phases, including ramps for wheelchair users as an essential part of a building's design. Similarly, closed captioning, originally intended to benefit people who cannot hear the sound from a television because of a disability, benefits many others (e.g., those in noisy bars, health clubs, or bedrooms when another person is sleeping) who do not have problems hearing.

Merely a decade ago, universal design for learning was the domain of a few instructional technology experts. However, given the rapid advances in technology and curriculum design, universal design is a reality that pervades schools and enhances individual teachers' delivery of content-area instruction, building in accommodations and making differences among students an ordinary part of the school day (McLeskey & Waldron, 2002). At Heritage High School, geometry co-teachers Anthony Long and Shana Watson have integrated a number of "special" universal techniques into their usual lesson plans. For example, they begin every class with a display of an advance graphic organizer of the lesson content. Guided notes help students keep up with the main points of the lesson, and calculators prevent calculation difficulties from interfering with conceptual understanding of the content.

Direct Instruction

Typically appropriate for learners of all ages, direct instruction (DI) refers to a set of specific teacher behaviors and curriculum materials that correlate with increased levels of student academic achievement. Known for its high degree of structure and predictability, DI contains three principal components: demonstration, guided practice, and independent practice. During the demonstration stage of a lesson, the teacher explicitly presents elements of the instructional material or models methods for applying a skill or solving a particular problem. Consider how students apply DI in secondary settings: In their geometry class Anthony Long or Shana Wheeler demonstrate explicitly the formula for determining the degree of an interior angle of a parallelogram when the degrees of three of the other angles are known. Using a direct instruction sequence, they present the formula and model the steps in solving several examples.

Guided practice is a closely supervised application of the demonstrated content supplemented by teacher cues, prompts, and corrective feedback. Often indistinguishable from interactive demonstrations, guided practice is most effective when students have numerous and varied opportunities to interact with the content of the lesson. Examples of guided practice activities in secondary content-area classes include small groups of students solving algebra or geometry problems on the board, working together to apply a chemistry or physics laboratory concept, or replying in unison fashion to questions about characteristics of governments.

One effective method of guided practice is having small heterogeneous groups of students apply science concepts in laboratory settings.

Independent practice typically follows guided practice, but only when students are ready to engage the content on their own. Teachers can and should deliver independent practice through creative instructional activities and cooperative group projects. Most content-area classrooms, however, typically rely on seat work and homework. Because many students spend as much as 70% of an instructional period in seat-work activities, it is essential that the activities be age and subject appropriate, be consistent with the goals of the lesson, have multiple response formats, and contain components that students can complete with a high degree of success (Gaffney, 1987). Like seat work, students should be able to complete homework assignments independently. Effective assignments emphasize information already learned and set the stage for the acquisition of new content. When integrating homework into lessons, teachers should ensure they do not use it to punish students or to replace school-based instruction (Cooper, 2001).

Guided Discovery Learning

The primary goal of guided discovery learning (GDL) is to teach students to be independent problem solvers, to learn the generic steps to scientific inquiry and logical thinking. By learning the generic process of problem solving, students can acquire and master information from a number of content areas. GDL instruction applies problem-solving strategies to new material and situations. Students learn specific content information through the introduction of novel problems requiring similar problem-solving strategies and involving new but similar information. In essence, with GDL, the problem-solving process supersedes any learning of specific content material (Rosenberg et al., 2006).

For students with disabilities included in content-area classes, the guided portion of GDL must be prominent. Teachers accomplish this by emphasizing different ways to solve content-specific problems. A model of instruction that carries many of these general features is proleptic teaching (Vygotsky, 1978). Teachers develop a strategy or problem-solving process through a natural dialogue with students, with students gradually taking over the steps and procedures involved in the task at hand (Paris & Winograd, 1990; Rosenshine & Meister, 1992). The role of the teacher is to provide necessary support structures, or *scaffolding,* as needed (Rojewski & Schell, 1994).

Cooperative Learning

As we detailed in Chapter 13, cooperative learning approaches vary widely in type yet share some common beneficial characteristics (e.g., Good & Brophy, 2003; Putnam, 1998; Slavin, 1999) including:

- **Positive interdependence.** The accomplishment of the group goal depends on heterogeneous, diverse group members working together *and* each individual attaining her goal.
- **Individual accountability.** All students are held individually accountable for their own learning as well as for their contributions to the group.
- **Cooperative skills.** Students practice social and cooperative skills that are commonly used in group activities, such as sharing materials, taking turns, helping one another, and encouraging others.

Teachers use cooperative learning frequently in Heritage High School, with secondary content-area co-teaching teams often selecting and sometimes adapting the following evidence-based applications.

Jigsaw. As fully described in Chapter 13, three to five students form heterogeneous groups. Each team member is assigned a part (piece) of the assignment (puzzle). Students from the different groups who are assigned to the same part form expert groups. The expert groups meet to review information regarding their part, determine the most important information, and then return to their teams. The teams then review the important information from each part and synthesize the information (Aronson, Stephin, Sikes, Blaney, & Snapp, 1978; Slavin, 1990).

Student Teams—Achievement Divisions (STAD). Students are arranged into heterogeneous teams of four to six. Following a pretest, the teacher presents content, and teams work together on worksheets, study guides, or other practice activities. Students take individual tests on the material, and scores are compared with their pretest scores to derive a gain score. The gain scores are averaged for a team gain score. Points are awarded for individual and team gains (Slavin, 1990).

Team-Assisted Individualization (TAI). The teacher determines students' skill levels and makes placement within an individualized skill sequence. Students complete worksheets daily and progress through the curriculum at their own pace. Peer team members help check responses on the worksheets. At the end of each unit of individualized instruction, students take a final unit test. Points are awarded for passing the unit tests, completing multiple units, and completing homework assignments (Slavin, 1990).

Learning Strategies

Learning strategies are a broad array of techniques that help students access and use higher-order secondary-content knowledge (Rogan, 2000). Strategies work because they focus directly on what students can do to improve their performance, allow for active student engagement in instruction, and promote the active creation of rules for using instructional presentations and materials. Effective strategies focus on content (what to teach) and design (how to teach) (Ellis & Lenz, 1996). The content of strategies includes explicit instructional steps that help students organize, store, and ultimately express elements of their lessons and activities. For example, with the DEFENDS writing strategy (see Strategy 14.2), teachers present a series of seven steps for writing persuasive essays: (1) Decide on goals and theme; (2) Estimate main ideas and details; (3) Figure best order of main ideas and details; (4) Express the theme in the first sentence; (5) Note each main idea and supporting points; (6) Drive home the message in the last sentence; and (7) Search for errors and correct.

| Strategy | Strategy 14.2 discusses expository writing. |

The design, or "how-to-teach," component requires teachers to model, lead, and test students in the acquisition of the strategies. This instruction usually consists of eight steps:

1. Teacher pretests and obtains student commitment to learn.
2. Teacher describes the new strategy.

3. Teacher models the new strategy.
4. Teacher and students verbally rehearse strategy steps.
5. Student practices on controlled materials.
6. Student practices on grade-appropriate classroom materials.
7. Teacher post-tests and obtains student commitment to generalize.
8. Student generalizes.

During strategy acquisition, steps are taken to facilitate generalization by having students apply learned strategies across content areas.

Pause & Reflect

Think back to your days as a secondary student. What learning strategies did you use in your content area classes? Which of the strategies did you find to be most effective?

Content Enhancements

Content enhancements are instructional techniques that teachers use to help academically diverse learners understand, store, and access secondary subject-area material. These techniques help teachers think about and organize content as well as present and explain difficult concepts to struggling learners. When using content enhancements, teachers ensure that (1) group and individual needs are met; (2) the integrity of content is maintained; (3) critical elements of content are translated in ways that promote learning; and (4) an instructional partnership exists between teacher and student (Lenz et al., 2004). As there are many different ways to enhance content, it is useful to think of content enhancements in three major categories: redesigning instruction and materials, devices, and routines (King-Sears & Mooney, 2004).

Redesigned Instruction and Materials. Educators usually design teaching sequences and instructional materials to match the profiles of "average" students. However, few if any students meet all elements of these profiles, and it is not unusual for teachers to find it necessary to adapt certain lessons or the materials they use. Earlier in this chapter, we talked about universal design for learning, a proactive way of making instruction accessible to all students by building supports and accommodations into the original mode of teaching. Although this is a preferable mode of adapting instruction, teachers sometimes must differentiate instruction or make adaptations to existing methods and materials. Teachers usually choose among nine types of instructional adaptations (see Table 14.1; Cole et al., 2000). The most frequently used adaptations tend to be the more obvious—adaptations in size (e.g., the number of items that a student is expected to complete) and time (e.g., time allocated for completing a task). However, other adaptations include the following: (1) adjust the difficulty level of lessons, (2) structure how students participate and provide responses, (3) provide encouragement and support, (4) recognize the individual student's success in large-group lessons, and (5) facilitate peer-driven, content-focused reciprocal questioning.

Devices. By *devices* we are referring to the range of concrete prompts and cues that help students understand content material and relationships among concepts. Graphic organizers, for example, are very useful for representing relationships between and among critical elements typical of content-area instruction. Graphic representations help make abstract concepts and complicated relationships (e.g., cause–effect, compare–contrast, hierarchy, cycle, etc.) concrete and tangible, allowing for easier application to the content being studied. Equally useful are mnemonic and key-word strategies (see Strategy 14.3), tools that help students with disabilities as well as other students to access content information when needed (Wolgemuth, Cobb, & Alwell, 2008).

Strategy 14.3 discusses mnemonic strategies.

Routines. A teaching routine is a series of integrated steps and procedures that guides the introduction and learning of content knowledge (King-Sears & Mooney, 2004). Some routines help teachers organize and present content that help students see both the big picture and details of what they will learn. Other routines serve as supports for teaching difficult concepts and operations. The primary purpose in using a specific routine is to proactively structure a segment of instruction in ways that identify and address potential obstacles to learning (Bulgren & Lenz, 1996).

Earlier, we introduced two universal design routines (the unit and lesson organizer routines) that help organize and present content. An example of a routine that assists in the actual teaching

Table 14.1   Nine Types of Adaptations

Adaptation	Definition	Example
Input	The instructional strategies used to facilitate student learning	Use videos, computer programs, field trips, and visual aids to support active learning.
Output	The ways learners can demonstrate understanding and knowledge	Students write a song, tell a story, design a poster or brochure, or perform an experiment.
Size	The length or portion of an assignment, demonstration, or performance learners are expected to complete	Reduce the length of report to be written or spoken, reduce the number of references needed, reduce the number of problems to be solved.
Time	The flexible time needed for student learning	Individualize a time line for project completion, allow more time for test taking.
Difficulty	The varied skill levels, conceptual levels, and processes involved in learning	Provide calculators, and tier the assignment so that the outcome is the same but with varying degrees of concreteness and complexity.
Level of support	The amount of assistance to the learner	Students work in cooperative groups or with peer buddies, mentors, cross-age tutors, or paraeducators.
Degree of participation	The extent to which the learner is actively involved in the tasks	In a student-written, -directed, and -acted play, a student may play a part that has more physical action rather than numerous lines to memorize.
Modified goals	The adapted outcome expectations within the context of a general education curriculum	In a written language activity, a student may focus more on writing some letters and copying words than composing whole sentences or paragraphs.
Substitute curriculum	Significantly differentiated instruction and materials to meet a learner's identified goals	In a foreign language class, a student may develop a play or script that uses both authentic language and cultural knowledge of a designated time period rather than reading paragraphs or directions.

Source: Adapted from Cole, C., et al. (2000). *Adapting curriculum and instruction in inclusive classrooms: A teachers' desk reference* (2nd ed., p. 39). Bloomington, IN: Indiana Institute on Disability and Community.

of concepts is the concept diagram (see Figure 14.2). Notice how the graphic explicitly guides students in considering similarities and differences among key elements of higher-order math. Keep in mind, however, that routines are complex and often require some degree of training and practice if they are to be implemented effectively. Routines will not be effective if they are simply distributed to students without adequate instruction. Detailed manuals are published by the Center for Learning at the University of Kansas, Center for Research on Learning (*http://www.ku-crl.org*), and extensive descriptions of these routines are available in the literature (e.g., Bulgren & Lenz, 1996; Bulgren, Schumaker, & Deshler, 1988, 1993; Lenz et al., 2004; Sabornie & deBettencourt, 2009).

Content Survival Strategies

The successful acquisition of content-area knowledge requires that students learn and apply a series of survival strategies. Four of the more important strategies are content-area reading, note taking, test taking, and time management.

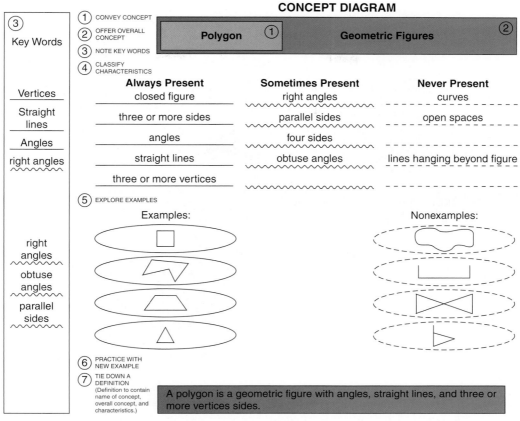

Figure 14.2

A Concept Diagram for a Math Lesson: Polygons

Source: Adapted from Gorman, J. A., & Lysaght, K. (1996). *Accommodating diversity in a general education math class in a middle school.* Presentation at Boston College, School of Education and from *The Concept Mastery Routine* by J. A. Bulgen, J. B. Schumaker, & D. D. Deshler (1993). Lawrence, KS: Edge Enterprises.

Content-Area Reading

For Susan Hill, Dean of Special Education at Heritage High School, one of the major challenges in providing secondary content instruction is that many students lack the reading skills to benefit fully from textbooks. Because a large part of secondary-content instruction involves the independent reading of textbooks, it is essential that teachers use a range of strategies to facilitate content-area reading for students with disabilities. Keep in mind that secondary textbooks contain more than just narrative text. Students must also be able to navigate through a series of maps, graphs, charts, and tables that augment and reinforce critical content (Sabornie & deBettencourt, 2009).

> ### Pause & Reflect
>
> What changes need to be made to current textbooks if they are to contain supports and accommodations for students with learning problems? Identify ways that technology can help provide these supports.

Providing supports for content-area reading requires a multifaceted approach including textbook exploration activities, intensive vocabulary instruction, comprehensive comprehension strategies, audio-texts, study guides and focused chapter questions, as well as the identification of supplemental Web-based resources (Conderman & Elf, 2007; Steele, 2007; Wood, 2001). For students with more severe challenges, teachers can, depending on the cognitive characteristics of students, replace and/or supplement text by priming background knowledge, using picture walks

Because textbooks are a large part of secondary instruction, it is essential that students learn strategies for successfully using textbook features that facilitate understanding and application of content.

Strategy Strategy 14.4 discusses content-area reading.

Strategy Strategy 14.5 discusses note taking.

(pictures that preview lesson content), and integrating think-alouds in their instruction (Gately, 2008). Detailed descriptions of several of these content-area reading techniques are provided in Strategy 14.4.

Note Taking

Students who have effective note-taking skills perform better on content-area assessments than those students who have difficulty with the process (Boyle, 2007). Unfortunately, few students receive direct instruction in how best to record the important points of classroom lectures and presentations. Many students with disabilities are at increased risk for failure because they are unable to negotiate the complex processes associated with recording their thoughts. Specifically, students with disabilities often have trouble deciding what points to record; keeping up with the constant flow of lecture material; shifting back and forth between the process of listening and writing; and reviewing the information they record (Porte, 2001; Suritsky & Hughes, 1996).

Teachers can develop, improve, and support note-taking skills in four general ways: (1) accommodations, (2) techniques that facilitate note taking, (3) directly teaching note taking, and (4) note-taking strategies (Suritsky & Hughes, 1996). Note-taking accommodations include using strategic forms and guided notes, which are explicit supports that cue the student to elements of the recording process. Techniques to facilitate note taking include teachers' changing the presentation rate of the lectures, using visual aids, and inserting questions and cues into their lessons. Direct teaching of note taking is the explicit delivery of lessons on how best to address content before the presentation, during the lesson, and after the lesson. Finally, using a specific note-taking strategy (e.g., LINCS and AWARE) involves the teaching and application of highly structured packages of note-taking processes. Detailed descriptions of these methods are provided in Strategy 14.5.

Test Taking

Traditional pencil-and-paper tests are the dominant method of measuring student performance in most content-area classes. Unfortunately, many low-achieving students including students with disabilities fail to use the effective testtaking strategies employed by their higher-achieving peers (Hong, Sas, & Sas, 2006). These students are not *test-wise*: They often fail to attend to test directions, lack persistence in considering multiple-choice options, and are easily misled by irrelevant and distracting information on the test form (Scruggs & Mastropieri, 1990). Because they tend not to use deductive reasoning, they fail to eliminate similar and absurd options when considering response options (Hughes, 1996). Similar to note taking, teachers can improve students' test-taking skills by providing accommodations on the test, directly teaching effective test-taking techniques, or employing a comprehensive test-taking strategy. Detailed techniques are provided in Strategy 14.6.

Pause & Reflect

Describe the feelings you experience when getting ready to take a "big" test. How can having a test-taking strategy reduce nervousness and anxiety and facilitate clear thinking?

Strategy Strategy 14.6 discusses test taking.

Time and Assignment Management

To succeed in content-area classes, students need to organize their time and efforts, ultimately completing homework and other assignments accurately and on time. One way students organize time and manage their assignments is by using planners and agenda books. These tangible organizers

Figure 14.3	Two Strategies for Assignment Management

TRICK BAG (Scott & Compton, 2007)
   T—Take out agenda book.
   R—Record assignment.
   I—Insert important details.
   C—Circle materials you need.
   K—Keep materials in homework folder.
   B—Be sure you can read it.
   A—Ask a partner to check it.
   G—Go put it in your backpack.

PROJECT (Hughes et al., 2002)
   P—Prepare your forms.
   R—Record and ask.
   O—Organize
      B—Break assignment into parts.
      E—Estimate the number of study sessions.
      S—Schedule the sessions.
      T—Take your materials home.
   J—Jump to it.
   E—Engage in the work.
   C—Check your work.
   T—Turn in your work.

provide a structure for listing and prioritizing assignments, as well as a way for scheduling short- and long-term academic activities and events (Scott & Compton, 2007). Unfortunately, too many students do not make full use of the planners because they have difficulty recording assignments, detailing the requirements of multicomponent tasks, and estimating the amount of time needed to complete tasks (Salend & Gajria, 1995). Other students just forget to use their planners and agenda books. As with the other content survival strategies, teachers can provide direct instruction and support for the use of planners for assignment and time management through strategic instruction (see Figure 14.3). For example, researchers found that the mnemonic strategy PROJECT increased homework rate completion, assignment quality, and grades among students with disabilities in inclusive content-area classes (Hughes, Ruhl, Schumaker, & Deshler, 2002).

Content-Area Instruction for Students with Severe Disabilities

Until recently, educators assumed that individuals whose measured intelligence fell below an IQ of 55 were incapable of content-area learning. This thinking has changed: Although students with severe disabilities will not acquire academic skills approximating the level of students with less severe disabilities, research has shown that many can benefit from access to the general education curriculum and strategically enhanced content instruction (Browder & Spooner, 2006). Encouraged by this research and spurred on by federal legislation requiring an increased focus on academic instruction, content-area instruction at some level is expected practice for students with severe disabilities (Westling & Fox, 2008).

> ## Pause & Reflect
>
> Where students with severe disabilities receive instruction remains highly controversial. In your view, in what setting should teachers deliver secondary-content instruction? What challenges must teachers meet in order to provide this instruction in general education classrooms?

What does this mean for general and special education teachers who already work collaboratively in inclusive content-area classrooms, but with students whose disabilities are less severe? In some respects, teaching content to students with severe disabilities requires many of the same processes used with other students. Units and lessons need to be designed and delivered with an understanding of curriculum, collaboration, and instructional methods if all students are to benefit from the instruction. Universal design principles that employ multiple means of presentation, expression, and engagement are necessary if students are to truly participate during lessons (Wehmeyer & Agran, 2006). Finally, working with peer tutors or friends without disabilities increases involvement with the content as well as fostering greater opportunities for social interaction (Carter, Cushing, Clark, & Kennedy, 2005).

Teachers' achievement expectations for students with disabilities may differ in depth and complexity from those for students without disabilities; however, expectations must be true to grade-level content (Browder et al., 2007). Consider how Dymond et al. (2006) developed a universally designed high school science course responsive to needs of all students including those with severe disabilities. Initially, the researchers developed a series of questions to address modification of key areas of curriculum and instructional delivery. The researchers made major changes to the course by adapting materials and modes of student participation, adjusting instructional delivery, and having alternate forms of assessment. Specifically, large-print reading material and laptops with Internet connections and LCD projectors were added to the more traditional materials. Students were given a range of choices of how they would like to participate, ranging from interactive lessons to hands-on activities, team projects, and peer tutoring. Finally, a range of assessments such as rubrics and checklists were used to evaluate student outcomes during presentations and hands-on work sessions.

As a result of the UDL process, general education and special education teachers began to collaborate more, shared more instructional responsibilities, and became more concerned that the students with severe disabilities participate meaningfully during instruction. Frequency of teacher interactions with students increased, and student participation in lessons grew from an afterthought to a part of the planning process. Although the greatest gains were in personal and social skills, Dymond et al. (2006) found notable gains in the understanding of the science content. Table 14.2 contains a series of action steps teachers can apply when redesigning secondary content for students with severe disabilities.

Table 14.2   Redesigning Content Lessons for Students with Severe Disabilities

Design Need	Action Steps
Curriculum	• Identify curriculum standards addressed and the big ideas to be taught. • Add and delete content to match the learning needs of students. • Sequence content appropriately. • Ensure content relates to outcomes that can be applied out of school.
Instructional Delivery/Organization	• Provide a variety of hands-on learning activities. • Ensure that activities allow for choice-making opportunities. • Allow for numerous opportunities for repeated practice. • Incorporate heterogeneous grouping arrangements. • Have explicit roles for all adults in the provision of academic and behavioral supports. • Program activities that call for a full range of student participation and responses.
Materials	• Incorporate assistive technology support to facilitate participation and understanding of material. • Modify instructional materials to make more concrete and functional (e.g., color-code equipment, label equipment with symbols, etc.).
Assessment	• Have multiple methods available to assess performance. • Allow students to choose assessment method. • Use assessment data to evaluate and refine instruction.

Source: Adapted from Dymond, S. K., Renzaglia, A., Rosenstein, A., Chun, E. J., Banks, R. A., Niswander, V., & Gilson, C. L. (2006). Using a participatory action research approach to create a universally designed inclusive high school science course: A case study. *Research & Practice for Persons with Severe Disabilities, 31*(4), 293–308.

Summary

Effective teachers can teach content in inclusive classes by understanding the learning characteristics of their students and working collaboratively to implement proactive strategies that support higher-order learning.

Student learning: What to expect

- Unlike their normally achieving peers, many students with disabilities included in content-area classes do not have the basic reading, writing, or math skills necessary for academic success.
- Students also have problems acquiring content due to organizational deficits, problems in self-regulation, and deficits in short- and long-term memory.
- As deficits are largely in skill and metacognitive ("the thinking about thinking") areas, content instruction must address both skills issues and strategic learning.

Prerequisites for inclusive content-area instruction

- Although state and local policy makers are prominent in the composition of subject-area curriculum, teachers remain central decision makers in how topics are emphasized and taught.
- As students vary in their ability to learn new information, teachers must decide which elements of their subject area are essential for all students to know.
- Planning pyramids help teachers decide which content is important for all students to learn, the content that most should learn, and the material that only some are expected to access.
- Content-area instruction in inclusive settings requires active collaboration among subject-area experts and special education learning specialists.

Models and approaches for instruction

- Universal design for learning, a proactive way of making instruction accessible for all students, minimizes the need to make adaptations in methods and materials after the fact.
- Direct instruction—known for its structure, predictability, and correlation with high levels of student achievement—comprises three principal components: demonstration, guided practice, and independent practice.
- Guided discovery learning focuses on applying problem-solving strategies to a range of subject areas and situations.
- Although they vary by type, cooperative learning approaches are defined by three common beneficial characteristics: positive interdependence, individual accountability, and cooperative practices.
- Learning strategies guide students as they interface with higher-order content material. Areas emphasized in the approach include what to teach (content), how to teach (design), and transferability across subject areas.
- Content enhancements are instructional techniques that assist all learners while maintaining the integrity of the subject-area material. The three major categories of content enhancements are redesigned instruction and materials; devices such as graphic organizers and mnemonics; and routines that proactively structure segments of instruction to avoid obstacles to learning.

Content survival strategies

- Because many students with disabilities have problems reading text, a multifaceted series of supports is necessary, including textbook exploration activities, intensive vocabulary instruction, comprehensive comprehension strategies, audio-texts, study guides and focused chapter questions, and supplemental Web-based resources.
- Students with disabilities included in content-area classes benefit from note-taking accommodations, techniques that facilitate note taking, and direct instruction in note-taking techniques and comprehensive strategies.

- Because many students with disabilities are not test-wise, explicit test-taking strategies can attain a true measure of academic performance.
- Students with disabilities can increase their time and assignment management through explicit instruction on how to use planners and agenda books.

Students with severe disabilities

- Although students with severe disabilities will not acquire the depth and complexity of subject-area curricula, they can benefit from strategically enhanced content instruction.
- Methods that maximize benefits for students with severe disabilities include universal design and working with peer tutors.

Addressing Professional Standards

Standards addressed in Chapter 14 include:

CEC Standards: (3) individual learning differences, (4) instructional strategies, and (7) instructional planning.

INTASC Standards: Principle 2—Provide learning opportunities to support the learning and development of all students; Principle 3—Create instructional opportunities for diverse learners; Principle 4—Understand and use a variety of instructional strategies.

Praxis™ II Standards: Knowledge-based core principles: Delivery of services to students with disabilities. Application of core principles: (1) curriculum, (2) instruction.

PUTTING IT ALL TOGETHER

With increased academic standards required of all students, more students with disabilities are being included in high-demand content-area classes and many arrive unable to respond to the academic demands. Teams of general and special education teachers are required to design and apply instructional procedures that simultaneously meet the individual needs of students with learning differences as they deliver engaging, challenging, and provocative lessons to entire classes.

To maximize your efforts, we recommend that you keep in mind the following factors—central to successful student outcomes:

1. **Content-area instruction in inclusive settings is a team effort** requiring the active participation of subject-area experts and special education learning specialists.

2. **The primary role of the content-area specialist is to select carefully the subject matter** that is essential for all students to learn and to format the material for access and acquisition; the role of the special education specialist is to provide supports and teach students the strategies and skills to enhance their effectiveness as efficient learners (Deshler & Putnam, 1996).

3. **When presented well, content-area subject matter is interesting, engaging, and motivating.** Consequently, if provided with opportunities and support for interacting with the material, students will respond positively and participate in class discussions and activities.

4. **Methods that support and enhance accessibility** such as universal design, content enhancements, and learning strategies can be integrated into classroom activities with little negative impact on the instruction of other learners.

5. **Remember the affective elements of teaching when providing specialized supports.** Encouragement, positive self-statements, and skills for coping with difficult situations should always supplement content and strategy instruction.

myeducationlab

We present a series of evidence-based strategies in the second half of this chapter (Strategies 14.1 to 14.6) in a step-by-step format so that you can use them in your classroom right away. In addition, in the following table, we identify some video clips, cases, and simulations that will allow you to experience these strategies (or complementary strategies) in a real classroom environment.

EFFECTIVE PRACTICE	MYEDUCATIONLAB CONNECTION	CONSIDER THIS
Strategy 14.1: Content Enhancements: Unit and Lesson Organizers	Go to MyEducationLab, select the topic *Instructional Practices and Learning Strategies*, and go to the Activities and Applications section. Next, go to the subsection *Developing Learning Strategies and Conceptual Understanding*, and watch the video entitled "Graphic Organizer."	As you watch the video and answer the accompanying questions, compare and contrast this graphic organizer and the accompanying cooperative activity with the discussion in Strategy 14.1. Do you think the graphic organizer and this activity (depicted in the video) are successful in helping all students access this content? Why or why not?
Strategy 14.2: Improving Expository Writing Across Content-Area Classes	Go to MyEducationLab, select the topic *Content-Area Teaching*, and go to the Building Teaching Skills and Dispositions section. Next, complete the activity entitled "Scaffolding in Literacy."	As you complete the activity and watch the videos, focus on the techniques these teachers use to teach and scaffold successful writing for their students. Although these students are in elementary school, they are receiving the basic instruction on how to improve their expository writing. Compare and contrast these strategies with Strategy 14.2.
Strategy 14.3: Mnemonic Strategies	Go to MyEducationLab, select the topic *Instructional Practices and Learning Strategies*, and go to the Activities and Application section. Next, complete the simulation entitled "Using Learning Strategies."	As you complete the simulation, reflect on the importance of learning strategies such as mnemonics in the general education classroom. Consider the usefulness of the strategies discussed in the simulation as well as in Strategy 14.3.
Strategy 14.4: Content-Area Reading	Go to MyEducationLab, select the topic *Reading Instruction*, and go to the Activities and Applications section. Next, go to the subsection *Comprehension*, and watch the video entitled "Context Clues."	As you watch this video and answer the accompanying questions, consider how you could adapt the techniques this teacher uses for older students using a textbook.
Strategy 14.5: Developing and Supporting Note Taking	Go to MyEducationLab, select the topic *Attention-Deficit/Hyperactivity Disorder*, and go to the Activities and Applications section. Next, read and analyze the strategy entitled "Split-Page Note Taking," then go to the topic *Intellectual Disabilities*, and watch the video entitled "Guided Notes Study Cards."	As you read and analyze the strategy and then watch the video, consider the similarities and differences between these two note-taking strategies. How do these strategies support the discussion in Strategy 14.5?
Strategy 14.6: Developing Effective Test Taking	Go to MyEducationLab, select the topic *Instructional Practices and Learning Strategies*, and go to the Activities and Applications section. Next, read and analyze the strategies entitled "Strategies for Taking Objective Tests" and "PIRATES Test-Taking Strategy."	As you read and analyze these strategies, compare and contrast the major components of these strategies with the discussion in Strategy 14.6. How would you use these strategies in your classroom to help students who are struggling with taking tests?

EFFECTIVE PRACTICES

In the remainder of this chapter, we describe six effective strategies, which we referred to previously in the chapter, to help you plan effectively to meet the needs of all students.

EFFECTIVE PRACTICE	TYPE OF STRATEGY/BRIEF DESCRIPTION	SPECIAL CONSIDERATIONS
Strategy 14.1: Content Enhancements: Unit and Lesson Organizers	A universal design instructional support that highlights unit and lesson content, how elements of the content are related, and the knowledge and assignments required for success.	Components of the organizers must be taught explicitly to mastery; without such instruction, students may be confused by the graphical components.
Strategy 14.2: Improving Expository Writing Across Content-Area Classes	The most important skills for writing thoughtful and informative narratives involve an awareness and strategic application of the three-stage writing process: prewriting, production, and reviewing.	Writing is very complex, and students need to understand that it is a process that cannot be completed thoughtlessly. Successful writing is focused, multiphased, and iterative, requiring considerable planning, adequate source material, and an organizational framework.
Strategy 14.3: Mnemonic Strategies	A versatile series of techniques that produce meaningful recall-enhancing connections that do not exist naturally in content.	Mnemonics can be a labor-intensive, time-consuming instructional activity, and the relative cost-benefit of using the technique needs to be monitored regularly.
Strategy 14.4: Content-Area Reading	A series of supports and strategies that assist students in understanding textbook content. Specific techniques include textbook exploration activities, adapted vocabulary, structured comprehension strategies, study guides, and visual maps.	The development of effective reading accommodations for secondary content can be challenging. However, the extent of text-driven content instruction necessitates that teachers devote time to the development of these supports and accommodations.
Strategy 14.5: Developing and Supporting Note Taking	To facilitate the coordination of the myriad skills required for effective note taking, teachers provide explicit instruction in specific techniques and strategies as well as infuse supports in their lessons.	The complexity of skills required for successful note taking may require that some students receive intensive practice in small groups with enhanced teacher guidance.
Strategy 14.6: Developing Effective Test Taking	A series of strategies that ensure that student test performance reflects true understanding including appropriate test accommodations and the direct teaching of test-taking skills and strategies.	In addition to teaching test-taking strategies, it is important to ensure that test accommodations provided are acceptable and appropriate for individual students.

Strategy 14.1

CONTENT ENHANCEMENTS: UNIT AND LESSON ORGANIZERS

Rationale and Research

The major concepts, activities, and requirements for a subject-area unit or lesson can be represented in a user-friendly graphic organizer. Both unit and lesson organizers contain elements of universal design and assist students with and without disabilities. Both organizers provide explicit visual supports reflecting (a) essential content; (b) how elements of the content are related and fit into the "big picture" of the task; (c) ways for self-monitoring progress; and (d) the knowledge and assignments that are required for success. A number of research efforts have demonstrated that students of teachers who use these organizers improve their academic performance.

Key References

Boudah, D. J., Lenz, B. K., Bulgren, J. A., Schumaker, J. B., & Deshler, D. D. (2000). Don't water down! Enhance content through the unit organizer routine. *Teaching Exceptional Children, 32*(3), 48–56.

Bulgren, J., Deshler, D. D., & Lenz, B. K. (2007). Engaging adolescents with LD in higher order thinking about history concepts using integrated concept enhancement routines. *Journal of Learning Disabilities, 40,* 121–133.

Bulgren, J., & Lenz, B. K. (1996). Strategic instruction in content areas. In D. D. Deshler, E. S. Ellis, & B. K. Lenz (Eds.), *Teaching adolescents with learning disabilities* (2nd ed.). Denver: Love.

Fisher, J. B. (1995). Searching for validated inclusive practices: A review of the literature. *Focus on Exceptional Children, 28,* 1–16.

Step-by-Step

(1) *Convert elements of the curriculum into tangible unit and lesson learning segments, determine relationships among the segments, and identify supports needed for students to learn segmented material.*

- Engage in ReflActive planning, and use the acronym SMARTER to guide actions.
  a. **S**hape the content: Focus on the material that is critical for all students to understand.
  b. **M**ap the critical content: Graphically represent connections between and among elements of the material.
  c. **A**nalyze difficulties: Determine the content that may prove difficult for students to understand.
  d. **R**each enhancement decisions: Decide how to best organize, sequence, and support instruction.
  e. **T**each strategically: Explicitly cue students to important information, and directly teach alternative ways to think about and apply the content.
  f. **E**valuate the enhancements, and **R**evisit the outcomes: Ensure that students can learn the material (Bulgren et al., 2007).

- Incorporate unit and lesson segments into organized graphic devices that students can readily understand.

(2) *Deliver direct instruction related to the various components of graphic unit and lesson organizers.*

- Explain the purpose of the organizer, and clarify actions that both students and teachers need to take to ensure successful learning.
- Focus on new vocabulary and the organization that links the elements of the content.
- Demonstrate graphically how content is organized, and relate to "big-picture" issues (Lenz et al., 2004).

(3) *Actively engage students in the continued use of the organizers.*

- Articulate cooperative teacher and student responsibilities when using the organizers.
- Cue components of organizers, demonstrating how they work with specific content, and regularly review effectiveness.
- Analyze student errors, and make adjustments in instruction.

Applications and Examples

Sample unit and lesson organizers are provided in Figures 14.4 and 14.5. The two examples represent how the unit, *Causes of the Civil War,* can be represented and how one lesson, *Economic Differences,* is organized. Pay particular attention to the many supports provided on the organizers. Specifically, the unit organizer shows how the current learning segment is related to previous and future units and graphically illustrates how elements of the unit are related. A schedule of activities is provided, and self-test questions related to the "big ideas" of the unit are prominently displayed. The lesson organizer reviews the big picture of the unit and provides a graphic representation of the content being presented, self-test questions, and lesson-related tasks.

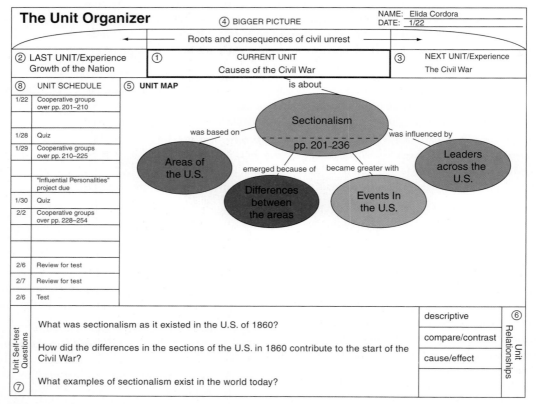

Figure 14.4

Unit Organizer

Source: Reprinted with permission from Bulgren, J., & Lenz, B. K. (1996). Strategic instruction in content areas. In D. D. Deshler, E. S. Ellis, & B. K. Lenz (Eds.), *Teaching adolescents with learning disabilities* (p. 437). Denver: Love. Copyright 1996 by Love Publishing Company.

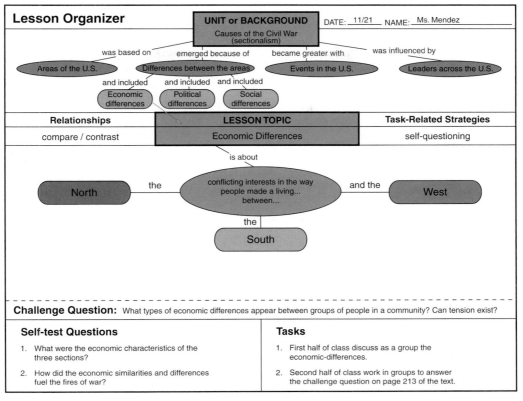

Figure 14.5

Lesson Organizer

Source: Reprinted with permission from Bulgren, J., & Lenz, B. K. (1996). Strategic instruction in content areas. In D. D. Deshler, E. S. Ellis, & B. K. Lenz (Eds.), *Teaching adolescents with learning disabilities* (p. 439). Denver: Love. Copyright 1996 by Love Publishing Company.

Keep in Mind

Unit and lesson organizers are excellent classroom applications of universal designs for learning. They are useful for most learners, as they correspondingly provide support for students with disabilities. For students with learning problems, however, it is important that elements of the organizers be taught to mastery. Without adequate explicit instruction and supervised practice, students may be confused by the interplay of the graphical supports and fail to use them.

Strategy 14.2

IMPROVING EXPOSITORY WRITING ACROSS CONTENT-AREA CLASSES

Rationale and Research

Expository writing is the primary way that secondary students communicate their conceptual understanding of subject-area content. In most content-area classes, students are expected to compose thoughtful, persuasive, and informational narratives that reflect their integration and synthesis of required content (Chalk, Hagan-Burke, & Burke, 2005). This type of writing is highly complex and demanding. To succeed, students must adhere to the mechanics of writing, as well as focus on organization, purpose, and communication of intent (Harris, Graham, & Mason, 2003). Unfortunately, many students with disabilities in content-area classes do not fully grasp the writing process and experience great difficulty when required to write narrative essays. Teachers of content-area classes likely will encounter students whose writing difficulties range from lower-order mechanical difficulties to higher-order organizational and conceptual problems. Fortunately, general and special education teachers can turn to a solid body of research that has improved the writing performance of students in content-area classes.

Key References

Chalk, J. C., Hagan-Burke, S., & Burke, M. D. (2005). The effects of self-regulated strategy development on the writing process for high school students with learning disabilities. *Learning Disability Quarterly, 28,* 75–87.

Ellis, E. S., & Colvert, G. (1996). Writing strategy instruction. In D. D. Deshler, E. S. Ellis, & B. K. Lenz (Eds.), *Teaching adolescents with learning disabilities* (pp. 127–207). Denver: Love.

Harris, K. R., Graham, S., & Mason, L. H. (2003). Self-regulated strategy development in the classroom: Part of a balanced approach to writing instruction for students with disabilities. *Focus on Exceptional Children, 35*(7), 1–16.

Monroe, B. W., & Troia, G. A. (2006). Teaching writing strategies to middle school students with disabilities. *The Journal of Educational Research, 100*(1), 21–33.

Schumaker, J. B., & Deshler, D. D. (2003). Can students with LD become competent writers? *Learning Disability Quarterly, 26,* 129–141.

Step-by-Step

1 *Have students develop an awareness of the writing process* by presenting the questions effective writers ask themselves when writing. Questions fall in three areas: prewriting, production, and reviewing (Ellis & Colvert, 1996).

- Prewriting
  - Who will read my work?
  - What is the reader's frame of reference?
  - Do I have enough information?
  - What is the theme of my effort, and what are the main ideas I want to express?
  - What details can I provide for each of the main ideas?
  - How can I best organize all of these details?
- Production
  - What more can I add to my effort?
  - Does each sentence make sense?
  - Does each sentence relate to the ones that precede and follow it?

- Reviewing
  - Did I tell the readers what I planned to tell them?
  - Are the paragraphs purposeful, coherent, and unified?
  - Is everything I wrote needed?
  - Did I fully convey my ideas?

2 *Directly teach students to be content-rich, strategic writers* by delivering Self-Regulated Strategy Development (SRSD) instruction (Harris et al., 2003):

- Step 1: Have students identify and generate the basic parts of an essay. Consider having students vocalize positive self-statements (e.g., "I can do this if I use a strategy") and practice the DARE mnemonic:
  - D—Develop topic sentence.
  - A—Add supporting detail.
  - R—Reject arguments from the other side.
  - E—End with a conclusion.

- Step 2: Discuss the writing strategy to be used, and set goals.
    i. Think, "Who will read this and why I am writing this?"
    ii. Plan what to say using DARE.
    iii. Write and say more. (Chalk et al., 2005)
- Step 3: Model the strategy using a think-aloud or self-instructional sequence.
- Step 4: Have students memorize the steps in the strategy.
- Step 5: Provide collaborative practice and support, shifting more of the writing and strategy use to the student.
- Step 6: Have students practice the strategy independently.

3 *Consider teaching a comprehensive writing strategy* such as DEFENDS to help students develop essays that stress a specific point of view (Ellis & Covert, 1996):

- **D**—Decide on goals and theme.
- **E**—Estimate main ideas and details.

- **F**—Figure best order of main ideas and details.
- **E**—Express the theme in the first sentence.
- **N**—Note each main idea and supporting points.
- **D**—Drive home the message in the last sentence.
- **S**—Search for errors and correct.
    - **S**—Set editing goals.
    - **E**—Examine essay to see of it makes sense.
    - **A**—Ask yourself if message is clear.
    - **R**—Reveal picky errors (capitalization, punctuation, etc.).
    - **C**—Copy over neatly.
    - **H**—Have a last look for errors.

Applications and Examples

Charts and tangible graphics are excellent ways of organizing expository writing. For secondary students who have to justify and support their ideas, a format that allows for structuring main and supportive ideas is useful for developing essay themes. A graphic tool adopted from Ellis and Covert (1996) is provided in Figure 14.6.

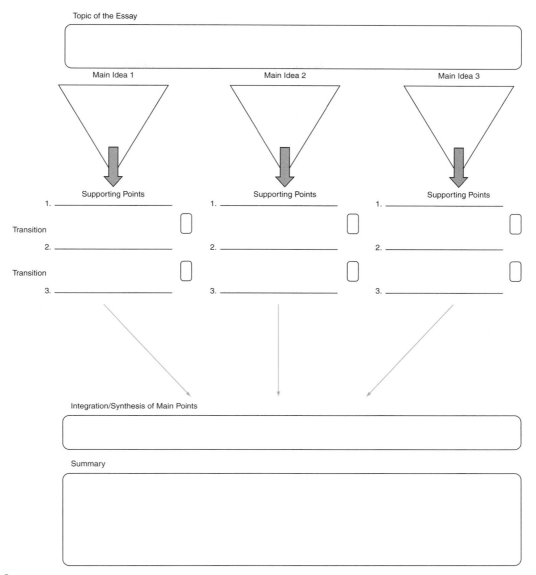

Figure 14.6

Essay Development Planning Tool

Source: Adapted from Ellis, E. S., & Covert G. (1996). Writing strategy instruction. In D. D. Deshler, E. S. Ellis, & B. K. Lenz (Eds.), *Teaching adolescents with learning disabilities* (pp. 127–207). Denver: Love.

Keep in Mind

When presenting writing strategies, it is imperative that students understand that it is a multiphased process that goes beyond just putting words to paper (or machine). Successful writers spend substantial amounts of time on structured prewriting activities such as planning, the gathering of source material, and content organization.

Strategy 14.3

MNEMONIC STRATEGIES

Rationale and Research

Remembering subject-area information and having ways of applying what one has learned are essential for success in school. Mnemonic strategies are procedures that enhance memory by forming associations that do not exist naturally in the content. Mnemonic techniques form associations by building meaningful connections to seemingly unconnected concepts by recoding, transforming, and elaborating on existing material (Hughes, 1996; Mastropieri, Sweda, & Scruggs, 2000). To readily retrieve the content, students need to be explicitly taught effective ways to input (or encode) information. Mnemonic instruction and materials have produced significant gains in content-area instruction for students with and without disabilities. Mnemonics are versatile techniques, easily implemented in secondary-content classes, and applicable to a wide range of subject-area curricula. They are not, however, a specific curricular approach, educational philosophy, or even a method of improving comprehension. Mnemonics simply help students remember things.

Key References

Hughes, C. A. (1996). Memory and test taking skills. In D. D. Deshler, E. S. Ellis, & B. K. Lenz (Eds.), *Teaching adolescents with learning disabilities* (pp. 209–266). Denver: Love.

Mastropieri, M. A., & Scruggs, T. E. (1998). Enhancing school success with mnemonic strategies. *Intervention in School and Clinic, 33*(4), 201–208.

Mastropieri, M. A., Sweda, J., & Scruggs, T. E. (2000). Putting mnemonic strategies to work in an inclusive classroom. *Learning Disabilities Research & Practice, 15*(2), 69–74.

Sabornie, E. J., & deBettencourt, L. (2009). *Teaching students with mild and high-incidence disabilities at the secondary level.* Upper Saddle River, NJ: Merrill/Pearson Education.

Step-by-Step

1 *Help students develop an understanding of mnemonics* by demonstrating how first-letter strategies help organize and retrieve information through the acronyms FIRST and LISTS (Hughes, 1996):

- FIRST is used to help design the mnemonic by:
  - F—Form a word.
  - I—Insert a letter.
  - R—Rearrange the letters.
  - S—Shape a sentence.
  - T—Try combinations.
  - Sample: HOMES = First letters of the Great Lakes (Huron, Ontario, Michigan, Erie, Superior)
- LISTS for making and designing lists:
  - L—Look for clues.
  - I—Investigate the items.
  - S—Select a mnemonic using FIRST.
  - T—Transfer information to a card.
  - S—Self-test.

2 *Demonstrate how keyword mnemonics enhance associations, making information to be learned meaningful:*

- Transform an unfamiliar concept to a word or phrase (keyword) that the student knows. For example, the keyword for barrister would be *bear*, represented in a picture of a bear acting as a lawyer (Mastropieri & Scruggs, 1998).
- Provide a strategy for and practice retrieval of the concept. When asked to define *barrister,* students should think of the picture of the keywords. This facilitates the association and assists in the retrieval of the definition.

3 *Promote generalization across subject areas* by teaching students to generate their own keywords using a specific strategy such as IT–FITS (King-Sears, Mercer, & Sindelar, 1992):

- I—Identify the term.
- T—Tell the definition of the term.
- F—Find a keyword.
- I—Imagine the term doing something with the keyword.

- T—Think about the term doing something with the keyword.
- S—Study what you imagine and think until you know the definition.

 4 *Actively teach independent mnemonic use:*

- Alert students as to the purpose of mnemonic strategies and how practice will improve academic performance.

- Model mnemonic use, and reinforce correct applications.
- Make explicit your thinking processes in developing and using the mnemonics; have students explain their own thinking when using the technique.
- Provide adequate opportunities for generalization across topics and subject areas.

Applications and Examples

Teachers have used keyword mnemonic instruction to help students with disabilities to learn SAT vocabulary words (Terrill, Scruggs, & Mastropieri, 2004). At the conclusion of a 6-week instructional period, students with learning disabilities learned 92% of the words taught with the mnemonic compared to only 49% of the words taught traditionally. Note how Terrill et al. (2004) connected vocabulary to keywords:

WORD	KEYWORD	MEANING	ILLUSTRATION
Abhor	Horrible	Regard with horror; hate deeply	A monster regarded with horror
Extant	Ant	Still existing	Ants continue to come to picnics over the years
Turbulent	Turtle	Violent, stormy	A turtle swimming through a violent storm

Keep in Mind

Like all instructional techniques, the effectiveness of mnemonic use should be monitored regularly. Specifically, mnemonics can be a time-consuming activity and the relative cost-effectiveness of the technique needs to be considered in terms of student outcomes. In some cases, the addition of keywords to an already burgeoning curriculum can frustrate students and actually detract from lessons and units. Also, several research efforts (e.g., King-Sears et al., 1992) indicate that teacher-provided keywords are more effective than requiring students to generate their own. With limited instructional time, decisions as to when to use mnemonics must be made judiciously, considering student characteristics and actual measures of performance.

Strategy 14.4

CONTENT-AREA READING

Rationale and Research

Large numbers of students with disabilities lack the reading skills to benefit fully from their subject-area textbooks (Gajria, Jitendra, Sood, & Sacks, 2007). A large part of secondary content instruction is textbook driven, and students are frequently required to use their textbooks in class and to complete their homework assignments. Textbooks across content areas have been simplified to adjust to students' lowered reading levels and short attention spans, and organizational features have been added to help students focus on essential content (Sabornie & deBettencourt, 2009). Still, many students with learning problems and disabilities fail to succeed with these resources. Teachers assist with content-area reading in a number of ways, including textbook exploration activities, intensive adaptation of vocabulary, structured comprehension strategies and study guides, as well as visual maps and think-alouds.

Key References

Conderman, G., & Elf, N. (2007). What's in this book? Engaging students through a textbook exploration activity. *Reading and Writing Quarterly, 23,* 111–116.

Gately, S. E. (2008). Facilitating reading comprehension for students on the autism spectrum. *Teaching Exceptional Children, 40*(3), 40–45.

Sabornie, E. J., & deBettencourt, L. U. (2009). *Teaching students with mild and high-incidence disabilities at the secondary level.* Upper Saddle River, NJ: Merrill/Pearson Education.

Steele, M. M. (2007). Teaching social studies to high school students with learning problems. *The Social Studies, 98*(2), 59–63.

Wood, J. W. (2001). *Adapting instruction to accommodate students in inclusive settings.* Upper Saddle River, NJ: Merrill/Pearson Education.

Step-by-Step

1 *Have students become acquainted with the critical features of their textbooks:*

- Explain the purpose of the text, and demonstrate how the organization of the text aligns with the sequence of course activities.
- Provide explicit instruction about specific features of the textbook including the table of contents, index, glossary, and organizational cues such as introductory overviews, paragraph headings, as well as specialized print and font alternatives.
- Demonstrate how content-related features such as charts, graphs, and other visuals augment narrative text.

2 *Provide enhanced support for new vocabulary:*

- Identify, list, and define all boldfaced and italicized words in assigned chapters.
- Provide students with lists, or word banks, of vocabulary words and their corresponding definitions. Schedule time for structured peer-based cooperative activities (e.g., flashcard practice) that promote understanding.

- Audio-record persistently difficult words and their definitions, and provide time for students to listen and apply them in practice activities.

3 *Teach structured comprehension strategies, and provide study guides:*

- Teach students to apply the learning strategy **SCROL** for increased success with their textbooks (Reid & Ortiz-Lienemann, 2006):
  - **S**—Survey: Review the headings of the assigned reading selection, and ask "What do I know about this topic?" and "What information will be presented?"
  - **C**—Connect: Determine how the headings in the chapter relate to each other.
  - **R**—Read: Read the headings, and attend to boldfaced or italicized words and phrases.
  - **O**—Outline: Record the headings, and outline the major ideas and supporting details without looking back at the text.
  - **L**—Look-Back: Review the text, and then check and correct outlines.

- Provide study guides to clarify text material.
  - Effective study guides can include succinct summaries of the content, graphic organizers representing relationships among sections of the reading selection, definitions of difficult vocabulary, and key questions.
  - Explain the importance of study guides, model effective use, and provide immediate assistance to students if and when required.

④ *Supplement text material with visual maps and think-aloud activities (Gately, 2008):*

- Prepare "story" maps that reflect the content of the reading selection.

- Ensure that story maps contain adequate background information as well as the actions and events currently being taught.
- Use arrows to reflect the direction of actions occurring in the reading selection.
- Have students think aloud, or talk through, the content presented on the visual map.
- Ask questions to ensure that students understand the content and the relationship among critical concepts presented in the reading selection.

Applications and Examples

Conderman and Elf (2007) developed an exploration activity for students to discover clues for using their social studies textbook. The activity, "A History Mystery," prompts students to access the basic and specialized features of the textbook. First, students must identify the name and author(s) of the text. Second, students find their way around the book by identifying the number of chapters and reviewing how features of the text (e.g., advance organizers, glossary, index, and different-colored text) help facilitate information collection and assignment completion. Most important, the activity provides frequent opportunities for students to practice application of the text's features, either independently or in cooperative workgroups.

Keep in Mind

Constructing effective content reading accommodations can be difficult and time-consuming. However, with secondary-content instruction in science, history, and math using text material on a daily basis, we recommend that teachers allocate sufficient time for these essential activities. Remember to save hard and electronic copies of all of your text adaptations, because you can likely apply them with other groups of students.

Strategy 14.5

DEVELOPING AND SUPPORTING NOTE TAKING

Rationale and Research

The ability to take notes in content-area classes requires students to coordinate a number of complex skills and cognitive processes including listening, auditory discrimination, short-term memory, prioritizing, and transcribing for later use. Moreover, when making use of their notes, students need to recollect what they represent about the important content of the lesson. The ability to take notes is critical in secondary-content classes. Several studies have found that active independent note taking results in increased class participation, improved recall of information, and higher rates of achievement. Unfortunately, many students with learning problems and disabilities do not take notes or rely on others (e.g., peers and teachers) to take notes for them or to provide them with preexisting "canned" products. Teachers promote and support independent note taking by providing accommodations, adapting their instructional delivery, and directly teaching note-taking techniques and comprehensive mnemonic strategies.

Key References

Suritsky, S., & Hughes, C. A. (1996). Notetaking strategy instruction. In D. D. Deshler, E. S. Ellis, & B. K. Lenz (Eds.), *Teaching adolescents with learning disabilities* (pp. 267–312). Denver: Love.

Boyle, J. R. (2007). The process of note taking: Implications for students with mild disabilities. *The Clearing House, 80*(5), 227–230.

Boyle, J. R., & Weishaar, M. (2001). The effects of strategic notetaking of the recall and comprehension of lecture information for high school students with learning disabilities. *Learning Disabilities Research and Practice, 16*, 133–141.

Lazarus, B. (1993). Guided notes: Effects on secondary and post secondary students with mild disabilities. *Education and Treatment of Children, 16*, 272–289.

Step-by-Step

(1) *Provide within-lesson adaptations and accommodations for note taking:*

- Decrease the speed of presentations and inject pauses during logical breaks in lessons.
- Integrate verbal prompts, cues, and questions that signal the need for note taking.
- Supplement presentations with user-friendly visual aids such as charts, tables, and handouts.
- Provide detailed outlines that (a) contain an advance organizer for note taking, (b) help students identify key information in the presentation, and (c) result in products for future use.

(2) *Directly teach students components of effective note taking:*

- Highlight note-taking preparation strategies such as securing a seat with a good view of the teacher, reviewing previous days' notes on the topic, identifying unfamiliar vocabulary, and having all necessary materials (e.g., paper, pencil).

- Demonstrate specific "in-lecture" note-taking skills such as (a) recognizing cues that signal important information; (b) using a personalized system of abbreviations; (c) selecting user-friendly frameworks for organizing and recording notes; and (d) paraphrasing critical information summaries.
- Model and provide practice in post-presentation activities such as reviewing, editing, and studying notes.

(3) *Provide intensive instruction in a comprehensive note-taking strategy:*

- The LINKS strategy (Suritsky & Hughes, 1996), provides students with instruction in specific note taking steps and practice activities:
  - L—Listen
  - I—Identify verbal cues
  - N—Note
  - K—Key words
  - S—Stack information in outline form

- The AWARE strategy (Suritsky & Hughes, 1996), teaches students note-taking skills needed before, during, and after the content presentations:
- A—Arrange to take notes by
  i. Arriving early
  ii. Taking seat front and center
  iii. Having materials
  iv. Noting date
- W—Write quickly, making sure to
  i. Indent minor points
  ii. Record some words without vowels
  iii. Abbreviate whenever possible
- A—Apply cues by
  i. Attending to all verbal cues
  ii. Recording cued lecture points
  iii. Accentuating cued material
- R—Review notes as soon as possible
- E—Edit notes, remembering to
  i. Add information not recorded
  ii. Add personal details

Applications and Examples

Figure 14.7 contains a sample strategic note-taking form. Pay particular attention to how the form focuses student thinking about the content as well as providing a structure to organize, use, and develop questions about the information.

Keep in Mind

Teaching and supporting note taking are appropriate instructional activities for most inclusive content-area classes. Some students with disabilities, however, will need additional practice to attain competence. One way of providing additional opportunities is to have small groups of students practice the various steps cooperatively, supplemented with teacher guidance and feedback.

Preclass Information

    Class or Lecture Topic: _____

    What Do You Know About Topic? _____

_____

_____

_____

During Class

    Put Class/Lecture Notes Here:

_____

_____

_____

_____

_____

_____

    List New Vocabulary Here:

_____

_____

_____

    List Questions and Things You Are Unsure of Here:

_____

_____

_____

After Class

    Write three to five main points of the lecture here:

_____

_____

_____

_____

    Identify areas in need of more information here:

_____

_____

_____

Figure 14.7

Strategic Note-Taking Activity Form

Source: Adapted from Weishaar, M. K., & Boyle, J. R. (1999). Note-taking strategies for students with disabilities. *The Clearing House, 72*(6), 392–395.

Strategy 14.6

DEVELOPING EFFECTIVE TEST TAKING

Rationale and Research

As students with disabilities participate in secondary-content classes, they will also be subject to rigorous performance assessments. Unfortunately, a large proportion of students with disabilities lack adequate test-taking skills and strategies. Several options are available for teachers to ensure that student test performance reflects true understanding of the material. First, teachers can provide test modifications and accommodations. Second, teachers can directly teach specific test-taking skills or a comprehensive test-taking strategy. Research has demonstrated that the teaching of techniques and strategies can raise scores on various types of classroom and school-based assessments.

Key References

Carter, E. W., Wehby, J., Hughes, C., Johnson, S. M., Plank, D., Barton-Arwood, S., & Lunsford, L. (2005). Preparing adolescents with high incidence disabilities for high stakes testing with strategy instruction. *Preventing School Failure, 49,* 55–62.

Hong, E., Sas, M., & Sas, J. C. (2006). Test-taking strategies of high and low math achievers. *Journal of Educational Research, 99,* 144–155.

Hughes, C. A. (1996). Memory and test taking skills. In D. D. Deshler, E. S. Ellis, & B. K. Lenz (Eds.), *Teaching adolescents with learning disabilities* (pp. 209–266). Denver: Love.

Thurlow, M. L., Elliott, J. L., & Ysseldyke, J. E. (2003). *Testing students with disabilities* (2nd ed.). Thousand Oaks, CA: Corwin.

Step-by-Step

(1) *Use a range of accommodations when assessing content-area knowledge and performance:*

- Setting accommodations: Change the location or environmental conditions of the assessment.
- Timing accommodations: Allow more time for the test, or alter how the time is organized.
- Scheduling accommodations: Change when the test occurs and how it is administered.
- Response accommodations: Change the format of how the student responds to items, and allow for use of assistive devices when appropriate.

(2) *Directly teach students to be "test-wise" when being assessed:*

- Demonstrate how to eliminate absurd and similar options on multiple-choice tests.

- Illustrate how absolute words such as *always* and *never* are options to be avoided on multiple-choice tests.
- Emphasize the importance of reading all instructions carefully and managing time during test situations.
- Illustrate how to make the immediate test environment conducive for success (arranging furniture, organizing workspace, aligning numbers on test with answer or bubble sheet, etc.).

(3) *Provide intensive instruction in comprehensive test-taking packages such as the ANSWER strategy for essay tests (described next).*

Applications and Examples

The ANSWER strategy (Hughes, 1996), a mnemonic systematic way of approaching essay items, uses the following steps and substeps:

A—Analyze the situation.
- Read the question carefully.
- Underline key words.
- Gauge the time you need.

N—Notice requirements.
- Scan for and mark the parts of the question.
- Ask and say what is required.
- Tell yourself you will write a quality answer.

S—Set up an outline.
- Set up main ideas.
- Assess whether they match the question.
- Make changes if necessary.

W—Work in details.
- Remember what you learned.
- Add details to the main ideas using abbreviations.
- Indicate order.
- Decide if you are ready to write.

E—Engineer your answer.
- Write an introductory paragraph.
- Refer to your outline.
- Include topic sentences.
- Tell about details for each topic sentence.
- Employ examples.

R—Review your answer.
- Look to see if you answered all parts of the question.
- Inspect to see if you included all main ideas and details.
- Touch up your answer.

Keep in Mind

A student's performance on content-area assessments is a function of what he has learned as well as how skillful or "test-wise" he is in navigating the test-taking process. One way to obtain an accurate measure of student knowledge in content-area classrooms is by providing test accommodations. Although the provision of accommodations during tests is believed to "level the playing field" for students with disabilities, teachers should carefully consider which accommodations are acceptable and appropriate for individual students. When teaching test-wise techniques or comprehensive test-taking strategies, it is not enough to merely present the mnemonic steps. Students who need test-taking strategies require explicit instruction, models of effective application, and ample opportunities to practice the process.

Effective Practices for All Students: Classroom Management

KEY TOPICS

After reading this chapter you will:

- Know the range of student behaviors (and misbehaviors) typical of most classrooms.
- Possess core readiness strategies that contribute to successful classroom management.
- Be able to apply "tiered" behavior management, a sequential system that
  - Addresses universal management concerns for most students
  - Makes use of functional behavioral assessments to develop individualized behavior intervention plans
- Employs a continuum of targeted interventions and wraparound supports for those students who do not respond to the universal management system
- Possess a series of guided step-by-step effective practices for the prevention and reduction of challenging student behavior.

chapter 15

Perspectives on Classroom Management

Interview with Eileen Walls, Behavior Specialist, West Hernando Middle School

At West Hernando Middle School, students manage their behavior by using their WINGS. WINGS is an acronym that refers to the school-wide expectations that form the core of the school's structured-management (or tiered-management) program. Students are required to (a) make *Wise* choices; (b) engage in *Innovative* learning; (c) accept *New* challenges; (d) engage in *Good* citizenship; and (e) demonstrate *Strong* positive behavior. According to Eileen Walls, the behavior specialist at West Hernando, "All teachers, at the beginning of the year, are charged with explaining what constitutes using one's WINGS. Each of the WINGS expectations is operationally defined and modeled so students know what specific classroom behaviors the teachers are looking for to reinforce." Teachers post the WINGS acronym in every classroom and hallway, as well as in the gym and cafeteria. Teachers also use it as a streamlined method for verbally reminding students to behave appropriately.

The WINGS program is an application of positive behavior supports (PBSs). Students are provided positive consequences when they choose to meet the behavioral expectations. In addition to receiving positive attention from adults, students who earn a set number of positive bookmarks—the tangible method of recording appropriate student behavior—can attend a kid-friendly movie with popcorn and a drink.

For students who have difficulty meeting the WINGS standards, teachers provide supports and reminders designed to redirect behavior. For those who continue to be inappropriate, teachers use a hierarchy of negative consequences to decrease future occurrences of specific misbehaviors. These negative consequences include brief lunch detentions, in-school time-out and suspension, and after-school detention. Each of these negative consequences provides opportunities to teach students replacement behaviors—alternative ways of addressing their behavioral needs—in socially and school-appropriate ways. Teachers provide a range of supports and interventions before removing any student from the learning environment. Like most PBS systems, the great majority of students at West Hernando respond positively to WINGS. A second tier of interventions is available for those students whose extreme and persistent patterns of misbehavior require specialized supports and interventions.

According to Ms. Walls, WINGS works because everyone in the school is involved in its implementation. "Everyone—paraeducators, custodians, front office staff, teachers, and administrators—is committed to the system and expects WINGS behavior from students." The initial data on this comprehensive behavior management system have been impressive. West Hernando has the lowest rate of discipline referrals and suspensions than any other middle school in the county. Ms. Walls credits the PBS team and its reliance on data-based decision making for these impressive outcomes. The team meets regularly, reviews the discipline data, and proposes changes as necessary. The team addresses problem areas and regularly provides staff members with updated booster sessions in classroom management techniques.

Introduction

Consider this nightmare experienced, in one form or another, by many beginning teachers (and even some veteran educators): It is the first day of school, and the first-period, sixth-grade language arts class is filing into the classroom. Rather than any semblance of order, most of the 27 students, nine with identified disabilities, run into the room and upset the neatly arranged materials prepared for distribution on your desk. When the students reach their seats, two of the tallest young men refuse to remove their headgear, claiming that they belong to a strict religious order forbidding the exposure of an uncovered scalp. When you distribute the course overview, two girls in the back of the room crumple up the papers and throw them across the room, claiming that they don't care about the work. After you've spent 10 minutes trying to restore order, three students move to the back of the room and seem to be throwing the handouts, now paper airplanes, out the window. The two boys with headgear issues are trying to sneak out the back door. To cap off this nightmare, the principal is at the front door inquiring about your willingness to accommodate the special needs of a new student with a severe attention-deficit disorder.

Rarely do nightmares like this approximate the behavior in actual classrooms. Still, levels of concern and anxiety about classroom management among teachers, particularly those new to the field, are quite high. This anxiety is not surprising, because the ability to manage student behavior is a clear marker of teaching success: Effective discipline, classroom control, and organizational skills are associated with positive student outcomes and increased teacher ratings. Conversely, one of the main reasons beginning teachers leave the field is poor or inadequate discipline in the classroom (Kauchak & Eggen, 2005; Vittetoe, 1997).

What types of behaviors do teachers in inclusive settings encounter? How do they manage simultaneously the range of generic problem behaviors typical of most developing students as well as the more intensive challenging behaviors exhibited by others with behaviorally involved disabilities (i.e., attention deficits, emotional and behavioral disabilities)? Many teachers, like those on the faculty of West Hernando Middle School and Heritage High School, actively address the behavior of all of their students by adopting an approach to discipline that is *systematic*, *proactive*, *supportive*, and *responsive*.

As noted by Eileen Walls in the "Perspectives" interview, being *systematic* means that effective discipline is much more than having a "bag of tricks." As we discuss later in this chapter, management is a tiered and sequential process that requires careful and logistical thinking about all school and classroom activities and events (Sprague & Walker, 2005). Being *proactive* means taking carefully considered actions (e.g., adjusting the traffic flow in hallways and the cafeteria, making use of specific transition cues) that minimize and often prevent the occurrence of problem behaviors. Being *supportive* refers to the range of positive teacher attitudes that drive successful behavior management activities. As Susan Hill, the Dean of Students at Heritage High School knows, successful classroom teachers convey genuine concern for students by (1) having periodic private interactions that reflect a desire to know and understand students individually; (2) employing verbal and nonverbal communication techniques that indicate civility, respect, and patience; and (3) willingly making adjustments that assist students in meeting behavioral expectations. Finally, being *responsive* refers to teachers providing positive recognition for students who behave as expected and a willingness to try a variety of interventions to redirect problem behaviors when they occur.

Student Behavior: What to Expect

A broad consensus exists as to what constitutes appropriate student behavior. Most teachers believe that self-control and cooperation skills minimize disruption and foster the self-discipline necessary for academic success (Lane, Givner, & Pierson, 2004). Consequently, similar to many teachers in our featured schools, you will want students to (a) comply in an appropriate fashion to teacher requests and academic tasks;

Pause & Reflect

What student behaviors do you believe are essential for success in the classroom? How would you convey your expectations to students?

(b) have impulse control; (c) deal with problems, anger, and negative feedback in developmentally appropriate ways; (d) be cooperative and courteous with peers; (e) stay attentive, involved, and productive during classroom activities; and (f) follow rules, recognizing that the contexts for different types of behaviors (Trenholm & Rose, 1981; Walker, 1995).

Obviously, you will not always experience these desired behaviors, and it is the teacher's job to address and redirect misbehavior. What types of discipline issues do educators typically encounter? The popular media would have us believe that most misbehaviors faced by teachers are severe—aggression, theft, and vandalism. Fortunately, this is not accurate. As is the case in our three featured schools, most school and classroom misbehavior is related to inattention to task, crowd-control issues during transitions, getting work accomplished in a timely fashion, and students acting "cool" by creatively testing limits. Specifically, the most common misbehaviors exhibited by students include tardiness, being unprepared, not attending, talking, calling out, and mild forms of verbal and physical aggression (Doyle, 1986; Kulinna, Cothran, & Regualos, 2006). Some students may even swear, run in the hallway, tell off-color jokes, and show arrogance toward and disrespect for peers and

adults. As we will discuss later, teachers can prevent many of these behaviors through proactive structuring of the school and classroom environment. Misbehaviors that are not preempted typically stop when they are brought to the attention of teachers, administrators, and/or parents.

Some students, however, exceed these mild forms of challenging behavior and repeatedly disrupt the flow of school and classroom events. Others respond defiantly when asked to participate appropriately in activities and hurt others both physically and emotionally when frustrated. The number of such students and the frequency of their behaviors often vary according to the levels of structure and consistency in specific schools and individual classrooms. Still, even in the most positive and structured schools and classrooms, you will encounter students who, for any number of reasons,

pose challenges because of their behavior. These students stand out from other students because of their *significant behavioral excesses* and *behavioral deficits*. Not surprisingly, many require supports that go beyond typical practice and could require individualized services outside the general education classroom.

When we speak of *significant behavioral excesses*, we are referring to behaviors that, because of their high rate, frequency, duration, or intensity, interfere with opportunities to achieve academic success and/or social competence. For example, consider the student who spends far too much time out of his seat or argues vehemently and relentlessly when being directed by a teacher. *Significant*

When it comes to classroom discipline, most teachers desire cooperative students who comply with teacher requests, have impulse control, and stay attentive, involved, and productive during classroom activities.

behavioral deficits refer to specific behaviors and actions students lack that are required for academic and social competence. For example, it is not unusual for teachers to note that several of their students lack appropriate social skills. Significant numbers of students with behavioral deficits in social skills simply don't know, or have not been taught, how to behave in certain situations; others may have acquired the skills but do not perform them at acceptable levels. When encountering students with persistent challenging behaviors, you will likely conclude that most troubling patterns of misbehavior are a dynamic combination of behavioral excesses and deficits.

Behavior Management Readiness

Pause & Reflect

Successful behavior management requires considerable planning and preparation. What steps would you take to get your classroom "management ready" before the arrival of your students?

Successful teachers' behavior management efforts begin long before students enter the classroom. Like the preparation efforts of a professional athlete or master craftsman, preparation of the work environment, organization of equipment, and mental self-preparation for the task at hand require considerable attention of the teacher. Specific critical areas of concern for teachers are (1) classroom organization; (2) effective instruction; and (3) creating a climate of care and respect.

Classroom Organization

Regardless of the subject area being taught or the age of the students, most classrooms are busy, energetic places that have a variety of instructional and noninstructional events occurring simultaneously for all students. For example, consider biology class at Heritage High School. During the fifth period, Gina Craun directs an active, hands-on laboratory class to 22 students who require intensive instruction if they are to meet the state's standards of learning. Eight of the students are conducting independent laboratory experiments. The remaining 14, having completed the experiments, are writing up their results. Six of these students have identified individualized education program (IEP) goals related to written expression. Denise Pohill, the special education teacher, therefore provides them additional supports and accommodations. At the rear of the room, a one-to-one instructional assistant from the "school within the school" program for students with behavioral needs monitors a student as he completes independent seat work.

Successful behavior management requires considerable planning and preparation before the arrival of students.

If you were to review a slow-motion video of a typical day in that classroom (or most other classrooms), you would see with pinpoint clarity how successful teachers recognize and address organizational pressures (see Table 15.1 for listing and definitions). Consider the following preventative practices that help address these ever-present demands:

- Arrange the physical environment.
- Value instructional time.
- Be prepared.
- Coordinate resources.

Arranging the Physical Environment. Successful behavior managers make effective use of the physical dimensions of their room, and arrange furniture and materials for accessibility, instructional effectiveness, appropriate social interactions, and safety. How teachers actually design

Table 15.1   Organizational Pressures of Classrooms

Organizational Pressure	Definition
Immediacy	Many events require immediate attention or action.
Publicness	Teacher is always on stage.
Multidimensionality	Classrooms are crowded and busy places in which limited resources are used to achieve a wide range of goals.
Unpredictability	Events in classrooms change daily, and many occurrences are difficult to predict.
History	Events that occur early in the school year set the tone for later happenings.
Simultaneity	Many things happen at the same time in classrooms.

Adapted from Doyle, W. (1980). *Classroom management*. West Lafayette, IN: Kappa Delta Pi.

the classroom varies as a function of (1) layout and location; (2) age, number, and behavioral profiles of the students; and (3) levels of supports required by students with disabilities (Paine, Radicci, Rosellini, Deutchman, & Darch, 1983; Rosenberg et al., 2006).

Valuing Instructional Time. Effective behavior management is contingent on treating instructional time as a valuable resource and, correspondingly, maximizing opportunities for teaching and learning. Specific strategies include (1) highlighting policies that encourage and reinforce attendance and punctuality; (2) ensuring that adequate time is devoted (and actually delivered) to task-relevant activities; and (3) conducting transitions between and among activities efficiently with little disruption.

Being Prepared. Teachers who are prepared have organized and easy-to-follow lesson plans, start lessons promptly, have materials close by, and keep to a consistent schedule. This preparation allows teachers to focus their efforts exclusively on the instructional and behavioral flow of their lessons.

Coordinating Resources. Effective behavior managers address the immediacy and connectivity of classroom events by developing time-saving organizational resources. Several of the more useful resources include (1) an IEP-monitoring procedure that promotes instructional support and accountability; (2) a substitute teacher packet that highlights the essential information one would need to teach and manage the class during short-term absences; and (3) a readily available resource guide of school and community services that can address critical needs presented by students and their families.

Effective Instruction

A major prerequisite for the success of any behavior management plan is the delivery of accessible and motivating instruction. Regardless of how interesting or topical a lesson might be, a precursor to disruptive behavior is student inability to understand academic content and frustration with the ways it is often presented. Rather than being perceived as being "dumb," some students, particularly those who have experienced repeated academic failure, find it easier to act up or be the class clown. During later interactions with peers, these

Pause & Reflect

Consider the relationship between instruction and student behavior. How can instruction that lacks supports and accommodations contribute to the disruptive behavior of students with learning problems and disabilities?

inappropriate behaviors are easier to explain than the lack of integration or problem-solving skills. Clearly, instructional supports and accommodations within the context of interesting, motivating lessons (e.g., those highlighted in Chapters 13 and 14) can reduce the frequency and intensity of disruptive behaviors.

A Climate of Care and Respect

Many of the guidelines for effective behavior management presented thus far are methodical, scientifically validated, systematic procedures applied in a seemingly mechanistic step-by-step fashion. Recognize, however, that these technical aspects of classroom discipline are only part of the process—clearly necessary, but not sufficient. The success of behavior management techniques is also contingent on the ways in which teachers communicate with their students. Similar to instruction, teachers deliver behavior management through a series of person-to-person interactions that involve a number of intangible (i.e., difficult to operationalize) dispositions, behaviors, and personal qualities (Rosenberg et al., 2006).

Behavior management efforts are enhanced when an authentic positive relationship exists between teacher and student.

Authentic Relationships. Most interpersonal relationships are built on trust and require adequate time to develop. Solid relationships between teachers and students typically grow from a foundation of brief contacts and interactions, such as greeting students at the start of the day and taking special interests in their interests and personal lives. Relationships evolve when teachers present themselves in engaging and appealing ways, revealing that they are considerate, ethical, friendly, enthusiastic, and caring. Helpfulness is a characteristic that most students value, particularly those who require additional academic and behavioral supports. Teachers demonstrate helpfulness by (1) highlighting the collaborative nature of classrooms; (2) emphasizing trust between themselves and students; (3) promoting positive and productive communication; and (4) teaching self-control strategies that help students take responsibility for their behaviors (Charles, 2002; Koenig, 2000).

Civility and Respect. *Civility* means being cognizant that our behaviors have consequences for others and anticipating what those consequences may be (Forni, 2002). *Respect* refers to the basic human right to be acknowledged and treated with dignity (Rosenberg et al., 2008). Teachers model civility and respect by (1) communicating through body language and a vocal tone that reflects support, patience, and understanding; (2) listening actively to students with appropriate eye contact; (3) having private interactions with students that reflect a genuine interest in their opinions, concerns, and well-being; and (4) communicating appropriate, positive expectations for student performance and behavior (Kauffman, Mostert, Trent, & Hallahan, 2002; Rosenberg et al., 2006; Thorson, 1996).

Pause & Reflect

Many believe that levels of civility and respect are decreasing among young people. How can educators demonstrate the importance of these behaviors in positive and nonpunitive ways?

Culturally Responsive Practices. Teachers communicate care and respect for all students by adhering to culturally responsive instructional and behavior management practices. These practices are built on the assumptions that one's culture influences perceptions and knowledge and aspects of that culture manifest themselves, directly and indirectly, during teacher–student interactions. Successful teachers maintain a healthy curiosity about cultural differences and are introspective about how their typical practices affect those from differing backgrounds. Keep in mind that this awareness and analysis are not excuses for student failure. Culturally responsive teachers believe they can help every student achieve and do so by reducing judgmental attitudes and reactions of those who struggle in school and highlighting examples of diverse students who succeed in school despite experiencing poverty, language differences, and/or disabilities (Ross, Kamman, & Coady, 2008).

Addressing Student Behavior: Tiered Management

As we noted earlier, successful behavior management in inclusive schools and classrooms requires the use of a systematic, tiered system of behavior management (Dwyer & Osher, 2000; Lewis & Sugai, 1999; Rosenberg & Jackman, 2003). Tiered systems (see Figure 15.1) allow educators to address the behavioral needs of all students by addressing universal, inclusive management concerns typical of most students and by using a continuum of individualized planning and interventions for those students who do not readily respond to elements of the universal management system.

Pause & Reflect

Why is it important to begin tiered management efforts at the universal level? Why not focus initial efforts on the most intensive interventions for students who are misbehaving?

In the first tier, often referred to as *universal inclusive practices and supports*, teachers emphasize classroom policies and processes (e.g., mission statements, rules, procedures, consequences for appropriate and inappropriate behaviors, crisis procedures, etc.). Approximately 80% to 85% of students respond positively to these universal practices. The second tier of interventions is for the 5% to 15% of students whose extreme, frequent, persistent patterns of misbehavior require targeted or specialized supports and interventions (Hawken & Horner, 2003). These targeted interventions are typically powerful, focused, school-based efforts designed to reduce frequent and intensive problem behaviors. Wraparound interventions are more intensive and extensive, involving the integrated efforts of a multidisciplinary team of professionals from both within and outside the school (Eber, Sugai, Smith, & Scott, 2002).

Universal Inclusive Practices and Supports

At the core of effective universal practices is a comprehensive management plan, an explicit representation of behavioral expectations and what happens when students either comply to or violate the standards. Generally, five core elements are included in successful plans: (1) mission statement, or statement of purpose; (2) rules, procedures, and behavioral supports; (3) surface management and consequences; (4) crisis considerations; and (5) documentation that makes the plan accessible to students, families, and colleagues (e.g., Curwin & Mendler, 1999; Lewis & Sugai, 1999; Nelson, 1996; Rosenberg & Jackman, 2003; Simonsen et al., 2008; Walker, Colvin, & Ramsey, 1995).

Mission Statement, or Statement of Purpose. A mission statement, or statement of purpose, is a brief declaration that represents your approach to teaching and learning with a particular emphasis on expected school and classroom behavior. Effective statements seek to inspire, have a positive focus, and reflect a respect for the dignity of all students and a commitment to helping students perform to their highest level (White, 1996).

Rules, Procedures, and Behavioral Supports. Rules and procedures communicate behavioral standards and expectations. Rules define acceptable behavior; procedures delineate the steps required for the successful completion of a task, activity, or operation. Well-articulated rules and procedures are particularly important for students who need explicit supports. Rules and procedures serve as discriminative stimuli and overt guides; teachers can use them to prompt and cue students throughout their daily multitasking. Rules and procedures also serve as specific behavioral targets that effective teachers reinforce with attention and praise.

Methods for developing and maintaining rules and procedures are presented in Strategy 15.1.

Strategy

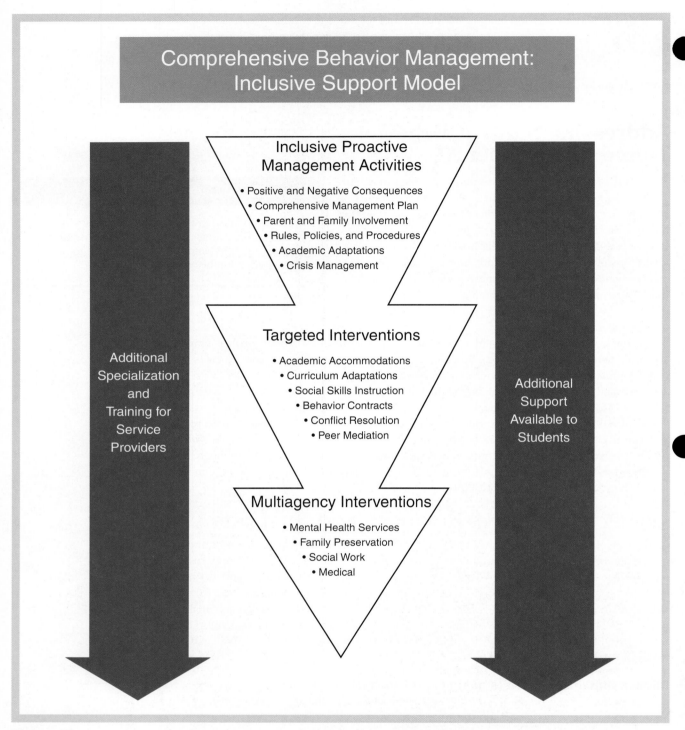

Figure 15.1

Comprehensive Behavior Management: Levels of Intervention and Inclusive Support Model

Sources: Adapted from Nelson, 1996; Rosenberg & Jackman, 1997; and Walker et al., 1996.

Reprinted with permission from Rosenberg, M. S., & Jackman, L. A. (2003). Development, implementation, and sustainability of comprehensive school-wide behavior management systems. *Intervention in School and Clinic, 39*(1), p. 13.

Surface Management and Consequences.

Rather than being authoritative and coercive, effective teachers structure their behavior management systems so students recognize that it is *their* choice to either comply or not comply with the stated expectations. As you can imagine, the way in which teachers respond to student choices has an enormous impact on subsequent student behavior. Typically, teacher responses to student behavior fall into three major categories: surface management techniques, consequences for rule and procedure compliance, and consequences for noncompliance.

Surface management techniques are the range of commonsense measures that address minor instances of misbehavior quickly, efficiently, and for the most part, with little disruption of ongoing instruction. Although the names for these techniques may seem novel and unusual, in action, they are clearly familiar. Generations of educators have been using surface management techniques, often in an automatic, intuitive fashion.

A major component of successful behavior management is having routines and procedures that guide students through school and classroom activities.

Consequences are teacher-initiated verbalizations and actions that follow students' behaviors, both appropriate and inappropriate. When employing consequences, it is important to consider their impact. For a consequence to be effective, student behavior must change. Teachers use positive consequences to increase levels of appropriate behavior and use negative consequences to reduce the frequency and intensity of troublesome inappropriate behaviors.

Unfortunately, some consequences, particularly those applied to student misbehavior, are delivered in anger and frustration, with little thought given to their influence on students' behaviors. One way to avoid this scenario is to apply consequences in an educative rather than vindictive fashion. Clearly, some classroom behaviors can get us angry, and instead of presenting consequences in a thoughtful manner, we may deliver them in a vengeful, almost menacing fashion. To minimize these situations, it is important to attend to our own feelings regularly and keep frustration and resentment in check (Curwin & Mendler, 1999).

Crisis Considerations. Fortunately, in most schools, crisis situations—instances when students present extreme physical and emotional behaviors responses—are rare. However, it is important for teachers to know what to do if and when such actions occur. The most challenging aspect of a crisis is that the student appears to have little or no control over the behavior, and management techniques and consequences designed to reduce problem behavior have little or no effect.

During the crisis, the primary task is to assist the student through the crisis in a safe, nonthreatening, and nonpunitive fashion as we maintain the safety of others in the immediate environment. The recommended course of action for schools is to develop crisis-response teams of four to five people who are trained in both verbal intervention techniques and safe, nonaversive methods of physical restraint (Johns & Carr, 1995). Other adults in the school are instructed in decision rules to determine if the team is to be called in as well as the code for accessing the team. However, when faced with a crisis, teachers should

1. Remain calm, remove dangerous items from the area, and send someone for assistance.
2. Avoid body language and verbalizations that escalate situations.
3. Instruct other students to vacate the crisis area.
4. Plan for the student in crisis to reenter class after the crisis (Albert, 2003; Johns & Carr, 1995; Jones & Jones, 2004).

> **Surface management techniques are presented in Strategy 15.2.**
>
> Strategy

Pause & Reflect

Why is it important that consequences, particularly those directed to inappropriate behavior, be delivered in an educative rather than vindictive fashion? What strategies can be used to help during these often stressful situations?

> **Developing consequences and delivering them with consistency are presented in Strategy 15.3.**
>
> Strategy

> **Methods for defusing confrontations and responding to dangerous behaviors are presented in Strategy 15.4.**
>
> Strategy

Although extreme physical and emotional student behaviors are rare, it is essential that teachers know what to do if such crisis situations occur.

Documentation for Access. Once you have developed the components of your comprehensive behavior management plan, it is essential to share it with students, their families, administrators, and related-service providers. Some school-wide teams and individual teachers create full-sized manuals that articulate the major components (mission statement, rules, procedures, consequences) of the management plan (see Dwyer & Osher, 2000; Jones & Jones, 2004; Rosenberg et al., 2006; Walker, Colvin, & Ramsey, 1995). Other schools develop user-friendly brochures and Web pages that highlight the major components of the plan. Figure 15.2 illustrates a sample brochure. Regardless of the format you choose, use of a summary checklist, such as shown in Figure 15.3, can ensure that your behavior plan presents the essential components in the correct manner.

Targeted Interventions

Even with the best planning and implementation of a well-conceived comprehensive management plan, some students (approximately 10% to 15% of the student population), with and without disabilities, will require additional school-based behavioral supports and accommodations. Targeted interventions are intensive actions directed toward chronic, repetitive, and pervasive problem behaviors presented by these students. Typically, the design of individualized targeted interventions involves completing a functional behavioral assessment (FBA) (described in the next section) and using the results to develop an individual plan of action. However, before engaging in the labor-intensive process of an FBA, it is often useful to engage in function-based thinking (FBT) and implement certain resource-efficient generic target interventions that researchers have found reduce a range of disruptive classroom behaviors (Hawken & Horner, 2003; Lewis, Sugai, & Colvin, 1998; Park, 2007). FBT and two interventions (check-in, connect, check-out systems and behavioral contracting) are detailed in Strategies 15.5 and 15.6.

> **Strategy**
>
> Strategies 15.5 and 15.6 present two targeted interventions: check-in, connect, check-out systems and behavioral contracting.

Functional Behavioral Assessment

For those students who do not respond to generic targeted interventions, teachers should conduct an FBA. The FBA is a powerful problem-solving process that identifies the function or purpose of an individual student's inappropriate behavior patterns. The results of the FBA provide a more precise road map for the design and implementation of methods that help students reduce their troubling behaviors and engage in alternative positive behaviors. Three key assumptions serve as the foundation for FBA process. First, all behavior, appropriate and inappropriate, is learned and supported by current environment conditions. Second, all behavior is purposeful, meaning that we all behave in ways that satisfy our needs or help achieve a specific outcome. Finally, FBAs are most effective when a team of professionals collaborate in the process (Carpenter, King-Sears, & Keys, 1998; Chandler & Dahlquist, 2002). Typically, these are professionals from diverse fields who provide input and suggestions from their areas of expertise. As a classroom teacher, you may be required to serve as case manager for the team, organizing the information and coordinating communication among team members.

> **Strategy**
>
> Methods for engaging in FBT and completing FBAs and behavior intervention plans are presented in Strategy 15.7.

Behavior Intervention Plans

Successful behavior intervention plans (BIPs) are characterized by (1) the simultaneous strengthening and reducing of targeted behaviors through the application of behavioral techniques, (2) direct teaching of social skills, (3) emphases on self-management and self-control, and (4) goals of student independence.

This is a sample of the consequences used in my class. For a complete list, please reference the student handbook.

Positive Consequences

(To Increase Appropriate Behavior)

- Line Leader
- Verbal praise
- Positive note home
- Positive phone call
- Stickers
- School supplies
- Healthy treats
- Lunch with teacher/administrator
- Extra computer time
- Homework pass
- Ice cream social
- Extended recess

Negative Consequences

(To Decrease Inappropriate Behavior)

Nonverbal cues/warnings
- Verbal cues
- Time-out with written reflection
- Loss of recess
- Note or phone call home
- Parent conference
- Office referral
- In-school suspension
- Out-of-school suspension

Mrs. Marquis's contact information:
Marquis@omail.com

We welcome your comments and feedback. Feel free to contact me by e-mail at any time or by phone after 3:00 PM and before 7.00 PM.

Plan for Success
Mrs. Marquis's Third-Grade Class

Parent Guide

2009–2010

Mission Statement

To provide a safe and nurturing environment, which fosters creativity, academic achievement, and cooperation. With the support of families, staff, and community members, our students will reach their full potential.

Please help us achieve our goals! Volunteer to be a class helper.

Rules for
Stars

Show respect;
Keep yourself to yourself.

Truly be prepared
for class.

Adhere to directions the
first time given.

Raise your hand, and
wait to be recognized.

Show up on time.

Figure 15.2

Sample Brochure for a Comprehensive Behavior Management Plan

Figure 15.3	Evaluative Measure to Assess Evidence of Quality School-Wide Manuals

How Evident? Read each statement and circle the most appropriate rating in regard to the manual being evaluated.

1—Not evident   2—   3—Evident   4—   5—Extremely Evident

Mission Statement	Rating
The mission statement clearly states a vision reflecting student outcomes.	1 2 3 4 5
The mission statement clearly states expectations for students.	1 2 3 4 5
The mission statement has direct, clear statements that are focused and behaviorally used.	1 2 3 4 5
Rules and Expectations	
The rules are stated positively and defined clearly.	1 2 3 4 5
There are six or fewer rules.	1 2 3 4 5
Rules are observable and measurable.	1 2 3 4 5
Rules are jargon free and age appropriate for students.	1 2 3 4 5
Supports for rule success are articulated (supports need to be in place prior to failure).	1 2 3 4 5
Positive Consequences	
Positive consequences can be implemented easily at both team and classroom level.	1 2 3 4 5
Positive consequences contain a balance of praise, nontangible reinforcement and tangible reinforcement that can be easily delivered.	1 2 3 4 5
The positive consequences include a mix of desirable tangible reinforcements and big ticket items (e.g., social and physical activities).	1 2 3 4 5
Negative Consequences	
The consequences are natural, logical, and have an established hierarchy (e.g., rule reminder, warning, action plan).	1 2 3 4 5
The consequences are related to mission statement, rules, and procedures.	1 2 3 4 5
The consequences preserve a student's dignity and help to promote an internal locus of control.	1 2 3 4 5
The negative consequences reduce instances of secondary gain.	1 2 3 4 5
Intervention for problem behavior is not viewed as a negative consequence (e.g., referral to guidance, SIT team).	1 2 3 4 5
Procedures	
Procedures are positively stated and are age appropriate.	1 2 3 4 5
Each procedure is developed in a logical, step-by-step fashion.	1 2 3 4 5
The terms used in procedures are simple (as short as possible), specific, and jargon free.	1 2 3 4 5
Procedures are observable and measurable.	1 2 3 4 5

Procedures promote increased efficiency and effectiveness of the instructional environment.	1	2	3	4	5
There are at least three different school procedures (e.g., hallway, bathroom, late, cafeteria, nurse).	1	2	3	4	5
Crisis Intervention					
Crisis is defined in terms of students.	1	2	3	4	5
There is a plan for responding to and dealing with a crisis.	1	2	3	4	5
Additional Factors for Success					
The plan outlines target dates for staff implementation, evaluation, and student and parent education.	1	2	3	4	5
The supports for student noncompliance clearly divide faculty and administrative expectations and responsibilities.	1	2	3	4	5
Members of the crisis team are identified, and a plan for responding to a crisis developed.	1	2	3	4	5
Rules are jargon free and can be readily understood by parents, staff, and faculty.	1	2	3	4	5
Guidelines promote, encourage, and recognize compliance of procedures.	1	2	3	4	5
Reflects that the school values positive behavior.	1	2	3	4	5
The faculty has created unique forms, checklists, lesson plans for teaching the plan, specific to the needs of their school.	1	2	3	4	5

Note: These statements reflect effective characteristics of a school-wide comprehensive behavior management plan.

Source: Reprinted with permission from Rosenberg, M. S., & Jackman, L. A. (2003). Development, implementation, and sustainability of comprehensive school-wide behavior management systems. *Intervention in School and Clinic, 39*(1), 10–21.

Strengthening and Reducing of Targeted Behaviors. When implementing behavioral intervention programs, the teacher's goal is to replace instances of disruptive classroom behaviors with more appropriate alternatives. This step requires that teachers implement techniques that simultaneously reduce and strengthen targeted behaviors. Increasing behavior involves the process of reinforcement. Positive reinforcement occurs when the presentation of an environmental consequence results in a corresponding increase in the frequency or intensity of a behavior. Negative reinforcement (often confused incorrectly with punishment) occurs when the removal of an unpleasant event results in an increase in the target behavior. Teachers have three behavioral options to decrease behavior: extinction, differential reinforcement, and punishment. The diversity of behavioral methods to strengthen appropriate classroom behavior and decrease problem behavior is summarized in Tables 15.2 and 15.3.

Pause & Reflect

Why is it important that BIPs focus on simultaneously decreasing and strengthening specific target behaviors?

Direct Teaching of Social Skills. Some students misbehave because they lack the specific behavioral skills to act productively in the school and classroom environment. For these students, direct instruction in such skills would improve social competence and reduce problem behavior. Some teachers provide instruction in social skills by using commercially prepared social skills curricula (e.g., the Skillstreaming series; Goldstein & McGinnis, 1997; McGinnis & Goldstein, 1997). These programs cluster specific skills into domains (e.g., dealing with feelings, friendship-making skills, coping skills) and provide instructional sequences for teaching the skills. Effective curricula typically include validated instructional components (e.g., direct instruction, modeling, coaching, reinforcement, controlled practice), assessment instrumentation, and the flexibility to

Table 15.2   Procedures for Increasing Appropriate Behaviors

Type	Definition	Advantages	Disadvantages
Edible	A primary reinforcer. Potency varies as a function of deprivation and satiation.	Potency with students who possess severe handicaps. Useful in establishing reinforcing properties of other events (e.g., praise, smiles).	Delivery disrupts classroom functioning. Difficult to dispense in busy classroom settings. Need to be constantly aware of student allergies.
Praise and attention	Conditioned social reinforcers that can be delivered verbally and nonverbally (e.g., smiles, winks, physical contact).	Easily and quickly administered. Unobtrusive during classroom activities. Little preparation required.	Because the reinforcement values of praise and attention needs to be learned, some individuals may not respond. Limited potency with inappropriate behaviors that have high secondary reinforcing properties (e.g., theft, substance abuse).
High-probability behaviors	The preferred activities of students can be used as reinforcers for low-probability behaviors. Using the knowledge of progress or results to reinforce a target behavior.	Schools have many desirable activities available. Powerful and cost free. Low probability of satiation.	Difficulty in delivering activity reinforcers immediately. Disruptions may occur during transitions between activities. Delivery mode tends to be all or none; little opportunity to portion out activities.
Performance feedback	Conditioned, generalized reinforcers whose strength is derived from items, activities, and desirable consequences they present.	Easily initiated in setting where performance criteria are explicitly stated. Low cost and motivating.	Effectiveness of feedback alone has been equivocal.
Tokens		Combat satiation in that a number of backups can be employed. Easily dispensed. Serve to bridge the period of time between the occurrence of a behavior and the delivery of a primary reinforcer. Allow for gradations of reinforcement.	Require effort in record keeping and other management activities. Fading of tokens often neglected.

Source: Reprinted with permission from Rosenberg, M. S., O'Shea, L. J., & O'Shea, D. J. (2006). *Student teacher to master teacher: A practical guide for educating students with special needs* (4th ed., p. 272). Upper Saddle River, NJ: Merrill/Pearson Education.

One method of directly teaching social skills, social stories, is presented in Strategy 15.8.

address the needs of individual students as well as small groups (Carter & Sugai, 1989; Sugai & Lewis, 1996). Other teachers choose to create their own activities to teach replacement behaviors.

Self-Management and Self-Control. The ultimate goal of any behavioral intervention is for a student to regulate his own behavior independently. Teaching self-management and self-control allows students in need of behavior change to assume larger roles in their behavior change efforts. Programs typically consist of three components: self-assessment, goal setting, and self-determination of

Table 15.3   Three Commonly Used Punishment Techniques

Type	Definition	Advantages	Disadvantages
Reprimand	A verbal statement or nonverbal gesture that expresses disapproval.	Easily applied with little or no preparation required. No physical discomfort to students.	Sometimes not effective. Can serve as positive reinforcement if this is a major source of attention.
Response cost	A formal system of penalties in which a reinforcer is removed, contingent upon the occurrence of an inappropriate behavior.	Easily applied with quick results. Does not disrupt class activities. No physical discomfort to students.	Not effective once student has "lost" all reinforcers. Can initially result in some students being more disruptive.
Time-out	Limited or complete loss of access to positive reinforcers for a set amount of time.	Fast acting and powerful. No physical discomfort to students.	Difficult to find secluded areas where students would not be reinforced inadvertently. May require physical assistance to the time-out area. Overuse can interfere with educational and prosocial efforts.

Source: Reprinted with permission from Rosenberg, M. S., O'Shea, L. J., & O'Shea, D. J. (2006). *Student teacher to master teacher: A practical guide for educating students with special needs* (4th ed., p. 273). Upper Saddle River, NJ: Merrill/Pearson Education.

reinforcement (Polsgrove & Smith, 2004). In self-assessment, a student reflects on her own behavior and determines if the behavior is inadequate or inappropriate. Second, the student identifies the behaviors required, sets goals, and selects strategies that help regulate behavior. Finally, through the process of self-determination, the student evaluates her performance and considers the nature and scope of reinforcement that she should receive to perform the target behavior.

Classroom implementation of self-management typically follows the following sequence. First, the teacher introduces the procedure by informing a student (or a small group of students) that it is important to keep track of the occurrence and nonoccurrence of his target behavior. The teacher then introduces the student to a cuing mechanism. This could be a "low-tech" tool such as a self-monitoring card or a technologically enhanced device such as a Palm Pilot (Kramer, 2004). Every time the student is cued, he should ask himself, "Was I engaging in the target behavior?" and mark the monitoring device appropriately. The instructor should model the procedures, and the student should practice initially to ensure that the student can reliably differentiate between the occurrence and nonoccurrence of the target behavior. Once the procedure succeeds in teaching a student to monitor and record his own behavior, procedures designed to teach the self-determination of reinforcement can begin (Rosenberg et al., 2006). When the student reaches an acceptable level of performance, it may be time to carefully wean the student from the external aspects of the procedure. However, if student performance begins to deteriorate, the teacher should not hesitate to resume using the external prompts. Most of us require self-management procedures for a variety of behaviors (scheduling, remembering specific tasks), and the appropriate use of external devices is natural to inclusive environments.

Wraparound Supports

A small percentage of students, usually no more than 1% to 3%, requires a series of intensive, highly structured behavioral supports that involve the coordinated efforts of families, educators, and community-based professionals. Educators often use the terms "wraparound" or "system of care" to describe these interventions because they reflect three essential elements associated with this type of service delivery. First, rather than conforming to existing service-delivery alternatives, these are integrated educational and community services designed to meet the unique needs of children and their families. Second, services are provided in the local neighborhood. Finally, services are responsive to the culture of the child and family. It is not unusual for wraparound systems of care to include professionals from the fields of mental health, medicine, social work, substance abuse, law enforcement, and vocational rehabilitation.

What do teachers need to know about wraparound programming, and how can they contribute to the success of such programs? First, recognize that the community school is the most effective place for service coordination. It is a centrally located setting that can provide convenient access to a range of services with reduced stigma (Cullinan, 2002). Second, use positive strength-based commentary during conversations with family members. This will help ascertain, with minimal defensiveness, the ideas, values, frustrations, and dreams family members have about their child. Clearly, to attain increased family participation and trust, members of the school community must project an encouraging and supportive attitude toward behavioral improvement. Finally, as a teacher recognize that you contribute to the school-based wraparound team process by (1) helping identify and prioritizing needs, (2) developing action plans and interventions, and (3) collecting data that assist in the evaluation of interventions (Duckworth et al., 2001; Eber, Sugai, Smith, & Scott, 2002).

Consider how Susan Hill, the Dean of Special Education at Heritage High School, participates in her school's system of care. Ms. Hill often facilitates the student support team, which is a group of administrators, teachers, and related service personnel who together consider the needs of students who require integrated social, behavioral, and medical supports in order to fully benefit from educational programming. The team serves as a focal point for reviewing student progress and responding to needs as expressed by the students and their families. Ms. Hill readily admits that this is challenging work: Services are difficult to access, and teachers experience an emotional toll in seeing so many families in pain and dire circumstances. Fortunately, she has witnessed many successes such as (1) securing needed mental health and therapeutic treatments for students and (2) accessing in-home social work support for several single mothers who were having difficulty managing the behavioral demands of their nonverbal and very active adolescents with developmental delays. Ms. Hill believes that much more work remains to be done. At the top of her list of frustrations are those few families who are reluctant to become involved in the process and tend to avoid contacts with school personnel. Ms. Hill is always looking for novel ways to increase involvement.

Summary

Effective teachers manage the behavior of all of their students by developing procedures that are systematic, proactive, supportive, and responsive.

Student behavior: What to expect

- Most school and classroom misbehavior is related to tardiness, inattention, crowd-control issues, and students' testing the limits.
- Students who exceed these mild forms of misbehavior stand out from their peers due to their behavioral excesses and behavioral deficits.
- Students with behavioral excesses engage in high rates and frequencies of disruptive behaviors that interfere with academic performance; those with behavioral deficits lack specific skills necessary for academic and social competence.

Behavior management readiness

- Successful behavior managers organize their environments by making effective use of the physical dimensions of their classroom, valuing instructional time, being prepared, and coordinating resources.
- An essential prerequisite for effective behavior management is the delivery of accessible, motivating, and supportive instruction.

- In addition to the technical aspects, successful behavior management is contingent on developing authentic relationships with students, modeling civility and respect, and employing culturally responsive practices.

Addressing student behavior: Tiered management

- Tiered management allows teachers to meet the needs of all students by first addressing universal concerns—the typical needs of most students—and then using a continuum of interventions for those students who don't respond to the system.
- At the center of universal practices is a comprehensive management plan containing five core domains: mission; rules, procedures, and supports; surface management and consequences; crisis considerations; and accessible documentation.
- Targeted interventions are intensive actions directed toward chronic and pervasive problem behaviors.
- For students who do not respond to function-based thinking (FBT) and generic targeted interventions, teachers may need to complete a functional behavior assessment (FBA) and develop a structured BIP.
- Successful BIPs focus on the simultaneous strengthening and reducing of targeted behaviors; direct teaching of specific skills; and student self-management and independence.
- A small percentage of students will require wraparound supports, intensive, highly structured supports that require the coordinated efforts of families, educators, and community-based health professionals.

Addressing Professional Standards

Standards addressed in Chapter 15 include:

CEC Standards: (3) Individual learning differences, (4) instructional strategies, (5) learning environments and social interactions, and (7) instructional planning.

INTASC Standards: Principle 2—Provide learning opportunities to support the learning and development of all students; Principle 3—Create instructional opportunities for diverse learners; Principle 4—Understand and use a variety of instructional strategies; Principle 5—Create learning environments to support student motivation, behavior, and learning.

Praxis™ II Standards: Knowledge-based core principles: Delivery of services to students with disabilities. Application of core principles: (1) curriculum, (2) instruction, (4) managing the learning environment.

PUTTING IT ALL TOGETHER

At times, particularly early in your career, you will find the process of managing student behavior challenging. You may encounter colleagues who hold flawed views of how best to manage behavior, parents who fail to respond to your well-intentioned efforts to address persistent troubles, and administrators who fall short in supporting your structured management system. If and when these events occur, it is best if you respond in a professional manner:

1. **Remain patient, keep things in perspective, and be aware of the big picture.** Schools are a microcosm of society, and you should not take it personally if events do not go as planned.

2. **Practice diplomacy.** Consider the perspective of those who you find frustrating, and identify the functions of their actions. Try to understand why they believe and act as they do, and seek to negotiate win-win resolutions to conflicts.

3. **Remain poised.** Your comportment during stressful and frustrating circumstances is a reflection of your competence and professionalism. Students look to adults as models of desired behavior, and they will learn from your actions.

4. **Reflect on your own actions, and get help when needed.** Consider how your own actions and belief systems contribute to the development and maintenance of challenging situations. Do not be reluctant to ask for help and support from friends and colleagues.

5. **Show your pleasure when helping your students.** We choose to teach because we enjoy it and derive satisfaction in seeing our students overcome challenges and grow socially. Recognize when challenges are met, and celebrate when students succeed as a result of your efforts.

myeducationlab

We present a series of evidence-based strategies in the second half of this chapter (Strategies 15.1 to 15.8) in a step-by-step format so that you can use them in your classroom right away. In addition, in the following table, we identify some video clips, cases, and simulations that will allow you to experience some of these strategies (or complementary strategies) in a real classroom environment.

EFFECTIVE PRACTICE	MYEDUCATIONLAB CONNECTION	CONSIDER THIS
Strategy 15.1: Developing and Maintaining Rules and Procedures	Go to MyEducationLab, select the topic *Classroom/Behavior Management*, and go to the Activities and Applications section. Next, complete the simulation entitled "Who's in Charge?"	As you complete the simulation, reflect on how developing rules and procedures (as discussed in Strategy 15.1) fit into a comprehensive behavior management plan.
Strategy 15.2: Surface Management Techniques	Go to MyEducationLab, select the topic *Classroom/Behavior Management*, and go to the Activities and Applications section. Next, read and analyze the case entitled "Hang in There," and answer the accompanying questions.	As you read and analyze the case, consider how you would use the surface management techniques discussed in Strategy 15.2 to help the struggling teacher featured in the case.
Strategy 15.3: Developing Consequences and Delivering Them with Consistency	Go to MyEducationLab, select the topic *Classroom/Behavior Management*, and go to the Activities and Applications section. Next, read and analyze the case entitled "Encouraging Appropriate Behavior."	As you read and analyze this case, think about how you can apply the step-by-step techniques discussed in Strategy 15.3 to the multiple instances of problem behavior addressed in the case.
Strategy 15.4: Defusing Confrontations and Responding to Dangerous Behavior	Go to MyEducationLab, select the topic *Classroom/Behavior Management*, and go to the Activities and Applications section. Next, complete the simulation entitled "Addressing Disruptive and Noncompliant Behaviors: Part 1."	As you complete the simulation, compare and contrast the strategies discussed in the simulation with those techniques highlighted in Strategy 15.4. Which techniques seem to be most effective in addressing these confrontational behaviors?
Strategy 15.5: Check-In, Connect, Check-Out Systems	Go to MyEducationLab, select the topic *Classroom/Behavior Management*, and go to the Activities and Applications section. Next, watch the video entitled "Schoolwide Positive Behavior Support."	As you watch the video and answer the accompanying questions, reflect on the similarities and differences between Strategy 15.5 and the school-wide PBS program discussed in the video.
Strategy 15.6: Behavioral Contracts and Strategy 15.7: Function-Based Thinking, FBAs, & BIPs	Go to MyEducationLab, and select the topic *Classroom/Behavior Management*. Next, go to the Building Teaching Skills and Dispositions section, and complete the activity entitled "Multilevel Motivation System."	As you watch the videos and answer the accompanying questions in this activity, consider how you might use these specific motivational techniques and strategies to complement the targeted interventions discussed in Strategies 15.6 and 15.7.
Strategy 15.8: Direct Teaching of Social Skills: Social Stories	Go to MyEducationLab, select the topic *Emotional or Behavioral Disorders*, and go to the Activities and Applications section. Next, watch the video entitled "Social Skills Lesson," and answer the accompanying questions.	As you watch the video and answer the accompanying questions, compare and contrast the social skills lesson presented in the video to Strategy 15.8. Are these strategies equally effective in teaching social skills? Why or why not?

EFFECTIVE PRACTICES

In the remainder of this chapter, we describe eight effective strategies, which we referred to previously in the chapter, to help you plan effectively to meet the needs of all students.

EFFECTIVE PRACTICE	TYPE OF STRATEGY/BRIEF DESCRIPTION	SPECIAL CONSIDERATIONS
Strategy 15.1: Developing and Maintaining Rules and Procedures	A universal design behavioral support that communicates and defines acceptable behavior and efficient routines associated with success in the classroom.	Rules and procedures must be taught explicitly as well as reviewed and practiced throughout the school year, particularly after breaks for holidays and vacations.
Strategy 15.2: Surface Management Techniques	Commonsense behavior management methods for minor disruptive behaviors, surface management techniques overlap with elements of teaching with little disruption to the instructional process.	Surface management requires an awareness of classroom activities and events, multitasking skills that increase with time and experience.
Strategy 15.3: Developing Consequences and Delivering Them with Consistency	A series of teacher-directed events and behaviors that are used to promote compliance to behavioral expectations and to reduce the frequency and intensity of inappropriate behaviors.	For classroom management systems to succeed, it is essential that students complying with expectations are recognized and reinforced for their efforts.
Strategy 15.4: Defusing Confrontations and Responding to Dangerous Behavior	A series of interpersonal communication techniques that can defuse confrontational situations and maintain the safety of students and staff.	Some students use the shock value of extreme behaviors to intimidate and coerce others. It is important to minimize instances of these students' attaining desired outcomes through such behaviors.
Strategy 15.5: Check-In, Connect, and Check-Out Systems	Targeted low-cost interventions that provide students with immediate feedback on behavior, supportive relationships with school personnel, and increased recognition contingent on improvements in appropriate behavior.	The success of check-in systems depends on the quality of adults who coordinate the program. Specifically, coordinators need to interact well with students, work closely with families, proactively address conflict, and believe that positive changes will occur.
Strategy 15.6: Behavioral Contracts	Formal documents that detail the elements of specific, realistic individualized behavior change initiatives.	Because contracts require students to wait for a specific "payoff," it is important to gauge how long students can maintain their behavior without tangible reinforcement.
Strategy 15.7: Function-Based Thinking, Functional Behavior Assessments, and Behavior Intervention Plans	A process designed to identify possible linkages between student behavior and the events and conditions in classroom and school environments; information identified is used to develop a behavior intervention plan (BIP).	Keep it simple and straightforward: The key element of functional thinking is to identify and intervene on factors that contribute to a student's inappropriate behaviors.
Strategy 15.8: Direct Teaching of Social Skills: Social Stories	Written from the student's perspective, social stories explicitly highlight a course of action that one could take when encountering a challenging social situation.	Social stories work best when they are implemented along with other methods of evidence-based social skill instruction including modeling, role playing, and practice in naturalistic settings.

Strategy 15.1

DEVELOPING AND MAINTAINING RULES AND PROCEDURES

Rationale and Research

Teacher expectations regarding classroom organization and behavior management are communicated most effectively to students through rules and procedures. *Rules* are explicit definitions of acceptable behavior in your classroom; *procedures* are the routines or series of behaviors that students follow in order to complete a task, activity, or operation such as eating lunch in the cafeteria or requesting a pass to the lavatory. When introduced correctly, rules and procedures prompt, motivate, and guide students to adhere to classroom behavioral standards.

Key References

Curwin, R. L., & Mendler, A. N. (1999). *Discipline with dignity* (2nd ed.). Alexandria, VA: ASCD.

Evertson, C., Emmer, E. T., & Worsham, M. (2006). *Classroom management for elementary teachers* (7th ed.). Boston: Allyn & Bacon.

Rademacher, J. E., Callahan, K., & Pederson-Seelye, V. A. (1998). How do your classroom rules measure up? Guidelines for developing an effective rule management routine. *Intervention in School and Clinic, 33*(5), 284–289.

Rosenberg, M. S. (1986). Maximizing the effectiveness of structured classroom management programs: Implementing rule-review procedures with disruptive and distractible students. *Behavioral Disorders, 11*(4), 239–248.

Rosenberg, M. S., O'Shea, L., & O'Shea, D. J. (2006). *Student teacher to master teacher* (4th ed). Upper Saddle River, NJ: Merrill/Pearson Education.

Step-by-Step

The steps for developing and maintaining rules and procedures are:

1 *Know local community and school district expectations regarding the behavior of students.* Consider the community context of your expectations for discipline. Design your classroom rules and procedures to be congruent with the prevailing legal requirement and school board expectations.

2 *Articulate the specific behaviors and procedures associated with success in your classroom.* Reconstruct these expectations into explicit statements that will enable you and the students to agree about the occurrence or nonoccurrence of the behavioral expectations.

3 *Involve students in the development of the rules and procedures:*
- Solicit input as to the importance of classroom rules and how they should be enforced.
- Generate procedural solutions for classroom processes that contribute to disruption and disorder.

4 *Keep rules and procedures accessible:*
- Limit the number of rules to five or six, and ensure that procedures are phrased in a task-analyzed, easy-to-follow sequences of steps.
- Keep the wording of rules and procedures simple and jargon free.
- Phrase rules and procedures positively rather than negatively, focusing on what students should do rather than not do.
- Provide supports for those students who have difficulty meeting expectations.

5 Maintain the potency of rules and procedures:
- Keep rules and procedures posted in areas where students can see them.
- Teach and provide extensive practice with rules and procedures during the first week of school.
- Model desired student responses, and provide booster sessions on the rules and procedures at regularly scheduled intervals throughout the school year.
- Monitor your own level of consistency in adhering to the classroom rules and procedures.

Applications and Examples

To assist in the development of rules, make use of the Rules Development Worksheet (see Figure 15.4) (Rosenberg et al., 2006), a format that allows for (1) the articulation of a general case rule, (2) the definition of the rule in your classroom or setting, (3) plans for teaching the rule, and (4) methods to provide supports for those students who have difficulty complying to the rule. We recommend that you use this format to fully develop each of your classroom rules.

Successful behavior managers also know how to facilitate the completion of daily procedural routines such as morning

Directions: List the school-wide rules in the first column. Think about what each rule will look like and mean in your classroom. Record these points in the second column. Next, list a variety of methods for "teaching the rule" to your students. Finally, generate a list of possible supports for helping *all* students achieve success with the school-wide rules in *your* classroom.

School-Wide Rule	Meaning of the Rule in My Class	Teaching the Rule	Available Supports
The students will be prepared.	The students will be in their seats at the ringing of the bell with books, writing tools, drills, and homework.	• Elicit rationale for the rule • Role-play "the prepared student." • Display "being prepared materials" visually.	1. Set up pencil & pen loaner box. 2. Praise students who are prepared. 3. Provide visual and verbal cues to prompt preparedness.

Figure 15.4

Rules Development Worksheet

Source: Reprinted with permission from Rosenberg, M. S., O'Shea, L. J., & O'Shea, D. J. (2006). *Student teacher to master teacher: A practical guide for educating students with special needs* (4th ed., p. 18). Upper Saddle River, NJ: Merrill/Pearson Education.

arrival, trips to the rest room, and transitioning to the cafeteria. Consider the following two sample procedures as possible models for use in your own classrooms:

Morning Arrival
- Students enter building after 8:15.
- Check schedule: A or B Day.
- Go to locker and retrieve supplies.
- Deposit all hats and personal items in locker.
- If you eat breakfast, report directly to cafeteria.
- When the warning bell rings, report directly to class.

- Upon arrival to classroom, complete your morning log.

CAFÉ (Care About Food Enjoy lunch) Procedures
- Join the END of ONE line, ONE time.
- Sit in your assigned area.
- Respect each other's space, feelings, and property.
- Use appropriate language and tone.
- Remain seated until the teacher signals for you to dispose of waste correctly and return to class.

Keep in Mind

For compliance to rules and procedures to maintain throughout the school year, it is essential to teach, practice, and reinforce them with regularity and consistency. It is also important to provide structured booster sessions at various times of the year, particularly after holidays and vacations.

Strategy 15.2

SURFACE MANAGEMENT TECHNIQUES

Rationale and Research

Surface management techniques are commonsense "stop-gap" methods that teachers use intuitively to deal with relatively minor instances of disruptive behaviors. The strength of these techniques is that they overlap elements of the teaching process and can be applied with minimal disruption to the instructional process. Although they are not a substitute for a well-planned comprehensive management program, they do allow teachers to return students to the instructional flow of the classroom with finesse, "withitness," grace, and sometimes, good humor.

Key References

Beck, M. A., Roblee, K., & Johns, C. (1982). Psychoeducational management of disturbed children. *Education, 102*(3), 232–235.

Kounin, (1970). *Discipline and group management in classrooms.* New York: Holt, Rinehart & Winston.

Levin, J., & Nolan, J. (2007). *Principles of classroom management* (5th ed.). Boston: Allyn & Bacon.

Long, N., & Newman, R. G. (1965). Managing surface behavior of children in school. In N. Long, W. Morse, & R. Newman (Eds.), *Conflict in the classroom: The education of emotionally disturbed children* (pp. 233–240). Belmont, CA: Wadsworth.

Step-by-Step and Applications and Examples

Surface management techniques are best viewed as a menu of alternatives in which specific techniques align with the intensity of the behaviors and match the presenting behaviors.

We identify presenting behaviors that are typically served by each technique and highlight how it is best applied.

TECHNIQUE	BEHAVIORS	APPLICATION
Planned ignoring	Minor attention-seeking behaviors such as pencil tapping or making noises.	When teachers do not feed in, or reinforce, a student's need for immediate gratification, minor disruptive behaviors will eventually stop.
Signal interference	Off-task behaviors such as talking with or annoying peers.	Use of nonverbal gestures, eye contact, noise, or body posture prompts students to redirect their inappropriate behaviors.
Proximity control	Minor disruptive behavior such as talking and socializing with others during task-oriented activities.	Close physical presence to the student serves to deter disruptive behaviors and promotes greater task orientation.
Changing the pace	Reduces off-task behaviors such as staring out windows, resting head on desk, and talking to neighbors.	Infusing the lesson with a game, personal anecdote, story, or even a change in vocal tone revitalizes lessons and keeps students attending to work.
Removal of seductive objects	Reduces the disruptive and off-task behaviors associated with task-irrelevant objects.	Objects that co-opt student attention are removed without incident and returned at an appropriate time.

TECHNIQUE	BEHAVIORS	APPLICATION
Interest boosting	Reenergizes a student's flagging interest (and corresponding inappropriate behavior) in activity.	Interest heightened by teacher noting the unique and challenging qualities of the activity as well as indicating personal interest in the content.
Tension decontamination through humor	Reduces tense or anxiety-filled classroom situations.	Diplomatic use of humor, mostly the self-deprecating type, can preempt confrontational and counterproductive situations.
Antiseptic bouncing	For a student who is on the verge of a potentially serious, highly disruptive behavioral event.	Safely and nonpunitively removing a student from the classroom (e.g., delivering a message to the school nurse, running an errand).

Keep in Mind

Some teachers develop a surface management routine rapidly and can orchestrate the overlapping nature of behavioral prompting, redirection, and interruption-free instruction instinctively, with little apparent forethought. Most teachers, however, require practice in this multitasking. With experience and time, successful teachers develop the seamless awareness of everything that is going on in the classroom, and they are characterized by their students as "having eyes in the back of their heads."

Strategy 15.3

DEVELOPING CONSEQUENCES AND DELIVERING THEM WITH CONSISTENCY

Rationale and Research

Consequences promote compliance to behavior expectations and reduce the frequency and intensity of inappropriate behaviors. Consequences work best when they (1) are clear and related to class rules and procedures; (2) possess a range or hierarchy of alternatives; (3) are natural and logical for the school environment; (4) serve an educative rather than vindictive function; and (5) are delivered with consistency and care.

Key References

Curwin, R. L., & Mendler, A. N. (1999). *Discipline with dignity* (2nd ed.). Alexandria, VA: ASCD.

Jones, V., & Jones, L. (2007). *Comprehensive classroom management: Creating communities of support and solving problems.* Boston: Pearson/Allyn & Bacon.

Rhode, G., Jenson, W. R., & Reavis, H. K. (1993). *The tough kid book: Practical classroom management strategies.* Longmont, CO: Sopris West.

Rosenberg, M. S., O'Shea, L., & O'Shea, D. J. (2006). *Student teacher to master teacher* (4th ed). Merrill/Pearson Education.

Sprick, R., Sprick, M., & Garrison, M. (1993). *Interventions: Classroom management strategies.* Longmont, CO: Sopris West.

Taylor-Greene, S., et al. (1997). School-wide behavioral support: Starting the year off right. *Journal of Behavioral Education, 7*(1), 99–112.

Step-by-Step

The steps for developing consequences and delivering them with consistency are:

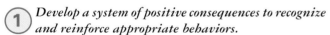

1 Develop a system of positive consequences to recognize and reinforce appropriate behaviors.

- Generate a menu of desirable products, actions, and events that can be integrated into the daily routine of the classroom. This menu can include
  - Privileges such as first choice of games, computers, and athletic equipment during free time
  - Certificates and awards recognizing periods of appropriate behavior and initiating positive social initiations toward others
  - Notes, phone calls, or e-mails home recognizing desired changes in behavior
  - Ways for students to be a class/teacher helper such as tutoring younger students, grading papers, or serving as a messenger
- Target the specific behaviors you seek to enhance or increase. A good rule of thumb when targeting is to ensure that the behaviors are consistent with class rules and procedures, overt, and easy to determine if they occur (i.e., contain movement).
- Ensure that you deliver points and tokens in a systematic and logically appropriate fashion. For some students

delivery of points can wait for the end of the instructional period; others, because of the intensity of the presenting behaviors, require more frequent recognition.
- Make sure to record points and tokens easily and accurately. Whenever appropriate, allow students to manage and keep track of their own points and tokens.
- Develop an array of desirable and school-appropriate back-up reinforcers. Have several activities or items that students can earn in a short period of time; highly regarded, larger items or events should require savings over time.
- Consider a response–cost system, a method for deducting points if students engage in intensive disruptive and aggressive behaviors.

2 Develop a hierarchy of negative consequences that provide a range of options to decrease rates of inappropriate behavior.

- Consider the use of least intrusive generic consequences that do not interrupt the flow of classroom activities. These include surface management techniques, indirect class reminders and restatement of the rules and procedures, and directed verbal reminders of expectations.

- Use, when necessary, more intensive directed consequences:
  - Allow the student a quiet time to calm down (work to make up).
  - Teacher-directed time-out.
  - Reflection time in class or other classroom.
- Refer students to the appropriate administrator for behaviors such as fighting and bullying; contact parents for design of a coordinated action plan.

(3) **Initiate a self-check system that promotes delivery of consequences with respect and consistency.**

- Stay close to the student and make direct eye contact, using a soft voice. Do not embarrass the student in front of peers. Always implement the consequence, and do not accept excuses or bargaining.
- Monitor your delivery of consequences, making sure that you maintain consistency, remain calm and professional, and are fair to all students in the classroom (not inadvertently picking on a few who act out).
- Avoid power struggles with confrontational students:
  - Be aware of how power struggles develop and entrap (Curwin & Mendler, 1999).
  - Be firm and anger free rather than defensive.
  - Do not give into coercion, whining, or emotionality.
  - Have a private discussion with the student about her frustrations and alternatives to her behavior.

Applications and Examples

Some teachers remain concerned that giving students rewards for appropriate behavior can be seen as "bribery." Consider using positive reinforcers that are natural to the school and classroom environment. Rhode, Jenson, and Reavis (1993) provide several suggestions in their classic resource, *The Tough Kid Book*. Here is a listing of several of the natural reinforcers:

- Being line leader, team captain, or paper monitor
- Helping the custodian, feeding the fish and other class pets, or serving as class messenger
- Tutoring younger students
- First choice of activity, art supplies, or PE equipment
- Free time with specific activities, favorite peers, or adults
- Lunch with principal or related service personnel

Keep in Mind

The delivery of consequences for enhancing rule compliance and decreasing instances of noncompliance is at the heart of successful behavior management. Unfortunately, many teachers deliver negative consequences far more frequently than positive recognitions. For discipline systems to be effective, it is essential to maintain a focus on positive behaviors; students who are doing the right things need to be recognized and reinforced. When delivering consequences to reduce inappropriate behaviors, it is critical to maintain an educative and professional manner instead of presenting an angry, menacing, and vindictive demeanor. Attend to your feelings when you are managing student behavior, and recognize that it is your professional responsibility to keep frustration and anger in check.

Strategy 15.4

DEFUSING CONFRONTATIONS AND RESPONDING TO DANGEROUS BEHAVIOR

Rationale and Research

Consider this strategy: "An ounce of prevention is worth a pound of cure." It is unlikely that you will have to deal with aggressive confrontational behaviors that threaten the safety of students and staff in your classroom. However, you should be aware of interpersonal communication techniques that can defuse some situations and of rapidly implemented procedures that maintain the safety of students and staff. Rather than fear these unfortunate circumstances, it is best to view them as manageable challenges and part of a complex process of assisting students in need and crisis. This type of mind-set is a prime example of a positive approach to the resolution of behavioral flare-ups and allows students in vulnerable situations to get the help and support they need, as others in the immediate environment are kept safe and secure.

Key References

Albert, L. (2003). *Cooperative discipline.* Circle Pines, MN: AGS.

Colvin, G., Ainge, D., & Nelson, R. (1997). How to defuse confrontations. *Teaching Exceptional Children, 29*(3), 47–51.

Johns, B. H., & Carr, V. G. (1995). *Techniques for managing verbally and physically aggressive students.* Denver: Love.

Jones, V., & Jones, L. (2007). *Comprehensive classroom management: Creating communities of support and solving problems.* Boston: Pearson/Allyn & Bacon.

Sprick, R., Sprick, M., & Garrison, M. (1993). *Interventions: Managing physically dangerous behavior.* Longmont, CO: Sopris West.

Step-by-Step

1 *Be aware of atypical signs of agitation.*
- Signs of agitation can include distractible behaviors such as darting eyes, nonconversational language, out-of-context outbursts, and intermittent starting and stopping several activities.
- Other signs include significant decreases in academic and social behaviors such as staring into space, withdrawal from typical peer groups and activities, and lack of eye contact.

2 *Attempt to defuse the confrontational or dangerous behavior.*
- Communicate your support and concern for the student by remaining calm and acknowledging the critical nature of the situation.
- Minimize chances of escalating the situation: lower your voice, slow your rate of speech, adjust your body stance, keep your arms at your side and avoid face-to-face positioning, and do not back the student into a corner (figuratively or literally).
- Allow the student to vent, but redirect the student to focus on current situation; do not respond to irrelevant comments.

- Provide students with choices (and limits) for resolution of the situation. Remind students that the choices have corresponding and varying consequences.

3 *Take charge of your own emotions.*
- Respond but do not react to the student's verbalizations and behaviors.
- Deal in the moment, yet be aware of the importance of maintaining the relationship.
- Release your emotions at the end of the situation.

4 *If the student escalates into physically violent or dangerous behaviors, engage in preplanned safety procedures.*
- Signal a room-clear, removing all other students from the immediate environment to a predetermined location with adequate supervision.
- Remove, or clear, the audience from the emotional event, thereby reducing the emotional intensity of the situation and the reinforcing properties of the behavioral event.
- Contact the school crisis support team (or designated individual) immediately to provide emergency physical restraint (only when deemed necessary) and crisis intervention procedures.

⑤ *After the event, complete all necessary follow-up procedures.*

- Maintain a running record of the event and any relevant antecedent and/or consequent actions.

- Notify parents or guardians of the event, and involve them in problem solving and intervention planning.
- Plan instructional efforts to teach the student alternatives to the problem behavior.

Applications and Examples

Defusing confrontations and managing physically aggressive behaviors involves minimization or avoidance of certain behaviors and verbalizations. To identify those actions that should be avoided, Albert (2003) surveyed teachers to determine actions that failed to work and even made things worse. Consider this list as behaviors to avoid when seeking to defuse confrontational situations:

Behaviors to Avoid

- Raising voice, preaching, and insisting on the last word
- Tense body language
- Sarcasm and degrading or embarrassing put-downs
- Questioning student's character
- Acting superior, and insisting on being correct
- Drawing unrelated persons into the conflict
- Backing the student into a corner
- Pleading, nagging, or bribing
- Bringing up unrelated events
- Commanding, demanding, and/or dominating communication style

Keep in Mind

Aggressive and confrontational student behaviors are frightening, and, although infrequent, teachers unfortunately must be aware of how to manage them. Some students have learned to use the shock value of extreme behaviors to intimidate and coerce others. These inappropriate behaviors are reinforced when peers and adults acquiesce to aggressive students' demands. The chain of aggression and intimidation can be broken when students learn that they cannot get desired outcomes through threatening and confrontational behavior.

Strategy 15.5

CHECK-IN, CONNECT, CHECK-OUT SYSTEMS

Rationale and Research

Check-in, connect, and check-out systems, sometimes referred to as *behavior education programs,* are targeted interventions for students who do not respond to typical classroom behavior-management prevention approaches. These low-cost approaches provide additional supports in the form of more immediate feedback on behavior, sustained positive relationships with school personnel, and increased positive attention contingent on positive behavior change. A number of research efforts have found that the system is an easily administered, cost-effective means of reducing the frequency of problem behaviors, particularly those that are initiated and maintained by peer and adult attention (e.g., Hawken & Homer, 2003; Lehr, Sinclair, & Christenson, 2004).

Key References

Crone, D. A., Horner, R., & Hawken, L. S. (2004). *Responding to behavior in schools: The Behavior Education Program.* New York: Guilford Press.

Lehr, C. A., Sinclair, M. F., & Christenson, S. L. (2004). Addressing student engagement and truancy prevention during the elementary years: A replication study of the Check & Connect model. *Journal of Education for Students Placed at Risk, 9*(3), 279–301.

Hawken, L. S. (2006). School psychologists as leaders in the implementation of a targeted intervention: The Behavior Education Program. *School Psychology Quarterly, 21*(1), 91–111.

Hawken, L. S., & Horner, R. H. (2003). Evaluation of a targeted intervention within a school-wide system of support. *Journal of Behavioral Education, 12*(3), 225–240.

Step-by-Step

(1) *Before the start of each school day, students identified as being in need of specialized behavior supports check in with a coordinator or monitor.*

- The coordinator/monitor, a paraprofessional or trained volunteer, must have the flexibility to check students in and out (approximately 10 hours per week).
- Successful coordinators/monitors interact well with students and believe they can succeed; work closely with families and other teachers; negotiate, compromise, and proactively address conflict; and apply solid organizational and recording skills.

(2) *During check-in, the coordinator or monitor:*

- Ensures students are prepared for the school day (e.g., necessary materials and completed homework assignments).
- Reviews the student's individualized daily progress feedback (DPF) form, an easy-to-complete feedback mechanism that allows teachers and other school personnel to

connect with students, prompt target behaviors, and rate student performance (see following sample on page 390).
- Dispatches students to class with good cheer, positive statements, and high expectations for meeting the day's goals.

(3) *Throughout the day teachers and other school staff:*

- Greet students and prompt appropriate behavior.
- Provide directed verbal feedback regarding behavioral goals.
- Complete the DPF form at natural transitions (e.g., hourly, end of instructional period, after lunch).

(4) *At the end of the day, the coordinator or monitor:*

- Computes student points and provides performance feedback.
- Gives students a copy of the DPF form for parents to review and sign.
- Enters student data into a database for weekly and monthly performance reviews.

Applications and Examples

A sample DPF form is provided below. Note how the teacher, paraeducators, and related-service provider have the opportu- nity to provide feedback on the identified goals throughout the school day.

Sample DPF Form Skeet Ulrich's Daily Progess Feedback Form				
PERIOD	**GOAL 1: USING APPROPRIATE LANGUAGE IN APPROPRIATE TONE**	**GOAL 2: KEEPING HANDS AND FEET TO SELF**	**GOAL 3: RAISING HAND AND BEING RECOGNIZED BEFORE SPEAKING OUT**	**SIGN-OFF**
Arrival/Morning Activities 8:10–8:30				
Reading Group and Follow-up Activities 8:30–9:45				
Written Language 9:50–11:00				
Speech/PE 11:05–11:45				
Lunch 11:50–12:30				
Math 12:35–1:35				
SS/Science/Activity Time 1:40–2:45				
End-of-Day Activities 2:50–3:10				

Keep in Mind

Teachers often use check-in, connect, and check-out systems in conjunction with token and point systems. It is there- fore essential that teachers plan programs with "fading" in mind. Teachers should view the fading of specialized supports as celebratory and should recognize appropriate behavior maintenance recognized through school and classroom events. For students who do not respond to these programs, teachers often need to conduct an in-depth functional behavioral assessment in order to supplement or adapt intervention procedures.

Strategy 15.6

BEHAVIORAL CONTRACTS

Rationale and Research

Behavioral contracts are formal, tangible documents that clearly specify the specific elements of an individualized behavior change program. They are advantageous because they allow students to work at their own pace and, most importantly, remain involved in the planning and ongoing monitoring of interventions. Well-planned behavioral contracts also guide students in realistic goal setting and help those who lack motivation to attain reasonable and worthwhile benchmarks.

Key References

Hall, R. V., & Hall, M. C. (1982). *How to negotiate a behavioral contract.* Lawrence, KS: H & H Enterprises.

Lovett, T. C. (1995). *Tactics for teaching.* Upper Saddle River, NJ: Merrill/Pearson Education.

Rhode, G., Jenson, W. R., & Reavis, H. K. (1993). *The tough kid book: Practical classroom management strategies.* Longmont, CO: Sopris West.

Sprick, R., Sprick, M., & Garrison, M. (1993). *Interventions: Goal setting and contracting.* Longmont, CO: Sopris West.

Step-by-Step

1 *Meet with the student to discuss the need for the contract and the advantages of mutual negotiation.*

2 *Define the specific behaviors required of the student.*
- State in positive, observable, and measurable terms all elements of the expected behaviors.
- Articulate contract criteria such as starting and ending dates as well as daily time periods and locations in which contract provisions will be enforced.
- Ensure that student goals are reasonable and attainable and, if necessary, open to renegotiation.

3 *Negotiate contract reinforcers.*
- Identify privileges that the student would like to attain.
- Negotiate a point system in which cumulative instances of appropriate behavior lead to the reinforcer.
- Consider adding in bonus clauses for exceptionally high rates of compliance to contract criteria.

4 *Formalize the contract.*
- Put all negotiated elements in writing.
- Sign the document.
- Share the contract with parents and school administrators.

Applications and Examples

A sample generic behavioral contract follows. Note that the contract (1) is stated in positive terms, (2) promotes success through modest gradations of behavior change, (3) provides frequent and predictable reinforcement, and (4) reflects that the conditions were developed through negotiations between the teacher and student.

This is a contract between_____*Mr. Toohey*_____and ___*DeJuan*___.

DeJuan _____ agrees to work on the following behaviors:

1. ____*Keeping Hands to Self* 20% more than current rate_____

2. ____*Completing Assignments 10% more than current rate*_____

3. _____

If the above conditions are met, DeJuan will:

__*Earn 15 minutes computer time during recess*_____

__*Earn 5 extra opportunities for the mystery motivator drawing at the end of the week*__

_____

_____

_____

_____

as a recognition for his successful efforts. If the terms of the contract are not met by the student, all recognitions will be withheld.

Signatures and date

____*DeJuan Smith*____   ____10/23____
Student   Date

____*Bill Toohey*____   ____10/23____
Teacher   Date

_____   _____
Witness   Date

We will review this contract on_____12/1_____ to reevaluate it.
                                                  Date

Keep in Mind

Because contracts work on a "delayed-payoff" system, you will need to gauge how long students are willing to go without reinforcement. Students' having to wait too long often dooms well-developed contracts. Also, during the negotiation phase, students are likely to overestimate what they can accomplish during the contract period. It is often necessary to review the behavioral criteria expected of students to ensure that modest degrees of success can be attained. Finally, like many behavioral techniques, contracts may take some time to "kick in." Some students will test the system and will need time to trust that the adults are truly interested in helping them succeed rather than just developing another technique for highlighting their shortcomings.

Strategy 15.7

FUNCTION-BASED THINKING, FUNCTIONAL BEHAVIOR ASSESSMENTS, AND BEHAVIOR INTERVENTION PLANS

Rationale and Research

Function-based thinking (FBT) is designed to serve the needs of students who are not responding to universal interventions but whose behaviors have not yet evolved to the point of requiring intensive intervention. When faced with students who repeatedly misbehave and fail to respond to typical management structures, teachers use FBT to consider the function of the presenting behavior and plan a classroom-based intervention accordingly. The goal is to identify possible linkages between student behavior and events/conditions in the immediate environment. FBT is not designed as a replacement for functional behavior assessments (FBAs); it is a less intrusive and user-friendly examination of how a student's behavior problem may be caused and sustained by classroom events (Hershfelt & Rosenberg, 2008; Park, 2007). Although similar in approach, FBAs are more powerful problem-solving processes that teachers use when students do not respond to FBT-based generic interventions. Often, FBAs require a team of professionals to collaborate in observation and data analysis. The outcome of the FBA process is the development of a behavior intervention plan (BIP) that focuses on the simultaneous strengthening and reduction of target behaviors identified by the FBA.

Key References

Center for Effective Collaboration and Practice. (1998). *Functional behavioral assessment.* Retrieved August 10, 2007, from http://cecp.air.org/fba/problembehavior/main.htm

Chandler, L. K., & Dahlquist, C. M. (2002). *Functional assessment: Strategies to prevent and remediate challenging behaviors in school settings.* Upper Saddle River, NJ: Merrill/Pearson Education.

Gable, R. A., Quinn, M. M., Rutherford, R. B., Howell, K. W., & Hoffman, C. C. (2000). *Addressing student behavior—Part III: Creating positive intervention plans and supports.* Washington, DC: American Institutes for Research.

Hershfeldt, P., & Rosenberg, M. S. (2008, November). *Beyond universal management: What developing teachers need to know about managing problem behaviors.* Paper presented at the annual conference of the Teacher Education Division of the Council for Exceptional Children, Dallas, TX.

Park, K. L. (2007). Facilitating effective team-based functional behavioral assessments in typical school settings. *Beyond Behavior, 17*(1), 21–31.

Scott, T. M., Liaupsin, C. J., Nelson, C. M., & Jolivette, K. (2003). Ensuring student success through team-based functional behavioral assessment. *Teaching Exceptional Children, 35*(5), 16–21.

Shippen, M. E., Simpson, R. G., & Crites, S. A. (2003). A practical guide to functional behavioral assessment. *Teaching Exceptional Children, 35,* 36–44.

Step-by-Step

① *Engage in FBT by using the ERASE strategy to understand the relationship between presenting problem behavior and the school/classroom environment* (Park, 2007).

- **E**xplain the presenting problem behavior by identifying it and specifying events that occur before and after it.
- **R**eason: Hypothesize what the student may be gaining or avoiding by the problem behavior. Specifically consider

antecedents to the behavior and the outcomes of the behavior. This leads to identification of possible functions (e.g., attention, avoidance, etc.) of the behavior.

- **A**ppropriate: Identify the appropriate behaviors that will take the place of the problem behavior. Ensure that the desired behaviors to be taught and/or reinforced serve the same function as the problem behavior but are suitable for the classroom environment.

- Support: Identify the instructional accommodations, behavioral interventions, and implementation supports necessary to prompt and sustain the developing appropriate behavior.
- Evaluate: Define criteria for success, and evaluate the success of your efforts.

(2) *For more intensive behavioral problems and those behaviors that remain unresponsive to generic targeted interventions, conduct an FBA.* Effective FBAs can be conducted through a five-step process (Center for Effective Collaboration and Practice, 1998; McConnell, Hilvitz, & Cox, 1998; Rosenberg et al., 2008; Ryan, Halsey, & Matthews, 2003; Shippen, Simpson, & Crites, 2003):

- *Step 1: Describe and assess the significance of the behavior.* Consider how much the student's behavior differs from classmates, whether it is chronic and a threat to others, and whether the behavior may be a function of a cultural difference.
- *Step 2: Refine the definition of the problem behavior.* Enhance your knowledge of the behavior by noting (1) when and where the behavior occurs; (2) the conditions (e.g., certain students present or during large-group instruction) in which the behavior occurs; (3) activities that occur both before and after the behavior; and (4) common setting events—situations or contexts that can influence behavioral events (e.g., when late to school, after missing breakfast).
- *Step 3: Collect and analyze information on the environment, setting demands, and possible functions of the problem behavior.* Employ multiple methods to collect information on the behavior and the student. Useful artifacts include archival records, evidence of academic work, interviews with parents and relevant school personnel, descriptions of instructional and social environments, and direct observations. Characterize the behavior of interest by function or whether the problem is a skill deficit (not knowing how to behave) or a performance deficit (knowing how to behave but not performing it under specific conditions).
- *Step 4: Generate a hypothesis statement and plan for intervention.* Develop a concise summary of information, focusing on factors surrounding the student's behavior, including both the antecedents and consequences. The hypothesis, a best guess as to why the behavior is occurring, guides the development of the intervention.
- *Step 5: Develop, implement, and evaluate the intervention plan.* Develop an intervention plan that includes positive behavior-change strategies, program modifications, and behavior supports necessary to address the problem behavior. Implement the plan with fidelity, and collect data consistently on the targeted behavior in order to evaluate the efficacy of your intervention plan.

(3) *Develop BIPs that simultaneously strengthen and reduce targeted behaviors* through the application of behavioral techniques, emphasize self-management and self-control, and lead to student independence. As suggested by Gable et al. (2000), plans should include activities that:

- Teach acceptable replacement behaviors that serve a similar function as the inappropriate behavior.
- Teach students to cope with typical and difficult-to-alter settings or events such as the physical arrangement of the classroom, scheduling, and classmates.
- Replace antecedents that may prompt the occurrence of the problem behavior with events that set the occasion for appropriate behaviors.
- Employ positive consequences that reinforce desired behaviors.

Applications and Examples

Albert (2003) provides a useful framework for understanding the functions or goals of student misbehavior. Students often choose to misbehave in order to get attention, exercise power, obtain revenge, or avoid failure. In Table 15.4, we define these functions of misbehavior and indicate how knowledge of these goals is the first step in designing successful interventions.

Table 15.4   Understanding the Goals of Misbehavior

	Attention-Seeking Behavior	Power Behavior
Active Characteristics	Student does all kinds of behaviors that distract teacher and classmates.	*Temper tantrums and verbal tantrums:* Student is disruptive and confrontive.
Passive Characteristics	Student exhibits one-pea-at-a-time behavior, operates on slow, slower, slowest speeds.	*Quiet noncompliance:* Student does his or her own thing, yet often is pleasant and even agreeable.
Students' Legitimate Needs	Positive recognition	Personal autonomy
Silver Lining	Student wants a relationship with the teacher (and classmates).	Student exhibits leadership potential, assertiveness, and independent thinking.

	Revenge Behavior	Avoidance-of-Failure Behavior
Active Characteristics	*Physical and psychological attacks:* Student is hurtful to teacher, classmates, or boh.	*Frustration tantrum:* Student loses control when pressure to succeed becomes too intense.
Passive Characteristics	Student is sullen and withdrawn, refusing overtures of friendship.	Student procrastinates, fails to complete projects, develops temporary incapacity, or assumes behaviors that resemble a learning disability.
Students' Legitimate Needs	Safety and security	Success
Silver Lining	Student shows a spark of life by trying to protect self from further hurt.	Student may want to succeed if can be assured of not making mistakes and of achieving some status. For some severely discouraged students, there is no silver lining.

Source: Reprinted with permission from Albert, L. (2003). *Cooperative discipline: A teacher's handbook* (pp. 178–179). Circle Pines, MN: AGS Publishing.

Keep in Mind

As you approach the FBT, FBA, and BIP processes, don't be overwhelmed by the variety of methods and the host of instruments, tools, and techniques used to obtain critical information. If you experience any confusion, remember that, regardless of the professional jargon employed, the key element in the process is simply *identifying factors that may contribute to a student's misbehavior.* Once identified, you can develop a realistic positive intervention plan that includes program modifications, direct instruction, behavior change strategies, and behavioral supports needed to sustain desired changes in behavior.

Strategy 15.8

DIRECT TEACHING OF SOCIAL SKILLS: SOCIAL STORIES

Rationale and Research

Social stories are short, simple narratives written from the perspective of the student. They explicitly highlight a course of action for students to take when they encounter challenging social situations. Typically, the stories comprise concrete, developmentally appropriate cues, thoughts, and responses typical of targeted social situations, using six specific types of statements:

- *Descriptions:* Information centering on contextual factors such as the setting, required actions, and participants
- *Directives:* Descriptions of desired actions in response to social cues or specific situations
- *Perspectives:* Descriptions of the feelings and reactions of others in the social situation
- *Affirmations:* Statements that reassure the student by reinforcing the desired action
- *Control statements:* Words that assist the student to recall important information
- *Cooperative statements:* Descriptions of how assistance will be provided.

Teachers use social stories to teach a range of social behaviors, including sportsmanship, appropriate greeting behaviors, reducing talking out during lessons, and minimizing frustration during homework time.

Key References

Crozier, S., & Tincani, M. J. (2005). Using a modified social story to decrease disruptive behavior of a child with autism. *Focus on Autism and Other Developmental Disabilities, 20*(3), 150–157.

Gray, C. A., & Garand, J. D. (1993). Social stories: Improving responses of students with autism with accurate social information. *Focus on Autistic Behavior, 8*(1) 1–10.

More, C. (2008). Digital stories targeting skills for children with disabilities: Multidimensional learning. *Intervention in School and Clinic, 43*(3), 168–177.

Sansoti, F. J., Powell-Smith, K. A., & Kincaid, D. (2004). A research synthesis of social story interventions for children with Autism Spectrum Disorders. *Focus on Autism and Other Developmental Disabilities, 19*(4), 194–204.

Toplis, R., & Hadwin, J. A. (2006). Using social stories to change problematic lunchtime behaviour in school. *Educational Psychology in Practice, 22*(1), 53–67.

Step-by-Step

① *Identify the target behaviors in need of intervention.*
- Assess behaviors needed by students for success in the classroom including getting along with others, controlling anger, following directions, responding to others, requests, and using free time appropriately.
- Consult family members to assist in prioritizing of social behavior needs.

② *Identify the key features of the problematic social situation.*
- Identify where the situation occurs, who is involved, and what occurs, as well as how it starts and ends.
- Survey teachers and relevant service providers to ascertain what is prompting and maintaining the problem behaviors.
- Interview the student regarding his views of the situation.

③ *Write the social story.*
- Create the story from the perspective of the student.
- Emphasize the behavioral steps needed to address the presenting social situation.
- Consider the comprehension level of the student and include descriptions, directives, perspectives, affirmations, control sentences, and cooperative sentences.
- Ensure that the emphasis of the story is on description rather than direction.
- Use pictures whenever possible.

④ *Evaluate the effectiveness of the social story.*
- Have the student respond to questions about what he will do the next time the situation occurs.
- Monitor the student's behavior in natural social situations.

Applications and Examples

Following is a sample social story adapted from Toplis and Hadwin (2006) to teach appropriate lunchtime behaviors. Note that elements of the story are more descriptive and affirmative than directive.

Sample Social Story: Things to Do at Lunchtime

The buzzer for lunch goes at ten past twelve. It rings three times. (Descriptive)

That means we go to our seats and sit down. (Descriptive)

When everyone at my table is sitting, our teacher tells us to go. We can wash our hands in the sink at the back of the room if we have been doing messy stuff. (Descriptive)

The locker area is busy with lots of children. We get our lunch boxes there. (Descriptive)

Some children are talking to each other. (Descriptive)

I try to walk past them and into the dining room. Sometimes I say "excuse me" and wait for them to move. (Directive)

I sit at table number three by the door. (Descriptive)

Eating lunch is good. (Affirmative)

Then it is time for play. Playtime is a good time to spread out and get rid of my energy that builds up when I am sitting. (Descriptive and Affirmative)

In the playground, many children run and shout. They are loud because they are having fun. (Descriptive and Perspective)

Keep in Mind

Although research on social stories has been generally positive, the database is just emerging, and additional research on the intervention is necessary (e.g., Sansoti et al., 2004; Toplis & Hadwin, 2006). Specifically, little data exists regarding the generalization and maintenance of the stories or how they are best implemented in inclusive classrooms. Consequently, social stories should not be the only social skills intervention that teachers use with students, and teachers should implement social stories in conjunction with other evidence-based practices (Sansoti et al., 2004).

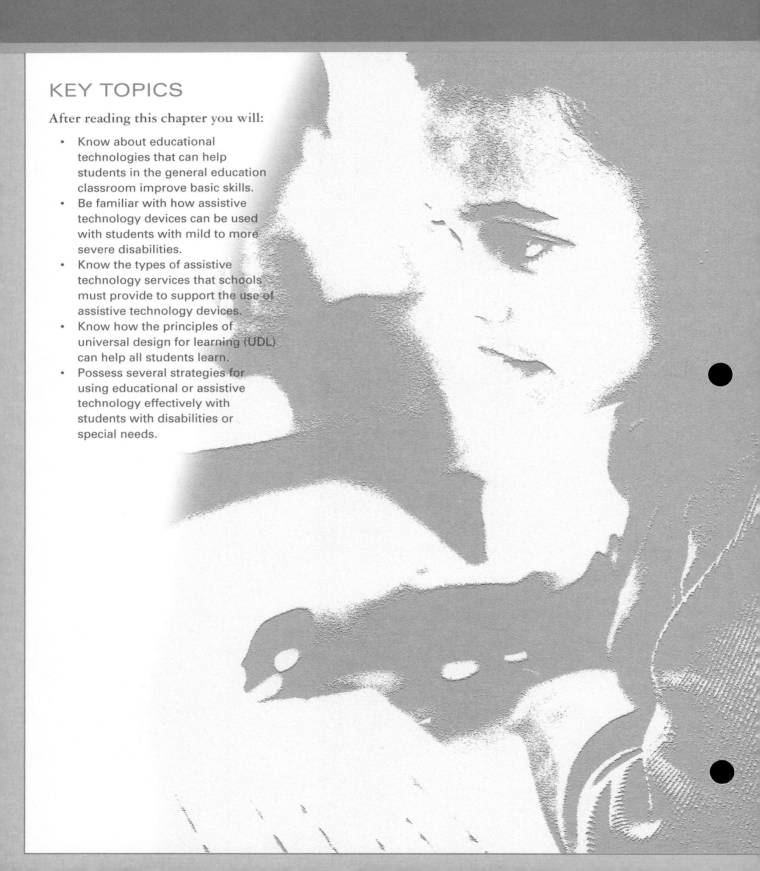

Using Technology to Enhance Inclusion

KEY TOPICS

After reading this chapter you will:

- Know about educational technologies that can help students in the general education classroom improve basic skills.
- Be familiar with how assistive technology devices can be used with students with mild to more severe disabilities.
- Know the types of assistive technology services that schools must provide to support the use of assistive technology devices.
- Know how the principles of universal design for learning (UDL) can help all students learn.
- Possess several strategies for using educational or assistive technology effectively with students with disabilities or special needs.

chapter 16

Perspectives on Using Technology to Enhance Inclusion

How Can Technology Help Meet the Needs of All Students?

Interview with Debra Bolinger, First-Grade Teacher, Mull Elementary School

Debra Bolinger is a big fan of educational technology. As a first-grade teacher at Mull Elementary School in Burke County, North Carolina, she has seen what educational technology can do for her students. Ms. Bolinger has been teaching for more than 10 years and has used technology in her classrooms for most of her career. Her interest in it, in fact, led to the pursuit and completion of a master's degree in educational technology at Appalachian State University in Boone, North Carolina.

Debra uses Reading Plus, a software program produced by Taylor Associates, designed to be used by students in grades K–12. Reading Plus provides a diagnostic assessment of a student's reading ability and then provides instruction for students in areas where they are weak. Key areas of instruction provided by the software include decoding, fluency, and comprehension.

Reading Plus was introduced in the Burke County school district by a local distributor about 9 years ago and subsequently was used at one school. Later, the program was introduced into other schools including Mull Elementary.

What Ms. Bolinger likes most about the Reading Plus program is the way it has affected students' reading scores, which she says "grew substantially" after the program was introduced. She says that the program "allowed the students to work at their individual levels. It has a very strong comprehension component." But she adds, "It is very important to know that for the success we experienced, the program must be monitored. It does not relieve the teacher of teaching responsibility; it just allows the reading instruction to be much more individualized." She has found that she can monitor about 10 to 12 students using the program at one time.

For students with special needs, or at-risk students participating in response to intervention, Debra says the program "most definitely" is a benefit. She does not claim that it answers all of a student's needs but explains, "It is the single best reading program I have ever used. However, it was only a piece of what we did; although, a very significant piece of our total program."

Clearly, Debra Bolinger will continue to see the advantages of educational technology and will use it to the benefit of her students for many years to come.

Introduction

Use of educational technology to help students learn to read, as the vignette about Debra Bollinger suggests, can be a powerful tool. But this may not be much of a surprise to you because today's world has simply become saturated with technology. We would guess that it's probably hard for you to remember a time without all the convenience brought to us by modern technology. We talk on our cell phones to friends and family between classes, watch Web-based presentations while sitting in the student union, listen to our iPods while exercising, and buy e-tickets online for a trip to a sunny place for spring break. We play electronic games with our fingers while sitting down and do arithmetic problems with calculators on our cell phones. MapQuest and the GPS on our dashboard mean never having to ask for directions again. People who used to earn a living typing term papers have mostly gone out of business, and if we don't have time to read, there are plenty of audio books that we can download and listen to while driving home.

New personal technology devices are appearing faster than we can learn how to use the ones we have, and the Internet puts just about every kind of information only a few mouse clicks away. Because technology makes so many tasks so much easier and faster, because we can do things sooner rather than later, and because so much of our work and play is of a higher quality, we readily pursue the benefits of technology. As Lee Ranie, Director of the Pew Internet and American Life Project, stated, "New gadgets allow people to enjoy media, gather information, and carry on communication anywhere. Wirelessness is its own adventure" (Ranie, 2007, slide 8). Ranie also noted:

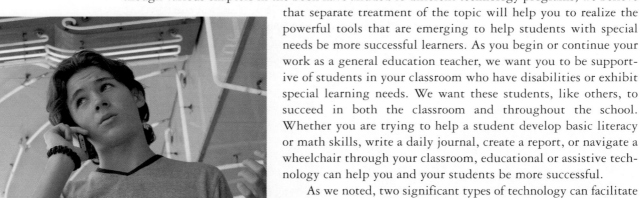

Pause & Reflect

What type of technology devices do you and your friends use? Do these devices and the connections they allow make your communication and learning easier? How would your student and social life be different without them? How would you survive?

- 88% of college students own cell phones
- 81% own digital cameras
- 63% own MP3 players
- 55% own video cameras
- 55% own laptops
- 27% own a PDA or BlackBerry
- 77% of college students play games online

Given the ubiquity of technology and the roles it plays in people's lives, it cannot be surprising that technology can also fill an important role in the lives and learning of public school students, especially those with special needs. For many of these students, technology can provide a shortcut to learning and participation that otherwise would be even more challenging without it.

Because of the rapid growth of educational technology and assistive technology, we believe that in a book on inclusion, a chapter devoted specifically to these topics is essential. Although various chapters in the book have alluded to different technology programs, we believe that separate treatment of the topic will help you to realize the powerful tools that are emerging to help students with special needs be more successful learners. As you begin or continue your work as a general education teacher, we want you to be supportive of students in your classroom who have disabilities or exhibit special learning needs. We want these students, like others, to succeed in both the classroom and throughout the school. Whether you are trying to help a student develop basic literacy or math skills, write a daily journal, create a report, or navigate a wheelchair through your classroom, educational or assistive technology can help you and your students be more successful.

As we noted, two significant types of technology can facilitate inclusion of students with special needs: educational technology and assistive technology. Additionally, instructional programs that incorporate universal design for learning (UDL) principles, which

Technology has made our lives very different.

can incorporate technology into the design of curricula, can also be very useful for enhancing student learning in inclusive settings.

Educational Technology

As you saw in the opening vignette about Debra Bolinger, she found that the reading software program called Reading Plus was a useful learning aid for many of her students. In fact, different types of educational technology can be useful for students with disabilities at various grade levels. Next we discuss the possible benefits of educational technology for some of the students you will teach.

Use of Educational Technology in General Education Classrooms

Educational technology in the general education classroom facilitates learning in several ways. For example, many students will use technology to gather information through the Internet, analyze data using spreadsheets, or create and share information using word processing and presentation software. When used effectively, technology can help learners direct more of their own learning, be more engaged in participatory and authentic learning processes, think more critically, and work more cooperatively with others (Bitter & Legacy, 2008; Jonassen, Howland, Marra, & Crismond, 2008). In this way, educational technologies support "meaningful learning when they fulfill a learning need—when interactions with technologies are learner initiated and learner controlled, and when the interactions with the technologies are conceptually and intellectually engaging" (Jonassen et al., 2008, p. 7).

> ### Pause & Reflect
>
> What role has educational technology played in your learning? Did you use specific software programs when you were in school? Have you often used word processing, presentation, or spreadsheet software for your academic work? And speaking of technology and education, how important is the Internet?

Using Educational Technology to Facilitate Inclusion

Many of the technology tools used by students without disabilities can be used in similar ways by students with disabilities. That is, many students with disabilities can work more effectively and efficiently when they use word processing programs, spreadsheets, presentation software, or the Internet. For example, one study found that adolescents with learning disabilities had fewer spelling errors and reading errors, and had better structure and organization in their written work when they used word processing software instead of writing with pencil and paper (Hetzroni & Shrieber, 2004). Other researchers have reported similar outcomes (e.g., Blackhurst, 2005; Hasselbring & Bausch, 2005; MacArthur, 2000; Wanzek et al., 2006).

When technology helps individuals with disabilities function more like those without disabilities, as found in the study by Hetzroni and Shrieber (2004), it is often considered to be *assistive technology*. It is thought of in this way because *assistive* technology is intended to bridge the gap between what a person *can* do and what he or she might *need* to do but cannot currently achieve. On the other hand, *educational* technology is intended to improve a student's knowledge or skills in many different curricular areas. As you can certainly imagine, assistive technology and educational technology often overlap. For example, word processing software can be considered assistive technology because it helps improve written output for a student with writing difficulties, as noted, but it might also help the student learn how to spell or use better grammar and thus be considered educational technology.

Later in this chapter, we will discuss programs that people with disabilities use as assistive technology. In the remaining portion of this section, however, we consider specific educational technology applications that are designed to help students with or without disabilities acquire and improve fluency in specific academic skills. You can use these programs to complement instruction in key academic areas. The technology that will be particularly useful might include drill-and-practice software, instructional games software, integrated learning systems, or combinations of these software packages (Bitter & Legacy, 2008). We hope you see how this technology can enhance instruction in basic skills, as discussed in Chapter 13.

Educational technology can enhance the acquisition of basic academic skills.

Types of Educational Technology. Drill-and-practice software provides learners with the opportunity to increase instructional time working on specific academic skills such as computing arithmetic answers, solving math word problems, or learning letter–sound correspondence. These software programs often use interesting formats to keep students' attention, present instructional items sequentially, and provide feedback either by telling the student the response is correct or by giving the student an opportunity to correct an incorrect response. Students can stop the program at any point and resume where they left off at their next session. Instructional games are similar to drill-and-practice software, except they have game formats and rules and allow students to compete with themselves or each other.

Integrated learning systems are more comprehensive instructional programs that educators may network throughout a school or school district. They are intended to incorporate instruction for an entire range of objectives tied to national, state, or district standards. According to Bitter and Legacy (2008), these systems are "generally intended to stand alone as a sole source of instruction" (p. 179). The material is presented in a linear format, and as with drill-and-practice software, the student may proceed at his or her own pace. The system manages data on student performance, and reports can be generated for teachers, schools, or school districts to monitor the progress of students. Although integrated learning systems software purports to offer complete instruction, most students, especially those with special needs, will need support from teachers in order to achieve academic success.

> **Strategy 16.1 discusses guidelines for teaching students to use educational technology.**

Teaching Students to Use Educational Technology. Many students with disabilities or special needs will enjoy working at a computer and will need little prompting to do so. It is important to realize, however, that most students will require initial instruction, modeling, and prompting in order to learn to use the software. Afterward, you may find that students can work independently on the computer for periods ranging from 10 to 20 minutes. Once you have learned for yourself how the software operates, you will be ready to introduce it to your students. Strategy 16.1 provides general guidelines for teachers to use when teaching students to use educational technology.

Reading and Math Educational Technology. Students with disabilities and special needs in regular classrooms will often need more intense instruction in two areas: reading and math. A number of commercially available, technology-based or -enhanced programs can help teachers in these areas. As noted in Strategy 16.1, these programs often can focus on the specific skill deficits of students and result in greater improvement than would occur without their use.

Pause & Reflect

Think about students you have known who have struggled with reading or math. What types of problems did they have? If you could design an instructional software program that could help them, what would it do? How would it help them?

Although we cannot tell you about all such programs, as a starter list, Figures 16.1 and 16.2 give you some examples of popular commercial technology products for teaching reading and math skills. You can investigate the Websites of these products in order to learn more about them.

As we said, products such as those listed in Figures 16.1 and 16.2 are quite numerous, and we could not hope to list or describe all of them. However, it will be beneficial for you to look in detail at instructional procedures used in some well-developed products. As you examine Strategies 16.2 and 16.3, you should realize that the producers of these products are attempting to offer applications that work in harmony with instruction provided by the teacher, and not as disconnected programs.

Figure 16.1	**Commercially Available Educational Software for Teaching Reading Skills**
Destination Reading Series (Riverdeep, web.riverdeep.net)	Four courses covering emergent literacy, phonemic awareness, fluency, comprehension, and vocabulary. For grades Pre-K–8.
The Waterford Early Reading Program (Waterford, www.waterford.org)	Offers self-paced, individualized instruction aligned with state and national reading standards. For grades Pre-K–2.
Headsprout Early Reading (Headsprout, www.headsprout.com)	80 individualized online lessons focusing on phonemic awareness, phonics, vocabulary, fluency, and comprehension. For grades K–2+.
PLATO Focus (PLATO, www.plato.com)	Uses print materials and educational technology to teach phonemic awareness, phonics, fluency, vocabulary development, and reading comprehension. For grades K–3.
Academy of Reading (Autoskill, www.autoskill.com)	Designed to help achieve rapid, permanent gains in reading and achieve skill mastery based on automaticity. Uses motivational principles to build fluency in foundation reading skills. For grades K–12.
LeapTrack (Leapfrog Schoolhouse, www.leapfrogschool-house.com)	Uses multisensory instruction, direct instruction, and high-interest nonfiction text to develop reading comprehension, word work knowledge, and vocabulary skills. For grades 3–8.
READ 180 (Scholastic, teacher.scholastic.com)	Provides individualized instruction in areas of phonemic and phonological awareness, fluency, vocabulary, comprehension, spelling, and writing. For elementary to high school.
KnowledgeBox (Pearson Digital Learning, www.PearsonDigital.com)	A digital learning system for reading/language arts, math, science, and social studies; designed to meet the varied needs of learners; offers materials across content areas. For grades K–6.

Strategy 16.2 outlines how to teach using READ 180, a program used to teach reading skills to students between the fourth and twelfth grades. You will see that the program provides a very comprehensive approach that not only uses technology but also requires direct instruction from the teacher and reading narratives from leveled readers.

In Strategy 16.3, we explain how to use PLATO® Achieve Now on PSP® (Mathematics) to improve students' math skills in different areas. The Achieve Now program is a recently developed product designed to present homework activities through a medium that many children and adolescents find entertaining, the PSP (PlayStation Portable). Although the centerpiece of this program is a piece of hardware that many young people today find entertaining, its success as educational technology depends a great deal on how well the teacher connects the game-based content to classroom instruction.

Strategy 16.2 discusses using READ 180 in the classroom.

Strategy 16.3 discusses using PLATO® Achieve now on PSP® (Mathematics) to improve homework performance.

What You Can Expect from Educational Technology

Teachers often use educational technology to complement or supplement instruction rather than replace it. This means that the students in your classroom with special needs will still require direct instruction in order to develop critical skills in reading, math, and other curricular

Figure 16.2	**Commercially Available Educational Software for Teaching Math Skills**
Achieve Now Mathematics (PLATO, www.plato.com)	Provides over 2,100 hours of instruction in math skills with over 1,000 learning objectives. For grades K–6.
Larson Pre-Algebra and Algebra (Larson Math, www.larsonmath.com)	This is online math software that covers middle school math topics including pre-algebra and algebra, and emphasizes skill building and problem solving.
iLearn Math (iLearn, www.ilearn.com)	Designed to provide individualized primary or supplemental instruction for students. For upper elementary grades (4 and 5) through high school.
Cognitive Tutor Algebra (Carnegie Learning, www.carnegielearning.com)	According to its Website, this product "uses students' intuitive problem-solving abilities to help them comprehend and master higher-order mathematical concepts."
Plato Algebra (Plato, www.plato.com)	This program includes 236 objectives for learning foundational skills and core algebra skills and includes tutorials and mastery tests. For students in middle school through high school.

areas. What you can expect from many educational technology programs, however, is an initial and periodic assessment of key skills, an opportunity to practice those skills, and an ongoing record of how students are progressing on skills. Programs will also often use thematic devices, graphics, and feedback to students to help motivate them to achieve the objectives of the program.

As a teacher, you may find that you have little personal choice in the software used in your classroom, at least as you begin teaching. Nevertheless, you should be knowledgeable about the desired qualities of educational technology programs. Strategy 16.4 offers a procedure for evaluating educational software that you will find helpful. We also encourage you to examine the Websites of specific products, keeping in mind that the technology producers want you to purchase their technology.

Many studies have evaluated the effectiveness of educational technologies, especially in the area of reading. Some of these studies have been supportive, but others have not (Bitter & Legacy, 2008). In one analysis of studies in which computers were used to help improve the reading skills of students with learning disabilities, Hall, Hughes, and Filbert (2000) found that students demonstrated improvement in 13 of 17 studies. In another review of literature, MacArthur, Ferretti, Okolo, and Cavalier (2001) found that computer programs were especially useful for teaching phonological awareness and decoding skills. Based on its review, the National Reading Panel concluded that "it is possible to use computer instruction for reading instruction" (p. 6-2) but did not feel the research at the time was conclusive about the overall effectiveness of educational software in reading (National Institute of Child Health and Human Development, 2000).

Although fewer studies have examined the effectiveness of educational technology in math for students with disabilities, they have been relatively positive. Hughes and Maccini (1997) found that drill-and-practice software was the most often-used type of program to teach math skills to students with learning disabilities and was generally effective.

In the largest study to date on the effectives of educational software, Dynarski et al. (2007), under contract to the U.S. Department of Education, focused on technology products that were used primarily to teach reading and math skills. Most of these are listed in Figures 16.1 and 16.2. The $10 million study included more than 9,000 students and evaluated the effectiveness of

Strategy Strategy 16.4 discusses evaluating educational technology.

reading software used in first and fourth grades, and math software used in sixth and ninth grades. Based on standardized test score results, the researchers concluded:

- Overall, the researchers found no differences between students who used the technology in their classrooms and those who did not.
- Reading scores for all first-grade students were better when class sizes were smaller.
- Fourth-grade students who spent more time using the reading software scored higher than students who spent less time.
- The researchers did not provide results for individual software products.

What can you conclude from these studies? Perhaps the safest conclusion is that educational technology is no panacea for student needs. Teachers should use educational software that has a good track record and appears to be effective, but should only use the technology with students under the appropriate circumstances. Strategy 16.4 will be useful to you as you evaluate individual software products.

It is important for educators to study and evaluate the quality of educational technology.

Assistive Technology

Whereas the purpose of educational technology is to help students learn or improve skills in areas such as reading and math, the purpose of assistive technology (AT) is to help students who lack specific skills or abilities engage in activities that they otherwise could not do or could not do very well. For example, a student who cannot read may listen to an audio book; someone who can't speak could use an augmentative or alternative communication (AAC) device; and a student who has poor writing skills could use word processing to write an essay.

Assistive technology devices vary greatly in their purposes and designs and may be used with students whose disabilities range from mild to severe. Unlike educational technology, which a school or school district may opt to use for its students, all students eligible for special education have a legal right under IDEA 2004 to be considered for an AT device and related AT services if these will help them meet their individualized education program (IEP) goals.

According to IDEA 2004, an AT device is "any item, piece of equipment, or product system, whether acquired commercially off the shelf, modified, or customized, that is used to increase, maintain, or improve functional capabilities of a child with a disability" (*excluding* "a medical device that is surgically implanted, or the replacement of such device"; IDEA 2004, Section 602). Additionally, the law does not simply recognize the importance of AT *devices* but also the critical need for providing AT *services* defined as "any service that directly assists a child with a disability in the selection, acquisition, or use of an assistive technology device." Figure 16.3 lists the AT services that schools can provide to help students use AT devices more effectively.

IDEA 2004 requires that, during an IEP session, the IEP planning committee must "consider whether the child needs assistive technology devices and services." This can be interpreted to mean that the IEP team must especially consider an AT device when reviewing the present level of performance, during the development of annual goals and objectives or benchmarks, and when determining the appropriate placement of a student (Parette & Peterson-Karlan, 2007).

An AT device that would better allow a student to function in a general education classroom would certainly merit consideration by the IEP team. However, the decision-making process for determining whether or not a specific AT device is appropriate for a student with a disability is complex. In Strategy 16.5, we provide a practical process for deciding about the appropriateness of specific AT devices and questions that the IEP team should answer when considering an AT device.

Strategy 16.5 discusses the assistive technology device decision-making process.

Strategy

Figure 16.3   Assistive Technology Services to Facilitate the Use of AT Devices

- Evaluate the needs of the student with disabilities, including a functional evaluation of the child in the child's customary environment.
- Purchase, lease, or otherwise provide for the acquisition of assistive technology devices by the student.
- Select, design, fit, customize, adapt, apply, maintain, repair, or replace assistive technology devices.
- Coordinate and use other therapies, interventions, or services with assistive technology devices, such as those associated with existing education and rehabilitation plans and programs.
- Train or provide technical assistance for the student or, where appropriate, the student's family.
- Train or provide technical assistance for professionals (including individuals providing education and rehabilitation services), employers, or other individuals who provide services to, employ, or are otherwise substantially involved in the major life functions of the student.

Pause & Reflect

If a technology device helps you do something that you cannot do without it, you might consider it an AT device. Recently, GPS navigational devices have become popular. Have you ever used one of these, and did it help you get somewhere? If so, you were using an AT device.

Thousands of AT devices are available, far too many to completely list, so the selection of the type of device a student may need, or a specific AT device, can be challenging. One way to determine the sort of device that would be useful is to consider different learning needs of a student and then think of the type of AT device that might be useful (Best, Reed, & Bigge, 2005; Wisconsin Assistive Technology Initiative, 2004). In the following sections, we discuss four broad categories of AT devices: those that are useful for helping students who have primarily academic weaknesses; devices to help students with more significant disabilities with communication; personal digital assistants to help students with various routines; and devices that can help students with daily living needs.

AT Devices to Support Academic Activities

Many students with disabilities can have greater success in learning academic content if they are supported with AT devices that help them do so.

Pause & Reflect

Do you prefer to read a book or to listen to an audio version? Can you imagine what you would choose if you experienced serious reading problems? E-books can open a big world to many people who have difficulty reading print due to learning disabilities or visual disabilities.

AT Devices to Support Reading. In the area of reading, technology may help students by providing them with visual and auditory supports. Technology can highlight certain words to improve visual discrimination, provide picture cues, and even convert written text to speech that the student can listen to. Using text-to-speech software, and compatible hardware, students can scan printed materials and read using digitalized speech, a great support for students with significant reading difficulties. Programs can also modify the speed of the reading, spell words for students, or even read in different languages or different voices. E-books and e-texts can be downloaded to help students with reading difficulties acquire content that they might otherwise not be able to access (Johnston, Beard, & Carpenter, 2007). Figure 16.4 provides a list of AT reading resources to assist students with reading difficulties.

AT Devices to Support Writing and Spelling. Technologies also can help students who have difficulty writing and spelling. If handwriting presents a challenge to students and it is important for the student to improve this skill, then various low-tech to high-tech approaches might be useful.

Low-tech strategies can help structure the student's writing environment to produce better handwritten work. For example, securing the paper with a clipboard or tape, providing clear boundaries with heavy lines, or adapting the writing tool by using pencil grips might be helpful. Occupational therapists can usually offer assistance to teachers to help in this area. If the student will be better facilitated by using a keyboard to write, the student can use a personal computer or portable word processor. Students can travel with these devices and use them to produce written work whenever necessary (Johnston et al., 2007).

E-books can be downloaded to make literature available for students with reading difficulties.

Besides circumventing handwriting problems, word processing can also be helpful in other ways. Many students with mild disabilities will have difficulty using spelling and grammar correctly to produce written documents. To help them overcome this challenge, word processing can provide spell checking and grammar checking and can facilitate editing a paper by providing tools such as cutting, copying, and pasting. Related hardware and software can also be helpful. Handheld devices can help students find and correct spelling errors and define words. Word prediction software aids students having difficulty spelling a word by providing several words that might be meaningful in the context of the sentence. The student can then look at the list of words and select the one that is most appropriate (National Center to Improve Practice, 1998). Technologies that are useful for helping students with spelling and writing appear in Figures 16.5 and 16.6. After you examine the types of products listed in Figures 16.5 and 16.6, look at Strategy 16.6, which explains how teachers can use word processing and related software when students have writing weaknesses.

> **Strategy 16.6** discusses using word processing and related software to support student writing.
>
> *Strategy*

AT Devices to Support Math. Students who have difficulty with mathematics can also be helped by AT devices. These devices can help students whose challenges are associated with completing calculations or who have difficulty with problem solving due to language and comprehension problems. Students who have difficulty functioning due to weaknesses in basic calculations may use calculators to help them circumvent these problems. Students who must focus on solving more complex word problems will often find that using calculators will allow them to focus more on reasoning and less on arithmetic operations. Figure 16.7 lists several AT devices that will help students who have difficulty with math. After reviewing the material that appears in Figure 16.7, look at Strategy 16.7, which includes several helpful tactics for teaching students how to use calculators.

> **Strategy 16.7** discusses teaching students with disabilities to use calculators.
>
> *Strategy*

Augmentative and Alternative Communication Devices

Some students, especially those with intellectual, physical, or multiple disabilities, require AAC devices to help compensate for their lack of verbal communication ability. Specially trained speech–language pathologists (SLPs) are best prepared to provide support for these students so they can learn to use these special AT devices. However, educators should also be aware of these students and their communicative needs and should know how to promote the use of the AAC devices so students can communicate effectively in natural environments.

Students can use a variety of AAC devices. They may range from being fairly simple (producing single words) to being capable of producing synthesized speech. Examples of AAC devices include the following:

- Communication boards or books with pictures, objects, letters, and/or words
- Eye-gaze boards or frames

Figure 16.4   Assistive Technology Reading Resources

Edmark Reading Program
http://www.donjohnston.com/
catalog/edmarkdtxt.htm

This software uses a whole word, multisensory approach to teach comprehension and recognition. Users of this software learn sight recognition and meaning of a word, practice comprehension, and use the word in story content. Repetition and short instructional steps are used.

Homework Wiz Plus and Speaking Homework Wiz
http://www.donjohnston.com/
catalog/homeworkd.htm

Franklin's nonspeaking speller and dictionary program helps students spell-check words and includes 40,000 basic definitions. Confusable Checker helps students distinguish homophones to make correct word choices. The Speaking Homework Wiz allows students to enter a word phonetically, then the correct spelling will be displayed along with an audio pronunciation of the word.

IntelliTools Reading: Balanced Literacy
http://www.intellitools.com/
Products/Balanced_Literacy

This is a nine-unit program that provides literacy instruction at the first-grade skill level. It incorporates reading, phonics, and writing. Included are 142 lessons, nine full-color storybooks, 212 phonics activities, a CD with more than 500 activities, and 27 structured writing exercises. This program uses a mouse and IntelliKeys.

Key Skills for Reading: Letters and Words
http://store.sunburst.com/Search.aspx?

Five multilevel activities provide animated practice. Students learn the order of the alphabet, to organize words and objects by initial consonant sounds, to identify short and long vowel sounds, and lots more. The program has clear auditory support to help in reading success.

Kurzweil 3000
http://www.kurzweiledu.com/
products_k3000win_features.asp

Kurzweil offers printed or electronic text for the computer screen with visual and audible assistance. The program includes many features to help with study skills, writing, and test taking. It adapts to each learning style. Kurzweil 3000 offers an audible assistant to help with spell-checking and word prediction as students type.

WYNN 3.1 Freedom Scientific's Learning Systems Group
http://freedomscientific.com

This software solution transforms printed text into understandable text and reads it aloud while simultaneously highlighting it.

Let's Go Read
http://www.sunburst-store.com/
cgi-bin/sunburst.storefront/EN/
Catalog/1244

Lessons offered in this software help students learn to read through interactive stories and sequenced lessons. Vocabulary skills are expanded, as is comprehension.

Picture It
http://www.slatersoftware.com/pit.html

This software includes more than 6,000 pictures that can be incorporated to text so that the reader can see picture-supported material to better understand the text. Students can listen to stories and read along with highlighted words.

Quicktionary II, Reading Pen II http://www.donjohnston.com/ catalog/quicktionarytxt.htm	These handheld scanners allow students to simply scan over a word that is not understood. The word is then read out loud back to the student and the dictionary definition is provided.
ScreenReader http://www.brighteye.com/texthelp.htm	Allows a PC to read out loud words that appear in any Windows-based application.
Recordings for the Blind and Dyslexic http://www.rfbd.org	RFB&D's library contains more than 104,000 titles in a broad variety of subjects, from literature and history to math and sciences, at all academic levels, from kindergarten through postgraduate and professional.
SoothSayer Word Prediction http://www.enablemart.com/ productdetail.aspx?store-10& pid-356&dept-22	Many features of this program help students type more accurately and more quickly. AutoType completes a word once the student starts to type it. SoothSayer can correct spelling errors and also comes with a built-in dictionary of more than 11,000 words. A speech voice option is available.
TextHelp Read and Write Gold http://www.brighteye.com/texthelp.htm	This software offers a range of helpful tools for special education in reading and writing. Some of these include word prediction, dictionary, spell-checker, RealSpeak voice providing a humanlike voice, and a pronunciation tutor.
WordSmith http://www.brighteye.com/texthelp.htm	WordSmith provides visual reinforcement and helps to develop recognition of new words and vocabulary through color highlights and reading of words, sentences, and paragraphs. WordSmith helps with pronunciation as it breaks words into syllables, and it includes a moving mouth to aid in more accurate speech. Also included are word prediction, spell-checker, thesaurus, and homonym support.
CAST eReader http://www.cast.org	This text-to-speech software tool is designed to support users who have difficulty reading.

Source: Reprinted from Johnston, L., Beard, L. A., & Carpenter, L. B. (2007, pp. 68–69). *Assistive technology: Access for all students.* Upper Saddle River, NJ: Merrill/Pearson. Used with permission.

- Simple voice-output devices (e.g., BIGmack, Cheap Talk, Voice in a Box, MicroVoice, Talking Picture Frame)
- Voice-output devices with different communication levels (e.g., 6 Level Voice in a Box, Macaw, Digivox)
- Voice-output devices with icon sequencing (e.g., AlphaTalker II, Vanguard, Chatbox)
- Voice-output devices with dynamic display (e.g., Dynavox, Speaking Dynamically with laptop computer, Freestyle)
- Devices with speech synthesis for typing (e.g., Cannon Communicator, Link, Write:Out Loud with laptop) (Best, Reed, et al., 2005)

Pause & Reflect

How would your life be different if you lost your ability to communicate? Would you want to find an alternative way to let people know what you want, what you need, or what you think? Do you see the importance of having AAC devices available for people with communication disorders?

Figure 16.5 | AT Spelling Resources

Quicktionary II http://donjohnston.com	This device translates and defines words and provides multilingual support. A pen is scrolled over the desired text and the device verbally announces and translates each word. The dictionary recognizes more than 300,000 words and expressions.
Speaking Spelling Ace Spelling Ace with Thesaurus Speaking Spelling and Handwriting Ace http://www.franklin.com	Franklin offers several handheld devices for correction of English-language spelling.
Language Master 6000 SF http://www.freedomscientific.com	This handheld dictionary offers full speech controls to read screens or speak individual words at controlled speeds. At 6 inches square, it has a large display option and QWERTY keyboard.
Homework Wiz Plus Speaking Homework Wiz http://donjohnston.com	These devices can be purchased as speaking or nonspeaking spellers and dictionaries. They offer spelling correction for about 50,000 words.

Source: Reprinted from Johnston, L., Beard, L. A., & Carpenter, L. B. (2007, p. 71). *Assistive technology: Access for all students.* Upper Saddle River, NJ: Merrill/Pearson. Used with permission.

Examples of specific AAC devices can be seen in Figure 16.8.

Finding an appropriate AAC device for a student and teaching him how to use it are only the beginning to helping the student to achieve communicative success. Many students with AAC devices will be more successful if they have support and instruction to use the device in the classroom and other areas around the school and community. Strategy 16.8 describes how a classroom teacher might be able to help a student using an AAC device learn to communicate more effectively.

> **Strategy**
> Strategy 16.8 discusses supporting students who use AAC devices.

Personal Digital Assistants

The appropriate AAC device can facilitate communication for many students with disabilities.

Many people use personal digital assistants (PDAs, also called palmtop computers) daily to help them manage personal needs. Depending on their specific capabilities, these devices can help with various chores such as managing an appointments calendar, writing documents, reading e-mails, accessing the Internet, or listening to downloaded books. Over the last several years, researchers have demonstrated that specially configured PDAs can help persons with intellectual disabilities perform various activities that they could do not alone or without extensive training (Wehmeyer, Palmer, Smith, Parent, Davies, & Stock, 2006). Although products such as these are currently not commercially available, they clearly show potential. One study provides an interesting example.

Individuals with intellectual disabilities used a palmtop computer called a Pocket Compass to help them decide what steps they should take on vocational tasks that required decision making. The Pocket Compass had been pre-programmed with audio and visual cues to remind participants what actions they should take (after initial instruction) at certain decision-making

Figure 16.6	**AT Writing Resources**	
Co:Writer http://www.donjohnston.com/catalog/cow4000d.htm	This program adds word prediction, grammar, and vocabulary to word processors. FlexSpell helps those students who spell phonetically by recognizing and predicting words consistent with the actual letters and sounds of the letters. Grammar support helps correct such errors as subject–verb agreement, spelling, customary word usage, and proper noun usage.
EZ Keys http://www.freedomofspeech.com/wordsplus.html	Uses dual word prediction that displays a table of the six most frequently used words that begin with the letters that the student types when beginning to type a word. EZ Keys provides alternatives to using a mouse: expanded keyboard, joystick, single and multiple switch scanning.
Gus! Word Prediction http://www.enablemart.com/productdetail.aspx?store-10&pid-576&dept-22	Improves typing speed by offering word completion and word prediction. Offers a list of words based on what keys the user has already typed. The list changes according to keys typed and then predicts the current and the subsequent words. This helps slow or one-finger typists. Abbreviation expansion, speech output, and dictionary are also provided.
WordQ Writing Aid Software http://www.enablemart.com/productdetail.aspx?store-10&pid-104&dept-22	This writing tool is used with standard word processors. It provides spoken feedback and suggests words to use through word prediction. Students can hear each word spoken so that it is easier to differentiate words. It is simple to use and transparent to all Windows applications.
Write:Outloud http://www.donjohnston.com/catalog/writoutd.htm	Immediate speech feedback is given as students type words, sentences, and paragraphs. Students can listen for proper word usage, grammar, and misspellings. Students with disabilities can correct their work independently from hearing and seeing what they write.
Draft:Builder http://www.donjohnston.com	This tool leads students through three key steps in creating a first draft: organizing ideas, taking notes, and writing the draft. The display gives students a framework to generate, manipulate, and connect ideas and information.

Source: Reprinted from Johnston, L., Beard, L. A., & Carpenter, L. B. (2007, p. 72). *Assistive technology: Access for all students.* Upper Saddle River, NJ: Merrill/Pearson. Used with permission.

points in the task. For example, when the individual had to make a decision, the computer displayed up to four pictures, each representing a different possible decision at the decision-making point. As the pictures were displayed, an audio instruction stated, "Touch the picture on the screen that matches the number shown on the second page of the invoice" (Davies, Stock, & Wehmeyer, 2003, p. 184). When the individual tapped the number, the program continued to provide audio and visual cues to direct the participant to the appropriate action. Davies and co-workers (2003) found that study participants using the Pocket Compass required fewer

Figure 16.7	**AT Mathematics Resources**
MathPad (IntelliTools) http://www.intellitools.com	MathPad enables students to do arithmetic directly on the computer. The program is ideal for students who need help organizing or navigating math problems or who have difficulty doing math with pencil and paper.
Access to Math http://www.donjohnston.com	Access to Math is the talking math worksheet program that helps students with organizing, sequencing, working in columns, and memorizing math facts. A worksheet generator lets you automatically create on-screen or printed worksheets to support individual learning needs.
Portable Calculator with Talking Multiplication Table http://www.independentliving.com	This small folding calculator performs standard arithmetic functions. When the key is pressed, followed by the number of the multiplication table the user wants to hear, it speaks the entire table.
GTCalc Scientific Calculator http://www.independentliving.com	This software offers a comprehensive range of scientific functions in logical groups for easy accessibility. Accessible features include input via keyboard or mouse with input and output spoken, large number display, a Mouse Talk feature that speaks the button captions, and four levels of screen magnification.
Talking Pocket Calculator http://www.independentliving.com	A small, thin, folding calculator with clear numbers on the number pads and on the monitor. All the setting functions speak, except the calendar, which is visual. Says numbers in units or digital.
Talking Texas Instruments Scientific Calculator http://www.independentliving.com	The features of this small scientific calculator include a learning mode for key identification that does not affect calculations. The key is announced when pressed. There is a choice of silent or talking operation. Tactile, large, functionally zoned keys, volume control, and earphone are included.
Big:Calc http://www.donjohnston.com	Six calculator layouts are available for this talking on-screen calculator. Font size and color adjust to increase visibility and figure ground discrimination.

Source: Reprinted from Johnston, L., Beard, L. A., & Carpenter, L. B. (2007, p. 74). *Assistive technology: Access for all students.* Upper Saddle River, NJ: Merrill/Pearson. Used with permission.

prompts from their support person, had fewer decision errors, and had fewer errors on completing the steps in the task.

AT Devices for Daily Living

Many additional AT devices can help meet a variety of daily needs. Many of these will be useful for students with physical or multiple disabilities. These include devices for mobility, such as powered wheelchairs or scooters; or for activities of daily living, such as adaptive eating utensils or adapted toothbrushes. To review many of the available AT devices that can be useful for students with disabilities, you can visit ABLEDATA at *www.abledata.com,* a Website that provides information about thousands of AT devices.

One of the most common AT devices used for daily living that teachers will encounter is a motorized wheelchair or other powered mobility device. These devices will often be used by students with physical or multiple disabilities and will allow them the freedom of movement similar to that experienced by other students. Strategy 16.9 provides a number of steps that a teacher should take when students require a motorized wheelchair.

Strategy 16.9 discusses supporting students who use motorized wheelchairs.

Strategy

How Effective Is Assistive Technology?

As you have seen from our discussion, AT devices are quite varied. This makes it difficult to evaluate them as a group and to draw any definitive conclusion about their effectiveness. We do know, however, that numerous case studies and single-subject design studies have reported positive findings when individual students with disabilities have used AT devices. These studies have included students with mild disabilities who have achieved greater academic success using AT devices (e.g., Hetzroni & Shrieber, 2004; Kim, Woodruff, Klein, & Vaughn, 2006; MacArthur & Cavalier, 2004; Montgomery, Karlan, & Coutinho, 2001; Wanzek et al., 2006; Williams, 2002) as well as students with more significant disabilities who have learned to communicate and control their environment using AT devices (e.g., Carey & Sale, 1994; Cavalier & Brown, 1998; Cosbey & Johnston, 2006; Daniels, Sparling, Reilly, & Humphry, 1995; Hutinger et al., 1996; Todis, 1996; Lancioni et al., 2002). It is safe to say that for individual students with disabilities, AT devices are likely to be more effective if they are selected and applied with care.

Universal Design for Learning

Universal design for learning (UDL) is a curriculum design process called for in IDEA 2004 that provides guidelines for designing curriculum in a way that will make it more accessible to more learners with various ability levels. UDL has become a more feasible practice because of advances in technology, specifically the availability of digitalized text.

Principles of UDL

One way to enhance the opportunity for students with disabilities to participate in inclusive classrooms and the general curriculum is to design a curriculum based on the principles of universal design. UDL principles begin with the notion that key elements can be varied to allow learning by students with a range of abilities. The Center for Applied Special Technology (1999–2007) proposed three essential qualities of a universal curriculum:

1. **Multiple means of representation:** Alternative means of presentation reduce perceptual/learning barriers and can adjust to the different ways that students recognize things. Digital format is the most flexible means for presenting curricular materials because it makes material transformable, transportable, and recordable.

2. **Multiple means of expression:** Students can respond with preferred means of control. Different strategic and motor systems of students can be accommodated.

3. **Multiple means of engagement:** Students' interests in learning can be matched with the mode of presentation/response; this can better motivate more students.

Pause & Reflect

UDL principles had their origin in architectural designs meant to accommodate people with different needs, such as cuts in sidewalks or ramps for wheelchairs, and Braille signs for blind people. While these designs are helpful to some, they are not meant to be detrimental to others. Can you think of other kinds of universal designs that could be helpful? Can you see the similarities between UDL and differentiated instruction (in Chapter 12)?

Applying UDL Principles

What does the application of UDL principles mean from a practical point of view? Essentially, it means that when designing curriculum, teachers should plan from the outset for variations in the

Figure 16.8 Examples of AAC Devices

Device and Company		Speech Output	Message Representation	Access (User Input)
Alpha Talker II (Prentke Romich Company)		Digitized speech	Combine symbols to create messages	Direct selection
Dec-Aid (Aptivation, Inc.)		Recorded speech	10-switch capacity	Direct switch
DigiVox 2 (Dyna-Vox Systems)		Digitized speech	Can use symbols, words, pictures, etc.	Direct selection
DynaVox 3100 (DynaVox Systems)		Synthesized speech and/or digitized speech	Dynamic display	Direct touch on the panel

Device and Company		Speech Output	Message Representation	Access (User Input)
LightWRITER (Zygo Industries)		Synthesized DECtalk	Type messages on the keyboard	Direct selection keyboard sensitivity can be adjusted
Macaw Series (Zygo Industries)		Digitized speech	Add your own symbols/ message overlays; up to 128 messages	Direct selection using the membrane keyboard
SuperHawk (ADAMLAB)		Digitized speech	Up to 72 message cells per page	Direct selection by the touch panel or plug in up to four remote switches
Vanguard (Prentke Romich Company)		DECtalk synthesized speech and digitized speech	Fully customizable; can use symbols, words, pictures, etc.; uses Minspeak technology	Direct selection with the touch panel, optical head pointing, or scanning with switches/joysticks

Source: Coping.org. (2006). Tools for coping with life's stressors. Retrieved on July 14, 2006, from http://www.coping.org/specialneeds/assistech/aacdev.htm DECtalk. Coping.org is a public service of James J. Messina, Ph.D., and Constance M. Messina, Ph.D. Reprinted with permission of James Messina.

design that will accommodate learners of different abilities. Consider the following examples from CAST (1999–2007):

- Pam, a student with learning disabilities for whom English is also a second language, uses CAST's eReader software to help her complete a reading assignment. eReader's spoken voice and synchronized highlighting features help her track words on a page, pace her reading, and associate the way a word looks with the way it sounds. After reading the story several times with the spoken voice option turned on and the highlighting speed set to slow, she turns the read-aloud feature off, increases the highlighting speed slightly, and reads the story again. In this manner, she works gradually to increase her reading comprehension and speed.
- Seth, a student with low vision whose word-comprehension skills are excellent, uses eReader to adjust the font, style, size, and color of digital text, background, and highlighting, to achieve maximum contrast and readability.
- Jeremy, a poor speller who does not enjoy writing, uses the auditory feedback offered by Don Johnston's Write:OutLoud software to engage in the task of writing an English composition. As he types his composition and it is displayed on the computer screen, the program reads it aloud by word, sentence, paragraph, or letter by letter, helping him to identify sentence-construction problems and spelling mistakes. When he misspells a word, it flashes on the screen, indicating his error. Using the program's talking spell checker, he calls up a list of suggested words to replace the misspelled word and, in the case of homonyms, short definitions to distinguish one word from another. Jeremy selects a word when its pronunciation (or definition) indicates it is the correct word, and completes the composition without spelling errors.

The CAST eReader and the more recent version, the AspireReader 4.0, were developed to facilitate reading by students who have deficiencies in this area. These products allow students to access text through digital talking books, Internet pages, and word processing through synchronized visual, auditory, and tracking feature functions. Other UDL products and services from CAST can be seen in Figure 16.9. These can help teachers design or adapt their own lessons based on UDL principles, develop digital books, and read unabridged literature.

Example of the Effectiveness of UDL Applications

Although e-books and similar technology-based products can be useful in implementing UDL principles, teachers should also consider other components of instruction and learning. Dymond and colleagues reported an example of a comprehensive instructional unit using UDL guidelines (Dymond et al., 2006). These researchers used the principles of UDL to design a high school science course that would be accessible to students without disabilities, students with mild disabilities, and students with more severe intellectual disabilities. The authors developed a set of questions to address as they redesigned traditional course lesson plans. The questions helped them consider how key areas could be modified including the curriculum, instructional delivery and organization of the learning environment, student participation, materials, and assessment. The major changes made to the course included the following:

Materials: Large-print reading material and laptops with Internet connections and LCD projectors were added to the more traditional materials.

Forms of student participation: Students were given choices of how they would participate. For example, active, interactive, and leadership types of participation were offered including more hands-on activities, team projects, and students teaching students.

Instructional delivery: A variety of instructional methods occurred during daily instruction including more student-directed instruction and technology-driven instruction.

Assessment: Forms of assessment increased including reading tests to students and using rubrics and checklists to evaluate students during presentations and hands-on work sessions.

Dymond et al. (2006) reported that as a result of the UDL process, many changes occurred in the teachers and their students. The general education and special education teachers began to

Figure 16.9 | UDL Products and Services from CAST

CAST UDL Lesson Builder™

The Universal Design for Learning (UDL) Lesson Builder is an interactive online tool that helps educators develop or adapt lessons that increase access to learning for all students based on UDL principles. UDL Lesson Builder walks educators through the process of customizing the curriculum to align standards and meet individual learner's needs. At each step, educators can read or hear explanations of the UDL principles behind each innovation. CAST developed UDL Lesson Builder, in cooperation with the Access Center (American Institutes for Research), as a free resource for educators. Copyright 2006 CAST. Please send comments or suggestions about UDL Lesson Builder to *lessonbuilder@cast.org*.

CAST UDL Book Builder™

The Universal Design for Learning (UDL) Book Builder is an interactive online tool that enables educators to develop their own digital books to support reading instruction for children aged 3–10. Here teachers can create, edit, and save universally designed texts that support diverse learners. Terry, an animated character, guides educators as they write text, choose images, and develop scripts for the prompts, hints, and models that will help build young readers' skills. CAST has developed UDL Book Builder as a free resource for educators to help increase all students' access, participation, and progress in the general education curriculum. Copyright 2006 CAST. Please send comments or suggestions about UDL Book Builder to *bookbuilder@cast.org*.

Thinking Reader®

Based on CAST's research into digital learning environments and the research of renowned reading experts, Thinking Reader provides students with instruction and practice in key reading strategies. Using unabridged core literature such as the novels *Roll of Thunder* and *The Giver,* this universally designed resource enables struggling readers to read the same high-quality books as their peers. In 2005, Thinking Reader won a prestigious 2005 Codie Award from the Software & Information Industry Association as the "Best Education Instructional Solution for Special Needs Students." It also won a 2005 Distinguished Achievement Award from the Association of Education Publishers.

Source: Product descriptions reprinted with permission from CAST. (1999–2007). Universal design for learning. Retrieved February 28, 2008, from http://www.cast.org/. Copyright 1999–2007 CAST.

collaborate more, shared more instructional responsibilities, and became more concerned that the students with disabilities be able to participate meaningfully during instruction.

Although UDL has existed for a number of years, it is still a developing and growing approach to designing instruction so that students at different ability levels can access it. It is notable, however, that many proponents of UDL view it as the basis of a new approach to instruction and are promoting UDL for universal applications in schools across the country (CAST, 1999–2007).

Summary

This chapter addressed the following topics:

The use of educational technology

- Educational technology products can be very useful to help students acquire specific knowledge or skills, especially for students with special needs, those who are at risk in school, or other students who require extra or more intense learning experiences.
- Educational technology can provide the student with the chance to work alone on different learning targets, engage the student more by providing dramatic graphics and performance feedback, and help the teacher monitor the student's skill acquisition.
- Numerous technology products can facilitate learning literacy and math skills.

The use of assistive technology

- Assistive technology (AT) devices are designed to help close the gap between what a student can do in a certain situation and what a student needs to do.
- AT devices can help students with mild disabilities or who are at risk achieve outcomes such as comprehending a written narrative by modifying the text or even translating written words into spoken words.
- AT devices for students with more severe disabilities include devices to help the students with tasks such as eating or mobility.
- According to IDEA 2004, school districts should provide AT devices to students with identified disabilities whenever a device may be needed to help them to achieve their IEP goals.

Principles of universal design for learning

- Universal design for learning (UDL) designs instruction so that it is accessible to all students.
- The use of UDL in curriculum and instruction can be facilitated with recent developments in technology.
- UDL is based on developing alternative ways to present instructional content, different ways for students to respond to the content, and multiple means for maintaining students' attention and participation.

Addressing Professional Standards

Standards addressed in Chapter 16 include:

CEC Standards: (3) Individual learning differences; (4) instructional strategies; (5) learning environments and social interactions; (7) instructional planning.

INTASC Standards: Principle 2—Provide learning opportunities to support the learning and development of all students; Principle 3—Create instructional opportunities for diverse learners; Principle 4—Understand and use a variety of instructional strategies; Principle 6—Use knowledge of communication techniques to support students; Principle 10—Collaborate to support student learning and well-being.

Praxis™ II Standards: Knowledge-based core principles: (3) delivery of services to students with disabilities. Application of core principles: (1) curriculum, (2) instruction, (4) managing the learning environment.

PUTTING IT ALL TOGETHER

One way to help students with special needs achieve their potential is to use existing technology as a component of universally designed instruction. You are undoubtedly familiar with an array of technology devices and the value they add to daily life. As a general educator, you will find that including students with disabilities in your classroom can be more successful if you and your collaborators in special education take advantage of different forms of technology. We suggest that to do so you reflect on the following suggestions:

1. **Learn about what is available.** Technology is so abundant it seems to be outdated before we can learn to use it. Knowing what is available therefore requires teachers to access information through the Web, read books or journals, attend conferences or workshops, or talk to their school district's technology consultant to keep up with newly developing products.

2. **Collaborate with others.** As we discussed in Chapter 11, collaboration with others is critical for successfully teaching students with special needs. All team members should be involved in identifying, selecting, and implementing the use of technology to ensure that devices will be used appropriately and in settings that will maximize potential.

3. **Focus on the student's needs.** We recommend the use of technology tools only when they contribute to the ability of the student to do something, or help the student learn better or faster. Although technology can be used for entertainment, in instructional settings, technology should help students achieve specific goals or perform important skills.

4. **Monitor students' progress.** Many educational technologies incorporate assessment probes into the program and create reports for teachers so they can assess students' progress. You should use these reports and modify instruction as necessary to improve your students' performance. With AT devices, you can observe how often the student uses the device, if the student uses it as designed, and if it helps meet the objective for which it was designed.

myeducationlab

We present strategies in the second half of this chapter (Strategies 16.1 to 16.9) in a step-by-step format so that you can use them in your classroom right away. In addition, in the following table, we identify some video clips, cases, and simulations that will allow you to experience some of these strategies (or complementary strategies) in a real classroom environment.

EFFECTIVE PRACTICE	MYEDUCATIONLAB CONNECTION	CONSIDER THIS
Strategy 16.2: Using READ 180 in the Classroom	Go to MyEducationLab, select the topic *Learning Disabilities*, and go to the Activities and Applications section. Next, watch the video entitled "Small Group Instruction," and answer the accompanying questions.	As you watch the video, focus on the three-part instructional element of this program. Compare and contrast the effectiveness of each of the instructional components. Which component do you think is most helpful for these students? Why?
Strategy 16.4: Evaluating Educational Technology	Go to MyEducationLab, and select the topic *Autism Spectrum Disorders*. Next, go to the Building Teaching Skills and Dispositions section, and complete the activity entitled "Instructional Software."	As you watch these two videos and answer the accompanying questions, think about how you might evaluate these two pieces of instructional software using the guiding principles discussed in Strategy 16.4.
Strategy 16.5: A Decision-Making Process for Selecting AT Devices	Go to MyEducationLab, select the topic *Inclusive Practices*, and go to the Activities and Applications section. Next, read and analyze the strategy entitled "Organization IS at Hand: PDAs in the Inclusive Classroom."	As you read and analyze the strategy, think about the decision-making process you would undertake (look at Strategy 16.6) when considering the use of a PDA in your classroom for specific students.
Strategy 16.6: Using Word Processing and Related Software to Support Student Writing	Go to MyEducationLab, select the topic *Content Area Teaching*, and go to the Activities and Applications section. Next, go to the Language Arts subsection, and watch the videos entitled "Scaffolding: Writing" and "Story Lesson," and answer the accompanying questions.	As you watch these videos, think about how you might use what you have learned in Strategy 16.6 to come up with a plan for these teachers to use word processing and related software as they support student writing.
Strategy 16.8: Supporting Students Who Use AAC Devices	Go to MyEducationLab, select the topic *Inclusive Practices*, and go to the Activities and Applications section. Next, watch the video entitled "An Inclusive Neighborhood School: Interview with Principal Jackson," and answer the accompanying questions.	As you watch the video and answer the accompanying questions, focus on the principal's discussion of the AAC devices they use at her school.
Strategy 16.9: Supporting Students Who Use Motorized Wheelchairs	Go to MyEducationLab, and select the topic *Physical Disabilities*. Next, go to the Activities and Applications section, and read and analyze the case entitled "Effective Room Arrangement."	As you read and analyze this case, focus on Level A— Case 2. This student has a medical condition that is characterized by fragile bones. Using Strategy 16.9 as your guide, how would you arrange this classroom environment if you had not only the student mentioned in the case but also a student who uses a wheelchair?

EFFECTIVE PRACTICES

In the remainder of this chapter, we describe nine effective strategies, which we referred to previously in the chapter, to help you plan effectively to meet the needs of all students.

EFFECTIVE PRACTICE	TYPE OF STRATEGY/BRIEF DESCRIPTION	SPECIAL CONSIDERATIONS
Strategy 16.1: Teaching Students to Use Educational Technology Programs	This classroom instruction strategy provides a step-by-step process for teaching students to effectively use educational software to improve basic academic skills.	A great deal of educational technology is available today that teachers can use to their advantage as a complement to direct instruction.
Strategy 16.2: Using READ 180 in the Classroom	A popular program that addresses critical reading skills for students in grades 4–12. This strategy provides an overview of how to use this program.	READ 180 will work best if teachers are adequately prepared to use it. Materials and workshops are available from the producer to teach teachers about the material.
Strategy 16.3: Using the Computer Game PLATO® Achieve Now on PSP® (Mathematics) to Improve Students' Homework Performance	Motivating students to learn math skills can be challenging. This strategy describes how this PSP-based game can help individual students in this area.	Although electronic games are more fun than more traditional approaches to learning, close teacher monitoring of assignments is still important.
Strategy 16.4: Evaluating Educational Technology	Will help teachers decide the value of various educational technology products. The step-by-step guide will better ensure that students will benefit from the selected program.	Although much educational technology software is available, it is not all equal. Careful review of different products will lead to a better selection for your students with special needs.
Strategy 16.5: A Decision-Making Process for Selecting AT Devices	Assistive technology can help students accomplish various tasks and assignments. But you must be able to decide what will be most effective for individual student needs.	Many students with disabilities can benefit from assistive technology, but much of it can be expensive. Teachers must always take care to select devices that students will use.
Strategy 16.6: Using Word Processing and Related Software to Support Student Writing	Offers guidance for teaching students with writing difficulties how to use word processing to produce better-written papers and reports.	Word processing allows many students with learning disabilities to better express their thoughts. An important tool for many teachers.
Strategy 16.7: Teaching Students with Disabilities to Use Calculators	Provides a step-by-step instructional process for teaching students to use calculators to solve math problems in school and in the real world.	There is some debate among experts as to the extent that students should use calculators to solve arithmetic problems, but for some students, they can be an important tool.
Strategy 16.8: Supporting Students Who Use AAC Devices	Relatively speaking, few students will require AAC devices to communicate. When the need arises, however, this strategy will help IEP team members select the best device for the student.	A few students with disabilities will require the support of AAC devices to communicate. Used correctly, these devices can enhance their ability to participate in daily life.
Strategy 16.9: Supporting Students Who Use Motorized Wheelchairs	Some students with special needs will require wheelchairs for mobility. This strategy helps teachers understand how wheelchairs operate and how to help students use them.	Students who use wheelchairs must learn how to navigate them in a way that helps them fit into the flow of daily life. A little instruction and direction may sometimes be necessary.

Strategy 16.1

TEACHING STUDENTS TO USE EDUCATIONAL TECHNOLOGY PROGRAMS

Rationale and Research

If you examine the research on the effectiveness of educational technology as a means to improving student learning, especially in the areas of basic academic skills, you are likely to see a mixed message. In a recent nationwide study in which reading and math instructional software programs were used with students across the country, the researchers concluded that the students in classrooms that used the programs performed no better on standard outcome measures than did students in classrooms where the programs were not used (Dynarski et al., 2007). In other studies, researchers have found more positive effects (Hall et al., 2000; Hughes & Maccini, 1997; MacArthur et al., 2001). Some experts have taken the position that further study is needed about these programs and their effects (National Institute of Child Health and Human Development, 2000). We suggest that certainly some students will benefit from educational technology, that some programs are better than others, and that the quality of direct instruction provided by the teacher will affect how well students benefit from the use of educational technology.

Key References

Dynarski, M., Agodini, R., Heaviside, S., Novak, T., Carey, N., Campuzano, L., Means, B., Murphy, R., Penuel, W., Javitz, H., Emery, D., & Sussex, W. (2007). *Effectiveness of reading and mathematics software products: Findings from the first student cohort.* Washington, DC: U.S. Department of Education, Institute of Education Sciences.

Hall, T. E., Hughes, C. A., & Filbert, M. (2000). Computer-assisted instruction in reading for students with learning disabilities: A research synthesis. *Education and Treatment of Children, 23*, 173–193.

Hughes, C. A., & Maccini, P. (1997). Computer-assisted mathematics instruction for students with learning disabilities: A research review. *Learning Disabilities: A Multidisciplinary Journal, 8*(3), 155–166.

MacArthur, C. A., Ferretti, R. P., Okolo, C. M., & Cavalier, A. R. (2001). Technology applications for students with literacy problems: A critical review. *Elementary School Journal, 101*, 273–301.

National Institute of Child Health and Human Development. (2000). *Report of the National Reading Panel. Teaching children to read: An evidence-based assessment of the scientific research literature on reading and its implications for reading instruction* (NIH Publication No. 00-4769). Washington, DC: U.S. Government Printing Office

Step-by-Step

(1) *Become knowledgeable about the program you are using.* Before exposing any of your students to the program, make sure you understand its features, how it operates, how the student uses it, and how the program directs the student through its activities. If staff development sessions are available on use of the program, take advantage of the opportunity to participate.

(2) *Identify appropriate objectives and activities within the software program.* The advantage of most educational technology programs is that they allow differentiated instruction for students with different skill levels. The program itself may identify specific student needs if a diagnostic component is built into it. Regardless, you will want the

student to focus on those areas of the program that will help meet academic needs.

(3) *Provide adequate supervision and support as each student begins to use the software program.* Each student must learn to use the program correctly to use it successfully. Students who are younger, who have less experience working on computers, or who have intellectual or learning disabilities likely will require more direct instruction and more support in using the program. This phase may take several sessions until the student is comfortable operating the program.

(4) *Maintain an awareness of students' level of comfort and frustration with the program.* If too many failures

occur, you should move the student to a lower level of the program to ensure more success. If the student is using different programs, proportionally distribute the student's time so that the student spends more time on the program that addresses the student's greatest need.

5 *Reinforce students for correctly using the software program.* You may reinforce correct use of the program by letting students engage in another preferred educational program, or you may let them play another computer game. Of course, you can also use more traditional types of reinforcement, such as extra playground time or token reinforcement. Many educational reading and math software programs have games built into them that are related to the learning objectives. Students may play these and still practice important skills.

6 *Monitor the student's progress in the program.* You need to examine the reports provided by the program and make sure the student is making adequate progress on the program's probes. If not, the student should not move forward in the program until better performance indicates that she should do so. The student may require more direct instruction from you to help her acquire some specific skills.

7 *Monitor the student's progress independently of the program's evaluation.* Performance on the program should not be assumed to equate with performance under other conditions, such as on curriculum-based evaluation in the classroom. Therefore, you should always have off-program tests to make sure the student can demonstrate skills under different conditions.

Applications and Examples

At Mull Elementary School, in Burke County, North Carolina, first-grade teacher Debra Bolinger discussed how she implemented the Reading First program produced by Taylor Associates (see *http://www.readingplus.com/*), which the district began using several years ago. She stated that she will

> usually begin with a modeling lesson on a computer monitor, and then they (the students) do a group lesson together. They may do two group lessons, or . . . may begin . . . to do an individual lesson. The teacher teaches each component separately and then once the students seem to understand, she begins assigning them lessons. They keep an individual paper record of their lessons.

There is also a very detailed teacher management feature that I can use.

Because Ms. Bolinger has been using the program for several years, she is already familiar with its structure and content. Obviously, the more familiar a teacher is with the software and the more she has used it with her students, the easier it will be for her to use it in the future. That is why Ms. Bolinger has already learned what it takes to ease her students into the content of the software. Her ability to effectively teach students how to use the program reflects their ability to use it to their greatest advantage.

Keep in Mind

Many of your students, like yourself, will already come to you with advanced computer usage skills. Their experience with different types of technology will be an advantage and may reduce the amount of time it will take them to learn how to use a program. Likewise, the quality and user-friendly features of a program can also affect a student's learning curve.

Strategy 16.2

USING READ 180 IN THE CLASSROOM

Rationale and Research

According to its Website,[1] READ 180 underwent an extensive research and developmental process that began in 1985 and continued through 1999. A recently produced *Compendium of Read 180 Research* (Scholastic, Inc., 2006), provided by the publisher, offers the results of extensive evaluation analyses and research conducted in school districts throughout the United States. Among the findings reported are the following:

- *All struggling readers need to be engaged and given incentive to learn to read.*
- *The READ 180® program and services are strongly aligned with the 15 elements (necessary to improve reading skills) cited in the Reading Next report* (Biancarosa & Snow, 2004).
- *READ 180, Scholastic's comprehensive reading intervention program geared for students reading below the proficient level in Grades 4–12, is the result of many years of educational research and development* (Scholastic, Inc., 2006, *Compendium of READ 180 Research*, pp. 4–5).

Key References

Charleston County School District. (2006). *Implementation of READ 180 (Reading Intervention Program) in CCSD Schools*. Retrieved May 21, 2008, from http://www.ccsdschools.com/CCSD_Reports/Program_Evaluation_ Reports/CCSD_Implementation_of_READ_180_July_2006.pdf

Hasselbring, T. S., & Bausch, M. E. (2005). Assistive technologies for reading. *Educational Leadership, 63*(4), 72–75.

Hasselbring, T. S., & Goin, L. I. (2004). Literacy instruction for older struggling readers: What is the role of technology? *Reading and Writing Quarterly, 20*(2), 123–144.

Scholastic, Inc. (2006). *Compendium of READ 180 Research*. Retrieved May 21, 2008, from http://teacher.scholastic .com/products/read180/research/pdfs/READ180_Compendium_6_26_06.pdf

Scholastic, Inc. (2008). READ 180. Retrieved May 21, 2008, from http://teacher.scholastic.com/products/read180/

Step-by-Step

1. *Become knowledgeable about the material.* READ 180 requires teachers to begin by studying the comprehensive teacher's material that comes with its product. The publisher offers teachers printed materials and also a 2-day staff-development session to learn to use its materials.

2. *Allocate adequate instructional time.* READ 180 is designed for use in 90-minute blocks of time per day, 5 days per week. During the 90-minute instructional period, the teacher uses the READ 180 materials to provide systematic instruction in reading, writing, and vocabulary.

3. *Start with whole-group instruction.* The first component of daily instruction includes 20 minutes of instruction to the whole class. Students then break into three smaller groups that rotate through three 20-minute small-group rotations.

4. *Divide the class into three small groups of comparable ability.* The small-group rotations include the following grouping patterns:
   a. *Small-group instruction:* The teacher works with one small group using the rBook and *Resources for Differentiated instruction.* In this group the teacher focuses on individual student needs and provides differentiated instruction.
   b. *Computer instruction:* In a second group, students use the READ 180 Software independently, which provides intensive, individualized skills practice.
   c. *Independent reading:* In a third group rotation, students build reading-comprehension skills through modeled and independent reading of the READ 180 Paperbacks and Audiobooks.

5. *End the daily instruction with whole-group instruction.* The 90-minute session ends with 10 minutes of whole-group instruction.

[1]READ 180 is produced by Scholastic, Inc. Much of the content reported here is based on the publisher's Website at http:// teacher.scholastic.com/products/read180/

6 *Evaluate individual and group performance.* The teacher can use the READ 180 built-in assessment to gauge the progress of each student. The results of the assess- ment allow teachers to group students for small-group instruction and to assign leveled READ 180 paperback books for independent reading.

Applications and Examples

In a recent report, the Charleston County School District (2006) described how several schools in its district used READ 180 and some of the results of its usage. Here is how the program was used in two schools:

In Chicora Elementary School, one fifth-grade teacher used READ 180 during her daily reading block. The teacher used the basal reader during whole-group instruction and then rotated only the lowest-performing students through the READ 180 stations. The remaining students worked on other reading-related projects during these rotations. Teachers at Goodwin Elementary School used READ 180 in the three fifth-grade classes during reading block. Goodwin had one full set of READ 180 materials and one partial set of ma- terials that the three fifth-grade teachers shared. The lack of materials made it challenging for all three teachers to fully implement READ 180. Two teachers therefore used the READ 180 materials to augment their reading instruction, primarily using the computer component of READ 180. The third teacher used all components of READ 180, imple- menting it in a fashion similar to that of the fifth-grade teacher at Chicora, using the basal reader during whole- group instruction, and then rotating the lowest-performing students through the READ 180 stations while the other students worked on other reading-related projects (Charleston County School District, 2006, pp. 1–2).

Keep in Mind

The value of READ 180 to students may depend on how well teachers are prepared to use it and how well they adhere to the recommended instructional practices. Teachers are likely to use the program more effectively if they have attended the in-service sessions provided by the publisher, are knowledgeable about how the instruction is to be provided, and can implement the program in the prescribed manner. Even so, there is always the chance of technical glitches occur- ring. Adequate technical support therefore should be available either from the publisher or from the school district's instructional technology department.

Strategy 16.3

USING THE COMPUTER GAME PLATO® ACHIEVE NOW ON PSP® (MATHEMATICS) TO IMPROVE STUDENTS' HOMEWORK PERFORMANCE

Rationale and Research

With the development of Achieve Now on the PSP (PlayStation®Portable) system produced by Sony, PLATO Learning is attempting to provide a medium to students in elementary and middle school grades that will motivate them to engage in learning math and other subjects. PLATO maintains that by providing the opportunity to learn math skills through a popular medium such as the PSP, students will be more likely to increase their learning time, increase family support for educational activities, and improve student attitudes and motivation.

At its Website, PLATO presents three evaluation reports (not true experimental studies) that show improvement in students' performance over time when the Achieve Now program was used. Because of other possible sources of influence, however, it is not possible to determine that the gains could be attributed solely or primarily to the product. Other researchers, however, have shown some support for the idea that students will learn more using computer games (see "Key References").

Key References

Ford, M., Poe, V., & Cox, J. (1993). Attending behaviors of ADHD children in math and reading using various types of software. *Journal of Computing in Childhood Education, 4*, 183–196.

MacKenty, B. (2006). All play and no work: Computer games are invading the classroom—and not a moment too soon. *School Library Journal, 52*(9), 46–48.

Ota, K. R., & DuPaul, G. J. (2002). Task engagement and mathematics performance in children with attention-deficit hyperactivity disorder: Effects of supplemental computer instruction. *School Psychology Quarterly, 17*, 242–257.

PLATO Learning. (2008). *PLATO® Achieve Now on PSP® (Mathematics)*. Retrieved May 23, 2008, from http://www.plato.com/Products/PLATO-Achieve-Now-on-PSP/PLATO-Achieve-Now-on-PSP-Mathematics.aspx

Step-by-Step

1. **Determine students' current skill level and needs.** In order to benefit the most from the Achieve Now program, the teacher will need to identify the student's current instructional needs and assign the appropriate lesson for the student.

2. **Review available lessons.** A variety of lessons are presented in game form for students to practice on the PCP. Sample games and their contents follow:

- *Cali's Geo Tools*™
  This is an open-ended program for practicing and mastering basic mathematics concepts. Various activities allow students to explore concepts of congruence, symmetry, and spatial relationships.
- *Math Gallery*™
  This provides multimedia mathematics manipulatives that allow students to acquire a concrete understanding of mathematics. Areas covered: geometry, measurement, probability, statistics, rational numbers, number sense, and computation.

- *P.K.'s Math Studio*™
  This collection allows students to master basic mathematics concepts by solving word problems, applying concepts and strategies to build expressions, and analyzing and discovering rules that govern patterns and functions.
- *P.K.'s Place*™
  This set of lessons provides practice in mathematics and problem solving. Areas covered are concepts of operations, experiments, number theory, computation, geometry, statistics and probability, and integration of concepts across strands (e.g., algebra patterns, estimation, and estimates).
- *The Quaddle Family Mysteries*®
  This program helps students develop their mathematics skills and become active problem solvers. Areas covered: concepts of measurement such as length, area, perimeter, weight and capacity, volume, time, and temperature.

- *The Secret of Googol*®
  These lessons help children develop a strong foundation in mathematics. Areas covered are geometry and spatial sense, concepts of whole numbers and groups, concepts of operations, computation, and problem solving.
- *Timeless Jade Trade*®
  This program engages students in concentrated study of mathematical concepts such as fractions, decimals, and percentages.
- *Timeless Math*®
  This is a series of mathematics challenges that broaden students' awareness of other cultures while strengthening their mathematics skills. Areas covered are rational numbers, concepts of operations, geometry and measurement, statistics and probability, relations, functions, and number theory.

(3) *Allow students to practice in the classroom. Observe students' abilities to use games appropriately.* Although many elementary and middle school students today can easily handle PlayStation technology, it will be important to allow them to practice the math lessons under supervision in order to ensure that they are attending to the problems and attempting to find the correct responses.

(4) *Create additional homework assignments.* Direct students to the appropriate lessons for homework assignments.

(5) *Probe students skills to ensure learning.* As with all academic learning activities, it is important that teachers use individual probes or curriculum-based assessments to assess student progress. Students may enjoy engaging with the programs and the PSP, but this does not guarantee that learning is occurring. To know this requires an independent evaluation.

Applications and Examples

Here is a report taken from the PLATO Learning (2008) Website describing how one school used the PLATO system: Holly Springs Intermediate served over 500 students in grades 4 through 6 and had a 97% African American student population. In 2002, Holly Springs began using PLATO Achieve Now, The PLATO Network, and PLATO eduTest Assessment in a special, grant-funded project. The school district selected 120 fourth graders to learn using The PLATO Achieve Now Program; students were pretested in September and post-tested in May. As part of the project, teachers attended staff development sessions to analyze pretest results and to determine greatest areas of need. Subsequently, The PLATO Achieve Now Program was aligned with the district's curriculum and the Mississippi State Standards. During the year, teachers provided direct instruction in the classroom, and students were allowed to check out PlayStations for use outside the classroom.

Keep in Mind

Students in elementary and middle schools are likely to find game-based activities on a PSP very attractive and fun to play. But you cannot think that learning will automatically improve when students are provided with these games. It is critical that teachers provide instruction in the classroom, that students know how to use the devices and can use them independently, and that you evaluate their learning in a traditional way.

Strategy 16.4

EVALUATING EDUCATIONAL TECHNOLOGY

Rationale and Research

Various educational technology programs allow students to work independently on computers to develop or improve basic skills. The advantage of this technology is that students can work on required skills while the teacher provides direct instruction to other students. As the student engages with the program, she is presented reading or math activities that require a response. Depending on the program, a variety of features may be included, such as attractive graphics, game-like formats, visual and auditory prompts, feedback to the student's responses, and directions for more practice. Programs can also monitor student progress and provide reports to the teacher on this progress.

The issue, then, is which program(s) to select. Usually, programs are not decided by an individual teacher but by a school district technology director working in concert with a district-wide committee. At times, however, you may need to play a role in the decision-making process or be asked to provide feedback about a program you are currently using.

Key References

Bishop, M. J., & Santoro, L. E. (2006). Evaluating beginning reading software for at-risk learners. *Psychology in the Schools, 43*(1), 57–70.

Bitter, G. G., & Legacy, J. M. (2008). *Using technology in the classroom* (7th ed.). Boston: Pearson/Allyn & Bacon.

Dynarski, M., Agodini, R., Heaviside, S., Novak, T., Carey, N., Campuzano, L., Means, B., Murphy, R., Penuel, W., Javitz, H., Emery, D., & Sussex, W. (2007). *Effectiveness of reading and mathematics software products: Findings from the first student cohort.* Washington, DC: U.S. Department of Education, Institute of Education Sciences.

Shakeshaft, C., Mann, D., Becker, J., & Sweeney, K. (2002). Choosing the right technology. *School Administrator, 59*(1), 34–37.

Step-by-Step

(1) *Determine classroom needs.* Identify which students will use the program, their ages or grade levels, specific skills they need more work on, their cognitive and learning abilities, any sensory and physical limitations, and their ability to interact with a program independently.

(2) *Determine if the program addresses classroom needs.* Note the grade levels the program covers, the objectives addressed, and if they are linked to national, state, or local standards.

(3) *Evaluate the interface design and user appeal.* Does it appear pleasant and engaging from your students' point of view? Does it enhance engagement rather than interfere with learning? Are the screen layouts, graphics, colors, and auditory stimuli pleasing, or might they detract from the content?

(4) *Consider the instructional design aspects of the program.* Determine if the program can diagnose current academic ability and if lessons are structured and presented in a systematic manner based on a hierarchy of objectives. Also assess the amount of practice the program allows and if it provides practice for skill generalization. Determine if the

program provides immediate feedback to students, if it monitors progress, and if it provides reports to the teacher.

(5) *Determine whether the program can be used in different locations.* Find out if the program can be used only in the classroom or if it can be transported to other places such as the computer lab or to the student's home.

(6) *Determine the technical features and requirements of the program.* Is the program Web-based or standalone? Will you have sufficient hardware and technical support? You will need to determine if you have adequate memory, workstation networking, or Internet connectivity. You should also find out if the vendor will provide training and technical support.

(7) *Look for information about the effectiveness of the program.* Look at the vendor's Website for reviews provided by professional organizations and for published studies in professional journals. Ask vendors to tell you who is using the program, and then contact these users. Ask about teacher satisfaction with the product as well as improvement in student performance outcomes.

Applications and Examples

Teachers who successfully incorporate educational technology into their instructional activities tend to do so in the following ways:

- They work with other teachers who are also using technology and are supportive of each other.
- They are supported by their schools and school districts and often supported by a technology coordinator or director.

- They receive adequate staff development and in-class support to help them use the technology.
- They often work for principals who are knowledgeable about technology and who provide leadership for its use.
- They generally have good relationships with their students and use effective classroom management practices.

Keep in Mind

Educational technology can add an important element to the instruction of students in many ways. Most importantly, the teacher needs to understand how the software works and in what ways it will address student needs. At that time, a valuable tool may be available to assist students with their academic challenges.

Strategy 16.5

A DECISION-MAKING PROCESS FOR SELECTING ASSISTIVE TECHNOLOGY DEVICES

Rationale and Research

Assistive technology (AT) devices can be useful to many students with disabilities; however, many times the student may not benefit from the device as intended. Several reasons can explain this lack of benefit: The device may not match the student's need, the student may not have the necessary skills to use the device, use of the device may not be acceptable to the student or the student's family, or the device may not operate as intended. For AT devices to be used most effectively, it is critical that the most appropriate device be found to meet the student's need in the context in which the student will use the device. Because so many devices exist, it may be tempting to simply select a device "off the shelf" or recommend a device because it seems as though it would be useful to the student. However, several authorities have noted the importance of undergoing a thoughtful and detailed process to find the most appropriate device and to put it into service with the student in a way that best ensures its correct use. Next we provide recommendations for correctly selecting and appropriately using AT devices.

Key References

Best, S. J., Reed, P., & Bigge, J. L. (2005). Assistive technology. In S. J. Best, K. Wolff Heller, & J. L. Bigge (Eds.), *Teaching individuals with physical or multiple disabilities* (5th ed., pp. 179–226). Upper Saddle River, NJ: Merrill/Pearson Education.

Parette, H. P., & Peterson-Karlan, G. R. (2007). Facilitating student achievement with assistive technology. *Education and Training in Developmental Disabilities, 42*, 387–397.

Parette, P., & McMahan, G. A. (2002). What should we expect of assistive technology? Being sensitive to family goals. *Teaching Exceptional Children, 35*(1), 56–61.

Todis, B. (1996). Tools for the task? Perspectives on assistive technology in educational settings. *Journal of Special Education Technology, 13*(2), 49–61.

Step-by-Step

(1) *Involve the IEP team in the decision-making process.* When considering the need for an AT device, the IEP team should collectively have enough knowledge to make a decision. At least one person on the team should have some knowledge about available devices, and other members of the team should have knowledge about the student's curriculum and functioning in different areas including physical ability, language development, and any other area that may be pertinent.

(2) *Determine the specific needs of the student.* The IEP team should select an AT device in response to clearly defined goals and objectives with the intention of enhancing skills.

(3) *Consider student characteristics and abilities.* Different AT devices have different levels of complexity and different use requirements that the IEP team should consider in light of the student's abilities. The team must take into consideration the student's intellectual, physical,

sensory, and social abilities. Whenever possible, the team should also attend to the student's preference for a device.

(4) *Determine where the student will use the device.* Although some devices may be appropriate for use in only one setting, others may be useful or necessary for several settings. The IEP team therefore must consider the transportability of the device, its size, and its durability, among other factors.

(5) *For AAC devices, determine with whom the device will be used.* The team should consider the targets of the individual when he uses an AAC device. If the target audience is limited, the select individuals can be instructed in the meaning of the signs, icons, or expressions that the device indicates. If the audience is broader, the production of the device must be relatively clear and unambiguous.

(6) *Determine how well the device must operate.* Consider how fast and durable a device must operate

and to what degree or breadth it must perform. A device in need of constant repair will not be often used or will soon be abandoned.

(7) *Consider practical constraints in acquiring the device, and determine if they can be adequately addressed.* Specifically, the team must consider different funding sources for the device, the availability of the device or equipment, and how long it may take to arrive. Team members should also consider who will teach the student to use the device and should interact with others, such as family members, about the use of the device.

(8) *Consider the response to the device within the student's family and cultural contexts.* Finally, the IEP team must give a great deal of thought as to how the AT device will affect the family of the individual with disabilities on a daily basis. The team should also consider how the student will use the AT device within the family and what effect it might have on family activities, routines, and resources.

Applications and Examples

The selection of an AT device requires an IEP team to consider many issues. As one authority stated, "to most effectively match assistive technology devices and services with any individual with a disability, team members must consider five parallel domains: (a) user characteristics, (b) family issues, (c) cultural factors, (d) technology features, and (e) service system considerations" (Parette, 1997, p. 271).

An often overlooked but important factor when selecting an AT device is the possible impact of a device within the family routine. For example, the device can affect communication within the family, change family member's roles and activities, and create new demands for family members. Additionally, many AT devices require parents or caregivers to learn how they operate and how to maintain them. This instruction of family members is considered an essential AT support service, but it requires additional time and effort on the part of family members.

Keep in Mind

AT devices can be very useful, but many such devices are sitting on shelves in schools and are not being used. Some are ordered and then never used; others are used briefly and then left on the sideline. This means there is a loss of both money and a student's potential—because the student did not use an appropriate device. Adhering to the guidelines presented in this strategy can help avoid these costly mistakes.

Strategy 16.6

USING WORD PROCESSING AND RELATED SOFTWARE TO SUPPORT STUDENT WRITING

Rationale and Research

Many students with learning disabilities have difficulty with written expression. When asked to write, they may try to avoid the task, and sometimes exhibit behavior problems, or simply not comply with the teacher's request. When they do try to work on a written assignment, they may not organize or plan their assignment very well; may produce written work full of spelling, punctuation, and grammatical errors; will likely use fewer words than their peers without disabilities and not vary their vocabulary; and then turn in an unedited, illegible paper.

Such outcomes as these may be avoided if teachers invest adequate time teaching students strategies to use word processing and related software to plan, create, and edit written products. Research has shown that when students use word processors to produce written documents, they tend to write more, have fewer errors, and produce written documents of higher quality (see "Key References," following).

Key References

Bryant, D. P., Bryant, B. R., & Raskind, M. H. (1998). Using assistive technology to enhance the skills of students with learning disabilities. *Intervention in School and Clinic, 34*(1), 53–58.

Hetzroni, O. E., & Shrieber, B. (2004). Word processing as an assistive technology tool for enhancing academic outcomes of students with writing disabilities in the general classroom. *Journal of Learning Disabilities, 37*, 143–154.

MacArthur, C. A. (2000). New tools for writing: Assistive technology for students with writing difficulties. *Topics in Language Disorders, 20*(4), 85–100.

Montgomery, D. J., & Marks, L. J. (2006). Using technology to build independence in writing for students with disabilities. *Preventing School Failure, 50*(3), 33–38.

Quenneville, J. (2001). Tech tools for students with learning disabilities: Infusion into inclusive classrooms. *Preventing School Failure, 45*(4), 167–170.

Step-by-Step

1 *Using selected software, teach students writing skills using the following steps:*

a. **Help students organize their written assignment.** Students can use programs such as Inspiration to help them brainstorm and create the major components of their writing assignment and synthesize the contents into related categories. Students need teacher instruction in how to create and complete their organization. Teacher-provided models and feedback on their creations will be helpful.

b. **Teach students to use word prediction to help with spelling weaknesses.** Word-prediction software allows students to type in the first few letters of a word and then offers the student a list of words to select to insert. The dictionaries included in many word-prediction software programs allow teachers to add custom words for special topics such as science projects.

c. **Use voiced text to allow students to review what they have written.** Voiced software converts written text into

spoken words and will often highlight the written text as the voicing of each word occurs. This process allows students to listen to their written work and make corrections as necessary.

d. **As students write, teach them to use spell checkers.** Spell checkers are not perfect, but they may be helpful to students. Problems with spell checkers include failing to identify words that are misspelled for their context (e.g., homonyms), not identifying the correct spelling of a misspelled word in the correction list, and the inability of the student to identify the correctly spelled word from the list. Teachers need to carefully monitor the use of spell checking in order to ensure correct usage.

e. **Encourage the use of a thesaurus to help students build and use different vocabulary.** A thesaurus offers students alternative vocabulary to help eliminate the overuse of certain words. However, teachers should carefully monitor the use of alternate words to make sure they fit the context of the written material.

f. **Help students review and edit their work using grammar checkers.** We all know that grammar checkers can be both a help and a hindrance. Students may use them to find errors, but sometimes they may work against the writer's purpose. If students use grammar checkers, the teacher needs to support students in understanding the grammatical error that is identified.

(2) *Evaluate the student's work, and provide feedback.* Feedback to the student should address the written product, the components of the product (organization, grammar, spelling, etc.), and the use of the software as part of the writing process. The teacher should point out areas of weakness to the student and provide opportunities to improve on those areas.

Applications and Examples

Here is how one student benefited from the use of AT software to facilitate writing:

> With the use of an organizational program, Joe is able to enter his research into a semantic web and then convert the web into an outline. Using the outline and a word-processing program, Joe pairs a verbal rehearsal strategy with word prediction. For each component of the outline, he generates a sentence aloud before typing it. He then uses the voice output feature to read back what he has written, at first, sentence by sentence, but then less often as his self-confidence grows. Once written, Joe uses the thesaurus to enhance the vocabulary of his report. With the help of a peer, Joe identifies words in his essay that are repeated frequently. He replaces these words using the thesaurus to assist him in identifying alternative word choices. Next, Joe uses the spell-check and grammar check features to produce a final product that contains fewer spelling and grammatical errors.

Source: Reprinted with permission from Montgomery, D. J., & Marks, L. J. (2006). Using technology to build independence in writing for students with disabilities. *Preventing School Failure, 50*(3), p. 37.

Keep in Mind

The software discussed here will not improve students' writing without sufficient direction from the teacher. For success to occur with writing, students need much practice with feedback. As students find that the software can accommodate their weaknesses, the quality of their writing content may improve. As with all learning, the more time invested in the process, the better the outcome.

Strategy 16.7

TEACHING STUDENTS WITH DISABILITIES TO USE CALCULATORS

Rationale and Research

Educators continue to debate the use of calculators by students learning math skills. One side takes the position that calculators can allow students to deal easily with simple calculations, focusing their mental energy more on using reasoning to solve problems. The other side maintains that students should learn basic arithmetic facts so they can apply them automatically when needed. Many experts feel the argument is not needed and maintain that while it is important for students to learn basic math facts, they also should be allowed to save time by using calculators (see "Key References," following).

For some students with disabilities, calculators are a helpful tool that allows them to overcome a serious weakness. Even though these students can often improve their math skills, the issue is often one of finding the correct answer in a short period of time. In these cases, their calculating abilities may be inadequate, so that without the use of a calculator, they may not be able to handle the immediate situation. A calculator, therefore (and sometimes a talking calculator), becomes an important AT device.

Key References

Huinker, D. (2002). Calculators as learning tools for young children's explorations of number. *Teaching Children Mathematics, 8,* 316–321.

Judd, W. (2007). Instructional games with calculators. *Mathematics Teaching in the Middle School, 12,* 312–314.

Mittag, K. C., & Van Reusen, A. K. (1999). One fish, two fish, pretzel fish: Learning estimation and other advanced mathematics concepts in an inclusive class. *Teaching Exceptional Children, 31*(6), 66–72.

National Council of Teachers of Mathematics. (2004). *Overview: Standards for School Mathematics: Pre-kindergarten through Grade 12.* Retrieved on December 15, 2007, from http://standards.nctm.org/document/chapter3/index.htm

Step-by-Step

1 **When students can memorize math facts, they should.** Many students with learning disabilities and other mild disabilities can learn math facts including addition, subtraction, multiplication, and division facts, and various drill-and-practice games will help them do so. Teachers, especially those teaching younger students, should not avoid teaching facts with an assumption that the students will always be able to use a calculator.

2 **Begin teaching the use of calculators as students learn math facts.** As students learn basic facts, teach them simultaneously how to use calculators. Create games that allow students to respond as fast as possible (in writing or orally) to math fact quizzes, then let them check their answers with calculators.

3 **Teach students to estimate the correct answers to problems.** Even when students use calculators, it is easy to make keying errors that lead to incorrect calculations.

For this reason, students should learn to estimate the answer when the problem uses large numbers. They can then compare their estimated answers to the calculated answers in order to determine if the latter are probably correct.

4 **Teach students to use appropriate operations (+, −, ×, ÷) to find answers.** If the value of the calculator is to help students find answers quickly, it is essential that they learn which math operations are necessary to solve particular specific problems. It is critical that students learn what math operations mean and when to apply them.

5 **Younger children can use calculators to play games to learn math functions and facts.** Allowing younger elementary-age students to play games with the calculator will help them learn the meaning of operations. These games should include items that can be manipulated while calculations are being conducted so that the children can see the relationship.

6 *Apply skills using calculators to solve word problems.* Solving word problems presents a great challenge for many students with disabilities. Teachers should place a great deal of focus on reading and understanding these problems and using calculators to solve them.

7 *Teach students to use calculators to in real-world applications.* Particularly as students grow older and must learn to operate in the real world, it is important for them to have practice using the calculator in community settings. At this time, it is also be important to focus on estimating.

8 *Some students benefit from talking calculators.* Students with visual problems and some students with learning disabilities benefit from talking calculators. These calculators allow the user to enter numbers (usually the keys are quite large and easy to see) and hear the answers to their calculations.

Applications and Examples

When working on skills with students using calculators, the first thing to remember is that the skills should not be dissimilar to skills being learned by other students. The best guide for teachers are the curriculum standards used for other students. Most states have such standards, and most often these are based on the standards of the National Council of Teachers of Mathematics.

Some students with disabilities are at a disadvantage in achieving higher-level standards because they lack basic skills that they have not been able to adequately master. For those students, the IEP team should consider the calculator to be an AT device that will allow the students to master these skills.

Keep in Mind

Even with calculators, many students with disabilities are at a disadvantage because of their difficulties in translating information provided in a word problem or in a contextual situation into knowing the math operations that they should conduct. The calculator is helpful in arriving at correct answers only if the students can enter numbers and operations appropriately. As with other skills learned by students with disabilities, practice is necessary for them to learn to use calculators effectively.

Strategy 16.8

SUPPORTING STUDENTS WHO USE AAC DEVICES

Rationale and Research

The development of augmentative and alternative communication (AAC) devices has opened up the door of communication for people who years ago could not express their needs, wishes, and thoughts. These devices range from something as simple as a board with small objects, pictures, or symbols for a student to point to, to a very sophisticated (and expensive) device that will produce completely synthesized speech when the person types letter keys, or touches words, symbols, or pictures.

The identification of an appropriate AAC device, the interface the individual will have with it, and the range of the vocabulary for the device are among the issues that the IEP team needs to address before a student can acquire and learn to use a device. This assessment process often is conducted by a speech–language pathologist (SLP) with specialized preparation. However, this person needs assistance from other key individuals, such as the classroom teacher, in making many of these decisions. Additionally, the SLP seeks the cooperation of these individuals in providing supports for the student using the AAC device so that the student will achieve improved communication.

Key References

Beukelman, D. R., & Mirenda, P. (2005). *Augmentative and alternative communication: Supporting adults and children with complex communication need.* (3rd ed.). Baltimore: Paul H. Brookes.

Downing, J. (2005). *Teaching communication skills to students with severe disabilities* (2nd ed.). Baltimore: Paul H. Brookes.

Hunt, P., Soto, G., Maier, J., Muller, E., & Goetz, L. (2002). Collaborative teaming to support students with augmentative and alternative communication needs in general education classrooms. *Augmentative and Alternative Communication, 18*, 20–35.

Kent-Walsh, J. E., & Light, J. C. (2003). General education teachers' experiences with inclusion of students who use augmentative and alternative communication. *Augmentative and Alternative Communication, 19*, 104–124.

TherapyTimes. (2006). *Back to school tips for AAC devices.* Retrieved May 29, 2008, from http://www.therapytimes.com/content=5601J64E48769C841

Step-by-Step

(1) *Develop a communicative rapport with the student.* The best communication is natural communication. Develop a comfortable rapport with the student so that your interactions do not seem strained or artificial. Always assume that the student can understand what you are saying, but at the same time, try to say what you mean in a way that is most likely to be understood. Having a good sense of humor and joking around are always good ways to build rapport.

(2) *Make sure the student has continued access to the device and that it is functioning appropriately.* Students who use an AAC device need to have as much access to it as possible, and the teacher should make sure that the device is working appropriately. It is not the teacher's responsibility to fix a broken AAC device, but it is important to let the SLP know if the device is not working as it should.

(3) *Encourage the student to communicate at natural times.* The more opportunities a person has to use an

AAC device, the better she will be able to do so. All teachers and other key people in the AAC user's environment should not let her fade to the communication background but should encourage her communication whenever the chance occurs.

(4) *Promote interactions with other students.* Interaction with peers is perhaps the best way to promote communication, and students with disabilities often improve their communication skills in contexts where peer interaction is promoted. However, because AAC devices can inhibit the initiation of communication, prompting peer interactions can be very important.

(5) *Ask open-ended questions, and encourage questions from the student.* Often, when people use AAC devices, others tend to limit the nature of verbalizations with them, for example, by asking yes or no questions. It is better for students if others ask questions or elicit comments that

might require them to stretch their ability so they can develop more elaborate responses.

(6) *Be aware of issues related to handling, maintenance, transportation, and storage of the device.* As we said, AAC devices can range from very simple to very elaborate. Those that are more sophisticated can be quite expensive to purchase and repair. It will be a good idea for you to understand any appropriate procedures and cautions that you should take when you must handle the device.

Applications and Examples

Chloe is a 10-year-old fourth grader with multiple disabilities. She uses a digitized AAC device that includes pictures of food and activities to state her wishes for snacks and different choices throughout the day. When it is time to make a choice, Chloe's teacher prompts her to look at her device and indicate her selection. If she does not respond, the teacher physically prompts her by moving her hand part of the way toward the board while asking her what she would like. When Chloe pushes the button, the communication device sounds out the word or the phrase that she has pressed, and the teacher (or others) responds. For example, if the teacher asks Chloe if she would like something to drink, Chloe responds by pressing the button for "juice, please" if she is thirsty. Other AT devices allow Chloe to participate in other ways during the day.

Keep in Mind

Having an AAC device does not mean that the student will be able to overcome all communication limitations, nor does it mean the device will be the sole manner in which the student communicates. As with other AT devices, an AAC device is only another tool that helps the student bridge the gap between current ability level and achieving a useful outcome. The efforts of the classroom teacher, along with the expertise of the SLP and the involvement of the family, increase the chance of a successful outcome.

Strategy 16.9

SUPPORTING STUDENTS WHO USE MOTORIZED WHEELCHAIRS

Rationale and Research

A person's ability to move around serves many important purposes. Early in life, movement is a critical part of learning and development, and young children who have limited mobility are at a disadvantage. Movement allows children to develop cognitive and perceptual abilities as well as communication and social skills. Impaired mobility therefore not only limits a child's movement from one place to another but has an overall detrimental effect on their general development.

Including students in wheelchairs in regular classrooms allows them to maintain their social relationships with their classmates and gives them the chance to participate in the general curriculum. Inclusion, however, may require that teachers are aware of accommodations for the student and some basic conditions necessary to facilitate the students' involvement and mobility. These are outlined in "Step-by-Step."

Key References

Best, S. J., Heller, K. W., & Bigge J. L. (Eds.). (2005). *Teaching individuals with physical or multiple disabilities* (5th ed.). Upper Saddle River, NJ: Merrill/Pearson Education.

National Institute for Rehabilitation Engineering. (2003). *Power wheelchairs and user safety*. Retrieved May 29, 2008, from http://www.abledata.com/abledata_docs/PowerChair-Safety.htm

Wadsworth, D. E., & Knight, D. (1999). Preparing the inclusion classroom for students with special physical and health needs. *Intervention in School and Clinic, 34*(3), 170–175.

Step-by-Step

(1) *Discuss the student's needs with a physical therapist, and evaluate your classrooms accommodations for the student.* Physical therapists (PTs) are key professionals who can help design classroom arrangements and conditions that can allow physical closeness and participation by students in motorized wheelchairs. It is also important for the PT to discuss with you any discomfort of the student so that he is not distracted from learning activities. In the classroom, the teachers should ensure ready access to all parts of the room, including centers and materials.

(2) *Monitor the student's position in the wheelchair, and be aware of comfort level.* The PT should provide you with instructions about the correct positioning of the student in the wheelchair, and you may need to monitor the student to make sure that this position is maintained. Sometimes it will be important for the student to be repositioned in order to be more comfortable.

(3) *Know when the student may leave the wheelchair and how to assist with the transition.* The student will sometimes need assistance to get out of the wheelchair and

into another position. At times, you, and perhaps another teacher or an assistant, may need to help the student move. The PT can provide you with instruction regarding the correct way to move someone.

(4) *Be aware of the basic operating procedure of the wheelchair.* You do not need to be a mechanic, but you should be aware of some of the basic parts and procedures that operate the wheelchair. At a minimum, you should know about the on-off switch, the chair lock, the control device used to direct the chair, the clutch for engaging the wheel, and the belt used to drive the wheel. Generally, in order for the wheelchair to move, plugs must be tightly plugged in, the brakes off, the clutch engaged, and the power turned on.

(5) *Make sure the student operates the wheelchair safely and correctly.* Like other students, those in wheelchairs will sometimes want to show off, move too fast, or not follow common classroom rules. Students in wheelchairs should know how to safely operate their wheelchairs and follow the rules for doing so.

Applications and Examples

When Jason was 4 years old, he was diagnosed as having Duchenne muscular dystrophy. The condition resulted in a gradual loss of muscle control and ultimately in the loss of Jason's ability to walk. Although his parents were devastated by his condition, they wanted to make sure that he remained a full participant in all life activities including school. At first Jason was mobile in a manual wheelchair, but as his arm muscles began to weaken, he required the use of a motorized wheelchair. Now 11 years old and in the fifth grade, Jason is involved as much as possible in regular class activities. He continues to have a positive output and is supported by his family, friends, and teachers. Jason's chair is an important form of assistive technology that facilitates inclusion.

Keep in Mind

While misbehavior may be occasionally acceptable, when the student is powering a device that may weigh up to 400 or 500 pounds, acting out can potentially cause serious harm to the driver or other students in the area. Students should be disciplined to be careful.

Glossary

Ability grouping: An instructional arrangement that allows students with common learning characteristics to benefit from targeted instruction.

Absence seizures: Also referred to as *petit mal seizures,* these seizures are very brief, lasting perhaps 1 to 10 seconds, with the person experiencing a loss of consciousness but otherwise remaining fixed in position.

Accommodations: Changes in curriculum, instruction, and/or grouping arrangements to meet the needs of students with disabilities in general education classrooms.

Acoustical amplification system: A device that serves to increase the volume and intensity of sound directed toward a student or group of students.

Adequate yearly progress (AYP): The No Child Left Behind Act mandates that all students make AYP. Each state defines AYP, which is intended to measure student progress and ensure that all students experience continuous and substantial growth in academic achievement.

Aggression: Physical or verbal attacks that use intimidation and manipulation to get one's own way.

Alternate assessments: The use of nontraditional methods of measurement to judge student performance.

Alternative grouping strategies: Used to support students who do not make adequate progress using whole-group instruction. Includes a range of small-group alternatives for instruction that reduce the number of students being taught and facilitate the use of effective instruction.

Alternative routes to certification: Nontraditional approaches to teacher preparation of varying length and intensity that circumvent traditional university training efforts.

Americans with Disabilities Act (ADA): An act that requires nondiscriminatory protection of civil rights and accessibility to physical facilities and applies to all segments of society with the exception of private schools and religious organizations.

Amphetamines: A type of stimulant medication used to treat the symptoms of attention-deficit/hyperactivity disorder (ADHD). Amphetamines include Adderall and Dexedrine.

Anxiety: Uncomfortable physical and mental signs of distress concerning our daily life challenges.

Applied behavior analysis (ABA): The application of the scientific method and behavioral principles to the observation, study, and modification of behavior.

Asperger's disorder: An autism spectrum disorder characterized by qualitative impairments in nonverbal behaviors, social relationships, interests, and social and emotional reciprocity, but, unlike autism, it involves no delays in language or cognitive development.

Assistive technology (AT): Technology that helps individuals with disabilities function more like those without disabilities by helping to bridge the gap between what a person can do and what he or she may need to do.

Assistive technology devices: Any item, piece of equipment, or product system used to increase, maintain, or improve functional capabilities of a student with a disability.

Assistive technology services: Any service that directly assists in the selection, acquisition, or use of an assistive technology device.

Asthma: A chronic lung condition that can result in attacks and difficult breathing, wheezing, coughing, excess mucus, sweating, and chest constriction.

Ataxia: A form of cerebral palsy characterized by lack of balance and uncoordinated movements.

Athetosis: A form of cerebral palsy characterized by involuntary muscle movements.

Attention-deficit/hyperactivity disorder (ADHD): "A persistent pattern of inattention and/or hyperactivity-impulsivity that is more frequently displayed and more severe than is typically observed in individuals at a comparable level of development" (APA, 2000, p. 85).

Augmentative/alternative communication (AAC): Simple or technologically advanced methods that support or enhance oral and mechanical modes of communication.

Autism spectrum disorders (ASD): ASD, also referred to as pervasive developmental disorders (PDD), are a group of developmental disorders that share common social, communicative, and stereotyped and ritualistic behavioral similarities, varying in age of onset and severity of symptoms. The group includes autism, Asperger's syndrome, pervasive developmental disorder—not otherwise specified (PDD-NOS), Rett syndrome, and childhood disintegrative disorder (CDD).

Autistic disorder: Sometimes referred to as early infantile autism, childhood autism, or Kanner's autism, it is characterized by marked impairments in social interactions and communication, and restrictions in activities or interests.

Autoimmune disease: A condition in which the body attacks its own cells due to an overactive immune response against substances and tissues normally present in the body.

Balanced instruction: In reading, *balanced instruction* means using components of both whole-language and phonics or skills approaches to instruction. This instruction in mathematics consists of an emphasis on both skills instruction and knowledge of underlying mathematical concepts.

Behavior intervention plan (BIP): An individual plan to improve a student's behavior based on an assessment of personal or environmental conditions hypothesized to influence the occurrence of the behavior.

Bilingualism: The ability to speak two languages. (*Multilingualism* refers to the ability to speak more than two languages.)

Blind: Lack of ability to see light and form.

Blindness: The condition of being without vision.

Bone tuberculosis: A rare condition in which an infectious disease (tubercle bacillus) attacks bones or joints.

Building-based support teams: Groups of professionals who work with teachers to address student academic or behavior difficulties.

Central auditory processing disorder: A disorder related to the processing of auditory information in the brain that is characterized by difficulty recognizing and interpreting sounds.

Cerebral palsy: A nonprogressive neurological disorder caused by brain damage before, during, or after birth that impairs a person's posture and movement ability.

Child find services: Services provided by a state to identify children with disabilities in order to provide them with educational and related services.

Childhood disintegrative disorder: Following 2 years of relatively normal development, the child develops a severe loss of functioning.

Chromosomal anomalies: A condition in which strands of chromosomal material within cells are not arranged in their normal pattern. Anomalies often result in syndromes such as Down syndrome.

Civil rights movement: A particularly active period from the late 1950s to the early 1990s that advocated for the application of the Bill of Rights to all disenfranchised persons, whether by race, gender, or disability.

Clubfoot: A congenital anomaly in which the foot points downward and inward.

Co-existing conditions: The co-occurrence of two or more disorders, disabilities, or diseases that are not caused by each other. Sometimes called *co-morbidity*.

Collaboration: Teachers' and other professionals' working together to achieve common goals.

Collaborative consultation: A formal process that includes (1) specific problem identification and goal setting; (2) analysis of factors contributing to the problem and brainstorming possible problem-solving interventions; (3) planning an intervention; and (4) evaluating the outcomes.

Collectivist cultures: Cultures in which working for the common good is more highly valued than individual achievement.

Communication disorders: Language disorders or speech disorders that interfere with communication.

Comprehension: Understanding and remembering what is read.

Conductive hearing loss: Locus of hearing loss in the outer and/or middle ear.

Congenital anomaly: A physical disability apparent at the time of birth.

Congenital hip dislocations (dysplasia): At birth, the ball at the top of the thighbone does not sit securely in the socket of the hip joint.

Consultant: A teacher (or other professional) who provides assistance to another teacher by problem solving possible solutions to a classroom problem.

Content disorders: See *semantic disorders*.

Content enhancements: Instructional techniques that help academically diverse learners understand, store, and access academic content.

Content maps: Visual representations that students may use to understand relationships among ideas or information. Maps explicitly present important information and make this content accessible to all students.

Continuum of services: A requirement of IDEA 2004; students with disabilities must be offered a continuum of placement options for service delivery, including both general education and special class placements.

Cooperative learning: Involves a range of strategies in which students work together to learn and to ensure that others in their group learn.

Core instruction: Instruction provided to the whole class based on the general education curriculum.

Co-teaching: When used in inclusive classrooms, co-teaching is defined as a general and special education teacher working collaboratively to share responsibility for instructing a diverse group of students in a single classroom.

Culturally and linguistically diverse: Backgrounds that are non–European American and, in some instances, non–English speaking, including African American, Hispanic, Native American/Alaskan Native, and Asian/Pacific Islander.

Culturally responsive classroom management: Built on the assumption that culture impacts people's perceptions, knowledge, and interactions, and that the impact of cultural assumptions is often implicit. Culturally responsive teachers strive to learn more about who they are, what they believe, and how their beliefs and experiences influence their perceptions of and interactions with students and their families from a range of cultural backgrounds. Teachers use this knowledge of self and others' cultural backgrounds to guide culturally responsive classroom management.

Culturally responsive teaching: Built on the assumption that culture impacts people's perceptions, knowledge, and interactions, and that the impact of cultural assumptions is often implicit. Culturally responsive teachers strive to learn more about who they are, what they believe, and how their beliefs and experiences influence their perceptions of and interactions with students and their families from a range of cultural backgrounds. Teachers use this knowledge of self and others' cultural backgrounds to guide culturally responsive teaching.

Culture: The values, beliefs, traditions, and behaviors associated with a particular group of people who share a common history.

Curriculum-based measurement: A systematic approach for monitoring student progress in reading, mathematics, writing, and spelling by directly assessing academic skills.

Curvature of the spine (scoliosis): Abnormal spinal growth with convexity to the right or left side.

Cystic fibrosis: A disease that affects major body organs that secrete fluids. It primarily affects the lungs and the digestive system.

Deaf: With a capital *D,* used to describe a particular group of people who share a language (American Sign Language) and a culture (Deaf culture).

Deaf-blind: Concomitant hearing and visual impairments, the combination of which causes severe communication and other developmental and educational needs.

Decibels (dBs): Unit of measure used to report degree of hearing loss.

Deinstitutionalization: The policy of releasing people, particularly those with disabilities of the mind, from institutions and into community settings.

Depression: A pervasive and insidious series of symptoms that influences mood, thought, and carriage.

Developmental aphasia: A language impairment that is assumed to be the result of some type of neurological dysfunction.

Developmental milestones: Characteristics and abilities of infants, toddlers, and children that commonly appear within a specific range of time (e.g., sitting up or rolling over).

Diabetes: A disease in which the body does not produce or properly use insulin to convert sugar, starches, and other food into energy.

Differentiated instruction: An approach to instruction that includes proactive planning to meet diverse students' needs. Differentiated instruction is student centered, based on student assessment data, and includes multiple approaches to content, process, and product to ensure that all students learn.

Diplegia: A physical disability in which the legs are more affected than the arms.

Direct instruction (DI): A systematic, explicit approach to instruction, often based on scripted instructional materials.

Dispositions: One's temperament or tendency, generally learned over time, to act or respond in a certain way, given a certain situation.

Distributed practice: The distribution of instruction or study of information over time. For example, it is often more effective to distribute the study of spelling words during 10-minute sessions over several days than massing practice over one or two longer periods.

Down syndrome: A condition due to chromosomal anomaly in which three chromosome strands (instead of two) occur at pair 21 (trisomy 21). Children with Down syndrome are usually smaller than average and have slower physical, motor, language, and mental development.

Duchenne muscular dystrophy: A commonly genetically inherited form of muscular dystrophy.

Dyslexia: A reading disability that is assumed to be the result of some type of neurological dysfunction.

Echolalia: Repeating words and parts of or whole sentences spoken by other people, with little understanding.

Educational technology: Technology used to facilitate learning academic skills.

Emotional and behavioral disabilities: Refers to students who exhibit inappropriate personal or social behavior that interferes with learning.

English-language learner (ELL): Includes students who are learning English as a second language or those previously called students with limited English proficiency.

Entrepreneurial supports: Supportive, self-sustaining, for-profit corporations built on the skills and interests of those with disabilities.

Epilepsy: A neurological condition that makes people prone to having seizures.

Ethnic group: A group in which individual members identify with one another, usually based on ancestry. Ethnic groups often share common practices related to factors such as culture, religion, and language.

Evidence-based instructional practices: Teaching approaches that have been repeatedly demonstrated through research to result in improved student learning.

Exclusion clause: Often included in the definition of learning disabilities to ensure that the primary reason for a student's academic difficulty is a learning disability and not another disability (e.g., intellectual disability or emotional and behavioral disability) or environmental conditions (e.g., poor teaching).

Explicit instruction: When instructional content is explicitly taught using systematic instructional methods, often based on behavioral theory.

Externalizing behavior problems: Overt manifestations of problem behaviors typically characterized by defiance and disruption.

Figurative language: A variety of figures of speech such as idioms, metaphors, analogies, similes, hyperbole, understatement, jokes, allusions, and slang.

Fluency: The rate and smoothness of reading, demonstrated by reading text quickly and accurately.

Fluency disorders: Interruptions in the normal flow of speech.

Form disorders: Problems in creating sounds used to make words and word parts.

Foster care: A state-run system of support in which children are removed from birth or custodial parents and placed with certified foster or stand-in parents under state authority.

Full inclusion: The perspective taken by some disability advocates that all students with disabilities should be educated in general education classrooms for the full school day.

Functional behavioral assessment (FBA): A systematic, highly structured method of gathering information to determine the purpose or function of observed behaviors.

Functional language: Communicating with a purpose, such as being able to communicate basic wants and needs.

Funds of knowledge: The cultural and experiential resources within a student's home that a culturally responsive teacher may use to provide effective, successful curriculum and instruction.

Genetic inheritance: A condition that is genetically transmitted from one or two parents to a child.

Grand mal seizure: See *tonic-clonic seizure.*

Graphic organizers: Visual representations or aids that may be used to organize and facilitate learning of information.

Hearing impairment: An impairment in hearing, whether permanent or fluctuating, that adversely affects a child's educational performance but that is not included under the IDEA definition of deafness.

Hemiplegia: A physical disability in which the limbs on one side of the body are more affected.

Hemophilia: A rare inherited disorder in which the blood does not clot normally and may lead to dangerously excessive bleeding.

Hyperactivity: A characteristic used to identify students with ADHD. Students who are hyperactive exhibit a high level of activity that is not appropriate in a particular setting and is not age appropriate.

Impulsivity: A characteristic used to identify students with ADHD. Students who are impulsive respond without thinking at a level that is not age appropriate.

Inclusion: Students with disabilities are included as valued members of the school community. This suggests that they belong to the school community and are accepted by others; that they actively participate in the academic and social community of the school; and that they receive supports that offer them the opportunity to succeed.

Individualist cultures: Cultures that value individual achievement and initiative and promote self-realization.

Individualized education program (IEP): A detailed, structured plan of action required by IDEA that informs and guides the delivery of instruction and related services.

Individualized health care plan (IHCP): A student plan that specifies health and medically related activities that must occur to maintain the student's health or to provide in the case of a medical emergency that may arise from the student's condition.

Individuals with Disabilities Education Improvement Act of 2004 (IDEA 2004): Landmark legislation, originally enacted in 1975 as the Education for All Handicapped Children Act, that guides how states and school districts must educate children with disabilities.

Insulin: A hormone that affects metabolism and other body systems. It causes the body's cells to take glucose from blood.

Intellectual disability: Subaverage general intellectual functioning, existing concurrently with deficits in adaptive behavior and manifested during the developmental period, that adversely affects a child's educational performance.

Internalizing behavior problems: Inwardly directed problem behaviors typically characterized by social withdrawal, anxiety, and depression.

Juvenile arthritis: A broad term that encompasses different types of chronic diseases that result in damage to the joints in children.

Juvenile diabetes: See *Type 1 diabetes*.

Language disorders: Conditions in which a person has difficulty sharing thoughts, ideas, and feelings completely, including disorders of form, content (or semantics), and use (or pragmatics).

Learning strategies: Approaches to planning, executing, and evaluating a task that enhance student learning. Learning strategies are learned and used naturally by some students and must be taught to others.

Least restrictive environment (LRE): A mandate of IDEA that requires that students with special needs are educated with children without disabilities to the maximum extent appropriate.

Legal blindness: A central acuity of 20/200 or less in the better eye with the best possible correction; is used to determine eligibility for various legal purposes such as taxation.

Leukemia: A cancer of the blood or bone marrow.

Limb deficiencies: Lack of fully developed arms or legs at birth.

Limited English proficiency (LEP): Describes individuals who do not speak English as their primary language, and who have limited ability to read, write, speak, or understand English.

Linguistic schema: A cognitive construct that allows for the organization of language information in long-term memory.

Litigation: A lawsuit or other action in the courts that seeks to resolve a legal disagreement about an issue.

Mediation: A voluntary process in which a qualified, impartial facilitator works with families and school districts to resolve issues related to the identification, assessment, and placement of a student with disabilities.

Mental handicap: See *intellectual disability*.

Mental retardation: See *intellectual disability*.

Metacognition: An awareness of thinking processes and how individuals monitor and use these processes.

Mixed hearing loss: Both a conductive and sensorineural hearing loss.

Mnemonic devices: Memory aids that teachers use to assist students in remembering information. For example, HOMES is a mnemonic device used to aid in learning the names of the Great Lakes (**H**uron, **O**ntario, **M**ichigan, **E**rie, and **S**uperior).

Motor speech disorders: Neurological conditions that affect a person's speech.

Muscular dystrophy: A progressive physical disability that results in ongoing muscle weakness.

Myelomeningocele: The most severe form of spina bifida; loss of sensation and muscle control occur in parts of the body below the lesion.

Negative reinforcement: The removal of events or activities following a behavior that serves to increase the rate of frequency or the behavior.

Nephritis: Inflammation of one or both kidneys.

Neurological disorder: A condition involving the nervous system.

No Child Left Behind Act (NCLB): Federal legislation requiring that states (1) assess student performance in reading, math, and science; (2) ensure that all students have highly qualified teachers; and (3) provide public school choice and supplemental services to students unable to meet adequate yearly progress (AYP) for 2 years.

Noncompliance: Instances when students choose not to respond to instructions or requests.

Normalization: Suggests that persons with disabilities should have the opportunity to live their lives as independently as possible, making their own life decisions regarding work, leisure, housing, etc.

Occupational therapists: A professional who works to improve physical skills that allow individuals to engage in purposeful activities such as using fine-motor skills related to daily living activities.

Occupational therapy: Delivered by an occupational therapist who has knowledge and skills similar to the physical therapist's but has an orientation toward purposeful activities or tasks such as the use of fine-motor skills related to daily living activities.

Orthopedic and musculoskeletal conditions: Conditions that affect bones or muscles within the limbs.

Osteogenesis imperfecta: A genetic disorder characterized by bones that break easily.

Paraeducator: A person who assists a teacher in a special education or general education classroom. Also called a paraprofessional, teacher assistant, or teacher's aide.

Peer-assisted strategies: Engage peers in supporting students using activities such as peer tutoring or peer buddy systems.

Peer tutoring: A series of grouping alternatives that allow same-age or cross-age peers to assist classmates who are struggling with specific academic content.

People-first language: Emphasizes that persons with disabilities are just that: people who happen to have a disability. This language is respectful of people with disabilities, puts the person first (*person with a disability,* and not *disabled person*), and avoids the use of negative terms (*handicapped, wheelchair bound, retard*) to describe people with disabilities.

Pervasive developmental disorder—not otherwise specified (PDD-NOS): Individuals who do not meet the criteria or the degree of severity that characterizes the four other disorders in the PDD group but who still show a pattern of impairments in social interaction, verbal and nonverbal communication skills, and stereotypical or restricted interests.

Petit mal seizure: See *absence seizure.*

Phonemic awareness: The ability to hear, identify, and manipulate sounds (phonemes) in words. Phonemic awareness is a basic prerequisite skill needed to use phonics in learning to read.

Phonics: The relationship between the sounds of oral language and the symbols (letters) of written language.

Phonological and articulation disorders: Difficulties using the mouth movement, lips, tongue, and voice box to produce speech sounds.

Phonological awareness: Understanding how oral language can be separated into smaller or component sounds and manipulated.

Phonological processing: The ability to use sound–symbol correspondences to sound out words. Many students with reading disabilities have problems with phonological processing.

Physical therapists: A professional who evaluates, plans, and develops interventions to improve posture and balance; to prevent bodily malformations; and to improve walking ability and other gross-motor skills.

Physical therapy: Provided by a physical therapist who evaluates, plans, and develops interventions to improve posture and balance; to prevent bodily misformations; and to improve walking ability and other gross-motor skills. The physical therapist works primarily with students who have significant disabilities.

Picture Exchange Communication System (PECS): An augmentative and alternative communication system that uses pictures to systematically teach people to initiate communication.

Picture walks: Using pictures to provide a preview of lesson content.

Poliomyelitis: An acute viral disease spread from person to person that can lead to muscle weakness and paralysis. Often referred to as "polio."

Pragmatic disorders: See *usage disorders.*

Pragmatics: The rules that govern and describe how language is used in different contexts and environments.

Prenatal causes: Conditions that result in a disability that originate before birth.

Proleptic teaching: A guided discovery model of instruction in which teachers provide a strategy and then allow students to apply the strategy to unique situations.

Prosthetic devices: Artificial devices or extensions used to replace missing body parts.

Pseudohypertrophy: A condition that appears in children with muscular dystrophy in which the calves seem to be growing larger.

Psychological processing: Often included as part of the definition of learning disabilities. A psychological processing problem suggests that an underlying psychological difficulty may cause an academic problem. For example, difficulty with phonological processing may contribute to a problem learning to read.

Quadriplegia: A physical disability in which all four limbs are affected as well as the trunk and the muscles that control the neck, mouth, and the tongue.

Regular Education Initiative (REI): A policy initiative formally introduced in the mid-1980s calling for general educators to become more involved in and responsible for the education of students with disabilities.

Replacement behaviors: A series of positive actions that help students achieve the same functions or outcomes as do the challenging behaviors of concern.

Resilience: Not an innate ability, but a capacity available to all students that results in successful adaptation in school (or other settings) in spite of threatening or challenging circumstances.

Response-to-intervention (RTI): An approach to the identification of special education needs that is based on the assumption that students who struggle academically should be identified with a learning disability only if they do not respond to effective and intensive levels of instruction. It is also a tiered service-delivery approach in which teachers provide more intensive levels of service to students only when lower levels of instructional intensity fail to succeed.

Rett disorder: A neurodevelopmental disorder characterized by seizures and mental retardation as well as a loss of functional or purposeful use of hands.

Rheumatic fever: An inflammatory disease that can develop as a complication of untreated or poorly treated strep throat.

Scaffolding: The temporary support that teachers give students as they learn academic content.

Screening: Determining whether a child has a broad set of behavioral characteristics that suggest the possibility of a disability and the need for further assessments.

Section 504 of the Rehabilitation Act: Civil rights legislation that provides protections for those whose disabilities do not match the definitions under IDEA, including communicable diseases; temporary disabilities; and allergies, asthma, or illnesses due to the environment. Under Section 504, a student has a disability if that student functions as though disabled. Section 504 extends protections against discrimination beyond schools to employment and social and health services.

Self-determination: Assumes that persons with disabilities will act as the primary decision makers in their lives and make choices free from undue influence.

Self-injurious behaviors (SIBs): These are behaviors such as hitting your own head or biting your own hand that can be potentially dangerous. They are sometimes exhibited by students with severe disabilities.

Self-management: A range of actions, such as self-instructing, monitoring, evaluation, reinforcement, graphing, and advocacy, by which a student can increase independence by increasing positive behaviors and skills.

Self-regulated strategy development (SRSD): A systematic approach to teaching students strategies for learning academic content, often in writing and mathematics.

Self-regulation: Strategies that students use to monitor and control their own behavior (e.g., to decrease inappropriate behaviors, increase appropriate behaviors, and/or increase academic accuracy and productivity).

Semantic disorders: Difficulty using specific words or word combinations required by language rules. Also called *content disorders*.

Sensorineural hearing loss: Locus of hearing loss in the cochlea, inner ear, or eighth cranial nerve.

Sensory disabilities: Visual disabilities, including blindness; hearing impairments, including deafness; and deaf-blindness.

Severe discrepancy: The primary criterion that educators use to identify students with learning disabilities in many states. Defined as a severe discrepancy between expected achievement (typically based on an IQ score) and actual achievement.

Sheltered workshops: Segregated facilities that provide noncompetitive training and employment opportunities for individuals with disabilities.

Sickle cell anemia: A disease in which a block in normal blood flow causes pain and can damage most organs. The condition is most common among those with sub-Saharan African ancestry.

Sickle cell disease: See *sickle cell anemia*.

Social stories: An instructional technique in which students create or interpret narrative or visual illustrations that reflect typical social encounters.

Social withdrawal: A tendency to spend excessive amounts of time in solitary activities with low rates of verbalizations and interactions with others.

Spasticity: A form of cerebral palsy characterized by stiff muscles.

Specific language impairment: A particular profile of language difficulty that an individual may exhibit; comprises various disorders.

Speech disorders: Conditions in which a person cannot produce speech sounds correctly or fluently, or has problems with his or her voice. Most common are phonological and articulation disorders, fluency disorders, voice disorders, and motor speech disorders.

Spina bifida: A break in the spinal cord that can leave a person with a loss of physical ability below the break.

Standard course of study (SCOS): A curriculum guide prepared by a local or state education agency that specifies learning objectives or benchmarks for subjects in all grade levels.

Standard English: A controversial term that is most often used to refer to the dialect of English spoken by educated people.

Stereotyped behaviors: Repetitive behaviors (e.g., hand flapping) seen among some individuals with disabilities.

Stereotypies: Also called *stereotyped behaviors,* these are repetitive behaviors (e.g., hand flapping) seen among some individuals with disabilities.

Stimulant medications: Frequently used to treat students with ADHD. These medications have been found to be highly effective for many students with ADHD because they increase attention and reduce restlessness. Stimulant medications include Ritalin and Concerta.

Supported employment: A range of supports that enable people with disabilities to work in natural environments.

Surface management techniques: A series of teacher-based actions that address minor instances of misbehavior with little disruption to the instructional environment.

Targeted interventions: Powerful school-based actions directed toward the chronic and persistent problem behaviors of those students who do not respond to school-wide methods of discipline and behavior management.

Teacher assistance team (TAT): A widely used form of building-based support that uses a systematic approach to identify student difficulties and generate possible solutions for referring teachers.

Time-out: A disciplinary behavior reductive technique in which a student is removed from a reinforcing environment following an undesired behavior.

Tonic-clonic seizure: Also referred to as a grand mal seizure, a seizure during which the person loses awareness, ceases to engage in any activity, loses consciousness, becomes stiff (tonic), and then engages in jerking (clonic) movements.

Type 1 diabetes: Also called juvenile diabetes or insulin-dependent diabetes; an autoimmune disease that destroys the cells in the pancreas that produce insulin.

Universal design for learning (UDL): A method of making curriculum and instructional activities accessible to all students by including supports and accommodations in the original design rather than making alterations after the fact.

Universal precautions: Guidelines provided by the Centers for Disease Control and Prevention to prevent the transmission of communicable diseases.

Usage disorders: Difficulty using language that is appropriate for the social context.

Visual acuity: Quality of ability to see, usually reported as a fraction (e.g., 20/20); the top number states the distance from the object, and the bottom number states the distance at which a person with normal vision could see the same object or figure that is 20 feet away.

Visual disabilities: See *visual impairment*.

Visual field: The area in front of a person that can be seen while looking forward and not moving the head.

Visual impairment: An impairment in vision that, even with correction, adversely affects a student's educational performance. The term includes both partial sight and blindness.

Vocabulary: In reading instruction, often refers to words that are quickly recognized in print. Also often called *sight vocabulary*.

Voice disorders: Inappropriate pitch, loudness, or sound quality during speech.

Voice-output communication aids (VOCA): Portable devices that allow people with difficulty in speech to communicate through the use of graphic symbols and words on computerized displays.

Working memory: Temporarily stores and uses information. Working memory allows an individual to see something, think about it, and then act on this information.

Wraparound interventions: Intensive interventions that are grounded in values of family empowerment and cultural competence, which typically require the coordinated and integrated efforts of teams of professional service providers.

References

Abbott, M., Greenwood, C., Buzhardt, J., & Tapia, Y. (2006). Using technology-based support tools to scale up the classwide peer tutoring program. *Reading and Writing Quarterly, 22*(1), 47–64.

Achenbach, T. M., & Rescorla, L. (2001). *Manual for the ASEBA school-age forms and profiles.* Burlington: University of Vermont, Research Center for Children, Youth, and Families.

Adkins, T. (2006). *Beliefs and practices of successful teachers of Black students: Case studies from secondary English classrooms.* Unpublished doctoral dissertation, Gainesville FL: University of Florida.

Albert, L. (2003). *Cooperative discipline: A teacher's handbook.* Circle Pines, MN: AGS.

Alexander, C., Entwistle, D. R., & Olson, L. S. (2001). Schools, achievement and inequality: A seasonal perspective. *Educational Evaluation and Policy Analysis, 23*(2), 171–191.

Allbritten, D., Mainzer, R., & Ziegler, D. (2004). Will students with disabilities be scapegoats for school failure? *Teaching Exceptional Children, 36*(3), 74–75.

American Academy of Pediatrics. (2000). Clinical practice guideline: Diagnosis and evaluation of the child with attention-deficit/hyperactivity disorder. *Pediatrics, 105*(5), 1158–1170.

American Academy of Asthma Allergy and Immunology. (2005). *Pediatric asthma: Feature article.* Retrieved July 1, 2008, from http://www.aaaai.org/

American Association of Colleges for Teacher Education. (2002). *Educators' preparation for cultural and linguistic diversity: A call to action.* Committee on Multicultural Education. Washington, DC: Author.

American Association on Intellectual and Developmental Disabilities. (2007). *AIDD/ARC position statement on sexuality.* Retrieved July 24, 2007, from http://www.aamr.org/Policies/pos_sexuality.shtml

American Association on Mental Retardation. (2002). *Mental retardation: Definition, classification, and systems of supports* (10th ed.). Washington, DC: Author.

American Federation of Teachers. (2006). *Let's get it right: AFT's recommendation for No Child Left Behind.* Retrieved August 14, 2008, from http://www.aft.org/nclbrecs.pdf

American Foundation for the Blind (AFB). (n.d.). *Quick facts and figures on blindness and low vision.* Retrieved August 30, 2005, from http://www.afb.org/Section.asp?SectionID=42&DocumentID=1374

American Psychiatric Association. (2000). *Diagnostic and statistical manual of mental disorders* (4th ed., text rev.). Washington, DC: Author.

American Speech-Language-Hearing Association. (2000). *Guidelines for the roles and responsibilities of the school-based speech-language pathologist.* Retrieved February 18, 2009, from www.asha.org/policy/

American Speech-Language-Hearing Association. (n.d.). *Hearing assessment.* Retrieved September 30, 2005, from http://www.asha.org/public/hearing/testing/assess.htm

Americans with Disabilities Act of 1990, Pub. L. No. 101–336, §2, 104 Stat. 328 (1991).

Anderson-Inman, L., Knox-Quinn, C., & Horney, M. A. (1996). Computer-based study strategies for students with learning disabilities: Individual differences associated with adoption level. *Journal of Learning Disabilities, 29*(5), 461–466.

Arick, J. R., Krug, D. A., Fullerton, A., Loos, L., & Falco, R. (2005). In F. R. Volkmar, R. Paul, A. Klin, & D. Cohen (Eds.), *Handbook of autism and pervasive developmental disorders: Vol. 2. Assessment, interventions, and policy* (4th ed., pp. 1003–1028). Hoboken, NJ: Wiley.

Aronson, E. (2004). Building empathy, compassion, and achievement in the Jigsaw classroom. In J. Aronson (Ed.). *Improving academic achievement: Impact of psychological factors on education* (pp. 213–227). Bingley, UK: Emerald Group Publishing.

Aronson, E. (2008). *Jigsaw classroom: Jigsaw in 10 easy steps.* Retrieved February 20, 2008, from http://www.jigsaw.org

Aronson, E., Blaney, N., Stephan, C., Sikes, J., & Snapp, M. (1978). *The Jigsaw classroom.* Beverly Hills, CA: Sage.

Artiles, A. J., Klingner, J. K., & Tate, W. F. (2006). Representation of minority students in special education: Complicating traditional explanations. *Educational Researcher, 35*(6), 3–5.

Austin, J. L., & Agar, G. (2005). Helping young children follow their teachers directions: The utility of high probability command sequences in pre-K and kindergarten classrooms. *Education and Treatment of Children, 28,* 222–236.

Autism Information Center. (2008). *Frequently asked questions: Prevalence.* Retrieved July 2, 2008, from http:/www.cdc.gov/ncbddd/autism/faq__prevalence.htm.

Axelrod, S. (1983). *Behavior modification in the classroom.* New York: McGraw-Hill.

Baca, L. M., & Cervantes, H. T. (2004). *The bilingual special education interface.* Upper Saddle River, NJ: Merrill/Pearson Education.

Baenen, N., Bernhole, A., Dulaney, C., & Banks, K. (2004). Reading Recovery: Long-term progress of three cohorts. *Journal of Education for Students Placed At-Risk, 2*(2), 161–181.

Baglieri, S., & Knopf, J. H. (2004). Normalizing difference in inclusive teaching. *Journal of Learning Disabilities, 37*(6), 525–529.

Baines, L., Baines, C., & Masterson, C. (1994). Mainstreaming: One school's reality. *Phi Delta Kappan, 76*(1), 39–40, 57–64.

Baird, G., Charman, T., et al. (2000). A screening instrument for autism at 18 months of age: A 6-year follow-up. *Journal of the American Academy of Child and Adolescent Psychiatry, 29,* 694–702.

Baker, S., Gersten, R., & Keating, T. (2000). When less may be more: A 2-year longitudinal evaluation of a volunteer tutoring program requiring minimal training. *Reading Research Quarterly, 35*(4), 494–519.

Banks, J. A. (1988). *Multiethnic education: Theory and practice* (2nd ed.) Boston: Allyn & Bacon.

Banks, J., Cochran-Smith, M., Moll, L., Richert, A., Zeichner, K., LePage, P., Darling-Hammond, L., Duffy, H., with McDonald, M. (2005). Teaching diverse learners. In L. Darling-Hammond & J. Bransford (Eds.), *Preparing teachers for a changing world: What teachers should learn and be able to do* (pp. 232–273). San Francisco: Jossey-Bass.

Barkley, R. (2006a). Comorbid disorders, social and family adjustment. In R. Barkley (Ed.), *Attention-deficit hyperactivity disorder: A handbook for diagnosis and treatment* (3rd ed., pp. 184–218). New York: Guilford.

Barkley, R. (2006b). Primary symptoms, diagnostic criteria, prevalence, and gender differences. In R. Barkley (Ed.), *Attention-deficit hyperactivity disorder: A handbook for diagnosis and treatment* (3rd ed., pp. 76–121). New York: Guilford.

Beirne-Smith, M., Patton, J. M., & Kim, S. H. (2006). *Mental retardation: An introduction to intellectual disability* (7th ed.). Upper Saddle River, NJ: Merrill/Pearson Education.

Bell, L. I. (2003). Strategies that close the gap. *Educational Leadership, 60*(4), 32–34.

Bempechat, J. (1998). *Against the odds.* San Francisco: Jossey-Bass.

Benard, B. (2004). *Resiliency: What we have learned.* San Francisco: WestEd.

Bender, W., & Shores, C. (2007). *Response to intervention: A practical guide for every teacher.* Thousand Oaks, CA: Corwin.

Benner, G. J., Nelson, J. R., & Epstein, M. H. (2002). Language skills of children with EBD: A literature review. *Journal of Emotional and Behavioral Disorders, 10,* 43–59.

Bennett, C. I. (2006). *Comprehensive multicultural education: Theory and practice* (6th ed.). Boston: Allyn & Bacon.

Best, S. (2005). Health impairments and infectious diseases. In S. J. Best, K. W. Heller, & J. L. Bigge (Eds.), *Teaching individuals with physical or multiple disabilities* (5th ed., pp. 59–85). Upper Saddle River, NJ: Merrill/Pearson Education.

Best, S. J., & Bigge, J. L. (2005). Cerebral palsy. In S. J. Best, K. W. Heller, & J. L. Bigge (Eds.), *Teaching individuals with physical or multiple disabilities* (5th ed., pp. 87–109). Upper Saddle River, NJ: Merrill/Pearson Education.

Best, S. J., Reed, P., & Bigge, J. L. (2005). Assistive technology. In S. J. Best, K. Wolff Heller, & J. L. Bigge (Eds.), *Teaching individuals with physical or multiple disabilities* (5th ed., pp. 179–226). Upper Saddle River, NJ: Merrill/Pearson Education.

Biancarosa, C., & Snow, C. E. (2004). *Reading Next—A vision for action and research in middle and high school literacy: A report to Carnegie Corporation of New York* (2nd ed.). Washington, DC: Alliance for Excellent Education. Retrieved March 4, 2009, from http://www.carnegie.org/literacy/PDF/ReadingNext.pdf

Biklen, D. (1985). *Achieving the complete school: Strategies for effective mainstreaming.* New York: Teachers College Press.

Bitter, G. G., & Legacy, J. M. (2008). *Using technology in the classroom* (7th ed.). Boston: Pearson/Allyn & Bacon.

Blackhurst, A. E. (2005). Perspectives on applications of technology in the field of learning disabilities. *Learning Disability Quarterly, 28,* 175–179.

Blinder, A., & Morgan, J. (2000). *Are two heads better than one? An experimental analysis of group vs. individual decision making.* Working Paper 7909. Cambridge, MA: National Bureau of Economic Research.

Bond, R., & Castagnera, E. (2006). Peer supports and inclusive education: An underutilized resource. *Theory into Practice 45*(3), 224–229.

Bondy, E., Ross, D., Gallingane, C., & Hambacher, E. (2007). Creating environments of success and resilience: Culturally responsive classroom management and more. *Urban Education, 42*(4), 326–348.

Books, S. (2007). Devastation and disregard: Reflections of Katrina, child poverty, and educational opportunity. In S. Books (Ed.), *Invisible children in the society and its schools* (pp. 1–22). Mahwah, NJ: Erlbaum.

Borman, G., & Hewes, G. (2003). Long-term effects and cost effectiveness of success for all. *Educational Evaluation and Policy Analysis, 24*(2), 243–266.

Borman, G., Dowling, N., & Schneck, C. (2007). The national randomized field trial of *Open Court Reading.* Retrieved March 12, 2008, from https://www.sraonline.com/download/News/PressRelease/National_OCR_Study.pdf

Boudah, D. J., Lenz, B. K., Bulgren, J. A., Schumaker, J., B., & Deshler, D. D. (2000). Don't water down! Enhance content learning through the unit organizer routine. *Teaching Exceptional Children, 32*(3), 48–56.

Boutot, E., & Bryant, D. (2005). Social integration of students with autism in inclusive settings. *Education and Training in Developmental Disabilities, 40*(1), 14–24.

Bower, E. M. (1960). *Early identification of emotionally handicapped children in school.* Springfield, IL: Charles C. Thomas.

Boyd, B., & Correa, V. (2005). Developing a framework for reducing the cultural clash between African American parents and the special education system. *Multicultural Perspectives, 7*(2), 3–11.

Boyle, J. R. (2007). The process of note taking: Implications for students with mild disabilities. *The Clearing House, 80*(5), 227–232.

Bransford, J. D., Brown, A. L, & Cocking, R. R. (Eds.). (2000). *How people learn.* Washington, DC: National Academy Press.

Bricker, D. (2000). Inclusion: How the scene has changed. *Topics in Early Childhood Special Education (TECSE), 20*(1), 14–19.

Broderick, A., Mehta-Parekh, H., & Reid, D. K. (2005). Differentiating instruction for disabled students in inclusive classrooms. *Theory into Practice, 44,* 194–202.

Browder, D. M., & Spooner, F. (Eds.). (2006). *Teaching language arts, math, & science to students with significant cognitive disabilities.* Baltimore: Paul H. Brookes.

Browder, D. M., Spooner, F., Wakeman, S., Trela, K., & Baker, J. N. (2006). Aligning instruction with academic content standards: Finding the link. *Research and Practice for Persons with Severe Disabilities, 31,* 309–321.

Browder, D. M., Wakeman, S. Y., Flowers, C., Rickelman, R. J., & Pugalee, D. (2007). Creating access to the general curriculum with links to grade-level content for students with significant cognitive disabilities: An explication of the concept. *Journal of Special Education, 41*(1), 2–16.

Brown, D. F. (2004). Urban teachers' professed classroom management strategies: Reflections of culturally responsive teaching. *Urban Education, 39*(3), 266–289.

Brown, L., Shiraga, B., & Kessler, K. (2006). The quest for ordinary lives: The integrated post-school vocational functioning of 50 workers with significant disabilities. *Research and Practice for Persons with Severe Disabilities, 31,* 93–121.

Brown v. Board of Education, 347 U.S. 483 (1954).

Bryan, T., Burstein, K., & Ergul, C. (2004). The social-emotional side of learning disabilities: A science-based presentation of the state of the art. *Learning Disability Quarterly, 27*(1), 45–51.

Bryant, D. P., Bryant, B. R., & Raskind, M. H. (1998). Using assistive technology to enhance the skills of students with learning disabilities. *Intervention in School and Clinic, 34*(1), 53–58.

Bryant, D., & Dix, J. (1999). Mathematics interventions for students with learning disabilities. In W. Bender (Ed.), *Professional issues in learning disabilities* (pp. 219–259). Austin, TX: Pro-Ed.

Buck, G., Polloway, E., Smith-Thomas, A., & Cook, K. (2003). Prereferral intervention processes: A survey of state practices. *Exceptional Children, 69*(3), 349–360.

Bulgren, J. (2006). Integrated content enhancement routines: Responding to the needs of adolescents with disabilities in rigorous inclusive secondary content classes. *Teaching Exceptional Children, 38*(6), 54–58.

Bulgren, J., Deshler, D. D. & Lenz, B. K. (2007). Engaging adolescents with LD in higher order thinking about history concepts using integrated content enhancement routines. *Journal of Learning Disabilities, 40*(2), 121–133.

Bulgren, J., & Lenz, K. (1996). Strategic instruction in the content areas. In D. D. Deshler, E. S. Ellis, & B. K. Lenz (Eds.), *Teaching adolescents with learning disabilities* (pp. 409–473). Denver: Love.

Bulgren, J., Schumaker, J. B., & Deshler, D. D. (1988). The effectiveness of a concept teaching routine in enhancing the performance of students with learning disabilities in secondary mainstream classes. *Learning Disability Quarterly, 11*(1), 3–17.

Bulgren, J., Schumaker, J. B., & Deshler, D. D. (1993). *The concept mastery routine.* Lawrence, KS: Edge Enterprises.

Bullis, M. (2001). Job placement and support considerations in transition programs for adolescents with emotional disabilities. In L. M. Bullock & R. A. Gable (Eds.), *Addressing the social, academic, and behavioral needs of students with challenging behavior in inclusive and alternative settings* (pp. 31–41). Arlington, VA: Council for Exceptional Children.

Burns, B. J., & Goldman, S. K. (1998). *Promising practices in wraparound for children with serious emotional disturbance and their families: Vol. 4. Systems of care: Promising practices in children's mental health 1998 series.* Washington, DC: Georgetown University, Child Development Center, National Technical Assistance Center for Children's Mental Health.

Burstein, N., Sears, S., Wilcoxen, A., Cabello, B., & Spagna, M. (2004). Moving toward inclusive practices. *Remedial and Special Education, 25*(2), 104–116.

Busch, T. W., & Reschly, A. L. (2007). Progress monitoring in reading: Using curriculum-based measurement in a response-to-intervention. *Assessment for Effective Intervention, 32*(4), 223–230.

California Department of Education. (2007). *Achievement gap charts.* Retrieved May 16, 2008, from http://www.cde.ca.gov/eo/in/se/agcharts.asp

Carey, D. M., & Sale, P. (1994). Notebook computers increase communication. *Teaching Exceptional Children, 27*(1), 62–69.

Carlson, E., Lee, H., & Schroll, K. (2004). Identifying attributes of high quality special education teachers. *Teacher Education and Special Education, 27,* 350–359.

Carnine, D., Engelmann, S., & Steely, D. (2003). *Corrective math.* Chicago: Science Research Associates.

Carpenter, S. L., King-Sears, M. E., & Keys, S. G. (1998). Counselor + educators + families as a transdisciplinary team = more effective inclusion for students with disabilities. *Professional School Counseling, 2*(1), 1–9.

Carr, E. G., Dunlap, G., Horner, R. H., Koegel, R. L., Turnbull, A. P., Sailor, W., Anderson, J. L., Albin, R. W., Koegel, L. K., & Fox, L. (2002). Positive behavior support: Evolution of an applied science. *Journal of Positive Behavior Interventions, 4,* 4–16, 20.

Carr, E. G., Horner, R. H., Turnbull, A. P., Marquis, J. G., McLaughlin, D. M., McAtee, M. L., Smith, C. E., Ryan, K. A., Ruef, M. B., & Doolabh, A. (1999). *Positive behavior support for people with developmental disabilities: A research synthesis.* Washington, DC: American Association on Mental Retardation.

Carter, E., & Hughes, C. (2005). Increasing social interaction among adolescents with intellectual disabilities and their general education peers: Effective interventions. *Research & Practice for Persons with Severe Disabilities, 30*(4), 179–193.

Carter, E., & Hughes, C. (2006). Including high school students with severe disabilities in general education classes: Perspectives of general and special educators, paraprofessionals, and administrators. *Research & Practice for Persons with Severe Disabilities, 31*(2), 174–185.

Carter, E. W., Cushing, L. S., Clark, N. M., & Kennedy, C. H. (2005). Effects of peer support interventions on students' access to the general curriculum and social interactions. *Research and Practice for Persons with Severe Disabilities, 30,* 15–25.

Carter, E. W., Wehby, J., Hughes, C., Johnson, S. M., Plank, D. R., Barton-Arwood, S. M., & Lunsford, L. B. (2005). Preparing adolescents with high-incidence disabilities for high-stakes testing with strategy instruction. *Preventing School Failure, 49*(2), 55–62.

Carter, J., & Sugai, G. (1989). Survey on prereferral practices: Response from state departments of education. *Exceptional Children, 55,* 298–302.

Cartledge, G. W., Gardner, R., & Ford, D. Y. (2009). *Diverse learners with exceptionalities: Culturally responsive teaching in the inclusive classroom.* Upper Saddle River, NJ: Merrill/Pearson.

Case, L., Harris, K., & Graham, S. (1992). Improving the mathematical problem-solving skills of students with learning disabilities: Self-regulated strategy development. *Journal of Special Education, 26*(1), 1–19.

Causton-Theoharis, J., Giangreco, M., Doyle, M., & Vadasy, P. (2007). Paraprofessionals: The "Sous-Chefs" of literacy instruction. *Teaching Exceptional Children, 40*(1), 56–62.

Cavalier, A. R., & Brown, C. C. (1998). From passivity to participation: The transformational possibilities of speech-recognition technology. *Teaching Exceptional Children, 30*(6), 60–65.

Center For Applied Special Technology (CAST). (1999–2007). *Universal design for learning.* Retrieved February 28, 2008, from http://www.cast.org/

Center for Applied Special Technology (CAST). (1999–2009). Retrieved August 8, 2007, from http://www.cast.org

Center for Effective Collaboration and Practice. (1998). *Functional behavioral assessment.* Retrieved August 10, 2007, from http://cecp.air.org/fba/problembehavior/main.htm

Chalfant, J., & Pysh, M. (1989). Teacher assistance teams: Five descriptive studies on 96 teams. *Remedial and Special Education, 10*(6), 49–58.

Chalfant, J., Pysh, M., & Moultrie, R. (1979). Teacher assistance teams: A model for within building problem solving. *Learning Disability Quarterly, 2*(3), 85–96.

Chalk, J. C., Hagan-Burke, S., & Burke, M. D. (2005). The effects of self-regulated strategy development on the writing process for high school students with learning disabilities. *Learning Disability Quarterly, 28,* 75–87.

Chamberlain, S. P. (2005). Recognizing and responding to cultural differences in the education of culturally and linguistically diverse learners. *Intervention in School and Clinic, 40*(4), 195–221.

Chandler, L. K., & Dahlquist, C. M. (2002). *Functional assessment: Strategies to prevent and remediate challenging behaviors in school settings.* Upper Saddle River, NJ: Merrill/Pearson Education.

Charles, C. M. (2002). *Essential elements of discipline.* Boston: Allyn & Bacon.

Charney, R. (2002). *Teaching children to care.* Greenfield, MA: The Northeast Foundation for Children.

Chawarska, K., & Volkmar, F. R. (2005). Autism in infancy and early childhood. In F. R. Volkmar, R. Paul, A. Klin, & D. Cohen (Eds.), *Handbook of autism and pervasive developmental disorders: Vol. 1. Diagnosis, development, neurobiology, and behavior* (4th ed., pp. 223–246). Hoboken, NJ: Wiley.

Cheney, D., & Bullis, M. (2004). The school-to-community transition of adolescents with emotional and behavioral disorders. In R. B. Rutherford, Jr., M. M. Quinn, & A. R. Mathur (Eds.), *Handbook of research in emotional and behavioral disorders* (pp. 369–384). New York: Guilford.

Clark, G. M., & Bigge, J. L. (2005). Transition and self-determination. In S. J. Best, K. W. Heller, & J. L. Bigge (Eds.), *Teaching individuals with physical or multiple disabilities* (5th ed., pp. 367–398). Upper Saddle River, NJ: Merrill/Pearson Education.

Clay, M. (1993). *Reading recovery: A guidebook for teachers in training.* Portsmouth, NH: Heinemann.

Clay, M. (2001). *An observation survey of early literacy achievement* (2nd ed.). Portsmouth, NH: Heinemann.

Coady, M., & Escamilla, K. (2005). Audible voices, visible tongues: Exploring social realities in Spanish-speaking students' writing. *Language Arts, 82*(6), 462–471.

Coates, R. (1989). The regular education initiative and opinions of regular classroom teachers. *Journal of Learning Disabilities, 22,* 41–56.

Cole, C., Horvath, B., Chapman, C., Deschenes, C., Ebeling, D., & Sprague, J. (2000). *Adapting curriculum & instruction in inclusive classrooms: A teachers' desk reference* (2nd ed.). Bloomington: Indiana Institute on Disability and Community.

Cole, C., Waldron, N., & Madj, M. (2004). Academic progress of students across inclusive and traditional settings. *Mental Retardation, 42*(2), 136–144.

Cole, R.W. (2001). *More strategies for educating everybody's children.* Alexandria, VA: ASCD.

Coleman, M., & Vaughn, S. (2000). Reading interventions for students with emotional/behavioral disorders. *Behavioral Disorders, 25*(2), 93–104.

Conderman, G., & Elf, N. (2007). What's in this book? Engaging students through a textbook exploration activity. *Reading and Writing Quarterly, 23,* 111–116.

Connor, D. (2006a). Stimulants. In R. Barkley (Ed.). *Attention-deficit hyperactivity disorder: A handbook for diagnosis and treatment* (3rd ed., pp. 608–647). New York: Guilford.

Connor, D. (2006b). Other medications. In R. Barkley (Ed.), *Attention-deficit hyperactivity disorder: A handbook for diagnosis and treatment* (3rd ed., pp. 658–677). New York: Guilford.

Connor, M. H., & Boskin, J. (2001). Overrepresentation of bilingual and poor children in special education classes: A continuing problem. *Journal of Children & Poverty, 7*(1), 23–32.

Cook, L. H., & Boe, E. E. (2007). National trends in the sources of supply of teachers in special and general education. *Teacher Education and Special Education, 30*(4), 217–232.

Coonrod, E. E., & Stone, W. L. (2005). Screening for autism in young children. In F. R. Volkmar, R. Paul, A. Klin, & D. Cohen (Eds.), *Handbook of autism and pervasive developmental disorders: Vol. 2. Assessment, interventions, and policy* (4th ed., pp. 707–729). Hoboken, NJ: Wiley.

Cooper, H. (2001). *The battle over homework* (2nd ed.). Thousand Oaks, CA: Corwin.

Cooper, H., Nye, B., Charlton, K. Lindsay, J., & Greathouse, S. (1996). The effects of summer vacation on achievement test scores: A narrative and meta-analytic review. *Review of Educational Research, 66*(3), 227–268.

Cooper, J. L. (2008). *Toward better behavioral health for children, youth and their families.* New York: National center for Children in Poverty, Columbia University. Retrieved May 14, 2008, from http://www.nccp.org/publications/pub_804.html

Copeland, S., Hughes, C., Carter, E., Guth, C., Presley, J., Williams, C., & Fowler, S. (2004). Increasing access to general education: Perspectives of participants in a high school peer support program. *Remedial and Special Education, 25*(3), 342–352.

Copeland, S., McCall, J., Williams, C., et al. (2002). High school peer buddies: A win-win situation. *Teaching Exceptional Children, 35*(1), 16–21.

Corbett, W. P., Clark, H. B., & Blank, W. (2002). Employment and social outcomes associated with vocational programming for youths with emotional or behavioral disorders. *Behavioral Disorders, 27,* 358–370.

Corbett, D., Wilson, B., & Williams, B. (2002). *Effort and excellence in urban classrooms.* New York: Teachers College Press.

Correa, V., Jones, H., Thomas, C., & Morsink, C. (2005). *Interactive teaming: Enhancing programs for students with special needs.* Upper Saddle River, NJ: Merrill/Pearson Education.

Correa, V., & Tulbert, B. (1993). Collaboration between school personnel in special education and Hispanic families. *Journal of Educational and Psychological Consultation, 4*(3), 253–265.

Corwin, M. (2001). *And still we rise: Trials and triumphs of twelve gifted inner city high school students.* New York: HarperCollins.

Cosbey, J. E., & Johnston, S. (2006). Using a single-switch voice output communication aid to increase social access for children with severe disabilities in inclusive classrooms. *Research and Practice for Persons with Severe Disabilities, 31,* 144–156.

Costello, J., Mustillo, S., Erkanli, A., Keeler, G, & Angold, A. (2003). Prevalence and development of psychiatric disorders in childhood and adolescence. *Archives of General Psychiatry, 60,* 837–844.

Council for Exceptional Children. (1999). *Universal design: Ensuring access to the general education curriculum.* Research Connections in Special Education. Arlington, VA: Author.

Council for Exceptional Children. (2007). *Position on response to intervention (RTI): The unique role of special education and special educators.* Arlington, VA: Author.

Coutinho, M. J., Oswald, D. P., & Forness, S. R. (2002). Gender and sociodemographic factors and the disproportionate identification of culturally and linguistically diverse students with emotional disturbance. *Behavioral Disorders, 27*(2), 109–125.

Cox, D. (2005). Evidence-based interventions using home–school collaboration. *School Psychology Quarterly, 20*(4), 473–497.

Coyne, M., Zipoli, R., & Ruby, M. (2006). Beginning reading instruction for students at risk for reading disabilities: What, how, and when. *Intervention in School and Clinic, 41*(3), 161–168.

Crawford, J. (2002). *Census 2000: A guide for the perplexed.* Retrieved November 27, 2005, from http://ourworld .compuserve.com/homepages/JWCRAWFORD/census02.htm

Crosnoe, R. (2001). Academic orientation and parental involvement in education during high school. *Sociology of Education, 74*(3), 210–230.

Cullinan, D. (2002). *Students with emotional and behavioral disorders.* Upper Saddle River, NJ: Merrill/Pearson Education.

Cullinan, D. (2004). Classification and definition of emotional and behavioral disorders. In R. B. Rutherford, Jr., M. M. Quinn, & A. R. Mathur (Eds.), *Handbook of research in emotional and behavioral disorders* (pp. 32–53). New York: Guilford.

Cullinan, D., & Sabornie, E. J. (2004). Characteristics of emotional disturbance in middle and high school students. *Journal of Emotional and Behavioral Disorders, 12,* 157–167.

Cummins, J. (2001). Assessment and intervention with culturally and linguistically diverse learners. In S. Hurley & J. Tinajero (Eds.), *Literacy assessment of bilingual learners.* (pp. 115–129). Boston: Allyn & Bacon.

Curwin, R. L., & Mendler, A. N. (1999). *Discipline with dignity* (2nd ed.). Alexandria, VA: ASCD

Cushman, K., & Rogers, L. (2008). *Fires in the middle school bathroom: Advice for teachers from middle schoolers.* New York: New Press.

D'Agostino, J., & Murphy, J. (2004). A meta-analysis of Reading recovery in United States schools. *Educational Evaluation and Policy Analysis, 26*(1), 23–38.

Dalston, R. M. (2000). Voice disorders. In R. B. Gillam, T. P. Marquardt, & F. N. Martin (Eds.), *Communication sciences and disorders: From science to clinical practice* (pp. 283–312). San Diego: Singular.

Daniels, L. E., Sparling, J. W., Reilly, M., & Humphry, R. (1995). Use of assistive technology with young children with severe and profound disabilities. *Infant–Toddler Intervention, 5,* 91–112.

Davies, D., Stock, S., & Wehmeyer, M. L. (2003). A palmtop computer-based intelligent aid for individuals with intellectual disabilities to increase independent decision making. *Research and Practice for Persons with Severe Disabilities, 28,* 182–193.

deBettencourt, L. (2002). Understanding the differences between IDEA and Section 504. *Teaching Exceptional Children, 34*(3), 16–23.

Delpit, L. (1995). *Other people's children.* New York: New Press.

Deno, E. (1970). Special education as developmental capital. *Exceptional Children, 37*(3), 229–237.

Deno, S. (2007). Curriculum-based measurement. In J. McLeskey (Ed.), *Reflections on inclusion: Classic articles that shaped our thinking* (pp. 221–249). Arlington, VA: Council for Exceptional Children.

Deno, S. L. (2003). Developments in curriculum-based measurement. *Journal of Special Education, 37*(3), 184–192.

Deshler, D. (2005). Adolescents with learning disabilities: Unique challenges and reasons for hope. *Learning Disability Quarterly, 28,* 122–124.

Deshler, D. D., & Putnam, M. L. (1996). Learning disabilities in adolescents: A perspective. In D. D. Deshler, E. S. Ellis, & B. K. Lenz (Eds.), *Teaching adolescents with learning disabilities* (pp. 1–7). Denver: Love.

Dettmer, P., Thurston, L., Knackendoffel, A. & Dyck, N. (2009). *Collaboration, consultation, and teamwork for students with special needs.* Upper Saddle River, NJ: Merrill/Pearson Education.

de Valenzuela, J. S., Copeland, S., Huaqing Qi, C., & Park, M. (2006). Examining educational equity: Revisiting the disproportionate representation of minority students in special education. *Exceptional Children, 72*(4), 425–441.

Doll, B., Sands, D. J., Wehmeyer, M. L., & Palmer, S. (1996). Promoting the development and acquisition of self-determined behavior. In D. J. Sands & M. L. Wehmeyer (Eds.), *Self-determination across the lifespan: Independence and choice for people with disabilities* (pp. 65–90). Baltimore: Paul H. Brookes.

Dore, R., Dion, E., Wagner, S., & Brunet, J. (2002). High school inclusion of adolescents with mental retardation: A multiple case study. *Education and Training in Mental Retardation and Developmental Disabilities, 37*(3), 253–261.

Doubt, L., & McColl, M. A. (2003). A secondary guy: Physically disabled teenagers in secondary schools. *Canadian Journal of Occupational Therapy, 70*(3), 139–151.

Doyle, W. (1980). *Classroom management.* West Lafayette, IN: Kappa Delta Pi.

Doyle, W. (1986). Classroom organization and management. In M. C. Wittrock (Ed.), *Handbook of research on teaching* (pp. 392–431). New York: Macmillan.

Duckworth, S., Smith-Rex, S., Okey, S., Brookshire, M. A., Rawlinson, D., Rawlinson, R., Castillo, S., & Little, J. (2001). Wraparound services for young schoolchildren with emotional and behavioral disorders. *Teaching Exceptional Children, 33*(4), 54–60.

Duhaney, L. M. G., & Salend, S. J. (2000). Parental perceptions of inclusive educational placements. *Remedial and Special Education, 21*(2), 121–128.

Dukes, C., & Lamar-Dukes, P. (2009). Inclusion by design: Engineering inclusive practices in secondary schools. *Teaching Exceptional Children, 41*(3), 16–23.

Duncan, G. J., Brooks-Gunn, J., & Klebanov, P. K. (1994). Economic deprivation and early childhood development. *Child Development, 65*(2), 296–318.

Dunlap, G., & Fox, L. (1999). *Teaching students with autism.* Reston, VA: ERIC Clearinghouse on Disabilities and Gifted Education. (ERIC Document Reproduction Service No. ED435148)

Dunlap, L., & Dunlap, G. (1989). A self-monitoring package for teaching subtraction with regrouping to students with learning disabilities. *Journal of Applied Behavior Analysis, 22*(3), 309–314.

Dunn, L. M. (1968). Special education for the mildly retarded—Is much of it justifiable? *Exceptional Children, 35,* 5–22.

DuPaul, G. (2007). School-based interventions for students with attention deficit hyperactivity disorder: Current status and future directions. *School Psychology Review, 36*(2), 183–194.

DuPaul, G., Barkley, R., & Connor, D. (1998). Stimulants. In R. Barkley (Ed.), *Attention deficit hyperactivity disorder: A handbook for diagnosis and treatment* (2nd ed., pp. 510–551). New York: Guilford.

Dwyer, K., & Osher, D. (2000). *Safeguarding our children: An action guide.* Washington, DC: U.S. Department of Education and Justice, American Institutes for Research.

Dymond, S. K., Renzaglia, A., Rosenstein, A., Chun, E. J., Banks, R. A., Niswander, V., & Gilson, C. L. (2006). Using a participatory action research approach to create a universally designed inclusive high school science course: A case study. *Research & Practice for Persons with Severe Disabilities, 31*(4), 293–308.

Dymond, S., & Russell, D. (2004). Impact of grade and disability on the instructional context of inclusive classrooms. *Education and Training in Developmental Disabilities, 39*(2), 127–140.

Dynarski, M., Agodini, R., Heaviside, S., Novak, T., Carey, N., Campuzano, L., Means, B., Murphy, R., Penuel, W., Javitz, H., Emery, D., & Sussex, W. (2007). *Effectiveness of reading and mathematics software products: Findings from the first student cohort.* Washington, DC: U.S. Department of Education, Institute of Education Sciences.

Eber, L., Sugai, G., Smith, C., & Scott, T. (2002). Wraparound and positive behavior interventions and supports in the schools. *Journal of Emotional and Behavioral Disorders, 10,* 171–180.

Eggen, P., & Kauchak, D. (2006). *Strategies and models for teachers: Teaching content and thinking skills.* Boston: Allyn & Bacon.

eHow. (1999–2008). How to use educational software for students with learning disabilities. Retrieved February 6, 2008, from http://www.ehow.com/how_2091734_use-educational-software-students-learning-disabilities.html

Ehri, L., Dreyer, L., Flugman, B., & Gross, A. (2007). Reading Rescue: An effective tutoring intervention model for language-minority students who are struggling readers in first grade. *American Educational Research Journal, 44*(2), 414–448. (Reading Rescue is a tutoring program that is used in some states which is similar to Reading Recovery).

Elbaum, B., Vaughn, S., Hughes, M., & Moody, S. (1999). Grouping practices and reading outcomes for students with disabilities. *Exceptional Children, 65*(3), 399–415.

Elbaum, B., Vaughn, S., Hughes, M., & Moody, S. (2000). How effective are one-to-one tutoring programs in reading for elementary students at risk for reading failure? A meta-analysis of the intervention research. *Journal of Educational Psychology, 92*(4), 605–619.

Elliott, S. N., & Busse, R. T. (2004). Assessment and evaluation of students' behavior and intervention outcomes: The utility of rating scale methods. In R. B. Rutherford, Jr., M. M. Quinn, & A. R. Mathur (Eds.), *Handbook of research in emotional and behavioral disorders* (pp. 54–77). New York: Guilford.

Ellis, E. S. (1993). Integrative strategy instruction: A potential model for teaching content area subjects to adolescents with learning disabilities. *Journal of Learning Disabilities, 26*(6), 358–383, 398.

Ellis, E. S., & Colvert, G. (1996). Writing strategy instruction. In D. D. Deshler, E. S. Ellis, & B. K. Lenz (Eds.), *Teaching adolescents with learning disabilities* (pp. 127–207). Denver: Love.

Ellis, E. S., & Lenz, B. K. (1996). Perspectives on instruction in learning strategies. In D. D. Deshler, E. S. Ellis, & B. K. Lenz (Eds.), *Teaching adolescents with learning disabilities* (pp. 9–60). Denver: Love.

Engelmann, S. (2001). *Reasoning and writing.* Chicago: Science Research Associates.

Engelmann, S., & Bruner, E. (2003). *Reading mastery classic.* Chicago: Science Research Associates.

Engelmann, S., Carnine, D., Bernadette, K., & Engelmann, O. (2003). *Connecting math concepts.* Chicago: Science Research Associates.

Engelmann, S., Hanner, S., & Johnson, G. (2008). *Corrective reading.* Chicago: Science Research Associates.

Epstein, M. H., & Sharma, J. M. (1998). *Behavioral and emotional rating scale.* Austin, TX: Pro-Ed.

Erwin, E. J., & Soodak, L. C. (2000). Valued member or tolerated participant: Parents' experiences in inclusive early childhood settings. *The Association for Persons with Severe Handicaps Journal (JASH), 25*(1), 29–41.

Escolar, D. M., Tosi, L. L., Tesi Rocha, A. C., & Kennedy, A. (2007). Muscles, bones, and nerves. In M. L. Batshaw, L. Pellegrino, & N. J. Roizen (Eds.), *Children with disabilities* (6th ed., pp. 203–215). Baltimore: Brookes.

Esquith, R. (2007). *Teach like your hair's on fire: The methods and madness inside room 56.* New York: Viking.

Evertson, C. M., Emmer, E. T., Sanford, J. P., & Clements, B. S. (1983). Improving classroom management: An experiment in elementary school classrooms. *The Elementary School Journal, 84*(2), 172–188.

Fahsl, A. (2007). Mathematics accommodations for all students. *Intervention in School and Clinic, 42*(4), 198–203.

Fairbanks, S., Sugai, G., Guarding, D., & Lathrop, M. (2007). Response to intervention: Examining classroom behavior support in second grade. *Exceptional Children, 73*(3), 288–310.

Fass, S., & Cauthen, N. (2007). *Who are America's poor children? The official story.* The National Center for Children in Poverty. Retrieved May 17, 2008, from http://www.nccp.org/publications/pub_787.html

Feldman, K., & Denti, L. (2004). High-access instruction: Practical strategies to increase active learning in diverse classrooms. *Focus on Exceptional Children, 36*(7), 1–12.

Ferguson, D. L. (1995). The real challenge of inclusion: Confessions of a "rabid inclusionist." *Phi Delta Kappan: The Professional Journal for Education, 77*(4), 281–287.

Fields, J. (2004). *America's families and living arrangements. U.S. Census Bureau.* Retrieved June 10, 2008, from http://www.census.gov/prod/2004pubs/p20-553.pdf

Fishel, M., & Ramirez, L. (2005). Evidence-based parent involvement interventions with school-aged children. *School Psychology Quarterly, 20*(4), 371–402.

Fisher, J. B. (1995). Searching for validated inclusive practices: A review of the literature. *Focus on Exceptional Children, 28*(4), 2–23.

Fisher, M., & Meyer, L. H. (2002). Development and social competence after two years for students enrolled in inclusive and self-contained educational programs. *Research and Practice for Persons with Severe Disabilities, 27*(3), 165–174.

Fletcher, J., Denton, C., & Francis, D. (2005). Validity of Alternative approaches for the identification of learning disabilities: Operationalizing unexpected underachievement. *Journal of Learning Disabilities, 38*(6), 545–552.

Fletcher, J., Lyon, R., Fuchs, L., & Barnes, M. (2007). *Learning disabilities: From identification to intervention.* New York: Guilford Press.

Florida Center for Reading Research. (2008). *Curriculum and instruction: Student center activities, grades K–1.* Retrieved May 13, 2008, from www.fcrr.org/Curriculum/studentCenterActivities.htm

Fombonne, E. (2003, January). The prevalence of autism. *Journal of the American Medical Association, 289*(1), 87–89.

Foorman, B. (2007). Primary prevention in classroom reading instruction. *Teaching Exceptional Children, 39*(5), 24–30.

Foorman, B., & Torgesen, J. (2001). Critical elements of classroom and small-group instruction to promote reading success in all children. *Learning Disabilities Research & Practice, 16*(4), 203–212.

Foreman, P., Arthur-Kelly, M., Pascoe, S., & King, B. S. (2004). Evaluating the educational experiences of children with profound and multiple disabilities in inclusive and segregated classroom setting: An Australian perspective. *Research and Practice for Persons with Severe Disabilities, 29*, 183–193.

Forness, S. R., & Kavale, K. A. (2000). Emotional or behavioral disorders: Background and current status of the E/BD terminology and definition. *Behavioral Disorders, 25*(3), 264–269.

Forni, P. M. (2002). *Choosing civility: Twenty-five rules of considerate conduct.* New York: St. Martin's Griffin.

Fox, N., & Ysseldyke, J. (1997). Implementing inclusion at the middle school level: Lessons from a negative example. *Exceptional Children, 64*(1), 81–98.

Freeman, S., & Alkin, M. (2000). Academic and social attainments of children with mental retardation in general education and special education settings. *Remedial and Special Education, 21*(1), 3–18.

French, N. (2003). Paraeducators in special education programs. *Focus on Exceptional Children, 36*(2), 1–16.

Friend, M., & Bursuck, W. D. (2006). *Including students with special needs: A practical guide for classroom teachers* (4th ed.). Boston: Allyn & Bacon.

Friend, M., & Cook, L. (2007). *Interactions: Collaboration skills for school professionals* (5th ed.). Boston: Allyn & Bacon.

Frost, L., & Bondy, A. (2000). *The picture exchange communication system (PECS).* Newark, DE: Pyramid Products.

Fuchs, D., & Fuchs, L. (1994). Inclusive schools movement and the radicalization of special education reform. *Exceptional Children, 60*(4), 294–309.

Fuchs, D., & Fuchs, L. S. (2006). Introduction to Response to Intervention: What, why, and how valid is it? *Reading Research Quarterly, 41*, 93–99.

Fuchs, D., Fuchs, L., & Burish, P. (2000). Peer-assisted learning strategies: An evidence-based practice to promote reading achievement. *Learning Disabilities Research and Practice, 15*(2), 85–91.

Fuchs, D., Fuchs, L., Thompson, A., et al. (2001). Peer-assisted learning strategies in reading: Extensions for kindergarten, first grade, and high school. *Remedial and Special Education, 22*(1), 15–21.

Fuchs, L., & Fuchs, D. (2001). Principles for the prevention and intervention of mathematics difficulties. *Learning Disabilities Research and Practice, 16*(2), 85–95.

Fuchs, L., & Fuchs, D. (2007). A model for implementing responsiveness to intervention. *Teaching Exceptional Children, 39*(5), 14–20.

Fuchs, L., Fuchs, D., Compton, D., Bryant, J., Hamlett, C. & Seethaler, P. (2007). Mathematics screening and progress monitoring at first grade: Implications for responsiveness to intervention. *Exceptional Children, 73*(3), 311–330.

Fuchs, L., Fuchs, D., Karns, K., Yazdian, L., & Powell, S. (2001). Creating a strong foundation for mathematics learning with kindergarten peer-assisted learning strategies. *Teaching Exceptional Children, 33*(3), 84–87.

Fuchs, L. S., Fuchs, D., & Hamlett, C. L. (2007). Using curriculum-based measurement to inform reading instruction. *Reading and Writing: An Interdisciplinary Journal, 20*(6), 553–567.

Fulk, B., & King, K. (2001). Classwide peer tutoring at work. *Teaching Exceptional Children, 34*(2), 49–53.

Furrer, C., & Skinner, E. (2003). Sense of relatedness as a factor in children's academic engagement and performance. *Journal of Educational Psychology, 95*(1), 148–162.

Gable, R. A., Hendrickson, J. M., & Van Acker, R. (2001). Maintaining the integrity of FBA-based interventions in schools. *Education and Treatment of Children, 24*(3), 248–260.

Gaffney, J. S. (1987). *Seatwork: Current practices and research implications.* Paper presented at the 64th meeting of the Council for Exceptional Children, Chicago.

Galea, J., Butler, J., Iacono, T., & Leighton, D. (2004). The assessment of sexual knowledge of people with intellectual disability. *Journal of Intellectual & Developmental Disability, 29*, 350–365.

Gallaudet Research Institute. (2005). *Regional and national summary report of data from the 2003–2004 annual survey of deaf and hard of hearing children and youth.* Washington, DC: Author.

García, S., & Ortiz, A. (2006). Preventing disproportionate representation: Culturally and linguistically responsive prereferral interventions. *Teaching Exceptional Children, 38*(3), 64–68.

García, S. B., Méndez Pérez, A., & Ortiz, A. A. (2000). Mexican American mothers' beliefs about disabilities. *Remedial and Special Education, 21*(2), 90–100.

Gardner, A., & Johnson, D. (1997). *Teaching personal experience narrative in the elementary and beyond.* Flagstaff, AZ: Northern Arizona Writing Project Press.

Gardner, J. E., & Wissick, C. A. (2002). Enhancing thematic units using the world wide web: Tools and strategies for students with mild disabilities. *Journal of Special Education Technology, 17*(1), 27–38.

Gardner, J. E., Wissick, C. A., Schweder, W., & Canter, L. S. (2003). Enhancing interdisciplinary instruction in general and special education: Thematic units and technology. *Remedial and Special Education, 24*, 161–172.

Gately, S. E. (2008). Facilitating reading comprehension for students on the autism spectrum. *Teaching Exceptional Children, 40*(3), 40–45.

Gay, G. (2002). Preparing for culturally responsive teaching. *Journal of Teacher Education, 53*(2), 106–116.

Gerhardt, P. F., & Holmes, D. L. (2005). Employment: Options and issues for adolescents and adults with autism spectrum disorders. In F. R. Volkmar, R. Paul, A. Klin, & D. Cohen (Eds.), *Handbook of autism and pervasive developmental disorders: Vol. 2. Assessment, interventions, and policy* (4th ed., pp. 1087–1101). Hoboken, NJ: Wiley.

Gersten, R., & Clarke, B. (2007). *Effective strategies for teaching students with difficulties in mathematics: Instruction research brief.* Reston, VA: National Council for Teachers of Mathematics.

Gersten, R., & Dimino, J. (2006). RTI (response to intervention): Rethinking special education for students with reading difficulties (yet again). *Reading Research Quarterly, 41*(1), 99–108.

Giangreco, M. F., & Doyle, M. B. (2002). Students with disabilities and paraeducator supports: Benefits, balance, and Band-Aids. *Focus on Exceptional Children, 34*(7), 1–12.

Giangreco, M. F., Edelman, S. W., Broer, S. M., & Doyle, M. B. (2001). Paraeducator support of students with disabilities: Literature from the past decade. *Exceptional Children, 68*, 45–63.

Giangreco, M. F., Smith, C. S., & Pinckney, E. (2006). Addressing the paraprofessional dilemma in an inclusive school: A program description. *Research and Practice for Persons with Severe Disabilities, 31*, 215–229.

Gillam, R. B. (2000). Fluency disorders. In R. B. Gillam, T. P. Marquardt, & F. N. Martin (Eds.), *Communication sciences and disorders: From science to clinical practice* (pp. 313–339). San Diego: Singular.

Ginsberg, M. G. (2005). Cultural diversity, motivation and differentiation. *Theory into Practice, 44*(3), 218–225.

Ginsburg-Block, M., Rohrbeck, C., & Fantuzzo, J. (2006). A meta-analytic review of social, self-concept, and behavioral outcomes of peer-assisted learning. *Journal of Educational Psychology, 98*(4), 732–749.

Goldstein, A. P., & McGinnis, E. (1997). *Skillstreaming the adolescent: New strategies and perspectives for teaching prosocial skills.* Champaign, IL: Research Press.

Gonzalez, N., Moll, L. C., & Amanti, C. (2005). *Funds of knowledge: Theorizing practices in households and classrooms.* Mahwah, NJ: Erlbaum.

Good, T., & Brophy, J. (2003). *Looking in classrooms* (9th ed.). Boston: Allyn & Bacon.

Good, T., & Brophy, J. (2008). *Looking in classrooms* (10th ed.). Boston: Allyn & Bacon.

Graham, S., & Harris, K. (2006). Cognitive strategy instruction. In C. MacArthur, S. Graham, & K. Harris (Eds.), *Handbook of writing research* (pp. 187–207). New York: Guilford.

Graham, S., Harris, K., & Larsen, L. (2001). Prevention and intervention of writing difficulties for students with learning disabilities. *Learning Disabilities Research & Practice, 16*(2), 74–84.

Graham, S., Harris, K., & MacArthur, S. (2006). Explicitly teaching struggling writers: Strategies for mastering the writing process. *Intervention in School and Clinic, 41*(5), 290–294.

Green, F., Schleien, S., Mactavish, J., & Benepe, S. (1995). Nondisabled adults perceptions of relationships in the early stages of arranged partnerships with peers with mental retardation. *Education and Training in Mental Retardation and Developmental Disabilities, 30*, 91–108.

Greenwood, C., Arreaga-Mayer, C., Utley, C., Gavin, K., & Terry, B. (2001). Classwide peer tutoring learning management system: Applications with elementary-level English language learners. *Remedial and Special Education, 22*(1), 34–47.

Greenwood, C., Delquadri, J., & Carta, J. (1997). *Together we can: Classwide peer tutoring to improve basic academic skills.* Longmont, CO: Sopris West.

Gregory, A. (2007). *African-American students and the discipline gap in high schools. UCAccord Public Policy Series. PB-014-0507.* Retrieved May 14, 2008, from http://www.ucaccord.org

Gresham, F. (2002). Responsiveness to intervention: An alternative approach to the identification of learning disabilities. In R. Bradley, L. Danielson, & D. Hallahan (Eds.), *Identification of learning disabilities: Research to practice* (pp. 467–519). Mahwah, NJ: Erlbaum.

Gresham, F. (2005). Response to intervention: An alternative means of identifying students as emotionally disturbed. *Education and Treatment of Children, 28*(4), 328–344.

Gresham, F. M., & Elliott, S. N. (1990). *The social skills rating system (SSRS).* Circle Pines, MN: American Guidance Service.

Gresham, F. M., & Kern, L. (2004). Internalizing behavior problems in children and adolescents. In R. B. Rutherford, Jr., M. M. Quinn, & A. R. Mathur (Eds.), *Handbook of research in emotional and behavioral disorders* (pp. 54–77). New York: Guilford.

Gresham, F. M., Lane, K. L., MacMillan, D. L., & Bocian, K. M. (1999). Social and academic profiles of externalizing and internalizing groups: Risk factors for emotional and behavioral disorders. *Behavioral Disorders, 24*, 231–245.

Griffin, H. C., Fitch, C. L., & Griffin, L. W. (2002). Causes and interventions in the area of cerebral palsy. *Infants and Young Children, 14*(3), 18–23.

Grinker, R. R. (2008). What in the world is autism: A cross-cultural perspective. *Zero to Three, 28*, 5–10.

Grossen, B., Coulter, G., & Ruggles, B. (1996). Reading recovery: An evaluation of benefits and costs. *Effective School Practices, 15*(3), 6–24.

Gruwell, E. (1999). *The freedom writers diary.* New York: Broadway Books.

Gudykunst, W. B., & Kim, Y. Y. (2003). *Communicating with strangers: An approach to intercultural communication.* New York: McGraw-Hill.

Gun Han, K., & Chadsey, J. (2004). The influence of gender patterns and grade level on friendship expectations of middle school students toward peers with severe disabilities. *Focus on Autism and Other Developmental Disabilities, 19*(4), 205–214.

Gureasko-Moore, D., DuPaul, G., & Power, T. (2005). Stimulant treatment for attention-deficit/hyperactivity disorder: Medication monitoring practices of school psychologists. *School Psychology Review, 34*(2), 232–245.

Gutiérrez, K., & Rogoff, B. (2003). Cultural ways of learning: Individual traits or repertoires of practice. *Educational Researcher, 32*(5), 19–25.

Haager, D., & Klingner, J. (2004). *Differentiating instruction in inclusive classrooms.* Boston: Allyn & Bacon.

Hall, M., Kleinert, H. L., & Kearns, J. F. (2000). Going to college! Postsecondary programs for students with moderate and severe disabilities. *Teaching Exceptional Children, 32*(3), 58–65.

Hall, T. E., Hughes, C. A., & Filbert, M. (2000). Computer-assisted instruction in reading for students with learning disabilities: A research synthesis. *Education and Treatment of Children, 23*, 173–193.

Hampton, E. O., Whitney, D. W., & Schwartz, I. S. (2002). Weaving assessment information into intervention ideas: Planning communication interventions for young children with disabilities. *Assessment for Effective Intervention, 27, 49–59.*

Handleman, J. S., Harris, S. L., & Martins, M. P. (2005). Helping children with autism enter the mainstream. In F. R. Volkmar, R. Paul, A. Klin, & D. Cohen (Eds.), *Handbook of autism and pervasive developmental disorders: Vol. 2. Assessment, interventions, and policy* (4th ed., pp. 1029–1042). Hoboken, NJ: Wiley.

Hanley, G. P., Iwata, B. A., & McCord, B. E. (2003). Functional analysis of problem behavior: A review. *Journal of Applied Behavior Analysis, 36*, 147–185.

Harden, B. J. (2004). Safety and stability for foster children: A developmental perspective. *The Future of Children, 14*(1), 3.

Hardman, M. L., & Mulder, M. (2004). Federal education reform: Critical issues in public education and their impact on students with disabilities. In L. M. Bullock & R. A. Gable (Eds.), *Quality personnel preparation in emotional/behavioral disorders: Current perspectives and future directions.* Denton, TX: Institute for Behavioral and Learning Differences at the University of North Texas.

Hardman, M. L., Rosenberg, M. S., & Sindelar, P. T. (2004). Preparing highly qualified teachers for students with emotional or behavioral disorders: The impact of NCLB and IDEA. *Behavioral Disorders, 29*(3), 266–278.

Harniss, M., Epstein, M., Bursuck, W., Nelson, J., & Jayanthi, M. (2001). Resolving homework-related communication problems: Recommendations of parents of children with and without disabilities. *Reading & Writing Quarterly, 17*(3), 205–225.

Harriott, W., & Martin, S. (2004). Using culturally responsive activities to promote social competence and classroom community. *Teaching Exceptional Children, 37*(1), 48–54.

Harris, K. R., Graham, S., & Mason, L. H. (2003). Self-regulated strategy development in the classroom: Part of a balanced approach to writing instruction for students with disabilities. *Focus on Exceptional Children, 35*(7), 1–16.

Harris, K., Graham, S., Mason, L., & Friedlander, B. (2007). *Powerful writing strategies for all students.* Baltimore: Brookes.

Harry, B. (2008). Collaboration with culturally and linguistically diverse families: Ideal versus reality. *Exceptional Children, 74*(3), 372–388.

Harry, B., Kalyanpur, M., & Day, M. (1999). *Building cultural reciprocity with families: Case studies in special education.* Baltimore: Brookes.

Hartshorne, N. (2001/2002). It sounds nice, but is inclusion really worth it? *Deaf-Blind Perspectives, 9*(2), 12–13.

Hasselbring, T. S., & Bausch, M. E. (2005). Assistive technologies for reading. *Educational Leadership, 63*(4), 72–75.

Hawken, L. S., & Horner, R. H. (2003). Evaluation of a targeted intervention within a schoolwide system of behavior support. *Journal of Behavioral Education, 12*(3), 225–240.

Hayes, L., Lane, H., & Pullen, P. (2005). *University of Florida reading initiative (UFRI): Tutoring for beginning readers.* Gainesville, FL: College of Education, University of Florida.

Heller, K. W. (2004). Integrating health care and educational programs. In F. P. Orelove, D. Sobsey, & R. K. Silberman (Eds.), *Educating children with multiple disabilities: A collaborative approach* (2nd ed., pp. 379–424). Baltimore: Brookes.

Helmstetter, E., Peck, C., & Giangreco, M. (1994). Outcomes of interactions with peers with moderate or severe disabilities: A statewide survey of high school students. *Journal of the Association for Persons with Severe Handicaps, 19*(4), 277–289.

Henderson, K., & Bradley, R. (2004). A national perspective on mental health and children with disabilities: Emotional disturbances in children. *Emotional and Behavioral Disorders in Youth, 4*(3), 67–74.

Hershfeldt, P., & Rosenberg, M. S. (2008, November). *Beyond universal management: What developing teachers need to know about managing problem behaviors.* Paper presented at the annual conference of the Teacher Education Division of the Council for Exceptional Children, Dallas, TX.

Hetzroni, O. E., & Shrieber, B. (2004). Word processing as an assistive technology tool for enhancing academic outcomes of students with writing disabilities in the general classroom. *Journal of Learning Disabilities, 37*, 143–154.

Hilton, A. (2007). Response to intervention: Changing how we do business. *Leadership, 36*(4), 16–19.

Hitchcock, C., Meyer, A., Rose, D., & Jackson, R. (2002). Providing new access to the general curriculum: Universal design for learning. *Teaching Exceptional Children, 35*(2), 8–17.

Hollins, E. R. (1996). *Culture in school learning: Revealing the deep meaning.* Mahwah, NJ: Erlbaum.

Hong, E., Sas, M., & Sas, J. C. (2006). Test taking strategies of high and low mathematics achievers. *Journal of Educational Research, 99*(3), 144–155.

Hoover, J. J., & Patton, J. R. (2008). The role of special educators in a multitiered instructional system. *Intervention in School and Clinic, 43*(4), 195–202.

Hoover, N. (2001). *Reading Rescue: A handbook for tutors.* Gainesville, FL: Literacy Trust.

Hoover, N., & Lane, H. (2001). *Preventing literacy failure through cost-effective tutoring: A report on outcomes in high-poverty and rural schools.* Paper presented at the annual meeting of the American Educational Research Association, New York.

Horn, L., Peter, K., & Rooney, K. (2002). *Profile of undergraduates in U.S. postsecondary educational institutions: 1999–2000.* Washington, DC: U.S. Department of Education.

Houghton Mifflin. (2006). *Reading intervention for early success.* Boston, MA: Author.

Houghton Mifflin. (n.d.). *Earobics.* Boston, MA: Author.

Howlin, P., & Asgharian, A. (1999). The diagnosis of autism and Asperger syndrome: Findings from a survey of 770 families. *Developmental Medicine & Child Neurology, 41*, 834–839.

Hughes, C., & Carter, E. (2006). *Success for all students: Promoting inclusion in secondary programs through peer buddy programs.* Upper Saddle River, NJ: Prentice Hall.

Hughes, C., & Carter, E. (2008). *Peer buddy programs for successful secondary school inclusion.* Baltimore: Brookes.

Hughes, C., Copeland, S., Guth, C. et al. (2001). General education students' perspectives on their involvement in a high school peer buddy program. *Education and Training in Mental Retardation, 36*(4), 343–356.

Hughes, C. A. (1996). Memory and test taking strategies. In D. D. Deshler, E. S. Ellis, & B. K. Lenz (Eds.), *Teaching adolescents with learning disabilities* (pp. 209–266). Denver: Love.

Hughes, C. A., & Maccini, P. (1997). Computer-assisted mathematics instruction for students with learning disabilities: A research review. *Learning Disabilities: A Multidisciplinary Journal, 8*(3), 155–166.

Hughes, C. A., Ruhl, K. L., Schumaker, J., & Deshler, D. D. (2002). Effects of instruction in an assignment completion strategy on the homework performance of students with learning disabilities in general education classes. *Learning Disabilities Research & Practice, 17*(1), 1–18.

Hughes, C., Guth, C., Hall, S., Presley, J., Dye, M., & Byers, C. (1999). "They are my best friends": Peer buddies promote inclusion in high school. *Teaching Exceptional Children, 31*(5), 32–37.

Hussar, W. (2005). *Projections of educational statistics to 2014* (33rd ed.). National Center for Educational Statistics. Report No: NCES 2005-074.

Hutinger, P., Johanson, J., & Stoneburner, R. (1996). Assistive technology applications in educational programs of children with multiple disabilities: A case study report on the state of the practice. *Journal of Special Education Technology, 13*(1), 16–35.

Hyman, S., & Towbin, K. E. (2007). Autism spectrum disorders. In M. L. Batshaw, L. Pelligrino, & N. Roizen (Eds.), *Children with disabilities* (pp. 325–343). Baltimore: Brookes.

Ideadata.org. (2007). Retrieved May 17, 2008, from www.ideadata.org

Idol, L. (2006). Toward inclusion of special education students in general education. *Remedial and Special Education, 27*(2), 77–94.

Individuals with Disabilities Education Act, Public Law 105-17. (1997). Retrieved August 27, 2007, from http://www.ed.gov/offices/OSERS/Policy/IDEA/index.html.

Individuals with Disabilities Education Improvement Act (IDEA) of 2004, Public Law 108-446 (2004). Retrieved November 24, 2008, from http://frwebgate.access.gpo.gov/cgi-bin/getdoc.cgi?dbname=108_cong_public_laws&docid=f:publ446.108

Institute for Children and Poverty. (2003). *Miles to go: The flip side of the McKinney-Vento Homeless Assistance Act. Fact Sheet.* Retrieved May 17, 2008, from http://www.icpny.org/PDF/reports/MilestoGo.pdf?Submit1=Free+Download

Institute for Children and Poverty. (2007). *Quick Facts.* Retrieved May 17, 2008, from http://www.icpny.org/index.asp?CID=7

Institute of Education Sciences. (2008). *What works clearinghouse.* Retrieved March 12, 2008, from http://ies.ed.gov/ncee/wwc/

Irvine, J. J. (2002). *In search of wholeness: African American teachers and their culturally specific practices.* NY: Palgrave/St. Martins Press.

Irvine, J. J. (2003). *Educating teachers for diversity: Seeing with a cultural eye.* New York: Teachers College Press.

Iverson, S., Tunmer, W., & Chapman, J. (2005). The effects of varying group size on the reading recovery approach to preventive early intervention. *Journal of Learning Disabilities, 38*(5), 456–472.

Jimerson, S., Burns, M., & VanDeHeyden, A. (Eds.). (2007). *Handbook of response to intervention: The science and practice of assessment and intervention.* New York: Springer.

Jitendra, A., Salmento, M., & Haydt, L. (1999). A case analysis of fourth-grade subtraction instruction in basal mathematics programs: Adherence to important instructional design criteria. *Learning Disabilities Research & Practice, 14*(2), 69–79.

Johns, B. H., & Carr, V. G. (1995). *Techniques of managing: Verbally and physically aggressive students.* Denver, CO: Love.

Johnson, D., & Johnson, R. (1974). Instructional structure: Cooperative, competitive or individualistic. *Review of Educational Research, 44*, 213–240.

Johnson, D., & Johnson, R. (1999). *Learning together and learning along: Cooperative, competitive, and individualistic learning.* Boston: Allyn & Bacon.

Johnson, D., Johnson, R., & Stanne, M. (2000). *Cooperative learning methods: A meta-analysis.* Minneapolis, MN: University of Minnesota. Retrieved February 14, 2008, from http://www.co-operation.org/pages/cl-methods.html

Johnson, D. W., Johnson, R., & Holubec, E. (1998). *Cooperation in the classroom* (7th ed.). Edina, MN: Interaction Books.

Johnson, G. O. (1962). Special education for the mentally handicapped: A paradox. *Exceptional Children, 29*(2), 62–69.

Johnston, L., Beard, L. A., & Carpenter, L. B. (2007). *Assistive technology: Access for all students.* Upper Saddle River, NJ: Merrill/Pearson Education.

Jonassen, D. H., Howland, J., Marra, R. M., & Crismond, D. P. (2008). *Meaningful learning with technology* (3rd ed.). Upper Saddle River, NJ: Merrill/Pearson Education.

Jones, E., & Southern, T. (2008). Academically gifted and talented. In M. Rosenberg, D. Westling, & J. McLeskey, *Special education for today's teachers: An introduction* (pp. 408–429). Upper Saddle River, NJ: Merrill/Pearson Education.

Jones, T. (2005). Twenty ways to incorporate diversity into your classroom. *Intervention in School and Clinic, 41*(1), 9–12.

Jones, V. (1993). Assessing your classroom and school-wide student management plan. *Beyond Behavior, 4*(3), 9–12.

Jones, V., & Jones, L. (2004). *Comprehensive classroom management: Creating communities of support and solving problems* (7th ed.). Boston: Pearson.

Justice, L. M. (2006). *Communication sciences and disorders: An introduction.* Upper Saddle River, NJ: Merrill/Pearson Education.

Kagan, S. (1994). *Cooperative learning.* San Diego, CA: Kagan Cooperative Learning.

Kame'enui, E., & Carnine, D. (1998). *Effective teaching strategies that accommodate diverse learners.* Upper Saddle River, NJ: Merrill/Pearson Education.

Kame'enui, E., & Simmons, D. (1999). *Toward successful inclusion of students with disabilities: The architecture of instruction.* Reston, VA: Council for Exceptional Children.

Kamps, D., & Greenwood, C. (2005). Formulating secondary-level reading interventions. *Journal of Learning Disabilities, 38*(6), 500–509.

Kampwirth, T. (2006). *Collaborative consultation in the schools* (3rd ed.). Upper Saddle River, NJ: Prentice Hall.

Kanner, L. (1943). Autistic disturbances of affective contact. *The Nervous Child, 2,* 217–250.

Kaplan K12 Learning Services. (2008). *SpellRead services.* Retrieved May 13, 2008, from http://www.KaplanK12.com

Kauchak, D., & Eggen, P. (2003). *Learning and teaching: Research based methods* (4th ed.). Boston: Allyn & Bacon.

Kauchak, D., & Eggen, P. (2005). *Introduction to teaching: Becoming a professional.* Upper Saddle River, NJ: Merrill/Pearson Education.

Kauchak, D., & Eggen, P. (2008). *Learning and teaching: Research-based methods* (5th ed.). Boston: Allyn & Bacon.

Kauffman, J. (1993). How we might achieve the radical reform of special education. *Exceptional Children, 60*(1), 6–16.

Kauffman, J., & Hallahan, D. (2005). *Special education: What is it and why we need it?* Boston: Pearson Education.

Kauffman, J., Lloyd, J., Baker, J., & Riedel, T. (1995). Inclusion of all students with emotional and behavioral disorders? Let's think again. *Phi Delta Kappan, 76*(7), 542–546.

Kauffman, J. M. (1981). Introduction: Historical trends and contemporary issues in special education in the United States. J. M. Kauffman & D. P. Hallahan (Eds.), *Handbook of special education* (pp. 3–23). Upper Saddle River, NJ: Prentice Hall.

Kauffman, J. M. (2001). *Characteristics of emotional and behavioral disorders of children and youth* (7th ed.). Upper Saddle River, NJ: Merrill/Pearson Education.

Kauffman, J. M., Mostert, M. P., Trent, S. C., & Hallahan, D. P. (2002). *Managing classroom behavior: A reflective case-based approach* (3rd ed.). Boston: Allyn & Bacon.

Kavale, K., & Forness, S. (2000). History, rhetoric, and reality: Analysis of the inclusion debate. *Remedial and Special Education, 21*(5), 279–296.

Kavale, K. A., Mathur, S. R., & Mostert, M. P. (2004). Social skills training and teaching social behavior to students with emotional and behavioral disorders. In R. B. Rutherford, Jr., M. M. Quinn, & A. R. Mathur (Eds.), *Handbook of research in emotional and behavioral disorders* (pp. 446–461). New York: Guilford.

Kennedy, C. H., & Shukla, S. (1995). Social interaction research for people with autism as a set of past, current, and emerging propositions. *Behavioral Disorders, 21,* 21–35.

Kilgore, K., Griffin, C. C., Sindelar, P. T., Webb, R. B. (2002). Restructuring for inclusion: Changing teaching practices (Part II). *Middle School Journal, 33*(3), 7–13.

Kim, A., Woodruff, A. L., Klein, C., & Vaughn, S. (2006). Facilitating co-teaching for literacy in general education classrooms through technology: Focus on students with learning disabilities. *Reading & Writing Quarterly, 22,* 269–291.

King-Sears, M. E., Mercer, C. D., & Sindelar, P. T. (1992). Toward independence with keyword mnemonics: A strategy for science vocabulary instruction. *Remedial and Special Education, 13,* 22–33.

King-Sears, M. E., & Mooney, J. F. (2004). Teaching content in an academically diverse class. In B. K. Lenz, D. D. Deshler, & B. Kissam. *Teaching content to all: Evidence-based inclusive practices in middle and secondary schools* (pp. 221–251). Boston: Pearson.

Kitano, M. K. (2003). Gifted potential and poverty: A call for extraordinary action. *Journal for the Education of the Gifted, 26*(4), 292–303.

Kleinfeld, J. (1975). Effective teachers of Eskimo and Indian students. *School Review, 83*(2), 301–344.

Klin, A., McPartland, J., & Volkmar, F. R. (2005). Asperger syndrome. In F. R. Volkmar, R. Paul, A. Klin, & D. Cohen (Eds.), *Handbook of autism and pervasive developmental disorders: Vol. 1. Diagnosis, development, neurobiology, and behavior* (4th ed., pp. 88–125).

Klingner, J. K., Artiles, A. J., & Barletta, L. M. (2006). English language learners who struggle with reading: Language acquisition of LD? *Journal of Learning Disabilities, 39*(2), 108–128.

Klug, B., Luckey, A., Wilkins, S., & Whitfield, P. (2006). Stepping out of our own skins: Overcoming resistance of isolated preservice teacher populations to embracing diversity in educational settings. *Multicultural Perspectives, 8*(3), 30–37.

Kochhar-Bryant, C. (2008). *Collaboration and system coordination for students with special needs.* Upper Saddle River, NJ: Merrill/Pearson Education.

Koenig, L. (2000). *Smart discipline for the classroom: Respect and cooperation restored* (3rd ed.). Thousand Oaks, CA: Corwin Press.

Koh, M., & Robertson, J. (2003). School reform models and special education. *Education and Urban Society, 35*(4), 421–442.

Kohl, F., McLaughlin, M., & Nagle, K. (2006). Alternate achievement standards and assessments: A descriptive investigation of 16 states. *Exceptional Children, 73*(1), 107–123.

Kollins, S., Barkley, R., & DuPaul, G. (2001). Use and management of medications for children diagnosed with attention deficit hyperactivity disorder (ADHD). *Focus on Exceptional Children, 33*(5), 1–24.

Kramer, C. (2004). *The effects of a self-management device on the acquisition of social skills in adolescent males with SED.* Unpublished doctoral dissertation, Johns Hopkins University, Baltimore.

Kulinna, P. H., Cothran, D. J., & Regualos, R. (2006). Teachers' reports of student misbehavior in physical education. *Research Quartely for Exercise and Sports, 77*(1), 32–41.

Kyle, D., McIntyre, E., Miller, K., & Moore, G. (2006). *Bridging school & home through family nights.* Thousand Oaks, CA: Corwin Press.

Ladders to Literacy. (2008). *Ladders to literacy outreach.* Retrieved May 13, 2008, from www.wri-edu.org/ladders

Ladson-Billings, G. (1994). *The dreamkeepers: Successful teachers of African American children.* San Francisco: Jossey-Bass.

Lancioni, G. E., Singh, N. N. , O'Reilly, M. F., Oliva, D., Baccani, S. & Canevaro, A. (2002). Using simple hand-movement responses with optic microswitches with two persons with multiple disabilities. *Research and Practice for Persons with Severe Disabilities, 27,* 276–279.

Lane, K. L. (2004). Academic instruction and tutoring interventions for students with emotional and behavioral disorders: 1990 to the present. In R. B. Rutherford, Jr., M. M. Quinn, & A. R. Mathur (Eds.), *Handbook of research in emotional and behavioral disorders* (pp. 462–486). New York: Guilford.

Lane, K. L., Carter, E. W., Pierson, M. R., & Glaeser, B. C. (2006). Academic, social, and behavioral characteristics of high school students with emotional disturbances or learning disabilities. *Journal of Emotional and Behavioral Disorders, 14*(2), 108–117.

Lane, K. L., Givner, C. C., & Pierson, M. R. (2004). Teacher expectations of student behavior: Necessary success in elementary school classrooms. *Journal of Special Education, 38*(2), 104–110.

Lane, K., Pierson, M., Robertson, E., & Little, A. (2004). Teachers' views of prereferral interventions: Perceptions of and recommendations for implementation support. *Education and Treatment of Children, 27*(4), 420–439.

Lang, H. G. (n.d.). *Science education for deaf students: Priorities for research and instructional development.* Retrieved August 28, 2008, from http://rasem.nmsu.edu/Pdfs/symposium/LANGrasemwhitepaper.pdf

Lawrence-Brown, D. (2004). Differentiated instruction: Inclusive strategies for standards-based learning that benefit the whole class. *American Secondary Education, 32*(3), 34–62.

Lazarus, B. D. (1993). Guided notes: Effects with secondary and post secondary students with mild disabilities. *Education and Treatment of Children, 16*(3), 272–289.

Lee, S., Palmer, S., Turnbull, A., & Wehmeyer, M. (2006). A model for parent–teacher collaboration to promote self-determination in young children with disabilities. *Teaching Exceptional Children, 38*(3), 36–41.

Lee, S., Yoo, S., & Bak, S. (2003). Characteristics of friendships between children with and without disabilities. *Education and Training in Developmental Disabilities, 38*(2), 157–166.

Lenz, K., & Deshler, D. (2004). *Teaching content to all: Evidence-based inclusive practices in middle and secondary schools.* Boston: Allyn & Bacon.

Lenz, K., Bulgren, J., Kissam, J., & Taymans, J. (2004). SMARTER planning for academic diversity. In K. Lenz & D. Deshler (Eds.), *Teaching content to all: Evidence-based inclusive practices in middle and secondary schools* (pp. 47–77). Boston: Allyn & Bacon.

Lerner, J., & Kline, F. (2006). *Learning disabilities and related disorders.* Boston: Houghton Mifflin.

Lesseliers, J., & Van Hove, G. (2002). Barriers to the development of intimate relationships and expression of sexuality among people with developmental disabilities: Their perceptions. *Research and Practice for Persons with Severe Disabilities, 27,* 69–81.

Levy, H. M. (2008). Meeting the needs of all students through differentiated instruction: Helping every child reach and exceed standards. *The Clearing House, 81*(4), 161–164.

Lewis, R. B. & Doorlag, D. H. (2006). *Teaching special students in general education classrooms* (5th ed.). Upper Saddle River, NJ: Merrill/Pearson Education.

Lewis, T. J., & Sugai, G. (1999). Effective behavior support: A systems approach to proactive school-wide management. *Focus on Exceptional Children, 31*(6), 1–24.

Lewis, T. J, Sugai, G., & Colvin, G. (1998). Reducing problem behavior through a school-wide system of effective skills behavioral support: Investigation of a school-wide social training program and contextual interventions. *School Psychology Review, 27,* 446–459.

Lindamood, P., & Lindamood, P. (1998). *Lindamood phonemic sequencing program (LIPS).* San Luis Obispo, CA: Lindamood-Bell Learning Processes.

Linn, A., & Smith-Myles, B. (2004). Asperger syndrome and six strategies for success. *Beyond Behavior, 14*(1), 3–9.

Lipkewich, A., & Mazurenko, R. (2008). *ABC's of the writing process.* Retrieved March 12, 2008, from http://www.angelfire.com/wi/writingprocess/

Longwill, A., & Kleinert. H. (1998). The unexpected benefits of high school peer tutoring. *Teaching Exceptional Children, 30*(4), 60–65.

Loveland, K. A., & Tunali-Kotoski, B. (2005). The school-age child with an autistic spectrum disorder. In F. R. Volkmar, R. Paul, A. Klin, & D. Cohen (Eds.), *Handbook of autism and pervasive developmental disorders: Vol. 1. Diagnosis, development, neurobiology, and behavior* (4th ed., pp. 247–287). Hoboken, NJ: Wiley.

Luckner, J. L., & Muir, S. (2002). Suggestions for helping students who are deaf succeed in general education settings. *Communication Disorders Quarterly, 24,* 23–30.

Maag, J. (2002). A contextually based approach for treating depression in school-age children. *Intervention in School and Clinic, 37*(3), 149–155.

Maas, E., & Robin, D. A. (2006). Motor speech disorders: Apraxia and dysarthria. In L. M. Justice, *Communication sciences and disorders: An introduction* (pp. 180–211). Upper Saddle River, NJ: Merrill/Pearson Education.

MacArthur, C. A. (2000). New tools for writing: Assistive technology for students with writing difficulties. *Topics in Language Disorders, 20*(4), 85–100.

MacArthur, C. A., & Cavalier, A. R. (2004). Dictation and speech recognition technology as test accommodations. *Exceptional Children, 71,* 43–58.

MacArthur, C. A., Ferretti, R. P., Okolo, C. M., & Cavalier, A. R. (2001). Technology applications for students with literacy problems: A critical review. *Elementary School Journal, 101,* 273–301.

Maccini, P., & Gagnon, J. (2005). *Math graphic organizers for students with disabilities.* Retrieved March 11, 2008, from www.K8accesscenter.org

Madden, N.A., & Slavin, R. (1983). Mainstreaming students with mild handicaps: Academic and social outcomes. *Review of Educational Research, 53,* 519–569.

Maheady, L., Harper, G., & Mallette, B. (2001). Peer-mediated instruction and interventions and students with mild disabilities. *Remedial and Special Education, 22*(1), 4–14.

Maheady, L., Mallette, B., & Harper, G. F. (2006). Four classwide peer tutoring models: Similarities, differences, and implications for research and practice. *Reading & Writing Quarterly, 22*(1), 65–89.

Mahoney, M. (Producer), Kern, R. (Writer), & Levin, P. (Director). (2003). *Homeless to Harvard: The Liz Murray story* (Motion Picture). United States: Patriarch Pictures.

Manset, G., & Semmel, M. (1997). Are inclusive programs for students with mild disabilities effective? A comparative review of model programs. *Journal of Special Education, 31*(2), 155–180.

Marks, D. (2005). *Culture and classroom management: Grounded theory from a high poverty predominately African American elementary school.* Unpublished doctoral dissertation University of Florida, Gainesville, FL.

Marston, D. (1996). A comparison of inclusion only, pull out only, and combined service model for students with mild disabilities. *Journal of Special Education, 30*(2), 121–132.

Martinez, R. S., Nellis, L. M., & Prendergast, K. A. (2006). Closing the achievement gap series: Part II. Response to Intervention (RTI)—Basic elements, practical applications, and policy recommendations. *Center for Evaluation & Education Policy, 4*(8).

Marzano, R., Pickering, D., & Pollock, J. (2001). *Classroom instruction that works.* Alexandria, VA: ASCD.

Masten, A. S., Best, K. M., & Garmezy, N. (1990). Resilience and development: Contributions from the study of children who overcome adversity. *Development and Psychopathology, 2*(2), 425–444.

Mastropieri, M., & Scruggs, T. (2007). *The inclusive classroom: Strategies for effective instruction* (3rd. ed.). Upper Saddle River, NJ: Merrill/Pearson Education.

Mastropieri, M., Scruggs, T., Graetz, J., et al. (2005). Case studies in co-teaching in the content areas: Successes, failures, and challenges. *Intervention in School and Clinic, 40*(5), 260–270.

Mastropieri, M. A., & Scruggs, T. E. (1998). Enhancing school success with mnemonic strategies. *Intervention in School and Clinic, 33*(4), 201–208.

Mastropieri, M. A., & Scruggs, T. E. (2005). Feasibility and consequences of response to intervention: Examination of the issues and scientific evidence as a model for the identification of individuals with learning disabilities. *Journal of Learning Disabilities, 38*(6), 525–531.

Mastropieri, M. A., Sweda, J., & Scruggs, T. E. (2000). Putting mnemonic strategies to work in an inclusive classroom. *Learning Disabilities Research & Practice, 15*(2), 69–74.

Mathes, P., & Denton, C. (2002). *Reading Recovery: Current practice alerts.* Retrieved March 12, 2008, from www.TeachingLD.org

Mathes, P., Grek, M., Howard, J., Babyak, A., & Allen, S., (1999). Peer-assisted learning strategies for first-grade readers: A tool for preventing early reading failure. *Learning Disabilities Research & Practice, 14*(1), 50–60.

Mattison, R. E. (2004). Psychiatric and psychological assessment of emotional and behavioral disorders during school mental health consultation. In R. B. Rutherford, Jr., M. M. Quinn, & A. R. Mathur (Eds.), *Handbook of research in emotional and behavioral disorders* (pp. 163–180). New York: Guilford.

Matuszny, R., Banda, D., & Coleman, T. (2007). A progressive plan for building collaborative relationships with parents from diverse backgrounds. *Teaching Exceptional Children, 39*(4), 24–31.

McConnell, M. E., Hilvitz, P. B., & Cox, C. J. (1998). Functional assessment: A systematic approach for assessment and intervention in general and special education classrooms. *Intervention in School and Clinic, 34,* 10–20.

McGinnis, E., & Goldstein, A. P. (1997). *Skillstreaming in early childhood: New strategies and perspectives for teaching prosocial skills.* Champaign, IL: Research Press.

McLean, M. (2004). Assessment and its importance in early intervention/early childhood special education.

In M. McLean, M. Wolery, & D. B. Bailey, Jr. (Eds.), *Assessing infants and preschoolers with special needs* (3rd ed., pp. 1–21). Upper Saddle River, NJ: Merrill/Pearson Education.

McLeskey, J. (Ed.). (2007). *Reflections on inclusion: Classic articles that shaped our thinking.* Arlington, VA: Council for Exceptional Children.

McLeskey, J., & Pacchiano, D. (1994). Mainstreaming students with LD: Are we making progress? *Exceptional Children, 60,* 508–517.

McLeskey, J., & Waldron, N. (1996). Responses to questions teachers and administrators frequently ask about inclusion. *Phi Delta Kappan, 78,* 150–156.

McLeskey, J., & Waldron, N. (2000). *Inclusive schools in action: Making differences ordinary.* Alexandria, VA: ASCD.

McLeskey, J., & Waldron, N. (2002, September). School change and inclusive schools: Lessons learned from practice. *Phi Delta Kappan, 84*(1), 65–72.

McLeskey, J., & Waldron, N. (2006). Comprehensive school reform and inclusive schools: Improving schools for all students. *Theory into Practice, 45*(3), 269–278.

McLeskey, J., Henry, D., & Axelrod, M. (1999). Inclusion of students with LD: An examination of data from *Reports to Congress. Exceptional Children, 65,* 55–66.

McLeskey, J., Hoppey, D., Williamson, P., & Rentz, T. (2004). Is inclusion an illusion? An examination of national and state trends toward the education of students with learning disabilities in general education classrooms. *Learning Disabilities: Research & Practice, 19*(2), 109–115.

McLeskey, J., Tyler, N. C., & Flippin, S. S. (2004). The supply of and demand for special education teachers: A review of research regarding the chronic shortage of special education teachers. *Journal of Special Education, 38*(1), 5–21.

McLeskey, J., Waldron, N., So, T. H., Swanson, K., & Loveland, T. (2001). Perspectives of teachers toward inclusive school programs. *Teacher Education and Special Education, 24,* 108–115.

McLeskey, J., & Waldron, N. L. (1995). Inclusive elementary schools: Must they cure students with learning disabilities to be effective? *Phi Delta Kappan, 77*(4), 300–303.

McMaster, K., & Fuchs, D. (2005). *Cooperative learning for students with disabilities.* Retrieved February 20, 2008, from www.teachingld.org

McMaster, K., Fuchs, D., & Fuchs, L. (2006). Research on peer-assisted learning strategies: The promise and limitations of peer-mediated instruction. *Reading & Writing Quarterly, 22*(1), 5–25.

Meadows, N. B., & Stevens, K. B. (2004). Teaching alternative behaviors to students with emotional and behavioral disorders. In R. B. Rutherford, Jr., M. M. Quinn, & A. R. Mathur (Eds.), *Handbook of research in emotional and behavioral disorders* (pp. 385–398). New York: Guilford.

Mercer, C., & Pullen, P. (2004). *Students with learning disabilities* (7th ed.). Upper Saddle River, NJ: Merrill/Pearson Education.

Miller, S. (2004). *Promoting sustained growth in the representation of African American, Latinos, and Native Americans among top students in the United States at all levels of the educational system.* National Research Center on Gifted and Talented (Report NO: RM04190). Retrieved May 21, 2008, from http://www.gifted.uconn.edu/NRCGT/nrconlin.html

Miller, S., & Hudson, P. (2007). Using evidence-based practices to build mathematics competence related to conceptual, procedural, and declarative knowledge. *Learning Disabilities Research & Practice, 22*(1), 47–57.

Milner, H. R., & Ford, D.Y. (2005). Racial experiences influence as teachers: Implications for gifted education curriculum development and implementation. *Roeper Review, 28*(1), 30–36.

Moll, L. C., Amanti, C., Neff, D., & Gonzalez, N. (1992). Funds of knowledge for teaching: Using a qualitative approach to connect homes and classrooms. *Theory into Practice, 31*(1), 132–141.

Montague, M. (2007). Self-regulation and mathematics instruction. *Learning Disabilities Research & Practice, 22*(1), 75–83.

Montague, M., Warger, C., & Morgan, T. (2000). Solve it! Strategy instruction to improve mathematical problem solving. *Learning Disabilities Research and Practice, 15*(2), 110–116.

Montgomery, D. J., Karlan, G. R., & Coutinho, M. (2001). The effectiveness of word processor spell checker programs to produce target words for misspellings generated by students with learning disabilities. *Journal of Special Education Technology, 16*(2), 27–41.

Montgomery, D. J., & Marks, L. J. (2006). Using technology to build independence in writing for students with disabilities. *Preventing School Failure, 50*(3), 33–38.

Mooney, J., & Cole, D. (2000). *Learning outside the lines.* New York: Simon & Shuster.

Morrison, G. M., & Allen, M. R. (2007). Promoting student resilience in school contexts. *Theory into Practice, 46*(2), 162–169.

Moses, H. (1990, June 22). *The Americans with Disabilities Act of 1990—Summary: American Rehabilitation.* Retrieved August 11, 2008, from http://findarticles.com

Multimodal Treatment Study of ADHD (MTA) Cooperative Group. (1999). A 14-month randomized clinical trial of treatment strategies for attention-deficit/hyperactivity disorder. *Archives of General Psychiatry, 56,* 1073–1086.

Munk, D. D. & Bursuck, W. D. (2004). Personalized grading plans: A systematic approach to making the grades of included students more accurate and meaningful. *Focus on Exceptional Children, 36*(9), 1–11.

Murdick, N., Gartin, B., & Crabtree, T. (2002). *Special education law.* Upper Saddle River, NJ: Merrill/Pearson Education.

Murray, J., Macomber, J. E., & Geen, R. (2004). *Estimating financial support for kinship caregivers.* Retrieved May 17, 2008, from http://www.urban.org/url.cfm?ID=311126

National Center for Education Statistics. (2005). *NAEP 2004 trends in academic progress. Three decades of student performance in reading and mathematics: Findings in brief.* Retrieved December 14, 2005, from http://nces.ed.gov/pubsearch/pubsinfo.asp?pubid=2005463

National Center for Education Statistics. (2007). *Percentage of gifted and talented students in public elementary and secondary schools, by sex, race/ethnicity, and state: 2002 and 2004.* Retrieved May 30, 2008, from http://nces.ed.gov/programs/digest/d07/tables/dt07_051.asp

National Center for Hearing Assessment and Management. (2008). *Universal newborn hearing screening fact sheet.* Retrieved August 25, 2008, from http://www.infanthearing.org/index.html

National Center on Student Progress Monitoring. (n.d.). *Review of progress monitoring tools.* Retrieved July 7, 2008, from http://www.studentprogress.org/default.asp

National Center to Improve Practice. (1998). *NCIP profile: How word prediction works.* Retrieved February 18, 2008, from http://www2.edc.org/NCIP/library/wp/How.htm

National Commission on Teaching and America's Future. (2003). *No dream denied: A pledge to America's children.* Retrieved December 13, 2005, from http://www.nea.org/goodnews/citation.html

National Council on Disability. (2008). *The No Child Left Behind Act and the Individuals with Disabilities Education Act: A progress report.* Washington, DC: National Council on Disability.

National Education Association. (2003). *The status of the American public school teacher 2000–2001.* Washington, DC: Author.

National Education Association. (2007). *C.A.R.E. Strategies for closing the achievement gaps.* Washington, DC: Author.

National Institute for Direct Instruction. (n.d.). *What is direct Instruction?* Retrieved July 30, 2008, from http://www.nifdi.org/#Tools

National Institute of Child Health and Human Development. (2000). *Report of the National Reading Panel. Teaching children to read: An evidence-based assessment of the scientific research literature on reading and its implications for reading instruction* (NIH Publication No. 00-4769). Washington, DC: U.S. Government Printing Office.

National Reading Panel. (2000). *Teaching children to read: An evidence-based assessment of the scientific research literature on reading and its implications for reading instruction.* Washington, DC: National Institute of Child Health and Human Development.

National Research Council & Institute of Medicine. (2004). *Engaging schools: Fostering high school students' motivation to learn.* Washington, DC: National Academies Press.

National Research Council. (2001). *Educating children with autism.* Washington, DC: National Academy Press.

National Technical Assistance Consortium for Children and Young Adults Who Are Deaf-Blind (NTAC). (2004). *National deaf-blind child count.* Retrieved August 16, 2006, from http://www.tr.wou.edu/ntac/documents/census/2004-Census-Tables.pdf

NCATE. (2006). *NCATE Unit Standards: Glossary.* Retrieved October 15, 2007, from http://www.ncate.org/public/unitStandardsRubrics.asp?ch=4 National Council for Accreditation in Teacher Education.

Neel, R. S., & Cessna, K. K. (1990). Behavioral intent: Instructional content for students with behavior disorders. In K. K. Cessna (Ed.), *Instructionally differentiated programming* (pp. 31–40). Denver: Colorado Department of Education.

Nelson, J. R. (1996). Designing schools to meet the needs of students who exhibit disruptive behavior. *Journal of Emotional and Behavioral Disorders, 4*(3), 147–161.

Neubert, D. A., Moon, S., & Grigal, M. (2004). Activities of students with significant disabilities receiving services in postsecondary settings. *Education and Training in Developmental Disabilities, 39,* 16–25.

Newcomer, P. L., Barenbaum, E., & Pearson, N. (1995). Depression and anxiety in children and adolescents with learning disabilities, conduct disorders, and no disability. *Journal of Emotional and Behavioral Disorders, 3*(1), 27–39.

Newman, L. (2007). *Secondary school experiences of students with autism: Facts from NLTS2.* Washington, DC: National Center for Special Education Research.

Nieto, S., & Bode, P. (2008). *Affirming diversity: The sociopolitical context of multicultural education* (5th ed.). Boston: Allyn & Bacon.

NIMAS at CAST. (2008). *What is the National Instructional Materials Accessibility Standard (NIMAS)?* Retrieved August 5, 2008, from http://nimas.cast.org/about/nimas

Nirje, B. (1972). The right to self-determination. In W. Wolfensberger (Ed.), *Normalization* (pp. 177–193). Ontario, Canada: National Institute on Mental Retardation.

No Child Left Behind Act. (2001). 20 U.S.C. 6301 et seq.

North Carolina State Board of Education. (2007). *North Carolina extended content standards.* Retrieved August 13, 2007, from http://www.ncpublicschools.org/curriculum/ncecs

Oakes, J. (1992). Can tracking research inform practice? Technical, normative, and political considerations. *Educational Researcher, 21*(4), 12–21.

Ochs, E., Kremer-Sadlik, T., Solomon, O., & Sirota, K. G. (2001). Inclusion as social practice: Views of children with autism. *Social Development, 10*(3), 399–419.

Oetzel, J. G., & Ting-Toomey, S. (Eds.). (2006). *The SAGE handbook of conflict communication: Integrating theory, research, and practice.* Thousand Oaks, CA: Sage.

Olley, G. J. (2005). Curriculum and classroom structure. In F. R. Volkmar, R. Paul, A. Klin, & D. Cohen (Eds.), *Handbook of autism and pervasive developmental disorders: Vol. 2. Assessment, interventions, and policy* (4th ed., pp. 863–881). Hoboken, NJ: Wiley.

Olson, L. (2005) AYP rules miss many in special education: More students left out of accountability ratings. *Education Week, 25*(4), 1, 24–25. Retrieved August 14, 2008, from http://web.ebscohost.com/

Orkwis, R., & McLane, K. (1998). *A curriculum every student can use: Design principles for student access.* Reston, VA: Council for Exceptional Children, ERIC Clearinghouse on Disabilities and Gifted Education.

Osher, D., Morrison, G., & Bailey, W. (2003). Exploring the relationship between student mobility and dropout among students with emotional and behavioral disorder. *Journal of Negro Education, 72,* 79–96.

Owens, R. E., Metz, D. E., & Haas, A. (2003). *Introduction to communication disorders: A life span perspective* (2nd ed.). Boston: Allyn & Bacon.

Paine, S. C., Radicci, J., Rosellini, L. C., Deutchman, L., & Darch, C. B. (1983). *Structuring your classroom for academic success.* Champaign, IL: Research Press.

Parette, H. P. (1997). Assistive technology devices and services. *Education and Training in Mental Retardation and Developmental Disabilities, 32,* 267–280.

Parette, H. P., & Peterson-Karlan, G. R. (2007) Facilitating student achievement with assistive technology. *Education and Training in Developmental Disabilities, 42,* 387–397.

Parette, H. P., Hourcade, J. J., & VanBiervliet, A. (1993). Selection of appropriate technology for children with disabilities. *Teaching Exceptional Children, 25*(3), 18–22.

Parette, P., & McMahan, G. A. (2002). What should we expect of assistive technology? Being sensitive to family goals. *Teaching Exceptional Children, 35*(1), 56–61.

Paris, S. G., & Winograd, P. (1990). Promoting metacognition and motivation of exceptional children. *Remedial and Special Education, 11*(6), 7–15.

Park, K. L. (2007). Facilitating effective team-based functional behavior assessments in typical school settings. *Beyond Behavior, 17*(1), 21–31.

Patrick, H., Turner, J., Meyer, D. K., & Midgley, C. (2003). How teachers establish psychological environments during the first days of school: Associations with avoidance in mathematics. *Teachers College Record, 105*(8), 1521–1558.

Patterson, G. R., Reid, J. B., Jones, R. R., & Conger, R. E. (1975). *A social learning approach to family intervention: Vol. 1. Families with aggressive children.* Eugene, OR: Castalia.

Paul, R. (2005). Assessing communication in autism spectrum disorders. In F. R. Volkmar, R. Paul, A. Klin, & D. Cohen (Eds.), *Handbook of autism and pervasive developmental disorders: Vol. 2. Assessment, interventions, and policy* (4th ed., pp. 799–816). Hoboken, NJ: Wiley.

Pavri, S., & Monda-Amaya, L. (2001). Social support in inclusive schools: Student and teacher perspectives. *Exceptional Children, 67*(3), 391–411.

Peña, E. D., & Davis, B. L. (2000). Language disorders in infants, toddlers, and preschoolers. In R. B. Gillam, T. P. Marquardt, & F. N. Martin (Eds.), *Communication sciences and disorders: From science to clinical practice* (pp. 409–436). San Diego: Singular.

Peck, C., Staub, D., Galucci, C., & Schwartz, I. (2004). Parent perception of the impacts of inclusion on their nondisabled child. *Research & Practice for Persons with Severe Disabilities, 29*(2), 135–143.

Pelham, W. (2002). *ADHD: Diagnosis, assessment, nature, etiology, and treatment.* Buffalo, NY: Center for Children and Families.

Pellegrino, L. (2007). Cerebral palsy. In M. L. Batshaw, L. Pellegrino, & N. J. Roizen (Eds.), *Children with disabilities* (6th ed., pp. 387–408). Baltimore: Brookes.

Pelo, A., & Davidson, F. (2000). *That's not fair! A teacher's guide to activism with young children.* St. Paul, MN: Redleaf.

Petry, K., & Maes, B. (2007). Description of the support needs of people with profound multiple disabilities using the 2002 AAMR system: An overview of literature. *Education and Training in Developmental Disabilities, 42,* 130–143.

Pfiffner, L., Barkley, R., & DuPaul, G. (2006). Treatment of ADHD in school settings. In R. Barkley (Ed.), *Attention-deficit hyperactivity disorder: A handbook for diagnosis and treatment* (3rd ed., pp. 547–589). New York: Guilford.

Pierce, C. D., Reid, R., & Epstein, M. H. (2004). Teacher mediated interventions for children with EBD and their academic outcomes. *Remedial and Special Education, 25*(3), 175–188.

Piers, E., & Harris, D. (1984). *The Piers-Harris children's self-concept scale.* Nashville, TN: Counselor Recordings and Tests.

Pinnell, G. (1989). Reading recovery: Helping at-risk children learn to read. *Elementary School Journal, 90*(2), 161–183.

Pivik, J., McComas, J., & Laflamme, M. (2002). Barriers and facilitators to inclusive education. *Exceptional Children, 69*(1), 97–107.

Pollitt, E. (1994). Poverty and child development: Relevance of research in developing countries to the United States. *Child Development, 65*(2), 283–295.

Polsgrove, L., & Smith, A. W. (2004). Informed practice in teaching self-control to children with emotional and behavioral disorders. In R. B. Rutherford, Jr., M. M. Quinn, & A. R. Mathur (Eds.), *Handbook of research in emotional and behavioral disorders* (pp. 399–425). New York: Guilford.

Porte, L. (2001). Cut and paste 101: New strategies for note taking and review. *Teaching Exceptional Children, 34*(2), 14–20.

Pottie, C., & Sumarah, J. (2004). Friendships between persons with and without developmental disabilities. *Mental Retardation, 42*, 55–66.

President's Committee on Mental Retardation. (1969). *The six-hour retarded child.* Washington, DC: U.S. Government Printing Office.

Pressley, M. (2002). *Reading instruction that works: The case for balanced teaching* (2nd ed.). New York: Guilford Press.

Pullen, P. C., Lane, H. B., & Monaghan, M. C. (2004). Effects of a volunteer tutoring model on the literacy development of struggling first grade students. *Reading Research and Instruction, 43*(4), 21–40.

Putnam J. (1998). *Cooperative learning and strategies for inclusion* (2nd ed.). Baltimore: Brookes.

Rainie, L. (2007). *The impact of technology on people's everyday lives.* Retrieved March 4, 2009, from http://www.pewinternet.org/PPF/r/107/presentationdisplay.asp

Rashotte, C., MacPhee, K., & Torgesen, J. (2001). The effectiveness of a group reading instruction program with poor readers in multiple grades. *Learning Disability Quarterly, 24*(2), 119–134.

Ravet, J. (2007). *Are we listening?* Stoke-on-Trent, England: Trentham Books.

Rea, P., McLaughlin, V., & Walther-Thomas, C. (2002). Outcomes for students with learning disabilities in inclusive and pullout programs. *Exceptional Children, 68*(2), 203–222.

Reed, V. A., & Spicer, L. (2003). The relative importance of selected communication skills for adolescents' interactions with their teachers: High school teachers' opinions. *Language, Speech, and Hearing Services in Schools, 34,* 343–357.

Reid, R., & Ortiz-Lienemann, T. (2006). *Strategy instruction for students with learning disabilities.* New York: Guilford.

Reiff, M. (2004). *ADHD: A complete and authoritative guide.* Elk Grove Village, IL: American Academy of Pediatrics.

Renaissance Learning. (n.d.). *Accelerated reader best classroom practices.* Madison, WI: Author.

Reschly, D. (2005). Learning disabilities identification: Primary intervention, secondary intervention, and then what? *Journal of Learning Disabilities, 38*(6), 510–515.

Reschly, D., & Hosp, J. (2004). State SLD identification policies and practices. *Learning Disabilities Research and Practice, 27*(4), 197–213.

Reutzel, R. (2003). Organizing effective literacy instruction: Grouping strategies and instructional routines. In L. M. Morrow, L. B. Gambrell, & M. Pressley (Eds.), *Best practices in literacy instruction* (2nd ed., pp. 241–267). New York: Guilford Press.

Reynolds, M., Wang, M., & Walberg, H. (1987). The necessary restructuring of special education. *Exceptional Children, 53*(5), 391–398.

Rhode, G., Jensen, W. R., & Reavis, H. K. (1993). *The tough kid book: Practical classroom management strategies.* Longmont, CO: Sopris West.

Rief, S. (2005). *How to teach and teach children with ADD/ADHD* (2nd ed.). San Francisco: Jossey-Bass.

Riggs, C. (2005). To teachers: What paraeducators want you to know. *Teaching Exceptional Children, 36*(5), 8–12.

Ritzman, M. J., & Sanger, D. (2007). Principals' opinions on the role of speech–language pathologists serving students with communication disorders involved in violence. *Language, Speech, and Hearing Services in Schools, 38,* 365–377.

Rivkin, S., Hanushek, E., & Kain, J. (2001). *Teachers, schools, and academic achievement.* Political economy working paper 09/01. Richardson, TX: University of Texas at Dallas.

Robins D., Fein D., Barton M., & Green J. (2001). The modified checklist for autism in toddlers. *Journal of Autism and Developmental Disorders, 31*(2), 131–144.

Rock, E., Fessler, M., & Church, R. (1999). Co-occurring disorders and learning disabilities. In W. Bender (Ed.), *Professional issues in learning disabilities* (pp. 347–384). Austin, TX: Pro-Ed.

Rogan, J. (2000). Learning strategies: Recipes for success. *Beyond Behavior, 10*(1), 18–22.

Rohrbeck, C., Ginsburg-Block, M., Fantuzzo, J., & Miller, T. (2003). Peer-assisted learning interventions with elementary school students. A meta-analytic review. *Journal of Educational Psychology, 95*(2), 240–257.

Rojewski, J. W., & Schell, J. W. (1994). Cognitive apprenticeship for learners with special needs: An alternative framework for teaching and learning. *Remedial and Special Education, 15,* 234–243.

Rorschach, H. (1932). *Psychodiagnostic: Methodik und Ergebnisse eines Wahrnehmungs-diagnostischen Experiments* (2nd ed.). Bern, Switzerland: Huber.

Rosenberg, M. S., Boyer, K. L, Sindelar, P. T., & Misra, S. (2007). Alternative route programs to certification in special education: Program infrastructure, instructional delivery, and participant characteristics. *Exceptional Children, 73,* 224–241.

Rosenberg, M. S., & Jackman, L. A. (2003). Development, implementation, and sustainability of comprehensive school-wide behavior management systems. *Intervention in School and Clinic, 39*(1), 10–21.

Rosenberg, M. S., O'Shea, L., & O'Shea, D. J. (2006). *Student teacher to master teacher: A practical guide for educating students with special needs* (4th ed.). Upper Saddle River, NJ: Merrill/Pearson Education.

Rosenberg, M. S., Sindelar, P. T., & Hardman, M. T. (2004). Preparing highly qualified teachers for students with emotional and behavioral disorders: The Impact of NCLB and IDEA. *Behavioral Disorders, 29,* 266–278.

Rosenberg, M. S., Westling, D. L., & McLeskey, J. (2008). *Special education for today's teachers: An introduction.* Upper Saddle River, NJ: Merrill/Pearson Education.

Rosenberg, M. S., Wilson, R. J., Maheady, L., & Sindelar, P. T. (2004). *Educating students with behavior disorders* (3rd ed.). Boston: Allyn & Bacon.

Rosenfeld, J. S. (2005). Section 504 and IDEA: Basic similarities and differences. *Learning Disabilities OnLine.* Retrieved November 29, 2005, from http://www.ldonline.org/ld_indepth/legal_legislative/edlaw504.html

Rosenshine, B., & Meister, C. (1992). The use of scaffolds for teaching higher-level cognitive strategies. *Educational Leadership, 49*(7), 26–33.

Rosenshine, B., & Stevens, R. (1986). Teaching functions. In M. C. Wittrock (Ed.), *Handbook of research on teaching* (3rd ed., pp. 376–391). New York: Macmillan.

Ross, D. D., Bondy, E., Gallingane, C., & Hambacher, E. (2008). Promoting academic engagement through insistence: Being a warm demander. *Childhood Education, 84*(3), 142–146.

Ross, D., Kamman, M., & Coady, M. (2008). Accepting responsibility for the learning of all students: What does it mean? In M. Rosenberg, D. Westling, & J. McLeskey (Eds.), *Special education for today's teachers: An introduction* (pp. 52–81). Upper Saddle River, NJ: Merrill/Pearson Education.

Rothstein, R. (2002). *Class and schools.* Washington, DC: Economic Policy Institute.

Rutter, M. (1978). Diagnosis and definition. In M. Rutter & E. Schopler (Eds.), *Autism: A reappraisal of concepts and treatment* (pp. 1–26). New York: Plenum.

Ryan, A., Halsey H., & Matthews, W. (2003). Using functional assessment to promote desirable student behavior in schools. *Teaching Exceptional Children, 35,* 8–15.

Ryndak, D. L., Morrison, A. P., & Sommerstein, L. (1999). Literacy before and after inclusion in general education settings: A case study. *Journal of the Association for Persons with Severe Handicaps, 24,* 5–22.

Sabornie, E. J., & deBettencourt, L. U. (2009). *Teaching students with mild and high-incidence disabilities at the secondary level.* Upper Saddle River, NJ: Merrill/Pearson Education.

Safran, J. S. (2002). Supporting students with Asperger's syndrome in general education. *Teaching Exceptional children, 34,* 60–66.

Safran, S., & Safran, J. (1996). Intervention assistance programs and prereferral teams. *Remedial and Special Education, 17*(6), 363–369.

Saint-Laurent, L. (2001). The SIO: An instrument to facilitate inclusion. *Reading and Writing Quarterly: Overcoming Learning Difficulties, 17*(4), 349–355.

Salend, S. J. (2006). Explaining your inclusion program to families. *Teaching Exceptional Children, 38*(4), 6–11.

Salend, S. J., & Gajria, M. (1995). Increasing homework completion rates of students with mild disabilities. *Remedial and Special Education, 16,* 271–278.

Salend, S., & Duhaney, L. (1999). The impact of inclusion on students with and without disabilities and their educators. *Remedial and Special Education, 20*(2), 114–126.

Salend, S., & Duhaney, L. (2005). Understanding and addressing disproportionate representation of students of color in special education. *Intervention in School and Clinic, 40*(4), 213–221.

Salend, S., Duhaney, D., Anderson, D., & Gottschalk, C. (2004). Using the Internet to improve homework communication and completion. *Teaching Exceptional Children, 36*(3), 64–73.

Salend, S., & Garrick Duhaney, L. (2007). Research related to inclusion and program effectiveness. In J. McLeskey (Ed.), *Reflections on inclusion: Classic articles than shaped our thinking* (pp. 127–159). Arlington, VA: Council for Exceptional Children.

Sanders, W., & Horn, S. (1998). Research findings from the Tennessee value-added assessment system (TVAAS) database: Implications for educational evaluation and research. *Journal of Personnel Evaluation in Education, 12*(3), 247–256.

Sanders, W., & Rivers, J. (1996). *Tennessee's value-added assessment system: A primer for teachers and principals.* Knoxville, TN: University of Tennessee Value-Added Research and Assessment Center.

Sanger, D., Maag, J. W., & Shapera, N. R. (1994). Language problems among students with emotional and behavioral disorders. *Intervention in School and Clinic, 30,* 103–108.

Sanger, D., Moore-Brown, B., & Alt, E. (2000). Advancing the discussion on communication and violence. *Communication Disorders Quarterly, 22,* 43–48.

Sanger, D., Spilker, A., Williams, N., & Belau, D. (2007). Opinions of female juvenile delinquents on communication, learning and violence. *Journal of Correctional Education, 58,* 69–92.

Santos, M. (2002). From mystery to mainstream: Today's school-based speech-language pathologist. *Educational Horizons, 80,* 93–96.

Scheffler, R., Hinshaw, S., Modrek, S., & Levine, P. (2007). The global market for ADHD medications. *Health Affairs, 26*(2), 450–457.

Scheurich, J. J., & Skla, L. L. (2003). *Leadership for equity and excellence.* Thousand Oaks, CA: Corwin Press.

Schirmer, B. R. (2001a). *Psychological, social, and educational dimensions of deafness.* Boston: Allyn & Bacon.

Schirmer, B. R. (2001b). Using research to improve literacy practice and practice to improve literacy research. *Journal of Deaf Studies and Deaf Education, 6*(2), 83–91.

Schrepferman, L. M., Eby, J., Snyder, J., & Stropes, J. (2006). Early affiliation and social engagement with peers: Prospective risk and protective factors for childhood depressive disorders. *Journal of Emotional and Behavioral Disorders, 14,* 50–60.

Schumaker, J., & Deshler, D. (2003). Can students with LD become competent writers? *Learning Disability Quarterly, 26,* 129–141.

Schumm, J. (1999). *Adapting reading and math materials for the inclusive classroom.* Reston, VA: Council for Exceptional Children.

Schumm, J. S., Vaughn, S., & Leavell, A. G. (1994). Planning pyramid: A framework for planning for diverse student needs during content area instruction. *Reading Teacher, 47,* 608–615.

Scott, G. S., & Compton, L. (2007). A new trick for the trade: A strategy for keeping an agenda book for secondary students. *Intervention in School and Clinic, 42*(5), 280–284.

Scott, K. (1999). Cognitive instructional strategies. In W. Bender (Ed.), *Professional issues in learning disabilities* (pp. 55–82). Austin, TX: Pro-Ed.

Scott, T. M., & Kamps, D. M. (2007). The future of functional behavioral assessment in school settings. *Behavioral Disorders, 32*(3), 146–157.

Scruggs, T. E., & Mastropieri, M. A. (1990). The case for mnemonic instruction: From laboratory research to classroom applications. *Journal of Special Education, 24*(1), 7–32.

Scruggs, T., & Mastropieri, M. (1996). Teacher perceptions of mainstreaming/inclusion, 1958–1995: A research synthesis. *Exceptional Children, 63,* 59–74.

Scruggs, T., Mastropieri, M., & McDuffie, K. (2007). Co-teaching in inclusive classrooms: A metasynthesis of qualitative research. *Exceptional Children, 73*(4), 392–416.

Semmel, M., Abernathy, T., Butera, G., & Lesar, S. (1991). Teacher perceptions of the regular education initiative. *Exceptional Children, 58*(1), 96–106.

Shakeshaft, C., Mann, D., Becker, J., & Sweeney, K. (2002). Choosing the right technology. *School Administrator, 59*(1), 34–37.

Shapiro, D. A. (1999). *Stuttering intervention: A collaborative journey to fluency freedom.* Austin, TX: Pro-Ed.

Shapiro, E. S., Miller, D. N., Sawka, K., Gardill, M. C., & Handler, M. W. (1999). Facilitating the inclusion of students with EBD into general education classrooms. *Journal of Emotional and Behavioral Disorders, 7*(2), 83–93.

Shea, V., & Mesibov, G. B. (2005). Adolescents and adults with autism. In F. R. Volkmar, R. Paul, A. Klin, & D. Cohen (Eds.), *Handbook of autism and pervasive developmental disorders: Vol. 1. Diagnosis, development, neurobiology, and behavior* (4th ed., pp. 288–311). Hoboken, NJ: Wiley.

Sheridan, S. M. (1997). *The tough kid social skills book.* Longmont, CO: Sopris West.

Shippen, M. E., Simpson, R. G., & Crites, S. A. (2003). A practical guide to functional behavioral assessment. *Teaching Exceptional Children, 35,* 36–44.

Siebelink, E. M., de Jong, M. D. T., Taal, E., & Roelvink, L. (2006). Sexuality and people with intellectual disabilities: Assessment of knowledge, attitudes, experiences, and needs. *Mental Retardation, 44,* 283–294.

Siegel, L. S. (2003). Basic cognitive processes and reading disabilities. In H. L. Swanson, K. R. Harris, & S. Graham (Eds.), *Handbook of learning disabilities* (pp. 158–181). New York: Guilford.

Silva, M., Munk, D. D., & Bursuck, W. D. (2005). Grading adaptations for students with disabilities. *Intervention in School and Clinic, 41*(2), 87–98.

Simonsen, B., Fairbanks, S., Briesch, A., Myers, D., & Sugai, G. (2008). Evidenced-based practices in classroom management: Considerations for research to practice. *Education and Treatment of Children, 31*(3), 351–380.

Sitlington, P. L., & Nuebert, D. A. (2004). Preparing youths with emotional or behavioral disorders for transition to adult life: Can it be done within the standards-based reform movement? *Behavioral Disorders, 29*(3), 279–288.

Skiba, R., Simmons, A., Ritter, S., Kohler, K., Henderson, M., & Wu, T. (2006). The context of minority disproportionality: Practitioner perspectives on special educator referral. *Teachers College Record, 108,* 1424–1459.

Skinner, D., Correa, V., Skinner, M., & Bailey, D. (2001). Role of religion in the lives of Latino families of young children with developmental delays. *American Journal on Mental Retardation, 106*(4), 297–313.

Skinner, D., & Weisner, T. (2007). Sociocultural studies of families of children with intellectual disabilities. *Mental Retardation and Developmental Disabilities Research Reviews, 13*(4), 302–312.

Slavin, R. (1977). Classroom reward structure: An analytic and practical review. *Review of Educational Research, 47*(4), 633–650.

Slavin, R. (1990). *Cooperative learning: Theory, research, and practice.* Upper Saddle River, NJ: Pearson Education.

Slavin, R. (1995). *Cooperative learning: Theory, research, and practice* (2nd ed.). Boston: Allyn & Bacon.

Slavin, R. (1999). Comprehensive approaches to cooperative learning. *Theory into Practice, 38*(2), 74–79.

Slavin, R. (2004). Built to last: Long-term maintenance of success for all. *Remedial and Special Education, 25*(1), 61–66.

Slavin, R., Hurley, E., & Chamberlain, A. (2003). Cooperative learning and achievement theory and research. In I. Weiner, W. Reynolds, & G. Miller (Eds.). *Handbook of psychology, Volume 7: Educational psychology* (pp. 177–197). Hoboken, NJ: John Wiley.

Slavin, R., & Madden, N. (Eds.). (2001). *Success for all: Research and reform in elementary education.* Mahwah, NJ: Erlbaum.

Slavin, R., & Madden, N. (2006). *Success for all: Summary of research on achievement outcomes.* Baltimore: Johns Hopkins University, Center for Data-Driven Reform in Education.

Smith, B., Barkley, R., & Shapiro, C. (2006). Attention deficit/hyperactivity disorder. In E. Mash & R. Barkley (Eds.), *Treatment of childhood disorders* (3rd ed., pp. 65–136). New York: Guilford.

Smith, K., & Geller, C. (2004). Essential principles of effective mathematics instruction: Methods to reach all students. *Preventing School Failure, 48*(4), 22–29.

Smith, T. E. C. (2001). Section 504, the ADA, and public schools. *Remedial and Special Education, 22*(6), 335–343.

Smith-Myles, B., & Simpson, R. L. (2001). Effective practices for students with Asperger's syndrome. *Focus on Exceptional Children, 34*, 1–16.

Smithgall, C., Gladden, R., Howard, E., Goerge, R., Courtney, M. (2004). *Educational experiences of children in out-of-home care.* Chicago: Chapin Hall Center for Children at the University of Chicago.

Snell, M., & Janney, R. (2000). *Collaborative teaming.* Baltimore: Brookes.

Soodak, L. C., Erwin, E. J., Winton, P., Brotherson, M. J., Turnbull, A. P., Hanson, M. J., et al. (2002). Implementing inclusive early childhood education: A call for professional empowerment. *Topics in Early Childhood Special Education (TECSE), 22*(2), 91–102.

Sperling, R. A. (2006). Assessing reading materials for students who are learning disabled. *Intervention in School and Clinic, 41*(3), 138–143.

Spina Bifida Association. (2008). Fact sheets. Retrieved September 3, 2008, from http://www.spinabifidaassociation.org/site/c.liKWL7PLLrF/b.2642343/k.8D2D/Fact_Sheets.htm

Sprague, J. R., & Walker, H. M. (2005). *Safe and healthy schools. Practical prevention strategies.* New York: Guliford.

SRA/McGraw-Hill. (2005). *Open court reading.* Columbus, OH: Author.

Stainback, W., & Stainback, S. (1984). A rationale for the merger of special and regular education. *Exceptional Children, 51*(2), 102–111.

Stecker, P. M., Lembke, E. S., & Foegen, A. (2008). Using progress-monitoring data to improve instructional decision making. *Preventing School Failure, 52*(2), 48–58.

Steele, M. M. (2007). Teaching social studies to high school students with learning problems. *The Social Studies, 98*(2), 59–63.

Stenhoff, D., & Lignugaris/Kraft, B. (2007). A review of the effects of peer tutoring on students with mild disabilities in secondary settings. *Exceptional Children, 74*(1), 8–30.

Stormont, M. (2007). *Fostering resilience in young children at risk for failure.* Upper Saddle River, NJ: Merrill/Pearson Education.

Storti, C. (1999). *Figuring foreigners out: A practical guide.* Yarmouth, ME: Intercultural Press.

Stronge, J. H. (2002). *Qualities of effective teachers.* Alexandria, VA: Association for Supervision and Curriculum Development.

Stump, C. S., & Bigge, J. (2005). Curricular options for individuals with physical, health, or multiple disabilities. In S. J. Best, K. W. Heller, & J. L. Bigge (Eds.), *Teaching individuals with physical or multiple disabilities* (5th ed., pp. 278–318). Upper Saddle River, NJ: Merrill/Pearson Education.

Sugai, G., & Lewis, T. J. (1996). Preferred and promising practices for social skills instruction. *Focus on Exceptional Children, 29*(4), 1–16.

Sun, Y. (2003). The well-being of adolescents in households with no biological parents. *Journal of Marriage and Family, 65*(4), 894–909.

Suritsky, S. K., & Hughes, C. A. (1996). Notetaking strategy instruction. In D. D. Deshler, E. S. Ellis, & B. K. Lenz (Eds.), *Teaching adolescents with learning disabilities* (pp. 267–312). Denver: Love.

Taylor, R., Richards, S. B., & Brady, M. (2005). *Mental retardation: Historical perspectives, current practices, and future directions.* Boston: Pearson/Allyn & Bacon.

Terrill, M. C., Scruggs, T. E., & Mastropieri, M. A. (2004). SAT vocabulary for high school students with learning disabilities. *Intervention in School and Clinic, 39*, 288–294.

Texas School for the Blind and Visually Impaired. (2007). *Dos and don'ts for teaching social skills.* Retrieved August 28, 2008, from http://www.tsbvi.edu/Education/do-dont-social-skills.htm

Thorson, S. (1996). The missing link: Students discuss school discipline. *Focus on Exceptional Children, 29*, 1–12.

Thousand, J., Villa, R., & Nevin, A. (2006). The many faces of collaborative planning and teaching. *Theory into Practice, 45*(3), 239–248.

Thuppal, M., & Sobsey, D. (2004). Children with special health care needs. In F. P. Orelove, D. Sobsey, & R. K. Silberman (Eds.), *Educating children with multiple disabilities: A collaborative approach* (2nd ed., pp. 311–377). Baltimore: Brookes.

Thurlow, M. L., Elliott, J. L., & Ysseldyke, J. E. (2003). *Testing students with disabilities* (2nd ed.). Thousand Oaks, CA: Corwin Press.

Tobin, T., Sugai, G., & Colvin, G. (1996). Patterns in middle school discipline records. *Journal of Emotional and Behavioral Disorders, 4*(2), 82–94.

Todis, B. (1996). Tools for the task? Perspectives on assistive technology in educational settings. *Journal of Special Education Technology, 13*(2), 49–61.

Tomlinson, C. (2001). *How to differentiate instruction in mixed-ability classrooms* (2nd ed.). Alexandria, VA: ASCD.

Tomlinson, C. A. (2005). *How to differentiate instruction in mixed-ability classrooms* (2nd ed.). Upper Saddle River, NJ: Merrill/Pearson Education.

Torgesen, J. (2000). Individual differences in response to early interventions in reading: The lingering problem of treatment resisters. *Learning Disabilities Research & Practice, 15*(1), 55–64.

Torgesen, J. (2002). Empirical and theoretical support for direct diagnosis of learning disabilities by assessment of intrinsic processing weakness. In R. Bradley, L. Danielson, & D. Hallahan (Eds.), *Identification of learning disabilities: Research to practice* (pp. 565–613). Mahwah, NJ: Erlbaum.

Torgesen, J., Alexander, A., Wagner, R., Rashotte, C., Voeller, K., & Conway, T. (2001). Intensive remedial instruction for children with severe reading disabilities: Immediate and long-term outcomes from two instructional approaches. *Journal of Learning Disabilities, 34*(1), 33–58, 78.

Traxler, C. B. (2000). The Stanford achievement test (9th ed.): National norming and performance for deaf and hard-of-hearing students. *Journal of Deaf Studies and Deaf Education, 5*(4), 337–348.

Trenholm, S., & Rose, T. (1981). The compliant communicator: Teacher perceptions of appropriate classroom behavior. *Western Journal of Speech Communication, 45*(1), 13–26.

Trumbull, E., Rothstein-Fisch, C., & Greenfield, P. M. (2000). *Bridging cultures in our schools: New approaches that work. Knowledge brief.* San Francisco: WestEd.

Tschannen-Moran, M., Woolfolk Hoy, A., & Hoy, W. K. (1998). Teacher efficacy: Its meaning and measure. *Review of Educational Research, 68*, 202–248.

Turnbull, H. R. (1993). *Free appropriate public education: The law and children with disabilities* (4th ed.). Denver: Love.

Turnbull, H. R., Stowe, M. J., & Huerta, N. E. (2007). *Free appropriate public education: The law and children with disabilities.* Denver, CO: Love.

Tyler, N., Yzquierdo, Z., Lopez-Reyna, N., & Flippin, S. S. (2004). The relationship between cultural diversity and the special education workforce: A critical overview. *Journal of Special Education, 38*(1), 22–38.

U.S. Census Bureau. (2006). *Annual estimates of the population by sex, race, and Hispanic origin for the United States.* Retrieved May 16, 2008, from http://www.census.gov/popest/national/asrh/NC-EST2007-srh.html

U.S. Census Bureau. (2007*). More than 300 counties now "Majority-Minority."* Retrieved May 17, 2008, from http://www.census.gov/PressRelease/www/releases/archives/population/010482.html

U.S. Census Bureau News. (2008). An older and more diverse nation by midcentury. Retrieved August 26, 2008, from http:// www.census.gov/Press-Release/www.releases/archives/population/012496.html

U.S. Department of Education. (2005). Assistance to states for the education of children with disabilities. *Federal Register, 70*(118), 34 CFR, Parts 300, 301, Amend. 304, Sec. 300.8.

U.S. Department of Education. (2006). *Individuals with Disabilities Education Act data.* Retrieved December 11, 2007, from https://www.ideadata.org/index.html

U.S. Department of Education. (2007). *Individuals with Disabilities Education Act (IDEA) data.* Retrieved October 15, 2008, from http://www.ideadata.org/

U.S. Department of Education. (2007). *Twenty-seventh annual report to congress on the implementation of the Individuals with Disabilities Education Act, Parts B and C.* Retrieved May 16, 2008, from http://www.ed.gov/about/reports/annual/osep/2005/parts-b-c/index.html

U.S. Department of Education. (2007a). *Final regulations on modified academic achievement standards summary.* Retrieved August 17, 2007, from http://www.ed.gov/policy/speced/guid/modachieve-summary.html

U.S. Department of Education. (2007b). Retrieved July 2, 2007, from http://www.ed.gov/about/offices/list/ocr/504faq.html

U.S. Department of Education. (2008). *No Child Left Behind provision gives schools new flexibility and ensures accountability for students with disabilities.* Retrieved November 10, 2008, from http://www.ed.gov/nclb/freedom/local/specedfactsheet.html

U.S. Department of Education. (n.d.). *History: 25 years of progress in educating children with disabilities through IDEA.* Retrieved October, 20, 2008, from http/www.ed.gov/policy/speced/leg/idea/history.html

U.S. Department of Education, Office for Civil Rights. (n.d.). *Questions and answers on disability discrimination under Section 504 and Title II.* Retrieved June 17, 2008, from http://www.ed.gov/about/offices/list/ocr/

U.S. Department of Health and Human Services. (2005). Mental health in the United States: Prevalence of diagnosis and medication treatment for attention-deficit/hyperactivity disorder—United States, 2003. *Morbidity and Mortality Weekly Report (MMWR), 54*(34), 842– 847. Retrieved February 9, 2009, from http://www.cdc.gov/mmwr/preview/mmwrhtml/mm5434a2.htm

University of Kansas. (1999–2005). *An introduction to classwide peer tutoring.* Retrieved on July 30, 2008, from http://www.specialconnections.ku.edu/cgi-bin/cgiwrap/specconn/main.php?cat=instruction&section=cwpt/main

University of Sheffield. (2008). *Teaching students with visual impairments.* Retrieved August 28, 2008, from http://www.shef.ac.uk/disability/teaching/visual/5_teaching.html

Unok Marks, S., Shaw-Hegwer, J., Schrader, C., Longaker, T., Peters, I., Powers, F., & Levine, M. (2003). Instructional management tips for teachers of students with autism spectrum disorder. *Teaching Exceptional Children, 35,* 50–55.

Unsworth, L. (1984). Meeting individual needs through flexible within-class grouping of pupils. *The Reading Teacher, 38*(3), 289–304.

van Garderen, D., & Whittaker, C. (2006). Planning differentiated, multicultural instruction for secondary inclusive classrooms. *Teaching Exceptional Children, 38*(3), 12–20.

Van Tassel-Baska, J., & Stambaugh, T. (2005). Challenges and possibilities for serving gifted learners in the regular classroom. *Theory into Practice, 44*(3), 211–218.

Vaughn, S., Bos, C., & Schumm, J. (2007). *Teaching students who are exceptional, diverse and at risk in the general education classroom* (4th ed.). Boston: Allyn & Bacon.

Vaughn, S., Gersten, R., & Chard, D. (2000). The underlying message in LD intervention research: Findings from research syntheses. *Exceptional Children, 67*(1), 99–114.

Vaughn, S., Hughes, M., Moody, S., & Elbaum, B. (2001). Instructional grouping for reading for students with LD: Implications for practice. *Intervention in School and Clinic, 36*(3), 131–137.

Vaughn, S., Linan-Thompson, S., Kouzekanani, K., Bryant, D., Dickson, S., & Blozis, S. (2003). Reading instruction grouping for students with reading difficulties. *Remedial and Special Education, 24*(5), 301–315.

Vaughn, S., & Roberts, G. (2007). Secondary interventions in reading: Providing additional instruction for students at risk. *Teaching Exceptional Children, 39*(5), 40–46.

Vellutino, F., Scanlon, D., Small, S., & Fanuele, D. (2006). Response to intervention as a vehicle for distinguishing between children with and without reading disabilities. *Journal of Learning Disabilities, 39*(2), 157–169.

Vittetoe, J. O. (1997). Why first year teachers fail. *Phi Delta Kappan, 58*(5), 429.

Voltz, D. L., Brazil, N., & Ford, A. (2001). What matters most in inclusive education: A practical guide for moving forward. *Intervention in School and Clinic, 37*(1), 23–30.

Vygotsky, L. S. (1978). *Mind in society: The development of higher psychological processes.* Cambridge, MA: Harvard University Press.

Wadsworth, D. E. D., & Knight, D. (1999). Preparing the inclusion classroom for students with special physical and health needs. *Intervention in School and Clinic, 34*(3), 170–175.

Wagner, M. M., & Blackorby, J. (1996). Transition from high school to work or college: How special education students fare. *Special Education for Students with Disabilities, 6*(1), 103–120.

Wagner, M., Blackorby, J., Cameto, R., Hebbeler, K., & Newman, L. (1993). *The transition experiences of young people with disabilities: A summary of findings from the national longitudinal transition study of special education students.* Menlo Park, CA: SRI International.

Wagner, M. M., Kutash, K., Duchnowski. A. J., Epstein, M. H., & Sumi, W. C. (2005). The children and youth we serve: A national picture of the characteristics of students with emotional disturbances receiving special education. *Journal of Emotional and Behavioral Disorders, 13*(2), 79–96.

Wahl, M. (2003). *What is early success?* Tallahassee, FL: Florida Center for Reading Research. Retrieved March 12, 2008, from http://www.fcrr.org

Wald, J., & Losen, D. J. (2007). Out of sight: The journey through the school-to-prison pipeline. In S. Books (Ed.), *Invisible children in the society and its schools* (pp. 23–38). Mahwah, NJ: Erlbaum.

Waldron, N. (2007). Teacher attitudes toward inclusion. In J. McLeskey (Ed.), *Reflections on inclusion: Classic articles that shaped our thinking* (pp. 161–187). Arlington, VA: Council for Exceptional Children.

Waldron, N., & McLeskey, J. (1998). The impact of a full-time inclusive school program (ISP) on the academic achievement of students with mild and severe learning disabilities. *Exceptional Children, 64*(2), 395–405.

Waldron, N., & McLeskey, J. (2008). Establishing a collaborative culture through comprehensive school reform. *Journal of Educational and Psychological Consultation,* in Press.

Waldron, N., McLeskey, J., & Pacchiano, D. (1999). Giving teachers a voice: Teachers' perspectives regarding elementary inclusive school programs (ISPs). *Teacher Education and Special Education, 22,* 141–153.

Walker, H., Colvin, G., & Ramsey, E. (1995). *Antisocial behavior in school: Strategies and best practices.* Pacific Grove, CA: Brooks/Cole.

Walker, H. M. (1995). *The acting-out child: Coping with classroom disruption.* Longmont, CO: Sopris West.

Walker, H. M., McConnell, S. R., Holmes, D., Todis, B., Walker, J., & Golden, N. (1983). *ACCEPTS: A children's curriculum for effective peer and teacher skills.* Austin, TX: Pro-Ed.

Walker, H. M., & Severson, H. H. (1992). *Systematic screening for behavior disorder (SSBD): User's guide and technical manual* (2nd ed.). Longmont, CO: Sopris West.

Walker, H. M., Severson, H. H., & Feil, E. G. (1995). *The early screening project: A proven child-find process.* Longmont, CO: Sopris West.

Walker, H. M., & Walker, J. E. (1991). *Coping with noncompliance in the classroom: A positive approach for teachers.* Austin, TX: Pro-Ed.

Wallace, T. (2003). *Paraprofessionals.* (COPSSE Document No. IB-3). Gainesville, FL: University of Florida, Center on Personnel Studies in Special Education.

Walther-Thomas, C., Korinek, L., McLaughlin, V., & Williams, B. (2000). *Collaboration for inclusive education.* Boston: Allyn & Bacon.

Wanzek, J., Dickson, S., Bursuck, W. D., & White, J. M. (2000). Teaching phonological awareness to students at risk for reading failure: An analysis of four instructional programs. *Learning Disabilities Research and Practice, 15*(4), 226–239.

Wanzek, J., Vaughn, S., Wexler, J., Swanson, E. A., Edmonds, M., & Kim, A. (2006). A synthesis of spelling and reading interventions and their effects on the spelling outcomes of students with LD. *Journal of Learning Disabilities, 39,* 528–543.

Ware, F. (2006). Warm demander pedagogy: Culturally responsive teaching that supports a culture of achievement for African American students. *Urban Education, 41*(4), 427–456.

Wehmeyer, M. L. (1992). Self-determination and the education of students with mental retardation. *Education and Training in Mental Retardation, 27,* 302–314.

Wehmeyer, M. L. (2006). Beyond access: Ensuring progress in the general education curriculum for students with severe disabilities. *Research and Practice for Persons with Severe Disabilities, 31,* 322–326.

Wehmeyer, M. L., & Agran, M. (2006). Promoting access to the general curriculum for students with significant cognitive disabilities. In D. M. Browder & F. Spooner (Eds.), *Teaching language arts, math, & science to students with significant cognitive disabilities* (pp. 15–37). Baltimore: Paul H. Brookes.

Wehmeyer, M. L., Kelchner, K., & Richards, S. (1996). Essential characteristics of self-determined behavior of individuals with mental retardation. *American Journal on Mental Retardation, 100,* 632–642.

Wehmeyer, M. L., & Metzler, C. A. (1995). How self-determined are people with mental retardation? The national consumer survey. *Mental Retardation, 33,* 111–119.

Wehmeyer, M. L., Palmer, S., Smith, S., Parent, W., Davies, D., & Stock, S. (2006). Technology use by people with intellectual and developmental disabilities to support employment activities: A single-subject design meta analysis. *Journal of Vocational Rehabilitation, 24,* 81–86.

Wehmeyer, M. L., & Schwartz, M. (1997). Self-determination and positive adult outcomes: A follow-up study of youth with mental retardation or learning disabilities. *Exceptional Children, 63,* 245–255.

Weiner, J. (2004). Do peer relationships foster behavioral adjustment in children with learning disabilities? *Learning Disability Quarterly, 27*(1), 21–30.

Weinstein, C., Tomlinson-Clarke, S., & Curran, M. (2004). Toward a conception of culturally responsive classroom management. *Journal of Teacher Education, 55*(1), 25–38.

Weinstein, R. (2002). *Reaching higher: The power of expectations in schooling.* Cambridge, MA: Harvard University Press.

Weinstein, S., & Gaillard, W. D. (2007). Epilepsy. In M. L. Batshaw, L. Pellegrino, & N. J. Roizen (Eds.), *Children with disabilities* (6th ed., pp. 439–460). Baltimore: Brookes.

Weintraub, F. J., & Abeson, A. (1976). New education policies for the handicapped: The quiet revolution. In F. J. Weintraub, A. Abeson, J. Ballard, & M. L. LaVor (Eds.), *Public policy and the education of exceptional children.* (pp. 7–13). Reston, VA: The Council for Exceptional Children.

Weishaar, M. K., & Boyle, J. R. (1999). Note-taking strategies for students with disabilities. *The Clearing House, 72*(6), 392–395.

Wenar, C., & Kerig, P. (2006). *Developmental psychopathology: From infancy through adolescence.* Boston: McGraw-Hill.

Werts, M., Wolery, M., Snyder, E., & Caldwell, N. (1996). Teachers' perceptions of the supports critical to the success of inclusion programs. *Journal of the Association for Persons with Severe Handicaps, 21,* 9–21.

Westling, D. L., & Fox, L. (2009). *Teaching students with severe disabilities* (4th ed.). Upper Saddle River, NJ: Merrill/Pearson Education.

Whitbread, K., Bruder, M., Fleming, G., & Park, H. (2007). Collaboration in special education: Parent–professional training. *Teaching Exceptional Children, 39*(4), 6–14.

White, R. (1996). Unified discipline. In B. Algozzine (Ed.), *Problem behavior management: An educator's resource service* (pp. 11:28–11:36). Gaithersburg, MD: Aspen.

Wiggins, G., & McTighe, J. (2005). *Understanding by design* (2nd ed.). Upper Saddle River, NJ: Merrill/Pearson Education.

Wilder, L. K., Dyches, T., Obiakor F. E., & Algozzine, B. (2004). Multicultural perspectives on teaching students with autism. *Focus on Autism and Other Developmental Disabilities 19*(2), 105–113.

Will, M. (1986). Educating children with learning problems: A shared responsibility. *Exceptional Children, 52*(5), 411–415.

Willard-Holt, C. (1998). Academic and personality characteristics of gifted students with cerebral palsy: A multiple case study. *Exceptional Children, 65,* 37–50.

Williams, S. C. (2002) How speech-feedback and word-prediction software can help students write. *Teaching Exceptional Children, 34*(3), 72–78.

Williamson, P., McLeskey, J., Hoppey, D., & Rentz, T. (2006). Educating students with mental retardation in general education classrooms: An analysis on national and state trends. *Exceptional Children, 72(3),* 347–361.

Wilson, B. L., & Corbett, H. D. (2001). *Listening to urban kids.* Albany, NY: SUNY Press.

Wilson, G., & Michaels, C. (2006). General and special education students' perceptions of co-teaching: Implications for secondary-level literacy instruction. *Reading & Writing Quarterly, 22*(1), 205–225.

Wingerden, C., Emerson, C., & Ichikawa, D. (2002). *Improving special education for children with disabilities in foster care.* Education Issue Brief. Casey Family Programs. Retrieved May 17, 2008, from http://www.fosterclub.org/training/upload/fosterclub_219.pdf

Wisconsin Assistive Technology Initiative. (2004). *The WATI assessment package.* Retrieved December 22, 2007, from http://www.wati.org/products/pdf/wati%20assessment.pdf

Wolfensberger, W. (1972). *The principle of normalization in human services.* Toronto: National Institute on Mental Retardation.

Wolff, J. C., & Ollendick, T. H. (2006). The comorbidity of conduct problems and depression in childhood and adolescence. *Clinical Child and Family Psychology Review, 9,* 201–220.

Wolffe, K. (2006). Teaching social skills to adolescents and young adults with visual impairments. In S. Z. Sacks & K. E. Wolffe (Eds.), *Teaching social skills to students with visual impairments: From theory to practice* (pp. 405–440). New York: American Foundation for the Blind.

Wolgemuth, J. R., Cobb, R. B., & Alwell, M. (2008). The effects of mnemonic interventions on academic outcomes for youth with disabilities: A systematic review. *Learning Disabilities Research & Practice, 23*(1), 1–10.

Wood, J.W. (2001). *Adapting instruction to accommodate students in inclusive settings.* Upper Saddle River, NJ: Merrill/Pearson Education.

Yeargin-Allsopp, M., Rice, C., Karapurkar, T., Doernberg, N., Boyle, C., & Murphy, C. (2003). Prevalence of autism in a US metropolitan area. *Journal of the American Medical Association, 289*(1), 49–55.

Yell, M. L., & Dragow, E. (2005). *No Child Left Behind: A guide for professionals.* Upper Saddle River, NJ: Pearson Education.

Yell, M. L., Rogers, D., & Rogers, E. L. (1998). The legal history of special education: What a long, strange trip it's been! *Remedial and Special Education, 19*(4), 219–228.

Yell, M. L., Shriner, J. G., & Katsiyannis, A. (2006). Individuals with Disabilities Education Improvement Act of 2004 and IDEA Regulations of 2006: Implications for educators, administrators, and teacher trainers. *Focus on Exceptional Children, 39,* 1–16.

Zentall, S. (2005). Theory- and evidence-based strategies for children with attentional problems. *Psychology in the Schools, 42*(8), 821–836.

Zentall, S. (2006). *ADHD and education: Foundations, characteristics, methods, and collaboration.* Upper Saddle River, NJ: Pearson Education.

Zigmond, N., Jenkins, J., Fuchs, D., Deno, S., & Fuchs, L. (1995a). When students fail to achieve satisfactorily: A reply to McLeskey and Waldron. *Phi Delta Kappan, 77*(5), 303–306.

Zigmond, N., Jenkins, J., Fuchs, L., Deno, S., Fuchs, D., Baker, J., Jenkins, L., & Couthino, M. (1995b). Special education in restructured schools: Findings from three multi-year studies. *Phi Delta Kappan, 76*(7), 531–540.

Zimmerman, B. J., & Dibenedetto, M. K. (2008). Mastery learning and assessment: Implications for students and teachers in an era of high-stakes testing. *Psychology in the Schools, 45*(3), 206–216.

Name Index

Abbott, M., 293
Abernathy, T., 21
Abeson, A., 33
Achenbach, T. M., 140
Adkins, T., 72
Agar, G., 142–143
Agodini, R., 406, 423, 429
Agran, M., 128, 334
Ainge, D., 387
Albert, L., 367, 387, 388, 394, 395
Albin, R. W., 125
Alexander, A., 313
Alexander, C., 62
Algozzine, B., 62
Alkin, M., 18, 290, 291
Allbritten, D., 44
Allen, M. R., 64
Allen, S., 293
Alt, E., 175
Alwell, M., 329
Amanti, C., 61, 68, 73
American Academy
    of Asthma Allergy
    and Immunology, 196
American Academy of
    Pediatrics, 111
American Association of Colleges
    for Teacher Education, 56
American Association on
    Intellectual and
    Developmental
    Disabilities, 131
American Association on Mental
    Retardation, 119
American Federation of
    Teachers, 44
American Foundation for the
    Blind, 179
American Psychiatric
    Association, 99, 101,
    102, 103, 111, 112, 154,
    155, 156, 157, 158
American Speech-Language-
    Hearing Association,
    172, 176
Anderson, D., 220
Anderson, J. L., 125

Anderson-Inman, L., 323
Andrews, A., 158
Angold, A., 103
Arick, J. R., 160
Aronson, E., 221, 291, 307, 308, 328
Arreaga-Mayer, C., 292, 293
Arthur-Kelly, M., 18, 118–119
Artiles, A. J., 60
Asgharian, A., 158
Austin, J. L., 142–143
Autism Information Center, 155
Axelrod, M., 85
Axelrod, S., 144

Babyak, A., 293
Baca, L. M., 60, 61
Baccani, S., 415
Baenen, N., 309
Baglieri, S., 57
Bailey, D., 63
Bailey, W., 144
Baines, C., 17
Baines, L., 17
Baird, G., 154
Bak, S., 18
Baker, J. N., 16, 128, 196
Baker, S., 310
Banda, D., 239, 240
Banks, J. A., 51, 65, 67, 70, 71, 72, 73
Banks, K., 309
Banks, R. A., 334, 418
Barenbaum, E., 143
Barkley, R., 101, 103, 105, 106, 112
Barletta, L. M., 60
Barnes, M., 83, 86, 87, 90
Barton, M., 154, 157
Barton-Arwood, S. M., 355
Bausch, M. E., 403 425
Beard, L. A., 408, 409, 411, 412, 413, 414
Beck, M. A., 383
Becker, J., 429
Beirne-Smith, M., 122, 123, 125, 130

Belau, D., 175
Bell, L. I., 23
Bempechat, J., 63, 64
Benard, B., 64, 67, 68
Bender, W., 84
Benepe, S., 131
Benner, G. J., 173
Bennett, C. I., 58
Bernadette, K., 290
Bernhole, A., 309
Best, K. M., 64
Best, S. J., 192, 195, 197, 200, 201, 408, 411, 431, 439
Beukelman, D. R., 437
Biancarosa, C., 425
Bigge, J. L., 192, 195, 198, 201, 408, 411, 431, 439
Biklen, D., 13
Bishop, M. J., 429
Bitter, G. G., 403, 404, 406, 429
Blackhurst, A. E., 403
Blackorby, J., 144, 146
Blaney, N., 291, 328
Blank, W., 146
Blinder, A., 210
Blozis, S., 290
Bocian, K. M., 143
Bode, P., 57
Boe, E. E., 45
Bond, R., 220, 292
Bondy, A., 161
Bondy, E., 60, 67, 68, 69
Books, S., 62
Bordin, J., 267
Borman, G., 305, 313
Bos, C. S., 66, 92, 229, 324, 325
Boskin, J., 60
Boudah, D. J., 339
Boutot, E., 18
Boyd, B., 63
Boyer, K. L., 45
Boyle, C., 155
Boyle, J. R., 332, 351, 353
Bradley, R., 141
Brady, M., 122, 123
Bransford, J. D., 322
Brazil, N., 273
Bricker, D., 35

Briesch, A., 365
Broderick, A., 271
Broer, S. M., 21
Brooks-Gunn, J., 56
Brookshire, M. A., 374
Brophy, J., 290, 291, 292, 293, 307, 308, 309, 328
Brotherson, M. J., 33
Browder, D. M., 128, 196, 333, 334
Brown, A. L., 322
Brown, C. C., 415
Brown, D. F., 68
Brown, L., 124, 130
Bruder, M., 220, 239
Bruner, E., 288
Bryan, T., 88
Bryant, B. R., 433
Bryant, D. P., 18, 87, 290, 433
Bryant, J., 314
Buck, G., 217
Bulgren, J. A., 92, 93, 329, 330, 339, 340, 341
Bullis, M., 146
Burish, P., 221, 296, 311
Burke, M. D., 343, 344
Burns, B. J., 146
Burns, M., 84, 313
Burstein, K., 88
Burstein, N., 18
Bursuck, W. D., 66, 220, 258, 260, 261, 281
Busch, T. W., 279
Busse, R. T., 140
Butera, G., 21
Butler, J., 131
Buzhardt, J., 293
Byers, C., 243

Cabello, B., 18
Caldwell, N., 22
California Department of
    Education, 50, 55
Callahan, K., 379
Cameto, R., 146
Campuzano, L., 406, 423, 429
Canevaro, A., 415

Canter, L. S., 277
Carey, D. M., 415
Carey, N., 406, 423, 429
Carlson, E., 24
Carnine, D., 92, 93, 290
Carpenter, L. B., 408, 409, 411, 412, 413, 414
Carpenter, S. L., 368
Carr, E. G., 125
Carr, V. G., 367, 387
Carta, J., 221, 311
Carter, E. W., 18, 22, 143, 221, 243, 244, 245, 334, 355
Carter, J., 372
Cartledge, G. W., 58
Case, L., 318
Castagnera, E., 220, 292
CAST (Center for Applied Special Technology), 128, 415, 418, 419
Castillo, S., 374
Causton-Theoharis, J., 235, 236
Cauthen, N., 52
Cavalier, A. R., 406, 415, 423
Center for Applied Special Technology (CAST), 128, 415, 418, 419
Center for Effective Collaboration and Practice, 393, 394
Cervantes, H. T., 60, 61
Cessna, K. K., 145
Chadsey, J., 18
Chalfant, J., 217, 231
Chalk, J. C., 343, 344
Chamberlain, C., 307
Chamberlain, S. P., 57, 62
Chandler, L. K., 141, 368, 393
Chapman, C., 329, 330
Chapman, J., 309, 310
Chard, D., 290
Charles, C. M., 364
Charleston County School District, 425, 426
Charlton, K., 62
Charman, T., 154
Charney, R., 70
Chawarska, K., 157
Cheney, D., 146
Christenson, S. L., 389
Chuin, E. J., 334
Chun, E. J., 418
Church, R., 87
Clark, G. M., 201
Clark, H. B., 146
Clark, N. M., 334
Clarke, B., 299, 300, 317
Clay, M., 292, 309
Clements, B. S., 69
Coady, M., 12, 60, 211, 365
Coates, R., 21

Cobb, R. B., 329
Cochran-Smith, M., 51, 65, 67, 70, 71, 72
Cocking, R. R., 322
Cole, C., 17, 18, 329, 330
Cole, D., 67
Cole, R. W., 70, 71
Coleman, M., 144
Coleman, T., 239, 240
Colvert, G., 343, 344, 345
Colvin, G., 142, 365, 368, 387
Compton, D., 314
Compton, L., 333
Conderman, G., 331, 349, 350
Conger, R. E., 142
Connor, D., 101, 111, 112
Connor, M. H., 60
Conway, T., 313
Cook, K., 217
Cook, L., 212, 215, 217, 227, 229, 230, 233, 235, 236
Cook, L. H., 45
Coonrod, E. E., 154
Cooper, H., 62, 327
Cooper, J. L., 62
Copeland, S., 54, 221, 243, 244, 245
Corbett, D., 63, 65, 70, 71
Corbett, H. D., 69, 71
Corbett, W. P., 146
Correa, V., 21, 63, 216, 219, 220, 227, 229, 230, 233, 239, 240, 241
Corwin, M., 56, 67
Cosbey, J. E., 415
Costello, J., 103
Cothran, D. J., 361
Coulter, G., 310
Council for Exceptional Children, 45, 128
Courtney, M., 53
Coutinho, M. J., 141, 415
Cox, C. J., 394
Cox, D., 220, 239
Cox, J., 427
Cox, S. G., 271
Coyne, M., 294
Crabtree, T., 33, 38, 42, 43
Crismond, D. P., 403
Crites, S. A., 393, 394
Crone, D. A., 389
Crosnoe, R., 72
Crozier, S., 397
Cullinan, D., 141, 142, 374
Cummins, J., 60–61
Curran, M., 68
Curwin, R. L., 365, 367, 379, 385
Cushing, L. S., 334
Cushman, K., 68

D'Agostino, J., 292, 309
Dahlquist, C. M., 141, 368, 393
Dalston, R. M., 171
Daniels, L. E., 415
Darch, C. B., 363
Darling-Hammond, L., 51, 65, 67, 70, 71, 72
Davidson, F., 73
Davies, D., 412, 413
Davis, B. L., 169
Day, M., 240
deBettencourt, L. U., 103, 330, 331, 347, 349
De Jong, M. D. T., 131
Delpit, L., 72
Delquadri, J., 221, 311
Deno, E., 31
Deno, S., 18, 90, 259
Deno, S. L., 275, 279
Denti, L., 91
Denton, C., 83, 310
Deschenes, C., 329, 330
Deshler, D. D., 86, 92, 93, 323, 330, 333, 337, 339, 340, 341, 343, 345, 347, 351
Dettmer, P., 227, 228
Deutchman, L., 363
de Valenzuela, J. S., 54
Dibenedetto, M. K., 259
Dickson, S., 258, 290
Dimino, J., 313
Dix, J., 87
Doernberg, N., 155
Doll, B., 132
Doolabh, A., 125
Doorlag, D. H., 57, 72, 73
Doubt, L., 196, 197
Dowling, N., 313
Downing, J., 437
Doyle, M. B., 21, 235, 236
Doyle, W., 361, 363
Drasgow, E., 40, 42
Dreyer, L., 309, 310
Duchnowski, A. J., 143, 144
Duckworth, S., 374
Duffy, H., 51, 65, 67, 70, 71, 72
Duhaney, D., 220
Duhaney, L. M. G., 34, 58
Dukes, C., 323
Dulaney, C., 309
Duncan, G. J., 56
Dunlap, G., 125, 160, 317
Dunlap, L., 317
Dunn, L. M., 31
DuPaul, G. J., 101, 103, 104, 106, 112, 427
Dwyer, K., 365, 368
Dyches, T., 62
Dyck, N., 227, 228
Dye, M., 243

Dymond, S. K., 16, 17, 22, 334, 418
Dynarski, M., 406, 423, 429

Ebeling, D., 329, 330
Eber, L., 365, 374
Eby, J., 143
Edelman, S. W., 21
Edmonds, M., 403, 415
Edrisinha, C., 158
Eggen, P., 11, 220, 288, 360
Ehri, L., 309, 310
Elbaum, B., 290, 292, 294, 309, 310, 312
Elf, N., 331, 349, 350
Elliott, J. L., 355
Elliott, S. N., 140
Ellis, E. S., 322, 328, 339, 340, 341, 343, 344, 345, 347, 351
Emerson, C., 53
Emery, D., 406, 423, 429
Emmer, E. T., 69, 379
Engelmann, O., 290
Engelmann, S., 288, 290, 296
Entwistle, D. R., 62
Epstein, M. H., 140, 143, 144, 173, 220
Ergul, C., 88
Erkanli, A., 103
Erwin, E. J., 33, 34
Escamilla, K., 60
Escolar, D. M., 192
Esquith, R., 67
Evertson, C. M., 69, 379

Fahsl, A., 317
Fairbanks, S., 314, 365
Falco, R., 160
Fantuzzo, J., 221, 292–293, 311, 312
Fanuele, D., 313
Fass, S., 52
Feil, E. G., 140
Fein, D., 154, 157
Feldman, K., 91
Ferguson, D. L., 35
Ferretti, R. P., 406, 423
Fessler, M., 87
Fields, J., 52
Filbert, M., 406, 423
Fishel, M., 220, 239
Fisher, J. B., 339
Fisher, M., 118
Fitch, C. L., 192
Fleming, G., 220, 239
Fletcher, J., 83, 86, 87, 90
Flippin, S. S., 45, 56
Florida Center for Reading Research, 295

Flowers, C., 334
Flugman, B., 309, 310
Foegen, A., 275, 279
Fombonne, E., 155
Foorman, B., 90, 294
Ford, A., 273
Ford, D. Y., 58, 66
Ford, M., 427
Foreman, P., 18, 118–119
Forness, S. R., 17, 140, 141
Forni, P. M., 364
Fowler, S., 243, 244, 245
Fox, L., 32, 124, 125, 126, 130, 160, 200, 243, 255, 333
Fox, N., 17, 18, 22
Francis, D., 83
Freeman, S., 18, 290, 291
French, N., 219, 235
Friedlander, B., 298, 315, 316
Friend, M., 66, 212, 215, 217, 227, 229, 230, 233, 235, 236
Frost, L., 161
Fuchs, D., 16, 17, 18, 33, 90, 221, 249, 279, 293, 296, 299, 300, 307, 311, 313, 314, 317
Fuchs, L. S., 16, 17, 33, 83, 86, 87, 90, 221, 249, 279, 293, 296, 299, 300, 311, 313, 314, 317
Fulk, B., 311
Fullerton, A., 160
Furrer, C., 72

Gable, R. A., 141, 393, 394
Gaffney, J. S., 327
Gagnon, J., 317, 318
Gaillard, W. D., 193
Gajria, M., 333, 349
Galea, J., 131
Gallaudet Research Institute, 179
Gallingane, C., 60, 67, 68, 69
Galucci, C., 18
Garand, J. D., 397
García, S. B., 62, 68, 70
Gardil, M. C., 138
Gardner, A., 295, 296
Gardner, J. E., 277
Gardner, R., 58
Garmezy, N., 64
Garrick Duhaney, L., 17, 18, 85, 291
Garrison, M., 385, 387, 391
Gartin, B., 33, 38, 42, 43
Gately, S. E., 332, 349, 350
Gavin, K., 292, 293
Gay, G., 51, 60, 62, 66, 67, 69, 70, 71, 73
Geen, R., 53

Geller, C., 300
Gerhardt, P. F., 162
Gersten, R., 290, 299, 300, 310, 313, 317
Giangreco, M. F., 21, 235, 236, 245
Gillam, R. B., 171
Gilson, C. L., 334, 418
Ginsberg, M. G., 51, 64, 68, 71
Ginsburg-Block, M., 221, 292–293, 311, 312
Givner, C. C., 361
Gladden, R., 53
Glaeser, B. C., 143
Goerge, R., 53
Goetz, L., 437
Goin, L. I., 425
Golden, N., 145
Goldman, S. K., 146
Goldstein, A. P., 145, 371
Gonzalez, N., 61, 68, 73
Good, T., 290, 291, 292, 293, 307, 308, 309, 328
Gorman, J. A., 331
Gottschalk, C., 220
Graham, S., 297, 298, 314, 315, 316, 318, 343
Gratcz, J., 217
Gray, C. A., 397
Greathouse, S., 62
Green, F., 131
Green, J., 154, 157
Greenfield, P. M., 58
Greenwood, C., 221, 292, 293, 311, 313
Gregory, A., 60
Grek, M., 293
Gresham, F. M., 83, 140, 143, 314
Griffin, C. C., 273
Griffin, H. C., 192
Griffin, L. W., 192
Grigal, M., 130
Gross, A., 309, 310
Grossen, B., 310
Gruwell, E., 67
Guarding, D., 314
Gudykunst, W. B., 58
Gun Han, K., 18
Gureasko-Moore, D., 103
Guth, C., 243, 244, 245
Gutiérrez, K., 59

Haager, D., 290
Haas, A., 169, 171, 173
Hadwin, J. A., 397, 398
Hagan-Burke, S., 343, 344
Hall, M., 130
Hall, M. C., 391
Hall, R. V., 391
Hall, S., 243

Hall, T. E., 406, 423
Hallahan, D. P., 9, 364
Halsey, H., 394
Hambacher, B., 67, 68
Hambacher, E., 60, 69
Hamlett, C. L., 279, 314
Hampton, E. O., 174
Handleman, J. S., 155
Handler, M. W., 138
Hanley, G. P., 125
Hanner, S., 290, 296
Hanson, M. J., 33
Hanushek, E., 286
Harden, B. J., 53
Hardman, M. L., 40, 45
Harniss, M., 220
Harper, G. F., 221, 275
Harriott, W., 69
Harris, D., 141
Harris, K. R., 297, 298, 314, 315, 316, 318, 343
Harris, S. L., 155
Harry, B., 59, 240
Hartshorne, N., 3, 4
Hasselbring, T. S., 403 425, 425
Hawken, L. S., 365, 368, 389
Haydt, L., 299
Hayes, L., 292, 310
Heaviside, S., 406, 423, 429
Hebbeler, K., 146
Heller, K. W., 194, 439
Helmstetter, E., 245
Henderson, K., 141
Henderson, M., 141
Hendrickson, J. M., 141
Henry, D., 85
Hershfeldt, P., 393
Hetzroni, O. E., 403, 415, 433
Hewes, G., 305
Hilton, A., 249
Hilvitz, P. B., 394
Hinshaw, S., 111
Hitchcock, C., 326
Hoffman, C. C., 393, 394
Hollins, E. R., 71
Holmes, D. L., 145, 162
Holubec, E., 307
Hong, E., 332, 355
Hoover, J. J., 45
Hoover, N., 292, 310
Hoppey, D., 14, 33, 35, 85, 86
Horn, L., 55
Horn, S., 286
Horner, R. H., 125, 365, 368, 389
Horney, M. A., 323
Horvath, B., 329, 330
Hosp, J., 82
Howard, E., 53
Howard, J., 293
Howell, K. W., 393, 394

Howland, J., 403
Howlin, P., 158
Hoy, W. K., 24
Huaqing Qi, C., 54
Hudson, P. J., 267, 300
Huerta, N. E., 33, 36
Hughes, C., 18, 22, 221, 243, 244, 245, 355
Hughes, C. A., 332, 333, 347, 351, 352, 355, 356, 406, 423
Hughes, E., 221, 243
Hughes, M., 290, 292, 294, 309, 310, 312
Huinker, D., 435
Humphry, R., 415
Hunt, P., 437
Hurley, E., 307
Hussar, W., 51, 211
Hutinger, P., 415
Hyman, S., 154, 155

Iacono, T., 131
Ichikawa, D., 53
Ideadata.org, 53, 54
Idol, L., 18
Institute for Children and Poverty, 53
Institute of Education Services, 295, 296
Institute of Medicine, 72
Irvine, J. J., 51, 64, 68
Iverson, S., 309, 310
Iwata, B. A., 125

Jackman, L. A., 365, 366, 371
Jackson, R., 326
Janney, R., 214, 231
Javitz, H., 406, 423, 429
Jayanthi, M., 220
Jenkins, J., 18
Jensen, W. R., 385, 386, 391
Jerman, P. L., 267
Jimerson, S., 84, 313
Jitendra, A., 299
Jitendra, A. K., 349
Johanson, J., 415
Johns, B. H., 367, 387
Johns, C., 383
Johnson, D. W., 291, 295, 296, 307
Johnson, G., 290, 296
Johnson, G. O., 31
Johnson, R., 291, 307
Johnson, S. M., 355
Johnston, L., 408, 409, 411, 412, 413, 414
Johnston, S., 415
Jolivette, K., 393
Jonassen, D. H., 403

Jones, E., 12
Jones, H., 21, 216, 219, 220,
    227, 229, 230, 233, 239,
    240, 241
Jones, L., 367, 368, 385, 387
Jones, R. R., 142
Jones, T., 71
Jones, V., 367, 368, 385, 387
Judd, W., 435
Justice, L. M., 169, 171, 172,
    173, 175

Kagan, S., 307, 308
Kain, J., 286
Kalyanpur, M., 240
Kame'enui, E., 92, 93
Kamens, M. W., 267
Kamman, M., 12, 211, 365
Kamps, D. M., 141, 313
Kampwirth, T., 214, 215, 228
Kanner, L., 154
Kaplan K–12 Learning
    Services, 296
Karapurkar, T., 155
Karlan, G. R., 415
Karns, K., 311
Katsiyannis, A., 44
Kauchak, D., 11, 220, 288, 360
Kauffman, J. M., 9, 16, 17, 33,
    42, 143, 364
Kavale, K. A., 17, 140, 145
Kearns, J. F., 130
Keating, T., 310
Keeler, G., 103
Kelchner, K., 131
Kennedy, A., 192
Kennedy, C. H., 143, 334
Kent-Walsh, J. E., 437
Kerig, P., 104, 105, 106
Kern, L., 143
Kern, R., 56, 67
Kessler, K., 124, 130
Keys, S. G., 368
Kilgore, K., 273
Kim, A., 403, 415
Kim, S. H., 122, 123, 125, 130
Kim, Y. Y., 58
Kincaid, D., 397, 398
King, B. S., 18, 118–119
King, K., 311
King-Sears, M. E., 329, 347,
    348, 368
Kissam, B., 323
Kissam, J., 92, 329, 330, 339
Kitano, M. K., 66
Klebanov, P. K., 56
Klein, C., 415
Kleinert, H. L., 130, 245
Kleinfeld, J., 68
Klin, A., 155

Kline, F., 86, 87, 88, 90
Klingner, J. K., 60, 290
Klug, B., 65
Knackendoffel, A., 227, 228
Knight, D., 260, 439
Knopf, J. H., 57
Knox-Quinn, C., 323
Kochhar-Bryant, C., 215, 220,
    225, 227, 229, 230, 239
Koegel, L. K., 125
Koegel, R. L., 125
Koenig, L., 364
Koh, M., 305
Kohl, F., 211
Kohler, K., 141
Kollins, S., 112
Korinek, L., 211, 214, 215, 216,
    229, 231, 232, 233
Kounin, J. S., 383
Kouzekanani, K., 290
Kramer, C., 373
Kremer-Sadlik, T., 155
Krug, D. A., 160
Kulinna, P. H., 361
Kutash, K., 143, 144
Kyle, D., 73

Ladders to Literacy, 296
Ladson-Billings, G., 68
Laflamme, M., 16, 17, 18, 22
Lamar-Dukes, T., 323
Lancioni, G. E., 158
Lanconi, G. E., 415
Lane, H. B., 292, 310
Lane, K. L., 143, 144, 217,
    231, 361
Lang, H. G., 183
Larsen, L., 297, 298, 315
Lathrop, M., 314
Lawrence-Brown, D., 66
Lazarus, B. D., 351
Leavell, A. G., 277, 278
Lee, H., 24
Lee, S., 18, 220
Legacy, J. M., 403, 404, 406, 429
Lehr, C. A., 389
Leighton, D., 131
Lembke, E. S., 275, 279
Lenz, B. K., 86, 92, 93, 323,
    328, 329, 330, 339, 340,
    341, 345, 347, 351
LePage, P., 51, 65, 67, 70, 71, 72
Lerner, J., 86, 87, 88, 90
Lesar, S., 21
Lesseliers, J., 131
Levin, J., 383
Levin, P., 56, 67
Levine, M., 162
Levine, P., 111
Levy, H. M., 271, 273

Lewis, R. B., 57, 72, 73
Lewis, T. J., 365, 368, 372
Liaupsin, C. J., 393
Light, J. C., 437
Lignugaris/Kraft, B., 292,
    311, 340
Linan-Thompson, S., 290
Lindamood, P., 296
Lindsay, J., 62
Linn, A., 157
Lipkewich, A., 296
Little, A., 217, 231
Little, J., 374
Lloyd, J., 16
Long, N., 383
Longaker, T., 162
Longwill, A., 245
Loos, L., 160
Lopez-Reyna, N., 56
Losen, D. J., 60
Loveland, K. A., 157
Loveland, T., 22
Lovett, T. C., 391
Luckey, A., 65
Luckner, J. L., 183
Lunsford, L. B., 355
Lyon, R., 83, 86, 87, 90
Lysaght, K., 331
Lytle, R. K., 267

Maag, J. W., 143, 175
Maas, E., 171
MacArthur, C. A., 403, 406, 415,
    423, 433
MacArthur, S., 298, 314,
    315, 316
Maccini, P., 317, 318, 406, 423
MacKenty, B., 427
MacMillan, D. L., 143
Macomber, J. E., 53
MacPhee, K., 18
Mactavish, J., 131
Madaus, J. W., 269
Madden, N. A., 18, 85, 221,
    305, 307
Madj, M., 17, 18
Maes, B., 124
Maheady, L., 112, 140, 142, 144,
    154, 156, 158, 221, 275
Mahoney, M., 56, 67
Maier, J., 437
Mainzer, R., 44
Mallette, B., 221, 275
Mamlin, N., 267
Mann, D., 429
Manset, G., 18
Marks, D., 60
Marks, L. J., 433, 434
Marquis, J. G., 125
Marra, R. M., 403

Marshall, L. H., 267
Marston, D., 18
Martin, J. E., 267
Martin, S., 69
Martinez, R. S., 45
Martins, M. P., 155
Marzano, R., 292, 307
Mason, L. H., 298, 315, 316, 343
Masten, A. S., 64
Masterson, C., 17
Mastropieri, M. A., 21, 22, 45,
    92, 93, 217, 218, 332,
    347, 348
Mathes, P., 293, 310
Mathur, S. R., 145
Matthews, W., 394
Mattison, R. E., 143
Matuszny, R., 239, 240
Maxson, L. M., 267
Mazurenko, R., 296
McAtee, M. L., 125
McCall, J., 221, 245
McColl, M. A., 196, 197
McComas, J., 16, 17, 18, 22
McConnell, M. E., 394
McConnell, S. R., 145
McCord, B. E., 125
McDonald, M., 51, 65, 67, 70,
    71, 72
McDuffie, K., 217, 218
McGinnis, E., 145, 371
McIntyre, E., 73
McLane, K., 326
McLaughlin, D. M., 125
McLaughlin, M., 211
McLaughlin, V., 18, 85, 211,
    214, 215, 216, 229, 231,
    232, 233
McLean, M., 121
McLeskey, J., 4, 14, 16, 17, 18,
    22, 31, 33, 35, 45, 85,
    86, 182, 211, 212, 215,
    216, 218, 220, 225, 291,
    326, 364, 394
McMahan, G. A., 431
McMaster, K., 293, 307, 311
McPartland, J., 155
McTighe, J., 92
Meadows, N. B., 145
Means, B., 406, 423, 429
Mehta-Parekh, H., 271
Meister, C., 327
Méndez Pérez, A., 62
Mendler, A. N., 365, 367,
    379, 385
Menlove, R. R., 267
Mercer, C. D., 86, 87, 347, 348
Mesibov, G. B., 163
Messina, C. M., 417
Messina, J. J., 417
Metz, D. E., 169, 171, 173

Metzler, C. A., 131
Meyer, A., 326
Meyer, D. K., 68, 69
Meyer, L. H., 118
Michaels, C., 218
Midgley, C., 68, 69
Miller, D. N., 138
Miller, K., 73
Miller, S., 55, 300
Miller, T., 292, 311, 312
Milner, H. R., 66
Mirenda, P., 437
Misra, S., 45
Mittag, K. C., 435
Modrek, S., 111
Moll, L. C., 51, 61, 65, 67, 68, 70, 71, 72, 73
Monaghan, M. C., 310
Monda-Amaya, L., 18
Monroe, B. W., 343
Montague, M., 300, 317, 318
Montgomery, D. J., 433, 434
Montgomery, E. J., 415
Moody, S., 290, 292, 294, 309, 310, 312
Moon, S., 130
Mooney, J. F., 67, 329
Moore, G., 73
Moore-Brown, B., 175
More, C., 397
Morgan, J., 210
Morgan, T., 317
Morrison, A. P., 18, 119
Morrison, G. M., 64, 144
Morse, W., 383
Morsink, C., 21, 216, 219, 220, 227, 229, 230, 233, 239, 240, 241
Moses, H., 43
Mostert, M. P., 145, 364
Moultrie, R., 217, 231
Muir, S., 183
Mulder, M., 40
Muller, E., 437
Multimodal Treatment Study of ADHD (MTA) Cooperative Group, 112
Munk, D. D., 260, 261, 281
Murdick, N., 33, 38, 42, 43
Murphy, C., 155
Murphy, J., 292, 309
Murphy, R., 406, 423, 429
Murray, J., 53
Mustillo, S., 103
Myers, D., 365

Nagle, K., 211
National Center for Education Statistics, 11, 51, 52, 53, 54

National Center for Hearing Assessment and Management, 178
National Center on Student Progress Monitoring, 275
National Center to Improve Practice, 409
National Commission on Teaching and America's Future, 56
National Council for Accreditation in Teacher Education, 213
National Council of Teachers of Mathematics, 435
National Council on Disability, 44
National Education Association, 56, 72
National Institute for Direct Instruction, 275
National Institute for Rehabilitation Engineering, 439
National Institute of Child Health and Human Development, 406, 423
National Reading Panel, 294
National Research Council, 72, 156, 158, 161
National Technical Assistance Consortium for Children and Young Adults Who Are Deaf-Blind, 179, 180
Neel, R. S., 145
Neff, D., 61
Nellis, L. M., 45
Nelson, C. M., 393
Nelson, J. R., 173, 220, 365, 366
Nelson, R., 387
Neubert, D. A., 130
Nevin, A., 218, 233
Newcomer, P. L., 143
Newman, L., 146, 161
Newman, R. G., 383
Nieto, S., 57
Nirje, B., 32
Niswander, V., 334, 418
Nolan, J., 383
North Carolina State Board of Education, 126
Novak, T., 406, 423, 429
Nuebert, D. A., 146
Nye, B., 62

Oakes, J., 291
Obiakor, F. E., 62
Ochs, E., 155
Oetzel, J. G., 58
Okey, S., 374
Okolo, C. M., 406, 423

Oliva, D., 415
Ollendick, T. H., 143
Olley, G. J., 159
Olson, L. S., 44, 62
Olson, M. M., 281
O'Reilly, M., 158
O'Reilly, M. F., 415
Orkwis, R., 326
Ortiz, A. A., 62, 68, 70
Ortiz-Lienemann, T., 349
O'Shea, D. J., 37, 253–254, 327, 363, 364, 368, 372, 373, 379, 380, 385
O'Shea, L. J., 37, 253–254, 327, 363, 364, 368, 372, 373, 379, 380, 385
Osher, D., 144, 365, 368
Oswald, D. P., 141
Ota, K. R., 427
Owens, R. E., 169, 171, 173

Pacchiano, D., 18
Paine, S. C., 363
Palmer, S., 132, 220, 412
Parent, W., 412
Parette, H. P., 407, 431, 432
Paris, S. G., 327
Park, H., 220, 239
Park, K. L., 368, 393
Park, M., 54
Pascoe, S., 18, 118–119
Patrick, H., 68, 69
Patterson, G. R., 142
Patton, J. J., 45
Patton, J. M., 122, 123, 125, 130
Paul, R., 160
Pavri, S., 18
Pearson, N., 143
Peck, C., 18, 245
Pederson-Seelye, V. A., 379
Pelham, W., 108
Pellegrino, L., 192
Pelo, A., 73
Peña, E. D., 169
Penuel, W., 406, 423, 429
Peter, K., 55
Peters, I., 162
Peterson-Karlan, G. R., 407, 431
Petry, K., 124
Pfiffner, L., 106
Pickering, D., 292, 307
Pierce, C. D., 144
Piers, E., 141
Pierson, M. R., 143, 217, 231, 361
Pinckney, E., 21
Pinnell, G., 309
Pivik, J., 16, 17, 18, 22
Plank, D. R., 355
PLATO Learning, 427, 428

Poe, V., 427
Pogoloff, S. M., 267
Pollitt, E., 56
Pollock, J., 292, 307
Polloway, E., 217
Polsgrove, L., 145, 373
Porte, L., 332
Pottie, C., 131
Powell, S., 311
Powell-Smith, K. A., 397, 398
Power, T., 103
Powers, F., 162
Prendergast, K. A., 45
President's Committee on Mental Retardation, 121
Presley, J., 243, 244, 245
Pressley, M., 294
Pugalee, D., 334
Pullen, P. C., 86, 87, 292, 310
Putnam, J., 292, 328
Putnam, M. L., 337
Pysh, M., 217, 231

Quenneville, J., 433
Quinn, M. M., 393, 394

Rademacher, J. E., 379
Radicci, J., 363
Ramirez, L., 220, 239
Ramsey, E., 365, 368
Ranie, L., 402
Rashotte, C., 18, 313
Raskind, M. H., 433
Ravet, J., 72
Rawlinson, D., 374
Rawlinson, R., 374
Rea, P., 18, 85
Reavis, H. K., 385, 386, 391
Reed, P., 408, 411, 431
Reed, V. A., 174
Regualos, R., 361
Reid, D. K., 271
Reid, J. B., 142
Reid, R., 144, 349
Reiff, M., 102, 103, 104, 106, 108, 109, 110, 111, 220
Reilly, M., 415
Rentz, T., 14, 33, 35, 85, 86
Renzaglia, A., 334, 418
Reschly, A. L., 279
Reschly, D., 82, 83, 295, 313
Rescorla, L., 140
Reutzel, R., 290, 291, 294
Reynolds, M., 32
Rhode, G., 385, 386, 391
Rice, C., 155
Richards, S. B., 122, 123, 131
Richert, A., 51, 65, 67, 70, 71, 72
Rickelman, R. J., 334

Riedel, T., 16
Riggs, C., 235, 236, 237
Ritter, S., 141
Ritzman, M. J., 175
Rivers, J., 286
Rivkin, S., 286
Roberts, G., 90, 313, 314
Robertson, E., 217, 231
Robertson, J., 305
Robin, D. A., 171
Robins, D., 154, 157
Roblee, K., 383
Rock, E., 87
Roelvink, L., 131
Rogan, J., 328
Rogers, D., 30
Rogers, E. L., 30
Rogers, L., 68
Rogoff, B., 59
Rohrbeck, C., 221, 292–293, 311, 312
Rojewski, J. W., 327
Rooney, K., 55
Rorschach, H., 141
Rose, D., 326
Rose, T., 361
Rosellini, L. C., 363
Rosenberg, M. S., 37, 45, 112, 140, 142, 144, 154, 156, 158, 182, 211, 220, 253–254, 327, 363, 364, 365, 366, 368, 371, 372, 373, 379, 380, 385, 393, 394
Rosenfeld, J. S., 42
Rosenshine, B., 288, 289, 327
Rosenstein, A., 334, 418
Ross, D. D., 12, 60, 67, 68, 69, 211, 365
Rothstein, R., 62
Rothstein-Fisch, C., 58
Ruby, M., 294
Ruef, M. B., 125
Ruggles, B., 310
Ruhl, K. L., 333
Russell, D., 16, 17, 22
Rutherford, R. B., 393, 394
Rutter, M., 156, 157
Ryan, A., 394
Ryan, K. A., 125
Ryndak, D. L., 18, 119

Sabornie, E. J., 142, 330, 331, 347, 349
Sacks, G., 349
Safran, J. S., 156, 162, 217
Safran, S., 217
Sailor, W., 125
Saint-Laurent, L., 273

Sale, P., 415
Salend, S. J., 17, 18, 34, 58, 85, 220, 291, 333
Salmento, M., 299
Sanders, W., 286
Sands, D. J., 132
Sanford, J. P., 69
Sanger, D., 175
Sansoti, F. J., 397, 398
Santoro, L. E., 429
Santos, M., 174
Sas, J. C., 332, 355
Sas, M., 332, 355
Sawka, K., 138
Scanlon, D., 313
Scheffler, R., 111
Schell, J. W., 327
Scheurich, J. J., 65
Schirmer, B. R., 180
Schleien, S., 131
Schneck, C., 313
Scholastic, Inc., 425
Schrader, C., 162
Schrepferman, L. M., 143
Schroll, K., 24
Schumaker, J. B., 92, 93, 330, 333, 339, 343
Schumm, J. S., 66, 92, 229, 277, 278, 324, 325
Schwartz, I. S., 18, 174
Schwartz, M., 131
Schwarz, P. A., 273
Schweder, W., 277
Scott, G. S., 333
Scott, K., 87
Scott, T. M., 141, 365, 374, 393
Scruggs, T. E., 21, 22, 45, 92, 93, 217, 218, 332, 347, 348
Sears, S., 18
Seethaler, P., 314
Semmel, M., 18, 21
Severson, H. H., 140
Shakeshaft, C., 429
Shapera, N. R., 175
Shapiro, C., 103, 112
Shapiro, D. A., 171
Shapiro, E. S., 138
Sharma, J. M., 140
Shaw, S. F., 269
Shaw-Hegwer, J., 162
Shea, V., 163
Sheridan, S. M., 145
Shippen, M. E., 393, 394
Shiraga, B., 124, 130
Shores, C., 84
Shrieber, B., 403, 415, 433
Shriner, J. G., 44
Shukla, S., 143
Siebelink, E. M., 131

Siegel, L. S., 87
Sigafoos, J., 158
Sikes, J., 291, 328
Silva, M., 260, 261, 281
Simmons, A., 141
Simmons, D., 92, 93
Simonsen, B., 365
Simpson, R. G., 393, 394
Simpson, R. L., 154, 160, 161
Sinclair, M. R., 389
Sindelar, P. T., 45, 112, 140, 142, 144, 154, 156, 158, 273, 347, 348
Singh, N. N., 415
Sirota, K. G., 155
Sitlington, P. L., 146
Skiba, R., 141
Skinner, D., 62, 63
Skinner, E., 72
Skinner, M., 63
Skla, L. L., 65
Slavin, R. E., 18, 85, 221, 291, 305, 307, 308, 313, 328
Small, S., 313
Smith, A. W., 145, 373
Smith, B., 103, 112
Smith, C., 365, 374
Smith, C. E., 125
Smith, C. S., 21
Smith, K., 300
Smith, S., 412
Smith, T. E. C., 43
Smithgall, C., 53
Smith-Myles, B., 154, 157, 160, 161
Smith-Rex, S., 374
Smith-Thomas, A., 217
Snapp, M., 291, 328
Snell, M., 214, 231
Snow, C. E., 425
Snyder, E., 22
Snyder, J., 143
So, T. H., 22
Sobsey, D., 194
Solomon, O., 155
Sommerstein, L., 18, 119
Sood, S., 349
Soodak, L. C., 33, 34
Soto, G., 437
Southern, T., 12
Spagna, M., 18
Sparling, J. W., 415
Sperling, R. A., 258, 259, 277
Spicer, L., 174
Spilker, A., 175
Spina Bifida Association, 195
Spooner, F., 128, 196, 333
Sprague, J. R., 329, 330, 360
Sprick, M., 385, 387, 391
Sprick, R., 385, 387, 391
SRA/McGraw Hill, 313

Stainback, S., 32
Stainback, W., 32
Stambaugh, T., 66
Stanne, M., 307
Staub, D., 18
Stecker, P. M., 275, 279
Steele, M. M., 331, 349
Steely, D., 290
Stenhoff, D., 292, 311, 340
Stephan, C., 291, 328
Stevens, K. D., 145
Stevens, R., 288, 289
Stock, S., 412, 413
Stone, W. L., 154
Stoneburner, R., 415
Stormont, M., 64
Storti, C., 58
Stowe, M. J., 33, 36
Stronge, J. H., 23
Stropes, J., 143
Stump, C. S., 198
Sugai, G., 142, 314, 365, 368, 372, 374
Sumarah, J., 131
Sumi, W. C., 143, 144
Sun, Y., 53
Suritsky, S. K., 332, 351, 352
Sussex, W., 406, 423, 429
Suter, D., 267
Swanson, E. A., 403, 415
Swanson, K., 22
Sweda, J., 347
Sweeney, K., 429

Taal, E., 131
Tapia, Y., 293
Tate, W. F., 60
Taylor, R., 122, 123
Taylor-Greene, S., 385
Taymans, J., 92, 329, 330, 339
Terrill, M. C., 348
Terry, B., 292, 293
Tesi Rocha, A. C., 192
Texas School for the Blind and Visually Impaired, 183
TherapyTimes, 437
Thomas, C., 21, 216, 219, 220, 227, 229, 230, 233, 239, 240, 241
Thompson, A., 293, 311
Thorson, S., 364
Thousand, J., 218, 233
Thuppal, M., 194
Thurlow, M. L., 355
Thurston, L., 227, 228
Tincani, M. J., 397
Ting-Toomey, S., 58
Tobin, K. E., 154, 155
Tobin, T., 142
Todis, B., 145, 415, 431

Tomlinson, C. A., 24, 253, 271
Tomlinson-Clarke, S., 68
Toplis, R., 397, 398
Torgesen, J., 18, 82, 293, 294, 313
Tosi, L. L., 192
Traxler, C. B., 180
Trela, K., 128, 196
Trenholm, S., 361
Trent, S. C., 364
Troia, G. A., 343
Trumbull, E., 58
Tschannen-Moran, M., 24
Tulbert, B., 63
Tunali-Kotoski, B., 157
Tunmer, W., 309, 310
Turnbull, A. P., 33, 125, 220
Turnbull, H. R., 30, 33, 36
Turner, J., 68, 69
Tyler, N. C., 45, 56

University of Kansas, 275
University of Sheffield, 184
Unok Marks, S., 162
Unsworth, L., 291
U.S. Census Bureau, 11, 51
U.S. Department of Education, 9, 12, 19, 20, 34, 35, 36, 41, 56, 83, 84–85, 104, 122, 126, 139, 155, 172, 176, 177, 178, 179, 194, 195
U.S. Department of Education, Office for Civil Rights, 251, 269
U.S. Department of Health and Human Services, 111
Utley, C., 292, 293

Vadasy, P., 235, 236
Van Acker, R., 141

VanDeHeyden, A., 84, 313
Van Garderen, D., 70
Van Hove, G., 131
Van Reusen, A. K., 435
VanTassel-Baska, J., 66
Vaughn, S., 66, 90, 92, 144, 229, 277, 278, 290, 292, 294, 309, 310, 312, 313, 314, 324, 325, 403, 415
Vellutino, F., 313
Villa, R., 218, 233
Vittetoe, J. O., 360
Voeller, K., 313
Volkmar, F. R., 155, 157
Voltz, D. L., 273
Vygotsky, L. S., 327

Wadsworth, D. E. D., 260, 439
Wagner, M. M., 143, 144, 146
Wagner, R., 313
Wahl, M., 314
Wakeman, S. Y., 128, 196, 334
Walberg, H., 32
Wald, J., 60
Waldron, N., 4, 17, 18, 21, 22, 85, 212, 215, 216, 218, 225, 291, 326
Walker, H. M., 140, 143, 145, 360, 361, 365, 368
Walker, J. E., 143, 145
Wallace, T., 235
Walther-Thomas, C., 18, 85, 211, 214, 215, 216, 229, 231, 232, 233
Wang, M., 32
Wanzek, J., 258, 403, 415
Ware, F., 68
Warger, C., 317
Webb, R. B., 273
Wehby, J., 355

Wehmeyer, M. L., 128, 131, 132, 220, 334, 412, 413
Weiner, J., 88
Weinstein, C., 68
Weinstein, R., 71
Weinstein, S., 193
Weintraub, S. J., 33
Weishaar, M. K., 351, 353
Weisner, T., 62
Wenar, C., 104, 105, 106
Werts, M. G., 22, 267
Westling, D. L., 32, 124, 126, 130, 182, 200, 211, 220, 243, 255, 333, 364, 394
Wexler, J., 403, 415
Whitbread, K., 220, 239
White, J. M., 258
White, R., 365
Whitfield, P., 65
Whitney, D. W., 174
Wiggins, G., 92
Wilcoxen, A., 18
Wilder, L. K., 62
Wilkins, S., 65
Will, M., 32, 85
Willard-Holt, C., 195
Williams, B., 63, 65, 70, 71, 211, 214, 215, 216, 229, 231, 232, 233
Williams, C., 221, 243, 244, 245
Williams, N., 175
Williams, S. C., 415
Williamson, P., 14, 33, 35, 85, 86
Wilson, B. L., 63, 65, 69, 70, 71
Wilson, G., 218
Wilson, R. J., 112, 140, 142, 144, 154, 156, 158
Wingerden, C., 53
Winograd, P., 327
Winton, P., 33

Wisconsin Assistive Technology Initiative, 408
Wissick, C. A., 277
Wittaker, C., 70
Wittrock, M. C., 289
Wolery, M., 22
Wolfensberger, W., 32
Wolff, J. C., 143
Wolffe, K., 184
Wolff Heller, K., 431
Wolgemuth, J. R., 329
Wood, J. W., 331, 349
Woodruff, A. L., 415
Woolfolk Hoy, A., 24
Worsham, M., 379
Wrightslaw, 269
Wu, T., 141

Yazdian, L., 311
Yeargin-Allsopp, M., 155
Yell, M. L., 30, 40, 42, 44
Yoo, S., 18
Ysseldyke, J. E., 17, 18, 22, 355
Yzquierdo, Z., 56

Zeichner, K., 51, 65, 67, 70, 71, 72
Zentall, S., 110, 111
Ziegler, D., 44
Zigmond, N., 18
Zimmerman, B. J., 259
Zipoli, R., 294

Subject Index

AAC. *See* Augmentative/alternative communication (AAC)

AAIDD (American Association on Intellectual and Developmental Disabilities), 119–120

ABA (applied behavior analysis), 160–161, 251, 441

Ability grouping
defined, 441
flexible, 256, 275
mixed-, 291–292, 304, 307–308
as tracking strategy, 290–291, 304, 305–306

ABLEDATA, 414

Absences, 196, 198

Absence seizure, 193, 441

Academic and cognitive performance
attention-deficit/hyperactivity disorder, 106
autism spectrum disorders, 158–159
communication disorders, 173
diversity and, 54–56
emotional and behavioral disabilities, 143–144
intellectual disabilities, 123–124
learning disabilities, 86–87
physical disabilities, health impairments, and multiple disabilities, 195–196
sensory impairments, 179–180

Academic content instruction, planning for, 256, 257, 266, 277–278

Academic success strategies
communication disorders, 174, 175
intellectual disabilities, 126, 128, 129–130
physical disabilities, health impairments, and multiple disabilities, 197–199, 200–201, 202–203
sensory impairments, 181–182, 183–184

Academy of Reading, 405

Access to Math, 414

Accommodations, 254, 332, 355, 441

Accountability, 41, 211, 212

Achievement gap, 54–56

Acoustical amplification system, 182, 441

ADA (Americans with Disabilities Act), 38, 43, 441

Adaptations, 260, 261, 266, 281–282, 330

Additions, speech, 171

Additive approach to culturally responsive teaching, 73

Adequate yearly progress (AYP), 41, 44, 441

ADHD. *See* Attention-deficit/hyperactivity disorder (ADHD)

African Americans
culturally responsive teaching, 72, 73
demographics, 51
discipline referrals, 60
emotional and behavioral disabilities, 141
supports for families, 63

Agenda books, 332–333

Aggression, 142, 441

Agitation, signs of, 387

Alphabetics, 295, 296

Alpha Talker II, 416

Alternate assessments, 44, 271, 441

Alternative grouping strategies, 290–292, 441

Alternative routes to certification, 45, 441

American Academy of Pediatrics, 102, 110

American Association on Intellectual and Developmental Disabilities (AAIDD), 119–120

Americans with Disabilities Act (ADA), 38, 43, 441

Amphetamines, 111, 441

And Still We Rise (Corwin), 56

Animals in the classroom, 262

ANSWER strategy, 356

Antiseptic bouncing, 384

Anxiety, 143, 441

Applied behavior analysis (ABA), 160–161, 251, 441

Articulation disorders. *See* Phonological and articulation disorders

Art therapists, 19

ASD. *See* Autism spectrum disorders (ASD)

Asperger's disorder. *See also* Autism spectrum disorders (ASD)
academic instruction, 159
age of onset, 158
characteristics, 152, 154
communication, 156
defined, 441
language instruction, 160
ritualistic behavior, 157
social-behavioral functioning, 160
social interactions, 157

Assessment. *See also* Functional behavioral assessment (FBA)
alternate, 44, 271, 441
formative, 272
nondiscriminatory, 37
procedures of speech-language pathologists, 170–171
self-, 373

Assignment management, 332–333

Assistive technology (AT), 407–415
defined, 403, 441
effectiveness of, 415
intellectual disabilities and, 124
planning basic skills instruction, 256

Assistive technology devices. *See also* Augmentative/alternative communication (AAC)
for daily living, 414–415, 422, 439–440
defined, 407, 441
math, 409, 414, 422, 435–436
personal digital assistants, 412–414
for physical disabilities, health impairments, and multiple disabilities, 196, 198
reading, 408, 410–411
selecting, 422, 431–432
to support academic activities, 408–409
writing and spelling, 408–409, 412, 413, 422, 433–434

Assistive technology services, 196, 407, 408, 441

Asthma, 193, 196, 197, 199, 441

AT. *See* Assistive technology (AT)

Ataxia, 192, 441

Athetosis, 192, 441

Atkins, Sue, 285

Attendance, 30

Attention, ensuring, 110–111

Attentional problems, and learning disabilities, 87

Attention-deficit/hyperactivity disorder (ADHD), 96–114
causes, 101
characteristics, 101, 104–106
co-existing conditions, 102, 104
defined, 99–100, 441
identifying, 100, 101, 102–103
instructing students with, 106–111

Attention-deficit/hyperactivity disorder
    (ADHD) *(continued)*
  learning disabilities and, 87
  medication for, 111–112
  outcomes, 101
  overview, 101
  perspectives on, 97–98
  prevalence, 101, 103–104
  Section 504 of the Rehabilitation Act, 12,
      101, 103, 104
  service delivery, 101, 104
  standards, 114
Attention-seeking behavior, 395
Attitudes
  positive teacher, 23–24
  toward inclusion, 21–22
Augmentative/alternative communication
    (AAC)
  assistive technology, 409, 411–412
  autism spectrum disorders, 161
  communication disorders, 175
  defined, 441
  examples, 416–417
  physical disabilities, health impairments,
      and multiple disabilities, 201
  supporting students using, 422, 437–438
Autism spectrum disorders (ASD), 150–164
  age of onset, 157–158
  causes, 153
  characteristics, 153, 156–158
  defined, 10, 153–154, 441
  identifying, 153, 154–155
  instructing students with, 158–163
  intellectual functioning, 158
  outcomes, 153
  overview, 153
  perspectives on, 151–152
  prevalence, 153, 155
  self-injurious behavior and, 158
  service delivery, 153, 155–156
  standards, 164
Autistic disorder, 154, 441. *See also* Autism
    spectrum disorders (ASD)
Autoimmune disease, 193, 441
Avoidance-of-failure behavior, 395
AWARE note-taking strategy, 352
AYP (adequate yearly progress), 41, 44, 441

Backup reinforcers, 144–145
Balanced instruction, 298, 441
Basic skills instruction, 255–256, 266,
    275–276
Behavioral contracts, 378, 391–392
Behavioral deficits, 361–362
Behavioral disabilities. *See* Emotional and
    behavioral disabilities (EBD)
Behavioral excesses, 361
Behavior intervention plan (BIP)
  classroom management, 368, 371–373,
      378, 393, 394

defined, 442
  intellectual disabilities and, 125
  planning, 251
Behavior management plans, 368, 369–371
Behavior management readiness, 362–365
Behavior performance and social skills
  communication disorders, 173
  physical disabilities, health impairments,
      and multiple disabilities, 196–197
  sensory impairments, 180
Behavior problems
  attention-deficit/hyperactivity disorder
      and, 105–106
  externalizing, 142–143, 443
  intellectual disabilities and, 125, 129
  internalizing, 143, 444
Behavior rating scales, 140
Behavior specialists, 251
Big:Calc, 414
Big ideas, 92
Bilingualism, 60–62, 442
BIP. *See* Behavior intervention plan (BIP)
Blacks. *See* African Americans
Blind, 177, 442
Blindness. *See also* Sensory disabilities; Visual
      impairment
  academic and cognitive performance, 180
  academic success strategies, 182, 184
  defined, 10, 176, 442
  legal blindness, 177, 444
  overview, 177
  prevalence, 178, 179
  social success strategies, 183
Bolinger, Debra, 401, 403, 424
Bone tuberculosis, 191, 442
Boys
  attention-deficit/hyperactivity disorder, 103
  autism spectrum disorders, 155
  emotional and behavioral disabilities, 141
Brain abnormalities, 101
Brain injury, 101
Brainstorming, 231
Brown v. Board of Education (1954), 33
Buckley, Melanie, 49–50, 65, 83
Building-based support teams, 212, 217, 442

Calculators, 414, 422, 435–436
Cali's Geo Tools, 427
Care and caring, 23, 67–70, 364–365
Carl D. Perkins Vocational and Technology
      Education Act, 38
Casserta, Krista, 29–30
Casserta, Sarita, 29–30, 45
CAST (Center for Applied Special
      Technology), 258
CAST eReader, 411, 418
CAST Universal Design for Learning (UDL)
      Book Builder, 258, 419
CAST Universal Design for Learning (UDL)
      Lesson Builder, 419

CBM. *See* Curriculum-based measurement
      (CBM)
Center for Applied Special Technology
      (CAST), 258
Centers for Disease Control and Prevention,
      199, 201
Central auditory processing disorder, 176, 442
Cerebral palsy
  academic and cognitive performance, 195
  classroom considerations, 199
  defined, 442
  early years, 121
  including students with, 189, 197
  as physical disability, 191
  speech, 201
  types, 192
Certification, alternative routes to, 45, 441
Charleston County School District, 426
Check-in, connect, and check-out systems,
      378, 389–390
Chicora Elementary School (Charleston
      County School District), 426
Child Find services, 178, 442
Childhood disintegrative disorder, 153, 442.
    See also Autism spectrum disorders
      (ASD)
Choral responding, 91
Chromosomal anomalies, 120, 121, 442
Civility, 364
Civil rights movement, 33, 442
Classroom arrangement, 260–262, 362–363
Classroom management, 358–398
  behavioral contracts, 378, 391–392
  behavior intervention plans, 368,
      371–373, 378, 393, 394
  behavior management readiness, 362–365
  check-in, connect, and check-out systems,
      378, 389–390
  consequences, 367, 378, 385–386
  diffusing confrontations, 367, 378,
      387–388
  functional behavioral assessment, 368,
      378, 393, 394
  function-based thinking, 378, 393–394
  perspectives on, 359–360
  rules and procedures, 365, 378, 379–381
  social stories, 378, 397–398
  standards, 375
  strategies, 377–398
  student behavior overview, 361–362
  surface management techniques, 367, 378,
      383–384
  targeted interventions, 365, 368, 378,
      389–392
  tiered management, 365–374
  universal inclusive practices and supports,
      365, 367–368, 369–371
  wraparound supports, 365, 373–374
Classwide peer tutoring (CWPT), 256,
      275–276, 293
Clifford, Joe, 4, 6–7, 9, 23, 25

Closed captioning, 326

Clubfoot, 191, 442

Co-existing conditions, 102, 104, 442

Cognitive performance. *See* Academic and cognitive performance

Cognitive skill deficits, 87, 124–125, 143

Cognitive strategy instruction, 304, 317–318

Cognitive Tutor Algebra, 406

Collaboration, 208–245

   collaborative consultation, 172, 218–220, 442

   collaborative teams, 216–217

   communication skills and, 226, 229–230

   components, 212, 226, 227–228

   content-area instruction and, 325–326

   co-teaching, 213–214, 217–218, 226, 233–234

   defined, 211, 442

   described, 211–213

   dispositions needed for, 213–215

   factors influencing, 210–211

   guidelines, 225

   home-school, 220, 226, 239–241

   intellectual disabilities and, 127

   with paraeducators, 219, 226, 235–237

   peer buddies, 221, 226, 243–245

   perspectives on, 209–210

   roles in inclusive schools, 212, 216–220, 227

   skills needed, 215–216

   as special education characteristic, 11

   with speech-language pathologists, 168, 174

   standards, 223

   strategies, 225–245

   students in, 220–221

   teacher assistance teams, 217, 226, 231–232

Collaborative consultation, 172, 218–220, 442

Collaborative teams, 216–217

Collectivist cultures, 58, 442

Communicable diseases, 42, 43

Communication. *See also* Augmentative/alternative communication (AAC)

   autism spectrum disorders and, 156

   collaboration and, 226, 229–230

   cultural dimensions, 59

   with paraeducators, 236

Communication disorders, 167–176

   causes, 170

   characteristics, 170, 173

   defined, 169, 442

   identifying, 169–171, 170

   instructing students with, 174–176

   outcomes, 170

   overview, 170

   perspectives on, 167–168

   prevalence, 170, 172

   service delivery, 170, 172

   standards, 186

   types, 169, 171

Complementary teaching, 233

Comprehension, 294, 295, 296, 442

Compulsory school attendance exceptions, 30

Concept diagrams, 93, 329–330, 331

Conductive hearing loss, 176, 442

Confidentiality, 40, 268

Conflict management, 215–216

Confrontations, diffusing, 367, 378, 387–388

Congenital hip dislocations (dysplasia), 193, 442

Consequences, 367, 378, 385–386

Consultants, 212, 442

Content-area instruction, 320–356

   autism spectrum disorders and, 161–162

   content-area reading, 331–332, 338, 349–350

   content enhancements, 329–330, 331, 338, 339–341

   content learning differences, 323–324

   content survival strategies, 330–333

   cooperative learning, 257, 278, 328

   direct instruction, 327

   expository writing, 338, 343–345

   guided discovery learning, 327

   learning strategies, 328–329

   mnemonic strategies, 338, 347–348

   models and approaches, 326–330

   note taking, 332, 338, 351–353

   perspectives on, 321–322

   prerequisites for, 324–326

   severe disabilities and, 333–334

   standards, 336

   strategies, 337–356

   test taking, 332, 338, 355–356

   time and assignment management, 332–333

   understanding curriculum, 324–325

   unit and lesson organizers, 338, 339–341

   universal design for learning, 326, 334

   working collaboratively, 325–326

Content disorders, 171

Content enhancements, 329–330, 331, 338, 339–341, 442. *See also* Mnemonic devices

Content maps, 92–93, 442

Contingencies, 145

Continuum of service, 15–16, 34–35, 442. *See also* Service delivery

Contribution approach to culturally responsive teaching, 73

Cooperative learning

   content-area instruction, 257, 278, 328

   defined, 442

   elementary instruction, 291–292, 304, 307–308

Coordinators, in behavior education programs, 389

Core instruction, 89–90, 442

Corrective Reading, 290, 296

Co-teaching

   collaboration, 213–214, 217–218, 226, 233–234

   content-area instruction, 325–326

   defined, 442

Co:Writer, 413

Crisis situations, 367, 378, 387–388

Cube activities, 272

Cues, 110

Culturally and linguistically diverse, 11–12, 56, 442

Culturally responsive classroom management, 64, 442

Culturally responsive teaching, 64–74

   care, 67–70, 364–365

   curriculum, 71–74

   defined, 442

   expectations, 70–71

   Heritage High School, 49–50

   pedagogy, 64–67

   resilience and motivation, 64

   respect, 364

   vignette, 70–71

Cultural perspectives on education, 59

Culture

   defined, 57–58, 442

   disability and, 62–63

   establishing connections, 57

   ethnicity and, 60

   impact on education, 58–59

   language and, 60–62

   mediation of school experience, 62–63

   norms and school, 58

   student outcomes and, 56–57

Curriculum

   content-area instruction, 324–325, 334

   in culturally responsive teaching, 71–74

   differentiated instruction and, 255

   learning disabilities and, 92–93

   life skills, 198

   physical disabilities, health impairments, and multiple disabilities and, 198

   severe disabilities, 334

   in special education, 9, 11

   substitute, 330

Curriculum-based measurement (CBM)

   defined, 442

   guidelines for using, 266, 279–280

   learning disabilities and, 90

   monitoring student progress with, 259–260, 276

Curvature of the spine (scoliosis), 193, 442

CWPT (classwide peer tutoring), 256, 275–276, 293

Cystic fibrosis, 193, 200, 442

Daily living, devices for, 414–415, 422, 439–440

Daily progress feedback (DPF) forms, 389–390

Danford, Cathy, 6, 247
Dangerous behaviors, 367, 378, 387–388
DARE writing strategy, 343, 344
Davis, Susan
    collaboration, 209–210, 213–214, 217
    learning disabilities, 87, 88, 89
Deaf, 176, 443
Deaf-blindness. *See also* Sensory disabilities
    defined, 10, 177–178, 443
    intellectual disabilities and, 180
    overview, 177
    prevalence, 178, 179
    service delivery, 179
Deafness. *See also* Sensory disabilities
    academic and cognitive performance, 180
    academic success strategies, 182, 183–184
    defined, 10, 176
    overview, 177
    prevalence, 178, 179
    social success strategies, 183
Dean, Susan, 24
Dec-Aid, 416
Decibels (dBs), 176, 443
Decision making, 212
Dedication, 23
DEFENDS writing strategy, 328, 344
Degree of participation adaptations, 330
Deinstitutionalization, 32, 443
Demographics
    attention-deficit/hyperactivity disorder,
        101, 103–104
    autism spectrum disorders, 153, 155
    communication disorders, 170, 172
    diversity, 51–54
    divide between teachers and students,
        56–63
    emotional and behavioral disabilities,
        139, 141
    ethnic groups, 51
    intellectual disabilities, 120, 122
    language, 51–52
    learning disabilities, 81, 84–85
    physical disabilities, health impairments,
        and multiple disabilities, 191,
        194–195
    poverty, 52, 53, 55
    sensory impairments, 177, 178–179
    special education, 53–54
Demonstration, 327
Depression, 143, 443
Destination Reading Series, 405
Developmental aphasia, 80, 443
Developmental delays, 10, 121, 122
Developmental milestones, 121, 443
DI. *See* Direct instruction (DI)
Diabetes, 193, 199–200, 270, 443, 446
Diagnostic and Statistical Manual of Mental
        Disorders, Fourth Edition, Text Revision
        (DSM-IV-TR), 100, 120, 155
Differentiated instruction
    classroom arrangement, 260–262

culturally responsive teaching and, 70
    defined, 24, 443
    getting to know students, 253–254
    grading adaptations, 260, 261, 266,
        281–282
    learning disabilities and, 90
    Level-1 planning, 254–255, 266, 273–274
    Level-2 planning, 255–258
    Level-3 planning, 258–259
    performance monitoring, 259–260, 266,
        276, 279–280
    planning for, 251, 253–262, 266,
        271–272
Difficulty adaptations, 330
DigiVox 2, 416
Diplegia, 192, 443
Direct instruction (DI)
    content-area instruction, 327
    defined, 443
    effective instruction and, 288, 290
    planning basic skills instruction, 256, 275
    unit/lesson organizers and, 339
Disabilities, multiple. *See* Multiple
        disabilities
Disability
    categories, 9, 10
    culture and, 62–63
    defined, 42, 43, 250–251
    ethnicity and, 53–54, 55
    parent expectations and, 62–63
Discipline referrals, 60
Discrete trial instruction (DTI), 160
Diseases, communicable, 42, 43
Dispositions, 23, 213–215, 443
Distortions, speech, 171
Distributed practice, 299, 443
Diversity, 48–75
    academic achievement, 54–56
    collaboration and, 211
    culturally responsive teaching, 64–74
    demographic divide between teachers and
        students, 56–63
    demographics, 51–54
    gifted and talented students, 66
    Heritage High School, 49–50
    overview, 55
    perspectives on, 49–50
    in special education, 53–54
    standards, 75
Dofka, Cathy, 11, 13
Down syndrome, 121, 443
DPF (daily progress feedback) forms,
    389–390
Draft:Builder, 413
Drafts, writing, 297
Drill-and-practice software, 404
DSM-IV-TR *(Diagnostic and Statistical*
        Manual of Mental Disorders, Fourth
        Edition, Text Revision), 100, 120, 155
DTI (discrete trial instruction), 160
Duchenne muscular dystrophy, 192, 443

Duclos, Michelle, 93, 230
Due process, 36, 37, 39
DynaVox 3100, 416, 417
Dyslexia, 80, 443
Dysplasia, 193, 442

EAHCA. *See* Education for All Handicapped
        Children Act (EAHCA)
Early Intervention in Reading (EIR),
        296, 314
Early Success, 296, 314
Earobics, 296
EBD. *See* Emotional and behavioral
        disabilities (EBD)
Echolalia, 156, 443
Edible reinforcers, 372
Editing, 297
Edmark Reading Program, 410
Educational technology
    defined, 403, 443
    evaluating, 406–407, 429–430
    to facilitate inclusion, 403–405
    in general education classrooms, 403
    planning basic skills instruction, 256, 276
    reading and math educational technology,
        401, 404–405, 406, 422, 425–428
    results from, 405–407, 422, 429–430
    teaching students to use, 404, 422,
        423–424
    types, 404
Education for All Handicapped Children Act
        (EAHCA). *See also* Individuals with
        Disabilities Education Improvement
        Act of 2004 (IDEA 2004)
    emotional and behavioral disabilities, 139
    evolution into IDEA 2004, 36, 38
    free and appropriate education, 30
    learning disabilities, 85
    parent advocacy, 33
EIR (Early Intervention in Reading),
        296, 314
Elementary instruction, 284–318. *See also*
        Elementary students
    attention-deficit/hyperactivity disorder,
        106–109
    autism spectrum disorders, 158–161
    cognitive strategy instruction, 304,
        317–318
    communication disorders, 174
    cooperative learning, 291–292, 304,
        307–308
    effective instruction in inclusive
        classrooms, 287–288
    emotional and behavioral disabilities,
        144–145
    intellectual disabilities, 126, 128–129
    learning disabilities, 88–91
    math instruction, 298–300, 304, 317–318
    peer-assisted learning strategies, 293, 296,
        304, 311–312

perspectives on, 285–286
physical disabilities, health impairments, and multiple disabilities, 197–202
principles and practices, 288–293
reading instruction, 293–295, 296, 304, 313–314
Reading Recovery, 304, 309–310
Self-Regulated Strategy Development, 298, 304, 315–316
sensory impairments, 181–183
standards, 301
strategies, 303–318
Success for All, 304, 305–306
tiers, 304, 313–314
writing instruction, 295–298, 304, 315–316
Elementary students
attention-deficit/hyperactivity disorder, 106–109
autism spectrum disorders, 158–161
communication disorders, 174
emotional and behavioral disabilities, 144–145
intellectual disabilities, 126, 128–129
learning disabilities, 88–91
physical disabilities, health impairments, and multiple disabilities, 197–202
sensory impairments, 181–183
ELLs (English-language learners), 51–52, 60–62, 443
Emotional and behavioral disabilities (EBD), 136–148
characteristics, 139, 142–144
communication disorders and, 173
defined, 139–140, 443
identifying, 140–141
including students with, 137–138
instruction for students with, 144–146
overview, 139
prevalence, 139, 141
service delivery, 139, 141–142
standards, 148
Emotional disturbance, 10
Employment, 130, 162, 446
Eng, Vicki
attitude toward inclusion, 21
effective instruction, 286, 303
learning disabilities, 79–80, 86, 88, 89, 91
student benefits from inclusion, 24
Engagement, 72–73, 90–91, 128, 415
English-language learners (ELLs), 51–52, 60–62, 443
Enthusiasm, 23
Entrepreneurial supports, 162, 443
Epilepsy, 193, 197, 199, 443
Equal protection, 36
Equity projects, 73–74
ERASE strategy, 393–394
Essay development planning tool, 345
Ethnic groups
culture, 60

defined, 443
disabilities, 53–54, 55
placement settings, 54, 55
poverty, 52
European Americans, 51
Evidenced-based instructional practices, 24, 110–111, 443
Exclusion clause, 82, 443
Expectations, 62–63, 70–71
Expertise, 212
Explicit instruction, 72, 294, 443
Expression, in universal design for learning, 128, 415
Expulsion, 39–40
Externalizing behavior problems, 142–143, 443
EZ Keys, 413

Fading, 390
Fairness, 23
Families. See also Parents
African American, 63
attention-deficit/hyperactivity disorder and, 101
working with, 220, 226, 239–241
FAPE (free and appropriate public education), 30, 33, 36, 37
Fast match of high-frequency words activity, 295
FBA. See Functional behavioral assessment (FBA)
FBT (function-based thinking), 378, 393–394
Feedback, 108, 372, 389–390
Ferguson, Dianne, 35
Ferguson, Ian, 35
Figurative language, 156, 443
FIRST mnemonic strategy, 347
Flexibility, 41–42, 213–214
Flexible ability grouping, 256, 275
Florida Center for Reading Research, 294
Fluency, 294, 295, 296, 443
Fluency disorders, 171, 443
Formative assessment, 272
Form disorders, 171
Forms
daily progress feedback, 389–390
daily report card, 109
Rules Development Worksheet, 380
Section 504 referral, 252
strategic note-taking, 353
teacher assistance team referral, 232
Foster care, 52–53, 443
Frames of reference, 215
Free and appropriate public education (FAPE), 30, 33, 36, 37
Friendships, 131
Full inclusion, 16, 33, 443
Full-time special education classrooms, 15–16

Functional behavioral assessment (FBA)
behavior intervention plans and, 251
classroom management, 368, 378, 393, 394
defined, 443
emotional and behavioral disabilities, 141
intellectual disabilities, 125
Functional disorders, 170
Functional exclusion, 30–31
Functional language, 156, 443
Functional skill instruction, 126
Function-based thinking (FBT), 378, 393–394
Funds of knowledge, 61–62, 68, 443
Furniture arrangement and spacing, 260
Future challenges, 44–46

Games, instructional, 404
Gender
attention-deficit/hyperactivity disorder, 103
autism spectrum disorders, 155
emotional and behavioral disabilities, 141
General education classrooms
attention-deficit/hyperactivity disorder and, 106–108, 110
in continuum of services, 15
educational technology in, 403
time spent outside, by disability, 34–35
General education teachers, 19, 267
Generalization, 125, 276
Generalized anxiety, 143
Genetic inheritance, 120, 121, 443
Gibson, James, 7
Gifted and talented students, 12, 55, 66
Girls
attention-deficit/hyperactivity disorder, 103
autism spectrum disorders, 155
Give one-Get one strategy, 91
Goals, 212, 255, 330, 373
Goines, Madge, 167–168, 189, 197, 247
Goodwin Elementary School (Charleston County School District), 426
Gordon, Margaret, 6
Grading adaptations, 260, 261, 266, 281–282
Graduation rates, 55, 56
Grammar checkers, 434
Grand mal seizure. See Tonic-clonic seizure
Graphic organizers, 92–93, 300, 326, 329, 443
Graphic tools, 344–345
Grouping students, 290–292. See also Ability grouping
Grover, Lisa, 24–25, 285, 286–287
GTCalc Scientific Calculator, 414
Guidance counselors, school, 19
Guided discovery learning, 327
Guided notes, 93
Guided practice, 327
Gus! Word Prediction, 413

Hallal, Lisa
    collaboration, 209–210, 213–214, 217, 244
    effective instruction, 287
    learning disabilities, 88, 89
    peer buddy program, 244
Hartshorne, Jacob, 3, 4
Hartshorne, Nancy, 3, 4
Headsprout Early Reading, 405
Health impairments. *See also* Physical
        disabilities, health impairments, and
        multiple disabilities
    academic and cognitive performance, 196
    behavior performance and social skills, 197
    defined, 193
    instructing elementary students with,
        197–202
    medications for, 196
    overview, 191
    prevalence, 194
    service delivery, 195
    types, 193
Hearing impairment. *See also* Sensory
        disabilities
    academic and cognitive performance, 180
    academic success strategies, 182,
        183–184
    defined, 10, 176, 443
    identifying, 178
    overview, 177
    prevalence, 178, 179
    service delivery, 179
    social success strategies, 183
Helpfulness, 364
Hemiplegia, 192, 444
Hemophilia, 193, 444
Heritage High School (Leesburg, Va.)
    achievement gap, 54–55
    autism spectrum disorders, 155–156, 157,
        158, 159
    classroom management, 360–361,
        362, 374
    content-area instruction, 321–322,
        323–324, 325–326, 328
    diversity, 49–50
    emotional and behavioral disabilities,
        137–138, 142, 144
    highly qualified teachers, 45
    intellectual disabilities, 117–118
    interview with parent, 29–30
    overview, 7–8
Highlighting relevant information, 110–111
Highly qualified teachers, 41, 42, 44–45
High school graduation rates, 55, 56
Hill, Susan, 8, 321–322, 331, 360–361, 374
Hispanics, 51, 83
Holly Springs Intermediate School
        (Miss.), 428
Homelessness, 53
Homeless to Harvard (movie), 56
Home-school collaboration, 220, 226,
        239–241

Homework Wiz Plus, 410, 412
Hospital, homebound, separate residential
        schools, and separate day schools, in
        continuum of services, 16
Huckaby, Margaret, 7–8
Humor, 384
Hyperactivity, 100, 105, 444
Hyperactivity-impulsivity, 99, 100, 105. *See
        also* Attention-deficit/hyperactivity
        disorder (ADHD)

IDEA (Individuals with Disabilities
        Education Act), 36, 38
IDEA 2004. *See* Individuals with Disabilities
        Education Improvement Act of 2004
        (IDEA 2004)
IEP. *See* Individualized education program
        (IEP)
Ignoring, planned, 383
iLearn Math, 406
Illinois Supreme Court, 30
Immediacy, 363
Impulsivity, 100, 105, 444
Inattention, 100, 104–105
Incidental learning, 124–125
Inclusion
    characteristics of effective programs,
        16–17
    concerns about, 33
    current status, 34–35
    defined, 3, 444
    educational technology and, 403–405
    evolution of, 31–35
    full inclusion, 16, 33, 443
    mainstreaming *versus,* 32–33
    perspectives on, 29–30
    research on effectiveness, 17–18
    standards, 27, 47
    teacher attitudes toward, 21–22
    as term, 16
Inclusion-support teams, 216
Independent practice, 327
Individualist cultures, 58, 444
Individualized education program (IEP)
    components, 249–250
    defined, 444
    IDEA 2004, 37, 38–39, 249–250
    planning, 249–250, 266, 267–268
Individualized Health Care Plan, 200, 444
Individuals with Disabilities Education Act
        (IDEA), 36, 38
Individuals with Disabilities Education
        Improvement Act of 2004
        (IDEA 2004)
    assistive technology devices/services, 407
    attention-deficit/hyperactivity disorder,
        101, 102, 104
    autism, 154
    components, 37–40
    continuum of services, 15–16

deaf-blindness, 177–178
deafness, 176
defined, 444
disability categories and definitions, 9, 10
emotional and behavioral disabilities, 139
health impairments, 193
hearing impairment, 176
home-school collaboration, 220, 239
individualized education programs,
        249–250, 267
intellectual disabilities, 119, 130
learning disability, 80, 81, 82, 83, 84
least restrictive environment, 14–16,
        36–37, 38
multiple disabilities, 194
orthopedic impairments, 192
principles, 36–37
special education outcomes, 44
universal design for learning, 415
visual impairment including blindness,
        176, 177
Infants, 40
Information
    access to, 40
    highlighting relevant, 110–111
Input adaptations, 330
Instruction. *See also* Content-area instruction;
        Differentiated instruction; Direct
        instruction (DI); Elementary
        instruction; Secondary instruction
    attention-deficit/hyperactivity disorder,
        106–111
    autism spectrum disorders, 158–163
    balanced, 298, 441
    basic skills, 255–256, 266, 275–276
    cognitive strategy, 304, 317–318
    communication disorders, 174–176
    core, 89–90, 442
    discrete trial, 160
    emotional and behavioral disabilities,
        144–146
    explicit, 72, 294, 443
    functional skill, 126
    intellectual disabilities, 126–132
    learning disabilities, 88–93
    needs, identifying, 266, 273–274
    physical disabilities, health impairments,
        and multiple disabilities, 197–204
    principles and practices, 288–293
    sensory impairments, 181–184
    severe disabilities, 334
    supplemental, 254
    systematic, 126, 200, 201
    Tier 1, 83, 249
    Tier 2, 83–84, 249, 314
    Tier 3, 84, 314
    units of, 257, 277
Instructional accommodations, 254
Instructional assistants. *See* Paraeducators
Instructional games, 404
Instructional planning, 248

Instructional support teams. *See* Teacher assistance teams (TATs)
Instructions, 106, 111
Insulin, 193, 444
Insulin-dependent diabetes. *See* Type 1 diabetes
Integrated learning systems, 404
Integrating, 216
Intellectual disabilities, 116–134. *See also* Multiple disabilities
    causes, 120, 121
    characteristics, 120, 123–125
    deaf-blindness and, 180
    defined, 10, 119–121, 444
    identifying, 120, 121–122
    instructing students with, 126–132
    multiple disabilities and, 194, 196
    outcomes, 120
    overview, 120
    perspectives on, 117–118
    prevalence, 120, 122
    service delivery, 120, 122–123
    standards, 134
Intelligence, 158
Intelligence tests, 122
IntelliTools Reading: Balanced Literacy, 410
Intensity, 9
Interactive planning, 258–259
Interest boosting, 384
Internalizing behavior problems, 143, 444
Intervention assistance teams. *See* Teacher assistance teams (TATs)
Interventions, targeted, 365, 368, 378, 389–392, 446
IT-FITS mnemonic strategy, 347–348
Itinerant teachers, 181

Jigsaw strategy, 307–308, 328
Juvenile arthritis, 193, 444
Juvenile diabetes. *See* Type 1 diabetes

KaplanSpellRead, 296
Kelley, Kelly, 127–128
Kennedy, Steve, 137–138, 142
Key Skills for Reading: Letters and Words, 410
Keyword mnemonics, 347, 348
King, Jill, 5–6, 247, 248–249
KnowledgeBox, 405
Kraun, Gina, 157, 159, 362
Kurzweil 3000, 410

Ladders to Literacy, 296
Language
    autism spectrum disorders and, 160
    culture and, 60–62
    demographics, 51–52
    figurative, 156, 443
    functional, 156, 443
    intellectual disabilities and, 124
    people-first, 13–14, 445

Language disorders, 169, 171, 444. *See also* Communication disorders
Language Master 6000 XF, 412
Larson Pre-Algebra and Algebra, 406
Latinos, 51, 83
Laws, 36–43. *See also specific laws*
LeapTrack, 405
Learning. *See also* Cooperative learning; Universal design for learning (UDL)
    differences in, 323–324
    guided discovery, 327
    incidental, 124–125
    observational, 124–125
    peer-assisted learning strategies, 293, 296, 304, 311–312
Learning disabilities, 78–95
    causes, 81
    characteristics, 81, 86–88
    defined, 10, 80, 82
    identifying, 81, 82–84
    instructing students with, 88–93
    outcomes, 81
    overview, 81
    perspectives on, 79–80
    placement settings, 81
    prevalence, 81, 84–85
    service delivery, 81, 85–86
    standards, 95
Learning Disabilities Act, 85
Learning strategies, 93, 328–329, 444
Least restrictive environment (LRE), 14–16, 36–37, 38, 444
Least-to-most prompting, 201
Legal blindness, 177, 444
Legal foundations, 36–43. *See also specific laws*
LEP (limited English proficiency), 444. *See also* English-language learners (ELLs)
Lesson organizers, 339–340, 341
Lesson presentation format, 258–259
Let's Go Read, 410
Letter recognition, 295
Letter-sound correspondence, 295
Leukemia, 193, 444
Level-1 planning, 254–255, 266, 273–274
Level-2 planning, 255–258
Level-3 planning, 258–259
Level of support adaptations, 330
Life skills curriculum, 198
Lighting, 260
LightWRITER, 417
Limb deficiencies, 193, 444
Limited English proficiency (LEP), 444. *See also* English-language learners (ELLs)
Lindamood Phonemic Sequencing Program (LIPS), 296
Linguistic schema, 444
LINKS note-taking strategy, 351
LIPS (Lindamood Phonemic Sequencing Program), 296
Listening skills, 229
LISTS mnemonic strategy, 347

Literacy skills, 180
Literature, 71
Litigation, 36, 444
Living arrangements, postsecondary, 130
Local control, 41–42
Long, Anthony, 325, 326, 327
Los Angeles Unified School District, 52
LRE (least restrictive environment), 14–16, 36–37, 38, 444
Ludwig, Tracey, 324, 325

Macaw Series, 417
Mainstreaming, 31–32
Management style, 59
Materials
    redesigning, 329, 330, 334
    selecting, 256, 258, 259
    storing, 262
Math
    assistive technology, 409, 414, 422, 435–436
    calculator use, 422, 435–436
    educational technology, 401, 404–405, 406, 422, 425–428
    elementary instruction, 298–300, 304, 317–318
    learning disabilities and, 86–87
    software, 406–407
Math Gallery, 427
MathPad, 414
Mediation, 39, 444
Medications, 111–112, 196, 446
Memory, 87, 447
Mental handicaps. *See* Intellectual disabilities
Mental health services, 62
Mental retardation. *See* Intellectual disabilities
Metacognition, 87, 323, 444
Mild hearing loss, 176
Mild intellectual disabilities, 121, 123, 125
Mild-to-moderate disabilities category, 9
Misbehavior, goals of, 395
Mission statements, 365
Mixed-ability grouping, 291–292, 304, 307–308
Mixed cerebral palsy, 192
Mixed hearing loss, 176, 444
Mnemonic devices, 93, 338, 347–348, 444
Moderate hearing loss, 176
Moderate intellectual disabilities, 121, 123–124, 125
Monitoring, performance, 259–260, 266, 276, 279–280
Monitors, in behavior education programs, 389
Morning arrival procedure, 381
Morphology, 171
Motivation, 23, 64, 88
Motor speech disorders, 171, 444

Mull Elementary School (Burke County, N.C.)
communication disorders, 167–168
overview, 5–6
physical disabilities, 189
planning, 247
response-to-intervention programs, 248–249
technology, 401, 424
visual disabilities, 181
Multidimensionality, 363
Multiple disabilities. *See also* Intellectual disabilities; Physical disabilities, health impairments, and multiple disabilities
academic and cognitive performance, 196
behavior performance and social skills, 197
defined, 10
instructing elementary students with, 200
overview, 191
prevalence, 194
service delivery, 195
Muscular dystrophy, 192, 199, 444
Musculoskeletal conditions. *See* Orthopedic and musculoskeletal conditions
Music therapists, 19
Myelomeningocele, 192, 444

National Center on Student Progress Monitoring, 279
National Instructional Materials Accessibility Standard (NIMAS), 258
National Reading Panel, 406
Native Son (Wright), 72
NCLB. *See* No Child Left Behind Act (NCLB)
Negative consequences, 385–386
Negative reinforcement, 158, 371, 444
Nephritis, 193, 444
Neurological disorder, 171, 444
NIMAS (National Instructional Materials Accessibility Standard), 258
Nirjie, Bengt, 13
No Child Left Behind Act (NCLB)
defined, 444
effective inclusive programs, 17
effective instruction, 287
elements, 40–42
special education outcomes, 44
teaching to the test, 64
Noise control, 261
Noncompliance, 142–143, 444
Nonverbal communication, 230
No-parent children, 53
Normalization, 13–14, 32, 444
North Carolina Department of Public Instruction, 5
Note taking, 332, 338, 351–353
Numbered Heads Together, 308
Nurses, school, 200

Objective personality measures, 141
Observational learning, 124–125
Obsessive-compulsive disorder (OCD), 143
Occupational therapists (OTs)
defined, 445
physical disabilities, health impairments, and multiple disabilities, 194, 197, 200
role, 19
Occupational therapy, 445
OCD (obsessive-compulsive disorder), 143
OHI (other health impairments), 10, 101, 102, 104
Omissions, speech, 171
One teach, one support model for co-teaching, 233
Organizational pressures of classrooms, 363
Orthopedic and musculoskeletal conditions, 193, 199, 445
Orthopedic impairments, 10, 191. *See also* Physical disabilities
Osteogenesis imperfecta, 193, 445
Other health impairments (OHI), 10, 101, 102, 104
OTs. *See* Occupational therapists (OTs)
Output adaptations, 330

Pace, changing, 383
Palmtop computers, 412–414
PALS (peer-assisted learning strategies), 293, 296, 304, 311–312
Paraeducators
defined, 445
in part-time special education classrooms, 15
role, 20
students with deafness or hearing impairment and, 182
working with, 219, 226, 235–237
Paragraph shrinking, 312
Parents. *See also* Families
advocacy by, 33–34
expanded options for, 41, 42
expectations of, 62–63
interview with, 29–30
participation in education, 37
role in education, 59
Parent Training and Information Centers, 38
Parity, 212, 227–228
Partner reading, 311–312
Partner strategies, 91
Part-time special education classrooms, 15
PBS (positive behavior support), 251, 359–360, 445
PDAs (personal digital assistants), 412–414
PDD-NOS. *See* Pervasive developmental disorder-not otherwise specified (PDD-NOS)
PECS (Picture Exchange Communication System), 161, 445
Pedagogy, purposeful, 49

Peer-assisted learning strategies (PALS), 293, 296, 304, 311–312
Peer-assisted strategies, 220–221, 445
Peer buddies, 221, 226, 243–245
Peer relationships, 131, 160–161
Peer tutoring, 256, 275–276, 292–293, 445
People-first language, 13–14, 445
Performance monitoring, 259–260, 266, 276, 279–280
Personal digital assistants (PDAs), 412–414
Personality measures, 141
Personalized grading plans (PGPs), 281–282
Pervasive developmental disabilities. *See* Autism spectrum disorders (ASD)
Pervasive developmental disorder-not otherwise specified (PDD-NOS), 153, 445. *See also* Autism spectrum disorders (ASD)
Petit mal seizure. *See* Absence seizure
PGPs (personalized grading plans), 281–282
Phoneme matching, 295
Phonemic awareness, 296, 310, 313, 445
Phonics, 294, 295, 296, 445
Phonological and articulation disorders, 171, 445
Phonological awareness, 294, 295, 296, 445
Phonological processing, 82, 445
Phonology, 171
Physical aggression, 142
Physical disabilities. *See also* Assistive technology (AT); Physical disabilities, health impairments, and multiple disabilities
academic and cognitive performance, 195–196
assistive technology for, 196
behavior performance and social skills, 196–197
defined, 191
instructing elementary students with, 198
overview, 191
perspectives on, 189
prevalence, 194
service delivery, 195
types, 192–193
Physical disabilities, health impairments, and multiple disabilities, 188–206
categories of students with, 190
causes, 191
characteristics, 191, 195–197
definitions, 191–194
identifying, 191, 194
instructing students with, 197–204
outcomes, 191
overview, 191
prevalence, 191, 194–195
service delivery, 191, 195
standards, 206

Physical therapists (PTs)
  defined, 445
  physical disabilities, health impairments,
    and multiple disabilities, 194,
    197, 200
  role, 19
  wheelchairs, motorized, 439
Physical therapy, 445
Picture Exchange Communication System
  (PECS), 161, 445
Picture It, 410
Picture walks, 331–332, 445
P.K.'s Math Studio, 427
P.K.'s Place, 427
Placement settings. See Continuum of service;
  Service delivery
Planned ignoring, 383
Planners (agenda books), 332–333
Planning, 246–282
  academic content instruction, 256, 257,
    266, 277–278
  basic skills instruction, 255–256, 266,
    275–276
  behavior intervention plans, 251
  co-teaching, 234
  curriculum-based measurement, 266,
    279–280
  differentiated instruction, 251, 253–262,
    266, 271–272
  grading adaptations, 260, 261, 266,
    281–282
  identifying instructional needs, 266,
    273–274
  individualized education programs,
    249–250, 266, 267–268
  instructional, 248
  perspectives on, 247
  response-to-intervention plans, 248–249
  schedule, 235–236
  Section 504 Plans, 43, 250–251, 252, 266,
    269–270
  standards, 263
  strategies, 265–282
  transition, 162–163
Planning pyramids, 257, 277, 278,
  324–325
Plants in the classroom, 262
PLATO Achieve Now on PSP (Mathematics),
  405, 406, 422, 427–428
PLATO Algebra, 406
PLATO Focus, 405
Pocket Compass, 412–414
Pohill, Denise, 157, 159, 362
Point systems, 390
Poliomyelitis, 191, 445
Positive behavior support (PBS), 251,
  359–360, 445
Positive consequences, 385
Positive reinforcement, 158, 371, 386
Positive teacher attitudes, 23–24
Postsecondary education, 127–128, 130, 163

Poverty
  academic proficiency and, 55–56
  demographics, 52, 53, 55
  ethnicity and, 52
  impact on students, 62
  student performance and, 11
Powell, Jennifer, 181, 189, 197
Power behavior, 395
POW strategy, 315, 316
Pragmatic disorders. See Usage disorders
Pragmatics, 160, 445
Praise, 107, 108, 372
Prediction relay, 312
Prenatal causes, 120, 121, 445
Preschoolers, 40
Prevention
  primary, 83
  secondary, 83–84
Prewriting, 296, 343
Primary prevention, 83
Probes, 280
Procedural safeguards, 37, 39
Procedures, 69–70, 365, 378, 379–381
Production, in writing process, 343
Profound hearing loss, 176
Profound intellectual disabilities, 121, 124
Progress graphs, 279, 280
PROJECT assignment management
  strategy, 333
Projective personality measures, 141
Proleptic teaching, 327, 445
Prompting, least-to-most, 201
Prosthetic devices, 193, 445
Proximity, cultural dimensions of, 59
Proximity control, 383
Pruess, Jon, 323–324, 325
Pseudohypertrophy, 192, 445
Psychological processing, 82, 445
Psychologists, school, 19, 251
PTs. See Physical therapists (PTs)
Publishing, 297
Punishment, 108, 373

Quaddle Family Ministries, The, 427
Quadriplegia, 192, 445
Quicktionary II, 411, 412

Reading
  assistive technology, 408, 410–411
  content-area instruction, 331–332, 338,
    349–350
  educational technology, 401, 404–405,
    406, 422, 425–428
  elementary instruction, 293–295, 296,
    304, 313–314
  hearing impairments and, 180
  learning disabilities and, 86
  peer-assisted learning strategies, 311–312
  software, 405, 406–407

Reading First, 424
Reading Intervention for Early Success,
  296, 314
Reading Mastery, 288, 290
Reading Pen II, 411
Reading Plus, 401
Reading Recovery, 304, 309–310
Reading Rescue, 310
Read 180 (software), 405, 422, 425–426
Recordings for the Blind and Dyslexic, 411
Recreational therapists, 19
Referrals, 60, 231, 232, 252
Regular Education Initiative (REI), 32, 445
Rehabilitation Act. See Section 504 of the
  Rehabilitation Act
Reinforcement
  attention-deficit/hyperactivity disorder
    and, 108
  negative, 158, 371, 444
  positive, 158, 371, 386
Reinforcers, 144–145, 372
REI (Regular Education Initiative), 32, 445
Repetitive behaviors, 157
Replacement behaviors, 141, 145, 445
Report cards, 108–109
Representation, in universal design for
  learning, 128, 415
Reprimands, 373
Resilience, 64, 445
Respect, 23, 69, 214–215, 364
Response accommodations, 355
Response cost, 373
Response-to-intervention (RTI)
  curriculum-based measurement and,
    259, 260
  defined, 445
  effective instruction, 287–288
  learning disability identification, 83–84
  North Carolina pilot program, 5–6
  planning, 248–249
  reading instruction, 313–314
  teacher roles and responsibilities, 45–46
Rett disorder, 153, 445. See also Autism
  spectrum disorders (ASD)
Revenge behavior, 395
Reviewing, in writing process, 343
Revising, as writing stage, 297
Rheumatic fever, 193, 445
Rhyme Recognition, 295
Ritualistic behaviors, 157
Routines, 69–70, 329–330
RTI. See Response-to-intervention (RTI)
Rules
  attention-deficit/hyperactivity disorder
    and, 106
  classroom management, 365, 378, 379–381
  warm defenders and, 69–70

Scaffolding, 72, 93, 327, 446
Schedule planning, 235–236

Scheduling accommodations, 355
School guidance counselors, 19
School nurses, 200
School psychologists, 19, 251
School-to-Work Opportunities Act, 38
Schoolwide assistance teams. *See* Teacher
    assistance teams (TATs)
School-within-a-school (SWAS) approach,
    137–138, 142
Scoliosis, 193, 442
SCOS (standard course of study), 248,
    254, 446
Scott, Laura
    attention-deficit/hyperactivity disorder,
        97–98, 99, 105, 106, 107, 109
    effective instruction, 285–286
Screening, 140, 154, 446
ScreenReader, 411
SCROL learning strategy, 349
Secondary instruction. *See also* Secondary
    students
    attention-deficit/hyperactivity disorder,
        109–111
    autism spectrum disorders, 159, 161–163
    communication disorders, 175–176
    emotional and behavioral disabilities,
        145–146
    intellectual disabilities, 129–132
    learning disabilities, 91–93
    physical disabilities, health impairments,
        and multiple disabilities, 202–204
    sensory impairments, 183–184
Secondary prevention, 83–84
Secondary students
    attention-deficit/hyperactivity disorder,
        109–111
    autism spectrum disorders, 159, 161–163
    communication disorders, 175–176
    emotional and behavioral disabilities,
        145–146
    intellectual disabilities, 129–132
    learning disabilities, 91–93
    physical disabilities, health impairments,
        and multiple disabilities, 202–204
    sensory impairments, 183–184
Second-language learners. *See* English-
    language learners (ELLs)
Secret of Googol, The, 428
Section 504 of the Rehabilitation Act
    attention-deficit/hyperactivity disorder, 12,
        101, 103, 104
    defined, 446
    IDEA 2004 *versus,* 12
    overview, 12
    provisions, 42–43
Section 504 Plans, 43, 250–251, 252, 266,
    269–270
Section 504 referral form, sample, 252
SED (serious emotional disturbance), 139. *See
    also* Emotional and behavioral
    disabilities (EBD)

Segregation, 31
Self-advocacy, 89, 91, 203
Self-assessment, 373
Self-concept, 59
Self-control, 145, 372–373
Self-determination
    defined, 446
    intellectual disabilities and, 127, 131–132
    normalization and, 13
    physical disabilities, health impairments,
        and multiple disabilities and, 203
    teaching self-management and self-control
        and, 373
Self-injurious behaviors (SIBs), 125, 158,
    197, 446
Self-management, 142, 372–373, 446
Self-Regulated Strategy Development
    (SRSD), 298, 304, 315–316,
    343–344, 446
Self-regulation, 295, 315–318, 446
Semantic disorders, 171, 446
Sensorineural hearing loss, 176, 446
Sensory disabilities, 176–184
    causes, 177
    characteristics, 177, 179–180
    defined, 176–178, 446
    identifying, 177, 178
    instructing students with, 181–184
    outcomes, 177
    overview, 168–169, 177
    prevalence, 177, 178–179
    service delivery, 177, 179
    standards, 186
Sentence structure and meaning, 295
Separation anxiety, 143
Serious emotional disturbance (SED), 139. *See
    also* Emotional and behavioral
    disabilities (EBD)
Service delivery. *See also* Continuum of
    service
    attention-deficit/hyperactivity disorder,
        101, 104
    autism spectrum disorders, 153,
        155–156
    communication disorders, 170, 172
    emotional and behavioral disabilities, 139,
        141–142
    ethnic groups and, 54, 55
    intellectual disabilities, 120, 122–123
    learning disabilities, 81, 85–86
    physical disabilities, health impairments,
        and multiple disabilities, 191, 195
    sensory impairments, 177, 179
Setting, changing, 111
Setting accommodations, 355
Severe disabilities, 333–334
Severe discrepancy, 82–83, 446
Severe hearing loss, 176
Severe intellectual disabilities, 121, 124
Sexuality, 131
SFA (Success for All), 304, 305–306

Sheltered workshops, 162, 446
SIBs (self-injurious behaviors), 125, 158,
    197, 446
Sickle cell anemia, 193, 199, 446
Signal interference, 383
Significant disabilities, as term, 9
Simultaneity, 363
Six-hour retarded child, as term, 121
Size adaptations, 330
Skill maintenance and generalization, 276
Skill synthesis, 125
SMARTER strategy, 339
Social action projects, 73–74
Social anxiety, 143
Social problems
    attention-deficit/hyperactivity disorder
        and, 105
    emotional and behavioral disabilities
        and, 144
    intellectual disabilities and, 125
    learning disabilities and, 87–88
Social reciprocity, 156–157
Social stories, 161, 378, 397–398, 446
Social success strategies. *See also* Behavior
    performance and social skills
    autism spectrum disorders, 161
    classroom management, 371–372, 378,
        397–398
    communication disorders, 174, 175–176
    emotional and behavioral
        disabilities, 145
    intellectual disabilities, 128–129,
        130–132
    physical disabilities, health impairments,
        and multiple disabilities, 200,
        201–202, 203–204
    sensory impairments, 182–183, 184
Social withdrawal, 143, 446
Social workers, 19
Software. *See also specific programs*
    drill-and-practice, 404
    math, 406–407
    reading, 405, 406–407
    word-prediction, 433
    writing, 422, 433–434
SoothSayer Word Prediction, 411
Spasticity, 192, 446
Speaking Homework Wiz, 410, 412
Speaking Spelling Ace, 412
Speaking Spelling and Handwriting
    Ace, 412
Special education, characteristics of, 9, 11
Special education teachers, 19
Specific language impairment, 173, 446
Specific learning disability, 10, 80, 82
Speech disorders, 169, 171, 446. *See also*
    Communication disorders
Speech-language pathologists (SLPs)
    assessment procedures, 170–171
    augmentative/alternative communication
        devices, 437

collaboration with, 168, 174
physical disabilities, health impairments, and multiple disabilities, 200
role, 19
service delivery, 172
Speech or language impairment category, 10, 172
Spell checkers, 433
Spelling Ace with Thesaurus, 412
Spelling assistive technology resources, 412
SpellRead Phonological Auditory Training, 296
Spina bifida, 192, 195, 199, 446
SRSD. *See* Self-Regulated Strategy Development (SRSD)
STAD (Student Teams-Achievement Divisions), 328
Standard course of study (SCOS), 248, 254, 446
Standard English, 50, 446
Standards
    aligning, 255
    attention-deficit/hyperactivity disorder, 114
    autism spectrum disorders, 164
    classroom management, 375
    collaboration, 223
    communication disorders and sensory impairments, 186
    content-area instruction, 336
    diversity, 75
    elementary instruction, 301
    emotional and behavioral disabilities, 148
    inclusion and its importance, 27
    inclusion and its past, present, and future, 47
    intellectual disabilities, 134
    learning disabilities, 95
    linking, 255
    physical disabilities, health impairments, and multiple disabilities, 206
    planning, 263
    technology, 420
Statements of purpose, 365
Stereotyped behaviors, 125, 157, 446
Stereotypies, 197, 446
Stimulant medications, 111, 446
Story maps, 350
Strategic planning, 254–255, 266, 273–274
Student assistance teams. *See* Teacher assistance teams (TATs)
Students. *See also* Elementary students; Secondary students
    benefits from inclusive settings, 24–25
    as collaborators, 220–221
    demographic divide between teachers and, 56–63
    getting to know, 253–254
    gifted and talented, 12, 55, 66

grouping, 290–292
    involving in IEP planning meetings, 267
Student support teams. *See* Teacher assistance teams (TATs)
Student Teams-Achievement Divisions (STAD), 328
Study guides, 350
Stuttering, 171
Substitute curriculum, 330
Substitutions, speech, 171
Success for All (SFA), 304, 305–306
Success Nights, 49, 83
Success strategies. *See* Academic success strategies; Social success strategies
Summer programs, 62
SuperHawk, 417
Supervision of paraeducators, 236
Supplemental instruction, 254
Supported employment, 162, 446
Surface management techniques, 367, 378, 383–384, 446
Suspension, 39–40
SWAS (school-within-a-school) approach, 137–138, 142
Syllables Segmenting and Blending, 295
Syntax, 171
Systematic instruction, 126, 200, 201

Tactical planning, 255–258
TAI (team-assisted individualization), 328
Talking calculators, 414, 436
Talking Pocket Calculator, 414
Talking Texas Instruments Scientific Calculator, 414
Tantrums, 395
Targeted interventions, 365, 368, 378, 389–392, 446
Tasks, structure and sequencing of, 111
TATs. *See* Teacher assistance teams (TATs)
Teacher aides. *See* Paraeducators
Teacher assistance teams (TATs)
    collaboration, 217, 226, 231–232
    defined, 446
    response-to-intervention, 249
Teacher assistants. *See* Paraeducators
Teacher insistence, 69–70
Teachers
    attitudes toward inclusion, 21–22
    behaviors in delivering instruction, 288–290
    characteristics, 22–24
    cultural background, 56
    demographic divide between students and, 56–63
    dispositions, 23
    general education, 19, 267
    highly qualified, 41, 42, 44–45
    itinerant, 181
    positive attitudes, 23–24

role in response-to-intervention, 45–46
    special education, 19
Teacher support teams. *See* Teacher assistance teams (TATs)
Teaching to the test, 64
Team-assisted individualization (TAI), 328
Teams, 212, 216–217, 442. *See also* Collaboration; Teacher assistance teams (TATs)
Team teaching, 233
Technology. *See also* Assistive technology (AT); Educational technology; Universal design for learning (UDL)
    perspectives on, 401
    standards, 420
    strategies, 421–440
    to support writing, 298
Temperature, classroom, 261
Territoriality, 215
Testing accommodations, 254
Test taking, 332, 338, 355–356
Textbooks, 331, 349–350
TextHelp Read and Write Gold, 411
Tham, Kristen, 117–118, 123, 125, 129
Thematic instructional units, 257, 277
Thesauri, 433
Think-aloud activities, 350
Thinking Reader, 419
Think-Pair-Share, 91, 308
Thumbs up strategy, 91
Tier 1 instruction, 83, 249
Tier 2 instruction, 83–84, 249, 314
Tier 3 instruction, 84, 314
Tiered activities, 272
Tiered classroom management, 365–374
Time, cultural dimensions of, 59
Time adaptations, 330
Timeless Jade Trade, 428
Timeless Math, 428
Time management, 332–333
Time-out, 43, 373, 446
Timing accommodations, 355
Toddlers, 40
Token systems, 144–145, 372, 390
Tonic-clonic seizure, 193, 446
Tracking strategy, 290–291, 304, 305–306
Training of paraeducators, 235
Transformative approach to culturally responsive teaching, 73
Transition planning, 162–163
Traumatic brain injury, 10
TREE strategy, 315
TRICK BAG assignment management strategy, 333
Trust, 214
Tutoring
    classwide peer, 256, 275–276, 293
    individual, 292, 304, 309–310
    peer, 256, 275–276, 292–293, 445
Type 1 diabetes, 193, 199–200, 270, 446

UDL. *See* Universal design for learning (UDL)
Unit organizers, 93, 339–340, 341
Units of instruction, 257, 277
Universal design for learning (UDL)
　content-area instruction, 326, 334
　defined, 446
　example, 418–419
　intellectual disabilities and, 128
　planning academic content
　　instruction, 257
　principles, 415, 418
　selecting instructional materials, 258
Universal inclusive practices and supports,
　365, 367–368, 369–371
Universal newborn hearing screening
　programs, 178
Universal precautions, 200, 201, 446
Unpredictability, 363
Usage disorders, 171, 446

Vanguard (AAC device), 417
Van Harssel, Casey, 159
Ventilation, classroom, 261
Verbal aggression, 142
Verbal communication skills, 229–230
Visual accessibility, 262
Visual acuity, 176–177, 447
Visual aids, 182
Visual disabilities. *See* Visual impairment
Visual field, 177, 447
Visual impairment. *See also* Blindness; Sensory
　disabilities
　academic and cognitive performance, 180
　academic success strategies, 182, 184
　defined, 10, 176–177, 447
　identifying, 178
　overview, 177
　prevalence, 178, 179

service delivery, 179
social success strategies, 183
vignette, 181
Vocabulary, 294, 295, 349, 447
Vocational education, 146, 162–163
VOCA (voice-output communication aids),
　161, 447
Vogler, Anne, 6
Voice disorders, 171, 447
Voiced text, 433
Voice-output communication aids (VOCA),
　161, 447

Walls, Eileen
　attention-deficit/hyperactivity disorder,
　　97, 99
　autism spectrum disorders, 151–152
　classroom management, 359–360
　effective instruction, 286
　student benefits from inclusive settings, 25
Warm demanders, 68–70
Washington, Booker T., 6, 244
Waterford Early Reading Program, 405
Watson, Shana, 325, 326, 327
Western Carolina University, 127–128
West Hernando Middle School (Hernando
　County, Fla.)
　attention-deficit/hyperactivity disorder,
　　97–98, 107
　autism spectrum disorders, 151–152
　classroom management, 359–360
　collaboration, 209–210, 213–214,
　　217, 230
　dispositions, 23
　effective instruction, 285–286, 287,
　　288, 303
　guided notes, 93
　inclusive education philosophy, 4, 9

learning disabilities, 79–80, 89, 93
overview, 6–7
peer buddy program, 244
student benefits from inclusive settings,
　24–25
teacher attitudes toward inclusion, 21
Wheelchairs, motorized, 415, 422,
　439–440
Whites, non-Hispanic, 51
Williams, Steve, 137–138, 142
WINGS program, 359–360
Wisconsin Supreme Court, 30
Word Identification, Memory Word
　Match, 295
Word-prediction software, 433
Word processing, 403, 409, 422, 433–434
WordQ Writing Aid Software, 413
WordSmith, 411
Work experience, 145–146
Working memory, 87, 447
Wraparound interventions, 146, 365,
　373–374, 447
Wright, Richard, 72
Write:OutLoud, 413, 418
Writing
　assistive technology, 408–409, 413, 422,
　　433–434
　content-area instruction, 338, 343–345
　elementary instruction, 295–298, 304,
　　315–316
　learning disabilities and, 87
　software, 422, 433–434
W-W-W WHAT=2 HOW=2 strategy, 316
Wyke, Becky, 6, 247
WYNN 3.1 Freedom Scientific's Learning
　Systems Group, 410

Zero reject, 36